Brave
or
Stupid

© 2014 Albatross Förlag AB

www.albatrossforlag.com

ISBN 978-91-981867-1-0

Authors: Tracey Christiansen, Yanne Larsson and Carl-Erik Andersson

Editors: Anita Larsson, Steve Strid

Graphic production: Brun Media AB

Cover by Steve Strid

Printed and bound by CPI Group (UK) Ltd, Croydon, CR0 4YY

www.braveorstupid.com

Contents

Contents

"Ships are the nearest thing to dreams that hands have ever made."

Robert N. Rose

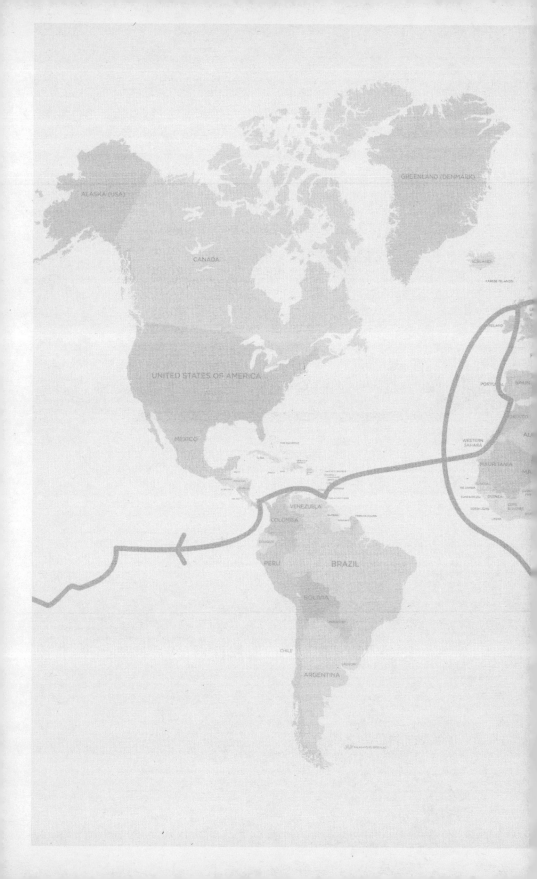

Our warmest thanks to our families, friends, supporters, kind strangers and helpful sailors who helped us throughout our expedition and enabled us to reach our goal. A journey of a thousand miles starts with a single step but ends with a million memories.

Yanne and Carl, Helsingborg, 2014

Chapter 1
The Ghosts of Omaha Beach

I t all started with a handshake: nothing fancier than that, no contracts with sub-clauses requiring signatures, witnesses and, heaven forbid, lawyers. It was just a brief clasping of hands. It was typically Swedish: brief and business-like, a couple of seconds at most, but it sealed a pact between us that would last more than eight years.

I often look back to that moment and wonder at the events that brought two committed landlubbers to a decision to sail around the world together, particularly as neither of us knew the first thing about sailing. In that respect, we bore little resemblance to our intrepid Viking forefathers. Add to that the fact that I was forty-something years old and had all my life suffered from such acute seasickness that the mere sight of a toy boat bobbing on a paddling pool would make my stomach lurch. So why on earth would I agree to a nautical global circumnavigation with a friend who knew even less about sailing than I did?

I grant you that the events leading to my handshake with Carl may have been fuelled by that feeling of bonhomie that steals over you after a good meal and a bottle of Bordeaux. An excess of wine may even have contributed to my agreeing to the scheme in the first place. And there was almost certainly the shadow of a hangover involved in the final decision-making process. But once Carl and I had shaken hands, that was it: the plunge into the unknown had been taken; the manly gauntlet to overcome my fear had been thrown down. The wheels were in motion and we were fully committed to the challenge of transforming our lives, leaving the security of well-paying jobs and the comfort of homes and families to risk everything.

The wine had been consumed at the top of a cliff overlooking the five-mile expanse of Omaha Beach in Normandy. It was here that the Allies arrived on 6 June 1944 to be thrown into one of the bloodiest battles of the Second World War. The conditions were against them from the start; the American landing craft had struggled against strong winds and rough waves, making it impossible for them to land at their planned sectors. Only two of the 29 support tanks made it to shore. Terrified young soldiers disembarked from the landing craft in deep water to discover unexpectedly strong defences. Those who didn't drown under the weight of the equipment they shouldered and made it to the beach, were cut to pieces by machine-gun and mortar fire from the Germans who lay hidden in the cliff tops.

Carl and I were now sitting at the top of such a cliff, basking in the perfect weather and admiring the view: an azure sea sparkled below a cloudless blue sky, the broad sandy beach stretched invitingly below us. It looked innocent and pure as if it had never known that day's unspeakable chaos and carnage. It was hard to believe that a drop of blood had ever sullied those brilliant golden sands.

Nevertheless, we both felt the ghosts of the past all around us; they'd been shadowing us on our cycle tour up to the bluff. As well as the museums, memorials and cemeteries, the Normandy coastline is dotted with poignant reminders of the fallen. Small plaques commemorate the number of soldiers who perished here, the distances between the plaques heartbreakingly short: eight hundred dead, three thousand dead, four thousand dead. The numbers are staggering; an estimated 425,000 Allied and German troops were killed, wounded or went missing during the Battle of Normandy. But it was only when we reached Omaha Beach itself that it really hit us: over a thousand American men had perished on the sands, most of them within the first hour of the landings.

We were sitting on the grass, quietly contemplating the scene below. We'd had a picnic of prawns and shared a bottle of red wine and were enjoying that pleasant mellow feeling you get after drinking in the sun. For a while Carl was lost in his thoughts and I in mine, but I'm certain we were both reflecting on life and death as we surveyed the landscape.

'Did I ever tell you about my father's old helmsman, Kurt Björkland? He took part in the D-Day landings,' I eventually said, breaking the silence.

'Really? And he lived to tell the tale?'

'He doesn't talk much about it, but apparently he enlisted in the British army and was one of the first to come ashore.'

Carl slowly shook his head. 'He was unbelievably lucky. Think of all those poor lads who didn't make it. Some of them weren't even in their twenties, and now here we are, two blokes in our fifties.'

'Speak for yourself,' I said. 'I'm only 43.'

Carl smiled briefly, then became serious again. 'Makes you think, though.'

'Certainly does. Kurt sailed around the world after that,' I said. 'Not just once but three times.'

'Everyone ought to do something like that.'

'Like what?'

'You know, follow your heart, fulfil your dreams. At least once in a lifetime.

Life's way too short. We spend too much time dreaming about what we want to do and never doing it. It may be a platitude, but it doesn't mean it's any less true.'

I agreed with Carl. We continued talking about how life was all work and no play, that life was over so quickly we barely got the chance to dream at all. And again we were quiet for a while, sombrely contemplating this. Then Carl broke the silence.

'I've got an idea, Yanne.'

'Yeah?'

'How about *we* sail around the world?'

I looked at him in astonishment. If he'd announced he was considering leaving his wife and three children to have a sex change and elope to Patagonia with the 30-year-old window cleaner, I would have been less appalled. My response, when I was finally able to regain the power of speech, was unequivocal.

'Are you nuts, Calle? I throw up on the 20-minute ferry ride between Sweden and Denmark. There's no way I'd survive puking my way around the world on a little matchstick boat.'

'It was just an idea ...,' Carl protested, throwing up his hands in defence.

'And a completely crap idea! Forget it!'

'I only thought ...,'

'Well, don't. And just in case it's slipped your memory, let me remind you that neither of us knows anything about sailing. I don't even like bloody sailing! Why would I start liking it now?'

My indignation at the preposterousness of the idea once vented, I cooled down enough to slap a somewhat subdued Carl on the back to show him I'd forgiven his foolishness. Me? Sailing around the world? Or even sailing? Was the man completely out of his mind? Carl and I had known each other for years. He should have known better than to even mention it.

We loaded our bikes with the remnants of our picnic, hoisted our rucksacks on our backs, left the cliffs and cycled inland towards Saint-Lô. Here, too, the Second World War had left its mark; the town was heavily bombed in 1944 and the church still bore the battle scars of the machine-gun fire. Carl and I each took a room at a *pension* in town. There, we ate dinner, enjoyed another fine bottle of wine and discussed our plans for the remainder of our cycling trip. Carl wisely avoided any further reference to sailing.

But damn it all if he hadn't planted the idea in my head. And the crafty old bastard probably knew it. That night I slept fitfully as Carl's words swirled like a fog in my head, 'Follow your heart, and fulfil your dreams.' Or was it the ghostly whisper of a young soldier who'd died on the sands of Omaha Beach reminding me to live life instead of watching it slip by? 'Life is short, make the most of the time you have.' I thought of Kurt Björkland and how he'd given his life purpose after the war. Life was full of risks, so why not decide to take the ones that made it meaningful. We only get one shot; I was already half way through my three score and ten and what did I have to show for it? Two failed marriages and a nine-to-five job to pay my mortgage. Hardly magical memories to take with me to the pine box that awaited. If my life lacked adventure, I only had myself to blame. So what was I going to do about it?

Carl was already sitting in the hotel restaurant, studying the map and eating a croissant, when I joined him for breakfast the following morning. Coffee was on the table and I poured myself a cup.

'That idea of yours,' I said. Carl looked up. I took a fortifying gulp of black coffee. 'Apart from the horrendous seasickness, it's not a completely brainless idea. Insane, yes; impossible, no.'

Carl put down his croissant. 'What's this? Are you still hung-over? I knew we shouldn't have hit the brandy last night.'

I grinned weakly. 'You're right. You should never make a decision with a hangover. Not that it would be the first time.' I sipped my coffee. 'But my father's always nagged me about learning to sail. I guess it's time to take a crack at it and show him I can do it.'

'Yanne, are you sure about this?'

'Kurt Björkland survived the Normandy landings and circumnavigated the world *three* times. He gave his life purpose; I need purpose in mine. What the hell, let's learn to sail. I mean, how hard can it be?' I hoped I sounded more confident than I felt.

Carl's grin was huge. 'You're on,' he said. And we shook hands over the table. That was the start of it: the beginning of a pact between two friends. 'Right,' he said decisively, rubbing his hands together as if keen to get started immediately, 'I guess we'd better get a boat.'

'And I'd better get some seasick tablets,' I said.

Carl's grin faded, he looked suddenly solemn. 'There's just one thing I'm a bit worried about,' he said.

'Just *one* thing?' There was a whole encyclopaedia of things I was already nail-bitingly, buttock-clenchingly concerned about.

Carl's face had turned the colour of uncooked pastry. 'How the hell am I going to tell my wife?'

Chapter 2

Auf Wiedersehen Berlin

I n general, we Swedish are slow to make decisions, but quick to implement them. It's an endearing national trait together with our penchant for flat-pack furniture and middle-of-the-road pop music. Carl and I, however, have always been quick to agree; we're inclined to go with our gut feelings, so the idea to circumnavigate the world swept over us with alarming speed and lack of control. As usual, we threw ourselves at the challenge: hearts first, brains last.

Carl and I go way back. We're both from the county of Skåne (Scania to English speakers) at the very southern tip of Sweden. It's an exceptionally flat landscape – think Norfolk flat if you're British, or Nebraska flat with a coastline if you're American – so we have endless open fields dotted with pic-turesque windmills, ancient castles and a surprising amount of golf courses given the length of our miserable winters.

I come from Helsingborg, a small town hugging the coast at the narrow-est point between Sweden and Denmark. On most days the Danish city of Helsingør (Elsinore) is visible, and fine weather might tempt you to swim the Öresund strait, the two-mile stretch of water that separates Sweden from Denmark, to Kronborg castle made famous by Shakespeare as Hamlet's bas-tion. Not that I'd recommend the swim: if the shock of the cold water doesn't get you, a ferry, cruise boat or tanker bearing down the Öresund towards Norway will. This particular stretch of water is one of three Danish straits connecting the Baltic Sea to the Atlantic Ocean via the North Sea and is there-fore one of the busiest waterways in the world.

Carl was born and bred further inland in the even smaller town of Eslöv, whose claim to fame is that it has Sweden's tallest wooden house, built, I assume, so people can admire the flatness of Skåne. Exciting stuff goes on here in Sweden, you know.

I first met Carl, however, in 1978, in former East Berlin during the days of Check Point Charlie and the Stasi. Germany was a strange place back then, desperately trying to shake off the shadow cast by the Second World War, yet still in its grip. The Berlin Wall was in its fourteenth year, and over a hundred people had already died breaching the border between East and West Berlin. East Berlin was an uninviting, purely functional place with regimented rows of imposing Soviet built concrete housing blocks dominating the cityscape: prisons have more charm.

Life behind the Wall was weird to say the least, especially to the many foreign workers who found themselves working in East Berlin on construction sites, as I did, in the late 1970s. I'd just turned 20 and had accepted a three-week job as an electrician on the construction of a hotel and department store. It was a huge job, worth 675 billion Swedish krona (approximately £80 billion at that time), an unheard of amount. Carl was 28 and project leader for the electrical department for which I worked. Twelve years later I finally left Berlin, having married, divorced and remarried. So much for three weeks.

I suppose I was seduced as much by the lifestyle I could afford as by the women I married. Foreign workers were exempt from the rules imposed on the East Germans, and the black market rate for our Western currency meant we could live like kings. I found myself a millionaire for the first and, unfortunately, last time. A bottle of imported champagne in a night club, for example, cost the equivalent of a can of cola in Sweden. Unsurprisingly, we drank it like water.

Despite my affluence, I was living in one of 50 caravans housing other Swedish workers parked on the Ostbahnhof car park. This was bordered by three colossal tower blocks, so tall they obstructed the sun after midday. Our commune of caravans became the entertainment equivalent of a third TV channel for the tower block residents, particularly in June when we celebrated midsummer in typical Swedish style with parties for 200 of our countrymen. And despite what you may have read, we Swedes know how to party, especially at midsummer. We bought supplies from the Intershop, the shop reserved for diplomats and those with hard currency, and provided at least 10 bottles of beer and a bottle of vodka per guest. We served great platters of pickled herring and smoked salmon, using huge oil drums to bake potatoes. The eating and drinking culminated in dancing around the midsummer pole erected in the middle of the car park and festooned with whatever greenery we could get our hands on, while belting out Swedish folk songs at ear-piercing levels. Bemused Germans hung out of their windows and watched with what must have been a mixture of amusement and envy from their concrete towers. Life was really tough for them; the shops were empty, as anything and everything people needed or enjoyed in Communist GDR was sent to Moscow: food, clothing, the lot. Meanwhile, we foreigners were cavorting decadently in their midst, flinging about our ill-gotten capitalist gains.

Mix into this the secret police and you have a surreal world. Stasi agents lurked on every street corner, spying on our activities. They keenly observed everything from the construction work to the antics at the parties and listened in on all our phone calls. If some poor sod said something stupid, critical or jokey, he'd find himself confronted by a couple of imposing types in dark overcoats and hauled off to a windowless hole for hours of questioning. One of our jobs was to run cables from 600 hotel rooms to a single control area where these faceless men could sit and eavesdrop to their suspicious hearts' content, scribbling frantically until they ran out of pages in their notebooks.

Both Carl and I were trailed by Stasi agents. It was rather like having a series of personal stalkers. I was followed by various dark-coated individuals at a discreet distance of 10 feet for only a year before they lost interest in me. Carl was observed more keenly because he travelled throughout the country to meet suppliers and was therefore followed most of the decade he spent in East Germany. The Stasi tried to nail him for something or other, but they didn't have a hope in hell. Carl was squeaky clean; he didn't attempt to smuggle anything in or out, not even banned magazines or books. Nevertheless, they made life awkward. After the Wall fell in 1989, Carl returned to the city and managed to find his file in the Stasi archives. It was nearly two feet thick: they'd observed and meticulously noted every tedious detail of his life: from where he ate and stayed to whom he met. Looking back, I feel slightly offended they didn't find me more interesting.

The crew working on the job was an uneven mixture of professionals and clowns – the majority being the latter – so it was astonishing we survived the experience. We were digging blindly in the middle of Berlin among unexploded bombs and high-voltage lines with neither drawings nor plans to guide us, all the archives having been destroyed. Instead, we had to put our faith in an odd bloke from northern Sweden who had an uncanny sense for detecting high-voltage lines. He would walk in front of the excavators with a metal rod, calling out when it was safe to lower the bucket; fortunately for him, and us, he never made a mistake. The quaint concept of workers' well-being and a department overseeing their health and safety was a thing of the future.

There were more than a few maniacs working on the sites and a lot of drinking on the job which made an already unstable situation even more volatile, in turn spawning a "so what?" attitude. This was partly the reason why Carl and I became friends – we were both horrified by this lack of professionalism. Young and newly trained as I was, I was still keen to learn and do the best job I could. Yes, you might call me a youthful idealist, but I was eager to climb the professional ladder. Carl was similarly focused; he was a meticulous project leader and a good boss who appreciated hard workers. Our respect for each other was mutual and we knew we could trust each other implicitly. We didn't socialize together much at the time, as Carl was living in a flat with his young family, whereas I was enjoying a bachelor life in my caravan. At least until I got married. It was only as our work together came to a close that Carl and I became better acquainted. He's a bear of a man with a hearty laugh, a voice like a Harley in full throttle and a lusty appetite. He became something of an older, gutsier brother to me. Overtly what you'd call a red-blooded man's man, his boisterous charisma also drew the ladies: a bonus for me, as being married Carl had to decline the come hither looks of the Teutonic blondes, leaving the field open for my more clumsy advances. By the time we returned to Sweden a decade later, we'd become friends for life who would go to the ends of the earth for each other.

What neither of us knew at the time was that one day we would do just that.

Chapter 3
Not Over the Hill ... Yet

I n 1997, Carl had reached a point in his life when he was supposed to be having a crisis: middle age. He was approaching 50, but he couldn't help wondering from what direction.

'Damn it all, Yanne,' he growled. 'For men of my age it seems you have two options: look old or look ridiculous.'

'Which look are you going for?' I asked.

'Neither. My wife won't let me do the first and my daughters have forbidden me from doing the second.'

'Well, I guess that means buying a snazzy sports car is out of the question.'

Carl shook his head ruefully, but grinned a moment later. 'True, but I can still have a snazzy sports bike.'

Knowing Carl as well as I did, I had a fairly shrewd notion that there was something about reaching a half century that was nagging at him: indeed, he'd confessed quietly to me of a growing yearning. I'd looked at him with alarm at this mention of yearning: many a middle-aged man has proved himself a bankrupt fool in an attempt to recapture his glory days with a young nubile beauty. My panic was allayed, however, when it became clear that Carl's burning desire was not to swing naked from hotel bedroom chandeliers with a buxom blonde, but to go for a bike ride.

Not that this was just any bike ride, you understand. Carl had always enjoyed the freedom afforded by a cycle tour and was planning more than a quick pedal down to the beach and back. Over the winter months, he'd tucked himself away in his study and poured over the literature that fed his fantasy: maps and travel guides of Europe. He was due to work his last day as CEO for the electrical department of PEAB and had six weeks holiday before he began his new job. He would finally have the opportunity to relive something he'd done years before as a much younger man when he'd dusted off his old army bike, packed a camping tent, some clean underpants and a bottle of whisky and spent a blissful week exploring his home county of Skåne and its stunning coastline.

This time the plan was bigger and better; the fact that he was older and slower didn't deter Carl at all. A week in Skåne was one thing, but he longed to go further afield. What I didn't know was that he'd planned a cycle route of Europe, starting from Elsinore on the north coast of Denmark, continuing through England and France and finally into Portugal. Lisbon was his goal, and he'd given himself six weeks to complete the journey. Had I known earlier, I would most certainly have tried to talk him out of it.

But the first I heard about all this was at Carl's fiftieth birthday party when he suddenly revealed his plans in a short, slightly slurred speech.

'I've heard the call of the open road,' he announced to the room. I rolled my eyes at the ceiling; what the hell was he thinking?

'Don't answer it,' some joker quipped.

'Bet you a bottle of whisky you won't make it as far as the Helsingborg ferry,' yelled another. There was raucous laughter from both the sober and the inebriated.

I got to my feet, swayed slightly and clapped Carl on the shoulder.

'Calle, you mad fool. Have you really thought this through? Apart from the god awful weather, consider the wear and tear on your arse!'

He smiled ruefully. 'You know how it is, Yanne. Once over the hill, you start to pick up speed. I want to make sure I set my own pace.'

'Yeah, but to Lisbon and back,' I may have slurred. 'What's so bloody marvellous about Lisbon?'

Carl shrugged. 'I don't know. I've just always felt there's something ... exotic about that city. Plus it'll be spring there.' He had a dreamy look in his eye that was almost pathetic, but damn it, if he wasn't serious. This wasn't some whim; he really needed to do this. Two gin and tonics later and the idea was rolling around my head that I should do it with him. He probably needed a co-pilot to help him navigate his way: or if not a co-pilot, then someone to ride shotgun in case of accidents or mishaps. At the very least he needed a sidekick. I decided that I should be that sidekick, and before I could stop my stupid, alcohol-muddled brain, I found myself addressing the room.

'Ladies and gentlemen,' I said in what people have since told me was a relatively commanding voice. 'I hereby announce that I will be accompanying Carl on his cycle tour through Europe.'

'Bloody fantastic!' Carl roared. He frantically shook my hand and clinked my glass to seal my offer with a speed that suggested he doubted my resolve would last the evening, never mind the journey. Meanwhile, the rest of the room started a sweepstakes on how quickly we'd give up.

Why is it that one's finest moments are never quite as fine on reflection the day after? I woke up at midday with that unsettling feeling you have when you know you've made a bit of a prat of yourself, but you can't recall exactly how or why. I was fairly certain I hadn't embarrassed myself on the dance floor, and I'd woken up alone, so more or less a good sign. But I couldn't shake the sensation that I done something I was already regretting even though I couldn't remember what it was.

When the events of the night finally filtered through my addled brain, my groan was loud and long. After a hearty brunch I began to feel better about it; after all, a cycle trip would be a way to get out of the working rut for a couple of weeks – that would be as much time as I could take off from the photo processing business my brother and I owned. I rang Carl to check our date of departure; no doubt I'd have a few weeks to prepare for the trip. For a start, I needed a bike, and maybe I should consider doing some light training.

'I'm thrilled you're coming with me, mate,' Carl said when he answered the phone.

'Wouldn't miss it,' I lied. 'So when do we leave?'

'The day after tomorrow.'

I laughed, such a joker that Carl. 'No, really.'

'Really, the day after tomorrow. Planning meeting at my house tonight. See you at eight.' And he slammed down the phone, leaving me stunned for a good half minute before I started doing that panic running thing cartoon characters do when they fall off a cliff and plummet to the ground.

But my word is my bond, and my handshake is as good as a signature on a notarized document, so I headed to my nearest cycle shop.

'And where are you cycling to?' asked the shop assistant.

'Lisbon,' I answered without enthusiasm.

The assistant rubbed his hands with glee and directed me to the top-end racing bikes with more gears than Carl had celebrated birthdays and prices to match. 'I'd suggest one of these. You'll also need this saddle cover, a good pump – this one's pricey but worth the money – a quality cycle bag and gloves. A helmet, of course. Oh, and I would recommend these cycle shorts and matching vest. Now what cycling footwear were you considering?'

'Hold on,' I said, steering the salesman back down the shop to the rack of cheaper city bikes. 'One of these will do. And I'm not wearing all that daft clobber. A pair of jeans with boxers underneath will do me just fine.'

The cycle salesman snorted derisively, believing he'd spotted a cheap amateur if ever there was, which of course he had. 'But you can't cycle in jeans.'

I fixed him with a bloodshot eye. 'When I was in the army, I cycled around southern Sweden and I didn't have fancy spandex shorts then, so I don't need them now. Furthermore, I'm not wearing anything that makes me look like an aerobics instructor.'

I chose a bike with seven gears and what I hoped would be a soft saddle. Right, so the equipment was sorted. But a small hitch in the plan was becoming horribly clear in the harsh light of day as I wobblingly peddled my new bike to my car. How in the hell was I going to cycle to Lisbon when I was barely fit enough to cycle to work? I pulled a muscle if I so much as sneezed.

Two days later, Carl stubbed out his last-ever cigarette, and we rolled our cycles onto the Helsingborg ferry to Denmark. Carl was as excited about his bike as a small boy getting his first two-wheeler. His company's parting present was a red Cannondale, a proper racing bike with a ludicrous number of gears which I suspected he'd never use, but with which he seemed thrilled as he lovingly stroked the handlebars. You're probably wondering why he didn't opt instead for a mantel clock, but cycling is popular in southern Sweden: remember that Skåne's a relatively flat county.

'Ah,' he said with a sigh of pure happiness. 'Finally, six weeks holiday and my first chance in 30 years to really get out of the rut I've been stuck in. Right, let's go. Lisbon here we come.'

The first day was utterly, numbingly miserable. The weather was shocking with snow storms and headwinds so strong we might as well have been pedalling backwards for all the progress we made. Neither of us was dressed for snow which pelted us in the face like well-aimed darts. We'd barely covered two miles in Denmark before I wanted to push Carl off his swanky bike and ride repeatedly over his prostrate body screaming, 'Why the hell couldn't you have taken up bloody marathon running like other middle-aged men!' Instead I put my head down, glared at the asphalt and shouted at myself, 'You bloody idiot! Nobody made you do this! You only have yourself to blame!'

Incidentally, anyone who would have you believe that Denmark is flat has either only seen it on a map, or is a deceitful, lying bastard. If you ever meet anyone who makes such a claim, disabuse them of that notion by whatever means you deem fit: preferably by insisting that they cycle the length and breadth of the damn country. They'll soon agree that the Danish landscape is as hilly as a ski resort. Carl and I were forced to cycle 60 miles uphill standing in the saddle all the way from Elsinore to the town of Hundested in eastern Denmark. My legs burned, and my pounding heart confirmed my suspicion that I was a wretched candidate for our tour de France.

Eventually, our struggle through the bad weather was rewarded with a hot meal and a warm bed. We checked into an inn at Hundested; thank heaven, at least Carl recognized that our camping days were over and that some creature comforts were essential: good food and rooms with ensuite bathrooms. The following morning, revived by a full Danish breakfast of fresh rolls, rye bread, herring, cold meats and cheese, we began another day's unhappy cycling with sleet lashing down in our faces like a storm of tiny knives.

I was beginning to regret not having bought the spandex cycling shorts. Furthermore, my "soft" cycle saddle felt increasingly like a small plank trying to wedge itself permanently between my buttocks – for the life of me, I cannot fathom how women manage to wear thongs. At the end of a day's cycling, my thigh muscles were shaking with exhaustion. I fell from my bike and tottered shakily about like a toddler; it was like learning to walk all over again.

We had a brief respite from the saddle for 20 hours on the ferry between Esbjerg and Harwich on England's east coast, allowing time for some sensation to return to my manly parts. We cycled into England and better weather; spring was bursting from every bush and tree, energizing us to pedal harder. Better still was the revitalizing power of the British beer which spurred us from pub to pub.

Then we arrived at Tilbury, a tired port on the north bank of the Thames where it seemed the sun dared not shine. I apologize to the good people of Tilbury – those of you who haven't abandoned it – but if ever there was a bleaker, more miserable place in twenty-first century England, I hope not to see it. Once a smart ship building city, Tilbury has not aged well; the buildings looked neglected, the people dejected. Never have I seen so much litter; empty beer bottles, plastic bags and overturned shopping trolleys blighting the streets. Gangs of youths hung about, smoking and glaring malevolently at passers-by. We avoided eye contact and pedalled furiously through the town and down to the old harbour where we checked into a small hotel and hid. Early the following morning, we slunk onto the ferry and crossed the Thames. Gravesend, on the other side, was a complete contrast: the sun shone and the air smelled fresh; couples taking their quiet Sunday strolls smiled pleasantly and waved to us as we rolled by. With renewed vigour and hope in our hearts, we began the journey down to Portsmouth to get the ferry to the continent.

Cycling through southern England was idyllic; the weather improved, the wind was helpfully at our backs and we enjoyed the best that England's fish and chip shops and pubs had to offer. We stayed in Portsmouth for two days to visit the naval base and Admiral Lord Nelson's flagship, *HMS Victory*. The oldest commissioned warship in the world, *Victory* was part of the fleet that twice defeated Napoleon Bonaparte's, an impressive testimony to Britain's naval achievements which even we seafaring Swedes could admire.

I should remind you here that the Swedish also have a proud history of shipbuilding, from Viking long boats to modern day racing yachts. Not that we've always been entirely successful with some of our vessels; we've had our fair share of disasters, one of which, the seventeenth-century warship *Vasa*, is an embarrassing example of massive ineptitude as well as proof that innovation is not always a good thing. In 1628, a splendid new warship commissioned by Gustav II, then King of Sweden, set sail on her maiden voyage out of Stockholm destined for the war with Poland. *Vasa* was a fearsome warship with a displacement of 1,210 tonnes and a hull built from more than a thousand oak trees. Her masts were over 160 feet high, carrying 10 sails with a total sail area a few feet shy of 1,400 square feet. She had 64 bronze cannon over two gun decks and could carry an army of 300 soldiers. Although designed as a fighting machine, she was a majestic craft decorated with hundreds of vividly painted baroque sculptures carved out of oak and pine, intended to reflect the power and the glory of the Swedish king. *Vasa*, so named after the ruling Vasa dynasty, required a crew of 150 men to sail her. She must have been an impressive sight, and excited Stockholmers lined the quay to witness her departure. As she proudly sailed out to the salute of cannon fire, men swarmed over her, hoisting sails and pulling ropes. The cheering crowds who'd gathered to see her must have thought this was the ship to beat all others.

Unfortunately, *Vasa* had barely sailed a single nautical mile before she promptly keeled over and sank. The crowds were still waving their kerchiefs when the ship heeled to port, and water rushed through the open gun ports, drowning at least thirty of the unfortunate crew. The ship's lack of stability was to blame; the ballast was insufficient in relation to the rig and the cannon. Fingers were pointed, the captain was arrested and released, but nobody was ever officially blamed for the catastrophe.

Surprisingly, despite the brouhaha surrounding the sinking of an expensive ship on her maiden voyage – the ill-fated Titanic got further – *Vasa* was more or less forgotten for the next three centuries and left to rot in the waters of Stockholm harbour. Eventually, in 1956, serious attempts to relocate the ship were made, and she was finally raised in 1961 after 333 years lost in the mud. After years of restoration, she is now housed in a splendid museum in Stockholm and continues to impress. Fortunately, Swedish boat builders have since learned to ignore the hubris of kings and concentrate on building ships that float – a necessary component for seagoing vessels. Not that the British should feel too smug about *HMS Victory*: her maiden voyage was in 1778, so 160 years had passed since the mistakes of *Vasa*.

From Portsmouth we crossed to Cherbourg where the eight forts guarding the harbour entrance are evidence both of the strategic importance of the port and a determination to keep the English out. We were on historic ground, the scene of tremendous battles during World War II when the German forces all but razed the city to prevent the Allied forces from using it.

Ah, how we loved France: the wine, the cheeses and the cured meats. I find myself salivating just thinking about it. We cycled out of Cherbourg, did some 20 miles and entered the picturesque town of Saint-Vaast-la-Hougue where we headed directly to the harbour, confident of finding a local quayside bistro specialising in the catch of the day. We did indeed find a splendid fish restaurant where I swiftly cast aside my metal steed, threw myself at an empty table and clicked my fingers to the garçon to bring us a bottle of chilled white and a large shellfish platter. Then we sat back and watched the world go by.

What I love about France is that the country and the people remain so unrepentantly French, indeed flagrantly so: men with Gauloise cigarettes dangling languidly from pouty lips as they talk; women chatting at the speed of express trains as they pick over the produce at the local épicerie; shoulder shrugging en masse. Everyone seemed to have stepped out of a Jean-Paul Belmondo film. I was slightly disappointed not to see a man in a stripped T-shirt with a string of onions around his neck, but the waiter had a pleasingly Gérard Depardieu nose, a Gallic honker clearly evolved over centuries to be able to assess the bouquet of a Beaujolais nouveau with one deep sniff.

We were just assessing the merits of the second bottle of wine when four Brits, boisterous types in sailing jackets and waterproofs, plonked themselves down at the table next to ours. We didn't think they looked like much initially, but appearances are deceptive; they turned out to be a doctor, a lawyer, a headhunter and a man who ran his own company, all of them so affable it was easy to fall into conversation. We eventually learned that they'd all learned to sail and once a year made a trip across the English Channel for a blokes' week. They sailed, drank too much, talked bullshit and let loose the way men without their better halves generally do. They laughed when we told them we were doing much the same but on bikes.

'You're not serious,' the doctor said. 'You're really doing this on pushbikes?' We nodded.

'Hell, if I had to travel on land, I'd have to travel by Bentley or Rolls,' the lawyer joked. 'Otherwise how would I pack everything I needed?'

'Easy, you just pack this,' I said, pulling out my credit card from my shorts' pocket. Lubricated with wine, we all howled with laughter.

'Can we have a look at your bikes?' the doctor asked.

'Sure,' Carl replied. 'I'll show you my bike if you show me your boat.'

It was a quick tour, even though Carl insisted on demonstrating all his gears. The Brits chuckled over my extensive luggage – some underwear, a toothbrush and a warm pullover – then we strolled down to the harbour. As Carl and I stood on the pier gazing at the yacht, a feeling began to creep over me. I wasn't sure what it was at first, but eventually I realized with dismay that it was envy: we were looking at a fabulous sailboat.

'Think what we could do with a boat,' Carl said in the awed voice of a man who has suddenly seen a heavenly light. Apparently, the feeling was catching.

'Well, for a start you wouldn't get blisters on your arse.' I said. 'But I'd rather have that than be seasick. That's even worse.'

'No, I'm serious. With a boat like this you could go for miles, using the wind instead of pedalling against it.'

'Well, you have a point there,' I conceded.

'And it's free.'

'A boat like this doesn't come free.'

'No, the wind is free. And look how much room there is.' Carl began to roar with excitement. 'Say you had a bigger boat, you could live on it... Do you get what I'm saying, Yanne? Think of the possibilities.'

I thought of them. 'Hypothermia. Drowning. Getting eaten by something with very sharp teeth,' I said dryly. 'Oh yes, the possibilities are endless.'

'Yes, but you wouldn't need anything else, no hotels or tents or eating at restaurants.' Carl was almost jumping with excitement, his arms were going like windmill sails. 'And you could see the world, Yanne. The whole world.' And Carl's eyes shone with that dreamy look again.

I blame those British yachtsmen; they put the idea in Carl's head. The following afternoon, as we were sitting on the bluff overlooking Omaha Beach, Carl popped the question and the next morning over breakfast in a small hotel in Saint-Lô, I found myself agreeing to sail around the world with him. We decided the date and exact time of departure there and then; we would set sail on 15 June 2002, at 15.00 hours, giving us five years to buy a boat and learn to sail it well enough to circumnavigate the world and hopefully not drown in the process.

A day later, I took the train back to Sweden; my two weeks were up and I had to get back to work at the photo shop. I was considerably fitter than at the start of the trip; my thighs now worked like well-oiled pistons, easily capable of cycling 80 miles a day, but I was beginning to develop a real cycle gait and walked as if I were on my bike even when it was chained to the nearest lamppost.

As for Carl, he never got to Lisbon. In order to escape a horrendous coastal storm, he had to change direction and head inland. He never reached his dream city by bike. Not that it mattered to him.

Why not, you ask, after all his meticulous planning and preparation?

Because he was planning a new route, a better route. As he merrily pedalled his way around France and back up to Sweden, the crafty devil was working out how to reach Lisbon by sea.

Chapter 4
So We Bought a Boat...

'Y ou did *what?*' Carl's voice boomed down the line. I held the receiver away from my ear. 'You did *what?*' he repeated.

'I've bought our boat,' I said lightly.

'I thought that's what you said,' he boomed again. 'What the hell, Yanne?'

'Yeah, I know. But while you've been away, I've been doing some research and ...'

'Holy crap, Yanne. I've barely taken off my bicycle clips, got through the front door and kissed the wife and you tell me you've bought a boat! Couldn't you have waited until I got back from France?'

'Yes, but Calle, the demand for these boats is huge; they're advertised one day and gone the next. If we really want to learn to sail, we've got to get a boat.'

'Look, give me a couple of hours. I'll come over to your place and we can discuss it.' Carl didn't so much hang up the phone as throw it across the room.

I looked around the kitchen in dismay; I doubted I'd have time to clear up before he arrived. Since my divorce I'd been living alone in my three-bed-room house. It wasn't that I'd let the place go – in fact, I'm usually quite tidy – but while Carl was still cycling from vineyard to vineyard in France, I'd become gripped with a fever: sailing fever. Free of the responsibilities of married life, I'd been able to devote myself to searching for the perfect boat and how to sail around the world. The kitchen had become the centre of operations for our expedition, and I was in peril of being crushed by the piles of sailing literature that had gradually accumulated on every available surface. There were Swedish and English sailing magazines, together with stacks of textbooks entitled *Sailing Techniques, Manoeuvres and Seamanship* or *Better Wind Management* and, alarmingly, *Emergency Care at an Accident Site*: I was being very thorough. There were numerous adventure books: one on sailing in Antarctica, another about rowing across the Atlantic, not that we were going to do either but it didn't matter; as long as there was a body of water in the title, I devoured everything and anything about crossing it. I was a man obsessed and it wasn't pretty.

I hadn't, in fact, bought a boat, but was very close to doing so having found something that suited our requirements near perfectly. With an unnatural amount of adrenaline coursing through my veins after making our solemn pact in France, I'd returned to Helsingborg and immediately set about search-ing for a 30-foot sailboat. With only five years to our sail date, we couldn't af-ford to waste time training with a small dinghy. We'd agreed to invest around 200,000 krona (approximately £19,000 / $31,000) on a practice boat, as we called it. I knew Carl wouldn't have time to hunt for boats, what with his new job, so I set myself the task. It was a labour of love and like most en-deavours associated with that emotion, it was demanding, maddening and nearly drove me to tears and drink. No matter how many sailing magazines I leafed through or how many enquiries I'd made about boats I'd spotted on the internet, we still didn't have our own. It was frustrating to read of other people's sailing adventures when we, aspiring round-the-world sailors, were still two landlubbers without so much as a rubber dinghy. No sooner had I agreed to look at a prospective boat, than I got a call saying it had been sold to another buyer. I'd sulk and kick the sofa for a bit, then return to ploughing through the yachting magazines.

Carl arrived and I showed him into the kitchen. He looked round the room, lifted a bushy eyebrow and nodded thoughtfully.

'You've got sails for brains,' he said. 'So tell me about this boat.'

'It's already gone,' I sighed and explained to him how due to the popularity of 30-foot sailboats I'd already missed out on two.

'I see,' said Carl. 'What about a berth? Have you looked into that yet?'

'No,' I said dumbly.

'Just as well you haven't bought a boat then,' Carl snorted. 'If you had, we wouldn't have anywhere to put it. We'd better go down to the marina and sign up for a berth.'

Like many harbours, Helsingborg's north harbour, can be very picturesque: sailboats sway gently on the sparkling water; a gentle breeze ruffles flags and makes wires clink softly against white masts; the sea beyond the harbour wall flashes golden in the sunlight. On a fine day, the towers of Hamlet's Kronborg castle can be seen in Elsinore across the waters of the Öresund. Meanwhile on their side of the sound, the Danes have a view of Helsingborg's imposing red brick city hall, our thirteenth-century watch tower, and the marina's smart yacht club, a white two-storey structure built in the same architectural style as the newly finished residential buildings. Restaurants and bars bustle with tourists. It's no wonder thousand-piece jigsaw puzzles feature summer har-bour scenes. Ah yes, the idea of messing about in boats is very tempting in such a setting.

A different week in June and the picture is less appealing: boats rock alarm-ingly on dirty grey waves; wires and wet ropes whip mercilessly against metal; the churning sea throws turbulent waves over the protective harbour wall; the Danish coastline has disappeared under a thick veil of slanting rain and mist. Notice the lack of jigsaws featuring scenes like these; you'd get seasick just doing the edges.

It was on such a day that Carl and I had braved the elements, staggering from office to office to register for a berth. Standing in a puddle of water dripping from our jackets, it occurred to me that conditions might be worse at sea.

'Crap weather, eh Calle? Do you think it gets much worse out there?' I jerked my head towards the Öresund. Carl studied the floor – I think he was forming a carefully phrased lie when harbourmaster Peter Sandberg greeted us.

'*Hej!* What can I do for you?' he asked.

'We're planning to sail around the world,' Carl replied with the slightly puffed-up attitude of a master seaman.

'Really?' The harbourmaster's smile was sceptical. 'I don't believe anyone in the 100-year history of Helsingborg Yacht Club has ever done that.'

'Well, we're going to,' I said, watching the sceptical smile grow broader. I glanced at Carl for backup.

'We're quite serious,' Carl said solemnly. 'We set sail on 15 June 2002, at 15:00 hours. So we need a berth.'

'I see.' The Harbourmaster smirked some more, then rifled in a cabinet for some forms. 'So how big is your boat?'

'Um, as of this moment we don't have a boat.'

'You don't have a boat?'

'Not as of this moment, no.'

'And which moment do you think you'll have a boat?'

'We're not quite sure. The fact is that we don't know how to sail.'

'You don't know how to sail? Just how many of you are attempting this … excursion?'

'Just the two of us,' I chipped in, maintaining as much dignity as I could in the face of such obvious disbelief.

I thought the man might actually pop a blood vessel he laughed so hard. Carl and I waited patiently for his mirth to subside. The reaction to the announcement that two confirmed landlubbers were planning to circumnavigate the world was becoming all too familiar. When I'd told my father of my plans, instead of slapping me heartily on the back and saying, 'That's my boy,' he'd got down on the floor and offered to help look for my missing brain cells, after which he'd lain on the carpet and cried with laughter. This I'd found deeply hurtful, mostly because I'd never in my life seen him so vastly amused. Carl's experience had been much the same; far from the fury he'd anticipated on telling his wife of our decision, he'd been greeted with a roll of the eyes and the assertion that he had as much chance of sailing around the world as of shagging Heidi Klum. Was our mission so impossible? Did we appear so inept? I didn't understand it; even complete strangers thought we had a severe case of missing marbles.

With great effort Peter wiped a tear from his eye and gave us each a pen and a form.

'Thank you for that,' he said. 'It's been such a dull day.' He repressed a chuckle and pulled himself together again. 'Right then, I can register you for club membership here, but I can't arrange a berth for your ... um, boat. You'll have to see Gertrud Stigfors about that. She'll be most ... interested in your plans.'

We left Chuckles the harbourmaster to laugh his head off and stomped through the puddles to find Gertrud Stigfors' office.

'You're in luck,' Gertrud said as we dripped onto her office floor. 'I do have a few free berths, but I think there'll be a real scramble for them when the harbour buildings are finished. Now, how big is your boat?'

'We don't have one yet,' Carl answered.

'Oh?' Gertrud's expression was one of polite curiosity. 'But didn't you say you were going to sail around the world. I don't believe anyone from Helsingborg has ever attempted that.'

'Yes, but we have to learn to sail first, so we're looking for a 30-footer,' I replied candidly. For a moment there was a battle between amusement and concern on Gertrud's face. Good manners won and her expression was pleasingly neutral as we completed the forms, shook hands and left the office. It was only spoiled by the echo of her tinkling laughter as we walked down the hall.

'Well, that went pretty smoothly, considering...,' Carl said cheerfully. 'We're members of the yacht club and we've got our own berth.'

'Yes, but no one damn well believes we're really going to do this,' I said morosely. 'Only Anders is taking us seriously.'

Of necessity, my brother had been the first to hear about our expedition. As he and I ran a photo processing business together, I'd had to negotiate not just a bit of time off work, but three years. Anders could have been the maggot in the apple of our plans, but after lengthy discussion we'd finally agreed that I could take off three years for the circumnavigation after which he would take the same amount of time. Carl had also got the green light to take a sabbatical from work. Now, all we needed to do was buy a boat.

Not as easy as we'd thought despite our relatively healthy budget. After narrowly missing out on the second boat, I was beginning to despair. I'd driven over two hours to see a boat, which on arrival turned out to have been sold.

Furious at having just missed it, I drove like Jeremy Clarkson back to Helsing-borg. It was eight in the evening as I arrived back in the city. On the off chance, I dived into a large supermarket to check if their order of sailing magazines had arrived. They had; I grabbed one off the rack, paid and rushed back to the car where I immediately started scanning the for sale ads. There it was, a 30-foot Scampi, and the phone number was for Lund, only 20 miles away. I whipped out my phone and dialled the number. The owner Lars answered.

'Your boat still for sale?' I shouted down the phone. No time for formalities or pleasantries.

'It certainly is,' answered Lars. 'It's a ...'

'I'll take it,' I panted. 'Just don't sell it to anyone else.'

'Don't you want to see it first?' Lars asked. 'The boat's in Vikhög harbour.'

'I'll be down tomorrow. The name's Yanne Larsson. See you first thing to-morrow, Lars.' I was damned if I was going to lose this one.

'So you say you're going to sail around the world?' Lars asked, doubtfully. He looked at his yacht with the same expression people usually reserve for their dogs or their first crush. The look he gave us was one of deep suspicion, but then he had every right to be wary of two blokes with a carrier bag of cash who seemed overly keen to buy something they didn't know how to operate.

'Yes, that's the plan,' Carl answered.

'Really?' Lars said. 'You might find it a bit on the small size for a circum-navigation.'

'No, we're going to use this one just to practise sailing.'

Lars looked us up and down and stroked his chin thoughtfully. 'Isn't this a bit on the large size for learning to sail?' Size seemed immensely important to Lars.

'We're no spring chickens, so we thought we'd just jump in at the deep end,' Carl said.

'Yes, sink or swim, as it were,' I added, before realising my unfortunate choice of words.

'Hmm,' said Lars. After an agonising pause, he waved his hand in the di-rection of his first love and said with clear reluctance, 'I guess you'd better come on board then.'

Veteran sailors will scoff at a 30-foot sailboat, but to us this was a big ship. We stood on deck and took in the number of ropes, sails, wires, winches and bewildering things we had no idea existed on a boat or elsewhere. I was on the verge of saying something clueless like 'the sails are a pretty colour,' but opted instead for saying something tougher and cleverer, or so I thought. 'Yes, I'm glad to see there are sufficient ropes and ... things.'

Lars winced. 'You'll soon learn, they're not called ropes.'

'How the hell are we going to cope with all this?' I hissed out of the corner of my mouth to Carl. 'We don't even know what any of this stuff is called.'

'Oh, don't panic. We can manage this,' Carl answered with more confidence than he probably felt. Carl's bluffing is as easy to spot as a politician's fake smile, and he did rather spoil it by asking to see the bedrooms and the kitchen.

We went below where Lars showed us the berths, the saloon, a very small toilet designed for a contortionist and an even smaller galley. Neither Carl nor I had any idea whether the boat was in good order or a good price. I could have been buying the Hubble telescope for all I knew about boats despite having immersed myself in sailing literature for the past few months. But the boat matched our budget, so after we sat in the cockpit and deemed it 'comfortable enough,' moved the tiller back and forth a bit and knocked on the side of the hull – although what we expected to hear I don't know – I looked at Carl and said, 'Yup, this will make a great practice boat.'

'Okay then, we'll take it,' Carl said.

'We agreed on 200,000 krona, right?' Lars asked. I started to open the carrier bag of cash wishing I thought to put it in a briefcase; it would have looked slightly more professional and less like a street corner drug deal.

'Let's say 195,000 krona.' Damn it all! Carl always insisted on haggling the price down. He hated paying the full asking price.

'No way, she's worth 200,000,' Lars answered. He narrowed his eyes, studied Carl and drew a deep thoughtful breath. 'But I'll let her go for 197,000.'

I held my breath: so close and yet so far. There was a long pause. Carl glanced at me; I communicated a look saying 'don't screw this up.'

'It's a deal,' Carl said. With relief I started to count out the cash with as business-like a demeanour as is possible when taking notes from a supermarket carrier bag.

Lars laughed nervously. 'Hang about. I can't take great wads of cash. You'll have to transfer the money to my account. But we can sign the purchase agreement now.'

'Fair enough,' Carl said. The contract was signed and sealed by all three of us and we shook hands. At last we had our practice boat.

Which we had no idea how to sail.

I turned to Carl. 'How the heck are we going to get it from Lund to Helsingborg?'

Carl shrugged. 'We'll find someone to help us,' he said.

Ever the bloody optimist, Carl.

Chapter 5
Losing our Virginity
June 1998 – Four years to cast-off

I was 44 years old and still a virgin: a sailing virgin that is. The sum total of my experience on a body of water was the few occasions my father had forced me out on a sailboat some 30 years earlier. 'You'll love it once you get your sea legs,' he'd said jovially. I'd thrown up from the moment we cast off from the dock to the moment I was carried, wretched and empty of all bodily fluids, back onto dry land. My father, who had captained his own ship for the merchant Navy and rounded the Cape of Good Hope over 90 times during his career, couldn't understand why the fruit of his loins would go green around the gills at the thought of a boating lake. I would start heaving if the wind rippled through a large puddle. His hopes of my following in his footsteps and having a seafaring career were completely dashed. I'm not sure he ever got over it.

Carl claimed he had more sailing experience than I had, and even reckoned he had a cast-iron stomach and didn't suffer from seasickness. I pointed out to him that lounging on the deck of a friend's sailboat, doing bugger all except sipping a glass of wine and enjoying the sound of waves gently lapping against the boat's hull did not constitute real seafaring know-how. Nor was motoring a dinghy over to Denmark on a beer run on a breezy day a real test of adverse sailing conditions. No matter how long we sat at a quayside bar, drinking beer while keenly observing other boat owners casting off and sailing out of Helsingborg marina, we still had no clue how to sail. Meanwhile our newly purchased Scampi was still sitting in Vikhög harbour.

We were beginning to think we'd have to enrol in a summer sailing school in a local harbour, but we were both too proud to do so: too proud and too old, the average age of the participants being eight, all confidently scooting about in little Jollyboats. The solution finally presented itself via the photo shop.

Anders and I advertised the business on one of Helsingborg's radio stations; as loyal customers we were invited to a sponsored event on *EF Language*, the yacht which had just won the Whitbread Round the World Race for the Volvo Trophy. The invitees would form the crew and be taught how to sail the boat. It was a brilliant opportunity; fortunately, I managed to wangle an invite for Carl.

We looked forward to our first real excursion on the water with a mixture of terror and excitement. Our skipper, Greger Östman, an experienced sailor who'd been hired to captain *EF Language* round Sweden with her crew of customers, put us through our paces from the start. He rushed around the yacht shouting instructions at other members of the crew while Carl and I stood on the deck trying to look busy by retying our life jackets. Everyone seemed to know what they were doing except for us. It was becoming clear just how inexperienced we were.

'Right, you two! Hoist the gennaker!' he shouted.

'What the hell is a gennaker?' I mouthed at Carl. He shrugged at me.

'The clue's in the name,' Greger said, spotting our confusion. 'You know what a spinnaker is, right?' Well, vaguely. I'd heard it mentioned on the TV coverage of the Volvo Ocean Race and knew it to be a huge balloon type sail. 'Right, so a gennaker's a cross between a genoa and a spinnaker.' This would have helped if I'd known what the heck a genoa was. Wasn't it a city in Italy? Greger saw our blank expressions and chuckled. 'Heard of a foresail? A mainsail? A jib?'

'Heard of them, don't know what to do with them,' Carl answered.

'It's going to take us a while to get to grips with all this,' I said. 'We're new to sailing.'

'You don't say!' Greger said with a grin. 'No worries, you'll know your spinnakers from your gennakers by the time I'm through with you.'

By the end of the day's sailing, we knew that and much more: we learnt that a genoa was a type of foresail that sits at the bow, in front of the mainsail; that a jib was another sort of foresail and a genoa is much larger. We discovered that when the 300-square metre gennaker on *EF Language* was hoisted, the yacht would shoot off like a bullet in what seemed to be completely windless conditions, teaching us the difference between apparent wind and true wind. We learnt about various sailing methods; beating, reaching and running, jibing and tacking. We paid careful attention to our first sailing lesson trying to remember all the terminology.

But the real thrill, the one that sent tingles of raw pleasure down our spines, was when Greger let us steer the boat. I was first up to the helm. To say I was nervous is an understatement. Sweat droplets started to bead on my forehead, my stomach turned watery. I smiled weakly against my fear, gripped the huge wheel as if my life depended on it and tried to steer as little as possible. The last thing I wanted to do was crash a prize-winning yacht into one of the ferries crossing the Öresund.

'Relax,' Greger said. I was anything but. I could understand why women giving birth feel the urge to throttle their well-meaning husbands who tell them to 'just relax' as they endure contractions while something the size of a watermelon forces its way out of a hole where a biro-sized thing went in nine months before. I clung, white-knuckled, to the helm. 'See how elegantly she slices through the water,' Greger said, slapping my shoulder. 'You're doing great.'

I gradually loosened my vice-like grip on the wheel, let it slide through my hands a little, watched the waves break softly against the bow, took a glance at the coastline and felt the wind rush on my face as we shot through the water. Amazingly, I hadn't crashed, I wasn't going to crash. I could do this. 'Yes! This is the life!' I shouted to the air. Then I blushed scarlet with embarrassment; my exuberant cry to the elements was really a bit naff. But when Carl's turn came to steer, I could see by his expression that he felt the same thrill as I had and wanted to shout it out loud. We both heard the call of the sea and were keen to answer it.

After our initiation, we went to the pub closest to Helsingborg's marina and hung out with the rest of the crew, talking like old salts dropping sailing jargon and words we'd never used before. There we plied Greger with drink to the point where we felt bold enough to ask him if he would consider helping us sail our boat from Vikhög to Helsingborg.

'Sure, happy to help,' he answered casually. Carl and I were mighty relieved to know we'd have someone on board who knew what the hell to do.

'Good to see you guys got your sea legs so quickly,' Greger said as we clinked glasses. 'A lot of first-time sailors get quite seasick out on the ocean.'

Seasick? How could I have forgotten? Strangely, I hadn't felt the need to throw up once. The mind is a curious thing; it seemed that having set my mind to conquering my fear of sailing, I'd also mastered my seasickness, at least temporarily. Could it be I was cured? It was too much to hope for, but would certainly make sailing round the world a heck of a lot easier if I didn't have to perpetually hang over the rail feeding the fish.

Chapter 6
Landlubbers No More

July 1998 – Three years,
11 months to cast-off

Think of all the official documents one person generates in a lifetime: the fundamental acts of being born or dying require numerous forms to be filled and papers to be stamped. Then there are all the formalities of identity and nationality necessitating passports, ID cards and so forth. Ownership brings with it reams of paperwork: bank accounts, credit card applications, loan applications, mortgages, property deeds, bonds, tax forms, ad infinitum. Then there is the multitude of licenses we are obliged to own in our lives: a license to drive a car, get married, go fishing, own a dog, operate machinery, drive a forklift truck, set up a stall on a street corner or sell wine at the school quiz night.

But strangely, you don't need a license to sail a 30-foot or even a 64-foot yacht. Yes, you generally need some paperwork to prove the boat is yours, but sailing around the Swedish coast or further out to sea is open to all and doesn't require a special permit. The same is true of British waters. Passage down one of Britain's inland waterways, however, calls for a boating license or registration. And thankfully, most countries now insist on proof of having completed some kind of boat safety course. But generally speaking, any moron with some money can buy a boat and sail off without anyone in authority stopping to ask whether he has the first clue what he's doing.

Carl and I were those morons. The ex-owner, Lars patted his beloved Scampi farewell with a misty eye and waved us off with a mutter loud enough for all to hear that we would probably run aground ten miles out to sea, which we certainly would have done had Greger not been with us. Keen not to sink our 200,000 krona investment, we sailed our Scampi under Greger's careful instruction and finally moored her in our berth at Helsingborg marina.

We'd christened our sailboat *Albatross*. This was the name I'd given my first company, cunningly chosen so it would appear first in the yellow pages and other alphabetical business listings. I was rather proud of the name, until I saw Greger's frown when I told him.

'*Albatross*? Interesting name,' he said. 'But you do know that legend says an albatross is the manifestation of the restless soul of a drowned sailor. That's why the bird is considered a bad omen.'

'I don't believe in all that superstitious claptrap,' Carl said firmly. 'This *Albatross* will be the start of something lucky for two living landlubbers.'

'Yes, well, let's just get her to Helsingborg first,' Greger said. 'Remember, I'm not sailing the boat for you, so think of this as your first real lesson. If you do exactly as I say, we'll get *Albatross* home in one piece.'

Greger took position well back in the stern and shouted instructions to us. Initially still unsure of which sail was which and whether starboard was left or right. As we left Vikhög, Carl and I were insufferably pleased with ourselves by the time we arrived in Helsingborg's marina. We were proper boat owners now and had successfully completed our maiden voyage with our first sailboat.

Then Greger left, taking with him our new found confidence. We spent a week eyeing up *Albatross* and waiting for the perfect sailing conditions. They'd been perfect all week, but we were nervous. No, make that stomach-churningly terrified about sailing by ourselves. What Greger had taught us was still all we knew about sailing. We'd been practising some of the sailing jargon, so we now knew better than to talk about bedrooms and the kitchen but rather referred to them correctly as berths and the galley. We'd read that the collective name for everything below deck was the cabin, and where you sat and chatted was the saloon. We'd learned that the wooden stick you steered the boat with was called the tiller, whereas on a large boat it was the wheel – not that we'd got that far yet. We knew our port from our starboard, our stern from our bow, our forward from our aft. We'd learnt the names of the sails, understood the difference between ropes, cables and wires, lanyards and halyards, could discuss jib furling and reefing systems. We now referred to hatches and stowage lockers, and we never went to the toilet but always to the heads. We could talk the talk, but we still hadn't sailed a sail.

It was a Saturday in July and sailing conditions seemed perfect; an idyllic, sunny afternoon with a wind so light it was almost imperceptible, one that hopefully wouldn't blow us off course and into the path of the seagoing traffic making its way up the Öresund towards Norway. Waving desperately and screaming, 'Stop! For the love of God, stop!' to a large tanker bearing down on us while we were fumbling with pulleys and sails would be as effective as trying to put out a fire at an oil refinery with a watering can.

We'd decided we needed a cheat sheet. I'd found a useful guide in a sailing magazine which broke down sailing manoeuvres into six easy lessons, the pages of which Carl was taping up around the instrument panel in the cockpit. We did our best to ignore the amused or concerned looks other boat owners gave us as they walked down the finger quay to their own sailboats.

I suppose they had every right to look alarmed. If you think about it, it's astonishing that sailing without a license is legal. I mean, would you get into a car with someone who said, 'Well, I haven't exactly driven by myself before, but I had a friend who sat in the back and told me how to work the gears. And don't worry; look, I've got the first couple of manoeuvres, turning left and right, taped to the glove box. And lesson three on stopping – sorry, I believe it's called "breaking" – is handily stuck to the sun visor. Now if you could just pass me lesson one, I can find out how to start the ignition and be off.' Wouldn't you just get out of the car and walk home instead? You'd refuse to let that person out on the roads. You might go so far as to insist that the person had taken numerous hours of instruction or have some kind of paperwork to prove their ability to operate a road vehicle, some kind of license to drive, say? But not so for sailing.

'Looks good,' I said, glancing around the cockpit. 'Now all we do is lick a finger, hold it up to the wind to check which direction it's blowing, then cast off and go.' I laughed nervously, as did Carl. He bit off another length of tape and secured the last page to the side of the cockpit. If the lessons blew away we'd be royally screwed.

'I thought we only needed the first two lessons,' I said anxiously. We'd planned to beat out to the open sea and then run back, which, on paper, looked relatively simple.

'Best to be prepared in case we're blown off course. We might accidentally go further than we think and need the other lessons,' Carl said.

'What do you mean, "accidentally go further than we think"?' I said, my voice rising a panicky octave as pictures of us scuttling towards Iceland crowded my brain.'

'Right, you man the helm and I'll untie us,' Carl instructed ignoring my question.

'Hold on, Calle, what do you mean "accidentally"?'

'Forget it, Yanne. We're more likely to get stuck in irons and end up going backwards than getting to Denmark.'

'Going backwards!' I squeaked. 'Calle, maybe we should just stay in the harbour today, wait until we can find another experienced sailor to show us the ropes.' I think I feared death by embarrassment as much as by drowning.

Carl eyed me narrowly. 'Come on, Yanne, just remember what Greger taught us. We can do this.'

'I bloody well hope so,' I muttered. 'Otherwise we're in for a very expensive dunking.

With a frantically beating heart, I started the engine. Carl untied the mooring ropes and we motored out of the marina at the speed of a slug on tranquilizers. Once out of the harbour, I cut the engine. It was the moment of truth: time to set the sails. The wind was faint but against us. Carl raised the mainsail, then the genoa, by which time the "faint" wind was blowing over 15 miles an hour. I threw a panicky glance at lesson one.

'The mainsail's flapping in the headwind. Sheet it in, Calle.' He jumped to it, the wind caught the sail and *Albatross* cut swiftly through the waves. We were sailing. We were sailing beautifully. Holy crap, we were sailing really fast. The rushing of the wind was loud. Just a minute, the rushing of the water was louder. We were leaning. We were leaning heavily, far too heavily. I could feel the spray on the back of my neck. I frantically glanced at the pages to my right.

'Calle, we're heeling too much! Loosen the sail!'

'Don't panic. She won't go over,' he shouted back cheerfully.

'Capsize. It's bloody well called '*capzise*',' I screamed. Strange how when on the point of disaster, I insisted on getting the sailing terminology right. 'Just loosen the bloody sail like Greger taught us!'

'Don't worry, we won't go over unless we're hit by a really big wave.'

'*Capzise*! Look out. I'm coming about.' I threw the tiller away from me, the boom swung across, Carl ducked and threw himself over to the other side of the boat to pull in the genoa.

'What manoeuvre was that?' yelled Carl. 'Tacking or jibing?'

'No bloody clue. We'll look it up later,' I shouted back.

Without any real understanding of what we were doing or how we were doing it, *Albatross* was zigzagging out on the dark blue waters. Wary of those life-threatening ferries scuttling backwards and forwards between Sweden and Denmark, we tried another lesson; we'd barely gone a quarter of the two miles to Denmark – with a strong arm you probably could have thrown a stone as far as we'd sailed – but we decided to come about, after carefully scrutinising our magazine pages.

'Ready to come about?' Carl said. 'Right, as I understand it, we turn away from the wind and push the boom over by hand ..., I think. Worst case scenario, we get wet.' He shrugged.

I could think of far worse scenarios but followed Carl's instructions, and we found ourselves doing something akin to jibing. Then we consulted lesson two, running, and let out enough sail to get ourselves back to north harbour. The sail billowed out and *Albatross* shot across the waves.

'This calls for a beer,' Carl said and we toasted to a successful first expedition, albeit a rather grandiose word for sailing less than two nautical miles.

'Fantastic!' I exclaimed, ecstatic to be above water and dry. 'Let's do it again!' So we spent the afternoon merrily going back and forth across the same stretch of water, inching out a little further each time. Not quite fully fledged yachtsmen, but on our way. We became more competent and confident with each passing weekend, working our way through our magazine lessons. After taking *Albatross* half way to Denmark –which seemed like dicing with death at the time – we felt brave enough to go further afield and sailed to Svinbåda, a small harbour some 25 miles up the coast from Helsingborg. 'Our first passage,' as Carl called it, took us a mere three hours, but we felt as if we'd sailed halfway around the world. We were extremely pleased with ourselves and cracked open a bottle of champagne in celebration.

The idea of competing in a race never entered our minds, but I swear I was goaded into it by two friends, Fredrik and Anders. Why is it that I always rise to a challenge?

'So on a scale of one to ten, how crazy are you?' Fredrik asked me over the phone. 'You say you're going to sail around the world and everything you know about sailing is from a few pages of a magazine.' He sounded unbearably cocky, which as an experienced yachtsman I suppose he had every right to be, but I found it infuriating.

'Fredrik, you and Anders may think you know everything but let's face it, you're no more than a couple of amateurs who paddle about the little island of Ven and do a bit of flotilla sailing now and again. Carl and I are in a whole different league; we're serious circumnavigators, planning to achieve something you guys don't have the balls to do. But don't worry, we'll be glad to give you a few tips when we get back.'

Fredrik snorted derisively. 'Have you ever sailed around Ven, Yanne? Have you even sailed as far as Ven? It's not as easy as you think. How about a race? Round Ven and back.'

'We could take you,' I said. *Who was I kidding?*

'Really? I wouldn't put money on it.' Damn Fredrick, he thought he knew it all.

'Why not? Make it worth my while and Carl and I will show you how it's done.' *Was there no stopping me?*

'Okay, loser pays for dinner and drinks ...as much as the winners can eat and drink.'

'You're on!' I said. *Why was I saying this? Why?*

'Don't be daft. We'll let you practise for a couple more years, then we'll race you.'

'We'll race you next weekend.' I'd lost all control of my mouth.

'Forget it, it wouldn't be a fair race. You barely know your port from starboard.'

'Next weekend,' I insisted. *Why, why, why?*

Carl asked me the same question. 'A fine bloody mess you've got us in, Yanne,' he said. 'We don't stand a chance. On the other hand, as underdogs no one expects much of us. It might just give us an advantage.'

'You're right, we've no hope in hell of winning,' I said. 'We've barely had *Albatross* a month and we still don't know how to use the spinnaker. That's in lesson six.'

'Well, I hope you're ready to pick up the tab, Yanne,' Carl said sourly. 'Don't you know what the first rule of gambling is: don't bet on something you know nothing about.'

The following Saturday we sailed down to Råå harbour, a few miles south of Helsingborg to meet our competitors. It was a windy day: a great day for racing, if you knew what the heck you were doing.

'Missed lunch today,' Fredrik said with a smirk as we shook hands. 'So I'm going to be pretty hungry after the race.'

Albatross sailed sedately out of the harbour with a northerly wind, looking less like a racing vessel and more like a diminutive galleon. Meanwhile, Fredrik and Anders raised their spinnaker which promptly caught the wind, ballooned out and catapulted them across the water at a furious pace, leaving us glumly in their wake. We watched them disappear round Ven's northern headland, giving them an easy half mile lead.

'Brilliant,' growled Carl. 'Bloody brilliant!'

I hoped Fredrik and Anders had small appetites; I was resigning myself to having only soup.

One of my favourite fables is that of the tortoise and the hare. The hare, in this case, didn't stop and have a snooze under a bush, but either our adversaries thought themselves invincible or Carl and I completely clueless. As we rounded the island and Råå was again in sight, we saw that they'd chosen to continue sailing with a full spinnaker and had set a course straight for land.

'Why the hell are they still sailing with their spinnaker up?' I wondered out loud. 'Surely they can't put that much distance between us?'

Carl's face darkened with determination. 'Arrogance. It's pure bloody arrogance. Come on, Yanne, if we close haul we can take them.'

Carl leaned so far out of the boat I thought he'd disappear under the waves as we heeled *Albatross* into the closest course she'd ever sailed under our ownership. If we surprised ourselves, it was nothing compared to Fredrik and Anders who saw *Albatross'* determined beating and lowered their spinnaker to set a direct course towards Råå harbour. Fortunately, we picked up a favourable wind out on the open water and needed to tack fewer times than our opponents. We sailed into the harbour with a healthy 20-minute lead, startling Uffe, a friend of Frederik's, who was waiting on the quay with a bottle of champagne at the ready. He was speechless when he saw *Albatross* slip effortlessly along the quayside.

'What the ...? Where are they? Did they sink?'

We'd finished mooring and were sipping the champagne when Fredrik and Anders eventually came in. We raised our glasses in an ironic salute.

'Better late than never,' Carl said. 'Sailing certainly works up an appetite, doesn't it?'

'By the way,' I said, 'don't you know what the first rule of gambling is: don't bet on something you know nothing about.'

That evening we made the ferry crossing between Helsingborg and Elsinore several times as we dined in the ferry's restaurant working our way through the menu and the wine list. By the time we'd racked up a 3,000 krona bill, we decided we'd punished Fredrik and Anders enough. They were gracious losers, picked up the tab and toasted to our beginner's luck.

'You know with your dumb luck, you just might manage to sail around the world,' Anders said, as we sipped our brandies and watched the sun sink, turning the sea golden and the sky pink. Sweden's short summer would soon come to an end and with it the sailing season. After our first brief taste of sailing Carl and I were hooked. It seemed we had overcome our fears and our seasickness, and we were keen to sail further afield and learn more. Carl and I were looking forward to concentrating on the theoretical side of sailing; we had enrolled for a skipper course in the autumn so we would have some idea of what we were supposed to do.

Beginner's luck wouldn't last long out on the Atlantic.

Chapter 7
The Things we do for Love

September 1998 – Three years, nine months to cast off.

According to my school reports, I wasn't the keenest student in class. My favourite subject as a schoolboy was woodwork because I wasn't required to commit anything to memory or do any homework. Carl, on the other hand, was something of a whiz kid at maths. Nevertheless, our different strengths were to prove complementary; I was pretty handy and could make repairs on board, and Carl would be able to calculate our position on the maps and charts once we were out on the open ocean.

I wasn't overly keen to recapture the days of the old schoolyard, but both Carl and I were aware of how inexperienced we were. Sure, we could fumble our way up the Swedish coast and back, but if we wanted to sail around the world and come back with our yacht and bodies in more or less the same condition as when we'd left, we had to hit the books. Unfortunately, it would take a couple of years to plough through all the courses we'd elected to do. We'd signed up for long distance courses to study the Coastal Skipper and Yacht-master Certificates; we were also taking a marine radio course and the SSB (Single Side Band Radio) certificate, and we would become marine mechanics, learn astronavigation and meteorology. Interesting though these courses were, it was tedious having to sit buried in textbooks every night knowing that *Albatross* lay bobbing on the water lonely and unmanned until spring.

A Swedish winter, however, is not conducive to sailing, even in Helsingborg where the weather is infinitely milder than in Stockholm, 350 miles away, where the waters of the lakes and inlets are still frozen into early May. Kiruna, the country's northern-most city in Lapland, is another 600 miles on from Stockholm as the crow flies, not that a crow would fly there as its wings would freeze and drop off. Kiruna's average daily temperature in January is minus 11 degrees Celsius, but can plummet to a bone chilling minus 21 degrees Celsius. Visitors to the city are drawn for the spectacular views of the northern lights, running with the huskies, and a stay in the Ice Hotel, a 60-room hotel which, as the name suggests, is built entirely of ice, from the walls to the furniture. In fact, so many people burn – if that is the right word – to experience eating and sleeping in subzero temperatures that the hotel website now boasts a small ice hotel in the summer offering "cold accommodation all summer long." I confess I have never understood the appeal, but then I'm the breed of Swede who regards skiing not as a sport but as a faster means of getting down a mountainside to the *après ski* activities.

We have our fair share of chilly spells in Skåne, when the Öresund ices over and the temperature can drop to minus 20 degrees Celsius, which is a cold so extreme that the tiny hairs in your nostrils freeze. As soon as you re-enter a warm environment, a mini thaw starts in your nose causing your nostrils to drip water onto the carpet. Yet, you'll still find people jogging along the seafront in deepest winter. As we airily say in Sweden, 'there's no such thing as bad weather, only bad clothing.' Despite this positive attitude to the inhospitable elements, we're still accused of being moody and pessimistic, but that's those northern Swedes for you. We southern Swedes are far more jovial, maybe because of our relative proximity to the Mediterranean. It may surprise you to learn that according to the World Happiness Report of 2013, Sweden ranked as the second happiest country in the world, which gave me a long and hearty laugh.

The straits between Sweden and Denmark no longer freeze over completely – the constant flow of ocean-going traffic prevents this – but several times over the centuries the Öresund has iced over. The Swedes and the Danes have been at each other's throats for centuries – we're rather like the English and the French in that regard – but a much narrower strip of water separates our counties. Political control of the Öresund has been an important issue in our histories. Subsequently one country has always been trying to control the other, with Denmark for the most part on the losing end. Between 1521 and 1814, there were 11 Dano-Swedish wars. The winter of 1658 was so cold that the Swedish army was able to walk across the frozen straits to Copenhagen. The citizens of the city woke up one morning to find themselves surrounded and the Swedish flag flying from city wall. Knowing the Danes, they probably shrugged and went back to sleep. Their long-term resentment, however, at the use of such a sneaky tactic may explain the existence of an ancient Danish law which states that if a Swede walks over the frozen straits to set foot on Danish soil, a Dane is permitted to beat him with a stick. Harsh but fair, I suppose, although the Danes really should have stopped sulking about being invaded by now.

During Carl's and my winter of discontent, I continued to devour books on sailing, circumnavigation or any form of paddling across a body of water. That winter was possibly as miserable as the one in 1658, making the following April's spring seem all the more glorious. With the lengthening spring days we could at long last participate in the evening regattas in the straits and finally take *Albatross* out at the weekends. We sailed across to Hornbäck, Elsinore and Gilleleje on the Danish side of the Öresund and along the Danish coast where we had cycled on our way to France the year before.

We'd had the Scampi for nearly a year when I started browsing through the sailing magazines on the hunt for a bigger boat. Although our departure date wasn't for another three years, I couldn't resist looking out for my dream boat. I can only compare my obsession to that of a woman who spends years searching for the perfect wedding dress before she's even met the man she eventually marries. It's more or less the same degree of insanity.

I knew exactly the boat I wanted, or rather we needed. Greger had advised us that the best boat for a circumnavigation was a Swedish built Hallberg-Rassy, the Mercedes of all yachts, known for it its quality and clean lines. The company had won numerous awards in the long distance cruising category, and the CIA had allegedly used a Hallberg-Rassy to spy on the Soviet Union in the Bering Straits outside Alaska in the 1980s. They were reliable cruising boats and unlikely to sink in the middle of the Atlantic unless we were very unlucky or completely incompetent.

I read the boat reviews with growing excitement and drooled over the various models on the Hallberg-Rassy website, lingering lustfully over luscious photos of elegant cruising vessels cutting crisply through exotic waters. These were gorgeous boats with sleek lines and solid hulls. If I glanced at other boats – and I admit, I sometimes did - it was not to be unfaithful, but only to confirm that a Hallberg-Rassy was truly the one. I'd also read a fascinating story on the website about yachtsman John Neal who owned a 42-foot Hallberg-Rassy with which he sailed round the world seven times. That, I decided, was the kind of boat we needed. I nearly burst into tears when I saw the price: to say it was beyond our budget was like saying Buckingham Palace was a bit on the expensive side for a town house. But bless the Hallberg-Rassy owners for adding a link to their website for pre-owned boats. I hit that link so many times over the course of the following six months I developed repetitive strain injury of the index finger and would find my hands twitching in my sleep.

Then in December, the miracle of Christmas came true. I rang Carl barely able to speak with excitement.

'Calle! I've found her! I've found her and she's beautiful. I can't wait for you to see her.'

'Oh, god.' Carl gave an audible groan. 'Not again. Yanne, how many times have I told you – just because you sleep with a woman, doesn't mean you're in love.

'No! I've found the boat!'

'We've got a boat.' Carl was confused. 'What do you mean? Did you lose *Albatross*? What the ...?'

'No, I've found the boat we're going to sail round the world in.'

'You're out of your mind. We've got more than three years before we head off.'

'Calle, we can't wait until the day we cast off to buy the right boat. Plus we'll need time to get to know her and work on her. Don't you think we ought to understand the boat inside and out before we attempt to cross the North Sea or the Atlantic?'

'Fair enough, I see the logic in that,' Carl said. 'So where is she?'

'In Germany.'

'I haven't got time to go to Germany this side of Christmas.'

'Calle, we'll lose this boat if we don't act quickly. I'm telling you, she's the one.'

'All right. Send me the link. I'll have a look at the photos.'

After studying the photos online, Carl agreed with me. She was a beautiful 42-foot ketch and as far as we could judge the only wart on her was the dodgy finish on the deck. As Carl couldn't make the trip with me to meet the German owner, I asked a friend, Bengt Larsson, to accompany me. What he didn't know about yachts wasn't worth knowing, and we valued his advice. We'd been very lucky buying the Scampi as blindly as we had, but this time the stakes were much higher, as was the price tag which was just shy of 1.5 million krona. Just to put this in perspective, the average monthly wage in Sweden at that time was around 21,000 krona.

Bengt and I drove down to Borgstedt, a small town located on the canal west of Kiel. There, we met the owner, Jürgen, who showed us where the ketch was neatly parked together with a hundred or so other boats in a huge hall. Jürgen watched as Bengt methodically inspected the hull, running his hands over the surface like a doctor examining a patient, pursing his lips and uttering the odd 'hmm' every now and again. Then he climbed on deck and examined every corner with the thoroughness of a forensic scientist.

'Flashlight,' he muttered to me. As I passed it to him, I half expected him to snap on a pair of surgical gloves. I, meanwhile, was raving like a lovesick Romeo about how beautiful she was. Yes, I'm a shallow man and I was attracted to her immediately. I sat in the enormous cockpit enjoying huge flights of fancy: Captain Larsson mans the helm, heroic Captain Larsson braves the stormy oceans, handsome Captain Larsson laughs in the face of the formidable Atlantic. Ha, ha, ha. I was practising my heroic, handsome look when Jürgen climbed on board. He coughed and gave me an odd look.

'Want to go below and check her out?' he asked.

We carefully stepped down the ladder into the cabin. Immediately to the left was a galley complete with gas stove and oven. A couple of feet in front of the stove was a small work area to lean against if you were cooking in gusty weather. The fittings, trim and stowage were all in a rich glossy mahogany. It felt as warm and comforting as a cocoon. In the middle of the cabin was a table that could be opened to provide more area for guests and seating that could easily be converted into beds once the table had been cleared. Small lamps, clocks and barometers were mounted along the walls and a large ship's bell hung in the galley. There was a work space for a navigation system and a computer. In the forward cabin were a berth, shower and toilet; the larger aft cabin had the same. This was the most beautiful and desirable boat I'd yet seen, and I wanted her with a keen lust I'd felt only a few times in my 44 years.

After a final inspection of the engine, Bengt turned to me. I held my breath; I wanted him to like her as much as I did.

'She's in fabulous shape, almost virgin condition. The engine room is as clean as an operating theatre.' *Oh, be still my beating heart!*

I called Carl immediately. 'Calle, she's bloody fabulous.'

'Yeah, and the boat?'

'Ha, ha. No, Bengt's checked her over. She's a fantastic boat. Just what we need, two berths so there's plenty of space for us to live comfortably. Bengt reckons she's strong and stable enough to handle whatever the Atlantic throws at us.'

'I don't know, Yanne. I still think it's too early to buy another boat.' My heart sank like a stone. 'Anyway, how are you going to fund your half of her? Can you put up that kind of money at the moment?'

My heart plummeted further at the reminder of the money. How was I going to find 750,000 krona? No bank would give me that kind of loan for a sailboat. My dream was slipping away. A sacrifice was called for if I was going to fulfil my ambition. I glanced again at the ketch. She was a beauty. Ah, what a fool will do for love.

'I'll sell the house,' I blurted out.

'What? Yanne, are you nuts?'

'No, I'll do it. I'll sell the house.'

'But where the hell will you live?'

'On the boat! I'll be a liveaboard.' I was roaring with excitement, a fire beating in my chest with the thrill of the idea. 'That way I'll be able to save enough money for the trip.'

There was a very long pause. I waited, after all Carl hadn't seen her and had to take my word on trust.

'Calle, it's our dream, so I'm willing to make the sacrifice.' I packed my voice with as much pleading as possible.

After a decade or two, Carl finally answered.

'Okay, Yanne. If you're really sure, then we'll buy the bloody boat. But try to get that German to varnish the deck. And beat down the price as far as you can. Only a fool pays the asking price.'

After the obligatory bargaining, I managed to haggle the price down a bit, but Jürgen frowned and shook his head at my suggestion that he varnish the deck – every experienced yachtsman knows that you don't varnish teak, but that was just one of the many things we didn't know. The slightly scuffed deck was a mere detail; we'd just spent an eye-watering 1.5 million Swedish krona, (approximately £113,000/$180,000), a huge amount to us. And I'd just agreed to trade my home for a completely different one. The question was, would I be able to sell the house in time to secure payment for our dream boat?

Chapter 8
And So We Bought a Bigger Boat

March 1999 - Three years, three months to cast-off

'Are you stupid or clinically retarded?' my father asked when I broke the news to my parents. Ah, not quite the reaction I'd hoped for.

'It's the only way to fund the boat. Surely you can see that,' I said. I'd guessed they weren't going to break out the champagne, but I hadn't expected them to be quite so negative about my selling my worldly possessions and living on a boat for the next three years.

If my parents took it hard, my girlfriend was even less enthusiastic. If you've ever tried to explain something to a woman using the line, 'It's me, not you,' you'll know how well that goes when you find yourself with your cheek burning from a well-aimed slap or the resounding slam of a door. Monika blinked at me for a moment.

'You're selling everything? The house? The car? And all your furniture?'

'Well, there's not much point in having any furniture if you haven't got a house to put it in, and I can hardly fit an oak dresser on a sailboat, can I?' I attempted a light hearted chuckle. Monika didn't chuckle with me.

'Listen, Yanne, I accept that you want to sail around the world, but now you're going to live on the damn boat for ..., well, for how long exactly? Forever?'

I'd told Monika of my intention to circumnavigate the world on our first date, which happened to be only a week after Carl and I had agreed on our plan. Come to think of it, my opening pickup line must have been on the unconventional side. 'Hi. Fancy having dinner with me next week? Oh, and just so you know, I'm planning to sail around the world, so I'll be a bit busy for a while and I'm not planning any long-term commitments.' I don't think Monika had ever fully believed I would go through with it, or maybe she'd quietly hoped to talk me out of it when I fell for her charms. Unfortunately, she hadn't realized how stubborn I was: I make a mule with a bad attitude appear compliant.

On reflection, I could appreciate that I was no longer the catch I had been when we'd first met. In fact, when I'd announced my plans to live on our new

Hallberg-Rassy, once we'd brought her from Germany to Helsingborg, many friends had wondered at my sanity. 'What the hell?' they muttered to each other. 'Why would a middle-aged man sell his house and possessions to live like a hobo on a boat at the marina?' People excuse, even encourage, this kind of behaviour when you're young, but find it cause for the therapist's chair when society deems you old enough to know better. But nothing was going to deter me from my goal, least of all people's opinions. Nevertheless, I didn't half get an earful of what everyone thought.

As soon as Jürgen agreed to sell the ketch to us, I advertised both the Scampi and the house for sale. The boat sold remarkably quickly; after only 30 minutes on the Swedish Boat exchange and mart homepage, an Austrian fellow named Helmut rang to buy it. The deal was done and my share of the money was deposited in the bank.

Selling the house proved more difficult: January went by without anyone asking to view it; February was agonizingly silent, and we were well into March before the estate agent finally rang me saying he had a potential viewer. I was at my wits end; everything depended on my selling the house, and the owner of the Hallberg-Rassy wouldn't hold her for much longer. I watched as the couple critically looked round my three-bedroom home. He stood with his arms folded, looking completely uninterested, while she opened all the cupboard doors with an air of faint distaste and examined the grout in the bathroom with a wrinkled-up nose. I almost fell over backwards when after no words between them, the woman turned to me and said, 'We'll take it.' The relief was so immense I nearly kissed her. I was another step closer to my goal.

On a cold day in early April, Carl and I set off in a minibus for Germany to collect my new home. We'd assembled a six-man crew of "believers" – friends who had faith that we could fulfil our dream. We were a motley but enthusiastic bunch: our mate Magnus would captain the yacht back for us, as he was the only person who'd sailed a vessel of this size before; then there was Andreas who'd spent many hours sailing with his parents and more importantly could work the GPS; there was Jan, a die-hard boat connoisseur; my brother Anders had joined us, as had Monika, who I hoped would see the folly of my ways once she'd spent some time with the other love of my life; lastly, there was Lennart, our minibus driver. What we lacked in experience and sailing know-how, we more than made up for in optimism and tuneless singing as the minibus rolled towards Kiel.

Jürgen was in the middle of launching the ketch as we arrived. As Lennart pulled the van over, I felt prickles of panic. What if Carl hated her? What if I'd made a horrible mistake?

We all piled out of the minibus and strode over to the quayside.

'Is this it?' Carl asked. I nodded mutely. He looked her up and down while I waited anxiously.

'Bloody hell!' he finally exclaimed, turning to me. 'Yanne! What have you done?' The blood froze in my veins. *Oh crap! What had I done?*

'That's not a sailboat!' Carl roared. He was in full throttle. 'That's a huge mother of a ship!' He walked her length, put his hands on his hips and stared up at her bow in awe. 'That's one hell of a fabulous ship! How on earth am I going to sail this mother by myself? What kind of speed can she do? What's her sail area?' I felt a smile steal slowly across my face. Carl liked her, confirmed by the fact he was talking without leaving any gaps. 'Yanne, can we really sail her? Seriously? Me? And you? I mean ...do you know what I mean?'

Relief swept over me like a cool breeze. Carl understood how I'd been swept off my feet. 'A stunner, isn't she?'

He punched my shoulder. 'I get it now. We make the greatest sacrifices in the name of love. Let's see her from the inside.' He admired all the features that had attracted me, rang the ship's bell and joked that I could ring mealtimes with it. He tested the berths, stood in the shower and opened and closed all the lockers. He stroked the interior mahogany trim and inspected the pristine engine.

'Well done, Yanne. Now this is a boat for life. This is home,' Carl said.

'Yup. I feel at home already,' I said.

'Just as well, this'll be your primary residence for the next six years.'

We both climbed on deck and on to the quayside again to admire her. Jürgen glared fiercely at us; he'd just grasped that we'd never sailed a boat of this size. Yet, here we were clambering all over his beloved ketch like it was an adventure playground. We were beginning to appreciate that boat owners were more protective of their yachts than mother tigers of their cubs. Jürgen wore the brooding look of the man who was reconsidering his decision. Carl tried to diffuse the tension of the situation, after all we'd only secured the boat with the deposit; the final payment hadn't yet changed hands, and Jürgen could still refuse to sell.

'How about we toast the deal with a glass of snaps?' Carl said bringing a bottle from the minibus with all the ceremony of bringing forth a peace pipe.

'Okay,' Jürgen warily agreed, 'but you'll have to help me rig the sails as per the agreement.'

This took the best part of the day. Nevertheless, it was an exceptionally good experience, as it gave us the chance to learn what all the wires and cables were for. When the mizzen was up, Carl rubbed his hands together and announced it was time to raise the Swedish ensign.

Jürgen gave him a look that clearly suggested he hadn't just fallen off the boat. 'You can only raise your flag when the cheque has cleared. The money must be in the bank,' he insisted dryly.

Mobile phones came out of pockets and numbers were dialled. I endured another tense moment: I was still waiting for the money from the sale of the house to be transferred. Once all parties had confirmation of payment, Jürgen gave a brief nod. The German ensign was lowered and Sweden's blue and yellow was hoisted as I popped the cork on a bottle of champagne. The boat was finally ours. More importantly, it signalled the end of my vagrant status: I had somewhere to live again.

'We intend to rename her,' I said to Jürgen once the Swedish flag safely confirmed the ketch was ours. 'We're going to call her *Albatross*.'

'What's wrong with the name *Schnubb*?' he asked with a frown.

Everything was wrong with the word *Schnubb*, but I didn't want to offend him by saying so. Instead I explained that as our first boat, *Albatross*, had been lucky for us, we wanted to use the same name for the sailboat with which we would circumnavigate the world.

'Yes, but the albatross was considered an unlucky omen for sailors, so in my opinion this is not a good name,' he insisted, clearly not concerned about offending Carl and me.

The following morning, the crew was mustered; the seven of us had to get *Albatross* home in one piece, although Jürgen intended to sail with us as far as Kiel as a final farewell. My stomach still lurched to think that Carl and I would have to handle a 42-foot yacht in treacherous oceans and wild weather. My father had a point when he'd feared for my sanity. Although our crew had people with more experience than ourselves, Carl and I needed to learn the ropes – the etymology of the expression was becoming abundantly clear to me – by doing most of the sailing ourselves. As I took the helm, I glanced at Carl who was dealing with the moorings and wondered if he felt as shaky as I did. The wind was blowing a brisk 30 miles an hour – force six on the Beaufort scale – as we sailed down the Kiel Canal.

'Shit! She's a big boat, all right,' I shouted. 'After the Scampi, it's like driving a double-decker bus.' Our second *Albatross* was reaching so much it felt as if she would dip her mainsail in the water. Everyone but Jürgen laughed; his doubts about our ability to take his beloved ketch around the world were written on his face. As he left us at the last lock on the canal, his parting words were, 'Sail very, very carefully.' I wasn't sure if he was talking to the crew or the boat.

In Kiel we made a booze run, loading *Albatross* so much she heeled at an angle of 20 degrees. We were prepared to take the risk as alcohol is extremely expensive in Sweden where a trip to *Systembolaget* – the government owned chain of liquor shops – once carried the same social stigma as popping into a local brothel. Sweden is historically part of the vodka belt and enjoys its binge drinking weekends as much as Britain, but our well-meaning government would like to cure us of this. Subsequently, any alcohol over 3.5 percent proof may only be purchased from *Systembolaget*. Prices for wine and spirits are toe-curlingly high and driving in excess of the legal blood/alcohol limit of 0.02 percent is punishable by firing squad – well, not quite, but I think some politicians are keen to propose this. Hence, you see Swedes panic buying when abroad, running amok in German supermarkets with trolleys piled high with bottles of hard liquor and scoffing liqueur chocolates.

Once we'd bought our supplies, we set a course for Denmark where we planned to stop off at three different harbours en route to Helsingborg. The April wind was perfect for putting our Hallberg-Rassy through a few paces. The boat was clearly in a different league from the Scampi and performed like the master-crafted vessel she was, slicing with ease and elegance through 10-foot waves. When the wind calmed, so did we, relaxing our pace to eat open faced sandwiches, drink beer or sip whisky. Carl and I were grinning so much our faces hurt; this was the life we'd imagined: a life of simple pleasures out on the open water. As we approached the suspension bridge spanning the Great Belt strait between the Danish islands of Zealand and Funen, we gathered the crew on deck. The bridge (not to be confused with the Öresund Bridge which features in the popular crime series *The Bridge*) is part of the 11-mile long fixed link across the channel, comprising of two bridges and a tunnel. It is a marvel of Danish engineering, boasting the world's third longest span at just under one mile and pylons that stretch 833 feet into the sky. The bridge is said to produce the most astounding echo, so the eight of us stood on deck and yelled long and loud to test the rumour. Carl and I grinned again at each other as we were rewarded with the echo of our joyous roar that followed *Albatross* as she slid out under the other side.

We continued our journey home exploring the features of our new boat; we tested the spinnaker which billowed out magnificently in the breeze, making *Albatross* flit over the water like a dragonfly. We tried our hand at night sailing – something Carl and I had been nervous about. We meandered merrily from harbour to harbour, stopping at the small Danish harbours of Spodsbjerg, Kartemunde and Gillileje, where we enjoyed new views, hot showers and good meals made all the more satisfying for having worked up a "sailor's hunger."

'This is what it's all about,' Carl said, as he poured generous glasses of Danish snaps and we surveyed the view. 'New destinations, new experiences, new people, new languages, new cultures. And I think this is the boat to take us there.'

I agreed with him; our three-day sail from Kiel to Helsingborg confirmed we'd picked the perfect boat; she responded well, she felt secure, she was already feeling like home: the realization of our goal was beginning to look more like reality and less like insanity.

Although we tried to affect modesty, both Carl and I must have been intolerably puffed with pride as we sailed our bigger and better *Albatross* into Helsingborg's harbour. Friends were waiting for us with champagne. Members of the yacht club stood on the bridge, some speechless and some envious as they caught sight of our new yacht.

'They've completely lost the plot,' someone said loudly.

I niftily navigated *Albatross* to the quayside, and Carl was ready with the mooring ropes. Fortunately, we didn't trip over anything or disgrace ourselves so we looked relatively competent. As we tied up, we noticed Helmut, the Austrian who'd bought the Scampi from us, struggling to rig the boat.

'Hi Helmut,' Carl said, waving cheerfully. 'Need some help?'

'No, I'm fine thanks,' Helmut said superiorly and loosened a strut. He was the type who having read something thought he knew it all and had been aghast when I'd told him we'd learnt to sail by trial and error rather than by theory and practice.

'Umm, Helmut, are you sure you wouldn't like some help there?' I'd noticed a potential problem.

'No. I know what to do, thank you.'

Now, it could have been our fault for distracting him, but our Austrian friend was about to make himself look like a total arse; he'd loosened the wrong strut with the result that the mast started to topple in the direction of the neighbouring boat.

'Shit!' Helmut screamed.

I looked at Carl. Carl shrugged. 'He said he knew what he was doing.'

One of Helmut's friends on the quay saw the panic and rushed along to help, but for him to climb on board, Helmut had to bring the boat closer to the landing-stage. He threw the motor into first gear, except that it wasn't first gear: it was reverse. As the friend stepped towards the boat, it shot away from him, and he dropped like a stone into the water. Chaos ensued; the friend thrashed about in the brink, and Helmut shouted Teutonic curses while trying to hold up the mast. The *Albatross* crew helpfully enjoyed the spectacle, doubling up and crying with laughter.

'Are you sure you don't need any help, Helmut?' Carl managed to ask without out smirking.

We hooted some more, pulled ourselves together and then fished the friend out of the water with a boat hook. Then we went on board the Scampi to help finish the rigging, which to his credit Helmut allowed us to do with good grace. A few moorings over, *Albatross* rocked regally on the water.

'Just wait till we get her out on home waters,' Carl said, with clear pride in his voice. 'We'll show them we're capable of sailing round the world.'

'Absolutely,' I said. 'We'll show them we're not half as stupid as we look.'

Chapter 9
Liveaboards
June 1999 – Three years to cast-off

After 15 years of living in a three-bedroom house, it was liberating to move down to Helsingborg harbour and onto *Albatross*. To be honest, I was tired of home ownership and all the work and worry that go with it. Most of all I was glad to finally be free of debt: you don't know the true meaning of poverty until you own your first home. Call me a cynical man, but we're all taken in by the Western dream of property ownership, as I had been when I'd left Germany and had put my foot on the first rung of that misery called the property ladder.

'The Swedish dream ruins many a marriage,' I would moan to Carl over a beer.

'Well, it certainly seems to be the ruin of yours,' Carl said dryly. 'You're on your second divorce.'

'There's never any money left for love; it's just work and drudgery and nothing else. Society traps you in a spiral of debt leaving you no time to do anything other than worry about the next pay check, the mortgage or the blasted car payments.'

So my shoulders felt lighter when I sold the house and the BMW. I was finally relieved of the burden of debt that had weighed upon me for over half my life. Not that moving house had been a picnic; I'd had to get rid of 15 years' worth of accumulated junk so that my belongings and I could fit in a sailboat measuring 42 by 12 feet. Renting a storage facility was too expensive for the possessions I wanted to keep, so I invested in a small one-room flat in the centre of Helsingborg where I could store all my boxes and some furniture I'd inherited; after all one day I would return and need somewhere to live – at least, if I didn't fall overboard and get eaten by sharks, captured by pirates or served up as the dish of the day by a cannibalistic tribe on a remote island in the South Pacific. I'd been alarmed to read that all three eventualities were not as unlikely as they sounded.

I moved onto *Albatross* with only the essentials: some cooking utensils, towels, a few books and my music collection of Frank Sinatra and Dean Martin. Yes, Frank and Dean are essentials. I threw half my clothes in a packing box and the other half I took with me.

I loved life at the harbour. I swopped gardening, cleaning and plumbing for working or taking it easy on *Albatross*. Instead of coming home from work and slumping on the sofa in a semi-coma in front of the mindless drivel on TV, I read more, learnt more, relaxed more. My life was more meaningful and harmonious. I was experiencing real happiness for which I didn't need the status symbols of an expensive lifestyle or a high-priced car. My contentment lay in looking forward to a life on the open sea, seeing the world and doing nothing more strenuous than lying in a hammock and reading a good book. Notice how completely I'd managed to weed out any thought of how much work there is to operating and sailing a boat around the world. But we'll get to that later. In the meantime, I was as blissfully ignorant of all that as a toddler is of paying taxes.

That summer, Helsingborg harbour was teeming with people as it always is during the warmer months. Swarms of Danes and other further-flung travellers gathered to party in the city, attracted by the cheaper prices offered on our side of the Öresund. There was always something going on at the harbour, and my "home" life was more rewarding than it had ever been before. Friends would often pop down to *Albatross* with a bottle of wine, and we'd sit in the cockpit and talk about everything from philosophy to politics.

But come the winter, the visitors died off like bluebottles. By the end of October, of the hundred berths in Helsingborg's north harbour, only four regulars were left; we were the so-called losers who lived fulltime on our boats: the liveaboards. We were a small family for each other, and I was its newest member.

"Wealthy Pete" – Rike-Per as we called him in Swedish – was the longest harbour resident; he'd been living on his boat for six years when I moved in. In his fifties and almost completely destitute, he displayed the most positive attitude of anyone without financial security I'd ever met, saying that he was "rich in experience."

Another harbour dweller was Martin, a divorcé in his late thirties, who'd moved onto his boat after his wife had kicked him out. The divorce had hit him hard, emotionally and financially, so he'd had no choice but to become a liveaboard. His four-year-old daughter Kajsa visited him weekly and thought it was cool that dad's home was on the water. Martin and I got along particularly well, and we spent a lot of time together, often entertaining Kajsa whom I promised to send a postcard from every country we visited.

The third resident was from northern Sweden. Ove was a white-haired genius aged 60; he was to teach me everything there is to know about boat mechanics. His boat *Freedom* was both his home and his workshop, a sloppy craft, 43 feet long with at least two tons of nuts, bolts and other unidentifiable metal bits scattered everywhere. It was a marvel it was still afloat. Ove was as poor as a church rat, as we say in Swedish, and as battered as his boat, but he could fix, weld and repair anything, as his home testified. He'd sailed from harbour to harbour and finally wound up in Helsingborg where he earned enough to keep him and his boat afloat by doing odd jobs around the harbour.

Living at the harbour certainly wasn't like sleeping under bridges like a tramp, particularly as being members of the yacht club we had the clubhouse at our disposal and it was here we spent our winter evenings. Helsingborg's marina clubhouse wasn't some dilapidated old shed so typical of some small harbours, but a spanking new building with all mod cons. Just inside the entrance was the harbourmaster's office, further down off the same corridor were the toilets, shower rooms and a sauna. On the floor above was a fully equipped kitchen and a superb living room with floor to ceiling windows offering fantastic views across the water towards Helsingør and Kronborg castle. The furnishings were homely: several tables were arranged around a huge open fireplace in the middle of the room, there were a couple of sofas, a TV and desktop computers. The knickknacks were typically yacht club themed: pennants from visiting boat clubs, model boats and artificial flowers decorated the place, but it was cosy, warm and modern and a great party venue. Best of all, we had all this to ourselves for the annual fee of only 300 kronor – the price of a bottle of house wine in a Swedish restaurant – the only restriction was that you couldn't sleep in the clubhouse.

My girlfriend had come around to my living on *Albatross* and realized it didn't mean my becoming a tramp. I still ran the business at the photo shop together with Anders, did my regular 13-hour day from seven in the morning to eight in the evening and looked presentable enough. I think many people had feared that my trading a house for boat would mean giving up personal hygiene, peeing in the harbour and refusing to shower. Monika was relieved to see that I still combed my hair, shaved, used soap and ironed my shirts, the same of which cannot be said for any number of homeowners.

Every weekend, or for as long as the evenings remained warm during the summer, *Albatross* was the meeting place for my friends and me. These were the moments I relished. I spent most of my evenings working on *Albatross*; there was plenty to do to prepare her for her circumnavigation. I never found living on the boat a hardship, not even in the winter when the wind was blowing 70 miles an hour and the waves were coming over the quayside. While the waters in the small harbours a couple of miles up the coast might ice over, Helsingborg's never did as the water circulated with the constant traffic of the ferries and other shipping. It could be minus 10 degrees Celsius outside, but it was toasty inside *Albatross* due to her thick hull and excellent insulation.

And strangely, even when it was blowing as if the wrath of Neptune was on us, I slept well in my berth, unaware that my home was straining at her moorings but soothed instead by the clink of the wires.

It was in this kind of weather that one night in early spring I was woken, not by the wind howling like a banshee outside, but by an elbow in the ribs; Monika had stayed over.

'Sorry,' I snuffled in my sleep. 'Was I snoring?' I rolled over.

'Yanne, listen. There's someone calling.' Another dig in the ribs. 'Yanne, can't you hear it?'

'It's *Albatross*; she's just creaking in the wind.'

'No, listen. There it is again.'

That time I did hear it: a faint cry, like the mew of a seagull, or the weak cry of a child.

I shot upright and glanced at the luminous numbers of the clock; it was four in the morning and still pitch black outside. I grabbed the torch I kept ready by the bed and ran out on deck in my boxers. I shone the torch in the direction of the water. Nothing. I swung the torch round wildly. There it was: a pale hand appeared briefly on the edge on the opposite pier and then slipped back into the darkness of the water. I shouted for Monika and ran towards where I'd seen the hand, calling to whomever to 'just hang on' as I ran. Of course they were hanging on; someone was hanging on for dear bloody life.

I reached the opposite pier and scanned the water for the hand. It had gone. Frantically, I shone the torch over the black water chopping against the pier posts. Then I saw white fingertips break the surface. I threw myself onto my stomach and lay over the edge of the pier, plunged my arms into the freezing water and found the hand. I grabbed it and pulled with a panic-fuelled strength I've never had in my life, neither before nor since, and lifted a body half out of the water. Monika was now beside me and together we pulled a man out of the harbour and onto the pier where he lay gasping like a landed fish.

A week before I wouldn't have known how to treat someone suffering from hypothermia, but fortunately I'd just completed a water survival course a few days earlier. We helped the man to *Albatross*, stripped him of his wet clothes, wrapped him up warm and pushed a rolled-up newspaper between his teeth to stop them from chattering so much he might bite off his tongue. I'd learnt not to massage our guest's arms and legs as this would cause the circulatory system to take cold blood from the surface into the body's core, resulting in a further temperature drop. Eventually, when he'd stopped shivering enough to speak coherently, the fellow told us that he thought he'd been in the water for over 15 minutes; seconds before I came along he'd lost the strength to hold onto the pier. At 65, he was a veteran seaman but had taken a tumble on the wet dock. He insisted he didn't want an ambulance, but he did want the chance to buy me a drink one day: in fact, he bought me several.

I can only recommend to any would-be sailors or even those of you who are experienced yachtsmen to brush up on your water survival and rescue skills. I was very glad to have saved a life, not because of the tremendous feeling such an act leaves you with, but because if the man had died due to my ignorance and ineptitude in an attempt to save him, I would never have forgiven myself. It was a keen reminder that the sea, even in the relative tranquillity of the harbour, is always treacherous. I would learn on more than one occasion of the enormous extent of its perils.

Chapter 10
Testing Our Metal
June 2000 – Two years to cast-off

S ailing is often defined as the fine art of moving slowly at great expense: we were just experiencing the tip of this costly iceberg. Wonderful sailboat though she was, there was a considerable amount of work to be done on *Albatross* in preparation for a three-year circumnavigation.

We started with the sails, ordering a new genoa, gennaker, staysail and mizzen sail from a sailmaker in Helsingborg harbour. The mainsail was good enough to keep, but we'd read that a third reef could be added. The old salts at the yacht club naturally made their opinions known about this.

'What the heck do you want with a third reef?' one asked after scrutinizing our activities. 'You won't have any sail left.'

'Well, we'll be crossing oceans where the winds are considerably more powerful than anything you might have experienced on the Swedish or Danish coasts,' I sniffed, affecting the tone of someone who knew what he was talking about. 'When you're sailing in hurricane force winds, you only need a third of a sail.'

'You might as well hoist a pair of knickers as use that,' the old salt said.

Harbours the world over are full of old boys giving unsolicited advice; this is why many sailors whistle, not as folklore suggests to rustle up a fair wind, but to block out the uninvited drivel spun by sailing has-beens. I ignored him with a hearty rendition of an Abba tune.

As well as the wind being stronger "out there," the waves were also bound to be significantly more powerful in some oceans, the North Sea and the Atlantic for starters, so we were advised to increase the angle of the sail at the front to avoid the sail filling with water and going down like a submarine. We also moved the staysail further aft where it would be more effective in strong winds.

One of the problems faced by yachtsmen is having enough electricity. We had a lot of equipment on board which devoured energy. The fridge, freezer and navigation lights were the main culprits, but all the instruments, the sonar, anemometer, speedometer, wind gauges, GPS, radio, water pump and lamps also depended on power. The generator could only draw so much in a head wind and wouldn't work at all in a tail wind. In order to ensure a steady power supply, we installed a wind generator aft on the mizzenmast and had two mounts installed in the stern which we intended to use later to hold solar panels.

Another problem long-distance cruisers will sympathise with is having enough water. The water capacity of the tank on *Albatross* was 600 litres, approximately 130 imperial gallons, certainly not enough for crossing the Atlantic. It's very easy to become dehydrated on the ocean, and as I had no wish to find myself in the unenviable situation of having to drink Carl's urine, or my own for that matter, we installed a watermaker. This entailed drilling a hole in the hull for a tube through which the salt water was fed into a machine which desalinated it into perfect fresh water. It was a fantastic gadget – if only it could be adapted a stage further for turning water into wine, we'd be laughing drunkenly. While not delicious drinking water, as it tasted too metallic, it was fine for showering, teeth brushing and cooking.

Having taken care of the sails, power and water, we turned our attention to the electronic gizmos which we hoped would make sailing life easier and the long crossings more interesting. Contact with the world on the ocean and the world we were leaving behind was essential, so we installed an Icon radio and bought desktop and laptop computers which we hoped would work until we reached New Zealand before the salt water destroyed them. We'd already learned that salt water will eventually bugger everything, so we made sure to get a guarantee that covered the computers worldwide so we could exchange them once we got to New Zealand. We planned to write and post *Albatross'* log online as often as we could so family and friends could chart our progress. We also installed a satellite phone so we could ring home from wherever we found ourselves in the world. This was something the women in our lives had insisted upon.

Safety was one of our primary concerns; naturally, we'd had lifejackets from the start and always wore them. For really rough weather, we bought Gore Tex gear and boots which cost an arm and a leg and a torso at over 10,000 krona each, but we knew they'd be invaluable. We also bought a man overboard lifebuoy and marked our names on our lifejackets. In the bottom of the cockpit we mounted two steel rings to which we could attach our safety lines, so we would always be safely harnessed when moving about the boat. We'd made a pact never to leave the cockpit – not even to take a pee – without wearing a lifejacket if one of us was below deck or asleep. And if a crew member couldn't manage to reef the sail alone, then he would have to wake the other. Safety was paramount because if one of us fell overboard in open water, the chances of being rescued were slim: turning *Albatross* around single handed to pull someone out of the water would be an impossible task in stormy seas.

As electricians, Carl and I were concerned to the point of paranoia about electrical storms; you're a sitting duck in open water where lightning can strike and bring down a mast for want of any other tall structure to serve as a conductor. With this worrying thought in mind we devised a lightning protection system to divert the current away from the mast. I rigged a copper track in the bottom of the boat to which were connected numerous cables, thus providing a direct path to ground. We'd also read that batteries could prove dangerous; if they shorted the boat could catch fire, so we fixed the main fuses for the battery cells. Changes were also made on deck. We invested in a new anchor and installed a windvane which would enable us to sail *Albatross* at night more or less single handed so one of us could get some rest.

When the sailing season finally returned after a long winter of discontent, Carl and I agreed we needed to log at least 5,000 nautical miles before beginning our circumnavigation. We clearly needed the practice and to find and solve any shortfalls in *Albatross* or ourselves. As yet, we'd had no experience of sailing in really rough weather and limited training in night sailing.

Subsequently, we made many weekend forays to Denmark with family and friends, sailing along the Rungsted coast and down to Tuborg. Participating in regatta racing and crewing on other boats was also invaluable. More experienced sailing friends were generous in giving time and advice with trips to Anholt (a Danish island in the Kattegat midway between Denmark and Sweden) to help get *Albatross* shipshape for the forthcoming adventure. The more nautical miles we had under our lifejackets, the more confident we felt.

But we still hadn't passed the real initiation test. After the new sails had been rigged, the installations completed and updated and numerous trips in our home waters, the moment had come.

'Right,' Carl said decisively. 'It's time to test your manhood, young Yanne. We may not like it but it can't be avoided. It's time to cross the North Sea.'

Carl and I had no intention of sailing around the world without having first ensured that we could cross a large body of water on our own, and the North Sea would be a good test of whether we could or couldn't. Although if we couldn't, it would mean ... well, it would mean that *Albatross* had lived up to her name, and we were lying on the ocean bed, which would be a bit of a blow to our hard sought confidence.

The North Sea is one of the toughest bodies of water for ships of any size or type. It's relatively shallow so the waves break more choppily and more frequently. The winter months see frequent gales and storms with ferocious winds; large inflows of Atlantic water meet the North Sea increasing wave amplitude, and storm tides threaten the coasts of the Netherlands, Belgium, Germany, Denmark and eastern England. It's much easier to capsize in this sea than anywhere else, and you have to admire the fortitude of the men who work on the fishing trawlers. The North Sea has swallowed many a ship, so it was with considerable trepidation that we decided to "have a go" at it.

First, we set a course for Heligoland, a half mile square triangle lying 45 miles off the coast of Germany. The island is as colourful as its history having been squabbled over for two centuries, passing through Danish, British and German hands. The British didn't treat the island very well, but used it mostly as target practise, bombing it to smithereens during the Second World War and rendering the island completely uninhabitable. In 1947, the Royal Navy went a step further by detonating 6,700 tonnes of explosives and creating one of the largest single non-nuclear detonations in history in an attempt to sink Heligoland. The "British Bang," as it was known, effectively reshaped the island but fortunately failed to sink it completely. The British continued to use the island as a bombing range until 1952 when it was finally restored to Germany who re-landscaped, rebuilt and resettled the island. Today Heligoland is a popular tourist destination for both its natural beauty and interesting military sites, including the U-boat base built by the Germans during the Second World War. No motor vehicles are allowed on the island, so the locals, of whom there are just 1,100, whizz about on push-scooters. Not that we saw any of this, we just read about it in the guide book. As it was pouring with rain, we didn't bother with a tour, but decided instead to rest up and brace ourselves for the long journey across the North Sea to Scotland the following morning.

It proved to be our toughest journey to date. The North Sea is not for the faint hearted. It tested our nerves, ability and stomachs, Carl's being less cast-iron and more soft-boiled than he'd realised. He spent much of the passage leaning over the rail with a face the colour of chalk. We got caught in a mother of a storm; the waves were worse than we'd anticipated, breaking over the bow with terrifying power; the windvane broke so we couldn't use the autopilot at night except by jamming the wheel and steering like the ancient mariners had in olden times. I must have shouted to Carl, 'We're sinking!' at least once an hour, with Carl shouting back, 'I don't care. I feel bloody awful!' We felt insignificant and powerless against the raw power of nature and the sight of the sea in all its terrifying wrath. But Albatross proved to be a steady and stable ship, and weathering the storm in the dark was good training. Remembering our sailing lessons, we reefed in the genoa, reduced the staysail and took down the mizzen sail. We left the mainsail up for the simple reason that it's essential to drive the boat, but by reefing in a couple of jacks and reducing the area of the sail made sailing somewhat smoother. We were grateful for all we'd learned through courses, books and sailing friends. It had been tough, but now we had some idea of what awaited us on the high seas, and we knew we'd be able to cope with anything the weather threw at us. Hopefully.

After three miserable days at sea, we gratefully reached Peterhead at the eastern most point on mainland Scotland. Our first sight as we slipped into the marina was a huge yacht.

'Wow,' I said to Carl as our heads simultaneously swivelled to admire her. 'Whoever owns her is a very lucky bastard.'

Not so. The water in the harbour was clear enough to see that the kelp covering the yacht's hull hung at least 12 feet below the water, an indication that she'd been there at least two years, the same amount of time the "lucky bastards" had been in prison. According to the harbourmaster, the yacht's owners had been caught smuggling drugs and were presently housed at Peterhead prison, an imposing Victorian facility set on the headland from where they could see their lovely yacht and rue the day they'd ever tested the Scottish harbour authorities. We later learned that HMP Peterhead was one of Scotland's toughest jails for long-term sex offenders, so the drug runners would not have been housed there. Nevertheless, wherever they were incarcerated, their fabulous yacht had since remained in the harbour and was now a meeting point for thirsty marina guests.

Peterhead's location means it has naturally been influenced by the sea and has always relied on fishing to ensure its prosperity. In 1987, it was Europe's largest white fish port, but today declining fish stocks and EU quotas present difficulties for the fishing fleet. The town wasn't particularly appealing, not helped by the red granite architecture which looked forbidding in the all-permeating drizzle. But now we had a broken windvane in need of repair. Although it had been a pain in the proverbial arse on the North Sea, we came to realize it was a propitious accident, teaching us that we needed always to have a spare blade. If our windvane broke out on the Atlantic, we'd be royally screwed. We just needed to find a handyman who could knock us up a few spares. After asking around at the harbour, a helpful fisherman suggested trying the village blacksmith. We jumped on our bikes and headed for the town where we were directed to McGregor-the-Smithy's house. A true Scottish beauty opened the door to us, pulling her dressing gown over her barrel body and growling without dropping the cigarette clamped between her lips, 'The mister's nay home. But there's tea in the pot if you'll wait.' At least we thought that's what she said as she shuffled us in to the kitchen and waved at the teapot on the table. She was as charming as Peterhead prison.

Casting a dubious eye over the sink full of dirty crockery, I declined the offer of tea and botulism. The missus slumped back on her shabby sofa, lit another cigarette and zapped the TV with the remote control. The room hung heavy with smoke, and Carl and I tried not to breathe in the fumes. Fortunately, the smithy returned and over his own cup of tea eventually grasped the problem despite a massive language barrier: he didn't seem to speak a language we'd ever heard before.

'A've nay stinless steel,' he said. 'A've no boot aluminium tay make it fir yee. Ha boot tha'?'

I should mention at this point that neither Carl nor I spoke very much English – unusual for Swedes, I know, but we'd both spent many years in Berlin, so German was our second language. It was only when we'd arrived in Scotland that it occurred to us we should have studied English along with our sailing subjects; we'd naively assumed we'd be able to muddle along. We were certainly more than a little muddled now. Not that two years of Cambridge proficiency in English would have helped us; the smithy's thick accent was as incomprehensible to us as the reason why women need so many handbags.

After much head scratching, a frantic round of charades and numerous stick figure drawings, the smithy took us to his workshop where he showed us that he didn't have any stainless steel, only aluminium if that would do us. We nodded happily to indicate that would do just fine, and he set to work.

It took McGregor-the-smithy a couple of days to create the parts for our wind vane, during which time Carl and I tidied up *Albatross* after her battering in the North Sea, visited the area and sat in the cockpit sipping whisky, studying the tides and reviewing all we'd learned. With the windvane fixed and an extra for back up, we were ready to sail back to Sweden. We'd survived one North Sea crossing: we hoped we could make it back. Lord knows, we didn't want a charmless Scottish town to be our last worldly view. There's a reason why the phrase "See Peterhead and die" is not a universal one. My apologies to the people of the town, but there was little that persuaded me to end my days there.

Chapter 11
So Which Way Round?
December 2001 – Six months to cast-off

'So you still think you can sail around the world, do you?'

Heavy sigh. 'Yes, we do.'

Shake of head. 'Well, you have no idea what you're in for.'

I don't know how many times my father and I had this conversation. Every time I saw him, he'd look at me, shake his head and mutter. He wasn't the only one to voice his doubts; there were many naysayers in Helsingborg's marina who said we were all talk and wouldn't make it further than France, but I liked to think these people were the sort who'd accuse Porsche owners of overcompensating. All the negative talk had little effect on us. If anything, it strengthened our resolve. Carl and I were as proudly stubborn as two middle-aged men can be. We never had any doubts about our project, but continued to slave determinedly at the daily grind in order to be ready for departure.

I freely admit I'd lost all heart in the photo processing business. At one time it had been an enjoyable challenge to start a new business and build up our client base from scratch. Anders and I developed over 45,000 rolls of film a year, as well as securing contracts for big print jobs for local businesses. But the grind was wearing me down, feeling increasingly like a means to a mortgage. Furthermore, I'd seen the writing on the wall; the digital revolution – that amazing but damnable digital camera – was well on its way and would have a significant impact on our trade. My interest shifted from the business to our forthcoming journey; it was the only thing I felt any passion for anymore, and I counted down the days to our departure with mounting exhilaration. Now that we'd become somewhat competent yachtsmen – I wouldn't go so far as to call ourselves proficient – the next step was to decide our route round the world.

Carl was in charge of planning the route: he liked pouring over maps and charts, so I trusted him to get us round the world the right way, as it were. Every couple of weeks we'd have a planning session on *Albatross*. I'd bought a steam cooker and was experimenting with different recipes with varying degrees of success. After testing my latest concoction, we'd uncork a bottle of red, spread out the maps on the saloon table whereupon Carl would wax lyrical about his latest ideas.

'I'm using this book,' he said, waving Jimmy Cornell's *World Cruising Routes* at me with the fervour of an evangelist with a Bible. 'The man knows what he's talking about, and it seems to me we should follow an expert's example. I mean, why reinvent the wheel?'

I nodded: sounded logical to me.

'Now the destinations are fairly straight forward but timing is crucial,' Carl continued. 'We're setting a course for New Zealand, right? But we don't want to end up stuck in the middle of the ocean during cyclone season, so we have to keep to a strict schedule to avoid that.'

As Carl had signed a contract for a leave of three years and wouldn't be allowed even one day over that, the return schedule was crucial: if we weren't back in time, he would have to leave the boat and fly home. However, with good planning we could take the three-year journey at a leisurely pace, stopping en route at islands that took our fancy. The whole experience was about leaving the stress behind, letting the journey take us: not us take the journey. Hence, our route followed the changing climate: as the winds shift with the seasons. According to Cornell's book, the best time to cross the Atlantic is in November when the favourable trade winds from Africa sweep in. By following his advice we wouldn't have to sail round the world with the wind against us. It was exactly what we were seeking and a perfect metaphor for how we wanted to free ourselves of life's crushing burdens: we would literally let the winds take us.

The first leg of the journey was of particular interest to us both: we'd read about the Classic Malt Cruise, a whisky trip down the Caledonian Canal which passes through some of Scotland's most spectacular scenery, visiting famous distilleries along the way. 'We've definitely got to do that!' Carl had said. He was preaching to the choir, whisky being nectar to this mortal. The passage would continue from Scotland to Ireland, then on to Spain and Portugal, thence across the Atlantic and through the Panama Canal. Once through the Canal, there'd be no turning back – from that point on you have to complete a circumnavigation to get home. Carl suggested we sailed to New Zealand where we would wait out the cyclone season. As later events proved, this was for me to be a life changing decision.

We were less certain about our route homeward; South Africa was on our list of "must see, must sail," but we were undecided whether to complete the journey home by sailing the Atlantic along the African or Brazilian coast; the latter was a much longer journey but enjoyed good winds, while there was a risk of becoming becalmed on the African side in the Horse Latitudes. We also planned to visit French Polynesia but hadn't decided on any specific islands. That was the beauty of sailing: there was room for flexibility and spontaneity, following recommendations of other cruisers and friends we met along the way. The more Carl and I discussed our route, the more tangible our dream became; it was within our grasp.

Once we'd nailed the route, we concentrated on the budget; this we had to analyse to the last detail to ensure we wouldn't go broke halfway around the world. My money from the sale of the house and car would be used first, as this was in a savings account; Carl's money was invested in stocks and shares which could still increase with a rising market, so this would be held in reserve until needed. We were financially sound as long as we were careful, but we wouldn't be living high life.

Food and drink were going to be our biggest expense; we could, however, save money by cooking and not eating out, although we agreed that on arrival in a new port after a long passage we would reward ourselves with a slap-up meal in a good restaurant to experience the local cuisine. Otherwise we hoped to catch enough fish to sustain ourselves, and buy cheap local produce and stock up on dried foods, such as pasta and rice, to cut costs. I was appointed head chef, as I love cooking and can swear as competently as any TV cook. Carl would take the role of galley slave and help clean up. As for booze, we would load up with cheap wine in Spain and Portugal before crossing the Atlantic. Carl suggested that if we became really strapped for cash, I could sell my body – mine being slightly less used than his, but as I pointed out, if prices were based on weight, we'd get more for his.

During our practice runs we'd settled into a routine of sorts: as I was generally a morning person and Carl was a night owl, it made sense to decide the watches based on this: I would take the morning watches and Carl, the nights, each watch being six hours long to allow us enough time to get a decent kip. I would sleep in the aft cabin: Carl would take the bed in the saloon. We'd take it in turns to keep the logbook and both take photos, but I would deal mostly with the radio. The pieces of the puzzle were falling into place.

As the final spring before our scheduled departure approached, I began to experience a severe case of excited panic. We'd spent a considerable time ensuring *Albatross* was ready for the high seas, but there was still a lot of work to be done. Every time we ticked off a job on our long list, two more were added. I began to loathe that never-ending list.

One March morning, I visited *Freedom* a few berths down from *Albatross* in the marina and called on Ove, my sailing tutor and technical mentor. He was one of the few people who, from the start, had been fully convinced that Carl and I would put our money where our mouths were and complete our journey. His confidence had given us confidence. I found him in his usual milieu bent over his workbench, his well-worn baseball cap askew over his white hair, his glasses sliding down the edge of his nose as he concentrated on whatever he was repairing. Most of the time he looked as if he was in need of repair himself. His jeans were worn, an old T-shirt strained over a full beer belly and I think the only pair of footwear he owned were his brown deck shoes. Both Ove and his boat had seen better days, but he seemed content for all that.

'Hej, Ove,' I called. 'Got a moment?'

Ove pushed his glasses up his nose, carefully put down his tools and grinned. 'Sure. What do you need?' He never failed to drop whatever he was doing to help us out. This time we needed his assistance to mount the GPS next to the wheel so we could see it in bad weather. We'd had a problematic sail from the Elbe estuary to the Kiel Canal when we couldn't see a damn thing, forcing Carl to shout in a very un-seaman-like way, 'Steer left, steer right,' the whole passage.

'See you've been busy,' Ove remarked as he climbed on board *Albatross*.

We had. Ove admired how Carl had replaced the wooden hatch opening into the cabin with two large pieces of Plexiglas. The solid wood had made it impossible to see each other unless we opened the hatch, which we couldn't do if the cockpit filled with water as we'd flood the cabin. Now we'd be able to keep an eye on each other during rough weather without having to open the hatch. We'd also put up a new sunroof over the cockpit so we wouldn't fry in the equatorial sun; it would also provide shelter from rain and wind. To give added protection at the sides, I'd sewn extra pieces of material that could be zipped on when the boat was heeling or we were sailing in rough weather. In the stern, we'd welded on mounts to hold fishing rods. I was very serious about fishing, particularly now that our lives might depend on what we caught. Hence, I'd invested in a Pen rod and reel, a mighty piece of equipment capable of landing anything up to 600 pounds. Carl had nearly choked at the price tag, but I'd whined about it at such length that he'd eventually thrown up his hands and barked, 'All right! Keep your damn fishing rod!' I was looking forward to trying my hand at deep sea fishing, curious about what we might catch: cooking mahi-mahi, marlin or cuttlefish would certainly test my culinary skills and Carl's so-called cast-iron stomach.

'Nice work,' Ove said as he admired our additions and alterations. Carl poured three snaps and we clinked glasses.

I cleared my throat. 'Ove, we have something to ask you.'

Ove smiled lazily. 'Ask away.'

'We know you can't join us on our circumnavigation, but we'd really like you on board when we make sail. You've believed in us from the start and helped make *Albatross* the boat she is.'

'We'd be honoured if you would join our crew for the first leg of the journey,' Carl added.

Ove's expression was unreadable behind the dark tinted glasses he wore when he wasn't at his workbench. He nodded slowly. We had no idea if he would accept our invitation or not. It wasn't that he didn't want to sail with us; it was that age old problem of lack of cash. Ove lived hand to mouth on the money he earned doing odd jobs in the harbour. If he did come with, we weren't sure how he'd get back to Sweden again. I doubted he had the funds to get to Denmark and back.

'Take your time and think about it,' I said.

He took all of three seconds to think about it. 'I've always fancied visiting Dublin,' he said. 'I'll see if I can get some time off.' *Time off what?* I wondered but didn't ask. 'After all, you'll need someone with you who knows a thing or two about boats or you'll sink before you reach Skagen.'

Oh, ye of little faith! What did I say about confidence?

Chapter 12
Worse Case Scenarios
April 2002 – Two months to cast-off

'**R**ight Yanne? Have you made a will? And if something should go wrong, have you decided what you'd like done with your ... um, remains?'
'What?'

I looked at Carl with horror. Like most men, I hate any talk of my demise, preferring instead to worry about it if and when the time comes, not really having ever stopped to consider that the time will come and when it does, it will definitely be too late to worry about it. In fact, I saw no point in making a will: I wasn't married, failure to return was not in the plan and I refused to pay unnecessary legal fees. I had two children who would inherit should the worst happen.

Despite my reticence to contemplate the worst, we needed to consider what to do should it arise. An awful lot could go wrong: starving if we were be-calmed on the ocean and ran out of fuel; pirates boarding the boat; burglars stealing anything we didn't lock down, and all kinds of injuries which could dispatch us if we didn't get medical attention quickly enough.

'In the event of ... well, how do you feel about guns?' Carl asked me.

I frowned. 'Best left in the hands of James Bond.'

'But what if we're boarded by pirates off the African coast?' Carl said. 'We'll need something better than a boat hook or a frying pan to wave in their faces, don't you think?'

Carl had raised a crucial question. There'd been an alarming increase in stories of private yachts being taken by Somali pirates who either killed or kidnapped the owners and crew. Somalia has had no functioning central government since 1991, allowing piracy to flourish off its coast. However, I doubted guns would make us feel more secure. The deciding factor was whether we'd be prepared to shoot first if we did have a weapon, otherwise there's no point in having one.

'What if you shot the wrong person? You could end up spending the rest of your life in a prison that would make Alcatraz look like a four-star hotel,' I said. End of discussion. Instead we mounted a blue light on the mast. Should an unknown boat approach us in the dark, we could turn on the light and possibly ward off any potential pirates by looking like a coastguard vessel. To avoid theft from the boat we installed a burglar alarm using several hundred feet of cable to cover all the openings. Vigilance was essential.

Equally alarming was the list of potentially life-threatening tropical diseases out there, some of which could do us in within a few hours of infection. Apart from all the usual ones associated with insects, air and contaminated water such as malaria, tuberculosis and cholera, there were some lesser known, but very unpleasant parasitic worms I wished desperately to avoid: hookworms and guinea worms caught by walking barefoot on contaminated soil; pinworms passed via poor hygiene; roundworms transmitted by eating unwashed vegetables and tapeworms contracted through contaminated beef, pork or raw fish.

'I wonder if it's possible to travel the world without physically touching the ground, anything or anyone and limiting my intake to only tinned food.' I said to Carl.

'That won't help you in the event of contamination. You could just as easily die from botulism,' he replied wryly.

We hastily booked four rounds of vaccinations at Lund hospital where a very nice doctor startled us further by listing another two dozen nasty diseases we might easily encounter. She kindly used up her whole prescription pad on medications which were filled out for a breathtakingly hefty sum. We staggered out of the pharmacy, loaded with carrier bags bulging with tablets and potions of all colours and sizes. We also invested in 50 syringes; if we did need medical treatment en route, we didn't want to risk receiving an injection in a hospital where syringes were washed and reused.

'But what do we do in the event of serious injuries?' Carl asked during one of our planning sessions.

Although I was getting weary of his "in the event of," I had to admit he had a point: injuries or wounds requiring something more than a sticking plaster could be fatal. Fortunately, a neighbour referred us to his son, a dentist who obligingly helped us out by giving us a special suturing needle and lessons on how to use it. We practised on leather and, while not the neatest surgeons, felt pretty competent should the need arise, which hopefully it wouldn't; we'd been told to suture a wound only as a last resort as the danger of sewing in bacteria is extremely high. Nevertheless, we had a ready supply of scalpels and were prepared to operate in the event of appendicitis – following a doctor's instructions via the radio. All things considered, this would be on a par with a video game player landing a 747 under the directions of the control tower. Moreover, as we possessed neither anaesthetic nor morphine, we'd be forced to operate Wild West style, subduing the patient with half a bottle of whisky and a rag between the teeth. We did have a supply of antibiotics but the best medicine could be found in the booze cabinet, brandy being a fine defence against most germs. The dentist also gave us some equipment for operating on teeth and a concoction which when mixed together could be used for packing a broken tooth. Nevertheless, both Carl and I made sure to have dental check-ups before we left.

During the spring of 2002, our every spare moment was spent preparing *Albatross* for her big adventure: the list of things to repair, clean or buy was interminable. We were both still working fulltime until the week of our departure; I was putting in extra hours at the photo shop, tying up loose ends so Anders could take over, and Carl was finishing up his last days at his job. We'd realized quite early on that we might be forced to set sail before we'd completed all the tasks on our list despite working frantically and even with help from Ove and other friends. We serviced the engine and changed the oil, replaced all the anodes and installed a shut-off valve in the sink, having discovered that when the boat was heavily loaded – as it had been on the booze run back from Kiel – water rose in the basins and flooded over; it would be ironic, not to say completely moronic, to sink from the inside. We fixed a line between the rudder and the keel to avoid getting fishing nets or lines tangled in the propeller – a typical problem off the coast of Spain and Portugal where longline fishing is common. Numerous cables and connections needed repairing, and the satellite phone connection had suddenly and inconveniently begun to malfunction.

Our departure date was fast approaching. Carl and I were so obsessed with getting everything done before we sailed we didn't have time to reflect how we felt about leaving our families and friends for three years. "Must panic" and "Reflect deeply on consequences of our decision" weren't on the list, so we didn't do them. It was essential, however, to lift *Albatross* out of the water to check the hull and perform some basic maintenance on her to ensure she would survive her time at sea. Two months before our departure, we sent her to a harbour up the coast to have her hull painted.

In the month before our departure, all of Helsingborg's harbour milled around us, forcing us to postpone doing essential jobs; people were constantly dropping by to chat, say goodbye or wish us luck, or give us a critical once-over and a barrage of unsolicited advice. We'd become local celebrities despite the fact that we hadn't yet achieved anything other than learning to sail and buying a boat. Nevertheless, the media had covered our story in both print and on the radio – not much had happened of late in sleepy Skåne.

Overwhelmed by all we had to do, we decided to take a few extra maintenance days in Skagen in Denmark and finish the preparations there in peace and quiet. One comfort was that we would have a couple of extra crew hands to help us: apart from Ove, my liveaboard neighbour Martin and my son Dino were joining us.

We had a last practice run around the island on Ven, a final opportunity to check all the sails and the equipment. Carl and I were both feeling confident, hopeful and eager to be off; we'd waited a long time for this and the moment was almost upon us. We were following our dream, something many people talk about doing, but never do. We could finally prove we were full of talk and action. We couldn't wait to see the looks of the people in the harbour when we finally cast off and set off for the big blue yonder.

Anyway, there was no going back now even if we'd wanted to: after all our talk, we'd never live down the humiliation.

Chapter 13
Anchors Aweigh!
15 June 2002

I took a last look around the one-room flat: not much of a home – *Albatross* was my home – but more of a storeroom with a hotplate, filled with furniture and boxes containing items from what I now considered my former life. All this belonged to the BC era: Before Circumnavigation.

The date was finally upon us and we were scheduled to hoist sail at 15:00 hours. There was no time for reflection or deep poetic thoughts, however, as Carl and I had a huge amount to do if we were to slip our moorings on time. I picked up the last of my things and quickly turned the key in the lock. I admit I felt prickles of panic as I left: I wouldn't see the flat for another three years, if all went well.

Goodbyes are never easy, particularly for those who are left behind. Carl and I were setting sail for new destinations, going somewhere, sailing off beyond the horizon, but our families would have an interminable wait with the troubling knowledge that what we were doing wasn't without its dangers. The evening before our departure, I threw a farewell party at the yacht club. I'd been determined to make sure it was a party to remember, full of good spirits. We ate, we drank, we laughed and the women in my life cried. I laughed heartily when my friends presented me with a book, the cover of which was a cleverly edited photo of my head in a toilet bowl with the caption "Farewell Yanne" printed above. The book was filled with photos and best wishes from friends and family, and messages such as "You're never sailing away from anywhere, you're always sailing to somewhere." My workmates had composed a photo of them all setting fire to the many posters of sailing boats displayed in the shop and captioned, "At last we can chuck out everything to do with boats!" On the final page were the words, "When you're fed up of the ocean, babes and booze, this album will remind you how great it is to work at the photo lab. Have a great trip."

I'd truly enjoyed my last evening in Helsingborg although I was well aware that Monica hadn't. We'd been together for five years, and in all that time I'd been planning the expedition, she'd never been fully convinced I would see it through. All the bedroom romps in the world couldn't or wouldn't keep me in Helsingborg.

'I can't believe you're really going,' she kept saying. Neither could I, but my reason for saying so was not the same as hers. Now that my departure was imminent, she was bereft at my leaving for three years. Who could say what would happen during that time.

Carl was struggling with the same problem: his wife, Eva, was finding it difficult to grasp that he would be sailing away from Sweden in less than 24 hours. While I was doing my best to be the hearty host, Carl sat down to a home cooked meal with his Eva and his youngest daughter, Erika. He told me later that it had been a subdued evening. Carl and Eva had been happily married for years, and although she had agreed to his plans and certainly wouldn't stand in the way of his dreams, she wasn't overjoyed at being left behind. She said her goodbyes to Carl that night; she told him she couldn't bear to be at the harbour the next day when he left.

As I said jokingly to Monica, it wasn't as if we were getting rid of the women that quickly: both Monica and Eva had arranged to fly out and meet us at different destinations en route, the first of which was Dublin. We weren't sailing off round the corner to be joined immediately by bikini-clad supermodels or consumed by cannibals.

It was a beautiful start to the day: the sky was pale blue and a friendly breeze fluttered the flags on the boats in the harbour: promising sailing weather. Carl was already on *Albatross* when I arrived.

'Sleep well?' I asked. Carl shook his head. I didn't need to ask why. I'd barely slept myself: nerves and excitement had kept me awake most of the night.

We were joined by Ove, Martin and Dino and started the race against the clock, running around at double speed and tripping over in our haste. There was the last of the provisions to load on board which typically took more time than we'd estimated. We'd bought piles of tinned goods: skinned tomatoes, green and white beans and lots of peas, as well as packets of dried soup and jars of sausages. We'd stockpiled spaghetti, rice, potato powder and dried milk. We'd also bought flour and yeast so we could make our own bread. We filled the freezer with mince and meat but no fish as we were relying on our fishing skills.

I also loaded boxes of clothes I rarely used onto the boat; I'd read in one of my many sailing books how you could earn quite a bit for used clothes in French Polynesia because shops on the islands were so few and far between. I'd had a thorough cleanout of things I didn't need and boxed up and stored clothes I wouldn't require, leaving only sailing gear and one smart suit with a good shirt and tie in case an out-of-the-blue invitation required more formal wear – well, you never know. How annoying would it be to receive an invitation to hobnob on some Hollywood star's yacht only to whine, "But I've got nothing to wear!" I'd also packed a good travel bag I'd bought on the Volvo Ocean Race, which I hoped to sell for ten times what I'd paid. Money was going to be very tight and I needed to supplement my income by any legal means possible.

The clock was ticking and we all worked frantically to get the boat loaded. However, as our departure time got closer, more and more people dropped by to say farewell and wish us luck, bearing presents and champagne. Some of the members of the Helsingborg Yacht Club arrived to present us with parting gifts: a book on Helsingborg and a smart set of bunting of forty international code flags with which yachtsmen decorate their boats on high days and holidays. Helsingborg Yacht Club was very proud of having its first round-the-world yachtsmen, although we hoped their pride wasn't premature. Ove took charge of mounting the code flags, claiming he knew all about putting them up. *Albatross* did look very well-dressed now with her festive flags. The popping of champagne corks added to the party atmosphere.

Excitement and apprehension now competed for first place in the mixture of emotions Carl and I were experiencing. For the last few weeks leading to this hour, we'd put aside any feelings of doubt or worry; we'd been too busy with our final preparations to give time to any misgivings. But as the last of our boxes and supplies were finally loaded, the knot in my stomach grew larger, the lump in my throat tighter. We were really on our way; this is what it had all been about: to leave the daily grind behind and experience life and all it had to offer; to go out and see the world beyond for ourselves, not merely view it through a box of wires and coloured lights or the shiny pictures of *National Geographic*; to live the dream and not sleep through it. Each harbour would be a new destination and every time we stepped onto a new shore we would toast the experience in style with a shot of snaps, a case of which had already been loaded.

'You've still no idea what you're in for,' my father said as he shook my hand. His hand suddenly looked a little frail although his grip was firm.

'Maybe not, Dad, but if I don't go, I'll never find out,' I said.

'True enough,' he said. 'Good luck, son.'

My mother hugged me. Monica flung her arms around my neck, crying so much I could feel her tears through my shirt.

'Come on, love,' I said. 'We'll soon see each other in Ireland.' This only made her sob louder than ever. God, it was tough saying goodbye. Carl's daughter, Erika, clearly felt the same: too tearful to say a final farewell to her father, she ran from the pier and hid. Ah, bless them, I thought, women succumb so easily to their feelings: we men are made of sterner stuff.

Helsingborg's city hall clock could be heard striking three; time was up.

Carl and I dashed around desperately trying to stow the last of our things. Ove cast off while Martin and Dino tidied the deck. The yacht club saluted our departure with a cannon shot and all the sails were hoisted. *Albatross* and her crew were finally off. The cacophony of cheers, screams and yells was tremendous as everyone shouted their last goodbyes and waved frantically. As *Albatross* proceeded out of the harbour, Monica ran to the end of the quay, tears streaming down her face. She lifted her arm in a final wave farewell, then let her arm drop as we slipped further out onto the waters of the Öresund.

It was then it hit me like a bus slamming into a wall: the multitude of emotions and fears I'd so carefully tucked away suddenly and completely overwhelmed me; my throat burned and fat tears began to run down my cheeks. I cried, I sobbed, I howled. I was crying for all I was leaving behind and for all the uncertainty of what lay ahead. Would I ever return? Would I see my friends and family again? Would I see my parents again? They were both in their mid-seventies and there was no guarantee that they would still be alive when I returned, or if I returned. My tears fell faster. I felt a hand on my shoulder. I looked round to see Carl; his cheeks were as wet as mine. Oh yes, we men are certainly made of sterner stuff.

'Man,' he croaked. He wiped his eyes with a sleeve. 'Leaving is much tougher than I ever thought it would be.'

'You can say that again,' I sniffed back. We both looked towards the harbour where the crowd was slowly dispersing. I could still make out a lone figure at the end of the pier, still watching us as we sailed towards Skagen and out of sight.

Chapter 14
First Man Overboard
15 June – 3 July 2002

Skagen – Arendal – Kristiansand

Experience: *Tacking in rough seas is an exhausting way to reach your goal; better to wait it out in harbour until the weather turns to your advantage.*

Tip: *"A sure cure for seasickness is to sit under a tree." Spike Milligan*

Many old and young salts will tell you that if you truly want to experience sailing without the trouble of going to sea, you should stand fully clothed in a cold shower while throwing the contents of your wallet down the drain – the results are the same: it's wet and expensive. But that's not even half the story. Add to your cold shower the entire contents of the kitchen cupboards and everything from your stomach, then for good measure chuck in books, maps, paperwork, cameras, cushions, towels, clothes – heck, just throw in anything that isn't nailed or glued down into the shower with you, stamp about on it for a bit and then you have an idea of rough sailing. Add to the above, 36 hours of being thrown against every available surface until you have lost the will to live, while cold salty water is pelted unremittingly in your face and *then* you'll have an approximate idea of the first leg of our circumnavigation.

It was not the best start.

Helsingborg was still in sight when the first lightning flash lit up the city. The sky grew black in a matter of minutes, the wind changed from friendly to ferocious, and the Swedish coast disappeared in a thick wall of mist and driving rain. This wasn't just a little summer squall: this was a merciless channel storm and we were in the thick of it. We reefed in the sails and braced ourselves, but it wasn't long before Carl said goodbye to his home-cooked farewell dinner, breakfast and lunch over the side of the boat. Dino and Martin quickly followed suit, turning a paler shade of green before disappearing below. Ove was a seasoned yachtsman and didn't succumb. As for me, well, it seemed I had finally conquered my seasickness, but I didn't feel like tucking into a three-course meal anytime soon. We'd anticipated some rough sailing on our circumnavigation; we'd just never imagined it would start within sight of our home port.

The sail to Skagen – the northernmost point of Denmark, a projection of land sticking like an index finger out between the Skagerrak and the Kattegat straits – usually takes less than 24 hours, but we were forced to tack against the wind the entire way. We finally limped into harbour on Monday morning, some 36 hours after leaving Helsingborg having completed 131 nautical miles of our 50,000-mile circumnavigation. We were all exhausted, our stomachs empty and our spirits extremely low: after all the fanfare of our departure, it was a miserable way to start three years of sailing.

If we felt and looked rough, *Albatross* looked even rougher: Ove, who had claimed to know so much about hoisting the bunting set of code flags, had forgotten to attach a lanyard to bring it down again, so we'd sailed through the storm with our festive flotilla flags raised; torn and tattered, they now looked like something a scarecrow wouldn't be seen dead in; the unusually large choppy waves which had thundered over the bow had ripped up the wood on the bowsprit; it looked as if a tornado had torn through the cabin and it smelled most unpleasantly of vomit which made Carl, Dino and Martin want to vomit more, not that they had anything left in them. Nevertheless we weren't going to let our routine tumble just because half the crew felt off colour; desperate as we were to head for the harbour showers, we first had to adhere to our ritual of drinking a "mooring snaps" on arrival at a new harbour. We got out the *Gammel Dansk* – which literally translated means "Old Dane." One gulp made new men of us. If you are unfamiliar with the drink, it's a bitters liquor matured with various herbs, spices and flowers, which might sound soft but goes down with all the smoothness of molten lead; Carl and I love it. Thus fortified in Viking style, I went off to plunder and pillage. In other words, I cycled to the local shop and bought fresh rolls, Danish salami and cheese. Damn, if that wasn't the best breakfast ever after 36 hours of not being able to even think about food without heaving.

Once recovered, we were able to start our repairs and complete the unfinished tasks on our list. The harbour was lively as always in the summer months; it's a popular tourist destination with young Danish families seeking beach holidays among the dunes or retired couples enjoying the art museum – the area was made famous by the Skagen painters. Many are lured to Skagen's very tip, a sandy headland known as Grenen, for the thrill of watching the North Sea collide with the Baltic. The meeting of these two great bodies of water produces the thrilling sight of clashing waves as they battle against each other on either side of the tip.

For many Scandinavians, Skagen is a haven for cheap beer, and the marina was crowded with enterprising moped owners making beer runs for visiting yachts. The lure of cheap drink meant that all the pubs were packed, so attempting to get to the bar was like to trying to break through a rugby scrum. Nevertheless, we bravely persevered: money was passed from hand to hand and our drinks passed back to us with only a few spills and I suspect the odd sip taken on the way.

We spent five days in Skagen making our repairs and getting *Albatross* ready for the North Sea, but we allowed ourselves a couple of days to explore the area and indulge and recover from two important celebrations. The first was Martin's birthday: he was turning 40 and we felt it necessary to make a fuss and drink to his health without pause, so back to the pub scrum it was.

The second cause for celebration was Midsummer Eve and I cannot stress enough to all you non-Scandinavian readers the significance of this custom to a native Swede. As Swedish winters are interminably long and summers all too fleeting, it's customary for the community to gather together and celebrate the summer solstice. Simply put, it's the best party of the year, if you're prepared to follow the simple rules below as laid down by centuries of tradition.

1. Erect a 20-foot pole in centre of village common, leaving enough space for guests to dance around. Attach two tractor tyre-sized rings to each side of pole: pole should now resemble something phallic attracting attention of entire neighbourhood.
2. Gather wild flowers and foliage, or if lazy, buy last-minute wilting bouquets at supermarket before closing time.
3. Decorate pole and rings with flowers by either mounting or dismantling pole.
4. Make garland of flowers to wear as crown if young maiden. If male, decide on degree of security of own sexuality, make flower crown, then wear or discard as appropriate.
5. Join with villagers/other revellers to dance and sing around phallic symbol, joyously belting out important Swedish national folk song, *Små grodorna* – "Little frogs." Hop around maypole in style of amphibian, singing immortal words, "Little frogs are funny to look at; they don't have ears or tails."
6. Gather at long unstable trestle tables and wobbly benches for a splendid smorgasbord feast of raw fish, pickled herring, salmon, hard-boiled eggs, potato salad and strawberries. Drink copious amounts of *brännvin* – literal translation of which means "burning wine," also accurate description of effect of named drink.
7. Continue singing, eating and drinking until vision becomes blurry, sun rises or it is pointed out that hot girls at opposite end of table are in fact one plain, middle-aged male hippy.

8. Rest under trestle table for a bit, wake two to twelve hours later with stabbing pain behind eyes, take favourite pain relief and regret participating in all of the above.

Fortunately, Midsummer celebrations are considered so important as to warrant a national holiday on the eve closest to the summer solstice and the day thereafter. It's the only period during the year when everything is closed in Sweden, presumably to allow the nation to recover from its collective hangover.

Danish festivities are different, however. Displaying the pyromaniacal tendencies of troubled teenagers, the Danes see Midsummer as the ideal opportunity to hold a huge public bonfire on top of which they set the effigy of a witch, harking back to the witch burnings of the sixteenth century. Then they get roaring drunk, sing ludicrous songs and cavort grotesquely around the fire, all of which seems downright pagan compared to the civility of our own Swedish revelries.

For want of a Midsummer pole and the space in which to erect it, we sat in *Albatross*' cockpit and feasted on the traditional fare of herring, new potatoes and generous amounts of snaps and Danish beer, breaking into song as the fancy took us, which it did with increments in direct proportion to the amount of "burning wine" drunk. From our position in the harbour we could see the flames billowing out from the huge bonfire further down the shore and hear the raucous singing of the Danes, which naturally we did our best to drown out: Ove louder than Carl, Martin, Dino and I put together. Eventually the sun disappeared into the sea and Midsummer Eve became Midsummer Day. We decided to lasso our berths while we could still find them.

A couple of hours later, the thumping noise in my head had become too irritating to sleep through. I groggily sat up and rubbed my temples, wondering at the persistency of the knocking noise in my right ear. It took me more than a few seconds before my befuddled brain worked out that the knocking wasn't in my ear at all but against the side of the boat. I woke Dino with whom I shared the cabin and we stumbled up on deck. We quickly discovered the source of the noise: a drunk had fallen into the water on the starboard side of the boat and had been knocking on the hull to alert us. *Bloody idiot*, I thought to myself. The idiot turned out to be none other than Ove who'd been clinging desperately to a mussel covered pier post. Together Dino and I used all our strength to hoist him out; it's not easy landing a 62-year-old, 220-pound drunk with a beer belly. The old fool was shivering uncontrollably, his hands bleeding profusely from cuts he'd sustained from the razor sharp mussel shells as he tried to hold on to the post. He was more than a little confused, peering myopically at us as he'd lost his glasses in the water. We wrapped a towel around his head and shoulders to keep him warm and got him into the cabin. By this time Carl had woken, disturbed by the movement of the boat and the shouting.

'Who the heck is the old witch?' he asked, squinting at Ove.

'More like an old git,' I replied. 'We found him overboard.'

Carl did a double take as he realized who it was. 'Holy crap! Ove? I didn't recognize you with the headdress and without your glasses. What the hell...?'

Ove swayed and clutched at his towel. 'Call of nature. I lost my balance and fell in,' he managed to say through chattering teeth. 'Bloody hell, it was cold in the water. Thank god you heard me, Yanne.'

Carl rolled his eyes. 'First port of call on a 50,000-mile journey and we already lose a man overboard. Unbelievable!'

'I'm getting quite good at pulling people out of the water,' I said, cheerfully. We stripped Ove of his wet clothes, wrapped him in a blanket and propped him up in a chair. The water survival course was proving to be very useful.

Martin and Dino left *Albatross* at Skagen to take the train back to Sweden and work, while Ove would continue with us; despite his mishap overboard, he was none the worse for wear and hopefully a little wiser for the experience. 'Yup, back to the grind,' Carl said unable to hide a smug smile at Dino's mention of going back to work: it was wonderful to think that for the next three years our work was sailing. Now that we'd checked off the remaining tasks on our list and *Albatross* was ready for the North Sea, we set a course for Peterhead. The wind was already gusting fiercely as we sailed out of Skagen, and by the time we'd rounded the head and were out into the Skagerrak straits, we were sailing against 50-mile an hour winds – nine on the Beaufort scale.

'We can't sail 470 nautical miles in this!' I shouted to Carl.

'You're right,' he shouted back. 'Let's cut our losses and make for Norway instead.'

We set a course for Kristiansand convinced that the wind would drop enough to get there fairly easily. Wrong again. During the night the wind and wave strength increased, forcing us to change course yet again. The following evening in the glow of an amber sunset we slid into the safety of Arendal harbour.

Paying harbour fees are a necessary evil when arriving in a new port, but even a swig of our mooring snaps of *Gammel Dansk* failed to take the sting out of the shockingly high Norwegian fees. The first thing we wanted to do was to pile into the shower and rinse off two days of salt water, but even a shower was expensive. The three of us would normally have piled into one shower together, but for some reason this was frowned upon in Arendal, so we reconciled ourselves to using the small shower cabins on *Albatross*; we preferred to use our own fresh water than pay the exorbitant shower fees. Picturesque though Arendal harbour is with its bustling town centre and colourful timber houses dotted around the hills, we were disinclined to stay longer and preferred to sail for Peterhead where the harbour fees and the beer were cheaper. We were also anxious not to miss our place in the Classic Malt Cruise. Although we'd budgeted plenty of time for getting to the start of the cruise at Oban, our current progress in the face of the adverse weather conditions made us aware that plans can easily go awry.

We set sail for Scotland again and for a third time were thwarted by the damn weather. 'It's June for crying out loud,' Carl kept yelling at the sky as we battled against the west wind. Bugger the romantic notion of letting the winds take us: they seemed intent on driving us back to Sweden. It was exhausting sailing and we had to give in, having travelled a mere 70 nautical miles to Kristiansand, the capital of Southern Norway. Once again as we drifted into the city's marina, the wind dropped, the sun glowed golden and the water looked as innocent as an ornamental pond. I was beginning to wonder just how we'd pissed off the weather gods.

We moored beside another boat which had also decided to take refuge from the storm: a 55-foot Amel, so new her sails were as stiff as starched hotel sheets. She was owned by three retired Texan airline pilots whose names I forget – something like J.R., Bobby and Beau Junior. All three claimed to have Scandinavian ancestors and like most Americans were desperate to explore what they believed was the home country. They'd pooled together to buy a French ketch which they'd picked up in La Rochelle and sailed over from France to explore Scandinavia. The youngest of them was 70 if he was a day. They were instantly friendly and invited us on board for a drink. We entered the saloon and gasped with admiration. It was a beautiful boat, but what astonished us was the fact that the cabin was packed floor to ceiling with cases of red wine on the portside, whisky on the starboard and in the middle was a stack of boxes marked "peanuts." Well, I assumed they needed something to nibble with the drinks.

'Ballast,' said 75-year-old Beau Junior as way of explanation.

'Ah, I thought she was lying low in the water,' Carl remarked.

'Yup, she sure is. But you're welcome to help us lighten the load, fellas,' J.R. waved a mottled hand to port and starboard. 'Pick yer poison.'

Our English may not have been fluent but we could understand that much. The Texans were as hilarious as they were generous and despite the language barrier and Texan accents so thick you could have spread them on toast, we roared at the stories of their days as pilots for Pan American, although many of their exploits may explain why the airline declared bankruptcy in 1991. We spent the next few days visiting Kristiansand with them and could only gawp with envy as all three displayed the energy and libidos of 20-year-olds; they were to women as catnip is to a domestic tabby. Clearly sex appeal has no age limit when it comes to charm and charisma. I still wonder if it was an integral part of the Pan Am pilot's training.

As Kristiansand is Norway's fifth largest city, we felt we should take a day or two to visit some of its sights while waiting for the weather to turn. The Texans loaned Ove a bike so we could all cycle around the area which is pleasingly quaint with pretty white wooden houses hugging the inlets and islands of the Archipelago. A statue in the centre of the city of King Christian IV of Denmark and Norway, founder of the city in 1641, portrays him as a distinctly stocky figure with a paunch stomach, cartoonish beard, hand on hip and sporting an oversized hat, all of which give him a slightly camp air, although he sired at least 24 children with his various wives and mistresses. He is to date Denmark's longest-reigning monarch racking up 59 years as king, during which time England saw the end of the reign of Elizabeth I and the entire reigns of both James I and Charles I. Unlike Charles I, who was executed for treason, Christian IV was an extremely popular king, despite or possibly because of his notoriety as being a hard-drinking king and his keen involvement in many a witch burning.

We cycled along the coastline some 20 miles before coming to Møvik Fort, one of the four coastal defence batteries that made up the Kristiansand artillery group, erected between 1941 and 1944 by the German Navy, using forced labour. As testosterone fuelled boys (ladies, look away now), we were curious to see the only remaining 380 millimetre Krupp gun in the world, one of the biggest cannons ever built. We could easily have stuffed Carl in the barrel but he wasn't keen. The gun barrel alone weighs 110 tonnes, measures 65 feet in length and has an impressive reach of 35 miles, meaning it could shoot shells the length of Greater London and still have five miles to spare. A sister battery was built in Hanstholm in Denmark on the opposite side of Skagerrak, so the two batteries could operate together to effectively block the allied forces' access to the sea routes to the Kattegat and the Baltic. (Okay, ladies, it's safe to resume reading.)

After four days we decided to weigh anchor and make our third attempt to sail straight west to Scotland. Early Sunday morning, we optimistically sailed out of Kristiansand on a pleasant breeze only to be battered about again out on the North Sea where the waves turned dark and menacing and the wind increased to 50 miles an hour. We reefed in and tacked hard through the foam. After two days of feeling as if we were sailing in a washing machine set on the cold wash programme, our old friend seasickness turned up. Carl disappeared to throw up everything he'd ever eaten, and Ove and I felt as perky as zombies. We kept three-hour watches and ate only crispbread, raisins and bananas for energy. The nights were long and it was extremity-numbingly cold. Worse still, the wind generator appeared only to generate electricity when we sailed against the wind; if we sailed with the wind, it registered zero. In an effort to conserve electricity, we had no heating in the cabin and had to sleep in our clothes. It was an even more miserable crossing than the first time.

Anyone who believes the old chestnut that "it is better to travel than to arrive" has never experienced the misery of low cost airlines or crossed the North Sea in a 42-foot ketch in violent weather. After four days of rough sailing, arriving in Peterhead seemed better than winning the lottery. The joy of tying up the boat, drinking our mooring snaps and showering off four days of salt and sweat was simply blissful. And having finally put the dreaded North Sea behind us, both Carl and I felt the weight of stress falling from our shoulders. Despite the unremitting wretchedness of crossing the North Sea, not once had either of us said, 'That's it, I've had it. Let's go back.' It simply didn't occur to us: there was so much to anticipate. We couldn't wait to round the next cape, corner or headland. A whole world of experiences lay before us: the world was indeed our oyster and we were just beginning to prise it open to peek at the treasures inside. What strangers would cross our paths and what sailing tales would we hear? We, too, were collecting our experiences, our own stories for life. We clinked our snaps glasses together and toasted "to life." We were finally living it instead of marking out the monotonous days to its end.

Chapter 15

In Search of Nessie

3 – 13 July 2002

Peterhead – Inverness – Fort William – Oban

Experience: *The Scottish are completely incomprehensible, but very generous and helpful.*

Tip: *Pack a phrase book for each country you're visiting or be prepared to mime more than Marcel Marceau.*

'Da ye want three pints a' heavy, pal?'
Ove looked at Carl who in turn looked at me. I shrugged. 'Don't ask me. I've no idea what he's saying.'

Carl masterfully gave it a shot. 'I would like to buy three glasses of beer, thank you,' he said haltingly.

The barman rolled his eyes at the ceiling as if he'd never met such monumental cretins in his life before. 'Aye, but da ye want heavy or pale?' We all pondered this, increasingly confused now that there appeared to be a choice involved, not that we had any idea what "heavy" and "pale" meant. In Sweden we order our beers by strength: light, medium and strong. My turn to have a go.

'We would like to buy three medium beers, thank you.'

'Medium? Are ye talking aboot steaks now? There's no medium. Listen pal, it's a pint or a half.' The barman plonked two tumblers on the bar, one large and one small, to demonstrate the sizes.

'Ah,' we all said. Now we were getting somewhere. 'Three glasses of pint, thank you,' I said cheerfully.

'Heavy or pale?' asked the barman, enunciating slowly and pointing to a selection of pumps. We considered the writing and pictures on each one. I waved at a tap at random.

'This,' I said. 'Three, thank you.'

'So ye want three pints a' heavy?' asked the barman. We nodded. 'Glad we finally got that clear,' he said sardonically as he filled the glasses. He set them on the bar top. 'Mud in yer eye, ye Abba freaks.'

'No, thank you,' Carl said with a plastic smile. 'I certainly don't want that mud pie,' he muttered to me. 'Sounds disgusting.'

If communicating in English was proving to be a challenge, understanding Scottish was darn near impossible – and we were definitely in Scotland, the decorations said it all: red and green tartan wallpaper, purple tartan curtains and a turquoise and black tartan carpet left us in no doubt of our location, but made me feel slightly nauseous even before I'd downed the four pints. The three of us initially wrangled with the language as determinedly as that Braveheart chap with the English, but eventually admitted early defeat: Ove pointed at things he wanted, Carl would smile and nod a lot, and I became astonishingly good at drawing. Having a conversation in Scotland was like one long game of charades. Once we found a phrase that worked, we stuck with it and so continued to drink pints of heavy; it was easier than trying to untangle the beers on offer at the next pub. Fortunately, we really liked "heavy" so it wasn't a setback. We naively agreed that the Scottish accent was probably the most difficult we'd have to decipher: we hadn't yet visited Belfast.

We stayed just a couple of days in Peterhead to prepare *Albatross* for her next stint. We'd experienced several awkward problems getting to Scotland: the low water pressure in the taps in the fresh water system was eventually solved by unclogging the outlet pipe in the water tank; the bilge pump seemed to be working overtime, indicating that we were taking in water somewhere but we didn't know where. As usual our "to do" list started to grow. We'd bought a couple of tyres and planks to rig together and mount on the side of the boat to act as fenders in the Caledonian Canal locks; these we smartened up by painting white. Then there was the washing: after 14 days of sailing, our clothes and bedding crackled with salt and sweat. We filled two large buckets with soapy water, hand-washed everything and hung our laundry out on the gunwale where it quickly dried in the sun which finally shone hot for the first time on our trip.

Repairs and washing done, we set sail late in the evening for Inverness. The sea was mirror calm and the night's sailing was wonderfully smooth. As we entered the Moray Firth and passed Fort George, we spotted seals basking on the rocks in the morning sun. Shortly afterwards, two acrobatic bottlenose dolphins appeared and played engagingly around *Albatross*. The Moray Firth is home to over 2,000 seals and is one of the best places on the British coast for observing dolphins and whales.

This was trouble free sailing, enabling us to relax and admire the scenery for the first time. Either I became a little too relaxed, or possibly I was nervous about negotiating the first lock on the Caledonian Canal, but as we approached Clachnaharry I took *Albatross* on the wrong side of a marker buoy and we juddered to a halt with a sickening thud: we'd run aground.

'Nice one, Yanne,' Carl called. 'What do we do now? Stay here on a bloody sandbank like a fairy on a Christmas tree and wait for high tide?'

Fortunately, we hadn't been going at speed when I hit the sandbank and we were able to motor ourselves backwards off it. Nevertheless, I felt a bit of a fool for sailing on the wrong side of the buoy: it was akin to driving on the wrong side of the road. Lord knows what kind of mess I'd make of getting through the 29 locks of the Caledonian Canal. If you're thinking this sounds rather wimpy on my part, then you've never been down the 118-mile Göta Canal in Sweden, the lock system of which is so vast and complicated it's nicknamed the "divorce ditch" because of the numerous break-ups which ensue between holidaying couples as they try to navigate the 58 locks by themselves. The fact that there is a reality series on Swedish television solely devoted to the antics on Göta Canal is testimony to the calamities endured by holiday sailors. More disturbingly, it provides proof of our increasingly desperate need to observe the mundane lives of our neighbours, as well as their own desire for their 30 seconds of fame, however humiliated that half minute may render them. I've watched, slack jawed, as couples have screamed abuse at each other: him steering their dream yacht while shouting instructions to his other half with a megaphone: her screaming back endearments such as, 'You're such an ass-hole, you can shove your bloody boat where the sun don't shine!' I hoped Carl and I wouldn't have to resort to the same kind of language to get us to Fort William at the other end of the Scottish canal.

At a mere 62 miles long, the Caledonian Canal is the little sister to the Göta Canal. The Scottish project, built to provide a short cut between the North Sea and the Atlantic Ocean, was inaugurated by Scottish engineer Thomas Telford in 1803 and opened in 1822. The Göta Canal opened a decade later, was designed by, guess who, Scottish engineer Thomas Telford. Ironically, although the canals were hailed as engineering triumphs, they were both commercially unsuccessful; by the time the Caledonian Canal was complet-ed, ship building had advanced with the introduction of larger hulled ships too big to navigate the canal. In Sweden, the arrival of the speedier railways quickly rendered the Göta Canal redundant.

Today, however, both waterways are used by pleasure craft and offer holiday-ing couples the catalyst for the divorce they've probably been heading towards since leaving the church. As we approached the first lock at Clachnaharry, I shook Carl's hand and said, 'Remember that we're good mates and whatever we say in the Caledonian Canal stays in the Caledonian Canal.'

We needn't have worried: the great difference between the two waterways is that the Caledonian Canal was mechanised in the 1960s and there are plenty of people to help you at the locks, all of which makes for a very pleasant experience. Even the dreaded Neptune's Staircase, a breath-taking eight-lock flight, making it the longest in Britain, was manageable, taking less than two hours to clear all eight locks and lowering us 64 feet. We shared a beer with a couple of lock keepers who, on recognising our Swedish flag, joked how the Vikings had stolen all the good-looking women.

'Want to see Nessie?' asked a large jovial type who looked as if he'd carried off more than a few women in his time.

'We know the story,' I said. 'There is no Loch Ness monster.'

'Aye, but Nessie does exist. She lives at home with me. And she's a big monster if ever there was one,' he roared, delighted with his own joke which no doubt he told a dozen times a day.

Of the 60-mile waterway, only 22 miles are man-made; the remaining 38 miles are made up of four lochs of the Great Glen: Loch Dochfour, Loch Ness, Loch Oich and the unimaginatively named Loch Lochy. When I say "only" 22 miles are man-made, bear in mind that those geography changing man-made stretches were dug out by navvies using only spades. *Only spades!* I reflected with awe on this astonishing achievement as we sailed through the mountainous heart of the Highlands. Given a spade and told to dig for the best part of 22 miles, I would have scraped out a shallow pit for myself and let my fellow navvies heap the earth back over me.

A glorious view opened before us as we sailed into Loch Ness, a body of water said to be deep enough to hold the fresh water from every lake in England and Wales put together, and so big it could fit beneath its surface every human on the planet three times over. There was certainly an eerie atmosphere to the loch; the water looked like black oil and I had no doubt it held secrets in its deep.

I wondered how all this monster business had originated. After some research I gathered that the first recorded sighting went back to the sixth century when an Irish monk had a run-in with a "water-beast" which he dispatched with a sign of the cross, much to the surprise of the witnessing Picts. Nessie hunting began in earnest in the 1930s after a string of sightings and murky photos were published, eventually leading to the suggestion that the monster was an extinct plesiosaur. Since then, investigation bureaus, sonar studies, submersibles and satellite tracking have been employed to find proof of a monster, but extensive research has yet to confirm its existence. Despite this, Nessie believers would adamantly assert scientists have yet to disprove the presence of their watery friend. Whatever the case, we all like a little mystery and I felt it would be a shame if the myth were completely debunked, so I scanned the water vigilantly, becoming slightly overexcited when I mistook a bit of driftwood for the neck of the monster.

As we entered Loch Linnhe, the landscape reached a dramatic crescendo with Britain's highest mountain, Ben Nevis, rising behind the town of Fort William situated in the glen below. The Ben, as it is fondly known by the locals, is 4,406 feet high and therefore a mere pimple in terms of height when compared to the big daddy of them all, Mount Everest at over 29,000 feet or even Mount Blanc at 15,781 feet. Nevertheless, much of the time the Ben is shrouded in cloud. Snow normally covers the gullies or north-facing cliffs even in summer. It's a strenuous walk to the summit, taking between seven to nine hours to make the ascent, so I genuinely applaud Clement Wragge, a seriously nerdy meteorologist who in the summers of 1881 to 1883 climbed the peak daily to make meteorological recordings and establish a need for an observatory on the summit. The observatory has long gone but people still love to run up and down the mountain side at breakneck speed; an annual race takes place every September, the 1984 record for which remains unbroken at one hour, 25 minutes and 34 seconds. I asked Carl and Ove if they fancied a climb to the top, but they were strangely reluctant.

'We don't want to be late for the whisky cruise,' Ove said anxiously, looking at his watch. As a keen whisky drinker – Ove called himself a connoisseur, but that's just a posh term for dipsomaniac – he, most of us all, was looking forward to the Classic Malt Cruise.

A warm Atlantic wind carried us the 35 miles from Fort William to Oban where the 14-day cruise was to start. We anchored that evening in the bay off the tiny island of Kerrera where we met up with another Helsingborg yacht, *CU@sea* owned by Anna-Karin and Per. The following morning we took the dinghy into Oban to complete our registration for the cruise. By then, the bay was full of sailboats of every size and origin: many flew British flags, but others had come from Ireland, France, Germany, Holland, Norway and as far-flung as the USA to converge at Oban. The town was swarming with guests keen to participate in the greatest whisky tour of them all.

We'd registered for the cruise online and our place among the hundred craft had been confirmed. The concept was wonderfully simple: the cruise was a mixture of sailing in company and solo exploration following an itinerary of distillery visits, whisky tastings and "nosings," social events ashore and rendezvous afloat. Boats were free to follow their own routes allowing us to explore as much or as little as we liked. Every few days the fleet would meet up to share their stories – or 'go on a fleet bender' as one British yachtsman put it. Carl, Ove and I debated the meaning of the word "bender," eventually defining it as drinking until the memory of the event is forever lost or paralysis sets in.

We'd been joined in Fort William by my daughter, Beatrice, and her German boyfriend Philipp, whom I hadn't met before and for whom the Classic Malt Cruise would be quite an initiation test. Registration fittingly took place in the Oban whisky distillery where the whole crew was equipped with caps and fleece shirts and we were given our first distillery tour. We all smiled and nodded very politely as our guide explained the process involved in the production of a Single Malt. But if I'm honest we understood one word in a dozen and were merely marking time until we got our first sample of Oban whisky, whereupon the smiling and nodding began in earnest sincerity.

The distillery offered further festivities that evening with a banquet for the 400-strong crew members and distillery representatives, aptly held in a 200-year-old whisky warehouse where the walls reeked with the aroma of barley. We stood agog at the sumptuous buffet of lobster, prawns, Scottish salmon, oysters, clams, herring in various pickled forms that would make a Swede tearful, smoked mackerel, roast beef, smoked ham, roast chicken and game pies. This was followed by a modest dessert of fresh raspberries and whipped cream, cakes and pastries, and then a cheese course in case you were still feeling a bit peckish. It was as if the organizers had taken the cookbooks of Mrs Beeton, Delia Smith and Jamie Oliver and decided to prepare every dish described within. All of this was served with wine and, of course, whichever whisky you cared to sample. Oh, and did I mention this was free to all the participating crews? The whole shebang was funded by the distilleries. God bless them, every one.

The last clear memory I have of the evening was the parade of visiting yachtsmen marching through Oban led by a Highland piper, his kilt swinging fetchingly in time to his piping as he marched us around the town and down to the harbour. I briefly recalled the story of the *Pied Piper of Hamelin* and wondered if it was all an elaborate con to ditch the tourists and nab a hundred boats. But with one arm around Beatrice's shoulder and the other around Philipp's, I merrily marched along. While we would never master the mangled vowel sounds of the Scottish dialect, we were ready to embrace the culture wholeheartedly. I quite fancied myself in a dress kilt, although I was still perplexed by the furry purse dangling around the groin area: a nifty pouch for your car keys or condoms? By the end of the evening, I was imagining myself 'laird of the manor' with a clan tartan of bright blue and yellow; I wasn't ready to abandon my Swedish heritage altogether.

Chapter 16
Whisky Galore!
13 – 28 July 2002

Oban – Tobermory – Canna – Talisker – Lochaline –
Craobh Haven– Loch A'Bhealaich – Port Ellen

Experience: *Sailing around the Scottish isles is like seeing the world when it was first made – beautiful, rugged and unspoiled.*

Tip: *The correct way to drink whisky: pour three fingers of whisky into a tumbler, add a little water to release the flavour of the malt. Do not add ice; ice is for polar bears.*

The opening evening of the Classic Malt Cruise in Oban is the last lucid memory I have of the trip. The rest is all shamefully fuzzy. Here's as much as Carl, Ove and I could piece together.

- Visited a lot of distilleries where we made sure to sample each and every whisky offered, no doubt out of an inherent sense of politeness towards our hosts.
- Carl sang a Swedish ditty and was complemented on the melodious quality of his voice. Fortunately, no one in the four hundred-strong crowd could understand the song's lyrics which were so filthy they would have made a Scottish rugby team blush.
- Attended a party hosted by the Talisker distillery in a marquee where we were all much impressed by the temporary toilets: as our photos show, these were no ordinary portaloos but a glorious installation in a marquee decorated with crystal chandeliers and gold taps in the basins and urinals. Here you could stand and urinate accompanied by the music of Wagner. As Ove remarked, 'I've never experienced such an elegant pee.'
- Woke up in Port Ellen with *Albatross*, crew more or less intact and thumping headache.

Chapter 17

Guinness is Good for You

28 July – 18 August, 2002

Bangor, Belfast – Howth –Dublin – Arklow

Experience: *Howth is an expensive tourist trap; it's cheaper to sail into Dublin itself and moor in the city's docklands. Rural towns are more welcoming than big cities: Arklow is a gem.*

Tip: *Never try kissing the Blarney Stone; the caretakers at the site of the stone pee on it the night before the tourists arrive and then watch and laugh as unsuspecting tourists contort themselves to kiss it. Always take note of the advice given to you by locals and visiting yachtsmen alike: they have a lot to share that's worth listening to.*

'We're here,' Ove said. He pointed to a green blip at the edge of the screen. I looked at Carl who rolled his eyes impatiently.

'Really?' Carl said. 'You're quite sure about that, are you, Ove?'

'Oh yes. We're definitely here.' Ove jabbed at the screen again oblivious to the heavy sarcasm in Carl's voice.

'Ove, are you quite sure you know how to use the radar?' I asked.

Ove gave me a look that could have curdled milk, a look that wondered how the student dare question the master. 'Certainly. I've sailed using radar more times than you've had a hangover. That's *Albatross*, there.'

It would have been laughable had it not been so dangerous. We were sitting ducks in the North Channel of the Irish Sea in the middle of a white fog so thick you could have painted a wall with it. Visibility was zilch: it was like trying to see through cream soup. All the more reason to know exactly our position and, more to the point, everyone else's. Seventeen million tonnes of goods are traded between Great Britain and the Emerald Isle making it a very busy waterway. I could hear the melancholy boom of fog horns out in the darkness but could see nothing, so it was vital to know our position on the radar. *Albatross'* radar was 12 years old and fairly basic. We'd found the scanner didn't work particularly well in either rain or in very high waves: boats would suddenly disappear off the radar screen leaving us to wonder if they'd been sucked into the sky by some mysterious force. In fog like this, however, in an otherwise calm sea, we could and had to use it to sail into a port with which we were unfamiliar, so we'd dusted it off and hooked it up.

Ove peered at the screen again. 'Yup, that's definitely *Albatross*, right there.'

Carl shook his head. 'Bloody hell, Ove, if it were up to you, we'd be mown down by a huge flipping oil tanker. *Albatross* is here!' He jabbed at the centre of the screen. 'Right in the middle. All the other dots around us are the boats we have to avoid.'

Ove took off his glasses, breathed on them, wiped them on the bottom of his sweater and put them on again. He looked closely at the screen and frowned. 'Ah, right. I see what you're getting at now. Well, yes, of course, that's us, right in the middle, there.'

I pulled Ove away before Carl gave him an earful. This was no place to have a shoving match. Although the sea wasn't particularly rough and the wind was light, we had no desire to fall in the waters around us, having read that the Irish Sea is the most radioactively contaminated sea in the world. On the Cumbrian coast lay the Sellafield nuclear reprocessing site which according to Greenpeace discharges "some eight million litres of nuclear waste into the sea each day, leading to contamination of seawater and marine life." That kind of statement doesn't encourage taking a dip in any kind of weather or sampling the local catch of the day. We'd long since hauled in the fishing line – not that we'd caught a damn thing with it anyway – but we half expected the sea to glow lurid green with luminous life or catch mutant fish with hair and limbs.

With the help of the radar and without Ove's misguided interference, we navigated our way safely into Bangor harbour. Once the fog lifted we could appreciate that Bangor was a cheerful little town, with rainbow coloured buildings poised on green slopes. I was most impressed by how clean and tidy the town was, even more so to read on a lamppost that the penalty for littering was £35 and strictly enforced. I wanted to pin a medal on the chest of the man who'd implemented this law: I'd noticed on our cycle tour through England three years earlier how blighted the country was by a massive litter problem; trees sprouted supermarket carrier bags and bushes bloomed with discarded beer cans.

We were curious to see Belfast after years of hearing about the Troubles, but were apprehensive about how dangerous it might be. We took the train into the city and were pleasantly surprised. Having been fed a media diet of a city under siege, we were overjoyed to observe this was not the case: it was not blitzed and bombed as we'd imagined, but was a capital trying to rebuild itself. Nevertheless, we realized very quickly over a pint of Guinness that the IRA was not a topic for idle banter with the locals. Having said that, conversation on any topic was going to be a challenge, as the Belfast accent was even harder for us to decode than the Scottish.

After a day of chores and waiting for the fog to lift, we set a course for Dublin. It was a pleasant sail; we were pushed by an obligingly brisk wind, scooting us into Howth on the peninsular of Howth Head north of Dublin Bay as a rosy dawn rose. Once a small fishing village, Howth is now a busy Dublin suburb, popular with tourists and with a correspondingly expensive marina. After catching up on some sleep and toasting to another new port with a glass of snaps, we took the train into Dublin to look for a cheaper harbour. Our plan was to stay in the area for two weeks; Eva and Monica were due to join us the following week when Ove would leave *Albatross* and return to Sweden.

The Dublin Docklands proved to be an ideal harbour with a floating dock for 10 boats and a high-fenced and well-guarded marina. Ever thrifty, Carl managed to negotiate a discount for our stay and we sailed *Albatross* into her new berth. Here, as well as everywhere else in Dublin, we noticed the huge investment taking place in rebuilding. The Dublin Docklands were following the example set by the regeneration of the London Docklands, and were being renovated and redeveloped with new office buildings, waterside homes, shopping areas, parks, cycleways, theatres, art galleries and an O2 arena, all at a cost of some €6.3 trillion. The project is still ongoing and has radically changed the face of the city.

The Docklands wasn't the only area leeching money. We were staggered by Dublin's apparent wealth: spanking new four-by-fours sped around the city; on the outskirts, gleaming housing developments were sprouting like white truffles. 'Who the hell is paying for all this?' Carl wondered.

'We are,' I said, choking with shock. I'd just got the bill for our meal.

Our sense of bonhomie was restored as we enjoyed a pint of the black stuff in *The Brazen Head*, Dublin's oldest pub.

'Ah,' Carl said and smacked his lips. He held up his glass of Guinness, admired it and took another gulp. 'Ah,' he said again with even greater relish than before. 'How about we sell the boat and run a pub here in Dublin, Yanne?' I was tempted, I truly was: such is the power of a great beer to change a man's mind, and Guinness is undoubtedly a great beer.

When in Rome, do as the Romans do. When in Dublin, visit the Guinness Brewery and immerse yourself in the pub culture which is alive and swaying. Before the smoking ban was introduced in Ireland in 2004, making it the first country in the world to institute an outright ban on smoking in workplaces, there were over a thousand pubs in Dublin alone, but this number has since shrunk to 666. Nevertheless, Dublin is still a Mecca for the pub aficionado. We decided we should make an inventory of them all – in the name of research, you understand. Unfortunately, pub closing time is officially half an hour past the stroke of midnight allowing us less time than we'd thought to complete our catalogue, but we tried, really, we did. We sampled old pubs, famous pubs and pubs blasting with live music so loud it made your ears bleed. As last orders were called, we found ourselves standing together with a bunch of locals, raising our pints of the black stuff and singing the Irish national anthem. I'd hoped to end the evening with a little harmless flirting with a lovely redhead, but it wasn't to be; the only redhead I met was a builder called Rory with more tattoos than teeth.

We felt it only right to continue our investigation of the drinking culture by going directly to the heart of it. The Guinness Storehouse, the interior of which is fittingly built in the shape of a pint glass, details the history of the brewery and the beer. There we feigned polite interest in the Guinness making process – we were really just there for the free pint, although at an entrance fee of €14, it hardly qualified as free. Nevertheless, the tour did raise some interesting facts. In 1759, Arthur Guinness signed a 9,000-year lease for the four-acre disused brewery at an annual rent of £45 per year making him a man who laughed long and heartily all the way to his local bank; Guinness is brewed in 49 countries worldwide and sold in over 150. Most is sold in Great Britain, followed by Ireland and, surprisingly, Nigeria. Ten million glasses are drunk every day around the world, and at one point the brewery paid its workers in Guinness. This last fact perked up Ove no end who asked if there were any positions open and when he might start.

It was as we ended the tour in the Gravity bar at the top of the building and were learning that it takes 119.53 seconds to pour the perfect pint – approximately 110 seconds too long after a lengthy tour – that I realised just how painfully broke Ove was. I nudged Carl as we watched him try to cadge another "free" Guinness out of our tour guide. Carl nodded at me over the creamy head of his own pint; he'd also noticed how Ove not only begged cigarettes from strangers in bars, but would even pick up discarded butts out of ashtrays; he clearly didn't have the means to buy himself a packet. While in Dublin, Ove celebrated his sixty-third birthday, and we took the opportunity to pay for his drinks and a meal out. Carl, in a spirit of unusual generosity, even treated Ove to one of his precious Havana cigars which he'd intended to bring out only after we'd crossed one of the "big ones," as we called the Atlantic and the Pacific Oceans. I've never seen a man take such pleasure in smoking a cigar. Ove put it to his lips with great tenderness and gazed at it between each puff as a lover would his lady. I think I spotted a tear in his eye as he finally ground out the tiny stub.

Dublin was Ove's last port of call with us; his daughter had paid his return flight to Sweden, and as Monica and Eva arrived we said goodbye to a man who'd become our mentor and an invaluable friend. *Albatross* felt strangely empty without his presence; it was as if he'd been a part of the boat, which I suppose in many ways he had, from his help in preparing her for her circumnavigation to giving me tips on repairs and mechanics. I would miss his companionship, his largess of spirit and, indeed, his largeness. And I worried about him. Both Carl and I thought Ove was careless of his own safety: it was as if he wasn't concerned whether he saw his sixty-fourth birthday or not. I wouldn't have gone so far as to say he had a death wish, but he didn't appear to value his life and took no efforts to ensure his own well-being. Take, for example, the time I pulled him out of the water in Skagen: it wasn't the first time he'd been rescued from the water and I doubted it would be the last, so it was with complete sincerity that as I shook his hand farewell, I said, 'Ove, take care of yourself.'

His white eyebrows lifted slightly above his dark glasses. 'You're the idiots who have to cross the Atlantic without my help. Don't worry about me.' He slapped me cheerfully on the back.

Our minds were taken off Ove's departure by the arrival of the women and we all enjoyed a bit of a honeymoon. Carl and Eva took off for the Irish countryside leaving Monica and me the boat for the weekend. I will only say that we didn't leave the cabin for two days. Then we rented a car and drove to Donegal where we stayed in cosy little B and B's, explored the countryside and visited ruined castles.

A week later, we bade farewell to our fairer halves with slightly fewer tears than had been shed in Helsingborg. Carl and I resumed our journey with real joy in our hearts; we'd become reluctant landlubbers and were eager to feel the rush of water below *Albatross*' keel again. We set a course sailing along the Irish coast, passing Tuskar Rock at Ireland's southernmost tip on the way out of St George's Channel, crossing the Celtic Sea and then sailing into the Bay of Biscay and onwards to Spain. We rolled up our sleeves, cast off and set sail on the outgoing tide; with good weather, we estimated the 750-nautical mile journey would take us three days. With bad weather, it might take a week.

But damn it all if we hadn't even sailed 25 miles before foul weather forced us to abandon our route yet again. Towards evening, the tide turned against us and the wind picked up, throwing up mean 30-foot waves, hungry to swallow up a 42-foot ketch. There was no way we could tack a course in this. We'd heard that 176 wrecks are listed for the Tuskar Rock; the likelihood of our being the hundred and seventy-seventh was high in rough weather, so we cut our losses and made for the safety of Arklow harbour.

The following morning it was still blowing hard from the south, sending clouds scuttling across a benign looking blue sky. Until the wind changed, we would have to resign ourselves to staying in Arklow. So we pumped up the tyres on the bikes and cycled towards the town, a very pleasing place lying at the bottom of a hill with a busy high street lined with quaint shops, and, of course, numerous pubs advertising Irish folk music. I was beginning to understand how things worked in Ireland; parties were held in the pubs rather than at home, where everyone from the legal drinking age of 18 to nonagenarians would pack themselves in for *ceoil agus craic*, which, as we had learned in Dublin, was Gaelic for "music and fun."

The town is divided by the River Avoca, crossed by the Nineteen Arches Bridge, which, according to a plaque on the structure, is the longest hand-made stone bridge in Ireland and therefore something of a landmark. But our goal was a fishing harbour we'd spied on the opposite side where an elegant 40-foot wooden sailboat was moored. Although our Reeds Nautical Almanac indicated that mooring in the fishing harbour was strictly forbidden, it seemed another boat owner had done so.

'If he can, so can we,' Carl reasoned. 'Let's find the harbourmaster.'

We promptly sought him out. Peter, an elderly gentleman, told us he'd taken a job in Skagen in Denmark after the Second World War and so knew our part of the world well. He was happy to chat, at considerable length, about his days in the war as a pilot, his liking for *Gammel Dansk* and the Skagen artists. Eventually our patience was rewarded when Peter allowed us to moor in "his" harbour at a fifth of the price of the marina. As Peter said with a wise shake of the head, 'We're a public facility and not here to make money like the private marina.'

Thrilled at the prospect of cheaper rates, we moved *Albatross* and moored up beside *S/Y Westernman*, the wooden sailboat. As we stood there admiring her, the skipper appeared on deck. A man in his mid-fifties, he was astonishingly tall with a shock of white hair, expressive bushy eyebrows and a full moustache that looked as if it belonged on a character from a Victorian melodrama. He caught our appreciative glances and grinned.

'Ahoy there,' he called in a round, plumy voice. 'Fancy a tour?'

We nearly fell overboard in our haste to accept his invitation. He introduced himself as Tom and his boat was a copy of a 1905 schooner. We didn't have to fake our admiration for *Westernman*; the schooner combined the magic of old-fashioned boats with the conveniences of new technology.

'Where does her name come from?' Carl asked.

'Interesting you should ask that,' Tom replied. 'It was the name given to nineteenth-century pilot cutters, the boats that guided foreign ships down the difficult waters of the Bristol Channel. The men who wanted to earn good wages had to be first out to the ships outside the channel to get the business, so the pilot cutters made fine racing yachts, still considered by many to be the finest sailing boats ever designed.' The tradition of racing pilot cutters continues a hundred years on with the annual Bristol Channel race. Our affable host explained how he'd given up sailing old classic boats, which require so much maintenance, after a back injury. *Westernman* was constructed in wood epoxy and was therefore completely impervious to water. 'All the benefits of a fiberglass boat, yet looks, smells and sails like the real thing,' he said proudly, gesturing left and right.

Tom, wife Ros and daughter Hannah, were on a three-month cruise to Lofoten in northern Norway, but he'd also been driven into Arklow on account of the bad weather. 'It's one thing to risk your own life,' he said with a frown, 'but it's quite another to risk that of your family's.' He told us how as a teenager he'd been pushed off by his father – a man who clearly had a sink or sail attitude – in a 22-foot gaff sloop on the Norfolk Broads to keep him out of mischief. 'Since then, I've never looked back,' he said with a wry chuckle. He and Ros had made their first long sail at the age of 24 to Brazil with less than £50 between them; four years later they returned with £70 in bonds. Although Tom and Ros had made numerous sailing expeditions together and had a wealth of experience – the extent of which Carl and I didn't as yet fully appreciate – they'd never attempted a circumnavigation. Tom's jaw dropped to his chest when we told him how we'd learned to sail and why.

'Well, you certainly deserve credit for ...,' he furrowed his bushy eyebrows as he searched for an appropriate word, '... courage. Sailing round the world without much knowledge or experience certainly isn't for the faint-hearted, and I have to admire your guts. But I completely understand your need to fulfil your dream.' The British are so polite: I got the feeling Tom really wanted to scream, 'Are you completely out of your minds, you Swedish nutters!' Instead he suggested we might like a few tips before we set off for Spain and forced his eyebrows back into their normal position.

The wind was still blowing from the south the following day forcing *Albatross*, *Westernman* and their crews to remain in Arklow. For want of anything better to do, Carl and I decided to test a few of the town's pubs, and we invited Tom to join us. We were sitting quietly in the gloom of the first watering hole when a man presented himself before Tom, saluted him and asked to shake his hand. Tom coughed modestly and shook hands; the man seemed reluctant to let him go.

'Mr Cunliffe, what an honour to meet you. I'm a huge fan,' the man stammered, fervently pumping Tom's hand up and down. 'Just wait till I tell them all at the yacht club how I met the great man himself.'

Carl and I looked at Tom with a mixture of bewilderment and renewed interest.

'Don't you know who you're drinking with?' the huge fan asked, noticing our expressions. 'This is Tom *Cunliffe*: this man is a sailing legend!'

'Well, I wouldn't go so far as ...,' Tom started to say modestly.

'What this man hasn't written about sailing isn't worth reading,' the fan continued.

Carl and I hadn't known it, but we'd been in the company of the British yachting journalist, author and broadcaster. Tom has built a huge career out of his passion for sailing: doing it, teaching it, writing articles and books, and talking about it on TV, on the radio or on the after-dinner speech circuit. We'd been in the presence of greatness and not known it, Tom being the down to earth, modest man he is. (Tom is still going strong on the media circuit. In 2010, he presented an award-winning six-part documentary series, *The Boats that Built Britain*, for the BBC and continues to publish sailing manuals and stories. Much as I'm not the star-struck type, in Tom's case I'm prepared to make an exception.)

It's a strange thing, but despite the fact that we were just at the tip of our iceberg of a journey of 50,000 miles around the globe, the world is indeed a small place. There we were, sitting with our pints in another small pub, putting the world to rights in our broken English, when a bloke sidled up to Tom.

'Tom Cunliffe? Do you remember me?' he asked with a faint but discernible German accent. I was beginning to wonder if Tom's fan club was based in Arklow. Tom's eyebrows knitted together. 'I'm Egon, from Bonn. I failed your celestial navigation course many times.'

Tom's eyebrows lifted in surprise. 'Egon! Of course, I remember you. I see you finally got the hang of English.'

It seemed Egon had failed the course so many times on account of his shaky English, he'd left a permanent imprint on Tom. Egon and his wife, Jeanette, had visited Ireland in the 1980s and fallen in love with Arklow where they'd since remained. After a couple of years in Ireland and tired of finding nothing but soda bread or supermarket thick white sliced for their sandwiches, they decided to open a bakery, specialising in good German bread using different varieties of wheat and grain. Initially, this proved to be a tough sell to the locals who viewed buying German bread akin to joining the Nazi party.

'As you can imagine,' Egon explained, 'the Irish were very suspicious of buying anything from someone they thought might decorate his house with portraits of Hitler and whose father had only visited the British Isles on bombing raids. But we persevered, and 17 years on we're still going strong. Would you like a tour of the bakery?'

We accepted: the wind was still unfavourable; it was raining hard and we had to wait it out, plus we were genuinely interested in the process, particularly as I was the baker on board *Albatross*. With dedication and belief in his product, Egon had built up a successful bakery with a staff of three and supplied shops in Dublin. And tasting his bread, we could understand why he'd been determined to bring his German baking skills to Ireland. There were whole grain rolls, dark rye bread loaves, spelt bread, hazelnut triangles and, yes, soda bread. 'Well, we'll never convert everyone,' Egon said with a resigned shrug. He treated us to lunch at the bakery and gave us two shopping bags loaded with loaves and rolls hot out of the oven. Now, we had bread to enjoy on our journey to Spain as well as tips for better baking.

Although it was still gusting heavily on Saturday evening, the forecast promised a high pressure front between Ireland and the Azores. Both crews of *Albatross* and *Westernman* decided to weigh anchor early on Sunday morning. Carl and I invited the Cunliffe family and Egon and his wife for a potluck meal on board *Albatross* where I tried to impress with a typical Swedish beef stew cooked in my pressure cooker. The seven of us squished around our saloon table, ate and drank while Tom gave us invaluable tips on how to navigate the next part of our journey.

'Watch yourselves as you enter waters on the border between Spain and Portugal; there's a river which is difficult to navigate, and there are fishing nets at the estuary mouth which you can get snarled in if you're not careful. But it's worth the trip; there are some stunning little fishing ports which are quite unspoiled and tourist free.

Carl had been making careful notes between sips of wine. He put down his pen. 'We really appreciate your expertise, Tom. This calls for a cigar,' he said with a broad smile. 'How about a Havana?'

'You don't have to twist my arm hard; I love a good cigar,' Tom said. Carl disappeared to look for the cigar box and I poured more wine. I nearly dropped the bottle when Carl's cry of fury reverberated long and loud, around the cabin. 'Ove, you bloody, thieving git!'

Not only had Ove left the boat, but so had every single one of Carl's precious Havanas left with him. Ove: gone, but certainly not forgotten.

Chapter 18

Brown Boxer Sailing in the Bay of Biscay

18 – 23 August 2002

Arklow - Camariñas

Experience: *Know and obey the international regulations for avoiding collision at sea. And hope that everyone else, including those who sail for a living, obey them, too.*

Tip: *To avoid the Bay of Biscay's wrathful seas, go west, sail down the Irish coast past Cork. From there, sail towards the deeper safer waters where there is a depth of 8,000 to 9,000 feet.*

The Bay of Biscay has always been feared by seamen with some of the most violent weather conditions of the Atlantic Ocean. While the average depth is around 5,000 feet, the continental shelf extends into the bay resulting in areas of shallow water creating surging water and treacherous waves. Add to that the June gloom, a dense fog which settles over the bay, as well as low pressure fronts which turn storms to hurricane strength, and you have a recipe for shipwrecks. Just consider the opening verse of this eighteenth-century song, *The Bay of Biscay*:

> *Loud roars the dreadful thunder, the rain a deluge show'rs;*
> *The clouds are rent asunder by lightning's vivid pow'rs;*
> *The night was drear and dark; our poor devoted bark*
> *Till next day, there she lay in the Bay of Biscay, O!*

It goes on like this for a few more verses, with the poor crew thrashing about in the water, clinging to the wreckage and fearing watery pillows, but I'm sure you get the idea. The lines above – set to a disconcertingly jaunty tune – were written over 200 years ago and you'd think that things would have improved since then. But even today, large vessels go down or collide in the area despite all the technological advances in navigation and improvements in weather forecasting. Our fears of crossing the North Sea seemed mild compared to those of sailing the Bay of Biscay.

'Just sail west,' Tom had advised. 'Get into deep waters, as deep as possible. Sail past Ireland, then head out to where the seabed is 10,000 feet below you. Deep water is safe water.'

We had two options: the first was to go west via Cork and from there take a south-westerly course to reach the safety of deep water as quickly as possible. The other was to head directly for Camariñas in northwest Spain. This was only possible if the good weather held as the forecast had promised it would. We decided therefore to plot a course for Camariñas and hoped the forecast was correct.

Reveille was at the ungodly hour of five in the morning; it was dark and still, eerily so after the last few days of wind we'd experienced. There wasn't a ruffle in the sails and we had to motor a southerly course towards Tuskar Rock with the tide against us. While we loathed wasting diesel, sometimes you have to reconcile using the engine to make any progress. In the afternoon, the weather forecast finally announced a high pressure front heading from the Azores to Ireland, bringing with it a feeble south-easterly wind. We hoisted all the sails and *Albatross* started to bob over the water at a speed of three to four knots. The GPS indicated another 590 nautical miles to our destination which we reckoned would take us five days. The sea was choppy and the swells made *Albatross* buck up and down like an unpleasant rodeo ride. It wasn't long before Carl was hanging over the side, saying goodbye to his breakfast.

That first night on the Celtic Sea was dark and lonely. We didn't see a single other vessel, it was as if we were the only boat in the world. On the second day, we passed the southwest tip of England; the Bishop Rock lighthouse on the Isles of Scilly was clearly visible on the horizon. Early Tuesday morning, we sailed into the northern shipping lanes at the mouth of the English Channel where we had to change course frequently to avoid merchant vessels, but *Albatross* ploughed on, and with the help of the tide we increased our speed to six knots. By late Tuesday night, we were out of the Celtic Sea and laid out our charts for the Bay of Biscay to study the coasts of France and northern Spain. We had finally reached deep waters where roaring depths of 10,000 feet lay dark and comforting beneath our keel. The wind increased and *Albatross* slid serenely over the water.

Carl and I had continued our routine of taking watch as determined by our personalities: being a day person, I would be up and bustling around *Albatross*, working and keeping a look out. On a night watch, however, there's really nothing to do in the dark except keep a look out. I realized, on reading

Carl's entry in the ship's logbook, that my sailing companion tended to wax lyrical when all alone at night. Consider this entry: "We dream, we fantasise. What does northwest Spain look like? Slowly but surely, we sail south; the winds are gentle and kind. The night is lit by a starry sky and a moon shines with a full light. What a wonderful feeling as the water rushes around the hull carrying you across the waves with the wind behind you and the darkness banished by the light from a billion stars."

All this from a burly electrician. Who knew he had such poetic sensibilities?

On the fifth day, we had to swap poetic sensibilities for balls of steel when we encountered a major problem: we were passing through the southern shipping lanes of the Bay of Biscay where huge 400,000-ton tankers were thundering past us. During our Coastal Skipper certificate course, however, we'd learnt the international rules for avoiding collision at sea, which would have been just fine if everyone else had read and adhered to them, too. The first big tanker swerved to pass on our stern, but later that day we spotted a tanker on a direct collision course with us. We frantically called them on the VHF radio but there was no reply. We could see the foam on the bow as the giant bore relentlessly towards us.

'Carl! What do we do?' I shouted. This was scary stuff.

'Remember our training,' Carl shouted back. *Training? What bloody train-ing?* I was so panicked I could barely remember my own name.

'Remember what our instructor, Carl Erik Liljefors, said.'

'What the hell did he say?' My mind had gone helpfully blank.

'Hold your course and steer like crazy until your boxers are brown!'

We disconnected the self-steering gear and hand steered, determinedly holding our course. The tanker thundered towards us. I was gritting my teeth so hard my jaw ached. Then with only half a nautical mile between us and certain disaster, the tanker crashed to starboard and passed our stern. The rush of the water as all 400,000 tons of her hurtled past us was deafening. *Albatross* was left rolling up and down in Goliath's wake.

I was furious. With today's radar technology, ships like these can accurately establish other boats' positions on the open ocean. There was no excuse for endangering a smaller vessel by ignoring maritime rules. 'Bloody bullying bastard,' I shouted, shaking my already shaking fist somewhat uselessly at the disappearing stern.

I'd almost stopped quivering by the time we sighted the Sisargas light-house a mile from Cape Santo Adrián, in the northernmost spot on the Costa da Morte. We were so close to Spain and our destined port of Camariñas, I could almost taste the tapas. The port is set four nautical miles into a bay protected by the impressive cliffs of Cabo Vilán, meaning Cape Villain, so called because its treacherous currents had resulted in many wrecks. We proceeded with extreme caution and tentatively headed into Camariñas marina in the moonlight. We moored up and drew a deep sigh of relief. It was two in the morning and we were exhausted. After five days of nail-biting sailing, it would be good to feel the solid ground of Galicia under our feet. With relief, we fell into our bunks and started snoring before our heads had hit our pillows.

Chapter 19
Viva España!
23 – 30 August 2002
Camariñas, Spain

Experience: *When in harbour, offering to help the locals in small ways, with anything from repairs to cleaning fish, is hugely appreciated and wins new friends, offering you an insight into how life is really lived by the local people.*

Tip: *To avoid flare-ups on open grills from meat and fat juice, first sprinkle a handful of coarse salt on the coals. Caution: the salt will spit back in your face when it hits the hot coals.*

D espite my exhaustion, I slept fitfully and experienced that sort of sleep where the real world invades and distorts your dreams. Mine were of tankers bearing down on me as I sat astride *Albatross* which suddenly transformed into a bobbing cork and swayed ferociously on waves that turned into whales. This was interrupted by Carl frantically tooting a fog horn and screaming, 'Remember your training! Brown boxers! Remember your training!'

Eventually I woke up in a tangle of sheets, checked my boxers weren't brown and realized that the tooting in my dream was in fact a real siren coming from the harbour. Carl and I opened the cabin hatch keen to see what was outside as neither of us had any idea what northwest Spain looked like. Sunlight flooded the cabin as we opened up the hatch. Blinking like moles, we climbed on deck and surveyed a small fishing village bordered by pale beaches and surrounded by green wooded mountain slopes.

Camariñas is located in the province of La Coruña in the heart of Costa da Morte, the coast of Death, named after the fatal Atlantic storms that have taken their toll on ships unfortunate enough to go down in them. While I wouldn't describe Camariñas as the most picturesque fishing harbour I've ever visited – and when the wind blew in the wrong direction, neither would I call it the sweetest smelling place on the globe – it isn't without its charms. The landscape is beautiful and the people were some of the most welcoming of any harbour we sailed into.

Our first stop ashore was Club Nautico, the marina clubhouse. We'd barely placed our brunch order and tasted our beers when we met port captains, Manuel and Pedro, two friendly locals in their fifties who'd had years of sailing experience during which they'd visited numerous countries including Sweden. They were effusive in their praise of Scandinavia.

'Ah, so many beautiful girls in Sweden,' Pedro said wistfully.

'Ah yes,' agreed Manuel with a happy smile, his dark eyes twinkling. 'They kept us very busy.'

We all raised our glasses to toast the loveliness of Swedish womankind. Sometimes I'm very proud to wave my nation's flag, and although I can take absolutely no credit for the attractiveness of our women, I enjoy basking in their reflected glory. A couple of beers later, Carl and I found ourselves volunteering to help Pedro and Manuel with the grilling at the annual clubhouse party the following evening.

We walked to the village to stock up on provisions; our freezer was depleted and we'd been living on tinned goods. As we strolled, it became clear that Camariñas was a working village specializing in two products: lace and fish. Lace-making is an age-old tradition throughout Galicia, but we learned that the true heart of the art is in Camariñas, renowned throughout Spain for the hand-made lace executed by the *palilleiras*, the lace makers. On this sunny August morning, women of all ages were sitting outside their houses and shops with their work cushions on their laps, their fingers deftly sending spools of cotton, pins and threads flying and clicking as they created bewilderingly intricate patterns. It looked more complicated than string theory and gave me a headache just watching.

The hobby of lace making arose out of the fishermen's wives' need to occupy themselves while their men were out at sea. However, the craft has become an important source of revenue for the local people, and it's estimated that more than 3,000 women work in the lace industry around the village. But the main economy depends on fishing with nearly 30 percent of Camariñas' population active in the fisheries section. This was the reason for the random sirens we'd heard; they announced the arrival of the sardine boats.

During our wanderings we got to know Manuel, the skipper of a fishing boat, the *Siro Segundo*. Manuel was a huge bear of a man with calloused hands the size of frying pans. In broken English, he explained the importance of the fishing industry in the region. The fleet would leave the harbour in the evening, hoping to return with a full catch in the early hours of the morning. The siren sounded three times as the boats returned, alerting everyone to take their positions to help unload the catch: the ice-machine was started; the forklift truck drivers revved their engines; the handlers and packers rushed down to the quayside, and the lorry drivers were on standby set to transport the night's catch to the distributors. Nearly everyone in the village was involved in the industry one way or another: their livelihood depended on it. I asked Manuel what would happen if he didn't catch anything.

'I think I must make the lace,' he said with a dry smile, contemplating his huge hairy hands. 'But I don't think I am so good at it.'

That Monday night as all eight fishing boats left the village, Carl and I held our breath, listening out for the alarm. The night passed quietly, no sirens sounded: no catch. Finally, on Tuesday morning the air was pierced by the happy shriek of the alarm. People streamed out of their houses, the entire village moving like a volcanic flow towards the harbour where there was a frenzy of noisy activity: trays of sardines were unloaded from the boats to be packed into ice and salt; forklift trucks whizzed about to load them onto waiting lorries; seagulls screamed and swooped to squabble over imperfect sardines jettisoned on the quay. The whole community was there to help. Those who couldn't assist commented on the proceedings; old watermen sagely dispensed useless nuggets of wisdom, and elderly women loudly criticised the activities and chastised children who got in the way. Carl and I helped out by fetching and carrying, for which Manuel generously rewarded us with two buckets of sardines to fill our empty freezer. We were thrilled: we still hadn't caught one blasted fish with my expensive fishing gear, but now we had sardines for many tasty meals to come.

That evening we enjoyed a potluck meal on the boat with Nicole and Yves Peron, a French couple from Brittany we'd met. As we sat on deck, savouring the freshly fried fish and heady Spanish wine, wisps of fragrant smoke rose from barbeques around the village: everyone was grilling sardines.

Early on Saturday morning we unloaded the bikes, rinsed them off with fresh water and oiled the chains. We cycled east towards La Coruña on a road that wound its way into deep valleys and up over steep hills. The interior of Galicia is green and rugged, composed of low mountain ranges with rivers running down wooded slopes towards the many rias, firth-like inlets along the coast. The topography is reminiscent of Norway with its fjords and valleys but with infinitely milder weather. Northern Spain is very different from the south where the flat beaches of the better-known Costas groan under the weight of pasty northern Europeans seeking sun, cheap booze and cheaper thrills. Carl and I cycled around small tranquil villages where the loudest noise was the crowing of a rooster or the bray of a donkey. The modernization brought by tourism hadn't worked its evil here: villages remained untouched and idyllic. It's hard not to fall for the charms of stone-built cottages where flowering eucalyptus trees and blackberry brambles cascade over low walls, and friendly chickens scratch pleasantly around the yards. Admittedly the houses looked basic at best, and the idyll only lasts as long as you forget the joys of power showers and convection ovens. Several buildings were of a puzzling design: long low rectangular constructions balanced on circular columns. On top of each column was a large flat stone, giving the illusion that the structure on top was too big for its supporting columns and was thus defying gravity. We debated their use.

'Chicken coop? Guest house?' suggested Carl.

I dismissed both ideas. 'No ladder for the chickens, and I wouldn't put even my ex-mother-in-law in there.'

We were still pondering this when we came across a wizened old man with a face like a walnut, languidly hoeing a patch of weeds around the base of one such house, the gables of which were adored with crucifixes and crosses. He smiled cheerfully at us, displaying an array of teeth which would have driven an orthodontist to tears. We started our usual dance of gestures and actions while shouting pidgin English at him, only to discover that he spoke English fluently, albeit with much whistling and sucking through his remaining teeth. He explained how he'd learned English during his time as a deckhand on a merchant ship and told us how he liked the Scandinavians and the Dutch, particularly the women, but had no time for the nose-in-the-air British, the arrogant French and the over-bearing Germans. He explained any number of things we hadn't asked about, clearly enjoying the opportunity to speak English, and leaning on his hoe as if it were a lectern. At length we learned that the constructions were *hórreos*, ancient granaries designed for storing and drying corn on the cob, elevated to prevent damp, with flat stones atop the columns to stop rodents getting to the corn. We had to admire the craftsmanship of the buildings: each had its own unique charm.

That evening we helped Manuel and Pedro grill fish for 70 guests. Forget your expensive gas grills with hoods, timers and warming plates: the lads filled three oil drum halves with firewood, lit the wood and allowed it to burn down to a glow. Then we laid out thick steaks of bonito – a hearty tuna-like fish – seasoned well with salt and crushed garlic, and grilled them until the meat started to fall away from the bones: simple, wonderful food served with wine, bread and bonhomie. That evening we made 70 new friends and returned to *Albatross* with a present of a large parcel of bonito for our freezer.

The secret to successful sailing is not just in the sailing itself, but in the ability to solve problems: the only thing you can be sure of at sea is that something on a boat will go wrong. Carl and I seemed to spend as much time repairing

Albatross as sailing her. Fortunately, we were both handy and we'd invariably fiddle with something until we got it right. It also helped that as electricians we knew a blue wire from a red one. Our ability in boat maintenance had drawn the attention of Bernt, a German on a boat moored beside us. After we'd exchanged the usual harbour-side pleasantries, he'd spent the morning staring at us in that frank rather unnerving way Germans have, to the point where we wondered if he was on the run for bludgeoning his sailing partner to death and was looking for a new one. Eventually, he approached us and asked if we would take a look at his autopilot which hadn't worked all season; he was finding it tough having to constantly steer by hand. Carl and I drew a sigh of relief and had a look. We twiddled this and that and got it working again.

'How much do I owe you?' Bernt asked.

Carl scratched his chin thoughtfully. 'A couple of beers and your company?'

'Done!' Bernt was so happy I swear he skipped down the dock. I'd never seen a grown man, much less a German, skip before. As most in the sailing community will know, there's a real sense of family among people with boats, and a spirit of helping out and passing on the favour is readily found. Nobody thinks to charge anybody for a helping hand; it's all about new friendships and sharing the experience.

Word got out around the harbour that the Swedes on *Albatross* were pretty handy, and we were approached by another customer. Dave was a London type with a spanking new 65-foot yacht and an outfit to match, but clueless about how to sail. Carl and I immediately dubbed him Lord Nelson. He'd bought the boat in Spain together with a couple of other friends, but they'd had a massive argument over something or other – probably who should be the first to wear the skipper's hat – and the other two had thrown their toys in the corner and flown back to London. Dave and his wife had found themselves stuck in Camariñas with a brand new boat and no idea how to get home, until they'd struck upon the bright idea of hiring an English bloke – due to arrive any day now – to skipper the boat back to Britain.

And so it was that one afternoon while the Lord and Lady had gone ashore for the day, we spotted a pale-bearded fellow in a cap, sailing bag over his shoulder, prowling around their yacht.

'Can we help?' Carl called to him.

'Hi, I'm Keith, here to skipper the boat for David,' he answered.

'They're out for the day, but come on board and have a drink with us while you wait.'

'Thanks guys. Don't mind if I do.'

Keith, a pleasant enough fellow in his late thirties, had quite a thirst on him and wasn't shy about accepting refills. Although during the course of the conversation, I wondered just how much experience he had, despite his claim that he'd sailed every ocean on the globe. He'd stared at our GPS and frowned.

'Never used one myself,' he said, waving his empty wine glass in the direction of the bottle. 'A sextant is all a real yachtsman needs.'

'Really?' Carl asked in a tone drier than the Gobi.

Not only had Keith vastly inflated his sailing résumé, but he was a lightweight when it came to holding his liquor. After listening to him brag about his ability to drink snaps, Carl slyly poured him a large measure of *Gammel Dansk* with the clear intention of shutting him up. While it didn't shut him up, it certainly slowed him down to the point where he was unable to speak clearly or use his legs. It was at this moment that Lord and Lady Nelson arrived back to find their new skipper undecided whether to greet them by puking on their shoes or passing out in the cockpit. The eventual choice of greeting was moot; Keith attempted to clamber onto their yacht but failed utterly to do so, losing his balance and landing with a splosh in the harbour, not filling his new employer with confidence in his choice of crew. I suppose Carl and I should assume a little of the blame for that.

The outcome was that Lady Nelson was furious with her husband for having hired a nitwit, and Carl and I ended up giving both Lord Nelson and Keith a short course in basic navigation and how to use the GPS. As we never heard from them again, I wonder if they got back to Britain in one piece, or if Keith is even now leading them in circles around the world, pointing at waves and saying, 'Ah, yes, I recognize this ocean: sailed it before, don't you know.'

On Wednesday we got up early to catch the bus to La Coruña which local people in Camariñas had recommended we visit. We felt we had to make the effort as they were clearly proud of their neighbouring city. It was certainly worth the bus ride. We strolled leisurely around the city admiring the architecture, in particular the Roman Tower of Hercules, symbol of the city and the oldest continuous working lighthouse in the world. Then Carl and I did something unbelievably touristy: we fell asleep on the beach. Or as Carl poetically wrote in the logbook: "We lay back in the warm sand and dozed to the sweet music of the Atlantic playing in the background."

But paradise is fragile; three months later while we were on the other side of the world, the *Prestige* tanker, carrying 66,000 tonnes of crude oil went down during a heavy storm, mere miles off the coast of La Coruña. Fuel washed up on beaches across northern Spain and parts of France, turning the white sands black and so devastating the fishing industry that it was brought to a complete standstill. As I write this, 10 years after the event, the trial is only now taking place in the city of La Coruña. I think of that lovely coastline polluted by oil and I worry, too, for our friend Manual whose livelihood depended on his sardine catch and whose hands were not made for lace-making.

Chapter 20
Pilgrims and Prawns
30 August – 5 September 2002

Portosin – Ria de Vigo, Las Islas Cies – Baiona, Spain

Experience: *Local Spanish markets are wonderful. Shop till you drop.*

Tip: *Sail longer stretches around the clock to rack up some miles. Stand off the coast to avoid fishing nets and trawlers.*

During our stay in Camariñas we'd built up our stamina by starting each day with a strenuous bike ride into the mountains. After a week, we felt fit and ready to sail again; the winds had calmed and we heard the siren call of the sea. It wasn't without a sharp pang of regret, however, that we bade farewell to this unspoiled gem of a village.

Our goal was to reach the Guadiana River, which forms the border between Spain and Portugal, which a Swiss couple we'd met had raved about. It was a long route, some 500 nautical miles but we'd planned to stop at a couple of different harbours on the way as the fancy took us. With a warm glow in my chest, I realized how lucky we were to be able to say things like, 'We'll go where the fancy takes us.'

Our first fancy was Portosin where, after much haggling, we begrudgingly paid the marina fees, although *Albatross* was shrinking significantly in length as the rate per foot was horrendously expensive. Portosin, once a small fishing village, now boasts an internationally famous water sports club and a new marina. It's subsequently acquired an exclusive reputation and attracts those with larger budgets than ours. I rustled up a dinner of fried sardines on bread with a salad soaked in hazelnut flavoured olive oil. We ate in the cockpit by the dwindling light and the gentle heat of the fading day. Carl and I agreed that the sardine was a wonderful little fish and we would never tire of eating them, which was just as well as we had a freezer full of them to last us for weeks.

The following morning we took the bus into Santiago de Compostela, the capital city of Galicia which boasts a plethora of historic buildings, the most significant of which is the thirteenth-century cathedral.

I'm not a particularly religious person – most Swedes aren't; surveys have shown Sweden to be one of the least religious countries in the world: less than 2 percent of the population attend church services. Compare this to Spain where 48 percent of people claim to believe in a supreme being and 22 percent go to church, most of whom I'm fairly sure were in Santiago's cathedral the day we visited. Despite, or maybe because of, my lack of faith, I can't help but find all this demonstrative religious pomp both fascinating and slightly appalling with its gory relics, weeping virgins and bleeding statues. We have only 16 cathedrals in Sweden, most of which look more like city halls than places of worship. Their interiors are restrained and formal, as if to say to the increasingly dwindling congregations, 'Just sit quietly on your pew and think about things, no need to make a fuss about it.' But that's Lutheranism for you. Catholicism, on the other hand, really goes to town and never more so than in the church architecture of Spain. Santiago de Compostela's cathedral screams, 'I'm a religious building! Genuflect, pray and wonder at God's glory. Repent miserable sinners! Oh, and by the way, don't forget to light a candle and buy a plaster Madonna on the way out.'

When first built, the Romanesque architecture of the cathedral would have been quite understated but over the passing centuries, Gothic and Baroque styles added more twiddly bits: elaborate towers, arches and domes, statues of saints galore, and carved scrolls and finials. The once simple Gothic interior was embellished in the seventeenth century with enough bling to blind you; the main altar is a riot of pink angels sporting strategically placed gold drapery, holding aloft an oversized gold canopy on which more pink angels cavort. A bejewelled statue of Saint James, which, I noticed, pilgrims hugged on arrival, stands at the altar. Because the shrine reputedly houses the saint's bones, the Camino de Santiago de Compostela has been an important pilgrimage route since the Middle Ages. Many of today's pilgrims complete their journey in ninth-century dress, carrying canes and bearing scallop shells, the emblem associated with Peter. Only those, however, who have travelled over 60 miles on foot may call themselves pilgrims and are awarded the coveted certificate testifying as much.

I admit I was hugely sceptical about this pilgrimage business. I wondered how many of the throng in the cathedral had made the journey for reasons of devotion, as it seemed to me that the majority of the pilgrims were hikers out for a bit of a ramble. More affluent types had booked their pilgrimage via websites offering 'VIP Camino' tours with exclusive accommodation at hotels along the way, or there were those on the 'Camino Lite' package where the last hundred kilometres (62 miles) were done at a more leisurely pace. Where was the sense of suffering and deprivation required to demonstrate true faith? But then I stopped sneering and reconsidered: the goal of a pilgrimage needn't necessarily be a shrine; it's about the spiritual journey. It's also about removing oneself from the daily grind and finding meaning in life: something which Carl and I, in our own way, were also undertaking and just as worthy of celebration. As I stood in front of the altar, watching the gathering pilgrims take their pews for a service of welcome, the cathedral's organ started up; the music swelled to a glorious, gusty crescendo, filling the air and making the rafters hum. I admit the hairs on the back of this poor sinner's neck stood up at the effect and my spine tingled.

Impressed though we were, Carl and I went in search of a religion we could more readily identify with: food. As it was Saturday, the Mercado on Praza de Abastos was in full swing. We literally followed our noses to find it; we could smell the cheese, fruit and seafood long before we found the market. This was a splendid affair of six huge hallways divided into areas selling meat, fish, vegetables and fruit: all the produce locally caught or grown by villagers who came into the city to sell it. Now, this was the altar of my worship. We stuffed our rucksacks with sweet smelling red peppers, tasty tomatoes, bunches of carrots, fragrant peaches, fat garlic bulbs, locally made cheese – the aroma of which made my taste buds sing in anticipation – cured ham, fish and red wine at prices that made me weep with gratitude.

Not completely satisfied with this bounty, Carl had started eyeing up the live chickens.

'What do you think, Yanne?' he mused thoughtfully. 'If we buy a cockerel and a couple of hens, we'd never be short of eggs. We can make a net cage for them and keep them on deck.'

'Crap,' I replied, immediately spotting the flaw in his plan.

'Well, there's no need to be rude,' Carl said looking wounded. 'It's not such a bad idea.'

'No, I mean, there'd be chicken crap all over the deck.'

'Hmm. I see what you mean. But don't you think it's worth considering?'

'Yes, I've considered it, and I still think it's crap.'

'I'll give you a chance to think about it some more, then,' Carl said in that nonplussed way of his.

Early on Sunday morning we slipped our moorings and headed out of Portosin some 50 nautical miles towards the Cies Islands in the mouth of the Ria di Vigo. Once an old pirates' haunt, Las Islas Cies are now an uninhabited national park, open to the public only in summer. We'd heard that the locals dubbed them the "Galician Caribbean," and as we sighted them in the early evening I could see why from the vista of snow-white beaches framed by slopes of pine and eucalyptus trees and bordered by sparkling turquoise waters. The Atlantic side on the west, however, was a complete contrast with dark waves slamming against granite cliffs, spraying foam high into the air.

The Cies Islands consist of three islands; we decided to drop anchor in the sheltered bay east of Do Faro ("Lighthouse Island") which is linked to Monteagudo, the island to the north, by a long crescent of powdery sand known as Praia das Rodas, a popular beach which regularly crops up on lists of the top 10 best beaches of the world. It was hot in the sun and as we packed away our winter clothes, we reflected, not without a sense of smugness, that our friends in Sweden would be getting their winter long johns out of storage: we were gradually heading south into tropical climes and wouldn't need our warm clothing again for another two years when we returned to Scotland. The view and the sun may have been Caribbean like but the water certainly wasn't: this was after all the Atlantic, and the water was so cold that a quick swim shrank my testicles to the size of peas.

In 2002, the Cies were made part of the Galician Atlantic Islands National Park, making them highly protected. Visitors are strictly limited to 2,200 a day and no cars or bikes are permitted. The islands are home to one of Europe's largest colonies of yellow-footed gulls, drawing approximately 22,000 nesting pairs each year, and fish are abundant in this particular ecosystem, hence the attraction for gulls and fishermen alike. Small fishing boats jostled for space along the island's cliffs, laying pots for lobster and crab.

We felt a Robinson Crusoe like sense of isolation as we walked along the fine white sand; the day trippers had left and we were alone to enjoy the tranquility, broken only by the incessant shrieking of the gulls. We ate dinner in the cockpit – chilled sardines with tomato and pepper salad, accompanied, of course, by a bottle of red wine. As the sun slipped away, a fresh evening breeze rippled across the water turning the evening chilly; we unpacked our winter clothes again, our sense of smugness somewhat dispelled.

The following day we hiked around the island, enjoying spectacular views from the lighthouse and marveling at the wealth of bird life until the wind turned south and a cold mist descended, forcing us to stumble back blindly through a chilly blanket of fog. It had changed from Caribbean-like warm to Scottish moors cold and damp in a matter of minutes. We decided to escape the mist and set sail for Nazaré, north of Lisbon, proclaimed by one website as "Portugal's most picturesque fishing village." I'm always skeptical of such claims but was prepared to give it a go, so we weighed anchor and sailed out into the open sea. After struggling to tack hard in vicious 30-mile per hour winds, we decided to take refuge in Baiona to await better weather and escape the cold porridge-like fog which had descended on us. We'd sailed only 12 nautical miles.

Happily, Baiona proved to be a pleasant stop: a pretty medieval town with a population of 11,000, it quadruples in the summer when the tourists invade. The marina was full and the streets were alive with shoppers lured by arty shops and seafood restaurants. We explored the alleyways and took the opportunity to stock up again on the kind of produce which makes my mouth water: fat shrimp, cured ham and garlic sausages, olive oil, vegetables and assorted wines. Our legs bowed under the weight of our rucksacks forcing us to walk slowly and rest at length on the way back in a couple of bars we thought worthy of investigating. That evening I fried the prawns doused in olive oil, crushed garlic and lemon juice. We ate them hot out of the pan, licking our fingers and slurping down an exquisite red wine which had cost us less than a bottle of mineral water would in Sweden.

So, we'd had to change our course again and at this rate we might never get to New Zealand, but I was learning to take each day, each weather pattern and port it drove us into as it came. There was no doubt: this sailing life was unpredictable, but so far it had been gloriously good.

Chapter 21
Tales of the River Bank

7 September – 4 October 2002

Lagos - Vila Real de Santo Antonio – Guadiana River – Ayamonte

Experience: *River sailing is not to be missed.*

Tip: *Invest in the best pair of binoculars you can afford, particularly with built-in HD stabilizing compass for taking position readings. Steiner is a reputable brand.*

'Any regrets?' I asked Carl. 'Are you quite sure about this?'
 'Absolutely,' he replied with a firm nod of the head.
 'But it was your dream city,' I pressed.
'Nah. I've got better dreams now.'
 I agreed wholeheartedly with him. We had the wonderful good fortune to live afloat, enabling us to enjoy the flexibility of visiting smaller harbours and not having to follow in the wake of cruise ships or the exhaust fumes of tour buses. I had always felt, rightly or wrongly, that Portugal's Algarve coast was similar to southern Spain's: one long tedious strip of high-rise hotels catering to Brits and Germans seeking cheap deals in the sun. Carl and I had no interest in such resort areas and decided to move on directly to the south of Portugal and the Guadiana River, a passage of approximately 500 nautical miles.
 On Friday afternoon, the sun finally broke through the fog that melted away on a faint northwest breeze. We weighed anchor and sailed out on the light wind, hoisted the gennaker and made good speed of six to seven knots, sailing past the steep rocky coastline of Lisbon early on Saturday. Then we set a course for Cabo de Sao Vicente, Portugal's southernmost cape, at one time considered by the Romans to be a magical place. It was here that the sun sank into the ocean, thus marking the end of their physical world. Looking up at the sheer cliffs looming 250 feet above the Atlantic makes you gasp. At the top stands one of Europe's most powerful lighthouses, the light from which can be seen nearly 40 miles away – just as well, as on Sunday night the wind died and we drifted into a dense belt of fog.
 Why is it that when one light bulb dies, two or three others immediately decide to follow suit? How do inanimate objects know to do this? And how

do they know to time it at that particular moment when you have no spares available, the shops are closed or you're stuck in the middle of nowhere? It's the same with batteries and plasters; you could be bleeding profusely from an artery during a power cut, but no amount of panic-fuelled rummaging in the "bits and pieces" drawer will produce anything other than dead torch batteries, a candle stump and an empty box of plasters.

The bulb for the light at the top of the mast blew. Minutes later, POOF! The bulb on the starboard light popped. Somehow Carl – and I'm almost certain it was Carl's job to get the bulbs – had forgotten to buy spares. We drifted in the fog, laying blame at each other's feet for a while, before reluctantly deciding we would have to put into Lagos to get "the blasted bulbs."

Lagos is perfectly pleasant, but we just didn't want to be there; it's an expensive lure for the affluent, reflected in its pristine marina and correspondingly high prices. For the first time we were grilled on arrival over our boat documents and crew paperwork with questions like, 'Where's your home harbour? Where was your last harbour? Where are you going next? Length of boat? Nationality of crew? Preferred sexual position?' (Well, not the last, but it wouldn't have surprised me.) I thought Carl would keel over and expire when we had to hand over €34 for a night's mooring at a pontoon berth.

'We're not staying longer than one night,' he growled. 'Bloody light bulbs!' he added, looking at me, as if *I* were responsible for *his* forgetfulness.

We sailed out of Lagos the following afternoon with light bulbs, clean laundry and new charts for the east side of the Atlantic; for the most part we'd been using the computer to navigate, but we were concerned that if this crashed on us – which it eventually would given the destructive nature of salt water – we would be left without any charts for that area.

It was approximately 70 nautical miles to Vila Real de Santo Antonio on the Guadiana River. We'd heard that navigating the river entrance was difficult due to its shallowness and shifting sandbanks. It was important, therefore, to make an approach two hours before or after high tide; we decided to sail through the night to catch high tide at five a.m. We made a good start with a brisk wind filling the sails and the sun warming our backs as we left Lagos. When the wind dropped later that evening, we hoisted the gennaker and sat back to enjoy the satisfying sensation of *Albatross* cutting cleanly and swiftly through the waves. We were keeping three nautical miles off the coast to keep clear of the fishing boats and nets, sailing was easy, and we felt confident of arriving at the river delta by sunrise. I went below, leaving Carl to keep watch and enjoy his lyrical musings.

'Shit, damn and hell!' So much for lyrical musings. I hastened on deck.

'Oh crap!' I immediately saw the problem: despite our best efforts to avoid them, we'd managed to wander into a massive maze of fishing nets and buoys which stretched as far as we could see in the moonlit ocean. Fortunately, we'd taken the precaution of fixing a line between the rudder and the keel to avoid getting fishing nets or lines tangled in the propeller, but even so, it took us over three hours to steer our way through. The delay nearly cost us: we arrived at the river estuary as a red sun was rising over Vila Real De Santo Antonio, an hour and a half after high tide, with our depth gauge indicating just six feet below the keel; we would never have been able to navigate it during low tide.

The Guadiana River is one of the longest rivers of the Iberian Peninsula at 510 miles, but is only navigable for small boats as far as Mértola, approximately 40 miles upriver. I read recently, however, that plans to dredge the river as far as Alcoutim have been approved, making it navigable in the future for larger ships.

Many of the yachts in the marina at Vila Real de Santo Antonio were moored for only a day or so to resupply before continuing up river. After being stung in Lagos, Carl was pleased to negotiate harbour fees down to €11 a day so we paid for two days to give us time to stock up. A cycle ride into the town revealed it to be a tidy place with white washed buildings and pristine squares. There we stocked up on fresh vegetables and fish from the local market. Then we returned to *Albatross* to tackle our "to do" list.

I was beginning to come to terms with the fact that owning a property of any kind – be it a house, a boat, an allotment, a car or a caravan – is the first step towards servitude: no matter what it is, there will always be a degree of cost and maintenance involved. The list had quickly developed into the "effing to do" list, and we were its slaves. We scrubbed the cockpit, checked the oil levels in the engine and generator, cleaned the filters in the shower and the bilge pump, rinsed the teak deck, put 400 litres (approximately 85 gallons) of fresh water in the tank and made various repairs to things that had come unstuck because of salt water damage. Our biggest problem was repairing our echo pilot, the forward sonar of which hadn't worked in some time, we'd assumed because of debris on the sensor. We discovered, however, that the sensor was damaged, probably by sailing into a hard object that had sheared off the edge. There was nothing to be done about it but order a new sensor.

The only chore I enjoy is cooking, and that evening we sat down to dinner of grilled tuna with avocado salsa and a red pepper, onion, tomato and garlic salad tossed in plenty of olive oil and balsamic vinegar. We'd splashed out and spent the equivalent sum of a can of Coke in Sweden on a good white wine with an amusing bouquet. By the second bottle, it was side-splitting and so were we.

For the next few days we let the tide gently roll us up the river, discovering a Portugal that had been little changed by the tourist boom but remained quaintly and peacefully untouched. The land rose and fell in craggy cliffs with scorched slopes of almond trees, wild rosemary, and lavender. Dotted here and there were the picturesque ruins of small abandoned cottages. Where the river irrigated the land, however, it was lush and fertile with thick banks of bamboo, orange, olive, and lemon groves. We found quiet places to anchor, from which to sit back and observe life on the river and marvel at the kaleidoscope of nature's colours: the iridescent blue of a kingfisher's head; the vivid yellow of a golden oriole; the bright orange and lemon of fruits peeking through green foliage; a vermillion sun slipping behind the mountains slowly softening the landscape and turning it magenta. As the purple twilight fell, we reached Foz do Odeleite, a small village where we anchored for the night. The wind died, and everything was still, bar the glimmer of stars through the velvet darkness. A small orchestra of nightingales serenaded us, and we finally fell asleep to the cicadas' hypnotic chirp. This was all very lovely until two dogs on either side of the river decided to argue ferociously over whether Spain or Portugal had the most annoying canines.

To cruise the Guadiana is to step back a century, and as we languidly meandered upriver, we felt the constraints of the twenty-first century tumble. We stopped looking at our watches and set our pace to that of the river's tides; we literally went with the flow.

Eventually, we arrived at the twin villages of Alcoutim in Portugal and Sanlúcar de Guadiana on the Spanish side. Our decision to tie up here for a few days was propitious: an English boat was just relinquishing the last of six moorings; the couple on board were leaving because of the din of the upcoming five-day fiesta. Undeterred by the possibility of noise – nothing could be worse than those damn dogs – but mostly attracted by the very reasonable €5 a day harbour fee, we paid for 10 days so we could finish the work on *Albatross* at a leisurely Portuguese pace.

Both towns on either side of the river are postcard picturesque, typical *pueblos blancos*: white houses with warm terracotta tiled roofs clustered against the hillside. To call them towns is a bit of a stretch. Sanlúcar de Guadiana has a population of only 400 people, a few sheep, a couple of cats and the town dog. In the twelfth century, it boasted a fine castle, the ruins of which could be seen at the top of the hill, and was a busy port in the first half of the nineteenth century from which rice, soap, lead and wood had been exported. The surrounding areas are renowned for the now abandoned Rio Tinto mines, reputed to be the oldest in the world and are, according to popular myth, the legendary mines of King Solomon.

For a small village, Sanlúcar was well served with two grocery shops, a bakery, a post office and a couple of small restaurants. Yet happily, technology seemed not to have trampled its way this far up the river: the baker used the same method and recipe for his bread as his grandfather; the post office was located in a tiny cottage and run by an equally tiny 95-year-old lady who wrote with a goose-quill pen and weighed my postcard to Kajsa on a pair of scales that looked as ancient as the postmistress. Her son, a spritely 73-year-old, delivered the mail on foot. Neither of them looked as if they planned to retire any time soon.

The serenity of old-world Sanlúcar was a complete contrast to Alcoutim where on Saturday night the fiesta began in earnest. We and six other people were ferried across the river to the Portuguese side in a small rowboat. I got the impression that the entire municipality of Alcoutim, all 3,500 inhabitants, had turned out to party and dance till dawn. We participated enthusiastically for the first night of revelries, but couldn't keep pace with the locals who started the show in the late afternoon and ended with a 30-minute firework display at seven the following morning. Their stamina was enviable. I'm pretty sure I spotted the 95-year-old postmistress and her son among the throng as we left exhausted an hour after midnight.

We spent almost a fortnight working on *Albatross*, enjoying our surroundings and getting to know some of the other visitors to the river. Most of the boats were British, but one morning we heard Swedish voices on the quay-side. We went up on deck to introduce ourselves – few Swedes sailed this far and it was always interesting to hear others' stories. Ingrid and Richard, a couple in their early sixties, had left Stockholm in the 1970s to live on their 27-foot sailboat, funding their lifestyle by sewing boat covers which they made on board. They had spent the greater part of their time in the Caribbean but had recently discovered the seductive waters of Guadiana. Our neighbours at Sanlúcar were Ludo and Lia from Holland with their dog Bram, and an English couple from Grimsby, John and Sandra. Both couples were in their fifties, retired and sailed fulltime, making Carl and I uncomfortably envious.

Our final excursion on this unspoiled river was a dinghy ride further north to the last navigable point of the Guadiana at Puerto de La Laja, a small Spanish hamlet of only 50 inhabitants. The small community had originally been established on a bend in the river to assist the shipment of ore from the mining industry in the province of Huelva in the late nineteenth century, but closed down in the 1950s when the mining crisis in the region led to the dismantling of the port facilities and the railway line that served it. We wandered around the village looking at the abandoned port and buildings with interest. It was as if the inhabitants had heard the call to leave and just plonked down their tools and walked away; machinery lay rusting in the grass. The sun was high in the sky, our throats were dry and a cold beer called, not that we'd seen anything resembling a bar. An elderly woman trotted down the street, a basket of groceries on her arm. In our pidgin Spanish we asked her if there was anywhere we could get a beer.

'Oh, no. There's no restaurant in Puerto de La Laja. But if you'd like a beer, come to my house,' she said. Well, that's what we understood. With a wave of her hand and a jerk of her head, she indicated we should accompany her to her home. We entered a tiny, marble-floored house with colourfully tiled walls. She gestured us to sit down and placed on the table two glasses and a litre bottle of beer, condensation pooling from the bottle as it hit the warm air. The beer barely touched the sides as it went down our parched throats. As polite Swedes, we tried to pay for our drinks, but the old dear was very upset that we should even suggest such a thing: we were her guests and there was no question of payment. As I said to Carl, 'Can you imagine such a thing happening in Sweden, even in a small village?'

Carl shook his head. 'Well firstly, nobody would make eye contact with you; if you did, they'd suspect you of being American or crazy, or both. Secondly, no-one would ever invite a stranger into their house. And thirdly, who in their right mind gives away beer in Scandinavia? So no, I can't imagine that ever happening in Sweden.'

Of course, it's quite possible that given our limited Spanish we completely misinterpreted what the señora had said. But if so, she showed remarkably little surprise when we followed her home and drank the beer she put on the table for her husband.

The following day as we sailed down river and towards Ayamonte, we began to re-enter the twenty-first century, passing under the suspension bridge between the Algarve and Andalusia, once more holding our breath as our 17-foot mast seemed to scrape the underside of the bridge. The roar of the traffic overhead was an intrusive reminder that we were back in the modern world with all its conveniences that often make life so inconvenient. So much of the world has been transformed by the bulldozer that it seems increasingly difficult to find places where the quality of life does not depend on the number of channels on your satellite TV or the speed of your broadband connection. Quite the reverse, technology and speed in this disappearing world were the enemy. We realized more and more how privileged we were: *Albatross* enabled us to glimpse the tranquil pockets of an older, simpler way of life that remain blissfully untouched by modern man.

Nevertheless, Carl and I were happy to take advantage of modern conveniences when necessary. Before setting sail for the Canary Islands, we needed to make a vital purchase, one that could make or break the whole circumnavigation: we needed wine, and nowhere were we likely to find better or cheaper wine than in Spain. As our funds were limited, drinking out was beyond our meagre budget, but that didn't mean we would have to give up the grape altogether. I'd given up my job, my house and car, even my girlfriend, but there were limits to the sacrifices I was prepared to make: a decent bottle of wine was not one of them. I didn't, however, drink any alcohol during a passage as I felt I needed to be in control at all times in case of emergencies.

After taking a tour of the local shops, we found some bargain wine sold in Tetra packs: perfect for storing on a sailing boat as the packs were light and wouldn't roll about like bottles. But before making a serious purchase, we felt we should do some methodical research; this consisted of a tasting session of 10 different wines. We started off seriously and soberly enough, even going so far as to make written observations on the quality of the wines, although surprisingly each wine seemed to taste better than the previous one. By the end of the evening, our nosing session had disintegrated into pure farce: any notes were illegible; more wine went up our noses than down our throats as we snorted with laughter at our own jokes, and we both fell asleep in the cockpit. I awoke at dawn with an uncomfortable crick in my neck to discover I'd used two empty Tetra packs as a pillow. I barely had enough spittle to swallow and felt as if I'd been beaten about the head with Thor's hammer. When Carl finally came to, we tried to piece together the evening and establish which wine was the best buy: they'd all been good as far as we could recall, which wasn't further than the third Tetra pack.

We cycled to the supermarket and loaded up seven shopping trolleys with wine and the odd item of food – well, we needed something to go with the wine – all but emptying the shelves. There were a few uneasy looks from fellow shoppers who probably wondered if we were celebrating our release from prison. While I paid the worried looking girl at the till, Carl looked for a large taxi, the driver of which was quite nonchalant about the first five trolley loads but started to panic when I rolled out the last two.

'*No es posible. Esto no es normal,*' he shouted frantically, clearly worried for his vehicle.

We explained in our limited Spanish that we would cycle in front of him to show him the way to the marina. When the driver saw the Swedish ensign on *Albatross*, it all became clear to him. '*Vikingos suecos!!*' he said throwing up his hands and laughing. Of course, only Swedish Vikings would need this amount of wine. Fortunately, our methods of procuring it had changed: our days of plunder and pillage were over, and we paid for our supermarket raids by credit card. And although Carl and I would often try to live up to our legendary ancestors by making a serious attempt to revel as if we were in Valhalla, we almost always regretted it the following morning. Viking in name but not always in nature.

Chapter 22
Unhappiness on the Happy Islands

5 October – 23 November 2002

Peurto de Morro Jable, Feurteventura – Puerto Mogán, Gran Canaria – Puerto Rico, Gran Canaria – Santa Cruz de Tenerife, Tenerife – Puerto de La Luz (Las Palmas), Gran Canaria

Experience: *Don't mention the war. Don't burn your arse. Don't eat dodgy sausages and never bathe in the harbour!*

Tip: *To fish while sailing, cast out a 60-foot line and let it trail in the boat's wake: the big fish will go for the bait.*

Question: *What is the definition of misery?* **Answer:** *Seasickness.*

We were barely 30 nautical miles into the 800 of the next leg of our journey when Carl turned a familiar shade of green. Moments later he was running for the railings and feeding the fish. He had my sympathy; I wasn't feeling too bright myself, but at least I'd overcome the diabolical nausea, stomach cramps, headaches and cold sweats that Carl was prone to. He'd tried various remedies, but looking at him now, it was clear none of them worked. It was hardly surprising in the swells we were currently experiencing: the sea was pushing us from all directions, rolling *Albatross* around in deep troughs and crests. There was no wind to fill the sails so we were trying to make any headway we could by using the engine, but the boat lurched and dipped alarmingly, causing our stomachs to lurch and dip alarmingly, too.

We usually found our sea legs after a couple of days and the unpleasantness would normally pass, but on the third day of sailing, I looked as perky as a corpse; my skin felt clammy and was as grey as a 1960s municipal building. Carl, who was now on the mend and craving eggs for breakfast, frowned at me. 'What's the matter with you?'

'I think I've got the flu,' I croaked. And as neuroscientists have recently proved, a case of man flu is neither myth nor laughing matter: self-pity aside, I was really ill. I immediately took to my bunk with a sniffled "sorry," a pitiful look and two toilet rolls, leaving Carl to man the helm 24 hours a day for the next three days. Fortunately, the wind was favourable and *Albatross* performed well in the rough waters, doing eight to nine knots and averaging 170 nautical miles a day. There were very few other ships in the vicinity so Carl was able to doze in the cockpit on and off and let the autopilot guide us. Our route went along the Moroccan coast, 60 miles out. There the wind turned, creating waves of 20 to 30 feet – think of something the height of a two-storey house coming towards you – but our Hallberg-Rassy rode the waves well. Here, the ocean bed lay between 8,000 and 9,000 feet below us, so the waves didn't break over us as they had in the North Sea and the Bay of Biscay.

Eventually, the wind dropped to a pleasant breeze and the sun glowed hot in a perfect blue sky. I rose from my sickbed and joined Carl on deck where we could relax, read and idle the time away. By night, we'd count the aircraft making their way to the Canary Islands, clocking a plane every 20 minutes. The Happy Islands were clearly happy for good reason: the tourist industry there was booming to the tune of 12 million visitors a year.

The island of Lanzarote had originally been our goal, but unwillingly to navigate an unknown port in hard swells and darkness, we decided to continue to the harbour of Puerto de Morro Jable on Fuerteventura, an additional 80 miles, which we reached shortly before sunset. The sun was fading fast as we hauled down the sails, drifted in and sought a mooring. Fortunately, a bloke with a thick accent helpfully shouted directions to an empty berth. He introduced himself as Gunter, a German who had settled in Fuerteventura after sailing round the world for five years. He spent his days operating a small fishing boat that he charted to tourists for fishing trips. Gunter was quite a character, an ebullient, hefty type aged around 55 with white hair and a matching spiky white beard. He was a friendly mine of information on harbour registration procedures, where to shop cheaply and where to buy fresh bread – something we were desperate for after living on dry crackers for five days at sea. We thanked him for his help over a cold beer and toasted to our successful arrival in a new port with a shot of *Gammel Dansk*.

The Canary Islands – so named because of dogs which may have roamed the islands and nothing to do with little yellow birds – consist of 13 islands of which Fuerteventura is the second largest and oldest, dating back 20 million years when it was formed during a volcanic eruption. All the islands are volcanic in origin with activity as recent as 2011 under the smaller island of El Hierro. I'm glad I wasn't aware of this at the time; I might have felt less relaxed during our stay knowing that lava was brewing under my feet.

Because of their volcanic origin, many of the beaches are black and the land-scape barren and lunar looking without any vegetation, apart from the lush grounds of the larger hotels whose imported greenery is kept meticulously manicured and watered at horrendous expense.

Morro Jable was at one time a small fishing village until popularized by German tourists drawn by the balmy climate, crystal clear waters and oppor-tunities for big game fishing. The Germans congregate in the resorts in the south and the British in the north of the island, clearly separated to avoid confrontations over deeply rooted issues of national pride such as football results and towels on poolside chairs. We were astonished by the amount of construction: the skyline was crowded with cranes in the process of erecting hotel complexes designed to cater for the tourists' every whim: customers need never set foot outside their fortified compounds to see anything of the local island life. They merely move from the all-you-can-eat breakfast buffet at the hotel to the marina to be bundled onto fishing boats for a day of sitting in a padded chair with an expensive rod at one elbow and a constant supply of beers at the other. For a fee of €500 they can fulfil their dreams of hooking an 800-pound tuna or blue marlin to boast about to their friends back in Berlin.

Gunter had been capitalizing on this way of making a living on *Albin*, his 30-foot boat but had encountered problems with its electrical system. He idly asked if we could help him out. Carl and I went along with our bag of tricks, and after some intensive work and only a few choice curses, we corrected the errors and got the system working smoothly again.

'That's fantastic!' Gunter raved. 'Man, you guys could make some serious money out here. I've had so-called experts charge €80 an hour, and you can imagine how many hours they bill me for by the time they've finished. How about an afternoon of fishing as payment?'

How could we say no? That afternoon we joined Gunter and his Spanish crew, José, Manual and Tomas on *Albin* to learn the joys of big game fishing. On board was some serious equipment: hefty fishing rods with reels the size of toilet rolls and squid-styled fish hooks the size of my hand for catching game up to 300 or 400 pounds, although truth be told I was a little alarmed at the thought of trying to land something twice my weight. With two 400-hun-dred horse power engines growling below us, we stormed westwards towards Jandia lighthouse on the southwest tip of the island where the Atlantic bed rises up several thousand feet into long narrow reefs. The sea rose in power-ful swells, sending the azure water into spectacular columns of white foam. Not waters for the faint-hearted, but skipper José seemed well acquainted with the reefs, steering his boat with a confident hand.

During the ride out, the Spanish crew had cast out two fishing lines 30 feet behind the boat, letting the hooks trail in the water which within a short time hooked us two bonitos and two tuna weighing 10 and 8 pounds respectively: hardly big game fish, but Carl and I had an embarrassing struggle to land these, used as we were to only hooking small Swedish cod.

José steered us round the headland and along the northwest coast where the volcanic cliff sides were razor sharp. At their base we glimpsed deep caves and tunnels eroded by the pounding water.

Carl nudged me and pointed at one of the wide tunnel openings. 'What do you think?' he asked in a low voice. 'Could have been an ideal place for a base, no?' I knew immediately what he was referring to: the mystery of the Villa Winter.

Now I love a good mystery as much as the next man, the next man being Carl who some years before had passed me a newspaper article about the possible existence of a secret German submarine base on Fuerteventura. A few miles inland lay the desolate area of Cofete where German engineer Gustav Winter had a huge villa built during the Second World War, the use of which is still the subject of rampant speculation. Why construct a villa in such a barren landscape, accessible only by sea or dirt track? And what was "Don Gustavo," as he was known by the locals, doing on the island instead of assisting his country in the war in Europe? An agreement had apparently enabled a large part of the Jandia peninsular to be declared a military zone, and Herr Winter was commissioned to carry out important "projects" in the area for the Third Reich using German workers for that purpose. Rumours suggest that the villa's tower had once served as a beacon for planes and submarines: a small landing strip between the sea and the villa support this idea, and the lava tunnels of Fuerteventura might have provided a subterranean submarine harbour; certainly, allied ships were often attacked by German subs around the island.

Another juicy theory is that the villa was used as a clinic for Nazi Criminals to receive plastic surgery before making their escape to South America. It was all the stuff of spy movies and I could well imagine Don Winter sitting in his swivel chair up in his tower, cat on lap, saying, 'So, Herr Bond, we met again. But before you die a most convoluted and painful death, let me explain my plan...'

Unfortunately, Carl couldn't resist asking Gunter if there was any truth to the story of a subterranean U-boat base. I thought Gunter might pop a blood vessel when he replied furiously, '*Das ist aber reine bullshit*! That's total bullshit.' His normally jovial face went a dark shade of pink, enhancing his white hair and eyebrows. He pointed to the portals in the rock around which the sea swirled. 'You really think that's the entrance to a submarine base?

And just how would you navigate anything in and out of the tunnels in these kinds of currents?'

'Well, I just wondered,' Carl said defensively. 'I once read something in a Swedish newspaper ...'

'Pah! And you believe everything you read in the newspapers, I suppose,' said Gunter. Fair point to Gunter: nevertheless, we were all a bit quiet after his outburst.

Harmony was restored as José let the boat drift and we relaxed, enjoying the hot glow of the sun on our skin. We happily accepted a cold drink of honey-spiced rum mixed with a splash of coke which enhanced our mellow mood. As the sun began to sink in the west, Gunter turned the throttle on full and we sped back to Morro Jable. We'd thought we'd got our catch for the day, but just before the entrance to the harbour, my line began to thrash and kick.

'Looks like a big one,' José said. I followed his advice and let out the line, reeled in and let it out again. After a 30-minute tussle, I finally hauled in a 60-pound wahoo. I was exhausted, but it was a satisfying end to the day and we could restock our freezer. A good swop for a little electrical know-how.

Our next port of call was Puerto Mogán on Gran Canaria, an easy sail of only 85 nautical miles. Fortunately, José had helped us reserve a berth here as many marinas were fully booked during October and November with boats on their way to the Caribbean. Our main reason for visiting Gran Canaria was to meet up with my parents who had flown into Puerto Rico from Sweden. My father wanted to check we hadn't sunk the boat, and my mother probably wanted to bring me clean underwear, make sure I was eating well and allay other such motherly concerns. For the next five days we had a typically touristy time together: splashing out on a fabulous meal at a fish restaurant recommended by Gunter; spending a couple of days reading and swimming at the beach where I burnt my back and a buttock I'd carelessly left exposed; renting a jeep and exploring the island with my parents and a couple of their friends, to the constant accompaniment of my mother offering sandwiches from the cooler she'd packed, and my father asking if I knew where the hell I was going.

Once away from the resorts, the interior of the island offers astonishing scenic variety: Gran Canaria isn't called the "Miniature Continent" for nothing. We went from the Sahara-like sand dunes of Maspalomas beach – and incidentally, Europe's unofficial nudist capital – to the lush valleys of orange, lemon and banana plantations and the craggy volcanic mountains at the island's heart. We hiked along the razor sharp cliffs of Altavista and marvelled at how the islanders had carved their homes into the mountain sides, chiselling out small doors and windows. The simplicity of such houses was a huge contrast to the development on the coast where the harbours teemed with "party boats," fishing boats and everything designed to squeeze as much money out of the tourists' pockets as possible.

As we had two women with us, the sightseeing inevitably culminated in shopping at a local market where haggling was long and hard, particularly from Carl who can haggle with the best of them. An unsuspecting hat trader met his match in Carl: the starting price was €35 but Carl eventually walked off with a hat and a satisfied grin for only €8. My father's own take on bargaining was, 'You have to haggle, it keeps them happy.'

'How so?' I asked.

'Well, if you buy the product at his initial asking price, he'll only be miserable for the rest of his life because he didn't ask for more money in the first place.' It must be nice to think you're doing someone a favour by beating their price down to rock bottom.

After five days on Gran Canaria, it was time to move on. We had a farewell dinner with my parents during which we tried hard not to discuss the fact that it would be over two years until I next saw them, or that in a few days we would soon be taking on one of the world's largest oceans, the Atlantic. My mother's eyes grew misty and my father was exaggeratedly cheerful as I said goodbye to them at the dock of Puerto Rico. Of our 50,000 miles, we'd sailed 3,500 in four months. We had a long way to go before we would meet again.

As we sailed to Tenerife, conditions got so rough I seriously wondered if I would ever see them again. We left Puerto Rico with a whisper of wind behind us and calm water ahead, but as we rounded the southwest tip of Puerto del Castillete, we could see the white foam on the wave crests two or three miles ahead of us. We strapped on our safety lines and reefed in, thankful we'd ignored the experts in Helsingborg who'd scoffed at our having a third reef on the mainsail and said it would be like sailing with a handkerchief; in these kinds of conditions, hoisting something the size of a thong would have done. Mountainous waves broke and crashed over the deck, leaving salt crystals which dried in the sun and twinkled like diamonds. Thanks to the windvane we kept *Albatross* on course but had to tack hard all the way to Tenerife.

Once in the marina of Santa Cruz de Tenerife, we spent a couple of days on terra firma, cleaning ourselves and *Albatross* thoroughly, as all three of us would be scrutinised by two exacting visitors: Monica and Eva were due to visit, and heaven forbid they find that we had become a couple of tramps with less than fragrant armpits. Salt water seemed to have penetrated everything so we washed the lot: bedding and tea towels, all our clothes, carpets and cushion covers. We trudged up and down the quayside, filling buckets of water to mop down *Albatross* until she looked brochure fresh.

As we made our umpteenth trip to refill our buckets, we passed again an odd looking boat, a huge rusting steel thing. We put our buckets down and studied it.

'What the heck kind of boat is that? Looks like a huge sardine tin,' I said.

'Or a very badly designed submarine with a rig,' Carl said. 'I'm surprised it's still floating.'

As we stood there musing how the boat could float, much less sail, a small, slightly built man with a grey beard longer than his shoulder length hair appeared in the cockpit. The owner turned out to be a remarkable 60-year-old from the Czech Republic whose colourful career had included stints as a lumberjack, adventurer, writer and filmmaker. Rudolf Krautschneider told us how he'd built his own boats, including the steel tub we'd been staring at. He'd sailed it from Poland to the Shetlands, the Falklands and Antarctica, often dodging icebergs en route. He'd also completed a circumnavigation via Cape Horn, in the process becoming something of a sailing legend in his home country – astonishing, really, coming from a landlocked nation without any seafaring tradition whatsoever. I'd never met such a charismatic man with a simple philosophy he seemed genuinely to adhere to.

'The man with a lot of money and a lot of time is a lucky man,' he told us over a beer. *Well duh*, I thought. 'And the man with no money but a lot of time is also a lucky man,' he continued. I said I supposed so, but whoever said money can't buy you happiness, doesn't know where to go shopping. Rudolf shook his head and said, 'Ah, but the man who has money but no time, that's the unluckiest man of all.'

'So which are you?' Carl asked.

Rudolf pointed to his rusting craft and grinned. 'Which do you think? By the way any proceeds from sales of my books go to my eight godchildren in the Czech Republic or repairs to the boat.'

We got the hint and bought an English copy of his book, *Around the World for a Feather*, thus contributing something towards one of the eight "godchildren," and left a lucky man polishing the rust off his boat. I believe he's still going strong, continuing to build boats, make documentaries and write books. I wonder how many more godchildren he has since sired.

Monica and Eva arrived to find Carl and myself tanned if not toned – my cooking was improving to the point where I could rustle up a three-course meal with a certain amount of aplomb. Monica and I rented a car and explored the island, leaving Carl and Eva to enjoy the boat. The idea was that after a week we would swop – the car for boat time that is, not the women. But when Monica and I returned and went on board *Albatross*, Carl seemed to be acting very strangely; he was mumbling incoherently and incapable of standing.

'What the hell, Calle,' I said, looking at my watch. 'It's not even nine in the evening. How did you get so drunk?'

Eva shook her head. 'He hasn't had a drop, Yanne. I don't know what's wrong with him. I'm seriously worried.'

'Jesus! Maybe he's had a stroke or something. We've got to get him to a doctor.' Carl was moaning incomprehensibly.

'He won't go,' Eva said. 'I've tried.'

'He has to. No question about it. Let's get him in the car.'

With a screeching of tyres, we raced to the nearest hospital where we were horrified to see a huge queue of people snaking around the reception. The only Spanish word I knew pertaining to the body was *corazón*, so I screamed this while dragging Carl to the front of the queue and pointing to his heart. He was immediately plonked on a trolley and disappeared through the emergency doors. Eva slumped in a chair looking ashen. We were concerned that if Carl didn't improve, we'd have to fly him home.

It turned out that Carl had been attacked by some particularly vicious bacteria resulting from food poisoning, probably picked up by eating a quayside chorizo. Fortunately, he was pumped full of antibiotics and was released the following day. His first words to me: 'I knew there was something dodgy about that salami.'

Sadly, what should have been something of a romantic holiday for Monica and me ended in an unpleasant breakup. I should have realised that my three-year absence would make our relationship hard to maintain, yet I hadn't understood the root of the problem: Monica was deeply jealous of Carl and had been since even before our departure, regarding him as a threat to her bond with me. Her antagonism towards Carl increased; they argued, then Monica and I argued. Finally, after one argument too many, I'd had enough. I was disappointed that Monica was unable to accept how determined I was to continue our circumnavigation and felt it best to part company. Although I regretted that it had to end, I have to admit my heart felt a little lighter knowing that I could see my goal to its completion without the encumbrance of a girlfriend who wasn't wholly committed to my cause.

It was now 13 November 2002. We were up early, making sail for Puerto de la Luz, Gran Canaria. It was a beautiful morning with the promise of a warm day and a cooling breeze. The air was pure and fresh and...

'Holy crap! What the hell is that smell?' Carl said, wrinkling his nose in disgust.

The stench was overwhelming, and so unpleasant it stung the eyes. I covered my nose and looked around. Carl was partly right: it was crap, but there was nothing holy about it. Our neighbouring boat, a 70-foot schooner out of

Turkey, was also up early, to secretly and illegally empty their toilet tank into the harbour.

'Damn stinkers,' I said. 'Couldn't they have used the pump out facility or waited until they got out to sea?'

Carl looked with horror at the flow of crap on the water. 'I swam in there yesterday,' he said. 'Remind me never to swim in port again.'

It just goes to prove that money doesn't buy you good manners. We left the harbour as quickly as possible to head for the fresh air of the ocean. As we entered Puerto de la Luz marina, we were greeted with a forest of masts; the marina was crowded with sailboats waiting for the start of the Atlantic Rally for Cruisers for which we had registered in the spring of our departure. We would be here for 10 days, preparing *Albatross* for our longest sail yet: 2,700 nautical miles across the Atlantic to the island of St Lucia in the Caribbean. Carl and I had made it this far without any major incidents – unless you count narrowly avoiding a collision with a tanker, life-threatening food poisoning and a breakup among incidents – but the Atlantic was our "big one" and we were both thrilled and nervous. The crossing was certainly risky; nevertheless, we were ready for the challenge. By now, we'd learned that we had a great boat in *Albatross*; she could take on the Atlantic and survive as could Carl and I. We weren't a bad team; we had our strengths and weaknesses and knew where we could rely on the other. Carl was good with maps and charts, and I could climb the masts like a nifty pirate. We were both mechanically minded and pretty capable handyman having been schooled by Ove,

Even so it would be comforting to have extra crew with us. I looked at Carl as we tied up at the dock. 'We're here. Let's make the call.'

'Okay. Think he'll be surprised we've got this far in one piece?'

'He taught us well. I reckon he'll be pleased.' I dialled the number. 'Hej! Greger. It's Carl and Yanne here in Gran Canaria. Guess what? We're on lesson six.' Greger's familiar chuckle filled my ear. 'Still want to sail across the Atlantic with a couple of amateurs? Well, pack your bags and get over here. We're on our way.'

Chapter 23
Crossing the Pond
24 November – 23 December 2002

Puerto de la Luz, Gran Canaria – The Atlantic –
Rodney Bay, St Lucia

Experience: *The Atlantic is NOT blue water sailing.*

Tip: *There are many seasickness remedies on the market – old salts suggest ginger root or pressure point wrist bands for quelling queasiness – but for those desiring an over-the-counter pill, Stugerón is often recommended by hard core seasick sufferers.*

L et's talk about the Atlantic. I'm going to be giving you some big numbers so do your best to keep your wits about you.

At 41,100,000 square miles, the Atlantic is the second largest of the world's five oceans, covering approximately a fifth of the Earth's surface. Put another way, it's nearly two and a half times larger than Asia. The ocean's average depth is 10,955 feet or if you prefer, four times the height of the Burj Khalifa in Dubai, the tallest building in the world. However, the greatest depth, the Milwaukee Deep in the Puerto Rico Trench, is 28,232 feet, just 800 feet short of being as deep as Mount Everest is tall. I've always wondered how such things are measured: I picture a man dropping a very long, heavily weighted tape measure off the side of a boat somewhere between the coasts of Africa and South America, but I've been told it's all done with echo sounding equipment on hydrographic ships. Anyway, my point is that the Atlantic is very big and very deep. And did I mention how dangerous it is? On average, the North Atlantic basin experiences 11.3 named storms per season, most of which develop off the coast of Africa near Cape Verde and move westward into the Caribbean Sea. I was alarmed to read that hurricanes were most frequent from August to November: the Atlantic Rally for Cruisers start date was 24 November, and we were heading for St Lucia in the Caribbean. 'Should we be worried?' I asked Carl.

None of this seemed to deter any of the 250 sailboats in Las Palmas: the marina was bustling with craft of all sizes and crews of all ages and backgrounds. Dinghies were flitting like dragonflies across the marina to pick up supplies, bring over crew and order last minute equipment. The air was filled with the clink of lines against masts, the flutter of sailcloth in the warm wind and above all the chatter of a thousand or more participants eager to join the sailing rally of a lifetime with talk of winds and waves, sails and speeds. Boats were individual hives of activity with skippers shouting orders, crews in colour co-ordinated T-shirts clambering and tripping over themselves, sails being furled and unfurled, hoisted and lowered. Every age and social group seemed represented from families with babies and dogs, to octogenarians. There were seasoned yachtsmen who were making their fiftieth Atlantic crossing, and there were virgins like ourselves. The old hands sat in their cockpits, calmly laying out three meals a day, wryly observing the panic of the nervous and uninitiated. But the excitement was contagious; it rippled through us from the moment we woke to the moment we fell into our berths.

We'd heard that the best way for the inexperienced to sail the Atlantic was to do so with the ARC as it offered the security of a large organisation which assisted and monitored all the boats taking part. We were most impressed with the ARC organisation; it covered everything from training seminars and security checks to the social aspect of the rally with happy hours and parties held at local bars where we got to know some of our fellow ralliers. The event was as much about the social atmosphere as about the sailing itself. By the end of the week, we felt as though we'd joined a very large family: albeit one without the questionable uncle who spends an unhealthy amount of time in his shed or the brother's dipsomaniac girlfriend, although having said that there were several questionable characters and more than a dozen old soaks.

One of the prerequisites of participating in the ARC is to pass a safety inspection, so we made sure to get ours booked for *Albatross* immediately to give us ample time to solve any problems or make repairs. Subsequently, a pedantic safety equipment inspector arrived with a clipboard and hefty checklist and spent a good hour prodding things with his pen while we anxiously looked over his shoulder wondering if we'd pass or fail. Most of the requirements are already installed on the average cruising boat, such as a VHF radio with external speaker, a bilge pump operable from on deck, clip-on jacklines and so on, all of which were listed in the ARC information pack. Nevertheless, we received a dishearteningly long list of recommendations, but they were all good points, and we were happy to comply with them. It was reassuring to know that following these measures might save our lives in the event of a catastrophe.

We knew *Albatross* was a reliable boat, but we hadn't yet appreciated the tremendous service offered by Hallberg-Rassy. Fourteen Hallberg-Rassy boats between 34 and 49 feet with home ports in Canada, Germany, Ireland,

Norway, Turkey, the US, the UK and ourselves from Sweden were taking part in the 2002 ARC. The company sent two reps, Per Arvidsson and Roland Olsson, to inspect all the boats and give additional advice where needed. They were a terrific help, giving *Albatross* a full examination from rudder to masthead and making several suggestions for improvements for smoother sailing. Later in the week, the company held a party for all the Hallberg-Rassy owners and crew where we met many international yachtsmen and women with whom we could exchange our experiences. We bonded like fast acting glue over our love of our boats.

One particular boat, *Girlsforsail*, drew our attention, not solely because the crew was made up of nubile women, but because they were sailing the sister boat to *Albatross*. The venture had been started by their skipper, a charismatic blonde called Annie, who, upon finding that women in the sailing world generally tended to be relegated to the kitchen, had set up a one-boat operation offering sailing packages for women. The "girls" were mostly affluent women in their thirties and while some of their crew may not have known how to sail, they all knew how to party. It wasn't long before we were betting a bottle of champagne over who would cross the Atlantic first. Carl and I thought we'd got it in the bag as the ladies' approach to sailing and boat maintenance seemed completely chaotic; they'd managed to leave England without their anchor, having been unable to raise it, and had freed themselves by taking a hacksaw to the chain, ditching both the chain and anchor in the mud of an English harbour. They'd spent much of their time in Puerto de la Luz hustling for a new anchor without success. Per had been in charge of inspecting their boat and after doing so had returned to *Albatross* looking slightly flushed.

'I've never seen anything like it,' he said, wiping his hand across his sweaty brow. I handed him a beer which he gulped down like a man in desperate need of resuscitation. 'It was like something out of a lingerie catalogue. I've never seen so many bras and thongs scattered about the place. What on earth do they need so much underwear for?'

I quietly wondered if it a been a ploy on the girls' part to put Per off his game. Even so, we could already taste that champagne.

Our own crew had increased by three: Greger had arrived from Sweden together with his father-in-law, Ulf Östman, who had been building his own boat for some years with which he'd hoped to cross the Atlantic. As his plan had never come to fruition, Greger asked if Ulf could join us. After all the help Greger had given us over the years, we were more than happy to welcome his father-in-law on board.

Our third crew member was a last minute addition. I'd spotted a handwritten notice on the marina gate which went something like, "Young clean man anxiously seeking Atlantic crossing to St Lucia. Willing to work hard and pay €1,000 for the experience. Call Tim." Both the reek of desperation and the money immediately attracted me: furthermore, a native English speaker would be a bonus as Carl and I still struggled to understand anything that came over the radio bar the word "Mayday!"– which, incidentally, derives from the French *m'aidez*, meaning "Help me!" We duly gave Tim Bateup, from Worthing in England, a call. Tim was studying for his Yachtmaster exam and needed 3,000 nautical miles under his belt to get his qualification: crossing the Atlantic would nail at least 2,800 of those miles. Unfortunately, he'd literally been left high and dry on two occasions when skippers who had promised to take him on as crew reneged on their deals, so he was thrilled to get our call, and after an interview conducted over a beer, we told him to stow his gear. I think he may literally have jumped for joy – he was that type. With Greger's experience, Ulf's knowhow, Tim's enthusiasm, Carl's stubborn optimism and my cooking, we felt we had a winning team.

Like all the other 249 boats taking part, we spent the final days before casting off buying supplies for the three-week crossing. We loaded *Albatross* with fresh vegetables, fruit, eggs and bread to the point where she lay four inches below the waterline. As head chef, I spent two or three hours making several hundred meatballs with which to stock the freezer: nothing hits the spot quite like a dish of Swedish meatballs, cranberry sauce and boiled potatoes when you've got your sea legs.

On a warm November day, 250 boats bobbed up and down at the start line. It was an impressive sight, and thousands of holiday makers and Las Palmas residents gathered to see us off, waving and cheering us on. There'd been an opening ceremony, a parade, speeches and local bands playing in the harbour. A frigate stood sedately at the head of the start line: a tug boat on either side spraying two vast cascades of water straight into the sky. We were all excited, but Tim put it into movement for us by jumping up and down on deck with all the fervour of a five-year-old who's been told he can have chocolate cake for breakfast. On the stroke of one o'clock, all the boats hoisted their spinnakers or gennakers. We were off. We waved and shouted good luck to other crew on boats we recognized around us. 'See you in St Lucia!' Tim shouted, and bounced up and down with the vigour of Tigger.

Carl and I grinned at each other. Here it was: the Atlantic. We were setting sail for a whole new continent, across the biggest stretch of water we'd yet navigated. I put my head back and took a deep breath; I wanted to taste the sweetness in that moment and keep the memory of it as long as I could.

The weather was perfect: a very weak wind ruffled the sails and the sun shone in a cloudless sky. We would sail south along the Gran Canaria coastline towards Maspalomas. It was a gentle start and other boats very quickly disappeared out of view. It didn't matter: we needed to get our sea legs after two weeks on land, and Carl took the opportunity to set the four-hour long watches for himself, Greger, Ulf and Tim. I was exempt from watches as I was responsible for doing any necessary repairs on *Albatross* and feeding the crew three meals a day.

Day 1

Our first day starts innocently enough and we bob happily along blown by a pleasant wind, but as we reach San Augustin so the wind dies. Further out to sea, we can see that the larger boats have taken down their spinnakers and are tacking hard. We lower our spinnaker and hoist the mainsail, stay sail and genoa. The sun slowly slides below the horizon, the wind picks up massively and a gale suddenly blows in from the south; the anemometer starts to swing between 35 and 50 miles per hour, and the previously pretty Atlantic crests increase to tower block-sized walls of water. Tim swaps enthusiastic jumping for looking worried. We reef in all the sails, reef in the mainsail to the third reef and brace ourselves for a night of being knocked about like a mouse being played with by a tiger. By midnight, despite a dose of the best seasickness remedy on the market, Carl, Ulf and Tim are leaning over the sides heaving in unison.

Day 2

The culmination of seasickness is reached with the last dry heave from Tim at sunrise. In the brightening dawn light, we can see that the boats have dispersed: only a dozen are in sight, all of which, like us, are having to tack sharply and battle waves up to 35 feet high.

We're all feeling wretchedly tired and lethargic and try to sleep when not on watch: a near impossible task with waves slamming against the hull like cannon balls and being tossed out of your bunk with every pitch and roll. It's impossible to use the stove in such conditions, so we have to make do with cold cuts and bread which our empty stomachs welcome once we grow used to the pitching and rolling.

The wind eventually turns north-eastwards and dies down to 25 miles an hour. *Albatross* sails from crest to crest at seven knots and we all draw a sigh of relief. Hopefully, this is the start of easier, stomach friendlier sailing.

Day 3

I should know better by now than to say these things. The ocean churns and boils, throwing up giant waves aft of us. Just before the waves break, *Albatross* is lifted 40 feet to the top of the wave crest where she is poised briefly before plunging down to ride the trough to the top of the next wave. When it isn't boxer-wettingly terrifying, it's unbelievably exhilarating.

With practise I manage to develop a technique of cooking hot food without endangering myself or setting fire to the boat in the process, although it demands the skills of a circus performer: balancing pots and spinning plates while clad in a costume of waterproof overalls and boots to avoid burning myself when the frying fat spits and spills from the stove. I'd like to see Jamie Oliver try to rustle up spicy meatballs for five in similar conditions.

Day 4

Northwest winds of 40 miles an hour continue to whip up turbulent waves, and I continue to cook three meals a day. We eat, sleep and keep watch. Either our bodies are beginning to accept the routine thrust upon them, or the travel sickness pills are finally working their magic. Tim turns out to be very handy with the radio and the social atmosphere of the rally continues at sea with the daily Radio Nets when crews log in to exchange fishing tips, discuss the rally and get advice. It becomes a feature of our day to log in and read our position in the rally, how far we've sailed and how many miles we're covering each day. Are we ahead of *Girlsforsail*? We're pleased to discover we're averaging 180 nautical miles a day. I think Ulf is pleased he isn't throwing up any more.

Day 5

As we are fast running out of meatballs and burgers, I try my hand at fishing again: mealtimes are the highlight of the day, challenging me to be more inventive with my concoctions, so a fresh tuna would make a welcome change.

I set up the fishing rod and reel in the stern and cast out 20 feet of line, baiting it with a squid hook just as Gunter showed us. Deciding that a watched kettle never boils, I leave the line and go about my chores. Darkness falls and most of us are trying to get some shuteye when Ulf, who is on watch, shouts, 'All hands on deck. We've got a big one!'

We drowsily put on our lifejackets and clip on our safety lines. The rod is bent in a curve and the line strains taut with whatever is biting, and whatever is biting looks as if it's monstrous. I grab the rod and try to reel in, but to my astonishment the rod bends further into a tight arc and suddenly snaps in half. The rod, reel, line and octopus hook all disappear below the surface. We all stare open-mouthed at the sea. The rod is supposed to bear weights of up to 400 pounds.

'Holy crap!' Carl says. 'What the hell was that?'

'Dinner for a month,' I reply sulkily. 'And now it's swimming around with my rod and reel.'

Day 6

If an army marches on its stomach, it stands to reason that a ship's crew sails on its stomach, too. Tim's enthusiasm for "crossing the pond," as he has taught us to say, is closely matched by his passion for food. No matter what I serve, he is effusive with gratitude. 'Marvellous,' he says about a meal. He never refuses seconds and, given half the chance would lick the pots with his tongue. He's a nice guy with a cast-iron stomach and taste buds that have yet to find anything unpalatable.

Day 7

We've settled into our routine and chores; *Albatross* is flying across the water like her namesake.

We shower every other day on the aft deck, securely lashed to a lifeline; lathering up and rinsing off all the dried salt on the skin is pure pleasure. Then we stretch out on the deck and dry out in the sun, gazing at the sky through half-shut eyelids and making pictures out of the clouds. The temperature is between 26 degrees Celsius by night and a pleasant 29 degrees Celsius by day.

Day 8

We are suddenly and brutally reminded of the dangers of the ocean and how sailing accidents are not rare. During the daily position report on the radio, we listen with growing horror to a general distress call from an ARC boat: a two man boat has lost a crew member overboard. The craft's position is given and boats in the area are asked to help search for the missing yachtsman. Although we aren't in the vicinity, we all scan the waves for the rest of the day, hoping we might spot the survivor but knowing in our hearts the unlikely probability of his being found alive in such rough seas. A melancholy mood settles on the whole crew: we all feel it could have happened to anyone of us.

Day 9

We listen to the radio all morning for reports of the previous day's tragedy. The victim, a father of two, was swept off his brother's yacht, still attached to his lifeline, when a huge wave hit the boat. His brother desperately tried to pull him back on board but struggled in the rough conditions. He later told his family by satellite phone that by the time he'd succeeded in getting his brother into the boat's dinghy, he was blue and not moving. Although other boats go to the area to assist, conditions prevent them from getting close to the ketch. The lone brother has turned the boat around and headed back towards Gran Canaria, but such is his difficulty in steering, that the Coast-guard advise him to cut the dinghy free so they can retrieve his brother's body in calmer conditions. We can only imagine how the poor man is coping. The final note to the story strikes a particular chord with Carl and me: the brothers were fulfilling a lifelong ambition of taking part in a transatlantic rally. Their dream became their nightmare.

Our technical problems on board *Albatross* seem insignificant in compari-son, but they keep us occupied; the control pendulum on the windvane rud-der has come off and is dragging in the water. Fortunately, we'd attached an extra line to the helm, otherwise we would have lost the pendulum with the rudder fin. After our experience in Scotland we had the foresight to have four extra pipes cut to the correct length, but the powerful wake exerts so much force on the replacement pipe that it snaps in two after only a couple of hours. We decide not to take any risks by tinkering with the rudder where massive waves are pummelling the stern; instead we lash the rudder securely so it doesn't get swept away and use the electric autopilot.

Day 10

During the afternoon, the strong north-easterly wind finally drops and the ocean calms. We slip over the gently rippling waves and at long last expe-rience true "blue water sailing." It has been a tough start and one sailor has paid the ultimate price for his dreams.

The GPS shows we've travelled 1,500 nautical miles to St Lucia: approxi-mately halfway. Carl, Ulf and Tim celebrate the fact we were on the home-stretch to the Caribbean with a bottle of champagne. Greger and I stick with water as we've both taken a vow of abstinence: we feel it's essential to have at least one person on watch who is fully in command of their faculties during the crossing. Tim generally drinks very little, but Carl and Ulf always have a bottle of wine with their evening meal.

The evening is incredibly beautiful: the sky seems bigger, the ocean infinite when you are just a lone boat and nothing else but the stars and the waves are in view. I sit in the cockpit and lift my eyes to the heavens and let my thoughts drift. A sense of absolute peace settles on me. This is my pilgrimage; here is my nirvana.

Day 11

The northwest wind persists at speeds between 20 and 30 miles an hour, so we hoist the gennaker and maintain a speed of seven to eight knots. The weather forecast warns of squalls: the rain clouds increase the wind strength and rain bursts from the sky for a few minutes before passing. Then we quickly lower the gennaker as the force of a large sail on the rigging is huge in these wind speeds. During the course of the day we practise and test several ways of bringing the sail down so we can act quickly in case of an emergency.

Day 12

Shower day for the whole crew. We line up on the aft deck, naked as the day we were born, and take it in turns to lather up and rise off with fresh water from the hand shower. Unfortunately, the hand shower we bought in a marine supply store isn't the best quality; the valve on the shower handle slips open and all 500 litres (110 gallons) of fresh water gushes out into the Atlantic Ocean unnoticed by any of us. With approximately 10 days left to our destination, this is a serious problem. Fortunately, we can run the water maker for 12 hours straight; the filtered water is as palatable as cabbage water but is fine for cooking and showering. From now on, whenever we finish showering, we make certain to detach the blasted handle afterwards.

Day 13

Powerful waves continue to roll in from the stern and lift *Albatross* like a child on a swing. Timing the waves, we find that the boat reaches a crest every seven seconds. We've all become quite accustomed to this regular motion, the shudder of the boat and the musical rattle of the cupboards' contents. I'm quite agile in the galley, poised on my toes like Fred Astaire to keep my balance, chasing vegetables and swiftly juggling pans on the gas stove which I secure with thick rubber bands to the stove rail to stop them from sliding and sloshing their contents over me or the cabin floor.

Greger displays a hidden talent: his cinnamon buns are even better than my mother's. The delectable aroma of fresh baking filters up from the galley to those on deck causing a near feeding frenzy as we scramble for the warm buns. Tim's judgement is: 'Really marvellous.'

We realize, however, that we are all putting on weight: we've been eating three three-course meals a day and are getting no exercise. Hence, I am instructed to prepare three courses for lunch only. *Ungrateful bastards*, I think. Tim, however, looks stricken at the idea of less food.

Day 14

Today we are treated to the company of a large whale on our starboard side swimming alongside us for the best part of half an hour, surfacing several times, blowing out of its spout and seeming to fix us with an inky eye. We consult a colour chart of dorsal fins we picked up from the ARC office in Las Palmas and are able to identify our friend as a long-finned pilot whale. Apparently, these whales – whose lengths run between 12 to 15 feet – are really dolphins and are very sociable. I like to think we amused our whale as much as he or she amused us.

Shortly before dusk, a pod of a dozen dolphins appear – clearly they've heard about *Albatross* from the pilot whale – and race the boat and each other, breaching the bow waves in their competition to be the first ahead of us. After a quarter of an hour they grow bored of their game and head out into the ocean.

'Come back and play soon,' I find myself saying wistfully to their departing fins.

Day 15

After mourning the loss of my expensive fishing rod, I buck myself up by improvising a new one made of fishing line attached to a piece of wire and hung on the stern rail with a tough leather strap. 'Let's see you try and take that,' I say to the ocean monsters.

It's the second Sunday in Advent, so we play Christmas carols on the CD player and sing along, our voices ringing out across the water as the sun slowly disappears into the sea. As darkness falls, we watch as the stars light up the sky and the moon shines a path across the ocean. It's at these times, when the sunset spreads across the horizon and the wind makes the waves dance on the immense stretch of water before us, that we enjoy the luxury of exploring our own thoughts: never have I felt so insignificant as against this great body of water. I have a sudden sense of how small I am in relation to the world around me and the sky above. Then my thoughts wander to the journey that's lead me here: the twists and turns of life that have brought me to where I am now. I think of all the choices I've made, the paths I've chosen, the decisions I've taken. If I'd opened a different door, if I'd turned left instead of right, bumping into different people on the way, would I be sitting on a boat in the middle of the Atlantic with three Swedes and an eternally hungry Brit; would I even be the same person, have the same character, haircut, likes and dislikes? Such philosophising inevitably leads to contemplating the future: it's too late to have any regrets about the paths already taken; what matters is choosing the road ahead, and that in itself is key: what matters? We talk about our hopes and dreams, fears and frustrations. Ulf is more determined than ever to finish his boat and sail it across the Atlantic, and Tim's goal is to go to Nashville and make a record.

'I don't want to become a singing sensation or anything like that,' he explains, blushing modestly, 'but I like writing songs and I think a few of them might be quite good.'

Carl and I agree that we feel privileged to have taken the chance to fulfil our ambition to sail around the world; we're on our way to giving our humdrum lives a shot of adrenaline, a kick start for a more meaningful end to our days.

But no matter how long I muse or how long we talk, the blasted fish still don't bite.

Day 16

Only the night before we'd been contemplating how lucky we are, and today over the radio we hear that the yacht *F2* sailed by our friends Peter and Sarah have experienced major problems: their rudder has become damaged, preventing them from steering from the helm and forcing them to hand steer: a near impossible task for a two man crew with more than a thousand nautical miles left to St Lucia. Carl and I had got to know them in Camariñas and know how much they have their hearts set on completing a transatlantic crossing.

'Let's hold our thumbs for them,' I say to Carl as we discuss it around the radio. Tim looks at me with a puzzled expression. 'It's what we Swedes do for good luck,' I explain.

'Ah,' Tim says. 'In England, we cross our fingers.' He demonstrates.

'And in Germany, you press your thumbs together,' Carl adds.

'Well, let's do all of them and we might have it covered,' I say.

That afternoon we receive a visit from two minke whales, 25 feet in size. They swim round us in a figure of eight pattern, disappearing under our keel on every circuit. It's strangely hypnotic to watch them as they smoothly slip around us. They tire of our company before we do theirs and swim on.

Despite using the so-called best fishing lure on the market, I still haven't caught anything, leaving me feeling somewhat foolish. To add insult to injury, when I haul in the line, I discover that the lure has been taken and spat out: these fish are hard to fool.

Day 17

No amount of finger gymnastics have helped Peter and Sarah and their German shepherd; we learn from the ARC daily position report that they've had to abandon ship: *F2* finally lost its rudder and started taking on water. The U.S Coastguard subsequently issues a warning that a stray ship is floating around in the southwest Atlantic. The vessel will probably sink within 24 hours. We are gutted for the couple, knowing how they'd given up everything to buy their 45-foot Hunter to sail around the world for five years. They'd described their boat as a "floating caravan" – ironically, it proved just as buoyant. They'd wanted to buy a Hallberg-Rassy, but it had been beyond their budget.

The weather reflects our melancholy mood; the sun glimmers weakly behind sullen-looking clouds, rain is in the air and the wind gusts menacingly, so we lower the gennaker and sail with the genoa, mizzen and mainsail, making brisk speeds of seven to eight knots. Our destination is now only 400 nautical miles away.

We check my improvised fishing rod and haul the line on board hoping to be rewarded with something edible; the hook, half the line and swivel sinker have gone. There must be some huge fish in the waters below: another reason not to fall in. Determined not to be outwitted, I try modifying my contraption, mounting a new hook and taping an empty tin can to the line which will clatter if anything takes the bait. Catching at least one fish on this journey has become a matter of honour: I'll be damned if something with only a handful of brain cells outsmarts me.

Day 18

There's a long loud rattle, then an ominous silence, followed by 'Damn it!' Greger's voice brings us all on deck. The roller-furling drum for the halyard on the genoa has broken: bad news in view of the fact that strong storms are chasing us from behind and we can no longer reef in the genoa. Carl and Tim lie precariously on the bowsprit and attempt to repair the drum as the breaking waves swirl around them. In light of recent events, we respect the power of the ocean more than ever and always wear our lifejackets and lifelines when on deck, so Carl and Tim are well secured. Nevertheless, mindful of what happened to another rally member, it's hairy just watching the two of them make the repairs so close to the waves. After a considerable time, they manage to repair the roller and we're able to lower and hoist the genoa again.

It's one of those testing days when if it can go wrong, it will go wrong. After flattering Greger into baking again for us, he acquiesces and is just about to transfer the cake batter to the baking tray, when an ill-timed wave jolts him off balance, throwing all the batter down himself and in the bilge: a huge waste of sugar and eggs and a royal pain to mop up. The second batch makes it successfully into the oven; the cake rises spectacularly and then suddenly sinks like a stone. Even so, we fight like alley cats to eat the burned remnants.

Tim was making coffee to go with the cake and sustained a massive burn on his index finger which swells to a blister the size of a party balloon; inevitably, it bursts, seeps vilely and has to be wrapped in a plaster and kept away from salt water: easier said than done. Even the simplest sort of cooking has become an extreme sport.

And my luck fishing doesn't improve: a large tuna teases us by taking the bait. As we rush to the stern and begin to pull in the line, the fish does an elegant summersault over the waves and gets away. There's a collective gasp of exasperation: what does it take to catch a blasted fish?

Despite the run of small but aggravating disasters, excitement is mounting: the GPS indicates only 299 nautical miles to St Lucia. We're looking forward to reaching a new continent after the longest passage we've ever made. Our sense of achievement is enormous, matched only by our feeling of pride: our spines are a little straighter; we all stand a little taller.

Day 19

With only one day left on our long voyage, our position in the race is looking surprisingly good: we're ahead of at least 100 boats. We've "given it some iron," as we say in Sweden, and haven't disgraced ourselves. In preparation for our arrival we scrub everything inside *Albatross* and make a laundry pile to rival that of a rugby team's after a month on tour. As Carl says, 'I've had to wear my underwear inside out and upside down for the last week.' Not a savoury thought.

Day 20

On the stroke of midday, Ulf shouts, 'Land ahoy!' On the horizon we glimpse a volcanic mountain rising majestically out of the blue. What an immense feeling of joy; all five of us cheer and dance around on deck. I can fully understand how those mariners must have felt when after months at sea, they finally caught sight of land and knew they were saved a death from drowning, starvation, disease or infection from injuries. Of course, some of those sixteenth and seventeenth century sailors jumped ashore only to be attacked by suspicious or hungry natives or catch some nasty disease. In 1528, the Italian explorer Giovanni da Verrazzano was killed and eaten by Carib natives in the Lesser Antilles. The fact that there is a suspension bridge in New York bearing his name is probably of little consolation to his spirit.

At 17:28 we cross the finish line at the entrance to Rodney Bay. *Albatross* has completed the ARC in 19 days, 4 hours and 28 minutes, sailing over 2,800 nautical miles at an average speed of 7.5 knots from Gran Canaria to St Lucia. We are the ninety-seventh boat to cross the finish line and place sixteenth in our class. Our crew and boat are intact, save for a few bruises, a bandaged finger and a dubious pong in the cabin.

We slowly enter Rodney Bay marina, taking unashamed pleasure in the applause of crews on other yachts and holiday makers sitting in harbour side restaurants. ARC representatives are on the quayside ready to welcome us with congratulations and a cool cocktail – Greger's and my first sip of alcohol in nearly three weeks and we bloody well deserve it, although I nearly take my eye out on the decorative umbrella in my haste to drink it.

Our crew left the following comments on the voyage to our logbook:

"Sailing the Atlantic was an awesome achievement that I wouldn't have missed for the world. I could never have imagined such beautiful starry skies by night and whales and dolphins by day. The first few days of sailing were tough and during my bout of seasickness, I wondered if it would last the whole three weeks. But then it passed, I got my sea legs and my confidence. I've had a wonderful trip. I regretfully travel home with Greger tomorrow."

Ulf Ostman.

"This voyage cannot be described; it has been an absolutely fantastic time. The boat and crew have worked without any problems. I hope to meet Yanne and Carl again on their journey around the globe. Now I'm going home for Christmas. Thanks Yanne and Carl."

Greger Persson

"Truly a dream come true! Crossing the Atlantic on Albatross was easily the best sailing experience of my life. The camaraderie of the crew was second to none and the food was excellent. I really feel that I've made some great new friends with the Albatross boys and look forward to seeing them again one day.

The experience was so good in fact that I am inspired to go on and chase another dream as soon as I leave the boat. I will think of Albatross and her crew when I am in Nashville and will remember the great times we all had together when I need future inspiration. Carl, Yanne, Ulf and Greger, thanks for a wonderful sail. You are the champions, my friends."

Tim Bateup

Tim did follow his dreams. He wrote to us later to say that he made it to Nashville and did indeed make a record with the help of a producer. The album, fittingly entitled *Seabillie, Toy Boat*, after his time with us, was later released on a small independent label in Britain. That dream fulfilled, Tim returned to his teaching career, met the love of his life and now sails his own boat on the South Coast of England. He didn't mention it but I assume he continues to enjoy his food.

Chapter 24

Chilling Out in the Caribbean

13 December, 2002 – 2 January, 2003

Rodney Bay, St Lucia – Soufrière, St Lucia –
Admiralty Bay, Port Elizabeth, Bequia

Experience: *Beware of anyone claiming to be a harbourmaster: many locals try to fleece unsuspecting tourists by asking for harbour or anchor fees. When negotiating prices, always check which currency you're dealing in.*

Tip: *Never jump around a volcano crater; the ground might not be as solid as you think.*

Every four years, the Olympic Games remind me that a country's national anthem was at one time chosen to eulogize the history and traditions of that nation. France's *La Marseillaise* stirringly reflects the bloody invasion of France by foreign armies, hence the rather gruesome lyrics about fearsome soldiers coming to cut the throats of the country's sons and companions; the words of the *The Star-Spangled Banner* were taken from a poem inspired by the successful American defence of Fort McHenry from the British and the sight of the flag flying victoriously above the fort, although the patriotic effect is somewhat negated by the fact it was set to a melody nicked from the English. The British national anthem is, of course, one of the best known throughout the world, but was probably a sycophantic attempt to praise the reigning monarch at the time of its writing in the eighteenth century.

And the Swedish national anthem? Can anyone other than a Swede name it? Hum the melody? No, I didn't think so. Entitled *Du Gamla, Du Fria* ("Thou ancient, Thou free"), it eulogises our country as being the most beautiful land upon the earth with its "mountainous north and meadows green." Any sniff of patriotic fervour, however, is conspicuously absent from the original, resulting in the addition of a couple of more nationalistic verses, squeezing in the name of the country and culminating in the lines: "I trade thee not for anything in the world. No, I want to live, I want to die in the North." The accompanying notes on how to sing it probably read "lugubriously" and "without irony."

I have absolutely no clue what St. Lucia's national anthem is about but assume it was written by a reggae artist or at the very least set to a relaxed reggae beat. Everything about our arrival so far had been laid-back: from the welcoming rum punch cocktail from the ARC representative as we stepped ashore, to the lack of haste at immigration. We quickly realized that we hadn't just arrived at a new continent but had entered a whole different pace of life: one where the words "'hurry'" or "rush" didn't feature in the language. In all the time we were in the Caribbean, I never saw anyone run or even walk briskly: people of all ages ambled, strolled, lolloped, meandered or shuffled.

We were shuffling now in an immigration queue that meandered with more bends than a wayward river. The two so-called officials behind their desks were so far off in the distance they could have been mirages. We could only speculate that they were officials because of the far-away twinkle of gold braid on their lapels. It was the first time *Albatross* and her crew had had to clear immigration as we'd previously only travelled within the EU. The authorities seemed to have all the time in the world, whereas we had less than a week on the island. I was worried we wouldn't get to the top of the queue before we had to leave again. Ninety minutes and several rounds of the immigration hall later, we stood before an official who clearly enjoyed the power of his pen-pushing roll and the authority to chuck anyone out of the country who might give him a bit of lip. We looked suitably humble as he nonchalantly flipped through our documents. On the whole, the authorities weren't particularly interested in their contents apart from the issue of visas and the cash they generated, and a local declaration form completed in quad-ruplicate. Our man tapped his ink pen and looked up at us.

'How much alcohol are you bringing in?'

'How much are we allowed?' Carl asked.

He shrugged. 'About one litre of spirits and two litres of wine.'

Good lord, I thought. The islanders had no idea of the drinking capacity of the Swedish. I thought it best to just come clean. 'We've got 300 litres of spirits and 700 litres of wine. Oh, and about 2,000 cans of beer,' I said.

The official put back his head and laughed, showing teeth as white as the inside of a coconut. He said something in rapid fire Creole patois to the other uniformed man who slapped his thigh and whooped with laughter.

Our immigration officer wagged a long dark finger at us. 'You shouldn't mess with da authorities, man. But dat's okay. I like a joke.' He looked slyly at us. 'And maybe you gotta a little bottle or two extra.'

'No problem,' I replied. 'White or red?'

'I like red,' he said, at which there was more chuckling before he finally stamped our documents.

As soon as we'd cleared customs, we delivered him his wine as promised, just to pre-empt any possible raid on the boat.

'As my mother always said, "Honesty is the best policy,"' I said as we strolled back to the harbour.

'Don't bank on that always happening,' Carl warned.

As we were to find out later, honesty was a flexible concept on the island and would have horrified my mother. St Lucia is strikingly beautiful, with green clad volcanic peaks, tropical rain forests and pristine white sandy beaches bordered by water so clear you'd think it had been specially filtered. Rivers flow from the island's centre down to the sea, irrigating fertile land holdings where crops of mangoes and avocados are grown. But the "green gold," as the banana crop is known, is the biggest source of revenue after tourism. Or was until recently: St Lucia's banana exports have declined by over two thirds over the last 20 years, and the number of banana farmers has fallen drastically by more than 85 percent as the industry faces stronger competition and lower market prices, resulting in rising unemployment and crime. Holiday villas and yachts have become obvious targets for theft, and although the marinas are well guarded, thieves enter by sea at night, sneak on board yachts and steal anything that isn't nailed down while the unsuspecting crews are sleeping off their rum punches.

Tourists, of course, are considered fair game by the locals whose haggling skills we discovered were second to none. Nevertheless, we remained fairly confident of our secret weapon, Carl. As we took a meander – we quickly fell in step with the local pace of life – taxi drivers and street vendors hustled us for business. 'A special price for you, my friend, only for you,' they called.

'If you believe that, you deserve to get ripped off,' Carl said through his teeth. The trouble with Carl is that he enjoys the challenge of the negotiation: the more exorbitant the starting figure, the more he'll haggle it down. Eventually, he was mighty pleased with himself when he struck a deal with a local taxi driver to drive us round the island the following day at the "special price" of 100 dollars.

At nine the next morning, we rolled off with a couple of cooler bags stocked with water and beer, heading south along the west coast. The road snaked up and down around the hills, swinging us from side to side until I felt slightly sick. We bumped through small villages where families were gathered on the verandas of their rickety-looking houses. The women were dressed in their Sunday best, having been to church that morning. I couldn't decide which were more colourful: their large hats, their clothes or their houses.

The buildings, tiny colonial type structures with louvered windows and clap-board sides, were perched on wobbly looking pillars and looked as if they'd been the victims of a paint factory explosion: every colour ever created was represented: lime green walls clashed with orange trimmed windows; mauve verandas collided with citrus yellow exteriors. Both villages and villagers were happy riots of colour. The streets were framed by open concrete ditches, deep enough to swallow a truck, where chickens pecked at rubbish tossed away by the islanders. My heart sank to see so much detritus. Plastic bottles, tin cans, polystyrene fast food boxes, blown-out tyres and rusting piles of abandoned cars and burnt-out trucks littered the streets.

'Where's the local pride to preserve the beauty of the island?' I wondered aloud.

'In the hands of the hotel and marina developers,' Greger answered.

Typically, there was a furious debate between Carl and the taxi driver about which currency they'd agreed on, with the driver insisting the price they'd negotiated was for American dollars. A compromise was eventually reached but Carl's complaints were heard the length and breadth of the island. As we stood atop a cliff overlooking Marigot Bay, a natural hurricane hole and frequently described as the most beautiful bay in the Caribbean, Carl grum-bled. As we bathed in the lagoon below Diamond Falls where the cascade's rocks were encrusted with green, yellow and purple minerals, he continued to whinge. And as we chose three splendid lobsters in the fish market in Sou-frière, he criticized my bargaining skills. He did, however, praise my cooking ability later that evening when I grilled the lobsters in a garlic butter sauce. His mood was undoubtedly mellowed by a bottle of white wine.

Greger and Ulf left *Albatross* a couple of days later, followed by Tim who had been convinced by his time with us that his pursuit of a music career was something not to be postponed any longer. He set off for Nashville with renewed confidence and a firm resolution to record his first album. We were sad to see the lads leave; we'd been a happy crew for nearly a month and had worked well together. Nevertheless, their berths were barely cold before we were approached by two new hopefuls: Charlotta Norén, a student from southern Sweden, was taking a sabbatical from her university studies and had been boat hopping her way to St Lucia. We liked her immediately; she was unpretentious, had a sense of humour and would fit in well. A day later, we were joined by Anders Bergqvist. He'd been working on the island installing telecommunications equipment for Flextronics AB but wanted to sail during his three-week holiday rather than return to the frozen north of Sweden. He clearly didn't subscribe to the words of our national anthem about living and dying in the North, and who could blame him?

Carl and I had remained in Rodney Bay specifically to attend the ARC awards party. Although many teams and crews had already left for home, 200 people gathered to eat, drink and celebrate a successful Atlantic crossing. We met the ladies from *GirlsforSail* and reminded them they owed us a bottle of champagne as we'd beaten them to Rodney Bay. Strangely, they'd forgotten this. *GirlsforSail* is still going strong and now have several boats taking part in the ARC every year. If ever you bump into one of the girls, please mention that Yanne and Carl are still patiently waiting for that bottle of Moet.

The following morning, despite a mild throbbing behind the temples after the awards party and a nagging worry that we may have said or done something more stupid than usual, we cast off with our new crew and sailed 35 nautical miles south along the island's coast to Soufrière, the former French capital of St Lucia. The small town sits in the shadow of the Gros and the Petit Piton mountains, two volcanic spires rising precipitously like jade-clad pyramids from the sea. Designated a UNESCO World Heritage site in 2004, the area also boasts the only drive-in volcano in the world, although this is actually a misnomer as it's only possible to drive within just a few hundred feet of the gurgling, bubbling mass, whereupon you have to proceed on foot around the crater. At one time it was possible to walk on the crater, but this was recently prohibited after an overenthusiastic guide attempted to demonstrate the safety of the crust by jumping up and down in it. His party of tourists watched in horror as he disappeared to his armpits in the bubbling mass. Fortunately, he was rescued and lived to tell the tale but suffered severe burns in the process.

We decided to spend the afternoon and night at Soufrière but as we neared the shore, we were approached by numerous local boats, all declaring themselves to be "port captains" and directing us to moor at their buoys for which we would receive a special rate.

'There's an astounding number of port captains for such a small port,' Carl growled darkly. 'We'll anchor off the beach.'

No sooner had we heaved out 150 feet of chain, than another "harbourmaster" approached us, shouting that sailboats were not permitted to anchor but had to attach a stern line to a palm tree on shore for a 40-dollar fee. After some heated shouting, we saw him off. Moments later, a small motorboat with a dreadlocked type in a Bob Marley T-shirt at the tiller and a lady so large I wondered how the boat managed to remain afloat zoomed up to us.

'Hello, my friend,' she beamed. 'Forty dollars for coral fee.'

'Piss off, my friend,' Carl said. He is not best known for his tact. The lady's jowly face fell faster than the Greek economy.

'You don't pay, we're gonna call da police,' she shouted, wagging a fat finger.

'You come any closer to our boat, we'll call the police, the coastguard and the St Lucia air and sea port authorities,' Carl shouted back. 'So piss off!' And she did. We were finally left in peace and snorkelled for the rest of the afternoon, discovering a world of colour and tranquillity below the surface of the water.

We were disappointed that paradise seemed to be overrun by locals trying to fleece the tourists, and this from a nation with the highest ratio of Nobel laureates of any sovereign country in the world: Sir Arthur Lewis won the Nobel Prize in Economics in 1979, and Derek Walcott received the Nobel Prize in Literature in 1992. We weighed anchor the following day and made a course for Bequia, bypassing St Vincent which we'd heard was controlled by local gangsters: heaven forbid Carl have a run in with one of them. Besides which we'd planned to celebrate Christmas in true Scandinavian fashion at a glögg party hosted by a Nordic expatriate, an event which draws many homesick Norwegians, Swedes and Danes to the island.

The tiny island of Bequia, meaning "island of clouds" in ancient Arawak, is still the largest in the Grenadines at seven square miles with a population of approximately 5,000 inhabitants. It's popular among cruising yachts and tourists for its pure waters, white shores and numerous dive sites; there are several wrecks and caves attracting a variety of sea life including Hawksbill turtles, lobsters and moray eels. We'd noticed that Anders, a qualified diving instructor, had stowed a huge locker of diving equipment, obviously keen to explore the dive sites. For my part, I was looking forward to catching and grilling the lobsters. During the sail, Anders managed some grilling of his own: his arse in his attempt to get an all over tan. None of us volunteered to apply the after sun lotion, and it was a couple of days before he could sit comfortably again.

Later that afternoon, we sighted Admiralty Bay, crowded with hundreds of boats flying Scandinavia ensigns. Clearly we weren't the only Swedes seeking our traditional Christmas fare of herring and glazed ham. Many of the yachts were festively decorated with flashing lights and artificial trees set up on the decks or in the cabins. Our little Father Christmas figure looked rather forlorn in the cockpit, but it was the only decoration we had. As the sun set slowly in the west just after six o'clock, the mercury showed a balmy 29 degrees Celsius. We clinked our glasses of snaps and looked at this year's Christmas landscape: steep verdant hills against a darkening indigo sky, gently swaying palm trees on white beaches and white hulls bobbing on turquoise water. If ever there was paradise on earth, this was it, I thought.

'Bloody hell, my buttocks hurt,' Anders said, breaking the tranquillity.

Like St Lucia and many other islands in the Caribbean, Bequia was wrestled over by the British and the French during the seventeenth and eighteenth centuries as each country sought to enjoy the wealth reaped from slavery and sugar cane. The island finally ended in the hands of the British in 1783: thus English became the official language and cars drive on the left. While tourism generates a substantial proportion of the island's income, Bequia still depends on the old traditions of boat building, fishing and whaling. It is one of the few places where limited whaling is still permitted by the International Whaling Commission. Natives of the island are allowed to catch a maximum of four humpback whales a year, which they rarely succeed in doing, using only traditional hunting methods of hand-thrown harpoons from small sailboats. A small whaling museum chronicles the local whaling history and the Whale Boner Bar and Restaurant in Port Elizabeth welcomes their guests with an entrance arch of two whale ribs.

Scandinavians celebrate Christmas on 24 December, so Admiralty harbour was buzzing with activity as many of the Nordic boats were gearing up for the most festive day of the calendar outside of Midsummer. After Christmas lunch on the boat, we made our way to the famous glögg party at the home of Mariann Palmborg on Mount Pleasant. For a Scandinavian, Christmas isn't Christmas without glögg. Similar to, but infinitely better than glühwein, it is a mulled wine made with red wine, port and brandy and flavoured with spices, raisins and almonds: the perfect cold-weather drink that sends a warming glow through the body. What more natural than to crave it in the tropical heat? Stockholm born Mariann started hosting a small glögg party in the 1990s for the few Scandinavians she knew. Her party's reputation has grown so much that now between 200 and 300 guests make their way to the island every year to join the festivities. The only requirement is to bring a bottle of red wine to add to the glögg pot and a cash donation for the local school for handicapped children. We could hear the party as we walked up the hill, and by the time we arrived, sweaty from our climb, the garden was heaving with a couple of hundred Scandinavians. Our entrance ticket was added to the simmering pot on the stove and in return we received a steaming mug of glögg. The Christmas atmosphere was further enhanced by a group of Norwegian children singing carols. We wandered around the garden, chatting to Danes, Norwegians and Swedes. The thing about Scandinavian languages is that they are similar but completely different as we've spent the last 10 centuries invading and occupying each other's countries. In one thing, however, we are absolutely united: the unassailable conviction that Christmas day falls on 24 December and the undying belief in the right to drink hot wine no matter what the temperature on the day.

The view from Mariann's house was magnificent, a picture perfect for a luxury holiday brochure: Admiralty Bay sparkled below, yachts shimmered in the light.

'*God jul,*' I said to Carl, raising my mug. 'Merry Christmas.'

'Definitely,' he said. 'To friends and family.' And as we drank our hot wine with the sun beating down through the palm fronds, I felt a mild pang of regret that I wasn't with my family, although I certainly was with friends.

During the week, we slipped into a happy routine of getting up at seven to swim to the beach where we would perform our morning exercises, hoping to turn ourselves into bronzed sculpted gods: the bronzed bit was coming along quite nicely in the Caribbean sunshine, but there was still work to be done on the sculpting side – we looked more pizza dough than cast bronze. We exercised on the white sands, doing stomach crunches and push-ups until one of us begged for mercy. Then we'd jog or walk along the shoreline, dipping in the turquoise waters every now and again to cool off. We gathered coconuts that had fallen during the night, and for want of anywhere else to put them, stuffed them in our swimming trunks and swam back to *Albatross* – the coconuts providing extra buoyancy. Back on board, we cracked them open with a hammer, drank the juice and ate the flesh. What a glorious way to start the morning.

As pretty as the island was above, the world below the water was even more beautiful. Anders offered to teach Carl to scuba dive - both Charlotta and I were already qualified divers. I have witnessed some inept sportsmen in my life, but never anyone as comically unskilled as Carl when it came to diving; I laughed so hard at Anders' attempt to get him under the water that Charlotta feared I would have an aneurism. Carl was kitted out, practised using his regulator, could clear his mask, knew how to operate his BCD, was familiar with his depth and contents gauges and knew all the underwater signs. But he just couldn't stay under the water; his arse refused to cooperate with the rest of his body and kept popping back up like a giant cork. The more weights we added to his diving belt, the more his backside seemed determined to stay afloat while the rest of him sank.

'He's got the most buoyant buttocks I've ever encountered,' Anders said, scratching his head. 'He's a human bullfrog. I just can't sink him.'

'Couldn't we just put weights in his swimming trunks,' I managed to suggest between guffaws of laughter.

'Don't be ridiculous. I've got plenty in my swimming trunks already,' Carl said without any trace of irony. And I laughed so hard I had to lie on the sand for a while, gasping like a stranded fish to get my breath back.

Eventually, with enough weight around his hips to sink a mature elephant,

Carl finally managed to descend a couple of feet below the surface; eventually, he got the hang of keeping his arse below his shoulders long enough to dive, but he was never a "natural" at the sport.

New Year's Eve was celebrated in style, in the company of other Scandinavians we'd got to know during our week on the island. After a meal of grilled lobsters, we stood on the deck, glasses in hand and counted down the seconds to 2003. Fireworks lit up the dark and exploded over the ocean.

'Ah, wonderful,' said Anders, looking up into the sky and tipping his head back to watch the high arc of a particularly dramatic firework. Another, yet more brilliant firework soared into the air, bursting into long glittering strands of blue and red. 'Fabulous,' he said, leaning back even further and falling backwards off the boat with a splash into the ocean.

Helpless with laughter and clumsy with drink, we fished yet another friend out of the water. This was getting to be a habit.

'Bloody fool,' said Carl as Anders stood spluttering and dripping on the deck. 'Wasted a whole glass of good champagne.'

Chapter 25
Small Islands, Big Changes
2 - 8 January 2003

Charlestown Bay, Canouan – Tobago Cays – Clifton, Union Island

Experience: *For successful fishing, slow the boat right down and when the fish bites let it exhaust itself on the line. Then all you have to do is reel it in and land it in a net.*

Tip: *Snorkelling around the Tobago Cays Marine Park is fabulous, but be careful not to disturb the delicate coral.*

The half-moon island of Canouan rises like a small green jewel out of the ocean, its continuous ribbon of sugar white beaches surrounding it like a necklace. At only five square miles and with a population of less than 1,200, it's one of the smallest inhabited islands that make up the Grenadines, a necklace of 32 islands and cays lying south of Saint Vincent and stretching 50 miles towards Grenada. We were beginning to feel as if we were sailing off the map, each island more remote and less populated than the last. Canouan, an Arawakan word meaning "turtle" or "turtle island," was a traditional Caribbean island with very little outside influence and had only one hotel at the time of our visit. Sadly, it has since been discovered, and a massive luxury resort offering golf courses, spas and casinos attracting very well-heeled vacationers has swallowed half the island. Such resorts are popping up faster than poisonous toadstools. While I can't blame people from wanting to visit paradise, I regret the need to build and stomp all over it. In our shrinking world, it seems to me that only the privileged few can afford the best views of it.

However, if you happen to have $500,000 to $100 million in spare change, there are at least 600 islands for sale in the world, a good many of them idyllic spots in the Caribbean. With the global financial crisis, there are bargains to be had. Of course, for an investment of $500,000 don't expect to get a building, fresh water access or electricity on your island, in which case you'd be better off buying a sailboat.

The 16-nautical mile sail from Bequia to Charlestown on Canouan was swift, owing to a brisk easterly wind. As we came out into the Atlantic, the swell increased and the waves slapped hard against *Albatross*' port side. Anders had baited the fishing line and was sitting by it patiently. Poor fool, I thought. How often have I dreamed of catching a fish that way?

'Are they biting?' I asked, trying hard to disguise the note of sarcasm in my voice.

'A lot of big fish seem to be swimming after it, but I think we're probably sailing too fast for them to take the bait.'

The words were barely out of his mouth when the reel started spinning and the line grew taut. We all rushed to the stern where the fishing rod was bent to breaking point.

'We've got to reduce speed,' Anders shouted. Charlotta rushed to reef in the genoa and the staysail while Carl steered *Albatross* into the wind, slowing her speed to just over a knot, as Anders and I fought to reel in whatever had bitten. Slowly, we reeled in the line; a very big fish was twisting and fighting on the hook.

'Anders, get in the dinghy and try and catch it in the landing net,' I shouted.

He jumped into the dinghy which we'd been dragging behind the boat and tried to force the fish into the net. And blast it all! The aluminium ring holding the net broke. It seemed we'd bought some cheap rubbish meant only for catching goldfish in the bath. The fish was thrashing with all its force and would tear itself loose at any second.

'I'm not losing this one,' I screamed. 'Hold on to it!'

Fortunately, Charlotta had the presence of mind to quickly pass Anders the big grab hook with which he nabbed the fish and heaved it aboard. It lay squirming futilely on the floor of the cockpit as we panted heavily. I didn't know who was more exhausted: the fish, or the crew.

'At last,' I said with a happy sigh. 'Our first fish.' It was a kingfish, weighing nearly 30 pounds. There was something deeply satisfying about having caught a fish I could cook and serve the crew. I did a quick calculation in my head and reckoned the fish would provide at least 20 steaks. I felt the strange urge to beat my chest with my fists and roar into the wind, 'I am man. See me catch food and feed my clan!'

Charlotta made a face. 'I'm a bit fed up of fish,' she said. 'I rather fancied meatballs for dinner.'

We continued towards Charlestown and anchored in the soft sand, a few hundred feet from the beach. That evening I marinated kingfish steaks in olive oil, garlic, lemon pepper and lime, then grilled and served them together with my patented *Albatross* fish sauce: béarnaise sauce spiced with

Sambal-Oeleck chilli paste and lime. The remaining fish head became a coveted prize for the local people: they swarmed like flies around our boat, beseeching us for the fish head.

'What will you do with it?' Carl asked.

'Boil it for soup,' one shouted.

'And what will you give us in return?' he asked. There was no answer and therefore no trade. No doubt they'd use the head to bait their lobster cages. Instead we kept it and put it on a large hook hung from a railing over the side of the boat. Who knew: I might get lucky and catch something else.

The following morning after our ablutions, I checked the line; it was strained to breaking point with something having a good go at the fish head. Anders and I quickly climbed back on deck; it took all our strength to haul in the line. To our great surprise, a whopping 40-pound stingray was hanging from the bait, floundering in the water. A distant cousin of the shark, sting-rays are not normally aggressive, unless provoked or threatened when they can become dangerous, using their whip-like tails as weapons. Even then, a stingray's sting is rarely fatal, most often resulting in a painful cut with swelling and muscle cramps from the venom. Steve Irwin, the Australian wildlife expert, was unfortunately killed when his heart was pierced by the serrated, poisonous spine of a stingray. We were taking no chances; we cut the rope and let the stingray swim away with the kingfish head between its jaws.

That evening, we decided to go ashore and walk through the village in search of an early evening beer. The sky was inky black after the sun had set and there were no street lights, so we walked through the velvety darkness to the accompanying chorus of crickets and frogs. Along the roadside were small houses no bigger than potting sheds, but further up in the hills were larger, more imposing residences, teetering precariously on 10-foot high pillars. There was no sign of any commercial activity in the village, so we asked a man, aged approximately 200 if he was a day, out smoking on his stoop, where we could get a beer. 'Up top on main street,' he said, and waved his half-chewed stogy in the general direction of the hill. The "bar" was housed in a small shed, battened together out of an odd assortment of mismatched planks and only standing because it didn't know which way to fall down.

'This must be it,' I said.

'Do you think it's safe?' Charlotta asked. It was a fair question, although I wasn't sure if she was referring to the possibility of the building's imminent collapse or the presence of gun-toting kingpins. We stepped inside; the de-cor was knock-it-together-with-nails style: makeshift wooden stools of arse polished driftwood were placed around two wobbly-looking tables; a naked light bulb swung from an alarmingly frayed cord in the patchy ceiling. It was completely empty apart from two generously proportioned young women whom we took to be our waitresses. We ordered three Carib beers and a soft drink for Charlotta.

'Busy tonight?' asked Carl.

The waitress looked around vaguely puzzled by the question. 'Everybody done spend dey money over New Year's,' she said with a soft smile. But impressed by our patronage, she thoughtfully put on the sound system for us, going to a rickety shelf that looked as if it would collapse at any moment and turning the knob on an ancient boombox. Distorted Reggae music blasted out from the speakers: Bob Marley, of course.

The next day we sailed 17 nautical miles to the Tobago Cays, an archipelago of five small uninhabited islands which are now the key element of Tobago Cays Marine Park, a 1,400-acre national park managed by the St Vincent and Grenadines government. The cays are famous for their deserted beaches and miles of perfect snorkelling and therefore draw an estimated 3,000 yachts a year to the area.

We set a southwest course towards the north tip of island of Mayreau, turning to make an approach from the west, this being the safest approach, and navigated with extreme care into the strait between the islands of Petit Rameau and Petit Bateau where the Atlantic waves break white and foamy against the reefs, making them easy to see. As we got closer to the islands, so the water turned from cerulean to teal to azure to turquoise. A kaleidoscope of colours and life was visible through the water below us and the ripples on the white sandy seabed 25 feet below perfectly clear. The strait between the two islands was approximately a hundred feet wide with a dozen boats already at anchor. We decided to do the same, refusing all persistent offers of assistance from the locals. Eager to participate in the underwater sightseeing, we immediately dived off the side of the boat.

Once under the satin surface of the water, it was easy to lose track of time and sense of place. Despite other yachts and the ever present local vendors, it was possible to luxuriate in total solitude in the coral gardens. The sun above illuminated the water like a super trooper, intensifying the colours and making the corals glow. I swam with schools of yellowtail snapper, chased parrot and trumpet fish, marvelled at the flash of iridescent blues and greens on queen angelfish, watched two smooth trunkfish blowing jets of water on the sand to uncover food, observed a chameleon-like sand diver change its colours to blend with the coral and was rewarded by finding a slow moving turtle gracefully paddling his way along the reef. I found myself smiling under water as this gentle creature allowed me to swim alongside him before tiring of my company and turning out to the open sea.

When we were gathered back on deck, we exchanged superlatives, finally agreeing that the Tobago Cays were one of the finest places to anchor in the world.

As plentiful as the fish were the "boat boys" who hovered at the cut between Petit Rameau and Petit Bateau, waiting to earn a generous tip by "helping" new boats anchor. As the Tobago Cays are the most visited anchorage in the Grenadines, there is a concentration of captive buyers; hence, a dozen vendors make the daily commute from Union Island to the Cays, selling ice and fresh bread in the morning, shifting their marketing focus in the afternoon to pitch T-shirts, shell jewellery and the catch of the day. Some of them provide a genuine service – albeit at an inflated price – while Carl felt others were only there to eye up the boat with a shopping list of their own. All of the boat boys who approached us looked greedily at the bikes chained to the guard rail and asked if they were for sale, to which Carl would always firmly shake his head and say, 'Sorry, my bike is my best friend and not for sale.'

Fortunately, Anders and Charlotta slept in the cockpit at night and were able to guard both the bikes and the dinghy; several boats had been robbed of theirs. It seemed it was common practice for the locals to silently slide up to a boat during the night, cut the dinghy's mooring line and let it float away on the current. The following day, a youth would arrive with a big smile, the "lost" dinghy and ask for a hefty reward of $500. We always took the precaution of hoisting our dinghy onboard and warned others to do the same. It was a better solution than sleeping with a machete under the pillow.

The boat boys continued to be a nuisance as we arrived at Union Island, one of the southernmost islands in the Grenadine chain and from where Anders would be leaving us to return to work. The island rises out of the ocean like an emerald pyramid, the archipelago's highest peak, Mount Tobai, piercing the clouds. As we headed carefully around the reef that protects Clifton, we were "escorted" by numerous local boats who insisted they were port captains and requested that we follow them to a mooring buoy available for a cheap rate payable in either American or East Caribbean dollars. Weary of their persistence, we didn't waste time or discussion but requested they sod off, no fee required. I wondered how many visiting boats were suckered into paying.

The village of Clifton is a nice little place with lots of small shops and several pleasant restaurants and hotels along the shoreline. But keeping to our budget, we chose instead to stock up on groceries at Lambi's Supermarket and Hardware store owned by Lambi, a large islander who was well travelled enough to stand his ground when we had the temerity to question his prices, retorting sharply, 'Don't complain about *my* prices! I've been to Sweden and I know how high the prices are there. You should be ashamed to charge so much!' We didn't dare complain again, particularly as he seemed to be the local kingpin; he also owned the large restaurant and boatyard next to his shop.

While at the yard, we got chatting to Werner, Agneta and Horst, a crew on *S/Y Franginpani*, a 49-foot Hallberg-Rassy out of Berlin. We readily accepted their invitation to partake of a cold beer on board. When they realized we knew something about electrics and diesel technology, Werner mentioned that their diesel generator didn't work. 'No problem,' we said. 'We'll take a look at it tomorrow.' After a few hours' work, we got the generator humming again, earning us dinner and Werner's eternal gratitude. In fact we earned a great deal more than that: Werner had sold the boat and was about to deliver it to its new owners, but thoughtfully kept back a generous treasure trove of expensive spare parts for use on *Albatross* which he gave us. We promised to keep in touch with them all and genuinely meant it.

Anders' time with us was up; he'd managed to buy a plane ticket to St. Lucia and we regretfully waved him off but had arranged to meet him again in a year's time in New Zealand for a month's sailing there. He left the following message in the logbook:

'A Christmas trip with two cheerful blokes from Skåne and a Boras-girl in a sailboat makes for the best atmosphere; five star food and drink every night. As Christmas neared its end, I was promoted from deckhand to sailor and had to escort the "officers" from the beach to the boat.
Good luck on your journey! With thanks. Anders'

And our thanks to Anders, too, for teaching Carl to scuba dive and providing me with one of the most hilarious sights I have ever witnessed; it still brings tears to my eyes whenever I think of it.

Chapter 26
Trials and Tribulations in Tobago and Trinidad
9 January - 23 February 2003

Crown Point, Store Bay, Tobago – Plymouth, Great Courland Bay, Tobago
– Portlandia Bay, Tobago – Charlotteville, Man O'War Bay, Tobago –
Chaguaramas, Carenage Bay, Trinidad

Experience: *The people of Tobago are friendlier and more welcoming than those on Trinidad.*

Tip: *Pay attention to insect bites; these can quickly become infected and turn very nasty if not kept clean. Bathe in a saline solution and don't scratch!*

With a reduced crew we set sail mid-afternoon for the island of Tobago, 115 miles south of Union Island. Our charts warned of strong cross currents, and we wanted to avoid the coral reefs of Grenada and the island of Carriacou while it was still light and we could see what we were doing. Nevertheless, it was a rough passage with 40-mile an hour head winds and waves that pounded the hull like cannon fire. Shortly before sunrise, we glimpsed Tobago, a long narrow island with a volcanic mountain range in the north, sloping to a flat landscape in the south. We were heading for Store Bay, the white sands of which looked as pristine and smooth as new sheets.

Tobago's turbulent past is reflected in many of its colourful place names that sound as if they've come straight out of a boy's adventure book: Bloody Bay, Pirates Bay and Man O'War Bay. From the moment Columbus set foot on the island in 1498, it was deemed up for grabs by whoever had the most accurate weapons to secure it, until The Treaty of Paris finally ceded the island to Britain in 1814. Consequently, the islanders speak English and their own English-based Creole. With a land area of 116 square miles, Tobago is the smaller of the two islands that make up the Republic of Trinidad and Tobago, but both their economies rely heavily on tourism which flourishes due to their idyllic beaches and excellent diving sites.

We liked Tobago immediately; the Tobagonians were polite and friendly, genuinely interested in where we came from and making us feel welcome on the island, not in how much money they could make out of us: a refreshing change from the so-called harbourmasters and boat boys of St Lucia and the Grenadine Islands.

Approximately 20 yachts were at anchor in Store Bay. Spotting a Swedish ensign on a mast, Charlotta introduced herself to skipper Bo on the *Golden Dolphin*, a 39-foot ketch out of Gothenburg. She did that that thing women do – eyelash fluttering or whatever – which make men impulsively gallant, and quickly secured herself an offer of a passage to Sweden when Bo sailed back there in April. Carl and I found ourselves also requiring the assistance of another member of the *Golden Dolphin*, although we didn't stoop to eyelash fluttering. We'd discovered a fuel leak in the diesel engine; precious oil was dripping from one of the injectors in the cylinder. This needed repairing by a specialist, it wasn't something we could patch up ourselves. Fortunately, Christer was an experienced engine mechanic, having worked at a Volvo workshop in Sweden, and was able to seal the leak for us. We frequently and providentially found ourselves the recipients of the kindness of strangers when in port.

Store Bay is a short walk from the airport and on Saturday evening we strolled over to meet our friend Max Engqvist off the plane from London; he would be joining *Albatross* for two weeks. Max exited immigration looking slightly wilted in the heat as only the day before he'd been skiing in northern Sweden where the temperature was -25 degrees Celsius. The balmy January temperature of 32 degrees that greeted him was a pleasant shock to the system.

We spent the next two weeks falling into step with the gentle local pace and leisurely exploring Tobago, meandering from bay to bay and observing life on the island. Great Courland Bay, better known as Turtle Beach because it is the nesting site of the endangered giant leatherback turtle, teemed with fish below the water and was crowded with fat pelicans with smug looks on their faces above. This was not a place to be a fish or have a phobia of birds. Hundreds of pelicans lined the mooring ropes of small fishing boats or circled the sky, waiting for the moment to plunge torpedo-like into the ocean to scoop up a beak full of fish. I could spend hours watching them, marvelling at their accurate fast and furious fishing technique.

We anchored in the bay and took the dinghy ashore to walk up and explore the village of Plymouth, the first English city captured from the Dutch in 1628 and the site of Fort James, one of the oldest colonial forts on the island. Tobago has plenty of old forts, each a reminder of the 32 times the island changed hands while European powers battled for its possession. Fort

James is a well-preserved building with manicured lawns and four cannons for us boys to play on. When we'd finished recapturing the fort, we wandered around the village, stopping to watch youngsters play an unruly game of 20 aside and argue ferociously in Creole, proving that while cultures may be very different, arguments about the offside rule in football are universal.

As the sun slipped lower in the sky and the temperature cooled a degree or two, a strange sound like a burglar alarm rose, gradually increasing in volume.

'What the heck is that?' I asked, wondering if the island was being randomly evacuated.

We happened to be standing outside a small wooden hut, no bigger than your average single garage. A woman came out and we asked her about the noise.

'Oh, that's just our frogs, starting their evening concert,' she said. Our voices drew the rest of the family out of the hut, all eight children ranging in ages from toddler to teenager. Cynthia explained that her daughter-in-law lived next door together with her one-year-old, in a house the size of a potting shed, the building quality of which would have kept me awake at nights. While the children stared wide-eyed at us and the chickens pecked around our feet, Cynthia told us something of her life. She worked nights at a hotel as a receptionist for an hourly rate of less than a dollar to make ends meet and worried that she wouldn't be able to support her children once the free school textbooks and meals were cut back, as the children's father didn't provide for his offspring. Nevertheless, despite her limited means, her children were neatly dressed and seemed healthy and happy. They crowded round me to marvel at their portraits on my digital camera, the girls hiding shy giggles behind their hands. Cynthia said she had to start cooking dinner: tonight, chicken in coconut broth. With expert swiftness, she grabbed one of the chickens from the street and promptly broke its neck: dinner would be ready within the hour.

We spent two nights anchored in tranquil Parlatuvier Bay where we tried our hand at lobster fishing. The entrance to the perfect crescent-shaped bay lies in a narrow gap in the reef and therefore proved a little awkward to navigate. Once in, however, the water was deep and calm. Charlotta, whom we had dubbed "the seal" because of her impressive free diving ability, swam down 50 feet to check that the anchor was securely embedded; we could see her through the clear water, a blonde streak as she pushed her way down to the seabed, finally streaming to the surface and emerging with a gasp, signalling "okay" with her thumb and index finger. Max and Charlotta put together our homemade lobster cage by sewing fishing net onto a stainless steel frame I'd constructed and Carl prepared the bait: a kingfish pressed into a large plastic bottle half. As darkness fell, we swam out with the cage and sunk it 30 feet down the side of a rock wall. The lobsters could feast overnight and we'd feast on them the following evening. I started sharpening my knives in anticipation.

Our disappointment was huge when the following morning we found our much battered lobster cage empty of both lobsters and bait. Determined to have our lobster supper, we salvaged the cage and re-baited it with some left-over Spanish sardines recovered from the bottom of the freezer and sunk the cage down deeper at 50 feet. The next morning, there was no sign of the lobster cage and the water bottle we'd used as a marker buoy had also disappeared. Who knew lobsters were so cunning? We weren't giving up and dispatched Charlotta to do her thing. After a few minutes of snorkelling back and forth, she suddenly plunged down and a minute later reappeared with the empty pot; the locals had most probably sabotaged our attempts at lobster fishing and cut our marker to the buoy.

Man O'War Bay at the north-eastern tip of the island has even deeper water, and we had to let out 200 feet of anchor chain before we were satisfied we were securely anchored. The bay's natural harbour played an important role in the development of the small fishing village of Charlotteville, although the village seemed relatively untainted by tourism. Lush rain forest sweeps down to meet the golden sands of the bay where local fishermen make their rounds in small open boats dwarfed by 50-horsepower outboard motors. The village was well served with a school, a medical centre, a library and a police station, the latter's slogan "For Your Protection and Service" on a sign outside the building, although recent articles in the Tobago News suggest that crime is on the rise and as the station closes at 4 p.m., the police are not protecting or serving as readily as the residents would like. It's a sad fact that where tourism increases so does a criminal element, ready to take advantage of the affluent visitor with their seemingly greater disposable income.

After nearly a month with *Albatross*, Charlotta left us to start boat hopping her way back home to return to her studies in Sweden. We would miss our seal. She left us a sweet note in the logbook:

'An unforgettable month has passed so quickly. Not only have I spent Christmas with the guys from Albatross, but we've shared diving, morning exercises, haggling duels at market stalls, night sailing, beach barbecues and constant fun, with deep conversations about love and other essentials thrown in. An enriching experience.'

Just Carl, Max and I were left. We continued to Batteaux Bay, near the village of Speyside, on the Atlantic side of the Island. Navigating was somewhat perilous as the entire bay is surrounded by a rocky ridge that extends from the shoreline to the Weather Rocks, which can just be seen protruding above the waves. Facing the ultimate Robinson Crusoe islands of Little Tobago and Goat Island, Batteaux reef is also known by divers as the Aquarium as it contains a wealth of fish and sponges and at that time was home to a dozen or more Atlantic Mantas which used to take up residence every winter. Goat Island is reputed to have been owned by Ian Flemming: indeed, when the four-hectare island and its two-storey house were offered for sale by its owner for $3 million in 2007, it was hyped to have been the place where the author gained inspiration for his Bond novels. However, Fleming's official biographer and members of the family deny that he ever had any connection to or owned any property on Tobago. Nevertheless, as we sailed around Goat Island it was very tempting to imagine a bikini-clad blonde emerging from the sea with a collection of conch shells and a villain with an enviable set of dentures being conceived there, even if the island's name didn't quite live up to the Bond franchise.

Max had to fly back to Sweden on Monday morning, so we left Batteaux Bay on Sunday to sail back south to anchor at Store Bay to be close to the airport. As we sailed the length of the island, we noticed the beaches, bays and harbours were eerily deserted; it was as if the whole island population had been lifted by aliens. It was only as we heard the bells ringing the end of service that we realized that the islanders had been in church. Later that evening, we were invited to join Sunday school. Initially, I was concerned we'd have to convert, but there was nothing religious about this Sunday school: a loud street party was held every weekend at Buccoo Bay where the revelries started with a local steel band. The festivities moved up several ear-splitting decibels towards midnight when competing discos blasted out reggae, hip hop and R&B from speakers placed in the street. We bought bottles of beer and shots of rum from a lady who'd set up a temporary bar out of a giant cooler, and sat on the plastic chairs provided to watch the Tobagonians dance and the local gigolos hustle the ladies. Buccoo is famous for its goat races that take place every Sunday during the summer. The sport, although I hesitate to call it that, started in the early 1900s, has proved so popular that a brand new stadium has been built purely for the purpose of racing goats.

Eardrums still ringing, we saw Max off the following day and as usual mourned the departure of a shipmate. But only two days later we made the walk back to the airport to welcome our friends Mats and Dorota from Sweden. Like Max, they exited the immigration hall stunned by the heat but rallied with a cold beer and dinner of grilled kingfish steaks once on *Albatross*. Mats and Dorota gave us all the latest news from Sweden while Carl and I scratched like two dogs with a severe case of fleas.

'Got some impressive insect bites there,' Mats said. Dorota rushed for the mosquito repellent.

'The sand flies are the worst,' Carl said, scratching both left and right legs simultaneously.

'Yes, they're so tiny you can't see the damn things, and the bites drive you crazy,' I agreed as I bent myself double to scratch a bite on the back of my thigh. 'The only perverse pleasure is to sit and scratch them.'

Dorota made a face. 'Didn't your mother tell you never to scratch a bite?'

'Try and stop me,' Carl said, scratching more fiercely than ever.

'Although, I have to admit my knee is very uncomfortable,' I said, bending it slowly. 'It feels ... crispy.'

Mats grimaced. 'Sounds like you've got gravel in there, that can't be good. You'd better take it easy for a couple of days.'

Dorota was right: our bites became infected, growing steadily larger and more painful until they looked like huge welts. I lay morosely on my bunk, listening to the advice of fellow sufferers on the VHF radio and watching my knee swell to the size of a watermelon and change in hue from pink to lurid magenta. 'Bugger this for a lark,' I thought and asked Mats to drive me to the hospital in Scarborough.

The hospital, a 16-bed establishment for a population of 50,000, was located next to Fort George in an old building which had originally served as the garrison hospital for the English army. Very little in the way of facilities seemed to have improved since the English had left; the beds, cabinets and furnishings were badly worn, and I would have turned and hobbled out had I not been incapable of doing so.

The facilities may have left a lot to be desired, but the treatment was first rate, although the doctor who initially examined me looked aghast at my knee and scurried off mumbling the worrying words, 'This is serious; I need to get a specialist.' A kindly 65-year-old professor of medicine arrived and was thrilled to meet a Scandinavian: he'd completed his medical studies several decades before in Oslo and was overjoyed to reminisce about his time in Scandinavia. Eventually, he stopped tripping down memory lane and peered at my knee.

'Hmm, nasty,' he said. 'Very nasty. Definitely infected.'

I was whisked away on a trolley, had my knee bathed in antiseptic and – look away now if you're squeamish – the professor took up a scalpel and in a practised motion made a neat slice in my knee; the disgusting yellow pus which flooded out could have filled a pint glass. The joint was X-rayed to rule out damage to the bone, and for good measure the professor ordered a chest X-ray as he'd noticed I had a nasty dry cough. Although the X-rays were clear, he insisted I stay for a few days for observation; to be honest, I'd been horrified by what had gushed out of my knee and put up only the weakest argument against staying. My main concern was the bill I'd receive when I finally left, the shock of which was more likely to be the death of me than the infection.

For a tiny two-ward hospital, it was a lively place. I was woken at five in the morning by the crowing of the resident rooster on the roof. This was followed by the arrival of the cheerful cleaning lady who mopped our ward and sang with a voice that could have put Witney Houston to shame. Breakfast of toast, tinned vegetables and a cup of tea was served at nine, and the professor and the doctor made their rounds at eleven. Lunch of chicken or fish soup was served at one and we had a brief respite before visiting hours when it seemed the whole island turned out to see the man in the bed next to me. George, a spirited 75-year-old with a face that looked as if it had been pickled in formaldehyde, had 13 children and over 50 grandchildren that he could recall: they all came to visit, bringing pots of food and hidden tots of rum, chatting incessantly at the tops of their voices, while the younger grandchildren played chase around the beds. I was a curiosity and my bed was surrounded by 20 children at a time, all staring at me and asking me very direct questions in that way only children do: 'Where is your family? Why are you so pink? What's wrong with you? Are you going to die?' and so on. Visiting hour was as exhausting as it was entertaining. Eventually, George's extensive family were rounded up and chased out when the hour ended so we could be served our last meal of the day: two slices of toast with more tinned vegetables. This daily routine was punctuated regularly by various ministers who dropped by for extended preaching sessions to save a sinner or two, the captive audience of weakened patients hovering near death providing them with the perfect pliable flock.

After five days, the professor deemed me fit to leave and I braced myself for the bill; it could be a serious blow to my finances. I was astonished when the professor clapped me on the back and shook his head. 'No, no. You're our guest here. Just please pay for the X-rays on your way out. And remember to take it easy for a few days.' Relief at not being bankrupted by a hospital bill competed with relief at being able to return to *Albatross*. I bought cakes for the nurses from the vendors outside the building and sent the professor a bottle of wine from *Albatross*. It would be remiss of me not to thank the government of Tobago and Trinidad for their generosity. And I was pleased to read that a new 100-bed hospital has just been opened, fulfilling a clear need for the island's population.

I returned to the boat several pounds lighter; why is it that wherever you go in the world the food served in hospitals is the least nutritious and worst tasting outside of school? However, a celebratory meal was already organized; Carl, Mats and Dorota had prepared an evening of food, friends, wine and cannons at Cambleton Battery, set high on a cliff with panoramic views of the northern entrance to the island. Monica and Kenneth from S/Y Q-coon joined the party, and we grilled freshly caught tuna steaks, sat on the warm rocks and watched the lowering sun set fire to the sea. Life was good again.

Mats and Dorota left us in the second week of January to fly back to the frozen north. They wrote the following in the logbook:

'What an amazing reception! After clearing passport control, we were greeted with a Stag, "The Man's Beer," which was followed by the shortest transfer time we've ever experienced: only five minutes to the boat! Yanne and Carl had prepared everything thoroughly for our visit and foreseen our inexperience as sailors. Yanne became ill and had to be admitted to hospital, so Carl had the job of sailing us around the island on his own. But everything has gone smoothly and we've felt so carefree. We're so grateful for the opportunity to sail with you and look forward to doing it again. Thanks guys. We wish you luck for the rest of your journey. Mats and Dorota.'

We'd been in Tobago for over a month and it was time to move on. On our final evening on the island, Monica and Kenneth invited us over to their boat for "Jansson's Temptation," a traditional Swedish casserole made of potatoes, onion, pickled sprats, bread crumbs and cream: a dish commonly included on a Swedish Christmas smorgasbord. It was Valentine's Day, but what did we care; it was a delicious meal washed down with beer and snaps, tasting even better after a week of toast and tea. We wished Monica and Kenneth the best and returned to *Albatross*. As we climbed on board, Carl winced.

'What's the problem?' I asked.

He pointed to his right calf which had ballooned to twice the size of his left. 'Damn insect bites,' he said. 'Don't worry, if it gets any worse, I'll see a doctor in Trinidad.'

After over a month of taking it easy and sleeping in, it was hard to rally ourselves for a dawn start. But it was liberating to be out on the ocean again, to be in a big blue space with an unbroken sky above and the sense of horizons receding. Carl sat back in the cockpit and nursed his leg while I put out the fishing line. During my stay in hospital, George had given me a couple of fishing tips and I was keen to try them out. Within a few minutes, I'd hooked and landed two hefty tuna: dinner was sorted.

Around mid-afternoon, we approached the island of Monos, one of the Bocas Islands which lie in the Dragons' Mouth between Trinidad and Venezuela. We changed our westerly course and sailed south into Boca de Monos and then passed Scotland Bay where the scenery was spectacular. It was like sailing in a Norwegian fjord with steep jungle covered mountains rising dramatically above us. In the quiet of the afternoon we could hear the call and screech of Howler monkeys from the verdant hillsides. We had arrived in Trinidad.

We lowered the sails and motored slowly towards Chaguaramas, a sheltered bay lying in the northwest peninsula of the island, west of the capital, Port of Spain. Chaguaramas is the most developed part of the island, leased in 1940 to the United States for the construction of a naval base. The base was also used during the early 1960s as an early warning radar and missile tracking site but was finally returned to Trinidad and Tobago in 1963. It is now home to a huge marina and is a haven for boats during the hurricane season and a Mecca for boat maintenance and renovation. We'd decided against staying in the marina, however, having read about recent oil spills; even as we passed we could see a depressing amount of debris in the long purple and green oil slicks on the water. Where man goes he more often than not leaves a trail of rubbish in his wake.

Our goal instead was Carenage Bay which lay around a small peninsula. We sailed past the two Diego Islands, one of which, Carrera, has been the site of a prison for the last 150 years where the punishment was hard labour quarrying stone. Although breaking quarry rocks is no longer the penalty de jour, the island still houses nearly 500 prisoners. Despite its description as more "correctional facility than penal colony," it looked as inviting as Alcatraz through our binoculars; indeed, the same fear of perishing in the dangerous currents in the waters around the island deters prisoners from swimming to freedom.

We entered the mirror-like Carenage Bay late in the afternoon and joined the two dozen other boats anchored there.

'Mooring snaps first,' Carl said setting out the glasses and the *Gammel Dansk* bottle. 'Business later.'

The following morning, we lowered the dinghy and went over to the sailing club where we readily paid the very reasonable fee of $25 a week for a mooring at a pontoon deck and use of the facilities. Fortunately, we'd cleared all our paperwork for *Albatross* at customs and immigration in Tobago and only had to walk, or in Carl's case limp, along Western Main Road to Chaguaramas marina to register at the port authority there.

I have to admit my first impression of Trinidad was disappointing: of the two islands that make up the Republic of Trinidad and Tobago, Trinidad was clearly the bigger, uglier brother that didn't give a damn about its sloppy appearance: the marinas, harbours, roadsides and walkways were clogged with rubbish, making the island look more tropical rubbish dump than tropical paradise. I became increasingly depressed at the quantities of fast food containers, plastic bottles and bags, disposable plates, paper, aluminium tins, food scraps and other debris we picked our way through. There seemed to be no attempt to contain the refuse by providing litter bins, and recycling is clearly light years away. Eventually, of course, much of this litter is blown out to sea where the marine life chokes on it: another paradise blighted by our waste.

Trinidad's real bread and butter is the oil industry. At night we could see the lights of an offshore rig twinkling like a Christmas tree, a blinking reminder that tourism was a poor second. Although crude oil production has fallen by half since it peaked in 1980, the island produces 135,900 barrels of crude oil per day – a mere blip on the scale compared with Russia's production of 10,210,000 barrels – but still impressive for an island slightly smaller than Delaware and a fiftieth of the size of the UK. Trinidad has earned a reputation as a major investment site for international business and has enjoyed a period of substantial economic growth, which may in part explain the Trinidadians rather blasé attitude towards tourism. Unfortunately, its proximity to South America means the island is a convenient transhipment point for drugs destined for North America and Europe. I suspect that at least a couple of the prisoners sitting it out on Carrera Island had secured their places for drug running offences.

One of the biggest draws to the island is the Carnival season, a serious business in Trinidad. The saying is that the party lasts all year: ten months spent preparing and gearing up in anticipation, a month celebrating, followed by a month of sobering and cleaning up. It seems to be to be a great excuse for a huge public booze up, as well as a reason to host a parade of elaborately feathered and sequined yet scantily-clad nubile young women which, please don't misunderstand me, I heartily endorse. Trinidad has one of the largest, and therefore loudest, carnivals in the world. During the month of March, the island pulsates and shakes to the rhythm of a hundred competing calypso bands, the noise of which can probably be heard in Tobago. Feeling too middle-aged for such an ear-splitting event, we were planning to sail on before the party got out of hand.

But first we had to take care of a few problems, not least of which was Carl's leg which had begun to take on the alarming appearance of rotting meat.

'That's it,' I said firmly. 'Time to see a doctor.'

'Give it a couple more days,' Carl protested weakly. 'It'll be fine.'

'Calle, you can't keep saying that! Your leg is turning black! If you won't see a doctor, I'll take a scalpel to it myself.'

'Fair enough,' Carl mumbled sullenly. I swear Carl is one hundred percent mule.

We took a taxi to a doctor's surgery in the capital. Doctor Anthony Davis examined Carl's leg, drew a heavy breath and said calmly, 'Well, it's a pity you left it so long. This is very serious. It looks as if gangrene has set in. There's a strong possibility we'll have to amputate.'

If I was shocked, you can imagine how Carl must have felt; the doctor might just as well have taken out a hacksaw there and then. Carl's face bleached white, he reeled sideways on the examination bed and I thought he might pass out. Neither of us said anything: I had no words; Carl was mute with disbelief. Eventually, he uttered one word: 'Shit.'

'Are you sure?' I said managed to say in a hoarse whisper to the doctor.

'Well, we could try a course of antibiotics, elevate the leg and bathe it in a saline solution if you prefer.'

'I prefer,' Carl managed to stammer weakly.

'But I'm really not convinced it will work,' the doctor said. 'The infection is probably too far gone for that.'

'I still prefer,' Carl said, looking stricken.

We duly left with strict instructions and a prescription for antibiotics and dressings. Carl immediately took to his berth on *Albatross*; we washed his leg with the saline solution, dressed it and rigged up a sling to keep it elevated. And by god, did we hold our thumbs and cross our fingers for the next week.

While Carl concentrated on not panicking about the possibility of losing a limb, I concentrated on getting the chores done on the "effing to do" list. Apart from the laundry and stocking up with supplies for our next stint, there was the never ending general boat maintenance to be done. I renewed our contract for SailMail, so that we could continue to have email contact with family and friends but realized during the process that our modem wasn't working and so had to return it to the German manufacturers and order a new one to be sent to Venezuela that we could pick up on arrival. Then there was the purchase and installation of a second generator which I oversaw with Carl shouting helpful but wholly unnecessary instructions from his bed of pain.

After a nail-biting week of watching Carl's calf change in size and colour from flesh-eating black to angry purple to a healthier shade of livid red, we visited Doctor Anthony again and nearly wept with relief when he gave Carl the good news that his leg was on the mend. He handed him a prescription for more antibiotics and gave us both a serious talking to. 'Be really careful, boys. Keep your wits about you.'

Here it comes, I thought, *the conversation about safe sex with local women.'*

The good doctor continued. 'The waters off the coast of Venezuela are patrolled by pirates, so stay at least 30 miles offshore and beware of any boat that approaches you. They mean business and can be very dangerous.'

He didn't mention anything about sex.

Trinidad was gearing up for carnival time and with the good news about Carl's health we were in a carnival spirit so we didn't mind the two 20-piece steel bands which set up near our dock and rowdily engaged in a battle of the bands from dusk until dawn. 'Fantastic music,' I said. The second night was less entertaining. 'Knock it off, boys,' I groaned as I stuck my head under my pillow in an attempt to block out the eternal hammering of sticks on steel pans as the dawn light rose. By the third night, my ears were hearing steel drums long after they'd stopped playing. I was ready to commit the first steel band massacre in history.

'That's it!' I screamed on the fourth night over a calypso version of *No Woman, No Cry.* 'I can't take another night of reggae, calypso, soca or any other bloody form of happy carnival music! I'd rather take my chances with the pirates. We sail for Venezuela tomorrow!'

Chapter 27
Beer, Bullets and Beautiful Women

23 February – 24 March 2003

El Morro, Puerto La Cruz, Venezuela – Oranjestad, Aruba

Experience: *Always offer your services for free: it helps make friendships and contacts with the local community, permitting you an insight into the country and culture that you'd otherwise miss.*

Tip: *Hire a local agent to facilitate the complicated clearing procedures with Venezuelan port authorities: it will save you both time and a massive headache.*

In March 2001, the Mirens, a retired Swedish couple, were enjoying a tranquil sail from Isla Margarita to the Venezuelan mainland when a local boat with four men came alongside them. The men boarded the yacht, shot Mr Miren in the stomach and put a knife to his wife's neck demanding jewellery and money; they destroyed the two VHF radios and systematically stole everything of value: binoculars, sunglasses, cameras, watches, snorkelling equipment, the portable GPS, lifejackets and alcohol. Fortunately, the Swedish couple lived to tell the tale, but the pirates were never apprehended. Sadly since then, violent attacks on private vessels have increased to such a degree that the number of foreign yachts visiting Venezuela has declined substantially, not only due to the threat of piracy but also because of the high crime rate, concerns over the unstable government, corrupt officials, high consumer prices and widespread shortages. Unfortunately, while bringing piracy into the public eye forces idle governments to take a stand, it also encourages pirates who kidnap crews to ask for increasingly higher ransoms. There is nothing swashbuckling or glamorous about pirates; they're just muggers with machetes or, worse still, guns.

'Bloody pirates,' I swore. 'Bloody murderous thugs. I'm sick of having to check every damn boat out there. It's like trying to spot the fleas on a greyhound.'

We were about 30 miles off the coast and heading towards Isla Margarita, hoping to reach it shortly before dark. But then the wind dropped and with it our speed to only four knots: we wouldn't make the island before morning and we were very apprehensive about any small boat we encountered. We studied each one with deep suspicion, ready to activate our blue light at the top of the mast in a vain attempt to look like a patrol boat. Luckily, the vessels appeared to be small fishing trawlers. Nevertheless, we were on edge all night and both kept watch; if a rogue boat did approach us, we weren't sure what we'd do having decided against stashing weapons on board. The best we could do was look tough and act rough: not much good against a man with a loaded weapon and bad intentions.

The sun rose and with it our spirits. To the west climbed the green velvet mountains of Isla Margarita, but in the end we decided to head directly south for the harbour at Puerto La Cruz, passing the island of Coche on the north and the Paria peninsula of Venezuela in the south, its wasteland of desiccated red hills indicative of several months lack of rain. The sky was blue and cloudless, and we lay back in the cockpit and enjoyed the sun as *Albatross* cruised ahead at a good speed of seven knots; even so, we still wouldn't reach Puerto La Cruz before sunset. The water at the stern glimmered like gold: a mahi-mahi on one of the fishing lines. We let it thrash there for a while until it was too exhausted to fight being hauled in. It had barely touched the deck before I had it in the frying pan for the evening meal.

As the sun lowered and coloured the sea vermillion, we approached the islands of Chimana Grande and La Borrachas, an archipelago of islands just north of Puerto La Cruz where we'd booked a mooring in the El Morro marina. It was in these waters that 48 oil tankers lay at anchor during the Venezuelan general strike of 2002 to 2003 when opposition to President Hugo Chávez was at its highest. Venezuela is the fifth largest oil exporting country in the world, and the oil lockout, the key element of which was the stoppage of production of the state oil company, crippled the nation at the time, leading to shortages in fuel and basic foods. Millions of protesters took to the streets of Caracas to petition for Chávez' resignation and demand early elections, but despite calls for him to be removed from power, he served second, third and fourth terms as president until his death from cancer in 2013. We were arriving on 25 February 2003, just two weeks after the strike had ended. What confused state would the country be in?

Puerto La Cruz is a large coastal city with an abundance of marinas, boatyards and nautical facilities. The canals and waterways that wind through the area closely resemble those of Venice and are as complicated to navigate if you are unfamiliar with the area. We arrived in the dark and fortunately found the entrance to the El Morro complex where our mooring at the hotel

Maremare was located. Carl took the helm and I was at the bow following a simple chart of the canal system. After 40 minutes, we arrived at our destination and with the help of a couple of night-watchmen were directed to our slip where we quickly tied up.

It's always exciting to get up early and watch the world come to life in a new harbour. We sat on deck and admired the marina we'd arrived at. About a dozen sailboats and 20 large power boats, the "pimp palaces" as we called them, were moored the length of the 600-foot long quay. Each boat had its own service pillar with connections to water, electricity, telephone, cable TV and the internet. A stone's throw from the quay was a pool with plenty of sun loungers, a grill and cocktail bar shaded by artfully placed palm trees, all at our disposal in our mooring fee of $15 a day. This included the two uniformed guards visibly armed with high calibre revolvers, shotguns and "don't try it with me" stares. We'd pre-booked the mooring via the internet as the marina would normally be heaving with cruisers at this time of year, but the recent strike and the spiralling crime rate had clearly deterred tourists. El Morro is Venezuela's favourite holiday resort and consists of canals bordered by brand new hotels, expensive villas and luxury condominiums, all purpose-built for the cruising and tourist community. The area is famous for its 60-mile stretch of beautiful beaches and is well placed being close to neighbouring Cuidad Barcelona. It's particularly popular with Canadians looking to trade their bitter winters for warmer climes.

Our port captain Patrick gave us a tour of the facilities and strict advice on staying safe in Venezuela. 'Security is the best here in Puerto La Cruz,' he said confidently, 'so you can feel quite safe. Nothing gets past our guards.' I didn't doubt it looking at the broken glass cemented into the tops of the walls surrounding the complex and the smug-looking security guards.

'What about outside the ...,' I hesitated; I was tempted to use the word "compound" but that sounded too much like a prison. 'What about outside?' I finally said.

'Well, you definitely shouldn't walk around Puerto La Cruz after dark, there are too many thieves,' Patrick advised. 'And during the day, don't carry cameras or wear anything expensive, no watches or jewellery. And just take a little cash for what you really need. Otherwise, it's no problem. Oh, and be careful crossing the road.'

The last piece of advice sounded like something my mother would say to me when I was in short trousers. A walk outside the marina later explained everything. The Venezuelan economy had been in decline over the last two decades with unemployment at nearly 15 percent and an inflation rate of approximately 20 percent per year, both of which had increased in the wake of the general strike. Inflation and basic necessity shortages hit the poor the hardest: great poverty increases crime, and the country had seen murder rates triple over a decade. Theft was so common that most shops had an armed guard at the door, residential properties were surrounded by high fences or walls topped with barbed wire so that residents and visitors could only enter their premises by passing through an armed barrier, and windows and doors were protected by iron grills, all of which made the houses appear more like detention centres than luxury residences.

As for crossing the road, we soon discovered why we had to be careful: most of the cars were ancient American jobs lacking headlights, number plates and often chassis; it seemed the only item a vehicle really required was an engine: indicators, windscreen wipers and brakes were deemed optional extras. But we learned that the real problem was the fact that most people behind the steering wheel didn't possess a legal driving license: these could be bought by bribing a driving instructor. And auto insurance was just a laughable notion. Furthermore, half the drivers behind the wheel of the junk mobiles were so drunk they couldn't see the road. The police might occasionally stir themselves to intervene at this stage, but even then money would exchange hands and the drunk was sent on his merry way. If the drunk driver wasn't prepared to pay the private fine, he might pull out a shotgun from behind the passenger seat and negotiations of a different kind would ensue.

'Holy crap!' Carl said, observing a chaos of rattling cars speeding and swerving on the city streets. 'We've come to the Wild West, with oilrig workers instead of cowboys and American gas guzzlers instead of horses.' We were so stunned we about turned and sought the safety of our tranquil enclosure, grateful for our smug-looking guards and barbed wire fences.

Every Wednesday evening, the hotel threw a cocktail party for the marina guests with an open bar and buffet, so the event was naturally well attended: crews scuttled out of their boats like cockroaches at the mention of free drinks. It was a great way to meet other people and we made several new friends, the most jovial of whom was an Austrian named Hans. He'd previously run his own construction company, but when the flood of cheap Polish labour into Austria pushed down construction prices, Hans decided to move to Venezuela, leaving his wife and family behind. For the last 15 years he'd earned a steady income as a handyman and "fixer" enabling him to enjoy a playboy lifestyle. He was quite the Teutonic character: a big personality with a big laugh, heftily built with a beer belly and a dark handlebar moustache, the ends of which he'd mischievously twirl. We dubbed him Kaiser Hansi.

'Electricians!' he exclaimed when Carl and I mentioned our professions. 'No, don't tease me. Do you know how rare a decent electrician is around here? As rare as a wirgin in a strip club, that's how rare! They don't know their red vires from their blues here! I'd trade my girlfriend for an electrician.'

'What do you need doing?' I asked.

'I've got a customer, a Cuban, needs a generator installing on his boat. It's a bastard of a job.'

'No problem. I'll give you a hand.' The free drinks had made me feel a good will to my fellow man.

'If you really mean it, I start at seven in the morning,' Hans said. 'Just radio *Holiday Charter* on channel 72 and I'll direct you to my place. It's easy to get lost in the canal system.'

I looked at my watch; it was nearly midnight. 'Okay, then. One more beer and we'd better call it a night if we're working tomorrow.'

At seven the following morning I was still drunk and pondering the miracle of how one beer can turn into many and my watch suddenly leaps ahead in time: we'd lurched back to *Albatross* shortly before dawn. I took the dinghy up and down the different canals calling on the handset and shouting out loud, 'Hansi, *wo bist du?* Hansi?' At least eight burly voices replied, more than one of them telling me to piss off and didn't I know what time it was. Eventually, I found the right Hansi, his eyes puffy and his moustache a little dishevelled.

'A man of his vord,' he said, clapping me on the back. 'I didn't think you'd turn up. But vot the hell are you doing here so fucking early!'

Installing the generator was a tough job and took us longer than Hans had expected, but after three days we'd sorted it and his customer was pleased enough with the work to offer Hans more business.

'Ve make a great team, Yanne,' he said. He took off his sunglasses and narrowed his eyes at me. 'Right, vot do I owe you for your help?'

I didn't need to consider this for long: I had a shrewd idea the best way to see Venezuela was with someone like Hans who almost certainly had connections and could show Carl and me the best places to visit.

'Just show me a good time, Hansi,' I said with a shrug.

'Ha! That's vot all the girls say,' Hans said with a throaty chortle.

Hans was as good as his word and not only showed us a great time but also helped us out with daily chores and difficulties. While I'd been working with Hans, Carl had been preparing the boat for the arrival of Eva, his daughter Jessica and her boyfriend Mats who would fly in from Caracas at eight o'clock on Friday evening. Hans drove us out to Barcelona airport to meet them, repeating all the way that the flight was sure to arrive three hours late as nothing ever ran to schedule in Venezuela. As a punctilious Swede, Carl had a problem believing this and insisted on being at arrivals at eight on the nose, but sure enough, the arrivals board said the flight was delayed.

'Told you,' Hansi said. 'Time keeping is not a priority here. Come on, I'll show you a place to get a pepper steak so juicy and tender you'll vant to ....' Well, I can't repeat what he said, but he drove us out to a shady industrial area where I was convinced we'd be carjacked. The "restaurant" – I use the term loosely as it made a motorway van selling builders' tea and dodgy burgers look upmarket – was hidden among dark warehouses. We were shown to a plastic table and chair set that had seen better days, and Hans instructed the waiter – an old man in a dirty T-shirt – to keep the beers coming. Three pepper steaks, as large and as plump as pillows were put before us. After one bite I was a man in love.

'Vot I tell you?' Hans said with a laugh. He was telling us a lot of things.

At 11 p.m. exactly, we returned to the airport where the flight was just landing. Hans and I stood back to let Carl greet his wife, daughter and future son-in-law Mats. It was a sweet reunion for a man and wife.

Through Hans we also became acquainted with Wolfgang from Germany and Patrick from England, both of whom worked in the transport industry with major clients in the oil sector. Wolfgang's favourite choice of transport was a huge speedboat with twin 200-horsepower outboard motors. They invited all of us on several trips to the outer islands where we fished, swam, snorkelled and dived around the coral reefs. On one occasion Hans suggested we left the women behind for a day, 'so ve men can do some serious fishing.' The serious fishing seemed to have less to do with fishing and more to do with serious drinking. Hans produced a Glock 17, a semi-automatic pistol he'd "obtained" from a local police officer, and we all took turns shooting targets in the ocean. Give a man a luxury speedboat, a shiny gun and some booze and suddenly he'll think he's James Bond. There we were, armed and dangerous, on our way to a party held on an island by a rich and slightly shady friend of Hans who'd apparently made his fortune as an investment broker. This bloke certainly had money to burn: his villa was all marble floors and scantily-clad supermodels draped fetchingly around the infinity pool; two hungry-looking Rottweilers with muscles like Schwarzenegger and studded collars kept guard; minions scuttled around bearing trays of champagne cocktails and canapés. It slowly occurred to me that South America was a favourite hiding place of the career criminal and I had an uncomfortable thought that our host was the sort who might have had his fingerprints surgically removed at Villa Winter on Fuerteventura to avoid being traced. Fortunately, I managed to keep my speculations to myself and not make any quips on the subject: those Rottweilers were probably hungry-looking for good reason.

Carl's daughter Jessica was less impressed with the state in which I returned her boyfriend. She rather unfairly blamed me for the fact that Mats was so drunk he was incapable of coherent speech for 24 hours and forbade him from playing with Carl's and my friends for the rest of their holiday. I blamed the boy's poor constitution.

During the second week of their holiday Jessica and Mats visited Isla Margarita, Venezuela's most popular tourist destination. The locals swarm there at weekends to take advantage of the island's status as a duty-free port. Isla Margarita is really two islands joined by a band of sand, mangrove forests and marshes that compose the Restinga National Park. Jessica and Mats returned with tales of the wonders of the flora and fauna. Carl and Eva meanwhile decided to explore further south and took a taxi to Cuidad Bolivar located on the banks of the Orinoco. They returned with stories of the history of the city and its culture. I spent the week working and playing with Kaiser Hansi and returned to *Albatross* with a hangover the size of Brazil.

Venezuela is undoubtedly a man's playground and as in many South American societies the concept of machismo is still an intrinsic part of the culture. You didn't have to be a crack anthropologist to observe how Venezuelan men regard married women and mothers as Madonnas and available single women as whores. The labelling on the local beer bottles said it all: one side displayed the name of the beer, the reverse featured a lady's pert, thong-clad bottom. Beer coasters for Regional beer featured images of breasts normally reserved for the pages of a men's magazine. Can you imagine the riots that would ensue if European breweries tried that kind of advertising? Nevertheless, there is no denying that Venezuelan ladies are very beautiful women. Indeed, the country's fairer sex has been voted the fairest sex in the world, holding six Miss World titles, beating out the UK and India with five, and the US and Sweden with three.

Venezuela is not attractive for this reason alone; for tourists with a strong currency it was phenomenally cheap, even more so for us Scandinavians. We bumped into Peter, a retired Swede in his sixties whom we'd met in Bequia and who'd just taken up residence in Venezuela. 'On an annual pension of 60,000 kronor, I can't afford to return to Sweden,' he said as we drank a beer in the cockpit of his sailboat. 'But here, I can live like a king,' A dark-eyed, long-legged beauty walked past us. 'Surrounded by nature in all its beauty,' Peter added.

'Ah, yes,' Carl sighed. Eva nudged him with a sharp elbow. 'The beaches are really stunning,' he said without missing a beat.

Eva, Jessica and Mats returned to Sweden, and Carl and I regretfully started preparations for our own departure. It felt strangely empty on *Albatross*: how quickly we'd become accustomed to being a family on the boat. We resumed our daily routine of chores and tackling the "effing to do" list. There was much to repair and complete before we set sail for Panama, not least of which was stocking up with supplies again. Kaiser Hansi proved invaluable once more, driving us around in his huge Chevy to get our bottle of gas refilled at a depot in Peuto La Cruz, showing us where to get the best deal on engine oil and taking us to a huge Cash and Carry warehouse, normally reserved for restaurateurs, where we stocked up on goods unavailable in the local stores. As we went through the cashier, armed guards were on the other side ready to check all our purchases against our till receipt.

'What the hell? Do they really think we're going to rip off a couple of tins of beans?' Carl asked. 'Why would we? These prices are a fifth of what we'd pay in Sweden.'

'They're not checking you,' Hansi said. 'They know the tourists can pay. They're checking the cashier isn't fiddling the till. This will take forever. Come on, let's get a beer.'

As we sat in a restaurant adjacent to the store and ordered grilled steaks and beers, Hansi entertained us with more colourful stories of his life in Venezuela.

'Nothing fazes me anymore,' he said. He told us about how robbers had broken into his house one night and held him, his new wife and children at knife point, tied them up and stripped the house of any valuables. They didn't take his boat from the dock only because they couldn't get it started: 'Tricky choke,' Hans said. 'But that's vhy I have a gun. If you have something to protect, it's the only vay to protect it.'

The guards had finished checking our till receipt long before we'd finished our meal; by the time we left the restaurant, 24 empty Regional bottles were neatly lined up along the bar, thong-clad bottoms all facing outwards. We loaded all our shopping into the Chevy and rolled along to the main entrance of Hotel Maremares where Hans ordered a guest car to take the shopping through the grounds to our slip. There were the inevitable protests from the porters when they saw the amount we intended to pack on the battery driven golf car. '*No es posible!* The car will break down under all this weight.'

'Bullshit!' Hans said. 'All this veighs far less than six obese Americans and their overveight suitcases. Don't vorry about it.'

The golf car seemed to worry; it ground slowly along, making protesting noises under the weight of the shopping, eventually arriving at *Albatross* where we feverishly worked to store it all. *Albatross* sank lower in the water than she ever had before.

A couple of evenings later, Hans introduced us to Curt, Franz and Heinz, Austrian friends of his, all of whom lived in Miami. They were particularly keen to check out a Swedish sailboat so we invited them on board *Albatross*. Curt was smitten and dropped such clunking hints about wishing to sail to

Panama that we felt compelled to invite him. That was before we realized he was a little odd. He had a business in the chemical industry and I wondered if he'd accidentally inhaled too much of his own product. We were discussing a stubborn sticky substance on the hull which we couldn't get off no matter what we used. Curt gave us a sample of one of his products.

'Use this,' he said, 'but very sparingly. Gets rid of all sorts of crap.' He lowered his voice, glanced around and murmured, 'And if you want to get rid of the old cow at home, use a couple of bottles.'

I looked at him blankly. 'Sorry, I don't follow.'

'I'm just saying,' Curt said, 'a couple of bottles of this could solve all your problems. Nothing but the gold teeth left.' His laugh didn't reassure me that he was joking, but it was too late to uninvite him to sail with us; I just hoped he was better at sailing than at repartee.

On our last night in port we invited Hans to dinner on board *Albatross* to thank him for all his help and friendship while we'd been in Venezuela. Hans was moved enough to stand up and give us a heartfelt, albeit it drunken, farewell speech.

Curt signed on early the following morning and we made ready to slip our moorings for the 300-nautical mile trip to Aruba, the start of our 1,000-mile journey to Panama. The harbourmaster Patrick waved us all off and we slowly motored through the canal system and out to the entrance to the Caribbean. The sun shone off the supertankers anchored five miles offshore, steel Colossi silently guarding the horizon, a reminder of the importance of crude oil in the world economy. Incidentally, the world's first successful oil tanker, *Zoroaster*, was designed by Ludvig Nobel, brother of the more famous Alfred Nobel, and carried its first load in 1878, a reminder that the Swedish have always been great innovators, although I'd probably agree that the development of flat-pack furniture was not one of our finest contributions to the advancement of mankind.

We set a course in the strait between the Venezuelan mainland and the island of Tortuga. A starboard wind helped us pick up speed and *Albatross* seemed to flit across the turquoise waters. I took a deep breath and filled my lungs with the ocean air; it was good to be sailing again.

Unfortunately, Curt didn't feel the same; he hadn't sailed in four years and was wretchedly seasick. We tried to persuade him to stay in the cockpit where he'd feel better in the fresh air, but he wasn't having any of it and stubbornly insisted on going to bed in the forward cabin, one of the worse places to be in rough weather. I looked at Carl as Curt shook his yellow face at our advice and disappeared below. 'Yup,' I said, 'those chemicals have definitely melted a few billion brain cells.'

That first day was a good sailing day; we racked up a fair distance of 152 nautical miles and caught several fish with a new fishing contraption: three hooks baited with colourful tin fish which we'd christened Fittipaldi because the speed of the float pulling the hooks after it reminded us of the famous Formula One driver, Emerson Fittipaldi. We also managed not to be mown down by any of the numerous supertankers we encountered during the night, thanks to our home-made radar reflector sitting in the mizzen mast. The second day we made less speed and on the third we only did 120 miles, which in fact suited us as we wanted to arrive at Aruba in daylight as we lacked any port descriptions and were unsure where we would moor.

Early on Monday morning we glimpsed the island of Aruba to the northwest. A 20-mile long courgette shaped island, it's the A of the ABC islands: Bonaire and Curaçao being the two other island territories that once formed the southwest part of the Netherlands Antilles. As we sailed along its southern coast, my dreams of an unspoiled Caribbean paradise went up in smoke together with the urine coloured clouds bellowing out of dozens of tall chimneys belonging to sulphuric plants, oil refineries and landfills that lined the coast. First impressions are hard to erase and I was hugely disappointed. Yes, we could see aquamarine lagoons and glimpse white sandy beaches, but they lay in the shadow of grim industrial plants belching yellow clouds into a perfect blue sky. Surely this wasn't Aruba? If it was, we'd just arrived at the island's equivalent of the rectum.

With expressions as sour as the vile looking smoke, we sailed north towards Oranjestad, the capital city. Two mammoth cruise ships the size of hotel complexes were moored in the lagoon, disgorging huge groups of tourists slowly shuffling along towards the port's duty free shops. The quayside was buzzing with vendors and agents flogging day trips, jeep safaris, Catamaran cruises, palm tours, pelican tours, submarine rides: you name it, someone was selling it.

We found a small marina in the inner harbour basin with slips for 30 boats and resigned ourselves to paying $40 a night but for which we were allowed use of the hotel facilities. The marina was attractive, close to the lush palms of Queen Wilhelmina Park, but it was hard to erase the memory of the recent blot on the landscape we'd sailed past.

We took a walk around and tried to fall in love with the place, but I would have needed a large dose of Viagra to get even vaguely excited about it. Oranjestad, the town built around the original Dutch military fortification, had a few colonial buildings in the centre which had been restored into colourful landmarks, but generally the town seemed to cater for duty-free shopping, while the area to the north seemed purpose built for the tourist industry, luring large Americans with even larger wallets to any one of the island's 36 casinos. The island also lacked the dramatic topography typical of the other Caribbean islands we'd visited, with their lush green mountains and hidden hurricane bays. Aruba has a dry climate and an arid, cactus-strewn landscape which, together with its 24-hour casinos, made it for me the Las Vegas of the islands. Although one thing I will say for Oranjestad is that every effort is kept to keep it clean, something other Caribbean islands could certainly emulate. When I saw a street cleaner with his broom and wheelie bin, Carl had to stop me from rushing over to shake his hand and offering to buy him a beer.

Curt had decided to sign off and not continue with us to Panama; we didn't make any attempt to dissuade him and that afternoon he managed to get a ticket to fly back to Miami the following day. Had it not been for the fact that we had Curt with us, I think Carl and I would have left Aruba the same day but we'd paid our mooring fees and so we spent the evening on *Albatross*, far from the madding crowd. From the cockpit we observed the filming of a scene from an action film; there were chases in motorboats, explosions, helicopters and fireworks like something out of a Bond movie. At least, I hope it was a film and not some gangland war raging as we blithely watched over a bottle of wine.

The following morning we cast off our moorings and headed for San Blas in Panama. Maybe we hadn't given Aruba a fair chance, there are beautiful beaches and bays to enjoy, but it was too commercial for us. Carl and I are Vikings after all, not shop-till-you-drop package tourists. We continued to seek, if not unchartered waters, at least islands less explored and cultures remote from our own.

Chapter 28
Pictures in the Sand
25 March – 4 April 2003

Isla Porvenir, San Blas, Panama – Cayos LosGrullos, San Blas, Panama

Experience: *Don't sail at night with the gennaker up.*

Tip: *Keep knives handy on deck and below for emergencies.*

'I'm telling you, man, don't go anywhere near the Colombia coast. Stay in deep water with 3,000 feet below your keel. Keep at least 50 miles between you and the coast off Barranquilla and Cartagena. You don't wanna go anywhere near there.' The uniformed official energetically stamped our numerous sheets of paper – thump, thump, shuffle, thump, thump, shuffle – and added them to his mounting pile of documents.

We were doing the tedious rounds of Customs and Immigration to clear out only 23 hours after arriving at Aruba, but the harbour officials were friendly and full of advice, especially when they saw we were sailing to Panama.

'And you definitely don't wanna try visiting Colombia,' our immigration man added. 'You just gonna get yourself killed just *thinking* about going there.' Thump, thump, shuffle, thump, thump, big smile. 'Thank you. And come back again to Aruba.'

We hadn't the slightest intention of leaving a footprint or bloodspot on Colombian soil: despite what some people thought, we weren't as stupid as we looked and were well aware of the propensity of the Colombian criminal class for kidnappings, armed robbery and general thuggery. The numerous executions committed by the minions of the drug cartels, as well as your daily street and gang related murders, terrorist activity and the new wave of "express kidnappings" were additional disincentives. Foreign offices around the world advised against all but essential travel, and we followed their advice without hesitation.

We'd been told that the stretch of water between Barranquilla and Cartagena was not only dangerous due to the numerous incidents of piracy, but also because of its treacherous currents and waves and was accordingly referred to as the Caribbean Cape Horn: if the pirates didn't get you, the waves probably would.

With this advice we started our 700-nautical mile long journey to Central America and quickly established our routine of watches and sailing duties. A couple of fishermen in Oranjestad had told us that there was some good fishing to be had in the waters west of Aruba, so I rigged up our Emerson Fittipaldi line and very quickly hooked a 15-pound kingfish. There'd been bites on the other two hooks but when I lifted them out of the water, all that remained were two wavy bits of steel: whatever had bitten had managed to straighten out the hooks and escape with the bait.

'We need bigger hooks and stronger lines,' I said to Carl. 'There are some fat fish out there with my name on them.' Although I was learning something new about the sport every day, the fish were still getting the better of me. A couple of days later, I landed a 35-pounder: a new record. I could gut and clean a fish faster than change my socks, and happiness was a full freezer. How my priorities had changed over the past year.

The wind strength was between five and seven miles an hour, so we sailed with a hoisted gennaker around the clock, averaging 130 nautical miles a day; at this rate, it would take us about five days to reach our goal. It was smooth blue water cruising, leaving us time to read, sleep or just gaze into the middle distance and let our thoughts drift on the waves.

With just the two of us for company, we often turned to the short wave radio for conversation. While we enjoyed the sense of tranquillity and inner peace during long periods of quiet sailing – and sometimes we wouldn't spot another vessel for days – it was good to connect with the world we could no longer see. There were several radio enthusiasts who regularly called us for a chat: people we'd never met and never would meet who wondered how our journey was going, where we were, where we were headed for, what the conditions were like and so on. They in turn entertained us with stories from their corners of the world. There was Carsten from Denmark who now lived in Panama, Gustav from Dalarna and Mats from Halmstad in Sweden, and Peder, another Dane who lived in the Canary Islands. Most of the radio amateurs were retired, and if they travelled vicariously through us, we heard about the rest of the world through them. Carl admitted to a stab of home-sickness when Mats in Halmstad told us that the spring flowers were in full bloom. 'Nothing is lovelier than a Swedish spring,' Carl said with a misty eye.

'Bollocks,' I said and waved my hand at the infinity of blues that stretched before us.

Apart from talking to radio hams on the SSB radio, we also used the VHF radio to call up other boats within a 50-nautical mile radius; most often we made contact with commercial boats: cargo carriers, tankers and containers whose captains and crews were happy to chat with tourist boats. 'What are you guys doing in this neck of the woods?' they'd ask. Sailboats this far out were rare, and they were invariably interested in our story and always wished us good luck for the rest of our journey. The only shipping company who refused to answer our calls was Maersk, one of the largest container ship operators in the world; their policy was clearly not to waste time chitchatting with private yachts.

SailMail was another essential means of communication. At midnight each night, we'd log into our account via the SSB radio and pick up our many emails; we had a surprising number of followers who read our ship's blog and wrote us encouraging messages, although I suspect there might well have been a sweepstake organized on when we'd give up, capsize or run out of money. Once the ladies learned that I was single, I gained something of a reputation, exaggerated naturally, and acquired a small band of loyal groupies. Of course, the emails we were most eager to read were those from our friends and family. We'd left Sweden 10 months earlier and still had more than two years before we'd see some of them again.

It was for this reason that we allowed ourselves the luxury of a phone call once a week. Carl and I celebrated Saturday nights at sea with a slap-up meal prepared by yours truly, lots of loud music – pop favourites and a bit of Sinatra – followed by a very brief call on the satellite phone. It was a weekly ritual which kept us and our families reassured and sane. It was eye-wateringly expensive, but there's nothing quite like hearing a loved one's voice, even if it was only to hear the loved one say, 'Hello? Are you there? Can you hear me? Hello? Is this working?' for the best part of the minute. Greger once called us, slightly the worse for wear I think, and burbled incoherently down the line. When we suggested he hang up because of the expense, he got quite defensive and ranted about how he 'could afford it, no bloody problem, mate.' When he got the bill, he realized we hadn't been exaggerating the cost and never called again: proof that it's not a good idea to drink and dial.

We were into our fourth day of sailing and felt confident enough to resume six-hour watches instead of the four we'd kept when closer to the Colombian coast. It's possible that we'd become too complacent out on the deep calm waters and we'd kept the gennaker hoisted around the clock. So when the wind suddenly and very violently picked up in the middle of the night, we weren't prepared for it. The wind filled the gennaker faster than a magician blowing up a balloon; the sail was at bursting point, almost lifting *Albatross* out of the water.

'Shit,' Carl shouted. 'This is bad. We've got to get the gennaker down.'

Easier said than done in a force nine gale: the pressure exerted on the gennaker and the lines made it impossible to release the sail. *Albatross* was heeling increasingly to starboard and waves were flooding over the deck. Serious case scenario: the gennaker would finally rip under the pressure and we'd lose a £2,000 sail. Worst case scenario: the gennaker would bring the boat down and sink us quicker than a diving submarine.

'No time to lose,' I shouted to Carl through the wind. 'Get a knife!'

Fortunately, we'd taken the precaution of mounting six razor-sharp boat knives in strategic places around *Albatross* in case of emergency: two in the cockpit, two in the middle of the deck adjacent to the mainsail and two in the stern; we also had folding knives attached to our safety harnesses. Here was our emergency: it was pitch black, clouds covered the stars and blocked out what little moonlight there'd been; the wind threatened to knock us off our feet and bounced *Albatross* up and down and side to side; waves slammed against the hull and bow. It was like trying to stand on a seesaw balanced on a carousel while the playground bully throws buckets of water at you. Carl grabbed a knife and half crawled to the gennaker and with a quick downward thrust cut through the line to the tack. The sail immediately fluttered out and hung there like a giant flag. We quickly released the spinnaker halyard and hauled in the sail. When we'd finally got the sails in, we lay in the cockpit, soaking wet and panting with exhaustion and relief.

'A bit too close for comfort, that,' I eventually said, once I had breath enough to speak. Although I could barely see Carl in the dim light, I knew from his heavy panting he was trying to agree. After that brush with disaster, we decided to sail with the genoa at night; it was easier to get down in a panic.

As we neared the San Blas archipelago, we adjusted our sailing speed to ensure arriving during daylight: there are numerous reefs around the small islands which don't always appear on the charts, so we would have to use the time-honoured navigation system called "eyeballing it." The wind had been fresh for the last few nights, but as the sun rose higher and warmed our backs, we could glimpse a small island on the horizon, which, were it not for the palm trees bending in the wind, could have been mistaken for the broad back of a whale.

The San Blas archipelago, or Kuna Yala as it is officially known, is one of the most picture perfect destinations we had yet visited, with 365 islands (one for each day of the year so they say) of blindingly white sandy shores, coconut palms and clear turquoise waters. It's a corner of the world where many of the uninhabited islands resemble those in comic cartoons: mere sand bars with a couple of titling palm trees. Approximately 10 percent of the islands are inhabited by around 50,000 Kuna Indians who continue to live their traditional lives in the face of the advancing twenty-first century. The Kunas, who once lived in what is now Colombia at the time of the Spanish invasion, migrated westwards towards the islands to escape mistreatment from their Spanish invaders, conflicts with other native peoples and the mosquitoes; I could certainly sympathize with the irksomeness of the latter.

We'd lowered the main and foresails and were carefully eyeballing our way towards Porvenir, the most westerly island of the Kuna Yala group and a full port of entry into Panama. Our first task on arrival was to complete clearance formalities, although looking at the lean-to buildings struggling to stay upright in the wind, it was hard to believe there was anything formal about Porvenir at all. Once through the outer reef, we were safe in the deep waters of the lagoon where three other boats, all from the U.S., were already anchored.

We'd barely dropped anchor before two local men appeared on the beach, waving their hats and shouting, 'Hola, hello, beinvenido.' Although the Kuna Indians have successfully resisted Hispanic assimilation and retained their own Native American language, Spanish is widely used, not that it would be of much use to Carl and me as our Spanish was limited to ordering beer.

We went ashore to the immigration building, one of three huts on the island, the other two being a hotel and a bar. I would have felt more comfortable entering the office in a hard hat: only hope seemed to be keeping the roof up. Porvenir is the economic and commercial hub of the Kuna Yala islands and boasts an airport, the runway of which had seen better days. No, strike that: I don't think it had ever seen a single good day; it looked like something a moon buggy would have trouble negotiating and certainly appeared to be several feet too short to accommodate anything but a toy plane; nevertheless, a light aircraft arrived daily from Panama bringing keen eco tourists to visit the island, their first experience of which was probably peeing their pants during landing.

We ducked inside the one-roomed building. Immigration centres are rarely luxurious, but this one was particularly sparse with a concrete floor, a single window without any glass in it – or frame for that matter – and thinly plastered walls. I supposed the light socket swinging from the ceiling had once held a light bulb but no longer: not that it mattered as a good deal of the ceiling had fallen down anyway. Two red plastic garden chairs were placed in front of a cluttered wooden desk piled high with papers, as was most of the floor area around the desk and along the walls. If this was the filing system, the secretary was in trouble.

'Hola, hello, bonjour,' said a voice. We looked around, puzzled; we'd assumed the room was empty. Then a small Indian, the height of a garden gnome, emerged from behind one of the piles of papers on the desk. He smiled genially at us. 'Bienvenido in Porvenir,' he said. 'Immeeegrashionee, youtishe, centre touristica y politzia departamento,' he said and indicated we should sit in a garden chair. After a moment's reflection we understood this was not only the immigration department, but the justice, tourist centre and the police department. Hence the reason for all the paperwork. We handed him our passports and boat documents, he banged on the keys of a 1920s typewriter for a bit and rubber stamped several beige papers which he added to the pile next to the table on the floor. '*Noventa y ocho* dollars,' he said, then seeing our blank looks he pointed to a figure on a corner of the desk: $98 for a three-month cruising permit. We exchanged money, shook hands and smiled a lot at each other.

Then Carl and I went to explore the island. This took all of 10 minutes. We had a look in the Hotel Porvenir on the corner of the airstrip. 'At least, it's convenient,' Carl observed. That's all it was: the plane probably touched down in your room and the noticeable lack of cement in the breeze block walls led me to wonder if the hotel was still under construction. The interior would have made a hermit's cave look cosier and better lit. If you didn't fancy one of the two worn mattresses on the sandy floor, you could always lie back in one of the hammocks, *if* you trusted that the nails embedded in the breeze block walls would support your weight. The bathroom, incidentally, was at the end of a wooden pier jutting out over the ocean.

We wandered on and passed the local constabulary hard at work protecting the community. Three Indians dressed in military uniforms, each armed with a hefty revolver, were engaged in guarding the one prisoner on the island: a local man who'd received a five-month custodial sentence for theft, not that I could imagine what there was to steal. Maybe *he*'d nicked the light bulb at the immigration office. His punishment was to clear the weeds on the sand next to the airstrip. His jailers were sitting in the shade of a leafy palm tree, taking it in turns to nap and ensure he didn't make a break for freedom out of the sunshine for the liberty and good times of the next island. In the evening, the prisoner strolled along to the police station/immigration office/tourist centre where he bedded down for the night after a hearty meal provided by the government. Ha! That'll teach him to be so light fingered.

'If this is prison, lock me up and throw away the key,' I said.

We learned this and more from the man who served us at the local bar: three walls of bamboo sticks and banana palm leaves which rustled in the wind. It was only recognizable as a bar because of the beer and spirit bottles neatly lined up along a breeze block wall and a hand written price list made from a ripped up cardboard box. Our bartender, a man aged somewhere between puberty and retirement, was incomprehensibly chatty; we smiled and nodded at each other, catching, if we were lucky, one word in a hundred. We finally resorted to drawing pictures in the sand to communicate with one another and got along famously, although it's quite possible he misinterpreted my stick picture of two women with a line drawn through each of them to show I had been twice divorced. The way he recoiled and gingerly handed me another beer leads me to think he believed I was a fugitive on the run for double murder.

Carl and I had all but sailed off the map to a place where life seemed to have changed very little over the centuries. The Kuna Yala archipelago was granted independence in 1925 and now consists of 49 communities scattered amongst the islands, governed by the Kuna General Congress. Each community has its own political organization led by a *saila*, a political and spiritual leader who memorizes the sacred songs of the history of the people and relates them to the community to keep their traditions and beliefs alive. Despite their repression by the colonial Spanish and later Panamanian governments, the Kuna Indians have managed to retain their culture for over 500 years by refusing foreign or Panamanian owned businesses or property on the islands. Few of the communities have running water: the water available on Porvenir was collected daily in water barrels by canoe from another island. The Indians make their *cayucos*, canoes, following an age old tradition: boys are taken to the forest to select the tree from which to make their first *cayuco*; they chop down a palm tree with a machete and spend long hours patiently hollowing it out. The result is a fast, stable craft approximately 12 feet long. These are generally paddled over short distances but for longer journeys a simple mainsail and jib are hoisted to increase speed and propel a fully loaded canoe. Cooking is still done over open fires, and most Kuna people favour sleeping in hammocks in communal areas inside their huts rather than on mattresses in private rooms. Yet some are hanging onto the edge of the twenty-first century: on the more populated islands, many have televisions which flicker into life when the generator starts humming in the evening, and some cayucos are powered by Yamaha engines. Despite these small encroachments of modernisation, Kuna families continue to be matrilineal; the bridegroom moves into the bridal home and takes his wife's last name as dictated by tradition.

The following morning while we were enjoying our breakfast in the cockpit, four *cayucos* appeared, each paddled by three diminutive women dressed as colourfully as exotic birds in their traditional Kuna costume of patterned blue skirts, red and yellow headscarves, beaded forearm bracelets and leggings, gold nose rings and finely sewn *mola* blouses, an important symbol of Kuna culture. The ladies pulled up alongside *Albatross* and quickly began pulling out a variety of wares from plastic containers, screeching like parrots in a mixture of Spanish and English. 'Look, senior. *Muy* nice. Give me five dollar.

Solamente five dollar.' They held up beaded jewellery, carved coconuts and starting draping examples of *molas*, a colorful textile art form, over the yacht's rails. I shook my head and waved them away with a smile. '*Non gracias, non gracias.*' But then feeling sorry for them I added the only other Spanish word I knew: '*Mañana.*' The women continued their sales pitch for a bit with dark pleading eyes and smiles as bright as their clothes, but I kept repeating *mañana* until they paddled off to the next boat.

'You fool, Yanne,' Carl said. 'They'll be back tomorrow alright.'

They were, and the *mañana* after that and the *mañana* after that, until eventually we felt too guilty to refuse – it was after all their main source of income. We bought a *mola* each from the ladies who arrived first on the fourth day. I've always been a bit of a pushover for a pair of dark brown eyes.

'*Hejsan Sverige!* Hi Sweden. Sweden is the best! Go Sweden!'

As a Swede, I whole heartedly approve of this rallying cry, but it seemed strange coming from the 41-foot Jeanneau Sun Legend sailing cruiser flying a French ensign which had just dropped anchor beside us: I wasn't aware the French liked anyone apart from themselves. But later as we were sitting at the bar, enjoying a cold beer and a stilted picture conversation with our bartender, we met the cruiser's owner and skipper. Jean-Charles Cuissard was probably in his late thirties and possessed boyish good looks and an appetite for off-piste adventure. He told us how he'd sold his software company in Toulouse and escaped to Panama where he had become so charmed by the Kuna that he'd started a new career in yacht charters in the San Blas archipelago. He spoke excellent English, Spanish and Kuna and we learned much from him about the way of life on the islands.

'Tell you what,' he said throwing his hands up with typical Gallic flair, 'come over to the boat and meet the rest of us tonight. We've got one of yours onboard.'

The "one of ours" was Karin from Blekinge, a county bordering Skåne. Karin had worked for eight years for SAS in Paris and on a wild whim had decided on a holiday with a difference with her French boyfriend. Early the following morning, she and her boyfriend would leave Jean-Charles' boat to fly back to Panama City and return to "the real world," as she said with a mournful look.

'Don't worry,' Jean-Charles said, stuffing a cigar in the corner of his mouth, 'the flight might not even leave. Half the time when they stop both engines, a propeller cuts out and they have to radio for a new battery.'

We watched and waved from the airfield – the strip of sand where the prisoner was lethargically plucking at the weeds – as Karin and her boyfriend boarded the plane. The pilot didn't bother to cut the engine of the Twin Otter as he hustled one set of passengers off the plane, another set on, grabbed a Coke from the bar and zoomed off again into the blue.

'Right,' said Jean-Charles. 'Follow me. Porvenir is just the transit island. I'll show you Los Cayos Grullos, a proper desert island. The snorkelling is fantastic there.'

We sailed beside Jean-Charles' boat some 20 nautical miles east to an island which looked absurdly like something Robinson Crusoe would have been cast up on: birds squawking in the palm trees bent by the wind appeared to be the only inhabitants on the island. We anchored in a tranquil lagoon and snorkelled in warm water over a reef where coral clusters glowed and bloomed like huge flowers below us and fish teemed around our feet. Later when we went ashore, we tramped through the thick jungle-like growth and were surprised to arrive at a mini metropolis of a dozen timber framed-houses with untidy thatched roofs where smoke swirled from open cooking fires and chickens strolled happily unfettered until nabbed for the pot.

That evening we gathered on the soft sandy shores with other island hoppers for a potluck supper. Carl and I contributed Kingfish steaks from the freezer and Jean-Charles arrived with a bunch of squirming lobsters he'd bought from an Indian in a passing *cayuco*. We met Tom and Mina Caulfield, an inspiring couple from California in their mid-seventies who'd been sailing the area for a quarter of a century. They told us how on their first excursion around San Blas, they'd ripped up their hull on the reef and watched as their brand new boat sank. 'We're a lot older, wiser and better insured since those days,' Tom said wryly. He was happy to give us tips on sailing to Panama, drawing a plan of where the reefs were; he also recommended we sail along a 500-metre wide strait between the mainland and Isla Grande where navigation was easier.

'When you reach the Panama Canal, stay south,' Tom said. 'Sail towards the yellow mooring buoy area where there's firmer anchoring. Otherwise it's like anchoring in tomato soup; you'll never get a hold.'

A couple of days later after some maintenance work on *Albatross*, we left Los Cayos Grullos. Jean-Charles was already on his way to Porvenir to pick up a new set of customers, but Tom and Mina and a small group of Indians waved us off, the children running up and down the sand and the women making a last attempt to sell us more *molas*. As the island receded and became a small green dot on the horizon, I wondered how time would change the islands and the Kuna who live on them. Here was a contented community that seemed at one with their surroundings and resistant to anything they'd seen on their televisions; their building materials came from the forest and they lived almost entirely on the crops they grew, the fish they caught and the crafts they sold. So I am saddened to read that the San Blas archipelago is threaten by the general rising sea levels as a result of global warming and the dire prediction by scientists that the islands will be completely submerged in approximately 40 to 60 years. I hope they're wrong: the Kuna Indians would have to return to Panama and live again on the mountains surrounding their sunken islands. Then this paradise would be forever lost.

Chapter 29

Red Devils and Baywatch Boys in the White Man's Graveyard,

5 – 24 April 2003

Colón, Panama

Experience: *There's no need to fear transiting the Panama Canal, but the canal authorities may deny transit if a yacht cannot maintain a minimum speed of 5 knots.*

Tips: *Salt water contaminates everything from food to electrical systems. Copper wires oxidize and connections fall apart, resulting in reduced conductivity, so we recommend always using marine grade tinned wire.*

In 1881, a French company financed by over 100,000 small investors began work on a canal that would cross the Isthmus of Panama to join the Atlantic and Pacific Oceans. Ferdinand de Lesseps, flush with success as builder of the Suez Canal, led the project and no doubt thought that constructing a sea-level canal half the length of the Suez would be a relative doddle, reckoning to complete the job for around $132 million in a little more than a decade.

When the Panama Canal finally opened in 1914, ownership of the project was in the hands of the United States, its total cost had tripled and a staggering 27,000 workers had died of diseases and accidents during the construction. Some 22,000 workers died during the French construction period alone which was beset by so many problems that the surviving workers nicknamed it the "White Man's Graveyard" and De Lesseps "The Great Undertaker."

But not for nothing is the Panama Canal lauded as one of the "Seven Wonders of the Modern World" by the American Society of Civil Engineers. Although a mere 48 miles long, the canal was one of the largest and most difficult engineering projects ever undertaken, cutting through tortuous terrain and requiring a series of three locks at each end to lift and lower ships 85 feet above sea level. The amount of earth and rubble amassed during its excavation was enough to bury Manhattan Island to a depth of 12 feet. Some of the material was used to create nearly 500 acres along the Pacific Ocean coast to build the town of Balboa but much was disposed of in the jungle. When the Panama Canal officially opened in August 1914, however, the world's attention was elsewhere: German troops were marching through Belgium towards Paris. One of the greatest engineering projects of all time and which had cost so many lives was eclipsed by World War One.

As we approached the entrance to the mother of all canals, Carl and I both fell silent, awed by the momentousness of our location. Look at it on a map and we had reached a line that cut north to south through the narrowest part of Panama. But as we followed in the wake of nearly a million ships to transit the canal, we saw it as the pivotal point in our journey, both geographically and mentally; it was our milestone, our Everest base camp, our moon landing before the walk, our marathon runner's wall; this was where we had to make the decision to continue or turn back. On the other side, lay the biggest daddy of them all: the Pacific Ocean. We'd already sailed 9,000 nautical miles but passing through the canal meant committing to 40,000 more. Could we do it? Could we take that magic step?

Looking around us, we weren't the only yachtsmen to have wavered at this watery crossroads; for many it seemed Panama was the end station. Here lay around 50 boats in various stages of disrepair, ranging from the slightly shabby to the all but completely disintegrated: abandoned or sold by owners who'd fallen out of love with either their travelling companions, with the idea of crossing another perilous body of water, or who just couldn't afford the transit fees. If ever you fancy picking up a cheap yacht, fly out to Colón and bag yourself a bargain; there are plenty to be had. Many crafty dealers make a good living buying boats for a song to repair and sell on for enviable profits. Those vessels that hadn't been sold were left to rot in the water and would be picked over by scrap merchants like crows over roadkill. This is where many yachts and dreams had come to die.

But not so *Albatross* and her crew. 'Let's finish what we've started, eh Calle?' I said as we passed a dilapidated 42-foot schooner covered in algae and grey mould.

'Yup,' Carl agreed. 'We finish or we go down sinking.' Well, not quite the phrase I would have chosen but I concurred with the "never-give-up" sentiment.

We'd anchored together with around 60 other boats near a major container harbour within sight of the entrance to the Gatún locks, the first set of three locks which rises 85 feet to the level of the Gatún Lake. Here we could observe huge freighters ploughing their way down towards the canal entrance, throwing up vast troughs of water that rocked us small sailboats.

In 1928, Richard Halliburton, American adventurer, author and bit of a wacko, decided to swim the length of the Panama Canal and therefore entered the record books for incurring the lowest toll in the history of the Canal, paying a mere 36 cents as he weighed only 150 pounds. Compare this to the average toll of around $54,000. Tolls for the canal are based on vessel type, size and the type of cargo. As a sailboat under 50 feet we could expect to pay around $500 for *Albatross*, excluding extra fees for lines and fenders, a canal inspection, clearance and security charges, agency fees and a buffer of $800 in case of "damage to the canal," although our possibility putting a bit of a ding in it seemed remote compared to that of a Panamax tanker. All this meant a paper trail around several offices, culminating in a bank queue where we handed over a credit card to cover the costs and were told we would have to wait 15 days to transit the canal: only three sailing boats a day are permitted to enter. If we wanted to skip the queue we could fork out an extra $2,800 and transit the next day. It was a no-brainer: we joined the queue and prepared to wait our turn.

Fortunately, we were kept busy. The following evening we were eating dinner in the yacht club in Colón where the prices were so reasonable it was cheaper for us to eat there than buy and prepare food ourselves. Although the state of the kitchen would have sent a health inspector screaming for the hills, the food was outstanding. Our cook was a wizened old man with Prince Charles sized ears, a single tooth that stood like a tombstone for all the other teeth he'd lost and an apron he wore every day for the two weeks we were there. For this reason alone we felt it best not to look too closely at the food. Even so, his *sancocho*, a chicken stew, made with a starchy root called *ñamé* and seasoned with a cilantro-like herb, was outstanding. I was halfway through a plate of this when the arrival of a man in a T-shirt emblazoned with the word "Helsingør" caught my attention. I hadn't expected to meet a near neighbour.

'*Hej du Dansk!*' I called. 'Hi Danish! What are you doing in Panama?'

The Dane shot me a gruff look. 'Bugger all! Not unless I can find an electrician in this blasted country.'

Carl and I laughed. 'Well, this is your lucky day. You've found two,' Carl said.

The Dane nearly knocked over the other plastic tables in his haste to get to ours. He held out his hand. 'Name's Knud. If you're having me on, I'll drop you in the Canal. But if you're really electricians, I'll buy you a beer.'

Knud was one of those types who'd invested in what he'd thought was a boat at a bargain price that he could turn over for a quick profit. The boat, a 39-foot ketch, had come by way of an unfortunate Danish woman who'd woken up one morning in the Caribbean to find her husband had disappeared overboard – he'd probably overbalanced while taking a pee over the side. The distressed woman had tried to sail the boat alone but had hit a reef and sunk it. An American salvage boat had rescued her and towed the ketch to Panama where Knud had bought it for peanuts. But like peanuts, everything was salted: the seawater had corroded all the electrics, and the boat was useless unless he could find an electrician. As this was a business venture for Knud, Carl and I agreed to work for him for $20 an hour, to be paid in cash at the end of every working day – Swedes are deeply suspicious of Danes when it comes to business. We agreed to start the next day and shook hands on the deal. As we left Knud, Carl and I counted our fingers to check the Dane hadn't nicked them during the handshake.

It was hot, filthy work in the Panamanian heat and we earned our money; it took us five sweltering days to rebuild the entire electrical system and recondition the engine. Fortunately, we had a good supply of tools and equipment on *Albatross* with which to complete the job. When we finally turned the ignition key and heard the engine purr as smoothly as contented house cat, we knew we hadn't lost our touch.

During our labours on the Danish boat we were entertained by the antics of a local man who materialized every day beside the boat to scavenge through the pile of debris Knud dumped on the quayside. We couldn't get our Swedish tongues round his name so we called him Kuna Kuna. At not quite four feet tall, he was probably one of the shortest men I've ever met, and had it not been for his leathery skin and deep wrinkles, I would have initially taken him for a child. Nevertheless, he was as cheerful as he was resourceful. One day he appeared sporting a pair of winkle-picker shoes. The fact that they were six sizes too big for him didn't deter him from strutting about in them as if he owned the canal, but the effect was similar to that of a toddler trying to walk in daddy's shoes: whenever Kuna Kuna took a step forward, the shoe got left behind. Eventually he solved the problem by stuffing the toes with wads of newspaper. He also found a pair of Mexican boots, but these were so long for his short legs he risked catching his testicles in the tops.

We had almost completed our work for Knud and were wondering how to kill time for the next week, when a Danish couple asked if we'd assist as line handlers on their canal transit: sailboats require a minimum of four line handlers, excluding the skipper and the pilot to make the passage. Annie and Steen Larsen on *S/Y Larsine* had been let down by promises of help and were desperate to find extra crew. Knud, Carl and I signed on. It would be an excellent way of getting experience of the lock system before making the transit ourselves. We'd heard a few horror stories of problems encountered by sailboats: lines slipping, boats turned sideways or getting caught in the powerful eddies created by the gargantuan propellers of the supertankers.

It was still pitch black as we got up at 3 a.m. to board *Larsine*. Steen motored out to the Flats where we joined two Dutch yachts and waited for our advisor who would help pilot us through. An hour after the allotted time, a boat arrived with three advisors, one for each boat, and we all headed towards the first set of locks where the three vessels would be rafted together. As *Larsine* was the longest of the three, we were instructed to take the "centre lock." We laid out the ropes and side tied the Dutch boats on our starboard and port sides. Then as a "threesome" we proceeded into the first lock, followed by a massive French container ship that loomed menacingly over us. The lock gates slowly ground to a close, sealing us in the dark depths of the lock. There was a moment's eerie quiet as we waited entombed within the concrete walls, then the lock started to boil as 22,000 gallons of water gushed from the bottom of the chamber and the boats started to rise: not a time to fall overboard as the monstrous whirlpools would surely suck anyone under. Although the chamber took only eight minutes to fill, there was plenty of time to kill, particularly for us in the middle boat; the line handlers on the port and sideboard boats were busy keeping the tension on the lines, while we were relaxed to the point of catatonic as only Steen had to man the helm allowing us time to admire the workings of the lock system. The sun was lightening the sky and Knud was already demanding a liquid breakfast as we entered the second lock. Annie put a prompt stop to any mutiny by producing a huge buffet breakfast that we ate in the cockpit and washed down with cold beers.

We emerged from the Gatún locks three hours later and 85 feet higher than we'd started. The genoa was hoisted and we cruised at a pleasant seven knots through the waters of Gatún Lake that would carry us for 21 miles of our transit. The lake, created by the building of the Gatún Dam across the Chagres River, was at its completion in 1913 the largest artificial lake in the world. It is essential for the canal's operation, providing the water for the locks; 52 million gallons of water is passed from the lake into the sea each year as approximately 14,000 vessels make their transits. The lake's surroundings and the hilltop islands, created by the flooding of the valley, are lush with jungle and home to billions of insects and several species of monkey that we could hear screeching but not see. The trip was a little enlivened, however, when we saw the ridged back of a crocodile, startling Annie who'd been sitting with her legs dangling over the side of the boat. Just say casually, 'Blimey, hope that crocodile over there doesn't take your legs off,' if you want to see someone move at the speed of light.

After navigating two more locks, we were lowered again to sea level and on the home stretch: the Pacific was in sight. But it was only as we sailed under the Bridge of the Americas that connects North and South America that we could truly say we were in Pacific waters. Steen moored on one of the numerous anchor buoys in the bay from which we took a water taxi to the dock. Annie and Steen would sail on, and Carl and I would make our way back to Colón to take *Albatross* through the canal, now reassured that it was not the nightmare transit we'd been led to believe.

We took the opportunity to stay overnight in Panama City, checking into a hotel Jean-Charles had recommended. We got a great room with a TV and ensuite bathroom: luxuries we hadn't experienced for a long time. No matter how much we tried to keep clean on *Albatross*, our clothes and skin always felt crumpled and slightly stiff with salt. I indulged in a hot soak and left an impressive ring of grime around the tub.

Panama City was sweaty, congested and the entire population of 880,000 seemed to be out on the street at the same time. The city is full of contrasts, standing as it is at the crossroads of two continents and two oceans. Casco Viejo, the old quarter with its crumbling French and Spanish colonial style buildings, struggles to maintain its identity against a dense skyline of glossy high-rise buildings reminiscent of Miami. We hopped on a *diablo rojo*, one of the red devils as the buses are known. What these old American vehicles lacked in suspension, they certainly made up for in gleaming chrome and paint jobs; every inch from the bumpers to the seats was decorated with graffiti-style artwork depicting whatever fantasy the artist had dreamed up during a spliff: anything and everything from Neptune battling a sea monster, Moorish castles and buxom wenches to logos calling for revolution, recycling or an end to drugs, all in spray-paint colours that made your eyes water. It was urban art on the move, but it didn't make the rides any more comfortable. Although we vainly gripped the sides of our seats, we became dizzy from being bounced around, and if the driver hit a pothole – which he frequently did – we were jolted so far out of our seats, our heads hit the ceiling and our teeth rattled. But it was a cheap way to see the city. Residents half-jokingly call Panama City the "Dubai of the Americas" due to the recent influx of foreign investment. Yellow cranes crowd the skyline, an indication of a boomtown fever. The dilapidated old town quarter is gradually being rejuvenated, and swanky hotels and upscale wine bars are popping up overnight like white truffles. The city is swopping its tattered old rags for an Armani coat.

After exploring the local markets, eating *ceviche* – a dish made from raw fish marinated in citrus juice and spiced with chilli peppers – from one of the many street stalls, and absorbing the sounds and sights, we eventually grew tired of the unremitting racket of the chaotic traffic and caught a comfortable bus back to Colón.

Although a mere eight miles separate Colón from Panama City, they are worlds and decades apart. After the vibrancy of Panama City, Colón was a depressing contrast; it would have made a Victorian slum in Dickens' London look attractive by comparison. The buses in the station were the smartest thing about the area. 'Better to live on a red devil than in a death trap like that,' I said to Carl, pointing to one of the crumbling buildings. Founded by the Americans in 1850 as the Atlantic terminus of the Panama Railroad, Colón at one time resembled New Orleans, elegant facades of colonial architecture gracing its centre. Now the wrought iron balconies and stylish verandas were disintegrating under a layer of toxic-looking black mould; roofs were patched with rusty corrugated metal sheets; doors had fallen off rusted hinges, and the streets were littered with the debris of a city that just didn't care or had given up the fight. In its heyday, Colón had been a thriving city with nightclubs and theatres. Now it was home to squalid brothels and drug dens. Riots in the 1960s had destroyed the city's municipal palace, and the dictatorships of Omar Torrijos and Manual Noriega had furthered the city's economic and social decline. 'Colón's a shit hole,' Carl said, putting it more succinctly than me. I pitied the children born into this; how could they ever escape.

If you arrive by cruise ship, you'll see the smart side of the city where the port buildings are regularly spruced up, but step down a side street where the buildings are being reclaimed by the jungle and it's a different story: one which tourists are warned against. Carl and I made regular forays into Colón, always on the lookout and not so stupid as to carry valuables or flash wads of cash about. Nevertheless, the canal authority guards would often try to turn us around with dark threats. 'Why do you want to go downtown, man? You just gonna get your throat cut.' We called them the "Baywatch Boys," clad not in red Speedos but bullet-proof vests over their khaki uniforms and wielding impressive firearms in holsters strapped around their hips and thighs. It was comforting to know that we had our own personal security staff, at least until we'd turned the corner and disappeared into the heaving throng.

After running from office to office to get our paperwork stamped for our transit down the canal we hit a sudden snag; transit had been cleared for 19 April, but it was only possible to have our papers stamped a maximum of 48 hours in advance of clearing out. The official behind the desk explained that over the Easter holiday every government office in Panama closed. We pleaded with him and he duly rolled his eyes and groaned about how he would have to travel to his office and get out his little rubber stamp especially for us – it was the usual question of how much to grease the palm that stamped your paperwork. As a result we found ourselves staring at a new departure date on 23 April, a delay of 120 hours. Not only did this mean that *Albatross* and her crew were now in Panama illegally, but we could no longer call on our German friends who'd promised to act as line handlers for us as they were flying back home. Michel, a Danish friend we'd made while in Colón, agreed to help but we still needed two new line handlers. Bulletin boards around the yacht club offered help for hire at $50 a person, and we'd almost caved into paying for a couple of guys when we bumped into two young backpackers: Brian from San Diego and his British sidekick, Teresa from London. They were in their early thirties and were travelling around South America, and although Brian had a bit of a hippy dippy hairdo, they looked as if they might fit our brief: holding on to a rope for 45 minutes and not screwing it up.

'Would you like to help us to hold a rope?' I asked in my best English.

Teresa looked at me doubtfully. 'As pick-up lines go, that's not the best,' she said.

We explained the job and Brian immediately asked, 'Yeah, but where are you heading after the canal?'

'The Galapagos Islands,' Carl answered.

'How far away is that?'

'About a thousand nautical miles. You could come with us.'

I could see Brian and Teresa weighing up the pros and cons of sailing a thousand miles with two Swedish men they'd never met before. 'Hmm. I'm not sure. We've never done any sailing. I've never even been on board a sail-boat,' Teresa said.

'Oh, it's quite safe,' I replied. 'We haven't sunk or lost a man overboard yet. And once you get used to the bad weather, the seasickness passes. And my cooking's pretty good. We may be Vikings but we don't use the skulls of our victims as wine glasses anymore.' As they stared at me, I realized that my words may not have sounded as reassuring as I'd thought. 'Anyway, you can check out our website,' I added hastily, handing Brian the address.

'We'll let you know,' he said carefully.

That evening they called us on the VHF radio and agreed to help us down the canal on the condition they could continue with us to the Galapagos Islands, assuring us that they had the funds for an onward flight once they'd left *Albatross*. So the following day, we did another round of paperwork with the authorities now that Brian and Teresa had signed on as crew; this would avoid problems when we arrived at the Galapagos Islands. Unfortunately, there was much puffing and shouting when we presented our documents.

'But, *señor*, you cannot be here! You should have left Panama three days ago.' Unpleasant visions of being the 'pretty blond Swede' in a Panamanian jail swam before me: curse my good looks. Luckily, Brian came to the rescue and in fluent Spanish sorted the problem. The documents were rewritten, rubber stamped from top to bottom and we were legal again.

'Just as well we've got Brian with us,' I muttered to Carl.

'Don't tell him that,' Carl muttered back. 'He'll want payment for interpreting for us.'

The bay was still dark when the crew of *Albatross* was woken by the shrill beep of the alarm at three in the morning. As we stumbled about the cabin getting dressed and making ready, a toxic stench stung our nostrils. I looked at Brian with concern; what the hell had that guy been eating? He looked right back at me. 'Man! What a stink! I'm going on deck for some fresh air.'

There was no fresh air on deck: we were enveloped in pitch-black smoke pouring from a 30-foot chimney. An incineration plant was located close to the harbour, only a few hundred feet from a poor neighbourhood: as if those with the lowest income in the shittiest housing didn't have it bad enough, poison was added to the air they breathed.

We were only too happy to raise anchor and head towards the Flats to meet our advisor and the two other boats we would transit with. Shortly after five, an elegant man dressed in a gleaming white shirt and Panama hat arrived and introduced himself as Henry, our canal advisor. He looked every bit the smoothie, but he turned out to be very amiable once we'd relaxed him with a couple of gin and tonics. At the Gatún locks we were joined by a boat from Switzerland and a catamaran from Germany. Carl was skipper and while Michel and I managed the lines at the bow, Brian and Teresa took those at the stern. Having done this before, Carl and I were smugly relaxed. Once in the Gatún Lake, Henry pushed us to do seven knots and make straight for the Pedro Miguel locks. We were making good speed when suddenly there was an ominous bang in the engine compartment and the horrendous smell of burning rubber. Carl immediately cut the engine and headed for a mooring buoy. For a very nasty moment the large freighter behind us looked as if it was in a direct collision line with *Albatross*; Henry went white as he radioed the freighter's advisor to slow their speed; Brain, with a presence of mind I hadn't reckoned for someone with a hippy hairdo, grabbed the mooring rope, dived in the water and lassoed the buoy with the accuracy of a rodeo showman. The danger was over and we were safely moored, but what had happened to our beloved Volvo Penta motor? Michel and I worked feverishly on the engine; fortunately, the damage seemed to be superficial and we were able to repair it and continue, although at a lower speed as we didn't risk pushing it too much. We finally exited the last of the Miraflores locks at 2 p.m., dropping off our advisor, who was slightly the worse for wear after several gin and tonics, and Michel who stepped aboard the German catamaran sailing to Balboa from where he would get a bus back to Colón.

'Right,' said Carl, rubbing his hands and looking purposefully at Brian and Teresa. 'Time to lose your virginity!' Teresa's blond eyebrows shot up in alarm. 'Your sailing virginity. Time to set sail on a big ocean, the biggest of them all. The Pacific!'

'Bring it on,' Brian said. I could tell he meant business: he'd put on a clean T-shirt and tied back his long curly hair in a ponytail.

Chapter 30
Paving Paradise
24 – 26 April 2003

Isla San Jose, Las Perlas, Panama –
Isla del Rey, Las Perlas, Panama

Experience: *If other cultures may seem strange to us, we seem equally extraordinary to them.*

Tip: *Even if you're a champion fisherman, buy something now and then from the locals; it's important to support them and establishes a basis for good relationships.*

S ome of the most renowned pearls in the world have been discovered from oysters lying on the seabed around the hundred or so islands that make up the Pearl Island archipelago in the Gulf of Panama. But *La Peregrina* is the most famous of them all. The perfectly symmetrical pear-shaped 55-carat jewel was found by an African slave in the mid-sixteenth century, for which he was rewarded with his freedom. It was owned by Philip II of Spain, Queen Mary I of England and Napoleon Bonaparte, to name but a few, before being purchased at a Sotheby's auction in 1969 by a very smitten Richard Burton as a Valentine's gift for Elizabeth Taylor. *La Peregrina* was sold at Christie's in 2011 for a record price of £7.1 million. Amazing, isn't it? All that for something a mollusc secretes around a parasite.

We had a pearl of our own with us: Teresa with her fair skin, blonde hair and blue eyes looked like Agneta from Abba and was a source of fascination to the Indians of the Archipiélago de las Perlas. But then Carl, Brian and I were proving to be just as interesting to the locals as the locals were to us, even if they didn't ask to *buy* any of us.

We'd sailed on a light breeze for 30 nautical miles to the privately owned island of San Jose, the archipelago's second largest island, which according to the census of 2000 had a population of only 10. We floated into a bay where the cerulean sea rippled at snowy white sands and a canopy of dense jungle and palm trees provided a lush backdrop. There wasn't a soul in sight or any trace that there had ever been; the sand was smooth and unmarked. The shoreline, however, was teeming with pelicans, waiting to scoop up the fish rolled by the surf onto the sand into their cavernous beaks. Dinner was served to the birdlife here.

The islands, named Islas de las Perlas by Vasco Nunez de Balboa owing to the many pearls found there, were first occupied by Indians who were unfortunately wiped out within two years of the arrival of the Spanish. Various Indian chiefs had cheerfully tried offering baskets of pearls to conquistadors who stepped onto the islands, but the unlucky locals were slaughtered for their welcoming efforts in such huge numbers that the Spanish had to import a new workforce to harvest the pearls. They looked to Africa, snatched several hundred people off its shores and shipped them off as slaves. It is their descendants who today populate the Pearl Islands.

We spent the day snorkelling and exploring the shoreline. The island seemed as fertile as the waters surrounding it. Coconut palms and sugar cane lined the beach where the vegetation was all but impenetrable; giant plants dwarfed specimens we knew from garden centres back home; trees rose 80 feet and higher. Wildlife was abundant, too, with deer, pigs, parrots, toucans and giant pigeons. The island is irrigated with rivers and springs and there are several waterfalls with falls of 60 feet. Better yet, unlike the Caribbean, it is out of the hurricane belt and there are no earthquakes. As island chains go, this was the perfect one to be marooned on. Apparently, I wasn't the only one to think so as only four months after our visit an American television crew thought the same, choosing one of the uninhabited islands for a series of the programme *Survivor*.

On the evening of our arrival we were visited by three local fishermen who shyly offered us lobster and squid they'd caught with their bare hands while free diving around the reefs. We invited them on board. Their smiles were wide as we passed round the beers, growing even wider when Teresa appeared; they ogled her with undisguised curiosity and there was fierce discussion in rapid Spanish. With Brian as our interpreter, we learned that they spent 10 days fishing around the islands, after which they would return to Panama City to sell their catch. We bought five large lobsters for the price of a chicken in Sweden and invited them to return the following day to share a beer with us again. It wasn't out of any philanthropic duty that we extended our invitation but an easy and entertaining way of learning far more about the islands and their inhabitants than any guide book or internet site could ever tell us. And we enjoyed their company. Plus, we couldn't catch a lobster if our lives depended on it, although I was becoming quite the expert at preparing shellfish and we dined well that night, watching the sun set golden as we sat back replete.

'Man, this sailing is pretty good,' Brian mused, releasing his ponytail. 'I could do this forever.'

Carl and I decided not to disillusion him with any yarns of terror on the high seas. Let him enjoy the moment; over a thousand miles of sailing to the Galapagos Islands would reveal to him how the ocean can wreak havoc on even the most robust constitution.

The fishermen returned the following morning with a seven-pound tuna in a bucket, becoming quite touchy when we tried to pay, insisting that we were their friends; they readily accepted a beer each in lieu of payment and their smiles flashed brighter when Teresa re-appeared on deck.

On the fishermen's recommendation, we sailed that afternoon around the headland to a crescent-shaped bay in which a secluded hotel nestled. As we pulled the dinghy up the beach, we were greeted by George Novey, a genial Panamanian and owner of the Hacienda del Mar resort, the island and Air Panama. As we sat sipping drinks and enjoying the spectacular views from the pool side, he told us about the island and how he'd created the resort.

'San Jose is almost totally covered with forest and there is very little here except for my lodge, an airstrip so my guests can fly here with my airline, and 60 miles of roads built by the U.S military during World War II. They used the island for training operations and chemical testing.'

'No wonder the fish are so big in these waters,' I said.

George laughed. 'Don't worry. All traces of the chemicals were removed long ago and the people are returning to live on the island. And just look at the fabulous nature and wildlife around you. The waters here are considered among the best fishing grounds in the world; we have black marlin the size of elephant. If you sit here long enough, you'll see sea turtles and humpbacked whales. I like to think of my resort as an eco-village by the sea. There's no TV or internet here; it's about connecting with the land and the sea.'

His sales pitch was certainly enthusiastic, and both his airline and resort are still going strong. I read recently that his current plans are to build luxury accommodations for use as second homes and new hotels for the wealthier ecotourist on a nearby island while keeping San Jose secluded. Despite his pledge that the development of the Pearl Islands will not exceed more than 25 percent of the area's virgin land and that measures will be taken to protect turtle, whale and dolphin habitats, I cannot help but wonder how much longer the islands will remain the unspoiled gems they were when we were lucky enough to visit them.

'How much for the woman?'

'Are you sure that's what he asked?' Carl frowned over his rum and coke.

Brian nodded. 'Absolutely. I think we could get a bidding war going here.'

S/Y Albatross
Hallberg-Rassy 42 E

From cyclists to sailors. It all started in France with a handshake, an alcohol-fuelled idea and a couple of bikes. Carl (with his beloved Cannondale) and I (the handsome fellow giving the thumbs up) seal our pact to sail around the world.

Liveaboard life is never dull. On winter evenings I was frequently joined onboard Albatross by boat neighbours Martin and Ove for cooking and conversation. Ove became a close friend and mentor, teaching me much about boat maintenance and sailing.

Not Arctic sailing but crossing the North Sea. Carl and I barely visible in our foul weather sailing gear during a passage over the most treacherous body of water in the foulest conditions we encountered on our journey.

Crucial supplies. Fearful that the watermaker might malfunction and we would be forced to drink our own urine, we ensured we had enough liquid onboard in the form of beer, wine and our favourite Danish snaps. Stowing it was another problem.

S/Y Albatross finally ready to set sail for a journey of nearly 50,000 nautical miles. Notice the bike lashed to the lifelines, the code flag bunting which didn't survive the first short passage and the deeply sceptical air of the two onlookers.

Sailing Scandinavian waters in the summer months can be idyllic: not so for us. Rough weather forced us to change our plans and put into Norwegian harbours where the weather immediately became benign, as it was here in Arendal.

What mysteries lurk below?
Albatross' prow points the way towards Loch Ness in the mountainous heart of the Scottish Highlands. Passage down the Caledonian Canal offers stunning views and inviting pubs.

Whiskies for nosing and a piper on the banks of a Scottish loch. I don't remember much beyond that other than a burning desire to own a castle or a distillery.

In Arklow we met British yachting journalist and author, Tom Cunliffe, who joined us on our exploration of Irish pubs. As thanks for his patient advice, we entertained him on Albatross.

Crucial catch. Sardine fishing is the lifeblood of the harbour town of Camariñas where the whole community turn out to help unload the night's fishing catch. Sadly, just months after our visit the industry was devastated by an oil tanker spill.

Feeling the stress slip away in La Coruña. Carl strips down to his boxers to gaze at the sea and reflect on our journey so far. Shortly after finishing the carton of wine, we fell asleep and snored loudly on the sand.

Always on the lookout for a bargain. Despite my protests, Carl contemplates buying chickens in Santiago de Compostela to keep onboard for a supply of fresh eggs.

Going with the flow on the Guadiana River. A narrow strip of water separates the Spanish town of Sanlúcar de Guadiana from the Portuguese town of Alcoutim, but both small communities enjoyed surprisingly rowdy fiestas.

Store it or drink it now? Carl in a tight spot storing supplies. In Spain we stocked up
on sailing essentials: beer, wine and olives.

Fantastic boat, fantastic service. We were as impressed by the service offered by the
Hallberg-Rassy team as by their boats. Per and Roland were on hand in Las Palmas to
check Albatross thoroughly before the start of the Atlantic Rally for Cruisers.

Neptune and his entourage. A carnival spirit prevailed the week before the Atlantic Rally for Cruisers with parties for all the participating crews. We bet the mermaids (a women's team on Girlsforsale) a bottle of champagne we'd place ahead of them. We're still waiting, girls.

Happy crew, happy boat. We collected various crew members but few as enthusiastic about my cooking as Englishman, Tim. An invaluable addition on our Atlantic passage, he could explain what was being said over the radio to a couple of linguistically challenged Swedes.

Dinner for a week.
During the first few months of our journey, I lost expensive equipment, lures and lines to some cunning fish before I got the hang of fishing. Anders and I struggle to land a kingfish in the Caribbean.

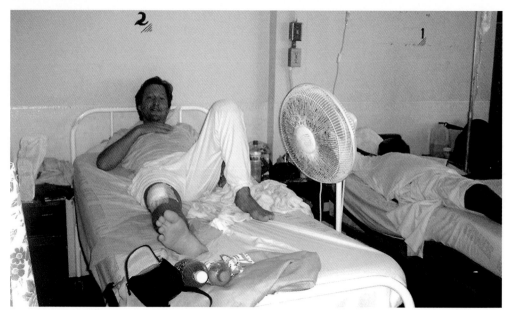

Beware the evil little sand fly. I spent a week in hospital in Tobago recovering from a nasty infection in my knee as a result of insect bites. Carl received an even more shocking prognosis when he was forced to visit a doctor in Trinidad.

Kaiser Hansi with his favourite libation. Austrian expatriate Hans showed us a taste of the playboy lifestyle enjoyed by affluent Venezuelans in Puerto la Cruz. Note the cheeky label on the beer bottle.

Never say mañana. The Kuna Indian women paddled their dugout canoes over to Albatross everyday hoping to make a sale. Eventually, those pleading brown eyes worked their charm and I bought a hand-embroidered mola.

No turning back. Three boats lined together approach the giant lock gates of the Panama Canal at the end of which lies the daunting vastness of the Pacific Ocean. The only way to get home is to complete a circumnavigation.

Robinson Crusoe's island was bigger.
This sandbar rising out of the clear blue
Caribbean Sea north of Panama is one
of the largest of the 365 islands of the
San Blas archipelago inhabited by
the friendly Kuna Indians.

Cleanliness is happiness. Always a joy to wash off the salt water after a long passage, we Swedes are quick to strip off publically as here in Colón, Panama. Notice the decaying boats behind me, abandoned by owners unable to make the transit down the Panama Canal.

A drop in the ocean. The hotel of Porvenir, San Blas, boasted ensuite facilities just a short walk from your bedroom hammock.

Not blue water cruising. We battled a week of heavy weather on the way to the Galapagos Islands, but Carl remained positive between bouts of seasickness.

Ecstatic at the Equator. After 11 months of sailing, we crossed the equator line and celebrated with a bottle of champagne, a couple of bottles of wine, a few beers, some brandies and a massive hangover the following day.

Brokeback horses. Our transport on the Galapagos Islands ensured I would never sire children again. Carl looks a natural in the saddle while my reluctant steed and I plod miserably behind.

Lunar landscape. Ascending the molten rock of the Sierra Negro volcano on Isabella, the clouds finally lifted to reveal the astonishing view.

Head for heights. I became quite agile at climbing the mast to fix the wind generator. Of course, this was best achieved when becalmed or safely moored in harbour.

What's in a name? The phallic lava turrets of the bay on Fatu Hiva inspired the original name of Bay of Penises until prudish missionaries tweaked the French spelling to change it to Bay of Virgins.

No mod cons. Some of the most delicious bread we tasted on our journey came from a simple charcoal-fuelled oven in Fatu Hiva, although the flavour may have been enhanced by the odd chicken pecking at the dough as it was left to rise.

The boys are back. Felix, André and Toma, a charismatic trio of fishermen on the tiny island of Raroia, taught us much about island life in French Polynesia.

Demigods of electrical repairs. The 126 people on Raroia had been eagerly awaiting our arrival; for seven weeks we were occupied repairing everything from toasters to the atoll's satellite dish.

The world is our oyster. Working side by side with the pearl farmers on the atoll of Raroia for a week, we learned to how the precious pearls are cultivated and extracted.

Black gold. As reward for helping on the island and as a token of their friendship, the Raroians generously allowed us to dive for these pearls.

Bounty of the sea. As Carl's increasing girth testifies, we ate exceptionally well during our stay on Raroia, learning to catch lobster and coconut crabs armed only with a stick and a rubber glove.

Shirts optional. The Chinese owned shop in Papeete, Tahiti, became a regular haunt where we dropped in to drink beers with the locals under the ever vigilant eye of Fu Manchu.

Duty-free happiness. Before leaving French Polynesia and crossing to New Zealand, we stocked up on vitals in Nuie where the favourable prices made Carl weep with joy.

Yet another perfect paradise.
Anchored off the Bora Bora Yacht Club (to the left) to admire views of straw-roofed huts jutting out over sparkling waters and Mount Otemanu rising dramatically in the centre.

Nothing peaceful about the Pacific Ocean. Sudden storms and squalls could sneak up on us without warning leaving no time for photo opportunities. This was taken moments before the deluge descended.

Vikings versus giants. My parents, nephew Linus and I join hands to demonstrate the circumference of a massive Kauri tree in Northland, New Zealand.

EQUATOR
2066 nm   3827 km

VANCOUVER
6225 nm

LOS ANGELES
5709 nm   AA

TROPIC OF CAPRICORN
659 nm   1220 km

LONDON
10490 nm   19271 km

SYDNEY
1165 nm   2160 km

TOKYO
4911 nm   8831 km

Lovers' leap.
My son Dino and girlfriend
Sofia at Cape Reinga where
the Tasman Sea clashes with
the Pacific Ocean. In Maori
mythology, the spirits of the
dead leap off the headland and
descend to the underworld.

Scene of seduction but who was doing the seducing? Opononi Beach on Hokianga Harbour is glorious by day, but I first saw it by moonlight in the company of Anita.

Mr Fix it. One of the keys to our success was that as handymen and electricians we learned how to do many of our own repairs. If you can't, be prepared to empty the contents of your wallet to the professionals in port.

Maintenance is a necessary evil. After two years of sailing, Albatross' hull was thick with plant growth necessitating having her lifted out of the water and high pressure sprayed.

Love's middle-aged dream with Anita.

Hands off! Our dinghy was worth risking life and limb for, which Carl did one night when thieves in Fiji tried to make off with it. A naked Viking crashing through the moon-lit mangroves is an alarming sight.

Calm before the storm on the way to Fiji. Kiwi crewman David complained that the fine weather made for an easy passage and wanted to experience 'real sailing' in tougher conditions. Be careful what you wish for.

Island hospitality. Ponipate (pictured top centre), chief of the island of Vivo, invited us to his home to lunch with his wife and six children. His 12-year-old daughter (beside me) had bravely identified the dinghy thieves.

Tempting but beware the teeth and tentacles. The waters around Thursday Island at the very Northern tip of Australia are dazzling but potentially deadly; sharks, crocodiles and the lethal box jellyfish lurk in the shallows.

'You're never too old.' Czechoslovakian resistance fighter and eternal romantic Aldis had survived torture and imprisonment in his homeland before escaping to Australia. Despite limited seafaring experience, he was sailing to Europe to be reunited with his first love he'd left some 40 years earlier.

Breakfast at the local with the locals. German expatriate, Dirk, was an eccentric with a special brand of humour who'd found a new life on Rodrigues together with his wife Birgit. His day started with a liquid breakfast before taking tourists on big game fishing expeditions.

Racing on Avanti around the Fairest Cape. The South Atlantic waters off Cape Town are bitterly cold, but the scenery is stunning. We were invited to participate in the Table Bay International Sailing week, a fierce and furious five-day event.

Packed to the gunwales. Celebrating surviving a day's racing with the Avanti crew onboard Albatross where we hosted dinner for twelve people. When not on Albatross, the Royal Cape Yacht Club was our home from home.

Surprising stamina for his age. Jonathan the tortoise, St Helena's oldest resident at 182, roams the grounds in front of Plantation House on the island of Napoleon's final exile. Jonathan is still going strong and enjoys regular sexual trysts.

My new family on their best behaviour. Anita and her two youngest children, Shaun and Antonia, joined us for a short reunion in the Azores – our penultimate stop before our arrival in Sweden. The children may have been sedated with ice cream to pose for this photo.

We were so overwhelmed by the huge crowd which turned out to welcome us at Helsingborg harbour that we forgot all sailing basics as we approached the quay.

'We did it!'
Drunk with jubilation and champagne, we try to express our joy and thanks to the crowd at Helsingborg harbour. We were probably completely incoherent.

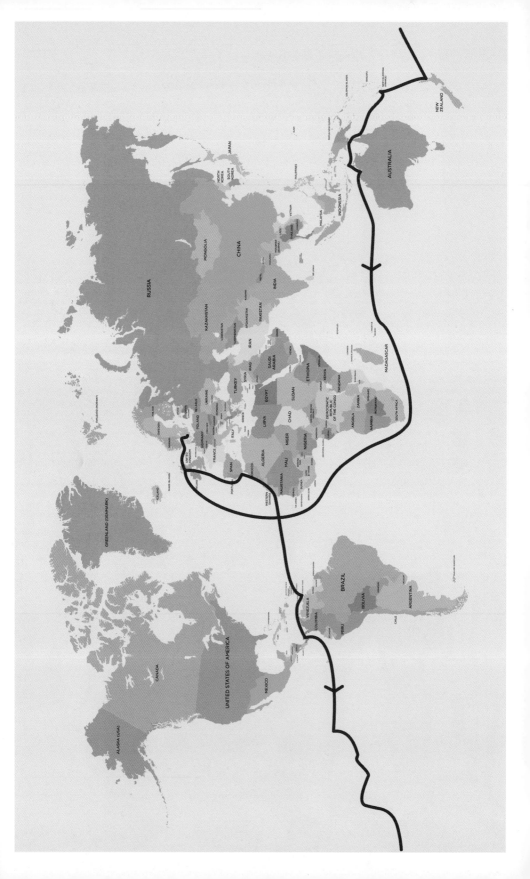

He jerked his head at the group of Indian men squatting on their haunches, clearly discussing us.

'And exactly how are they going to pay for her?' I asked. 'With chickens? Fish?'

'Don't be ridiculous,' Carl snorted. 'Lobster would be better. Ask for twenty lobster.'

'Lobster or chickens. It doesn't matter,' exclaimed Teresa. 'I'm not for bloody sale!'

'Are you sure, Teresa? You might get your own island out of it,' Brian said. Teresa shot him a look that spoke volumes, mostly consisting of expletives.

It was Saturday night and we'd been invited to a party on Isla del Rey by Miguel and Roheljo, two fisherman from the village of Esmeralda where we'd anchored earlier that day. As usual we'd asked the welcoming committee on board *Albatross*, handed out the beers and got the locals chatting, Brian translating as fast as he could between us. Isla del Rey was the largest island in the archipelago and the fishermen's home village of Esmeralda boasted a population of a thousand African Indians.

'We have our own school for children up to year six,' Miguel said. 'With four classrooms and a white teacher who is married to a local girl.' I couldn't tell which he was most proud of, the four classrooms or the novelty of having a white teacher.

'Yes, I myself have a wife and six children,' Roheljo said proudly.

'Pah,' Miguel said dismissively. 'That's nothing. Not like Hero.' We asked who Hero was.

'Hero has 13 wives and over a hundred children,' replied Roheljo, taking off his baseball cap as if in honour of the man.

'Holy crap!' Carl said. 'One wife's enough! Don't the 13 wives argue all the time?'

'Not at all,' Roheljo said. 'All the wives live on different islands and Hero visits each one at a time. If one wife is in a bad mood, he just paddles his canoe to the next island and finds one in a better mood.'

'That man's libido must be the size of Panama,' Teresa muttered.

'Yeah,' agreed Carl. 'Not to mention the size of his...,'

'Canoe,' Miguel said. 'He has a very big canoe. He has to catch a lot of fish.'

'I'm surprised he has the energy,' I said with reluctant admiration. 'So what do the other people of Esmeralda do for fun?'

'We drink beer and have cock fights,' Brian translated.

'Well, we know who wins those,' Carl said dryly.

'And on Saturday we have the village party. You must come,' Miguel said warmly, looking pointedly at Teresa.

'Yes,' Roheljo agreed. 'There's music and beer and dancing.'

So here we were, in a bar come motor repair workshop next to an island version of the village hall from where ear-numbingly loud reggae was being played for a group of gyrating adolescents. It doesn't matter where you go in the world, loud music in a dark room will attract loose-limbed, hormonally rampant teenagers. We were sitting at a plank that served as the bar, wrinkling our noses at the twin smells of grilled fish and rotting sewage, and peering through the dim light of a 20-watt bulb at our bartender/bouncer. His head was as round and smooth as a snooker ball and his eyes glinted as hard as crystal as he weighed up whether a customer had drunk too much and would therefore require evicting from the premises. Should the drunk prove reluctant to go, Snookerball could call for backup, the local reinforcements being the village policeman, somewhat overdressed in my opinion in a camouflage uniform, gleaming military boots and ostentatiously armed with a revolver in a hip holster. For "light" confrontations, he carried a hefty wooden nightstick which he twirled like a cheerleader's baton. Should the backup require more backup, the officer had a police cadet at his side, dressed in dark-blue overalls and equipped with handcuffs. I hadn't seen so much obvious security since the marina in Venezuela: what the hell goes on at the Saturday night rave-ups in sleepy, smelly Esmeralda, I wondered. Having said that, the cadet rather spoilt the effect by handcuffing his right hand to his belt and dropping the key in the dusty floor of the bar where he spent several minutes groping for it in the gloom.

'Four beers,' Carl said to Snookerball.

'No beers,' replied Snookerball. 'All sold out. Only white rum. One litre for five American dollars.'

'Okay,' Carl said. 'One litre of rum and four cokes.'

'No coke,' replied Snookerball. 'All sold out. Buy at the supermarket next door.'

'Well, I don't suppose there's any chance of ice and lemon then,' I said. We took a cautious sip of rum. I haven't had an oesophagus since.

'Man!' squeaked Brian, wiping the tears from his eyes. 'No wonder the Indians called it firewater; that burns all the way down.'

I went next door to the supermarket – a plastic-roofed room with shelves on the back wall displaying bags of rice and toilet paper. The centrepiece was a rusted Pepsi refrigeration unit which obviously hadn't worked since the 1970s. I bought four small bottles of warm cola and returned to the bar where Miguel and Roheljo had arranged a circle of eight wooden pallets into a configuration of table and chairs especially for us, the guests of honour.

'We don't get many visitors to our island,' Roheljo said. 'And they certainly don't stay in the village so everyone is very curious about you. Please, tell us about where you live.'

We drew a small crowd of locals interested to hear about Sweden. There were confused looks when we described the weather: try explaining snow to people who have only ever lived in a tropical climate where the temperature never dips below 21 degrees Celsius.

'How can you live so close to the North Pole?' a man asked us, shaking his head in bewilderment. 'Aren't you afraid the polar bears will eat you?'

'I want to know about your woman,' said another, pointing at Teresa. 'Do you have to share her?' Brian laughed as he translated for us.

'So how many wives do you have in the North Pole?' another local asked.

'Just one,' answered Carl.

There was much puzzled shaking of heads to this. 'That's not enough. You need more than one. What if you get tired of her?'

Carl turned to me. 'Do you want to explain divorce, Yanne?'

An old guy in his mid-sixties and as thin as a twig tapped Brian on the shoulder. 'Is the woman for sale?'

Teresa shook her head. 'Not that again,' she sighed. The old man shrugged and walked off. 'He's old enough to be my grandfather.'

'That was Hero,' Miguel said reverently.

'I guess the old guy has still got plenty of lead in his pencil,' Carl muttered.

The effects of the fire water became clear when towards midnight a few of the locals started to get rowdy. Snookerball refused to serve them more rum, leading to heated debates over the plank of wood. The village cop and his cadet stepped up, brandishing the nightstick and handcuffs as a reminder of what might happen if the troublemakers didn't go quietly. Most of them looked a bit shame-faced and staggered out, except for one Indian who put on a massive show of bravado, possibly in a misguided attempt to make a play for Teresa, by vehemently insisting that he was perfectly sober. This might have worked had he not walked straight into the door frame, knocking himself to the floor. He lay stunned for a moment, then got to his feet and made a second, successful attempt to exit. I could only admire his fortitude; had I received such a whack on the head, I would have been prostrate till morning.

On Sunday, Roheljo and his uncle gave us a tour of the village. As we walked around, we gathered a trail of half-dressed children of various ages who giggled whenever we turned around and winked at them. When we stopped to admire their school they all became very vocal, each one wanting to show us their classroom, which of the rickety desks they sat at and pointing out which of the coloured pictures taped to the wall was their masterpiece. When Teresa sat at a desk, one little girl put out a hand to gently stroke her hair and asked why it was the colour of the sand. They each peered at our faces and asked Roheljo if all foreigners' eyes were blue. When I took photos and videoed the children, they shrieked with incredulity when they saw themselves on the digital camera, clambering over me in their attempts to get a better view of themselves. We were as astonishing to them as the acts in a travelling circus. When I handed out a bag of lollipops, I had all the charm of the Pied Piper; never have I known such blind adoration.

Roheljo invited us to his house, a single-storey, breeze block building with a corrugated metal roof attached with rope to a wooden framework resting on the windowless walls. This was home for him and his wife and six children; he was immensely proud of it. We were humbled when he and the children loaded us with fresh fruit for our trip, coconuts and pineapples they'd gathered for us that morning in the jungle. The people with the least to give were the most generous in giving what little they had.

A surprisingly large band of children and adults saw us off that afternoon, waving and shouting their farewells from the beach. 'Come back again,' they called. I certainly hope to do so, but I wonder what sort of changes will have taken place in the decade since we were there. The potential of the Pearl Islands as a beach resort and leisure destination is quickly being realised. As I write, a group of European investors has begun work on a huge residential development of 500 waterfront homes, an airport, marinas and luxury amenities on Isla Viveros, the island just next to Isla del Rey.

They're paving paradise and putting up parking lots everywhere.

Chapter 31
Staggering in Darwin's Footsteps
27 April – 17 May 2003
Isla Isabela, Galapagos, Ecuador

Experience: *Sailing the route between the Pearl Islands and the Galapagos takes much longer than anticipated: expect to spend at least 500 miles tacking against headwinds.*

Tip: *In the words of Sir Francis Chichester: "Any damn fool can navigate the world sober. It takes a really good sailor to do it drunk."*

A fter two days, Brian finally emerged from his forward cabin looking as haggard as I've ever seen a man. His complexion looked bleached, his eyes were puffy slits and his long hair hung in greasy rat tails, even his beard looked ill.

'Feeling better?' Carl asked.

'Man, I hope so,' Brian groaned weakly. 'Cos if I'm going to feel worse, please just push me overboard now and end my misery.'

'Yup,' I said. 'This certainly isn't blue water sailing, but it'll pass.'

Brian rubbed his forehead with a shaky hand. 'Dear god, when? You said that days ago.'

Teresa passed him a cup of tea and patted him gently on the back. 'Poor boy,' she said. 'But look on the bright side, Brian.'

'I can't. It hurts my eyes too much.'

'You're physical proof that there is life after death.'

'I have to disagree,' I said. 'Look at him. He's clearly one of the undead.'

'He's only got himself to blame,' Carl said without sympathy. 'I told him to go easy on the brandy.'

Brian winced at the memory. 'I thought I could comatose myself and sleep through the weather. It was a kill or cure remedy. But now I can't tell the difference between the hangover and the seasickness.'

The first five days had certainly been a test of endurance, doing battle with

30-mile an hour head winds ever since we'd left Isla del Rey resulting in having to tack almost constantly. Brian and Teresa had had the worst of it, sleeping in the forward cabin where, as Brian said they were "bounced around like a kernel in a popcorn machine." It was tedious, heavy sailing and we'd had to run continuous watches. On the seventh day, sulky clouds gathered and a deluge poured from the sky, the wind increased even more and the waves grew in strength and size.

'Do boats like these sink often?' Teresa shouted over the wind and the slashing rain.

'No,' I shouted back. 'Usually only once!' Teresa didn't find my nautical humour amusing.

The elements eventually abated making sailing less hellish and more harmonious, so the following evening we were finally able to relax and swop life stories over a good meal and a bottle of wine. Teresa, who'd just turned 31, explained how she'd become a backpacker relatively late in life. She worked as a secretarial temp, taking jobs for six months and then travelling for the rest of the year. 'It's the perfect balance of work and sanity,' she said. She and Brian had hooked up in Costa Rica two years earlier. Brian, a Californian native, had earned a lucrative living as a computer programmer, but had woken up one day to find himself 30 years old with the complacent attitude and fat stomach of a prematurely middle-aged man who worked too hard, ate crap and saw only the tarmac to the office and back. So he'd quit his job, sold his luxury house and took to backpacking fulltime, travelling to Costa Rica to learn Spanish and lead a healthier, less consumer dependent lifestyle. He was a bit of a whiz kid with a huge memory for numbers which he'd put to dubious use with a bunch of computer nerds, amassing a fortune playing professional blackjack and breaking the casino banks.

'But those days are over,' Brian told us. 'I've always been the black sheep of the family, refusing to follow in Dad's footsteps, dropping out of college and all that. I'll never go back to a permanent job, either. It's all about simple pleasures now.'

'Hear, hear,' I said, refilling their wine glasses and raising my glass of water. 'To simple ... Shit!'

'Strange toast,' Teresa said. 'Is that typically Swedish?'

'No, look!' I said slamming down my glass and pointing to the cabin. Water was seeping up through the cabin floor.

Carl got to his feet. 'What the hell?' We both raced for the cabin. Water had already filled the void under the deck and was gushing over the wooden planks; we were clearly taking in a lot of water, but from where?

Carl and I looked at each other. 'The engine compartment!' we said simultaneously.

'Brian! Teresa! Get down here, bring the torches,' Carl shouted.

In the torchlight we could see that water was pouring through the area where the propeller shaft runs through the hull: the shaft was out of place and to our horror we realised that two bolts in the port engine mounts had broken in half. Of the four rubber pads each held in place by a bolt, only two were left which could not keep the engine in position in the rough conditions of the Pacific.

This was serious: we could sink.

'Hell! This must have happened when we were pushing the engine so hard in the Panama Canal, when we thought it was just a problem of the straps holding the hose in place,' I said. The bolt at the front must have broken long before; we hadn't realized the severity of the problem back in Panama.

'What the hell are we going to do?' Carl said, his voice rising in a panic uncharacteristic of him. 'We can't replace the bolts to remount the engine; we haven't got any more with the same thread.'

'The first thing to do is reduce our speed,' I ordered. Carl, Brian and Teresa shot up on deck to lower the sails while I rummaged frantically through our bag of assorted bolts we'd been given by Werner and Agneta, the German friends we'd helped on Union Island in the Caribbean. 'Please, let there be a couple of M14 bolts, just a couple,' I prayed. Of course, there weren't. But, praise Neptune, there were two M12 bolts that could do the job instead.

The next problem was lifting out an engine weighing half a ton and repositioning it to replace the bolts: a task which required the herculean strength of a team of young bodybuilders. Fortunately, just before leaving Sweden, our friend Nils-Gunnar had wandered along to *Albatross* one day and tossed us a strong strap able to take weights up to ten tonnes, saying to us, 'You never know, it might be useful.' Together with a large plank of hardwood which we'd salvaged in the Caribbean, we managed to hoist the engine into more or less the right position. Carl and I lay on our stomachs and slowly worked out the old bolts while Teresa held the torch and Brian manned the pump so we wouldn't sink in the meantime. Teresa was looking slightly tearful at this point, wondering if she'd ever see land again. Nobody said it but we were all thinking it: 'What if? What if this doesn't work? We're a thousand miles from land and what if we can't fix this?' The unspoken what-ifs hung over us like the sword of Damocles, the worst of them all being 'What if we sink?

The horizon was beginning to lighten as we finally restarted the engine. We watched, every muscle clenched with dread that all our efforts had been for nought. The drive shaft engaged and rotated without problems. We all drew a very heavy sign of relief.

'And that's the definition of cruising,' I said.

'What's that?' Brian asked, wearily putting down his bucket.

'Fixing your boat in exotic locations,' I replied. Teresa gave me a wobbly smile.

After the water deities had done sporting with us, we were rewarded with clear skies, a hot sun and a smooth ocean. Our moment of panic was over and we celebrated being above the water rather than below it.

'Right, this is more like it,' Teresa said emerging from the cabin in a bikini and sunglasses. 'Now, where are the dolphins frolicking on the waves like you promised me? If I don't see any dolphins, I'll never buy anything from IKEA again!'

'No dolphins as yet, but look,' I said, pulling up the fishing line. 'I've just hooked a squid. Something different for lunch today.'

Teresa looked at the large gelatinous mass on the hook with disgust. 'Really? Yanne, are you sure that's edible? It looks like something from a sci-fi movie.'

'Well, I've never cooked one before, but I'm sure I can do ... something with it.'

'And to think I was a committed vegetarian before I left Panama,' Teresa sighed.

Once I got rid of the ink sack and cleaned and chopped the squid, I sautéed it quickly in garlic and olive oil. 'What do you think?' I asked everyone as they chewed uncertainly on it. Brian smiled. 'Marvellous!' he said.

At 9:10 p.m. on 8 May 2003, we sent champagne corks flying over the deck of *Albatross*. We had just crossed the Equator, a momentous occasion, which required celebrating by following a tradition which has changed little since the eighteenth century: the age-old ritual of Crossing the Line in which "pollywogs" – crew who have not crossed the Equator before –take part in an initiation ceremony and undergo various tests to the satisfaction of the "shellbacks" – crew who have already crossed the Equator. We were all in fact "pollywogs," a detail we didn't mention to Brian when we threatened to shave him of all his body hair. In navies around the world, many a poor young seaman loses his eyebrows and pubic hair during an equatorial crossing.

The party atmosphere on *Albatross* grew more spirited, enhanced by the champagne and Abba's *Dancing Queen* ringing out from the CD player. I broke my self-imposed ban of not drinking alcohol during a passage, had a couple of glasses of the bubbly, and we danced like devils in the cockpit: after all, you don't have to be Swedish to agree that *Dancing Queen* is one of the greatest songs of all time. Brian and Teresa agreed that Abba was a terrific group, so we agreed to open more champagne and toasted to that. We agreed on and toasted to many things: that we should play some Frank Sinatra; that we should open a couple of bottles of wine; that Carl and I sang *My Way* even better than Frank; that the dolphins swimming beside *Albatross* were sent by Neptune himself on this propitious occasion; that a glass or two of brandy would go down well; that we should all follow our dreams and to hell with the rest of the world; that we should have a few beers. And when Teresa announced that her dream was to pole-dance naked on deck using the mast as the pole, three red-blooded males fell over themselves in their rush to agree with her. While her modesty didn't prevail, safety did: we insisted she at least wear a lifejacket and clip on her lifeline.

The following morning, we felt a bit blurry as we gingerly emerged to a scene of post-party debris: champagne and wine bottles, beer cans and an empty brandy bottle rolled around the cockpit. Carl had fallen asleep, or more accurately passed out, on watch, but fortunately *Albatross* had been on autopilot in calm seas so we'd come a hundred nautical miles closer to our destination without mishap. Brian and Teresa finally appeared, both clutching their heads and blinking like moles in the watery sunlight.

'Great night,' Teresa whispered, wincing as she spoke.

'I can't remember a damn thing about it,' Brian said.

Teresa gave him a look that could have stopped a Sherman tank. 'Well, I can. You threw up, said you hated me and gave me a long list of all my faults.'

'Oh, right,' Brian said, looking unconcerned. 'Good times, then.'

We'd expected the temperature to rise around the Equator but instead it dropped several degrees; we were in the cold waters of the Humboldt Current which flows along the west coast of South America from southern Chile to northern Peru. It supports an abundance of marine life, already evident in the variety and quantity of fish I was catching and our frequent sightings of dolphins, rays, seals and sea lions. Nights were clear, allowing us to admire the magical constellation of the Southern Cross and the burning tail of a comet as it fell through the heavens.

Finally, after a mixed voyage of 13 days we sighted the Galapagos Islands. As we sat on deck, watching them come into view, my sense of excitement increased: five years ago they had just been dots on a map, a destination very few are fortunate to reach, and now here I was: sailing the very waters which had brought a 26-year-old British scientist to the islands in 1835, where he started a process of research that would lead him to many of his conclusions in *On the origin of the Species by means of Natural selection*. To think that I would be walking in Charles Darwin's footsteps was strangely thrilling to this middle-aged electrician. It was my equivalent of "See Naples and die," except I wanted to see a giant tortoise and live another 40 years.

Located where three ocean currents converge, the 19 islands of the Galapagos are relatively young, sprouting only five million years ago out of the Pacific from a suboceanic lava vent on the ocean floor. They've been dubbed "a unique living museum and showcase of evolution," due in part to their isolation and the ongoing seismic and volcanic activity. We were heading for Isabela, the largest and youngest island at only a million years old and one of the most volcanically active places on Earth. We anchored in the stunningly clear bay on the south-eastern edge of Isabela next to the port village of Puerto Villamil, the island's only settlement, and took the dinghy ashore where we were welcomed by a committee of sea lions slumbering on the beach and the dock. They lifted their heads briefly at our arrival, then curiosity satisfied they went back to sunning themselves. As we climbed onto the dock, a female sea lion lazily flicked her long eyelashes at me and gave a happy grunt before curling up again cat-like on the wooden bench normally reserved for tourists awaiting their tour boats. I swear she was smiling.

There were several sailboats in the harbour; Villamil has become a popular stop catering for tourists visiting the living laboratory of the Galapagos. The residents of the village traditionally earned a living either through agriculture or fishing, but over the years the government has attempted to curtail fishing and increase tourist-based activities: a contentious move which resulted in violent confrontations in the 1990s and 2000s between locals and the Galapagos National Park service, including the capturing and killing of giant tortoises by the fishermen in an attempt to obtain higher sea cucumber quotas.

Teresa gave a contented sigh as we stepped ashore. 'At last, solid ground,' she said. I thought she might drop to her knees and kiss the sandy streets. After days of being battered and bruised in the "popcorn cabin," she and Brian decided to look for land-based accommodation and found a room with balcony for just $8 in a two-storey breeze block house on the main street, actually the only street and probably at that time the only so-called hotel.

We cleared in *Albatross* with a sociable harbourmaster and then meandered down the street to get a feel of the place, greeted by locals with friendly smiles and welcoming handshakes. When Darwin arrived on *HMS Beagle*, the islands were unpopulated, inhabited only by animals who had no fear of humans having never encountered them. A Dominican friar, Tomás de Berlanga, officially discovered the Galapagos in 1535, when strong currents accidentally drove his ship towards the islands. His written account describing the giant tortoises, the hostile topography and the difficulty of finding water indicates he was not much impressed with the place. Over the following five centuries, the islands attracted Spanish buccaneers, whalers, fur sealers, fishermen, scientists, colonists and finally tourists, all of whom have affected the flora and fauna, wreaking extensive changes on the delicate ecosystem. The increase in tourism has, of course, led to a surge in the islands' human population, increasing from 2,000 in 1960 to over 30,000 in 2010, many of the new residents drawn by the money to be made from the all the trappings that accompany the tourist industry.

Although Isabela is the largest island, it has a small population of 2,200 inhabitants. Joseph was one resident who'd moved from Peru to Villamil to make his living as a guide, taking tourists on tours of the volcanoes that make up Isabela. The island's seahorse shape is the result of the merging of five large volcanoes into a single land mass. His tour rates suited our wallets, so we booked an excursion with him for the following day. Together with the Finnish crews of two sailboats out of Helsinki, we clambered onto the back of a small truck on which we bumped towards the centre of the island. As we climbed higher leaving the lush coastline behind, we were greeted by a terrain of rust-red earth and ash-coloured Palo Santo trees. Feral goats grazed on the scrub and watched us with disinterest as we bounced past. The air grew heavy with rain, and clouds descended to meet us as we ascended. After about eight miles, Joseph stopped the truck by a field where a few bow-backed horses nibbled at the greenery. We all climbed out and stretched.

'So, do we hike the rest of the way to the volcano?' I asked.

Joseph laughed. 'Non, is too far to Sierra Negro. We have new transport here.'

The only transport I could see were the horses which looked as if they dated from Darwin's time. 'Oh crap!' I said.

'What's the problem?' Carl asked. 'Never ridden before?'

'Never needed to. Never wanted to. I'll go back to *Albatross* and get the bike.'

'*Non, non,*' Joseph said, bringing forth a sad-looking beast with the blank eyes of a depressive and a back so curved it had practically caved in. 'He is very kind horse. His name is Colorado.'

I looked at Colorado the kind horse and Colorado looked at me. He immediately recognized a coward when he saw one and bared his yellow teeth: it was not a kind smile.

'I think my horse is broken,' I protested to Joseph. 'Or hung-over.'

Carl looked at the horse with a quizzical eye. 'Don't worry, Yanne. I'm not sure that animal even qualifies as a horse.'

All the Finns were eagerly climbing on their animals, so it was a matter of pride that as a Swede I showed no fear and did so, too. Colorado allowed a couple of thin blankets and a cushion to partly fill the hollow of his back and reigns of rope were tied around his neck. I tentatively patted his side. 'I don't like this anymore than you do, my friend,' I confided to him. With Joseph's help I was hoisted over. Once on, the poor beast's back caved even lower so my sneakers were all but scraping the ground. I had a suspicion I would be carrying Colorado the kind horse back if we ever made it as far as the volcano.

Colorado wasn't so much obedient as ready for the glue factory – he reluctantly plodded forward without the will to do anything else than follow the horse's arse in front. The trail was a well-worn path through espino, a spiny bush on whose red berries Darwin's finches feasted, but the landscape became increasingly barren as we climbed higher. After two hours of being jostled along, I was mighty relieved when we dismounted and tethered the horses in the shade of a large tree. I'm not sure who was in more pain: Colorado or me, although Colorado's nether regions certainly must have felt better than mine. I feared my testicles would never be fully functional again. I could, however, appreciate why John Wayne had walked in that peculiar way of his.

The final two-mile ascent up the gentle sloping sides of the Sierra Negra was on foot. It felt like climbing on the surface of the moon: a landscape of barren molten rock hardened into whirls where lizards scurried and the occasional lava cactus flower bloomed. As we neared the top, the acrid smell of sulphur stung our noses. We were now at an elevation of 3,670 feet and on the rim of the second largest volcanic caldera in the world. As we gathered on the edge, the gods smiled on us and allowed the clouds to part as if to showcase the view in all its wonder. The six-mile diameter caldera resembled a huge upturned soup bowl where steaming fumaroles indicated how volcanic gases had found escape routes via tiny cracks or long fissures. Rather worryingly, the cauldron appeared to sizzle and bubble as if the volcano was coming to the boil again.

'Um, how often does it erupt?' I asked Joseph.

'Sierra Negra? Last time he erupt in 1979. See, many lava rivers to the ocean.' He pointed to black paths that cut through the terrain towards the north coast. 'He erupt every 20 years so maybe...' Joseph shrugged as if to indicate it was just a matter of minutes before the next eruption.

I looked at Carl anxiously. 'I hope it's not too soon.'

'I'm sure they have some kind of monitoring system in place,' Carl said.

Yes, they do, but despite GPS monitoring on Sierra Negra, there was no advance warning of the eruption in October 2005 when the volcano blew so violently it sent an ash cloud 25,000 feet high and lava fountains of nearly 1,000 feet tall. Fortunately, there was no loss of human life, although 1,200 acres of National Park land was engulfed in the ensuing lava fires.

The return journey started out briskly; Colorado was a different horse on the downward trail; it was as if he'd shaken off his hangover and found the will to live again; he even attempted to canter, inducing screams of pain from me and the belief that I would never sire children again. A bucket of oats was the explanation for Colorado's renewed lease on life. When Joseph produced bottles of cold beers from a cooler, I immediately shoved mine between my legs; I was not the only one to do so. I have not ridden a horse since, nor will anything or anyone ever induce me get back in the saddle.

The Galapagos Islands are named after its famous saddleback-shelled tortoises, as *galápago* means "saddle" in Spanish. I'd been looking forward to seeing these giants, and Isabela is home to more wild tortoises than all the other islands. Joseph explained how Isabela's topography created natural barriers for the slow-moving tortoises. Their inability to cross the lava flows and other obstacles resulted in the evolution of several different sub-species of tortoise. Shell size and shape vary between populations: on islands with humid highlands, the tortoises are larger with domed shells and short necks, whereas on islands with dry lowlands, the tortoises are smaller with "saddleback" shells and long necks. It was these differences which contributed to Darwin's development of his theory of evolution.

Unfortunately, the tortoises' lack of speed was almost their doom as visiting pirates and whalers gathered them for food – apparently their meat was just too delicious to resist; William Dampier, a seventeenth-century British pirate based on the Galápagos islands, described them as "extraordinary large and fat, and so sweet, that no pullet eats more pleasantly." Even *HMS Beagle* left from the Galápagos with over 30 adult tortoises on deck, not for scientific study as one would have thought, but as a source of fresh meat for the Pacific crossing. Their numbers thus declined from over 250,000 in the sixteenth century to just 3,000 in the 1970s. Happily, conservation efforts have resulted in a programme to release captive-bred juveniles onto the islands, and it's estimated that their numbers exceeded 19,000 at the start of this century.

We were advised not to get too close to the tortoises, there's no need to as they're certainly big enough to observe, reaching weights of over 880 lbs – approximately the weight of a Harley Davidson and its rider combined - and lengths of nearly six feet. They truly are remarkable creatures and together with the marine iguanas are reminders that our prehistoric past is not so far behind us. Sadly, the most famous tortoise of them all, 'Lonesome George,' passed away in 2012 at the relatively young age of a hundred. Great hopes had been placed on George's reproducing as he was the last surviving Pinta tortoise, but a mate was unfortunately never found for him. With his death, another subspecies has disappeared forever.

We spent a couple of days exploring this zoo without cages, virtually tripping over the wildlife. May is a particularly good month to be on the islands and Nature entertained us with colours, displays and performances not to be found anywhere else in the world: flame red Sally Lightfoot crabs scuttling sideways over dark lava rocks; the sea pink with flamingos poising like models on elegant legs; black marine iguanas thawing out in the sun, all but invisible against the black rock on which they lay; the courtship dance of the aptly named Blue Footed Boobies, doing high kicks with their feet of a such an intense blue they looked as if they'd been dipped in Dulux paint. But of all the animals, surely the sea lions were the most endearing with their long eyelashes and smiling mouths. They gambolled like puppies in the water; one even swam up to the jetty with a stick.

But nature is as cruel as it is beautiful. We watched aghast as a sea lion pup flopped over to a female who languidly flicked it into the air with a flipper. Female sea lions only take care of their own, so orphans are doomed. A male sea lion was bellowing in pain from large bite marks, no doubt the result of fighting a dominant male. The males compete for females with an aggression I'd not seen since a pub brawl in Peterhead.

Despite employment provided by tourism, many locals still made their living in 2003 by harvesting sea cucumbers – then a legal occupation. These worm-like echinoderms live on or near the ocean floor and feed on tiny particles. Young fishermen risk their lives free diving up to depths of 120 feet to pluck these animals off the seabed. They are then dried, salted and sold to Asia where they are highly valued for their supposed curative and aphrodisiac properties. However, these marine equivalents of earth worms perform an important role in the ecosystem of the Galapagos, and when overfishing caused their numbers to plummet, the Ecuadorian government imposed a ban on all sea cucumber fishing in 2005. This inevitably led to poaching and a rampant black market. A pound of sea cucumbers changes hands on the islands for approximately $1, but will fetch up to 80 times as much in a shop in Seoul or Hong Kong. We came across a group of fishermen unloading their catch from a small boat. One young man proudly showed me a sea cucumber, a rubbery spotted mass which I wouldn't have eaten dried, pickled or doused in a champagne sauce. The odds of it enhancing my sex life seemed as remote as my enjoying it as a starter.

As we wandered, stopping at the iguana crossing –the only controlled crossroads in town – I considered how much damage we were doing as visitors to this Eden. What kind of footprint were we leaving just by passing through? The Galapagos Islands are one of the most fragile environments on Earth, but it is also one of the fastest growing economies in South America due to the explosion in tourism over the last decade. Clearly the increased population puts a strain on the environment. Conservation groups are doing their best to curtail its effects while at the same time recognising that responsibly managed tourism is an important source of income for Ecuador. Not that everything can be blamed on the twenty-first century visitor; pirates in the eighteenth century introduced goats, donkeys, pigs, dogs and cats to the island, all of which have taken their toll on the endemic species resulting in the extinction of several. However, luxury hotels offering rooms at $300 a night, rooftop Jacuzzis and boutique shops are being built to accommodate tourists: a far cry from Teresa and Brian's simple room. The ecotourist is advised to shun such upmarket places and go more local to curb the necessity for the building of yet more luxury accommodation.

In 2007, the islands were added to UNESCO's List of World Heritage in Danger because of threats posed by invasive species, unchecked tourism and overfishing. Fortunately, in July 2010, the World Heritage Committee decided to remove the Galapagos Islands from the list because it decided significant progress had been made by Ecuador in addressing these problems.

But back in 2003 as I watched a feral cat stalk fledglings and rats scurry over a small rubbish heap, I wondered even then what Darwin would say if he could see his Eden a century on. I'm sure he would be gravely concerned for the survival of all Earth's species.

Chapter 32
The Coconut Milk Run
18 May – 10 June 2003

The Pacific

Experience: *Sailing the Pacific is like being in a horror movie; at the beginning everything seems quite normal, but you know that something evil lurks under the surface. Eventually, all hell will break lose.*

Tip: *Don't eat everything you catch.*

"'The Pacific Ocean is the largest of the world's five oceans,'" I read out loud to Teresa and Brian. "'It covers an area of approximately 60 million square miles. It is larger than the total land area of the world and about 15 times the size of the United States.'"

Teresa looked up from packing her rucksack. 'Well, that's 60 million good reasons not to continue.'

'Sure?' Carl asked. 'You're going to miss some of the world's most beautiful destinations by leaving *Albatross*.'

"'Its average depth is 2.8 miles,'" I continued reading, "'but the deepest known point in the ocean is the Mariana Trench which plunges to a depth of nearly 7 miles.'"

'Cool,' said Brian.

'No, not cool,' Teresa said dryly. 'Just very deep.'

'It says here that due to the depth of the Pacific Ocean, tsunamis can reach speeds of 450 miles an hour. Bloody hell, that's the same speed as a jet aircraft.'

'Impressive,' Brian said.

'Still not tempted?' Carl asked.

Teresa zipped up her backpack with a final flourish. 'Definitely not. I'll take my chances on a plane across the Andes over a possible tsunami any day.'

'Oh, come on,' I said. 'Ferdinand Magellan called it the "peaceful sea" because of its favourable winds so it can't be that bad.'

Brian shook his head. 'I'm with Teresa. Anyway, our plan was always to head to Peru, but we're sorry to leave you guys.'

Carl and I were certainly sorry to see Teresa and Brian sign off. We'd enjoyed their company for the last month, but they'd decided to continue by boat to the neighbouring island of Santa Cruz and from there fly to Ecuador and then on to Lima. We always felt a little flat losing new friends, particularly as we were facing our longest voyage yet when Carl and I would be a crew of only two. I'd been quietly speculating who would be the first to give into the urge to push the other over the side.

Carl and I agreed on most things and on the whole we rubbed along without too much friction despite having quite different personalities: Carl is bluff and speaks his mind to the point of extreme bluntness while I'm generally less forthright, tending instead to mutter darkly and fume about my grievances. But if there was one subject that made me furious enough to want to plunge a knife into his back or leave him bound and gagged on a barren rock in the middle of the ocean, it was on the subject of sailing with full sails. Whenever Carl was on watch, he would let out the sails so *Albatross* heeled in the wind, which is just fine if you want to get somewhere fast, but unreasonable if you don't want to be tipped out of your narrow berth because the boat is at an angle of 65 degrees. I spent many hours gripping the edge of my bunk, digging my fingernails into the wooden sides only to relax, drop off briefly and find myself rudely pitched onto the floor again. I'd fume, mutter darkly for a bit, then finally stomp up on deck and scream, 'Reef the bloody sails in, you old fool.' And the old fool would shrug and say in a gruff voice, 'My watch, my decision, Yanne. We'll never get anywhere if you reef in all the sails. We might as well be sailing with a hanky.' All of which would lead to a tussle over the ropes and bellowing abuse at each other. But our rule was whoever was on watch was captain and the captain had the last word. Carl refused to see my perfectly valid point, although I suspect he sometimes did but refused out of sheer stubbornness to admit I was right. When we changed watch, I'd immediately reef in the sails only for Carl to let them all out again as soon he took over. We still argue about it 10 years on. There's a lot to be said for single-handed sailing.

Speaking of which, the first solo circumnavigation was completed in 1898 by 54-year old American Joshua Slocum who sailed out of Boston in a decrepit 37-foot oyster dredger which he'd rebuilt himself. His book *Sailing Alone around the World* describes some wild adventures including being chased by pirates in the Mediterranean, running aground at Uruguay, tortuous sailing through the Straits of Magellan, battling hurricanes in the Pacific Ocean and navigating the reefs of Tobago without any charts because they'd been eaten by his pet goat which he called "the worst pirate on the whole voyage." After three years and a journey of 46,000 miles, Joshua entered the history books as the first man to complete a solo circumnavigation. And his navigation equipment to achieve all this? Just the stars and cheap tin clock: a far and humbling cry from today's circumnavigators who are armed with enough electronic gizmos to launch their own satellites. The goat, incidentally, did not make it all the way round but was eventually given to a man with a large pot and a gleam in his eye.

Since leaving Panama, Carl and I had gradually taken to heart the "don't worry, be happy" approach to life favoured by small island residents. With each additional mile between us and Sweden, we seemed to shed another layer of stress, becoming more relaxed than a hippy after a marijuana breakfast. We worried far less about completing all the jobs on the "effing to do" list and *mañana* became not just our catch phrase but our philosophy. Even so we were still vigilant when it came to boat safety, knowing it is better to be over than ill prepared, so we used our last couple of days in the bay off Puerto Villamil to check *Albatross* thoroughly and buy supplies for the forthcoming voyage of 3,200 miles. If all went well, we would see land in about three weeks: if it didn't, who knew when or if we'd walk on terra firma again.

Looking at the pile of groceries we'd amassed on the pavement outside the small shop, it appeared as if our main concern was starving to death. We certainly weren't going to die of scurvy: we'd bought 20 coconuts from a local farmer and a bunch of green bananas the length of an ironing board; around the cabin, we'd suspended pineapples and peppers on ropes to ripen, looking like weird Christmas decorations; we had sweet potatoes, tomatoes, cucumbers and eggs en masse. We nearly sank the dinghy as we attempted to get the load back to *Albatross*.

Carl and I were doing what is disparagingly called in some sailing circles "the Coconut Milk Run," meaning that we'd chosen the easy way to cross the Pacific, i.e. from east to west. Our goal was to follow the route with the best weather and the most reliable trade winds, bouncing from the islands of the Marquesas, the Tuamotus, French Polynesia, the Cook Islands and Tonga before sailing to New Zealand where we would wait out the cyclone season. While the weather varies from season to season, this route avoids as far as possible the South Pacific Convergence Zone where the frequency of extreme weather is greater.

While diehard sailors sneeringly call it the Coconut Milk Run, it's still not a voyage for the timid. The distances are vast and when something goes wrong there's no assistance handy. If you happen to be within lucky reach of land, the island ports are small and marinas with adequate service facilities are few and far between. Boats can become stuck in remote locations awaiting spare parts or even a boat specialist to be flown in to make vital repairs. Nevertheless, such is the siren call of the South Pacific that every year there are estimated to be approximately 400 yachts attempting the Coconut Milk Run because it is an astonishing journey across the ocean, chasing sunsets and being pursued by sunrises.

That's *if* Carl doesn't insist on sailing with full sails the whole time, and *if* I don't push the stubborn old fool overboard before we arrive at the Marquesas. As we weigh anchor and head out into the open Pacific, the odds are even against. But as we sail towards our first sunset, a pod of around 20 dolphins appear and entertain us with their graceful acrobatics. We feel it's a good omen.

Day 1

We set up the fishing gear at the stern and soon see two grey fins cutting through the water towards the bait. The sharks swim in intimidating figures of eight around us as that music from *Jaws* goes round my head. It looks disconcertingly as if they are eyeing us up more than the bait.

Day 2

Something has taken the bait and half the line in the night, no doubt one of the sharks. Call me a coward but I'm very reluctant to put my hands anywhere near the surface of the water after that. Later in the afternoon, we come upon a super-pod of several hundred dolphins chasing down a shoal of fish. The sea is alive with leaping dolphins, their gleaming silver skins catching the light. It's magical. Nature puts on the best shows.

Day 3

It's lonely out here so we're quite excited when we sight our first boat after three days of sailing: a large fishing trawler which gives us a wide berth.

We've now settled into our routines and have established the watches; I take the watch from 18:00 to 00:00, then Carl takes over until 06:30.

Day 4

I've just slipped into a sensational dream about cavorting with Miss Venezuela when Carl hoists all the sails and I am rudely pitched out of my bunk. I grab the frying pan, stomp up on deck, clobber him with the frying pan and throw his inert body over the side where the previous day's sharks enjoy a feeding frenzy.

Well, not really, but I'm sure some readers were hoping for a bit of murder and mayhem. Carl did hoist all the sails, *Albatross* keeled and pitched me out of bed and I did look thoughtfully at the frying pan before climbing back into my bunk and resigning myself to clinging to the sides as usual. I began to envy Joshua Slocum and his goat.

Day 5

The nights are cloudless and a universe of stars lights the ocean. We watch the arc of a satellite as it orbits the Earth over the equator. Every night we tune in to listen to Karsten in Panama who gives us valuable information on the weather. Dedicated radio hams like him volunteer their time to track the Pacific crossings of small boats. Their invaluable contribution adds to the security and comfort of an undertaking like this. We join the roll call every night and give our position and information about our course, speed and local weather observations. It's an enjoyable ritual to listen to the other check-ins and hear about the progress of fellow yachtsmen. We learn how other Scandinavian friends have turned homeward from the Caribbean and are heading for the Azores via Bermuda. Karsten warns us that a low pressure front will be followed by bad weather.

Day 6

We spend the morning clearing the deck of dozens of flying fish that fell like rain during Carl's watch. We use some of the smaller fish to bait the fishing hooks.

One of my few hidden talents is the ability to sew, having learnt during a brief career as a shoemaker, so I get out the sewing machine to repair our Swedish ensign which has got very tatty. Then for want of anything else to do, I make matching blue covers for each of the four winches in the cockpit. Then I rustle up a cover for the compass. Carl whets the Gotland sandstone and sharpens all our knives. Is it just my imagination or do I detect a malicious glint in his eye as he does so: I'd just reefed in the sails when he announced he thought the knives were too blunt. *Too blunt for what?* I wonder.

Day 7

Sunday: a day of rest, but it isn't as the generator begins to fuss. We discover that the drive belt has come off. We fiddle and curse at it for a while and eventually replace the drive belt.

Day 8

The mercury is creeping up again as we move west. Warm winds from the southeast increase our speed to eight knots. We finally take down the gennaker which has been up for six straight days, hoist the genoa and the staysail and hold a steady course. We relax and read.

Day 9

At sunrise we check the line and find a 10-pound dorado which will feed us for a couple of meals. In general, we eat very well: breakfast and lunch consist of fresh salads made from the fruits we bought at Puerto Villamil; dinner is the catch of the day with pasta or boiled potatoes cooked in the energy efficient pressure cooker. Carl praises my cooking effusively and I put away the frying pan thinking to myself, 'You'll never know how close you came...'

Day 10

I get out the sewing machine and make a cover for the outboard motor. I wonder if I should make a matching cover for Carl...

Day 11

The wind lulls during the night, but as the sun rises a light breeze picks up and so we raise the spinnaker for the first time. It looks and feels glorious as the wind billows out the sail and we fly over the waves.

To change the routine a little, we decide to make pancakes for breakfast following Carl's daughter's recipe. After gorging on half a dozen pancakes with fruit and syrup, we lie back in the cockpit enjoying the sound of the lapping of the waves against the hull.

Day 12

We hook a two-foot eel-like creature on the line so ugly it would give Freddy Kruegger nightmares. We have no desire to cook it, so we throw it back in the ocean with a shudder of revulsion. God knows from what depths that has risen.

Day 13

The wind is still favourable and we sail 170 nautical miles today, our furthest distance in one day to date. The windvane self-steering system continues to work well: the increasing wind pulls *Albatross* to port but the self-steering gear adjusts the course.

Saturday night is our bandstand night when Carl and I take it in turns to play our favourite music. We reminisce at length over some of the golden oldies: such is the power of a song or a piece of music to bring back memories from when we were younger with a clarity so keen we can both relive all those feelings of excitement, awkwardness and anticipation of those years as if it only moments ago.

Day 14

Sunday: the sun shines from a clear blue sky, the wind is fair and we relax with our books.

Day 15

We enjoy an extra hour today as we have to turn back the clock one hour for every fifteen degrees west we go. We are now 120 degrees west and 10 hours behind Sweden (DST).

In the afternoon the weather turns threatening; the ocean begins to swell and the early whispering wind increases to a deafening roar. The waves grow fiendishly tall and swells increase them to the size of hills. This so-called peaceful ocean is anything but. As the wind strength increases, we make the sails smaller, then smaller still. We triple-reef the mainsail and the jib looks like a handkerchief corner. *Albatross* is lifted high on these white-tipped monsters and surfs the crests, but now and again, BOOM, one slams against the side of the hull making the mast shudder.

Day 16

The weather continues to batter us although the wind dies down a little. We sight a freighter on the starboard side that is having a rough time of it, ploughing east in the winds. We're grateful we don't have to tack in these enormous waves. The freighter disappears up and down in the huge troughs: now you see her, now you don't.

Day 17

The weather calms and the sun rises against a clear blue sky, washed clean and fresh by the distant storm. During the night, a giant fish eats our bait, hook and all. We set up a new hook with bait made from a rubber glove with two angry fish eyes drawn on the palm part. This works surprisingly well and we catch a large dorado weighing 13 pounds which I fillet for the freezer. Now that we are approaching French Polynesia, we need to be careful about which fish we eat as some are toxic. Ciguatera is a very nasty form of food poisoning caused by eating reef fish whose flesh is contaminated with toxins from eating smaller fish who feed on poisonous coral or algae. Ciguatoxin is odourless, tasteless and heat-resistant so contaminated fish cannot be detoxified by cooking. Of course, if Carl continues to hoist all the sails ...

Day 18

So much for the fine weather: rain showers, squalls and gusting winds chase us all day.

Day 19

Today, 6 June, is Sweden's national day so in a burst of patriotic fervour Carl and I salute our nation's flag and sing *Du gamla, du fria*, bellowing out the lines 'Yes, I want to live, I want to die in the North' with particular irony seeing how we are in the South Pacific. Our triumphant chorus is accompanied by a cloud burst and it pours with rain for the rest of the day. It seems the weather gods have a sense of irony, too.

I construct a new signalling device to alert us when a fish bites by attaching an empty beer can on a thick rubber band which is released when the line is stretched taut by a biting fish and clangs against the anchor mounted on the aft. The noise wakes even Carl who snores like a Harley.

Day 20

The wind has abated and the waves are calm so we raise the spinnaker and sail a straight course towards our goal: the island of Hiva Oa. With only 392 nautical miles left to go, we feel like we're home free. It's a glorious day of blue water sailing; the Pacific is finally living up to its name. The beer can alarm sounds and we land a magnificent dorado. The freezer is packed solid.

Day 21

We turn back the clock another hour as we complete another 15 degrees to the west.

Our speed is slowing and we realize that *Albatross*' hull has accumulated a lot of algae and shells; it looks like lush farmland at the waterline. We'll need to scrape the hull thoroughly when we next get into port.

Day 22

The GPS displays only 140 nautical miles to Hiva Oa; we should make land with just one good day's sailing. Unfortunately, the weather gods read my mind and send strong squalls and gusting winds. Sailing in this is one thing: cooking is another, becoming a test of agility and endurance mastered by few. We have a hankering for pancakes so Carl disappears to whip up a batch. When I hear swearing so appalling it would make a TV chef blush, I know there's been an accident. I check below and see Carl standing in a pool of batter; sticky yellow liquid drips down the cabin walls and from the ceiling.

'Are the pancakes done yet?' I ask. Carl makes a noise at me like a grizzly bear about to attack. I leave him to clean up.

Day 23

At 09:15 we finally sight land in the west: the Marquesas Islands glimmering like emeralds on the horizon. We open a couple of cold beers and clink our cans together.

'Here's to French Polynesia and a voyage well done,' I say.

'And to not killing each other in the process,' Carl says.

'I never even thought about ...,' I begin, but the guilty expression on my face belies my attempt at denial.

Carl shakes his head and smiles. 'What? You think you're perfect, mate? There were times I was ready to smoother you with my pillow, you moody bastard.' He takes a gulp of his beer. 'And your bloody snoring is louder than the generator.'

Chapter 33
Crazy Pigs in the Land of Men
10 June – 10 July 2003

Atuona Baie, Hiva Oa, – Baie des Vierges, Fatu Hiva – Baie de Taiohae, Nuku Hiva, The Marquesas Islands, French Polynesia

Experience: *Sell, trade or swop any junk you have no use for: used clothes, makeup, bags and books will all be appreciated by the inhabitants on these remote islands.*

Tip: *Keep the hull clean below the waterline as organism growth will slow speed. But remember to use only phosphate-free and biodegradable cleaning products sparingly so that excess detergents do not enter the water.*

'If there is paradise on earth, it is here, it is here, it is here.' When Amir Khusrau Dehlavi, a prolific Persian poet wrote those words in the fourteenth century, he was describing his beloved Kashmir, but his words seemed just as fitting for the idyllic scene Carl and I were presently gazing upon.

Fatu Hiva's Baie des Vierges (Bay of Virgins) momentarily robbed us of the power of speech: it was stunningly beautiful. I know I've raved at length about many picture-perfect views but this was jaw-droppingly wonderful. And before you accuse me of hyperbole, let me say that novelist Robert Louis Stevenson, artist Paul Gauguin and singer-songwriter Jacques Brel would have agreed with me: they also succumbed to the sultry charms of French Polynesia's Marquesas Islands; Gauguin and Brel are both buried on one of the sister islands, Hiva Oa. We drew breath, closed our mouths and I got out the camera, knowing full well that even the most gifted photographer would be unable to capture the magnificence of such a view: the play of light on the water and land has to be seen.

We had arrived at the most remote archipelago in the world, 15 volcanic lumps in French Polynesia discovered and named by a Spanish explorer in 1595, now owned by the French. Called in the local language, "the Land of Men," the islands seem anything but that: a land-that-time-forgot landscape of verdant green rainforest suggested that the islands were uninhabited, claimed only by creeping vegetation. The Bay of Virgins on Fatu Hiva, where we had anchored, is bordered on both sides by huge rock formations rising straight out of the water like green skyscrapers over 1,000 feet in height; the mountains behind are lush with impenetrable forest contrasting with a strip of white sand beach and the translucent turquoise water. The phallic looking lava turrets clearly inspired the original name of the bay, Baie des Verges, (Bay of Penises) but horrified missionaries were quick to make this appellation more chaste by tweaking the spelling, thus renaming it Baie des Vierges.

The water around the islands wasn't just inviting, it absolutely begged us to dive in but we knew better: when we'd first arrived at island of Hiva Oa two days earlier, we'd anchored in Atuona Bay and plunged straight off the deck. During our 23-day voyage, we'd taken the chance now and then while the sea was at its most calm to slow *Albatross* down as much as possible so we could take a dip, but we'd always been nervous of sharks; one of us would remain on deck and frantically scan the ocean for a tell-tale fin while the other swam in panicky circles. So it was blissful after more than three weeks at sea to luxuriate in water as warm as consommé. It was only when we went ashore to the village to clear in, that we learned how islanders and crews from the other yachts in the bay had been placing bets on how long we'd last before a tiger shark rolled in to pick one of us off. We'd mistaken their frantically waving for an enthusiastic welcome.

The population of the islands suffered greatly as a result of the diseases brought by Western explorers, decimating it from over 78,000 inhabitants in the eighteenth century to a little over 4,000 by the beginning of the twentieth. Although the population now lies at approximately 8,500, no island has more than a couple of thousand inhabitants, so most of the villages on the islands are mostly one-shop, one-church, two-goat places, where chickens, ducks and puppies run in and out of one-room houses and pigs are kept on long leashes until dispatched for a holiday feast; the "street" chickens belong to the village and are fair game for anyone's cooking pot. We were astounded by the abundance of fruit; trees seemed to drip with limes, oranges and enormous grapefruit. Bushes, shrubs and palms drooped with papayas, breadfruit, guavas, bananas and coconuts. The Polynesians are a seafaring people, famous for their navigation and unique boat designs: the catamaran, a double canoe, is in fact an ancient Polynesian invention; they were built 100 to 150 feet long to carry hundreds of people from one island group to the next. The individuals who paddled these canoes across the vast stretches of the Pacific never suffered from scurvy, a cause of death for many a European sailor, as they loaded their vessels with vitamin C rich citrus fruits.

The Marquesas are very different from the Galapagos Islands: there are no giant tortoises and few birds to admire; there are no coral reefs to attract the variety of fish found around other atolls, although there are plenty of sharks. The pleasure was in meeting the residents of the islands and discovering their traditions and culture. No one passed us without giving us a smile and we felt ourselves to be more guests than tourists. Many offered us fruit in exchange for whatever we had, requesting children's clothes, make-up, medicine and alcohol. Alcohol, however, is strictly forbidden on the islands as the islanders have a very low tolerance level and quickly become loopy on a shot of anything stronger than cough medicine. Nevertheless, they gently pestered us on the off chance we might be ignorant of this fact. While we refused to sell them alcohol, we did rummage around *Albatross* and fill a sailing bag with old jeans, shirts, pens and assorted bits and bobs. Everything went like butter in the sun and we returned to the boat with armfuls of food. We also sold the sailing bag to a merchant in the village for a payment of cash and onions. Items such as cars, fuel, medicine and anything that can't be made on the island is brought on a cargo ship every two to three weeks, but between deliveries the Polynesians enjoy trading for whatever their visitors will swop. However, I drew the line at trading a pair of jeans for a pig, much as a pork chop would have been a welcome change from fish for dinner.

The most sophisticated business on Fatu Hiva was the bakery, located in the least sophisticated building on the island that looked more like a dilapidated chicken coop than a bakery. We'd placed an order for three loaves of bread the previous evening and arrived the following day to find three large loaves waiting for us, as perfectly browned as swimwear models and tasting better than any bread we'd had on our journey so far. It was astonishing what the baker could produce from a wood-fired stone oven with a recycled sheet of metal for a roof. We promptly ordered three more loaves for the following day.

'I give you chicken and pig; you give me whiskey, rum, bullets and sexy cards.' It was not the sort of deal I expected to conduct with an elderly grey-haired man, the owner of a small plywood-built shop that looked as if a strong gust of wind would blow it to the next island. We were buying pasta and flour when he surprised us with his request. I shook my head, knowing the sale of alcohol was not permitted on the islands, but the 'sexy cards'? I could only surmise that the supply of porn was low and a "striptease" pack of playing cards satisfied a certain demand. The best I could have offered was the label from a bottle of Venezuelan beer featuring a pert pair of buttocks, but I worried it might lead to a riot.

'Why do you need the bullets?' Carl asked, while I was still pondering which came first: the chicken or the porn.

'There are many crazy pigs in the jungle,' the shop owner replied with a frown. He explained that the traditional way of catching a wild pig was to stalk it, corner and attack with a large hunting knife, hoping that the animal wouldn't suddenly turn on you. Unfortunately, the feral pigs were beginning to outnumber the humans. Although guns were illegal on the island, there was a demand for ammunition for the weapons hidden under mattresses or in the palm-frond roofs to keep the swine population under control.

'Sorry,' we shrugged. 'We can't help you.'

'A pity,' said the old man with a sad smile. 'And I suppose you don't know anything about fixing that,' he added, pointing to a dusty fax machine.

'Now, there we can help you,' I said. We earned a couple of chickens in return for our expertise.

It wasn't long before our reputation preceded us and we were sought out by Sopi and Serge, brothers who invited us to their home/workshop/gallery where they showed us their tiki carvings. Polynesian tiki statues have been a symbol of power for centuries in the South Pacific; archaeological remains of stone statues featuring deities with large eyes, wide grinning mouths and larger-than-life male members –possibly the reason for the grinning mouths – litter many of the islands. We bought two small wooden carvings and left with numerous electrical items that we promised to repair. Sopi had entrusted us with a nineteenth-century book from which he wanted us to scan and enlarge several pages of tattoo patterns. He wrapped the book in a clean cloth as lovingly as if it were the Gutenberg Bible and pressed it into my hands, saying in French, 'Please, promise me you will not show anyone this book. It is most precious.'

The ancient tradition of tattooing is still highly prized amongst the people of Oceania; techniques and motifs date back 2,000 years, and each island within French Polynesian has its own unique designs, making it possible to identify a person's origins based on their tattoos. Within Polynesian societies, the master of tattooing was a highly trained and esteemed individual who determined not only the designs but who could be tattooed and when. It was considered a spiritual calling and the master's lifestyle was therefore restricted to avoid tainting himself or his work lest he offend the gods and his gift of tattooing be taken away. I'd always associated tattoos with Popeye or hairy bikers, but as we rubbed shoulders with the islanders, I began to have a new respect for the art: the complex geometric designs and polygonal symbols carried stories and meanings well beyond the "I love Mary" type. As our taxi driver around the island of Nuku Hiva said when I asked him about the intricate markings covering his chest and arms: 'A necklace can break, my house may fall down, but my tattoo is a jewel that I will take to my grave.' I could now appreciate why Sopi and Serge were concerned about the book of tattoo patterns. When we gave the brothers the printed enlargements, they fell over us with gratitude, rewarding us with a large tiki carving, two drawings made on tree bark and their eternal friendship.

During the nineteenth century, the Catholic Church played a major role in destroying native culture by attempting to subdue "the savages" by banning tattooing, native dress, dancing, drumming and other religious practices. Fortunately, native culture is undergoing a healthy revival, although the islanders remain deeply Catholic. Tattooing is making a comeback and the native Marquesan language, still spoken at home, has been added to the school curriculum. Ironically, the pagan traditions of drumming and dancing that the missionaries tried so hard to stamp out are now integral parts of Easter holiday festivals. The hypnotic thumping of drums lured us off the boat one evening to a volleyball court-sized clearing where approximately fifty teenage girls and boys were practising an ancestral dance, shaking hips, grass loin cloths and tail feathers as they performed the Haku manu, the bird dance. As fifty voices chanted in unison, hands pounded on hollowed-out tree-trunk drums and lithe figures whirled before us in the moonlight, I wondered at the missionaries' determination to eradicate a whole culture: I would have joined it in a drumbeat.

Midsummer Eve was upon us again; we'd left our families over a year ago and were nearly 14,000 nautical miles from home. *Albatross* was the lone boat anchored in Fatu Hiva's Bay of Virgins, all our neighbouring boats having sailed on, but we knew we'd catch up with them sooner or later; it's a small sailing community this far off the grid and we would keep bumping into each other. It was our first midsummer without our usual Swedish fair of herring, potatoes, strawberries and drunken mischief, but we grieved the lack of them only very briefly: homesickness was becoming an unfamiliar feeling. Here we were watching the midsummer sun turn the volcanic peaks orange recalling their lava-formed past, while in Sweden loved ones were rubbing the sleep from their eyes as they got up for a new day, moaning about how it was the wettest summer since the previous year.

We set a course northwest the following day for Nuku Hiva, the largest island in the archipelago. It was a surprisingly tough sail with 35-mile an hour winds whipping up swells and colossal waves that broke over *Albatross* and filled the cockpit on several occasions.

'This is as bad as the North Sea,' Carl shouted as another torrent of water crashed over the deck and into the cockpit. When the darkness finally lifted, we could glimpse the peaks of Nuku Hiva through their necklace of clouds. We sailed into the deep U-shaped cove of Taiohae Bay, the inlet of which is protected on each side by a rocky island, and anchored beneath towering green mountain peaks shivering with silver waterfalls. The island has a rugged terrain; steep cliffs plunge down to the sea and jagged ridges separate deep valleys. There are no reefs or lagoons surrounding the island, so the ocean pounds on its windward coasts. The lifestyles and livelihood of the 2,600 inhabitants are greatly influenced by the island's remote location and environment.

The main town of Taiohae, the administrative and economic capital of the Marquesas, still has a sleepy South Pacific feel, but nevertheless looked relatively prosperous for a small island community. We were mildly surprised to see some residents zipping about in spanking new four-wheel drives.

We set off on foot to explore, but friendly drivers stopped to offer us rides up and down the steep mountain sides in the back of their pick-up trucks. We pilfered limes from the trees that grow throughout the island, found numerous over-grown stone platforms, testament to Nuku Hiva's first settlers 2,000 years earlier, and admired dramatic waterfalls and astonishing views when not shrouded in clouds and rain.

The only fly in the ointment was the ferocious no-no fly, indigenous to the Marquesas and most common on Nuku Hiva. This vicious little horror breeds in the freshwater streams and pools which appear so tempting to the salty sailor after a long passage. Unlike a mosquito which pierces the skin with a neat hypodermic needle, the no-no fly takes a sizeable bite out of the skin, creating an itchy welt. We'd learnt our lesson after the sand flies in the Caribbean so we lathered on the repellent. I would have gladly wrapped myself in several layers of plastic film to avoid getting bitten.

The islands were undeniably beautiful with some of the most stunning views we had seen to date on our journey. Yet it is the memory of the people we encountered throughout our journey that stay with me: friendly smiles from all, beautiful brown-eyed children ready to laugh and make faces for the camera, generous hospitality from those with little to give. We made new friends among the islanders and other travellers alike. A *boules* evening was arranged in the village and all the crews of the visiting yachts in Taiohae Bay were invited to participate; every single one came, bringing something to eat and drink for this impromptu party where we exchanged our sailing stories in broken French, stilted English and whatever smattering of other languages we'd picked up. Many of the faces were familiar; some of them we'd met during our journey from Europe, but others were new: crews of American sailboats who'd sailed from Alaska, Canada and the United States.

We were all ages, shapes, colours and sizes. But one thing united us all: sailing off the grid to these Islands of Men had fulfilled an ambition in each of us.

Chapter 34
Catching Crabs
in the South Seas
10 July – 12 August 2003
Raroia, Tuamotu, French Polynesia

Experience: *Don't rush. Stay in the places you visit and get to know the people there. Good friendships with the locals create some of the longest lasting memories.*

Tip: *Always check the gender of the person flirting with you.*

I was looking at limp sails. As any man knows, limpness is a frustrating condition and I was frustrated now.

We were becalmed. After two days of brisk sailing, all trace of wind had completely vanished, leaving us to gaze morosely at a motionless ocean; nothing moved, not a ripple, not a cloud as far the eye could see. The air was still, the water glassy and the sun hot. We didn't need the anemometer to know we were in the doldrums, but despite myself I kept checking it; each time the numbers were still stuck at zero. We were at least 200 nautical miles from land and there was nothing to be done but wait. And wait. And wait.

'Relax,' Carl said, peering over the top of his book. 'The wind will come back. Go for a swim. At least we can spot the sharks more easily when the water's so calm.'

'I can't relax when I don't know how long I have to relax for,' I said. 'We've been drifting for 16 hours already. And with no wind, there's nothing to power the generator. Who knows how long this could last.'

In the golden age of sail when a ship was becalmed for more than a day, a rowboat was launched to pull it into an area of wind: an exercise in futility if ever there was as a rowboat of six or eight men might manage to move the ship 10 miles or less in a day. It did, however, serve to keep an otherwise idle crew busy and I suppose deprive them of the energy to mutiny. I stood on the deck, scanning the horizon for a tell-tale wisp of cloud and calling upon the winds like King Lear, but there was no blowing of winds nor cracking of cheeks, until the following day when the wind came back with a vengeance.

'Are you kidding me?' I shouted to no one in particular. 'From zero to hurricane force in an hour?' The sails, which had been hanging so loosely, were now straining to burst in the 50-mile an hour winds, so we reefed in and reefed in again and rode the breaking waves. Now we had energy to waste with the generator working overtime. The following day, we reduced the sail even further to lower our speed; we were aiming to arrive at the difficult strait in the atoll of Raroia at 10 a.m. the next day so we could sail in on the slack and navigate the reef.

Raroia is an oval-shaped atoll in the Tuamotus chain in French Polynesia, located 465 miles northeast of Tahiti. There is only one navigable waterway leading to the central lagoon that few sailboats bother to visit. Tourism isn't much developed on the atoll, one of the reasons that drew us here, as well as the fact that in 1947 Thor Heyerdahl became stranded here with his craft Kon-Tiki after a 101-day journey from Peru.

Like most Scandinavians, I was familiar with the story of the voyage of the Kon-Tiki, an anthropological expedition mounted by Norwegian Thor Heyerdahl to prove the feasibility of ancient sea routes between South America and Polynesia. The six-man, one-parrot crew of the Kon-Tiki, a balsa raft lashed together with hand-woven line, left Peru and sailed west, carried along on the Humboldt Current for over 4,300 miles before crashing onto a reef at Raroia. Fortunately, the crew and the parrot made it safety to land. Bengt Danielsson, the only Swede in the crew, later settled on the atoll together with his wife for three years during which time he wrote several books, including *Raroia: Happy Island of the South Seas*. We wanted to investigate just how happy the island was.

If, of course, we could get onto it. Another fabulous South Sea paradise was calling us across water so clear and sparkling it could make me poetic. For five days we lay alone anchored between two reefs buffeted by gale force winds. We didn't dare leave *Albatross* despite being anchored fore and aft as she was dancing and twisting in the gusts. Our concerns were that the anchors weren't dug down deep enough, that they would drag, that ropes would chafe and snap, that a swell would carry our beloved bird off, so we stayed on board. Janne on *S/Y Noah af Stockholm* radioed us and recommended crossing the lagoon, another eight nautical miles, to anchor on the east side of the atoll where there was more shelter, but we didn't want to chance "doing a Kon-Tiki" and crashing on the reef, so we stayed put. The wind generator produced electricity as never before and the watermaker was in full swing, so we were sitting windswept but pretty and on our own. The crew of *Noa af Stockholm* radioed us every day to swop news and remind us that the islanders were waiting for us. Janne had told them a Swedish boat with two electricians/mechanics would be arriving any day. Apparently, the Raroians were queuing up with items they hoped we could repair.

But meanwhile, like a needy girlfriend *Albatross* was demanding care and attention. We used the five days to catch up on boat chores, having found that despite constant maintenance there was always work to be done, although we were becoming progressively less pedantic about being slaves to the "effing to do" list. We took the time to read up on the island, keen to know what awaited us when we finally did set foot ashore.

Raroia belongs to the Tuamotu Archipelago, the largest chain of islands and atolls in the world covering an area of the Pacific Ocean approximately the size of Western Europe. Originally settled by Polynesians, the French claimed and colonized the Tuamotus during a frenzy of Catholic missionary activity in the 1880s. They have remained under French administration ever since; hence, the inhabitants of Raroia, a total of 126 people in 2003, speak the local language of Pa'umotu and French. Although our French was improving, Carl and I were still linguistically challenged, back to nodding and smiling. The main settlement on Raroia was the town of Guarumaoa where there was an elementary school; children had to travel to the larger island of Makemo to attend secondary school. This was the most remote place with the smallest population we had yet visited, making Fatu Hiva with its population of 550 look crowded and cosmopolitan in comparison.

By Thursday, the weather had improved enough for me to take the dingy ashore while Carl stayed on board *Albatross* "just in case." Garumaoa was a short one-road village with 20 or so simple buildings squeezed between the coconut trees, the largest of which was the pristine white-washed church. It took me one minute to walk through the town to the lagoon where I came across a man hitting an outboard motor with a spanner.

'*Un* problem?' I asked. At least the word "problem" was more or less the same in French. After a few words and a lot of gesturing, I managed to understand that André, a muscular, smooth-chested fellow in his late thirties, was a fisherman whose livelihood lay in his fishing boat. Unfortunately, he hadn't been able to get the motor to work for a couple of months and his only recourse had been to punish it by clobbering it with a hammer now and again. His face lit up like the sun when I said Carl and I could help him out the following day.

I turned back to the beach and the reef to the west and got talking, or gesticulating, to Felix, a spear fisherman who stood poised on a rock stabbing at the ocean and tossing fish into a bucket beside him as easily as if he were picking flowers. When I introduced myself and told him I was from Sweden, he nearly dropped his spear on his foot and shook my hand vigorously, his dreadlocks bouncing merrily. '*Je suis très content de vous voir. Nous vous avez attendu avec impatience*,' he said. Never had our arrival been so keenly anticipated. Our reputations as repairmen had clearly preceded us; I just hoped we wouldn't let them down. Imagine the frustration you feel when you're waiting for the washing machine repair man to arrive during that six-hour window, only for him to say he'll have to order the parts and come back next week. The villagers had been waiting months and their income depended on the help we could give them. The pressure not to disappoint was growing.

I returned to *Albatross* loaded with fish and a list of jobs Felix had given me. Carl went ashore and returned some hours later with a corked bottle of the local hooch and a lopsided grin.

'And just where have you been?' I demanded peevishly. 'Dinner is ruined.'

'You'll never guess who I met?' he slurred with a sheepish smile. 'The only French Polynesian in the South Pacific who can speak Swedish.'

It turned out Carl had been warmly received by the village chief Rondo who'd assisted the author Bengt Danielsson and his wife when they lived on the island in the 1950s. Rondo was advancing in years but still remembered plenty of Swedish, in particular numerous swear words which he used liberally in conversation, suggesting that Bengt might have been a bit of a foul-mouthed grump. Rondo and his friends also had several items in need of repair which Carl had promised we'd look at when we could. At this rate we could spend half a year on the island just fixing things.

Felix lived in a two-room house on the outskirts of town together with two friends, Toma and Fiu. All three had come from the Marquesas three years earlier to work for André on the pearl farms where the precious black pearls were harvested and processed. A decent boat with a working outboard motor was essential for their job; if we couldn't repair theirs, they'd have to return to the Marquesas. Felix, Toma and Fiu were a cheerful trio and clearly loved their way of life. Their accommodation was very basic – I've seen more luxurious one-man tents: they slept on mattresses on a rough-finished concrete floor and stored their clothes in a cardboard box which doubled as a table. The kitchen was furnished with a gas stove and a plywood table on which three cooking pots and some plates were arranged. There was no running water in the house, or on the island for that matter, but water was drained via a hose from a water butt on the roof. Nevertheless, these young men were no tramps: everything was tidy and their clothes clean. I wondered that they chose to live in such a small, remote community. Here were three men in their prime whose good looks and muscled torsos could have got them the pick of women. Felix, in his late twenties, was the youngest, with movie star looks, big brown eyes, a beguiling smile and long rock-star hair that would have drawn women to him like Playboy bunnies to Hugh Hefner. Hell, I was attracted to him: clearly, I'd been on the boat too long with Carl. The boys had a six-week break at Christmas, during which they went back to their families on the island of Tahuata, a boat journey of more than three days in favourable weather.

Carl and I looked at the first engine and quickly determined that the errors were in the electrical system and the starter. While I worked on the electrics, Carl took apart the engine, cleaned all the parts and put it back together again. We drew quite a crowd, all apparently impressed that we had a range of tools other than just a hammer and chisel. By evening, we'd reassembled the engine and were ready to do a test run. The crowd had swelled to most of the village, the pressure was on. 'The moment of truth,' Carl muttered and turned the ignition key: nothing happened. There was a collective sigh of disappointment in us. Damn! What had we done wrong? '*Pas de problème,*' we bluffed. We took the engine apart again, checked the wires and carbon rods and by chance found our error, put it back together and started the engine. The crowd which had started to drift away came running back again when they heard the smooth humming of the motor; they all cheered and applauded. We'd managed to pull the rabbit out of the hat after all and the boys' jobs were saved. Beer bottles clinked all round and we sat down to a celebratory dinner of fish and rice prepared by Felix. We ate under the begging eyes of three large dogs, two puppies and a very small kitten. 'Don't worry,' Toma said, 'they live well on all the scraps we feed them. Nothing goes to waste.' Over dinner, the boys asked us if we could help them with other items that needed repair: their diesel generator had broken down, the stereo didn't work and the satellite receiver had no audio. Could we take a look at another motor boat? Then there was the deputy chief's generator which didn't work properly: the list went on. Carl and I agreed between ourselves that we would do what we could for as long as we could.

Although over 9,000 miles as the crow flies separate Raroia from France, the islanders were as immersed in French culture and traditions as strongly as if they were in the heart of Paris, maybe more so because the island wasn't diluted by expatriates or foreign immigrants. So we were a little bemused to find ourselves invited to the island's Bastille Day celebrations on 14 July. The party was attended by all 126 inhabitants, Carl and myself for a day of football, boules, javelin throwing, barbequing and beer drinking; I never understood the reason for the javelin throwing part of the festivities: it seemed to me an incautious mix of pointed missiles and alcohol. Nevertheless, we joined in with the preparations.

It's customary in South Pacific cuisine to bake bread and slow-roast meat in an underground oven, for which a large pit measuring approximately five by eight feet and three feet deep was dug in the sand. The bottom of the pit was lined with a foot of coral stone that was heated up by burning a layer of wood on top. When the flames died and the embers glowed, a large mesh basket filled with individual parcels of woven palm leaves containing meat, chicken and dough was lowered into the pit. This was then covered with a layer of leaves, upon which were placed large jute bags, two panels of corrugated steel and half a foot of sand. All this was prepared the night before the festivities so that the food slowly cooked overnight and was ready for the village feast the following day. When the oven was opened, the sweet aroma of freshly baked bread and the spices of the meat summoned everyone to the feast faster than a dinner gong.

It was a jovial party even before the beer started flowing. Tahitian music played on a boombox; children ran around, clapping and dancing; the ladies had dressed for the occasion with crowns of bright exotic blooms. The most striking lady at the party wore the largest crown of red flowers to match a vivid floral dress and scarlet lipstick. She seemed quite enamoured with Carl, flirting outrageously with him: winking at him one moment, then acting coy and demure the next. 'Be careful, Calle,' I said to him as I watched with amusement his increasing embarrassment at his admirer's attentions. 'You've already got one wife.' After a few beers, the village beauty eventually staggered off to relieve herself against a palm tree with equipment not possessed by any lady I've ever met. There was applause and affable laughter as she adjusted her dress, smoothed her hair and wove her way back to the ladies' table. Even in a society as small as this, there was room for all sorts and all sorts were tolerated. I think the only judgement passed by her peers was that she overdid the lipstick a bit.

By the end of the day, Carl and I felt as if we'd known everyone on the island for years, from the local fuzz who couldn't hold his beer, to the five guys with homemade guitars who set up in the small town hall and played music so mellow Elvis himself would have sat back to listen. Goosebumps prickled down my skin as guitar chords blended with the sound of the waves rolling onto the shore.

André, Felix and Toma were keen to test drive the newly repaired engine and invited us to join them for a day on the lagoon snorkelling and harpoon fishing. Like many of the atolls of Tuamotu, the economy of Raroia is based on fishing, copra cultivation and pearl farming. Our lagoon, as we were beginning to think of it, had an area of 225 square miles and supported 15 pearl farms. As we sped across the water, shifting patches of bright blue and turquoise sparkled before us, indicating where the coral reef rose and fell: a perfect feeding ground for fish, both friendly and fierce. Toma cut the engine in the middle of the lagoon near the reef edge and André handed out the harpoon guns.

'*Restez près de nous.* Stay close,' he said. '*Et faites attention aux requins. Il y a beaucoup de requins.*' I'd just jumped in the water, harpoon gun in hand when I heard the word "requins" but what did it mean again? Rocks? Currents?

'Sharks?' asked Carl, with a leg hovering over the side of the boat. 'Il y a sharks?'

'*Oui*, sharks, requins,' nodded André. Brilliant! Here we were harpooning fish which would bleed in the water: catnip for sharks.

'Well, the water's so clear, you'll see the sharks coming early enough to panic,' Carl said optimistically. Ironically, Carl was in charge of the catch box, to which any shark worth his dorsal fin would be immediately drawn as it was the bloodiest place of all.

Both André and Felix were excellent free-divers and took off after a huge fish 40 feet below; Felix fired his harpoon, struck it and hauled it to the surface and flung the fish to Carl who threw it in the catch box. I was unpleasantly aware of the sharks swimming lazily below, keeping watchful slanty eyes on us. When they became too curious and swam towards us, André whipped his right hand up and down in the water which seemed to dissuade them from coming closer. Eventually, I forgot about the sharks and got the hang of using the harpoon, managing to spear one fish in a dozen. But the catch box was getting full enough to splash blood on the surface of the water and lure the sharks. Carl had a nasty "brown boxer" moment when a shark made a beeline for him. He propelled himself through the water and threw himself onto the reef, waved to Toma on the boat and screamed, 'Empty the catch tray!'

We took the catch to the boys' house and Felix prepared dinner. The smaller fish were cut into chunks and left to marinate in lime juice, coconut milk and spices for 30 minutes. This was eaten as a salad to accompany an aromatic fish stew served with boiled rice. Simple but wonderful food, and there was no doubting the freshness of the fish.

One of the main commodities on Raroia which drives the economy is copra, the kernel of the coconut. Long used by Pacific island cultures, it was a valuable product for merchants in the mid-eighteenth century and today is primarily a smallholder crop. Copra was originally grated and ground, then boiled in water to extract coconut oil but today the process is simplified and the copra is crushed. We saw long neat stacks of coconut halves drying in the sun; after two days the meat can be removed from the shell with ease and the shells are left to dry for another three to five days whereupon they are packed into jute bags and shipped to a distribution centre in Tahiti. Copra meal is used as a fattening fodder for horses and cattle as it is high in oil and protein, and the oil is used in the cosmetic industry. It's extremely labour intensive work and will never make the Raroians rich; back in 2003, they received less than a dollar per kilo for their trouble.

With only one general store on Raroia, however, the islanders had little opportunity to spend their money. The store's shelves would become increasingly empty with each passing week until the monthly arrival of the supply boat, the appearance of which caused great excitement. The first we knew of it was when we became aware of a general dash out of houses towards the small quay one morning.

'What's happening?' Carl asked a large man lumbering down the village road.

'*La bière est arrivée*,' he panted and jogged on. Ah, beer! Hence the rush. We followed him to the quay where most of the village had already amassed to help with the unloading process, receive packages or greet friends arriving from Tahiti. A large freighter was anchored offshore and boats were buzzing backwards and forwards loaded with provisions. Pallets were unloaded onto the dock with the aid of the island's digger, driven by the policeman. Then everyone bustled to help sort and stow the goods, chatting and laughing. The beer, washing detergent, sweets for the children and toilet paper had finally arrived: all was well again. When everything was finally unloaded, the motor boat returned to the freighter, this time disturbingly overloaded with villagers wanting to visit the ship's large store where they could buy extras. The only way of boarding the freighter was to climb up a rope ladder dangling down the ship's side, but young and old were scaling it like determined ants. Somewhere in the fray was Carl's "lady friend" keen to buy new eye shadow.

Communication between us and the locals had been made somewhat easier by the friendship of 29-year old Henri who acted as our interpreter; he spoke excellent English having spent three years in New Zealand. He was a conscript in the French Foreign Legion, something I connected with Beau Geste, the desperate on the run looking for a new identity and the lovelorn trying to dull the pain of rejection. But Henri laughed when I asked whether he was on the lam or heart-broken.

'No, the Legion doesn't accept hardened criminals anymore, but recruits must assume a new name on joining and only speak French, even for swearing and there's a lot of that.'

'So why join?' we asked him. Surely not for the brutal training regime, fighting to the death or the salary of only £1,000 a month?

'For a shiny new rifle, a white hat, a French passport and good wine,' Henri replied. 'The legion has its own vineyards in Provence and after three years, I can apply for French citizenship, and I get a full pension after 15 years in the Legion. I've already served eight so by the time I'm 36, I can retire to Raroia.'

Henri was due to return to his unit in France after visiting his uncle on the island: another excuse for a village party and we were invited to the feast to which I promised to bring a video I'd made of the Bastille Day celebrations. We arrived to find a small TV set up on a table in the garden with the whole family, including dogs, cats and a 350-pound black pig named Pata-pata, patiently waiting for us, keen to view the film before the food was served. The video was greatly appreciated; children and adults alike loved seeing themselves on screen, even the pig laughed. It was a fitting farewell to our friend and interpreter Henri who gave us a standing invitation to visit him at the Foreign Legion garrison in southern France. I was surprised to hear they were allowed visitors.

Like many atolls in the Tuamotus, the Raroians depend on pearl farming, which has largely replaced copra and fishing as a source of revenue in the South Pacific. We'd been on Raroia a week when the factory manager of a small Chinese owned pearl farm situated a few miles south of our lagoon, a young girl named Jessica, asked if we could repair their electrical system, essential for operating the water pumps and drills required in the pearl farming process. Felix took us out along the lagoon to a remote peninsula in a sheltered bay between the corals. On the way we passed an oyster farm, the green-purple shells visible through the clear water.

'Oh look, a turtle,' said Carl, pointing to starboard. 'He's a big one.' Carl was right; the turtle's shell must have measured over three feet. As we leaned over the side to get a better view, the boat's engine was cut and there was a sudden splash as the skipper dived into the water armed with a harpoon. He re-emerged a few minutes later and hauled himself back into the boat with a sour look on his face, clearly annoyed at having missed. We later learned that turtles are considered pests in this part of the world because they eat the oysters in which the black pearls are grown.

Pearl farming is an arduous process for both oyster and farmer; the latter may either use divers to collect mature oysters to use for pearl cultivation, or they can be raised from scratch. Young seed oysters are caught, kept in underwater rearing lines and washed with a spray hose every three months to prevent algae from killing the oysters. When aged between three and five years, they are ready for cultivation, whereupon each oyster is taken from the water, fixed to a support and held open with forceps. A "grafter" uses a scalpel to insert a graft that acts as an irritant causing the oyster to secrete the nacre which forms the layers of a pearl. Normally, it takes another 18 to 24 months to grow a pearl but only 5 to 10 percent of oysters implanted will produce a perfect pearl: hence their high value; the price for an individual pearl can range from $50 to $2,500 depending on its size, lustre, colour and purity. However, the prices for "black gold," as the black pearls are known, have dropped over the years from $100 per gram in 1985 to less than $5 in 2010 due to overproduction of low-quality pearls.

Jessica, her husband Gerard and half a dozen workers lived on the small farm – a house perched on posts in the shallows of the reef – throughout the year, returning to their villages every other weekend. One of the divers, Natua, spoke English well enough to explain the problem about the generator to us, but we quickly established that the main fault lay in the diesel generator. Unfortunately, it needed a part that had to be ordered, so we had to make a return trip a week later. After several hours stripping down the machine and fitting the part, there was a familiar moment of nervous anticipation. Would it work? Carl and I exchanged anxious glances but were rewarded by the satisfying roar of the generator as it sprang to life. Jessica hugged us, the men patted us on the back and there were smiles of gratitude all round. Our halos glowed with having helped out.

As the saying goes, "Give a man a fish and you feed him for one day: teach a man to fish and you feed him for a lifetime." Similarly, we tried to show the workers at the pearl factory where common faults occurred in their machinery and how these could be avoided, so they could make their own repairs or avoid them altogether. As thanks for our help, we were invited to join the factory's annual outing: a trip to the uninhabited island on the eastern side of the atoll where the Kon-Tiki had finally ended its voyage. There, half of the group put together different grills while the rest of us were dispatched to catch something to cook on them. The snorkelling was extraordinary and if you missed harpooning the fish you were aiming for, you were sure to hit one behind it or next to it: never had the term "shooting fish in a barrel" seemed so appropriate. The food was slow cooked as we sat on the sand, drinking beer and talking over the sound of the waves rolling over the reef, our appetites becoming ever more piqued by the scent of the palm wood-infused fish, although the sweet cloud of marijuana was enough to give anyone the munchies. The islanders were heavy weed smokers, which may explain their relaxed attitude to life, and they grew a crop in the middle of the island for their personal use. Better to mellow out on a couple of herbal cigarettes than becoming aggressive on hard liquor, we thought – not that Carl and I smoked anything, apart from what we inhaled after sitting in a haze of dope. That evening Carl and I finally had the opportunity to use the hammocks we'd bought in the Galapagos; we strung them up between two palm trees and slept that night like a couple of slightly stoned middle-aged mariners.

It would be the last of the fine weather for a while: the following week, the wind rose to 45 miles per hour and after blowing fiercely for four days, a mooring rope on *Albatross* broke, in the process sinking an excellent stainless steel hook we'd used and couldn't replace. We noted the positions but it was too deep for me to free dive down to make a search. Felix and Toma immediately offered to fetch it.

'No way, it's nearly 60 feet down.'

'*Pas de problème,*' Toma said. They both took a deep breath and dived off the bow. Carl and I watched anxiously as they pushed their way towards the bottom. A few minutes later, they both shot out of the water.

'*Cinq barracuda énormes,*' Felix gasped as they climbed back on board. Barracuda can be more aggressive than sharks and the boys didn't want to risk being bait. The following morning Taputu and his fishing crew came in from night fishing. Upon learning of our problem, the whole crew flung themselves in the water, determined to help. Taputu retrieved the hook and that evening we invited the fishing crew to celebrate with us over a bottle of rum; they were happy to accept.

After a few days, the weather calmed again and the boys invited us to go coconut crab hunting. Intrigued, we hopped in their boat to head for the north of the island. Here the terrain was thick with low bushes and palms; the coral sand looked as if it had been used for target practise, pitted with holes dug out by the crabs. Felix gave me a stick and a rubber glove. '*Pour les trous,*' he said.

'You want me to stick this down a hole?' I asked, examining my stick for special features: there weren't any. Felix demonstrated his patented coconut crab-catching technique – if you can call it a technique. First, you poke the stick down the hole to check if the crab is in; if he is, then you stick in your rubber-gloved arm, tussle and grunt for a bit and hook him out. Bear in mind that coconut crabs can grow up to over three feet in length, leg to leg. Furthermore, the crab has earned its name from its ability to climb palm trees to pick coconuts which it opens to eat the flesh. For this purpose, nature has equipped the crab with the perfect tools: two very powerful, vice-like pincers. We were equipped with a twig and a washing-up glove; the odds were not in my favour. Call me a coward, but I wasn't keen to engage in a battle with something over half my size with large secateurs for hands.

'What if it pinches me?' I asked.

Toma pulled an expression of pain. '*Aie, ça fait du mal!*'

André explained that if this should happen, the crab probably wouldn't let go; the trick to persuading the crab to loosen its grip was to tickle the soft parts under its body. I doubted I'd remember this while I was howling in pain. For the first few holes, I pretended all the crabs were out: I really didn't fancy putting my hand down there. Eventually, I gathered my glove and decided that the element of surprise was key; I quickly felt about with the stick, thrust my hand down the hole, grabbed whatever was there and flung it out behind me. *Et viola!* A two-foot bright orange crab. I'm not sure who was most astonished, me or the crab. I was thrilled with my catch; mostly, I was thrilled not to have lost a limb.

After bagging a few crabs, we moved on to lobster hunting. The reef extended from the shore for 600 feet or so before ending in a wall which dropped down to the sea bed. In the wall were large hollows inhabited by lobsters. The technique for ferreting them out was the same as for the crabs: rubber glove on, thrust arm in, drag out unwilling lobster. No messing about with lobster traps as we'd done in Tobago. We completed the seafood hat trick when we sighted a large school of fish teeming in less than a foot of water. The boys' method was again simple, yet effective: they pelted the school with large coral stones and picked out the stunned fish. We took our catch back to the boys' cabin and dined like kings, throwing the scraps over our shoulders to the dogs, puppies and increasingly fat kitten.

We'd been on Raroia for nearly six weeks and it was time to move on. Before we did so, we tweaked and serviced any machinery we could: who knew when another boat might pass this way, never mind one which had on board a couple of electricians. One of our last jobs was to fix the satellite dish. For want of a long, stable ladder, I was hoisted up 30 feet on the bucket of the island's digger to work my magic. The problem was relatively simple and I really didn't deserve the praise and thanks showered on me, but the fact that the islanders could now receive their favourite French programmes was no small feat.

In the last few days before weighing anchor, André took us to his oyster farming grounds where we dived to bring up dozens of sacks of oysters. Then Felix and Toma taught us how to extract the coveted black pearl from the oyster shell, cutting the pearl out of the muscle which was then rinsed clean. Even though Carl and I as novices were slow at the work, we still managed to harvest a large handful of gleaming green, purple and silver pearls, only a few of which were perfect. We proudly showed our work to André.

'*Pour vous,*' he said. '*Pour vous remercier pour tous vos efforts.*'

It was too generous of him to give us this: there were nearly a hundred pearls. 'We can't accept,' Carl said. 'It's really not necessary.'

'*Mais si,*' André insisted. '*C'est nécessaire pour tout le travail. Pour tout votre amitié.*'

And so we accepted, for friendship's sake.

Leaving Raroia was like saying goodbye to family; we'd become one of them, worked beside the oyster farmers, the pearl harvesters and the fishermen. We'd learnt so much in our short time here: how to harpoon fish; how to catch crabs and lobsters with our hands; how to make copra, how to cultivate oysters and extract the precious black pearls from their shells. We learnt again how the generosity of some people far outweighs their means, and that material possessions count for very little towards experiencing life to the full. The people of Raroia showed us the meaning of happiness on the Happy Island. It fully deserved its appellation. Long may it last.

Chapter 35
Beers with Fu Manchu
13 August – 16 September 2003

Papeete, Tahiti – Marina Taina, Tahiti – Cooks Bay, Moorea,
The Society Islands, French Polynesia

Experience: *World affairs are best discussed shirtless while sitting on an upturned beer crate.*

Tip: *An informative sailing guide to Polynesia is "Charlie's Charts of Polynesia" by Charles and Margo Wood.*

The sun was just peeking over the horizon as we made *Albatross* ready for departure. All the sails were prepared, the dinghy was pulled up and tethered on board, the diving platform was raised and the anchor slowly winched up. Most of the village of Guarumaoa were standing on the shore to see us off. I don't know which weighed heaviest: the anchor or my spirits, knowing that we probably wouldn't return; we would only pass this way once. It was like leaving family. But I had to smile when I saw that the village transvestite had dressed with extra care and was regally sporting an extraordinarily voluminous crown of flowers, even by her standards, in honour of our departure. She blew us fervent farewell kisses: we waved back.

The Pacific Ocean is a serious body of water, the size of which we were only just beginning to understand with this our third leg of our journey across it. To put into context its vastness, consider that every continent on Earth would fit inside the Pacific and still leave room to squeeze in another South America. But on this sail, we were doing a mere ant-sized hop of 450 nautical miles. Our destination: Tahiti.

Ah, Tahiti. The very name evokes images of translucent turquoise lagoons, sun-drenched sandy beaches and native maidens drenching themselves all over me. My images of the island had been formed by Paul Gauguin's paintings, ones in which it seemed the natives lived only to sing and make love at the drop of a grass skirt. I knew I had to put my hedonistic Gauguin dreams aside much as I fancied the idea of a nubile Tahitian girl fulfilling my every whim the moment I stepped ashore.

But the real Tahiti? Carl and I knew very little about it other than what we'd read in guidebooks and on the internet. The turtle shaped island is made up of two volcanic mountain ranges, Tahiti Nui is the larger part joined by the isthmus of Taravao to the peninsula of Tahiti Iti. It is the largest of the Society Islands which also include Bora Bora, Raiatea, Taha'a, Huahine and Moorea. Tahiti's 127,000 strong population is mostly Polynesian in ancestry, and French is the official language although Tahitian is widely spoken. We were heading for the Papeete, the capital of French Polynesia and the only port with a customs office where we could make inward clearance.

The Tuamotus were originally dubbed the "Dangerous Islands" by French explorer Bougainville because of the challenge of navigating around the coral atolls; look at a satellite picture and they resemble a flotilla of opaque jellyfish. Despite our charts and electronic aids, we had to spend a lot of time on deck keeping an eye out, particularly in the passes between the atolls where standing waves, caused by water rushing out of the lagoons, could be formidable. As we'd discovered before, it was essential to time our arrival and departure with slack tide or at least a favourable interval with plenty of water below the keel. It was tricky maintaining our course, particularly at night in the strong winds, but on the third day of sailing we sighted Mount Orohena, Tahiti's highest mountain rising over 7,000 feet above sea level, its green peak piercing a circle of clouds. By dusk we had arrived at the north of the island, passing Point Venus where Captain James Cook observed the transit of the planet Venus in 1769.

We were sailing in the wake of some big names in seafaring history: Captains Wallis, Cook and Bligh had all passed this way, each anchoring in Matavai Bay where they would have seen the rugged mountain peaks and black sand beaches Carl and I now admired. The sea captains were welcomed by local chiefs and their families. We, on the other hand, were greeted by a seven-building Radisson complex that had claimed most of the beach in the relentless march of so-called progress. The verdant hills were liberally dotted with luxury villas: small white palaces clinging to the steep sides. The beaches were full of tourists at play, and the bays were teeming with jet skis and motorboats zigzagging over the water and buzzing like angry dragonflies. Tahiti had clearly become a seductive resort for the rich and famous, a fantasy destination for honeymooners and a playground for those who can afford $600 a night for a "typical" thatched over-water bungalow jutting out into the palm-fringed lagoon where glass floors allow you to see the fish without having to get wet and breakfast arrives by boat. It was all a brusque contrast after the simplicity of life on Raroia.

After sailing a few miles along the outer reef, we were carried serenely forward on the long ocean swells towards Papeete. The Society Islands have become the new Hawaii for surfers due to the fact that the surf generally breaks over the coral reef a mile from shore, giving surfers a good long ride. One surfing website states that back in 1777 when Captain Cook observed a man in Tahiti riding the waves in his canoe, he noted, "I could not help concluding that this man felt the most supreme pleasure while he was driven so fast and so smoothly by the sea." This is regarded as a call to surfers everywhere.

The sun was skimming the sea as we entered Papeete harbour where we made our way to the quay alongside Boulevard Pomare, a busy avenue in the centre of the town. Here we moored stern to dock between a small sailboat and a Goliath. Once all the ropes were secured and we'd hooked up to the electricity outlet, we sat back in the cockpit to savour a chilled gin and tonic and the sights and sounds of Papeete. The harbour was busy with cargo freighters, copra ships and cruise ships. The quay was only a few steps from the market, banks, restaurants, offices and repair workshops, and the pavements were overflowing with cafés, shops and bars. We hadn't been in such a large metropolis since leaving Panama in April, four months earlier, so we were slightly shell-shocked by the bustle and noise after our six weeks of tranquillity in the village of Guarumaoa.

But we got over that when we bought baguettes and French cheese for breakfast the following morning from a small bakery. It had been a long time since we'd eaten cheese, and I like cheese in the same way I like to breathe. We were slowly resigning ourselves to re-entering the busy world, although it might take another couple of days before I could handle sitting in a café or tackle shopping in a crowded supermarket.

We discovered that the Goliath, a modest boat measuring 170 feet, on our port side was owned by Jim Clark, one of the founders of Netscape which, you might recall, was the dominant web browser in the 1990s before losing 90 percent of its usage share in the browser wars. But clearly Jim was doing all right: a nine-strong crew were feverishly at work on the *Hyperion*. One of the crew members told us Jim "sailed" via his office computer in the States: navigation and autopilot were controlled by satellite. If ever there a time to question whether size mattered, now was it: *Albatross* looked like a flea in comparison; Jim, incidentally, didn't invite us on board for drinks, even though we did our utmost to hang around on deck looking available.

But when it comes to cleaning a boat, smaller is better. Our laundry pile threatened to collapse and smoother us, so for two days we washed everything in sight, hanging our laundry on deck, over the guard rails and from the boom, no doubt blighting the view for Jim and his crew on *Hyperion* and generally lowering the tone of the place.

'Hi guys. Are you taking in washing now?' a familiar voice called. It was Titta, a Finnish girl we'd got to know in the Galapagos where she'd crewed on *Zara*, a yacht out of Helsinki. She'd signed off on Nuko Hiva and made it to Tahiti on the cargo ship that did the rounds of the islands in French Polynesia. She'd managed to find a new skipper, Henry, to crew for on a yacht sailing for Thailand in September and had some time to kill.

'Come along and meet my new skipper,' she said. 'I know he'd love to pick your brains about sailing.'

Henry had worked for many years in France, but had spent the last five years on Tahiti where he ran a computer company. He was currently putting the finishing touches to realizing his dream of sailing around the world, having bought *L'Arlésienne* a year earlier, so he welcomed our tips on planning a passage and boat maintenance. In return he shared his local knowledge and helped us locate strange little shops to source new diodes for the two generators from Raroia. Henry had a noisy small Renault van, and he packed Carl and me between boxes in the back where we sat looking out the small windows like the family dogs as we lurched around the narrow streets of Papeete.

To conclude our business with the generator repair from the pearl factory on Raroia, we sought out the owner, Paul Yo. Paul was a Chinese man in the teatime of his life who'd worked in the pearl farming industry for many years. He knew our services had been a real bargain – we asked only $2,000 for rebuilding the generator, probably a fifth of what he would have been charged elsewhere. He welcomed us to his home, a large house with extensive gardens and pool clearly built with the profits of his long career, making me wonder briefly if we should have charged more. Like most Chinese operated businesses, it was a family affair, and as Paul gave us a tour of his home, we came across his wife and son, sitting cross-legged on the marble floor, sorting and grading pearls.

'Pearls are easy to steal,' Paul said, 'so I only trust my wife and son to grade them.' Our host told us that 98% of all pearls were exported to wholesalers in Hong Kong and Japan who then sold them to dealers in Europe and the U.S. Even so, Papeete was jammed with jewellers with shop windows crammed with pearl jewellery. Apparently, a cartel functioning in French Polynesia maintains artificially high prices via a strict certification system and the agreement from pearl farmers that production remains at a certain limit.

Papeete has a small but thriving town centre, but there's little of real interest for tourists except the jewellery shops, a monument or two and some restaurants. After two months of living on a diet of fish, rice, coconuts and tinned goods, I was thrilled to find markets selling meat and fresh vegetables. 'Ah, meat,' I sighed with a carnivore's joy as I lingered lovingly over cuts of beef and lamb. Poor me, so bored of eating lobster and crab, I would have traded Carl for a pork chop. The warm air was full of foody smells that made my stomach churn in anticipation of culinary delights. We noticed how people around us were eating, licking their lips or wiping the corners of their mouths. Rounding a corner, we suddenly entered the equivalent of a car boot fast-food sale: dozens of worn-out old Citroëns and Toyotas were parked bumper to bumper, doors open to reveal hotplates on backseats or boot spaces with mini pizza ovens. There was fried chicken on grills, spicy noodles in woks, the joyful sounds of sizzling and the exotic tang of spices in the air. This was where the Papeete locals thronged to eat: a good sign meaning the food was authentic, cheap and unlikely to send us scurrying to the nearest bathroom.

At the end of the week, we took a meander south to the Taina Marina, a mile from Papeete. We strolled along the coastal path lined with idyllic looking luxury bungalows with prices only the Hollywood elite can afford; we could have bought another boat for a week's stay at one of the resorts. Taina Marina was inside the reef and well protected from the swells, and the bay looked calm and inviting. We decided to leave the hectic bustle of Papeete and sailed the five nautical miles to the bay where we could lie undisturbed on the waves and work on *Albatross*. Her hull had become slick with oil residue, but working in the polluted waters of Papeete harbour didn't appeal to us. Yachts sailing from and to Marina Taina must request permission to cross the airfield axis east or west 10 minutes before doing so as the runway to Papeete airport is built on a large coral reef parallel to the coast. Otherwise it's quite unnerving to be gently pootling along when suddenly the wheels of an Air New Zealand airbus zoom a few feet from your mast.

We dropped anchor outside the marina and spent our time doing maintenance work. Setting off to circumnavigate the world may be liberating, but as any boat owner knows, you'll always be a slave to boat maintenance, unless of course, you are Jim Clark and have staff.

On 26 August, we celebrated my birthday with an impromptu party on *Albatross* inviting Titta and Henry over from his sailboat *L'Arlésienne* and Henning from his Danish boat *Kuta*. Occasionally, we build bridges with the Danes if only to remind them that the Swedes won most of the battles between our two nations. Henning was in his fifties and had been a supervisor in a sugar refinery before losing both his job and his wife in a bitter divorce. He told us how he'd sat and stewed about how crappy his life was before pulling himself together and using his severance pay to sail to the Caribbean. He was still a little raw about past events, but he could now glimpse the light at the end of the tunnel, his confidence in himself having been boosted when he managed to cross the Atlantic single-handed.

As good Swedish citizens we were keen to vote in the Swedish elections. In 2003, a referendum was held on the introduction of the Euro. We duly registered at the Swedish Consulate in Papeete, managed by a friendly Frenchman. The consul hadn't received any instructions from the Swedish Embassy in Paris about absentee voting, but he immediately dashed off an email and promised to contact us as soon as he had a voting kit, making it sound like something which came in press-out pieces to be assembled with glue.

On our walk to the consulate, we'd noticed a small grocery shop directly opposite a large, two-storey supermarket. Always keen to support the underdog, Carl and I decided to pick up a few basics from the small store. As we entered, it was like stepping back into the nineteenth century: in the dim of the interior we could see a dark wooden counter separating shelves of carefully arranged tinned goods from the customer; trays below the counter displayed a random assortment of bric-a-brac: sweets, pencils, rubber bands, plastic toys, envelopes and fishing lure. It was part corner shop from my youth, part Chinese emporium hit hard times. Dust motes hung suspended in the sliver of sunlight that shone through the chink in the door. The air lay heavy and smelled as if it had been trapped in a tin for a decade or more.

'*Fermez la porte! Fermez la porte !*' a thin, reedy voice said sharply.

I'd initially assumed the shop was empty, but as we penetrated the gloom, a Chinese man shuffled into view around the counter. He was shirtless with the sagging chest of an older man, although he had a suspiciously dark head of hair for a man whose nipples were travelling towards his waist. He hauled himself up on a stool behind the counter, knees and hips creaking like the hinges on a rusty gate, folded his arms and peered at us like the insidious Dr Fu Manchu assessing a rival.

'*Que est ce que vous voulez?*' he demanded abruptly.

'Um. *Deux bières?*' I asked, feeling slightly intimidated.

'*Bière est là bas,*' Fu Manchu said, pointing to a refrigerator chest which hummed quietly at the side of the shop.

As we crossed over to the unit, we became aware of another pair of eyes glinting at us like a cat. A liver-spotted Chinese woman who hadn't seen her eightieth birthday for at least a decade sat on a stool, back ramrod straight like an empress on a throne, her head turning slowly to observe everyone in the shop. We helped ourselves to two Hinano beers and went to Fu Manchu to pay. He looked up from his handwritten ledger without a smile and snapped, '*Buvez ici?*' We nodded that we'd drink the beers in the shop: hell, it was too mysterious to leave; it was like being thrown into the middle of a Raymond Chandler novel.

'*Buvez ici, buvez en sac,*' the Chinaman said, handing us two small plastic bags and indicating we should use these to hide the beer bottles to disguise the fact we were drinking alcohol in his shop. He pointed to a darker corner to the right of the counter. '*Buvez là bas,*' he said, and we did as we were told under the watchful eye of the Empress who looked as if she didn't know whether to dispatch us with spider venom or snake bite. Having grown used to the gloom, our eyes adjusted enough to pick out other customers standing around the periphery of the shop, taking discreet swigs from their camouflaged bottles. In our corner were three old men, two shirtless and all sitting on upturned beer crates where they were chatting in a mixture of French and Mandarin. We lifted our plastic bags in greeting and were welcomed into the conversation.

This was clearly the place where old characters and eccentrics came to tell their stories and eventually die. There was Pierre, a handsome fellow in his early eighties who still had a roguish smile about his mouth. With his dark sunglasses and porkpie hat, he reminded me of one of the grumpy old men from *The Muppet Show*. He told us colourful stories of his experiences in the restaurant he'd run for 50 years in French Polynesia. Marlon Brando had been a regular guest since the 1960s following his role in *Mutiny on the Bounty* which had been filmed in Tahiti. Brando would often flee media attention and seek the tranquility of the South Pacific, in particular in Tetiaroa, a 13-island chain 35 miles from Tahiti which he purchased in 1967 and intended to develop. There was much talk of the actor's plans to build a small eco-friendly hotel reliant on solar energy and wind power. A year after our conversation with Pierre, Brando died, his plans unfulfilled, but his eight surviving grandchildren united to see the actor's wishes achieved; *The Brando*, a 35-villa, six-star resort, opened in 2014 to a resounding 'kerching!' that no doubt helped to unite the grandchildren to see poor old granddad's dream come true.

One beer led to another, and another after that. We perched on upturned buckets or bottle crates and listened to the old guys' stories of life in the Society Islands. Fascinated, Carl and I became regular customers at the store, dropping in on the pretence of buying toilet paper or matches, but ending up in the corner with a beer in a plastic bag under the ever watchful eye of the Empress. With each visit, we delved deeper into the store, turning dim corners to discover another small chamber where a different group of drinkers sat with contraband beers, scrutinizing us before deciding we were "safe." It wouldn't have surprised me to find Fu Manchu running an opium den at the back or the Empress masterminding a Chinese slave racket, bundling girls into laundry baskets and the back of a waiting van bound for Shanghai. Or would Lotus Blossom slink through the beaded curtain to weave her deceptive charms on two naïve middle-aged Swedish blokes? I furtively hoped so.

After a week of daily patronage, we finally gained entrance to the inner sanctum, having worked our way through numerous chambers in the store, emerging out the other side. The loyal regulars – the innermost circle of the circle – met in the store's backyard, a junkyard where defunct electrical items gathered to rust; old fridges, cash registers from the 1920s, broken televisions, radios and ovens lined the walls. The club members sat gingerly on armchairs and couches through which stuffing and metal coils were making their escape. God knows what was growing inside them. Upturned shopping carts, obviously pilfered from the supermarket across the road, housed roosters, used, so one old bloke told me, in cock fighting competitions from which the Empress and her son won "big" money: not that any of their winnings were being invested in property renovation. At one end of the yard was a large brick oven and grill where the Empress cooked Chinese dishes, the contents of which were unidentifiable. She frowned as she silently stirred her pots, casting suspicious glances at us when we laughed too loudly. I never once saw her smile.

Amid all this mess, we sat on our beer crates and discussed world affairs with our drinking buddies, interrupted every so often by the crowing of a rooster. It was the strangest version of a British Pub we were ever likely to come across.

'We need something like this in Helsingborg,' I said to Carl.

The locals included Daniel, a Polynesian who had just turned 75 and spoke impeccable English. He had a thick head of hair, brown button eyes and a chest severely affected by gravity – shirts were optional amongst the drinkers throughout the store. He told us how he'd signed up in the U.S. Navy in 1942 on hearing that the Japanese had bombed Pearl Harbour, and enjoyed a career in the Navy, using it as a means of personal travel to visit ports around the world. Daniel had been fortunate enough never to have come into active duty against the Japanese and had spent the Cold War avoiding conflict with the Soviet naval forces. He had come out of the forces unscathed and now lived a quiet life, visiting the store every day to escape the wife by volunteering to get the shopping and returning several hours later empty handed after sinking a few beers with his friends.

The best of the scrubby furniture, a rickety office chair missing a castor wheel, was accorded to the most senior among us: Sing Ling Hung, a 93-year-old Chinese man, held court. His grandfather had emigrated from China and settled on Tahiti in the late nineteenth century. Despite having a face as wrinkled as an old scrotum and trouble with his sight, he still had a boyish twinkle in his good eye and that eye was for the ladies. If he heard a young woman's voice in the shop, he'd squint intensely in her direction and nod approvingly if he liked what he saw. Sing had been a tailor up until his eyesight had begun to fail, and his penchant for clothes was still keen: he was always dapperly dressed in a neat dark suit and crisp cotton shirt. In fact, he was the only one of us who was fully dressed no matter how hot or humid the day.

At the beginning of September we returned to the Swedish consulate to vote. In the whole of French Polynesia, we were only four Swedes who had registered to do so. Incidentally, despite most political parties in Sweden being in favour of adopting the Euro, the "vote 'yes' campaign" ultimately failed with 55.9 percent of the public voting against the proposal.

Eva arrived in the first week of September to visit Carl, and I felt like a third wheel. They'd booked a few days in an exotic bungalow on the southeast coast of Tahiti, leaving me alone on *Albatross* to contemplate where my relationships with women had gone wrong. By the time they returned, I still hadn't come to any useful conclusions.

With Eva on board, we had planned to pootle around and explore the islands; our destination was Moorea, a volcanic heart-shaped island located nine miles northwest of Tahiti, the scenery of which was said to be spectacular. It didn't disappoint: it was dazzling. A wide, shallow lagoon surrounds the island where mountains graze curls of clouds. As we entered the long finger of Cooks Bay, the surrounding peaks were so lush and verdant they looked as if they'd been digitally enhanced. The writer James Michener called Moorea "a monument to the prodigal beauty of nature," and was apparently so inspired by its scenery that he based the mythical island of Bali Ha'i in *Tales of the South Pacific* on this South Seas jewel. The island's stunning scenery draws many honeymooners, but we noticed that several properties were empty, looking virtually abandoned: 9/11 had taken its toll on tourism from the United Sates: nevertheless, a large cruiser lay at anchor and the quayside was crowded with passengers awaiting their buses to take them around the island.

We anchored in the bay and for a few days we indulged our inner hedonists: kicking back, swimming and snorkelling in Evian-clear water, occasionally taking a lazy stroll on land to admire pastel-painted houses tucked into the fern-softened landscape, watch hummingbirds hover over hibiscus, and inhale the heady perfume of frangipani and jasmine: a little taste of nirvana that was over too quickly for Eva who reluctantly had to return to the real world. She left us the following in *Albatross'* logbook:

"It is with sadness in my heart that I leave Albatross, Yanne and Carl Erik. I especially want to thank Yanne for his excellent cuisine; he created many memorable meals in Albatross' kitchen.

'My beloved Carl Erick has been my guide here in these romantic South Sea islands. I return home with many fond memories of this paradise."

As Carl read out Eva's message, he shook his head sorrowfully, clearly touched by his wife's words.

'Four years,' he said. 'Four years we've had this boat, and she still calls it a bloody kitchen!'

Chapter 36
Savage Islands, Friendly Islands, a Coconut and a Kingdom
17 September – 22 October 2003
Bora Bora – Rarotonga – Alofi, Niue – Tonga

Experience: *The French Polynesian islands are exceptionally beautiful with great variety between the islands but very pricey: stock up with supplies beforehand.*

Tip: *Try to be a cardboard free boat to discourage unwanted pests, or you may feel the revolting crunch of something under your feet in the dark.*

So there I was, perched on a rickety stool at a tiny kiosk bar in Bora Bora drinking a cold beer and chatting with a few of the locals when I mentioned that I'd just sailed from Tahiti.

An old boy as dark skinned as a prune took a swig of his beer and said, 'Tahiti? I've got a friend on Tahiti.'

'Oh, yes? What's his name?' I asked idly.

'You wouldn't know him,' the local laughed. 'In fact, I doubt Daniel's still alive. He's older than me.'

'Daniel? Not Daniel who joined the U.S. Navy in 1942 and drinks in the Chinese shop?'

'Well, I don't know where he drinks, but he was in the American Navy.'

After a few more specifics, we established it was the same Daniel. 'What are the chances of you knowing my friend, Daniel!' the old guy said, laughing so much he nearly fell off his stool. 'You must come and eat with us.'

What were the chances indeed? If you've been paying attention, you'll have noticed how many times I've mentioned the vastness of the Pacific Ocean, so the odds of my bumping into a friend of a friend in a bar on an island some 160 miles away was fairly remote and therefore cause for celebration. I immediately accepted his invitation despite my reservations about the menu: as a special treat, Daniel's long-lost friend and his buddies were proudly treating me to a sea turtle supper.

In Tahitian tradition, turtles are a culinary delicacy and fetch premium prices despite the fact they are protected. Conservation groups do their best, but it's hard to stop the Polynesians from seeing sea turtles as anything other than pests or a delicious main course, so the locals continue to hunt and serve turtle at Tahitian feasts and celebrations. I was torn: my friend was honouring me by entertaining me with the best he could offer, but I was reluctant to eat the graceful creatures I'd spent hours swimming with in lagoon waters so clear I could see every grain of sand. The turtles were completely endearing: as curious and friendly as any islander we'd met, and I've always had strict rules about eating anyone I've been introduced to. So how could I sit down to tuck into a friend I'd swum with only that morning?

My reluctance evaporated with my first mouthful: it was the most succulent meat I've ever tasted, as tender as young lamb but with a slightly fishy flavour that reminded you this had been a sea creature. My relationship with turtles was forever changed. But before you judge me too quickly, let me say that was the first and last time I've ever been served turtle, and I wouldn't dream of hooking one into my net on the sly, delicious though they may be.

Bora Bora: another name that conjures images of tranquil lagoons of kaleidoscopic coloured fish, and straw-roofed huts jutting out over sparkling waters lapping at bone-white powdery beaches. It was all that and then some. When we visited, development had not yet started to boom. The island is relatively small at just over 18 miles in circumference, but its steep landscape gives it a dramatic impact. Rising from the lagoon like a medieval tower, Mount Otemanu dominates the view from almost any anchorage. Although the island has no cities – its largest village and main port, Vaitape, is home to a few shops and restaurants – there is a tiny airport located on Motu Mute receiving daily Air Tahiti flights from Papeete and other Tahitian islands. During World War II, the United States used the island as a military supply base, constructing seven naval cannons around the island to protect it against possible attack, which it happily never saw. Of the 7,000 men who were stationed on Bora Bora, many chose to remain at the close of the war – well, who wouldn't? Those who left for the miserable climes of New Jersey are probably still kicking themselves.

While it might be unusual to happen upon another islander's drinking buddy, it's common to bump into other expatriates of the small floating community as you hop from island to island, leading to an informal village atmosphere. We would exchange news over a mooring buoy as you would gossip with your neighbours over the hedge.

'Where's the young couple who were with you in Islas de las Perlas?'

'Oh, they left us at the Galapagos, didn't fancy sailing 3,000 miles across the Pacific.'

'Did you hear about Fred?'

'The guy with the girlfriend and the dog on the 50-footer out of California? What about him?'

'Girlfriend left him in Tahiti. Took the dog, too.'

'No! Is he okay?'

'Really upset. He adored that dog. Said he can always get a new girlfriend.'

And so the stories go around from boat to boat as we make new friends and bump into old. But invariably there's a good group of people who help each other out whenever we cross paths. So it was when we arrived in Bora Bora. Twenty or so yachts were already moored in the bay, one of which we immediately recognized: *Tico Tico*, a Danish boat we'd last seen in Tahiti. The skipper, Bengt, came over to us in his dinghy and helped us moor *Albatross* to a buoy. We had a lot in common with Bengt; he'd also had very little sailing experience when on a sudden whim he decided to take a sabbatical from his veterinary practise and sail around the world together with his wife. He had a Danish friend on board, Carsten, who was keen to dive, so Carl and I invited him to join us the following day when we explored the lagoon off Motu Toopua, a tiny, deserted coral island. There is so much aquatic life in the clear shallow waters around the motus that you don't really need to be a diver to enjoy the sea, but we kitted up anyway: at least you feel slightly more equipped to deal with the sharks, of which there are many. Sadly, Bora Bora was devastated by cyclone Oli in early 2010, destroying several hotels and much of the coral on the southern reef.

Our next hop was a four-day, 500-nautical mile journey away to Rarotonga, one of the 15 volcanic lumps that make up the Cook Islands. It was our first rough ride in some time and it took us by surprise. Our sea legs were a bit wobbly after our extended stays on Raroia and Tahiti. Fortunately, we hadn't lost our knack for catching fish and using a new fishing hook and thicker line, we managed to hook a 50-pound dorado, our biggest catch to date.

With a land area of less than 100 square miles, the Cook Islands seem like mere pebbles thrown into an area of ocean stretching over 690,000 square miles. They were not discovered by the famous English captain after whom they are named, but by Spanish explorers in the sixteenth century, nearly 180 years before James Cook's arrival in 1773. Cook, however, was the first to chart the group. In fact, Cook's greatest achievements were proving where land was not. He wrote, "I, however, have made no very great discoveries, yet I have explored more of the Great South Sea than all that have gone before me." He originally dubbed them the Hervey Islands in honour of a lord of the Admiralty – no doubt a sweetener to get more funding for future voyages – but 50 years later a Russian cartographer renamed them the Cook Islands in the late explorer's honour. Europeans more or less ignored the islands until the 1820s, when English missionaries set about expanding their flock with a rigorous policy of spreading the word around the South Pacific that it was better to love one's fellow man than eat him. It's testimony to their efficacy that many of the islanders remain strict Christians today.

We arrived at Rarotonga, the youngest but most populous of the Cook Islands, just after sunrise and made for Avatiu harbour which we'd been told was relatively sheltered. Apparently, the harbour has since undergone a huge realignment and has been dredged, giving it more draft for larger yachts but also making it more exposed to the north winds; however, it's a better alternative to mooring in the open ocean where the holding is poor and gusting trade winds can make for a very rough anchor.

Of these tiny islands, Rarotonga was surely the jewel in the crown with its blend of Polynesian culture and spectacular beauty. Yet again, we would have to suffer an idyllic climate, National Geographic cover scenery, and people with genuine smiles and gentle temperaments. Would we ever tire of the sight of gracefully arcing palm trees on snow white sands or craggy green mountains outlined against topaz skies?

Check in was quick and relatively painless with the help of an amicable harbourmaster who took care of every detail, although we did have to surrender our nuts for burning. This is not a euphemism: coconuts carry flies which attack other fruit bearing trees, and as insecticides are not used in the atolls, customs officials are vigilant about banning any nuts transported from other islands.

We gained several new crew members while we were in Avatiu: Carsten whom we'd met in Bora Bora on Bengt's boat *Tico Tico* was a welcome guest on *Albatross*. Bengt and his wife were continuing to Fiji but Carsten had made his way to Rarotonga; he'd been unable to find a hotel so we invited him on board. He drove buses for a living, scrimping and saving so he could travel to an exotic destination once a year. This year's journey was anything but a busman's holiday: a five-stop airline ticket around the South Pacific. He regaled us with stories of his adventures, reminding Carl and I that there was still a lot of world to explore that didn't require a banker's salary to do so.

Our other crew members were less welcome but adamantly refused to leave: cockroaches had invited themselves on board and were partying like teenagers: they helped themselves to our beers, raided the fridge, climbed into pots on the stove, hung around the sugar bowl waiting for a fix and would surprise you by creeping out of the pages of a paperback as you settled on the toilet for a contemplative read. But nothing was as revolting as that nasty crunch under your feet as you stumbled in the dark for a midnight pee. We tried everything short of getting a gecko to be rid of them, but roaches are cunning little bastards. It's a fact of life that boats in humid climates will attract these pests no matter how clean you keep your craft; they often board when you are tied alongside other boats; they hide out in grocery bags and boxes, getting high on glue. We tried to clear the cabin of as much cardboard as possible only to find them feasting on the adhesive in the binding of books. When Carl found one working its way across a rum label in search of more glue, he was outraged. 'That's it! They are not joining us for cocktails!' he shouted furiously. 'Yanne, get your tap shoes on!' While La Cucaracha played over the loudspeaker, I stamped my way around the cabin in my one pair of hard-soled shoes, leaving unpleasant splats around the decked floor.

While in harbour we got to know Captain Jimmy, the skipper of the *Lady Marie*, a 6o-foot fishing boat. He explained how he and his crew fished for tuna using satellite data to track schools of bluefin tuna for which they received $70 a kilo on the Japanese fish market. I recall wondering even then in 2003 how much longer it would be before tuna stocks were in trouble from overfishing. Pacific bluefin tuna are the largest of the species and are prodigious swimmers; built for speed, they can cross the Pacific Ocean in less than a month and can dive more than 4,000 feet. But they can't outrun the fishing boats: advanced fish-finding gadgets allow fishermen to track their ever-sparser populations, which seems a wholly unfair advantage to the fishermen. Nevertheless, tuna remains one of the world's most sought-after fish, and although their stocks have declined sharply, the Japanese are still determined to have their sushi and eat it. In 2013, a 489-pound bluefin tuna was sold for a record $1.7 million at a Tokyo auction, making an ounce-sized mouthful of sashimi worth over $200 per bite. Campaigners are fighting for tighter controls on fishing quotas of the tuna, considering it to be rarer than the tiger. I hope Jimmy and his crew have moved on to more sustainable sources of fish.

Another boat of interest was the *Bat'Kivshchyna*, a Ukrainian tall ship out of Kiev. Captain Dimitro Birioukovitch had set off with limited funds on an expedition to promote interest in the Ukraine as an independent European country. His enthusiasm had captured the public imagination, and the ship and crew had been warmly received around the world, including in the United States where its arrival had received huge media attention. The dedicated Ukrainians had travelled around the world seemingly on pure determination and ingenuity, raising funds to continue their mission by turning the

Bat'kivshchyna into a gift shop when in port, selling fake fur hats, fridge magnets and nesting wooden dolls of American presidents. 'We are discofering the vorld and the vorld is discofering us,' Captain Birioukovitch said with a bright smile. His optimism was infectious; he'd never lost faith in the three years since leaving Kiev, not when the ship ran aground losing a chunk of its keel, nor when storms in the Mediterranean shredded the mainsail, nor when the radio broke in the middle of the Atlantic, triggering a two-week ocean-wide hunt by the Coast Guard. There were certainly no luxuries on board, and the crew survived mainly on potatoes and carrots, but their enthusiasm seemed infinite.

Weary of picturesque lagoons, we decided to lather ourselves in mosquito repellent, pack our rucksacks and take a hike up one of the well-marked trails into the mountains. The island was formed by a giant volcano that collapsed in on itself a few thousand years earlier to create its present circular form. We sweatily tramped along a trail through the bush towards the peak of Te Rua Manga, commonly known as the Needle because of the summit's shape: a near vertical cylinder of rock 200 feet tall. A chain and a couple of old ropes at the base suggested we might want to haul ourselves to the very top, but I didn't feel the need to flirt with danger; furthermore, the view from where we collapsed in a damp heap was impressive enough; the low clouds parted long enough for us to admire the panoramic view of the island and its coral reef.

We continued down the trail on the other side, passing Rarotonga's lone waterfall down which only a trickle of water ran, and on towards the village of Vaimaanga, famous now only for the failure of what should have been the most fabulous resort on the island. In 1987, an Italian construction firm was engaged to build a luxury 200-room hotel, financed by an Italian government-owned backer and an insurance company, while the Cook Islands government agreed to guarantee the loan. By 1993, approximately $50 million had been spent and 80 percent of the hotel was finished, but amid alleged mafia-related corruption, the project went bust, nearly bankrupting the country as it faced a $100 million liability bill. The "No Trespassers" sign lay trampled in the boggy field and chickens pecked around the site, so Carl and I walked through the ghost hotel, wondering that the resort had come so near to completion yet had been so entirely abandoned. Luxurious bathroom suites, air-conditioning units and light fittings were overgrown with creepers and vines weaving their way into the rooms like the tentacles of a science fiction beast. For a tiny country with a population of only 14,000 which earns half its income from tourism, completing the project must be in its economic interests; indeed, over the last decade there have been various attempts by New Zealand developers to do so, but at the time of writing there are still no plans to complete the building. It seemed a horrendous waste of money and potential.

Later in the week, we welcomed Staffan Wikström on board. Staffan was a friend of Carl's and would be sailing the 2,000 nautical miles with us to New Zealand, if he ever got over his jet lag having travelled for 72 hours from northern Sweden to Roratonga. He was pumped and excited to join us although he'd never sailed before and was blissfully ignorant of that perpetual misery known as seasickness. We broke him in gently with a relatively short first passage to Niue, the world's smallest independent nation some 600 nautical miles to our west.

Niue, known locally as "the Rock," maybe a miniature state at only 100 square miles, but is one of the world's largest uplifted coral islands, boasting astonishing tunnels and caves both under the land and the sea. Lying on the direct route from French Polynesia to Tonga, it has become a popular stop for westbound yachts for its hospitality, excellent diving and when the season is right, whale watching. The island is situated on a humpback whale migratory path; between July and October an influx of whales calve and nurse their young in Niue's sheltered bays. It was early October and we were hoping to see something of these gentle giants.

As we left Roratonga, the sky was moody with heavy clouds, but a weak wind left *Albatross* lurching drunkenly on the swells. Virgin sailor Staffan went a clammy grey but hung determinedly on to the contents of his stomach. On the third day, the wind picked up with a vengeance and scuttled us briskly along. We sighted land in the west after five days of sailing and headed for the west coast to the capital of Alofi to secure a mooring buoy. They don't call it "the Rock" for nothing: there was no possibility of anchoring anywhere near Niue's shorelines, as most of the ocean bed around the island consists of scoured rock or broken coral. As we approached the break in the reef, the wind gusted so suddenly and with such strength that we were unable to jibe back; the result was a tear in the mainsail the size of a window. After Carl and I had used all the swear words in our vocabulary, we shrugged and accepted that "shit happens." After all, we'd been relatively lucky and hadn't suffered too much damage during our 18-month journey.

As we tied up, we tried radioing to arrange clearance but it was Sunday: the pubs were shut and everyone was in church. 'Ah, what the heck,' we said. The clear water begged us to dive in and we did.

Niue rises out of the sea, small but perfectly formed, a terrain of steep limestone cliffs along the coast with a central plateau rising to 200 feet above sea level. The population when we visited was less than 1,200 people – fewer than the number of students at most secondary schools in Sweden – as many migrate to New Zealand. Yet, it was a rocking little place with a country club, a nine-hole golf course, a VIP lounge at the airport and parties at the weekends that would rival the London or Manhattan club scenes.

James Cook was the first European to sight Niue, naming it the "Savage Island" because as legend has it, the natives who met him and his crew appeared to have blood stained teeth. In fact, the red of their teeth was most probably caused by their diet of the native red banana. The island's current name means "behold the coconut," I suppose because a visually challenged Polynesian paddling a dugout canoe glimpsed the island from afar and shouted 'Oh, look, a coconut!' and the name stuck.

On Monday morning we were just about to put the dinghy out to go over to the customs office when a small boat with three customs officials came alongside *Albatross*. An ebullient type, dripping with an unnecessary amount of gold braid from his shoulders, was the first to come aboard. He puffed out his chest like a fat pigeon and started ranting about how we'd committed a crime by entering the country without permission from the authorities. His two colleagues exchanged wry glances, clearly used to this behaviour.

'Don't worry, Yanne,' Carl said out of the corner of his mouth, 'I'll handle this.'

I should have known better than to let him, but he'd already started trying to out puff the customs officer before I could protest. Consequently, I became the bemused witness to the rare male dance of prowess performed by the Swedish tourist versus the Polynesian official. It wasn't pretty. Later that afternoon, *I* had to appear at the customs office for a scolding and to pay a hefty fine. I sat contritely before the pompous pigeon as he read out the list of our transgressions, but in the end my penitent demeanour convinced him to reduce the fine. The fat pigeon continued to keep a watchful eye on Carl and me, having marked us as gangster style yacht owners who would rip off the church collection plate given half a chance. I thought his head would spin 360 degrees and explode when Carl casually sauntered in front of the customs office window and took a prolonged pee off the side of the quay. Another reason never to swim in the harbour.

The customs man was the only unpleasant person we met in the whole of the South Pacific. We stayed at Niue only briefly as the wind veered to the south and *Albatross* was tossed around on her mooring like a plastic duck in a Jacuzzi; it was very unpleasant trying to sleep in such heavy swells.

We sailed on to Tonga, a journey of 300 nautical miles. We'd managed to repair the hole in the mainsail with spinnaker tape, glue and machine sewing a horizontal seam along the tear, but the ocean was so violent we wondered if the cyclone season had started earlier than normal. This was not sailing for wimps; the house-high waves slammed against the hull and threw up columns of blue water which pounded over *Albatross*; we unfurled the genoa by two thirds and were thrust over the water at a speed of eight knots. Trying to sleep was damn near impossible with constant pitching and rolling, and waves sounding like cannon fire every time they hit the port side. But we were sailing fast and before we knew it had crossed the date line, jumping from Thursday into Saturday.

On the second night we passed over the Tonga Trench; it was strangely eerie to think we had over 35,000 feet of water below us, and impossible to imagine that this depth is comparable to the height at which planes fly. The 850-mile long Tonga Trench is second only in depth to the Mariana Trench where a slot-shaped depression called the Challenger Deep takes the prize for the deepest known point in the Earth's sea floor at a depth of 35,814 feet: 6.78 miles if you can get your head more easily around that number. I admit I can't. The pressure under this weight of water is extreme: equivalent to one person trying to support 50 jumbo jets. And yet divers are constantly tempted to try this out. The current depth record for open circuit scuba diving is held by Pascale Bernabé, who in 2005 descended to 1,082 feet, the equivalent of the height of the Eiffel Tower. Deep diving is a risky hobby: exposure to excessive depths can cause a collapse of the lungs, cardiac arrest, blackouts, decompression sickness and, at worst, death. I get a nose bleed just thinking about it.

After two days sailing we sighted land: the kingdom of Tonga, another name to play havoc with the imagination. Of the 176 islands that dot the map like raisins, only 36 are inhabited and some of these have only a scattering of houses and a small church. Tonga was dubbed the "Friendly Islands" due to the cordial reception James Cook received on his first visit there. According to William Mariner, however, an Englishman who lived on Tonga 30 years after Cook's arrival, the chiefs had wanted to kill the captain during the gathering, but couldn't agree on how to do so. A case of too many cooks? Nevertheless, the Tongans reputation for generous hospitality lives on.

We'd set a course for Tongatapu, the main island, to explore the wonderfully named capital of Nuku'alofa, which translated means "abode of love." As usual we had to weave our way around hull-shredding coral reefs before we could get into the harbour where we put out 50 feet of anchor chain; the wind was still fierce but the constant heavy swells were lessened by the protection of the surrounding coral reefs. Staffan had brought a bottle of *Gammel Dansk* so we could reinitiate our custom of drinking a "mooring snaps" on arrival. It was a relief to take a breather after a frantic sail of 48 hours. Once again, we'd arrived on a Saturday afternoon when it wasn't normally possible to check in, but a friendly immigration officer arrived later that evening and after suitable lubrication in the form of a couple of whiskies, sorted out our paperwork. We were thus able to leave the ship and go ashore, which we otherwise wouldn't have been able to do until normal working hours after the weekend. On Monday morning, a customs officer arrived and leisurely checked *Albatross*, insisting with a sorrowful smile that we relinquish our remaining onions and potatoes as transporting fresh vegetables to Tonga was strictly forbidden.

We found everything about Tonga to be friendly and unhurried. This is due in part to the heat and the size of the people: the archipelago has the fattest population on the planet with 92 percent of all over-30s overweight or obese, caused by overeating and the national love of suckling pig and lamb belly accompanied by carbohydrate-rich root vegetables. When we visited Nuku'alofa, it was home of the late King Taufaahau, the world's largest monarch of the world's smallest kingdom. He cut a gargantuan figure, weighing over 430 pounds, although he took part in a national fitness campaign and lost a third of his weight before his death in 2006.

Tonga's motto is "Where time begins," but we found it to be where time stopped, at least on Sunday; the capital was deserted and everything was closed, and I half expected tumbleweed to roll down the empty streets. The explanation: the whole nation was at church. The Tongan Visitors Bureau claims that the kingdom boasts more churches per head of population than anywhere else on earth. It is certainly true that as we wandered about Nuku'alofa, the place hummed with hymns and harmonies; a day of rest is enforced by law on Sunday.

Monday saw a return to the normal hustle and bustle of the city. The Nuku'alofa yacht club was buzzing with Tongans and tourists eager to tune into the fifth Rugby World Cup for which Tonga had qualified. While many Tongans still live in village communities and adhere to traditional customs, one influence of New Zealand is highly visible: rugby is taken as seriously as religion. Ultimately, the small South Pacific countries of Fiji, Samoa and Tonga were knocked out early in the competition by the rugby superpowers, with England going onto to take the cup from Australia, cause for massive celebrations the length and breadth of Britain. As Swedes, Carl and I found it a bewildering sport, featuring a team of overweight thugs who spent most of the game trying to shove another man's head up his own team member's arse while ignoring the loaf-shaped ball being hidden in the arms of a guy belting down the pitch towards the biggest goal I'd ever seen. The only comparable blood sport in Sweden is ice hockey – a game for serious hooligans who try to club each other into a coma with sticks, although they have the sensible luxury of being protected by a considerable amount of gear. Still, maybe the fascination of rugby would become clear after our sojourns in New Zealand and Australia.

In an attempt to learn more about Tonga and local life, we booked a trip around the island with Eddie, a jocular taxi driver we'd got to know. He was proud to show off his island and insisted our first stop be Tonga's National Museum and Cultural Centre to learn about his country's heritage. The museum's displays were sparse, enthusiastic missionaries having destroyed anything inappropriately pagan. Somewhat more interesting was the Ha'amoga 'A Maui, a stone trillithon dating back over 1,200 years standing in the middle of a park; think Stonehenge but on a much smaller scale: i.e. just two standing coral slabs supporting a 40-ton horizontal slab and without the attending hordes of Japanese tourists plodding around it. We dutifully took photos but failed to get really excited about it.

Eddie then steered us to his old school, Tupou College, a Methodist boys' institute which claims to be the oldest secondary school in the Pacific Islands at 150 years old. This strict Etonian type boarding establishment where the boys were smartly dressed in school uniforms seemed an anomaly on an island where men generally wear traditional woven waist mats and go bare-chested. Eddie explained that all schools in Tonga were run on religious principles; nevertheless, the single most important subject on the curriculum appeared to be rugby.

After touring the west of the island where the terrain rises sharply and the Pacific has carved out channels in the rock through which the ocean is forced into huge cascades, Eddie recommended we visit the Flying Fox Sanctuary. We heard the bats before we saw them; thousands hung in the casuarinas trees that lined the road, squeaking and screeching, stretching their wings and twisting their fox-like heads as they marked our approach. Considered the official property of the king, they are protected and only royalty may hunt them. It seemed to me that they were more likely to terrorize the human population than vice versa when at nightfall they swept down from their trees to fly off in search of fruit or to suck the nectar from flowers. Fruit bats have been found to act as harbours for numerous diseases harmful or even fatal to humans, so I ask you, who's in need of protection from whom?

Our final visit was to the Royal Palace of Nuku'alofa which looked much like a very large Victorian cricket pavilion with its white painted clapboard façade and ornate trellises. Eddie warned us not to touch the surrounding wall as it was sacred. It seems Tongan royalty love their pomp and ceremony even more than the crown heads of Europe. Tongan coronations feature offerings of tapa cloth, between 70 to 80 pigs gutted and stuffed with banana leaves, and drinking kava out of a coconut shell. The presentation of kava, a mildly narcotic drink made from ground pepper plant root, acknowledges a person's authority, although the drink itself is very potent and can have a psychoactive effect. An interesting way to come to the throne: high on root juice.

As we returned to *Albatross*, suitably seeped in culture, the weather was becoming tempestuous and the barometer was plummeting alarmingly quickly. We stocked up on fresh fruit and vegetables at the local market, and watched the weather closely. As soon as the storm subsided, we would set sail for New Zealand where we planned to hunker down for the season. As the wind raged about *Albatross* and we bounced about the cabin, Carl and I anxiously wondered if we'd already missed the boat. The conditions were ripe for a tropical cyclone.

Chapter 37
And then all
Hell Breaks Loose...

22 October – 04 November 2003

The Pacific Ocean

Experience: *An experience richer and a mainsail poorer.*

Tip: *Don't panic! Don't panic! I said, 'DON'T PANIC!'*

The British are famous for their ability to make conversation about the weather ad nauseam; in Sweden we make jokes about it. Two English sailors sink their yacht and are marooned on separate desert islands. After two years, they are rescued and joyfully reunited. Their first words to each other? 'I say, old boy, what was the weather like on your island?'

But an Englishman's interest in the weather is nothing compared to the obsession for the subject shown by the sailing community; it was endlessly discussed up and down the quay. The storm had abated and the sun was shining in an innocent blue sky. If any of us were going to make it to New Zealand before the cyclone season, we needed to make sail in the next few days or the weather window would close. Timing was essential; crews of every sail, fishing or cargo boat in Nuku'alofa were debating when to go: was it now or never?

There was also a lot of talk about a small yacht which had disappeared on the way to Fiji. The story was being passed up and down the quayside like a game of Chinese whispers. A Danish couple had apparently set off, enjoyed fine sailing and maintained daily radio contact with a Swedish yacht. But when their Swedish friends hadn't heard from them or been able to contact them, they raised the alarm. Unfortunately, the Danish couple had made a critical mistake: they'd failed to tie their EPIRB – the distress radio beacon – to their boat. An Australian frigate located the beacon but found no boat in the vicinity. Looking for a small yacht in the Pacific is like searching for a needle in a haystack the size of France, but their rescuers didn't give up. By using the Swedish boat's last radio contact with the Danish couple, measuring currents and prevailing winds, they calculated the boat might have drifted to a certain reef. They headed directly for that point. Astonishingly, they found the couple perched on the highest point on the reef in water up to their waists. Their yacht had capsized in rough weather and they'd been stranded on the reef for four days, hanging on to the slim hope that they'd be found. Our jaws dropped in horror when Carl and I discovered the couple in question was Bengt and his wife from *Tico Tico*.

It was a bit too close for comfort and certainly scared everything out of our bowels – but for the grace of God and all that. However, while our confidence was shaken, our faith in our Hallberg-Rassy wasn't; the Danish boat had been far less stable than *Albatross*. Nevertheless, I found myself whistling "I will survive" as we made ready to sail. Carl and I pepped each other up: 'Can't be as bad as the Atlantic,' Carl would say. And I'd reply, 'Nah! It's only 1,100 nautical miles to New Zealand.' Repeat this sort of stuff enough times and eventually you fall for your own bravado. We agreed we'd be just fine.

And for the first seven days we were; the biggest problem was avoiding the coral reefs as we left Tonga and having to tack against a light wind; if we had to tack all the way, it would turn a 1,100-mile journey into a 1,800-mile chore. But what the heck, we'd have to take it easy. The fishing was good and I showed off my cooking skills to Staffan with infinite varieties of fish suppers.

'180 degrees longitude and 25 degrees latitude,' Carl announced one afternoon.

Staffan looked up from gazing at the waves. 'What's so significant about that?'

'We've sailed exactly halfway around the world,' Carl replied with a pleased grin. 'So far, so good.'

On the seventh day the wind faded like an echo and we struggled to maintain three knots an hour. Nevertheless, it was beautiful blue water sailing. We reclined in the cabin and watched low cumulus clouds scuttle across the sky as *Albatross* lazily slid onwards, wafting us to sleep with the rhythm of waves lapping against the hull. We hadn't seen another ship in our week-long sail. We were totally alone in the vastness and I wondered again at the sanity of those who undertake to sail it alone. I can only assume that the men and women who attempt to row single-handed across the Pacific must be a very special kind of crazy. Despite the odds against them, and no doubt friends and family trying to get them the appropriate therapy to dissuade them, to date nine people have successfully rowed the Pacific solo, most of them British, which must surely say something about that nation's psyche. The first person to cross the width of the Pacific propelled purely by muscle power was Londoner Peter Bird who left California on 23 August 1982 and rowed for

294 days until he arrived at the Great Barrier Reef in Australia, making me feel a massive underachiever as I lay indolently on my bunk reading of his exploits. Sadly, Bird must have felt his solo accomplishment not impressive enough as in 1996 he attempted to row the more difficult west to east journey across the Pacific; he never completed his journey: his capsized boat was found by the Russian Rescue Centre who picked up his emergency signal, but of Peter there was no trace.

'So far, so good.' Carl should never have tempted the weather gods by saying that out loud, because on the eighth day without any warning at all almighty hell broke loose. Dawn had risen but the sun was obscured by an innocent-looking white cloud accompanied by a cold south-easterly wind that blew us steadily along. Shortly after seven in the morning, Carl handed over the watch to me; we exchanged a couple of grunts and Carl crawled to his bunk to get some shuteye. I went on up deck, coffee cup in one hand, book tucked under my arm. I took a sip of my coffee, read a paragraph of my book and nonchalantly glanced at the horizon and immediately threw both cup and book aside: in the matter of a couple of minutes, the horizon had turned coal black as a massive cloud unfurled itself the width of the horizon, whipping up the sea into a violent frenzy as it sped towards us. And it was bringing two angry companions with it: sudden violent wind and lashing rain, both intent on full destruction. This was going to get very messy.

I raced to the wheel, struggling to stay upright in the force of the wind which was already trying to wrestle me into an early submission, while simultaneously huge raindrops were punching me furiously about the face. *Albatross* was already careening out of control, slewing to one side and heeling badly. There was no time to call Calle or Staffan; Christ, at this rate, we'd turn broadside before I even got to the wheel. It was crucial to turn the boat into the wind to keep from broaching. I was already soaked to the skin, salt water stung my eyes and *Albatross* was leaning at such an incline that the mast was perilously close to touching the water as the wind picked up wave after wave to throw over us. The cockpit was filling fast. I threw myself at the wheel and planted my feet on either side of the base, then using my whole upper body, I grappled with all my strength to steer into the oncoming wind.

Meanwhile Staffan was thrown off his feet in the cabin below and was being tossed from side to side like a Frisbee. Carl, who'd just fallen into a deep dreamless slumber, was brutally awoken by sea water suddenly pouring through the starboard hatch and into his open mouth. After a brief thought along the lines of 'What the bloody hell is Yanne doing?' he registered the hammering wind and rain, quickly closed the hatch and shot through the cabin as naked as the day he entered the world. As he opened the cabin hatch, so water from the cockpit poured in. Recognising the severity of our situation, he forced his way towards me to help at the wheel. No clothes, no life vest, no time. The mainsail had become a giant bucket and was filling with water: it would sink us if we couldn't steer the boat into the wind.

'I can't steer her,' I shouted through the pelting rain, stating the obvious as one does in a crisis.

'We've got to release the sail,' Carl screamed back as he struggled to loosen the rope. The sail flapped out and I turned the wheel to right *Albatross*. At exactly the same moment the wind and rain died as if they had never been. Nothing. Not a murmur. Carl and I looked at each other in total confusion. My soaked hair hung in my eyes. Carl stood blinking in bewilderment, his nakedness conspicuously incongruous.

'What the bloody hell was that?' called a voice from below: a slightly shaken Staffan.

'Did you see the anemometer?' Carl said. 'The needle was bent all the way over. It must have been blowing over 80 miles an hour.'

'But where did it go?'

'More to the point, where did it come from and will it be back?'

'Well, we'd better get that sail down before it comes back. And for God's sake, get a lifejacket on.'

The words were barely out of my mouth when the wind blew up with renewed vengeance as if to strike me down for my impudence. It snuck up on us from behind, picked up the mainsail which had been hanging limply on the mast, and with Zorro-like speed slashed it into three pieces. The storm toyed with us for a while, threw us about and knocked us down for an hour or so before growing bored and rolling out over the sea in search of another boat to bully, leaving us stunned and gasping for breath like newly landed fish.

'That Magellan fellow clearly never sailed through anything like that,' I said later. 'There was nothing peaceful about that!'

We were still licking our wounds two days later when the Royal New Zealand Air Force flew overhead. Spotting us, they made radio contact to recommend that we lower our sails because of cyclones and violent weather.

'We haven't got any flipping sails,' Carl answered. 'And we've just come through a blasted cyclone.'

From then on, we decided to sail without the mainsail, but put up the mizzen and the genoa when the wind calmed to 25 miles an hour. We had just 300 miles left to our destination. On our eleventh day of sailing, we finally sighted the Hen and Chicken Islands, two rocky wildlife sanctuaries 25 miles south-east of Whangarei on our horizon. We had almost made it but would wait until morning to enter the harbour. We decided instead to anchor in

Smugglers Bay. As Carl dropped the anchor, Staffan popped the cork on a bottle of chilled champagne and we toasted to each other under a crisp, clear starlit sky: we had sailed through a blender and survived. Moreover, land-lubber Staffan had endured some very rough weather and never shown any signs of seasickness – the smug devil.

Sometimes you have to go through hell to get to paradise.

Chapter 38

Love in the Land of the Long White Cloud

5 November 2003 – 7 May 2004

Auckland and Opua, North Island, New Zealand

Experience: *If the engine sounds strange when idle and there is a lot of vibration, check the engine bolts.*

Tip: *Save as many major repairs as you can until you get to New Zealand where marinas specialize in boat maintenance at very competitive prices.*

My expectations were higher than a 1960s hippy on his drug of choice as we approached New Zealand's North Island, so I felt mildly deflated as we sailed into Whangarei harbour. It wasn't that I was expecting a group of All Blacks performing a *haka* on the quay in honour of our arrival or a display of synchronised bungee jumping by Maori women with tattooed chins, but of all our arrivals in ports since crossing the Atlantic this was the most mundane; we were simply ignored. Whangarei harbour, approximately 80 nautical miles north of Auckland, offers a wide range of repair facilities making it a popular port of call, so we were just one of hundreds of yachts seeking a cyclone mooring in a storm. After enjoying our minor celebrity status as the demigods of electrical repairs on our visits to South Pacific islands, Carl and I were just another couple of tourists on a boat. We were back in civilization – well, more or less: there was still that business of rugby.

Not that the New Zealanders weren't warm and welcoming people; in fact I've never encountered folk who seemed so genuinely pleased to meet us. We were assisted with clearing in by harbour master, John, who firmly but amicably advised us not to even think about going ashore until *Albatross* had been cleared by Customs and biosecurity. Whangarei's main marina facility is located in the Town Basin in the centre of town where pristine buildings and restaurants lined the quayside. As we tied up at our allotted mooring at pontoon B, a familiar aroma filled my nostrils.

'What's that wonderful smell?' I wondered aloud.

Carl inhaled, then frowned. 'Hmm, I know it, but I can't place it.'

Staffan laughed. 'You guys have been sailing around coral islands too long. That's the smell of fresh-cut grass!'

I was faintly surprised that New Zealanders needed to mow their lawns at all, having a quaint idea that as sheep outnumbered the human population by 20 to one, every family had a couple of animals in the garage for the sole purpose of cutting the grass. I've since learned that this ratio has shrunk considerably in recent years as a gradual decline, driven by lower wool prices and competition from dairy and forestry activities, has resulted in the number of sheep shrinking by 7 million over the last five years to 31.2 million. With New Zealand's human population standing at approximately 4.5 million, this gives a ratio of around seven sheep – give or take a chop – to each person; lamb featured heavily on all restaurant menus, as did beef.

Not that we minded: one of the first things we did, after taking long hot showers, was to indulge in a steak dinner that would have made a cardiologist weep for our arteries; it was our reward for having lived mostly on fish on our journey halfway around the world. The local supermarkets were similarly a meat lover's fantasy, and with prices 50 percent lower than in Sweden we could afford to clog our arteries for good.

We would be here for six months in *Aotearoa*, as New Zealand is called in Maori, meaning "land of the long white cloud," and had a great deal of work to do on *Albatross*, the least of which was repairing our shredded mainsail. But before we hunkered down to the "effing to do" list, the length of which would have exceeded my stretched-out small intestine, we decided to rent a car for a few days so Staffan could see something of the area before returning to the frozen north. As the most road-savvy among us, I volunteered to negotiate driving on the left hand side.

The confusing thing about New Zealand – apart from the mysteries of rugby and driving on the left – is that it is so very British in character. Here we were, over 11,000 miles from Great Britain and yet there were many aspects of this southwest Pacific country which were so British it might as well have been wearing a bowler hat and carrying a rolled-up copy of *The Times* under its arm: a pot of tea for one with milk was a standard menu item and the rolling landscape of Northland with its sheep-dotted hills could have been cloned from a postcard view of Scotland or the Lake District. But turn a corner and there was a burly Maori gentleman with intricate facial and upper body tattoos bent over his Kauri wood carving.

From Whangarei we drove west towards Dargaville – causing only the odd pileup and confusion at roundabouts when I would veer into oncoming traffic

– a township established during the height of the Kauri timber trade on the edge of the Northland Wairoa River. Kauri, a huge coniferous species of tree native only to New Zealand, once covered much of North Auckland before its popularity as a versatile timber from which large, unblemished planks could be produced, led to its virtual destruction. Nowadays, Kauri forests are closely guarded by the New Zealanders and their regeneration throughout the region is increasing. For the most part, however, the area of Northland now supports a happy balance of dairy, beef, sheep and agricultural farming. We stopped and gawked at a cattle auction which seemed as furious an event as a rugby match but with prettier bovine. Animals were squeezed into pens over which long planked walkways allowed potential buyers to view the livestock. The noise of a thousand bellowing animals and burly famers shouting prices at each other would have intimidated the toughest headbanger at a heavy metal concert. I caught Carl looking thoughtfully at a group of heifers. 'No way,' I yelled sternly at him before he suggested that fresh milk would be a bonus on a long crossing. Fortunately, bidding was machine gun fire rapid and completely incomprehensible; nevertheless, we made sure to leave before Carl's fingers started to twitch: that man can never resist a bargain.

We decided to stay overnight in Kaitaia, a town positioned between trees and tourism, each taking a small room in a rather antiquated inn where we were greeted by an equally antiquated but delightful lady who showed us to our rooms, the décor of which was very feminine with pillow cases with ruffles and ribbons, and bowls of potpourri on every available surface. I felt as if I'd invaded a nine-year-old girl's bedroom.

The town's name Kaitaia, meaning "plenty of food" – kai being the Maori word for food – turned out to be particularly apt, as that evening we ate at a restaurant which seemed to be directly supplied by the local cattle auction we'd visited that afternoon. I don't recall the exact name of the restaurant, but it was something like "The All-You-Can-Eat Meat Place," which was more or less the only fare on the menu, together with pots of tea for one and jugs o' beer. The restaurant looked like a Disneyfied Wild West fort, built of rough logs and raw planks. Our waitress looked as if she'd been built out of logs as well and was a walking reason not to order the "all-you-can-eat meat platter." But she was as friendly as she was round and beamed pleasantly as we ordered our steaks.

'And how do you like us Kiwis?' she asked.

'Oh, yes, we like kiwis,' I answered. 'But you can also buy them in Sweden, you know.'

If our waitress' smile faltered a little before she disappeared to get our jugs o' beer, we didn't notice: we were gawking at the size of the steaks being served at the table next to us. Staffan, a desperate carnivore, was rhapsodic when a T-bone steak the size of a coffee table was placed before him. We waddled out a couple of hours later with contented smiles, stomachs bulging like Sumo wrestlers and cholesterol levels off the charts.

The following morning, we squeezed ourselves into our rental car and drove 15 minutes to Ahipara, where a strip of sand called Ninety Mile Beach starts. It's closer to 60 miles long but there wasn't anyone to quibble with over the missing 30 miles. In fact, there wasn't anyone at all: it was deserted when we arrived, although I was bemused when ten minutes later a tour bus came speeding down the beach like something out of an action movie, followed by a second coach intent on overtaking the first; Ninety Mile Beach is also classed as a highway and tour bus drivers regularly show off their skills on the hard beige sand.

Staffan eyed the speeding buses thoughtfully. 'Can we do that?'

'Do you want to dig us out if we get stuck in the sand?' I asked.

'Didn't the rental guy say something about not being covered for driving on the beach?'

Carl was right, we weren't covered for being stranded on the sand dunes. It is, however, possible to drive the length of the beach in the right conditions all the way to Cape Reinga at the north-western most tip of the North Island. We drove the safer, and insurance covered, State Highway 1 and arrived at the cape's viewing point at the base of the lighthouse where we watched the Tasman Sea to the west meet the Pacific Ocean to the east: an eternal clash of waves and foam, resulting in spectacular explosions of spray and spume. No wonder the Maori give this place special significance: according to mythology, the spirits of the dead travel to the cape to leap off the headland and descend to the underworld to return to their traditional homeland of *Hawaiki*.

Over 1,000 years ago, the Maori people paddled their canoes from their ancestral homeland of *Hawaiki* to the land of the long white cloud. Fourteen percent of the population is Maori, and their language and culture influence all aspects of life on New Zealand; their ancient beliefs are recognised and respected by New Zealand's leaders today. For example, a recent road project was modified to avoid disturbing a *taniwha* (water monster) when Transit New Zealand was persuaded to alter its plans so that the swamp in which the water monster was said to reside remained undisturbed. The Maori culture is rich with stories and legends, much like those of the native Indians of North America or the Aborigines of Australia, and like theirs long suppressed through colonisation by the white man.

So our next stop, Waitangi in the Bay of Islands on the east coast, was particularly significant, for this was where New Zealand's founding document was signed in 1840: the Treaty of Waitangi, an agreement between the British Crown and the Maori that established British law throughout the country. Billed as a "must-do" by the New Zealand tourist board, we did it, dutifully making appropriate noises of awe in front of the world's longest war canoe and looking suitably solemn when the guide told us about the terms of the treaty. Our chatty guide asked us how we were enjoying life amongst the Kiwis. We smiled and nodded and said, 'Yes, they're delicious.'

'I don't get it, why do they keep asking us about fruit?' Carl said.

I groaned out loud as sleepy neurons woke up and whirled about in my brain. 'How stupid are we? They're not talking about fruit at all!'

'No?'

'No! They're talking about the kiwi bird. Of course, they don't eat it; it's their national bird!' All was clear. How we chuckled at our misunderstanding.

Although to Swedish eyes New Zealand is a relatively new country, it offers much to see and do. After a week of touring the region of Northland, we'd barely glimpsed the tip of the iceberg. As we would be hibernating here for six months, it was the perfect opportunity to explore more of the country with visiting family and friends. First to arrive were my parents and my nephew Linus, so on Monday we made the 80-nautical mile sail to Auckland to meet them.

Auckland, known fittingly as the city of sails, is New Zealand's largest and most populated city, enviably ranked tenth in the Economist's world's most liveable cities index in 2013. Not that Aucklanders would seem to care; they appeared to be the most laidback, agreeable bunch of people I'd ever encountered. I put their geniality down to the proliferation of wine bars on every street corner and to the fact it is one of the few cities in the world to have harbours on two separate major bodies of water. We'd been advised to go to Bayswater Marina in the northern basin, which offered wonderful views of Waitemata Harbour, the America's Cup Village and Auckland Harbour Bridge. We decided to hole up there for the season as the facilities were outstanding and the marina was well secured.

The relaxed buzz of Auckland quickly seduced us, and a city built around life on the water is idyllic for a boat owner, so it's no surprise that one in three Auckland households owns a boat. During our stay in 2004, people were still raving about the America's Cup win in 2000 by Team New Zealand and mourning its loss in 2003 to Switzerland. Considered by many to be the oldest sporting trophy, Aucklanders were delirious with pride to have taken back the cup from the Americans in 1995. It's a difficult trophy to win and in the 163 years since the first race off England, only four nations have claimed it. If Aucklanders weren't gibbering about the last race, they were fervently speculating about the next.

If ever there was a place for buying or fixing sailboats, Auckland was it. On the bridge next to us was a 60-foot solid teak ketch, the asking price for which was a steal compared to European prices. 'It's a fantastic bargain,' Carl kept saying, gazing longingly at the ketch. His pain at not being able to take advantage of such a good deal was pitiful to witness.

But we had to attend to the boat we already owned. Our shredded mainsail was in desperate need of repair after the accident in the horrendous squalls we'd encountered on the way to New Zealand. We were spoilt for choice for sailmakers, but happened upon a terrific man who repaired and reinforced our sail for a fraction of what it would have cost in Sweden. We also invested in new lifejackets that would automatically inflate when they hit the water. And as we would be spending the next six months in the waters around New Zealand, we decided to cancel our original insurance policy and take out new insurance with a local company, saving us a great deal of money.

Staffan's time on *Albatross* had come to an end and with a deep sigh he returned to winter in Sweden, leaving us the following kind words in the logbook:

"It is with great sadness that I sign off after six weeks and just over 2,200 nautical miles. The experiences of the South Pacific islands and New Zealand have been fantastic with sailing ranging from beautiful – sunsets and calm seas while we enjoyed fresh fish and good wine – to nightmarish times with deadly force cyclones that have thrown themselves upon us, requiring great skill, courage and probably more than a little luck to cope with.

I commend Yanne and Carl-Erik for their good seamanship, but also for their great skill in preparing varied fish dishes. Most of all, however, I will miss their good humour and camaraderie. I will long remember this adventure."

We spent our first week in port tidying the boat and preparing our bikes which the Pacific salts had all but ruined, pulling them apart, removing the rust and cleaning the parts. After an hour's frustration I threw down my rag and spanner like a petulant toddler. 'Bugger this,' I said. 'It'd be a damn sight easier to buy a new bike.' I stomped off to the nearest cycle shop and forked out NZ $290 for a good quality bike including delivery to the marina where the ever-stubborn Carl was surrounded by all three hundred pieces of his Cannondale.

'Come off it, Calle,' I said as I watched him fiddle with brake callipers and tweezers. 'Don't be so tight. Buy a new one and save some time.'

Carl looked at me with hurt in his eyes. 'This beauty is too close to my heart, Yanne. This is the bike that started our whole venture. This is the bike that took me half way to Lisbon. This,' by now he was thumping his chest with his fist, 'is the bike that gave new meaning to my life. This is the bike that saved not just me, but you too, Yanne.

'Bloody hell, you're not sleeping with it!'

'No, but in the future I'm stowing her below deck. The weather and the sea are just too hard on her.'

Bored, I left him to his thousand-piece puzzle and peddled off on my new bike.

While cycling around the city was good exercise and relatively easy to do, we realized that to get further afield we really needed to invest in a car: renting one for six months was out of the question, so when we spotted a car for sale on our tours around the marina, we skidded our bikes to a stop and after kicking the car's tyres a couple of times called the owner. A quick test drive around Auckland and some amicable negotiating later, we were the owners of a 1986 Mitsubishi Mirage which, while it wouldn't get me any dates, would at least get us around for six months.

It was certainly perfect for touring the North Island with my parents and nephew. We packed ourselves off and went where the fancy took us, staying overnight in small bed and breakfast places where we were always greeted with genuine friendliness. We did the usual tourist sites, the Kauri parks and museums, as well as taking a "must-do" jetboat ride down the Waikato River to within a few feet of the Huka Falls. Linus, an adventure junkie if ever there was, had spotted the brochure's compelling lines "enjoy the most thrilling ride of your life" and insisted we give it a go. We thus found ourselves kitted out in lifejackets and helmets and gripping for dear life onto the handrail of the seat in front of us as we hurtled down the river at torpedo speed.

'Pretty good,' Linus said indifferently, clearly jaded by too many amusement park rides. 'But I wouldn't say it was the *most* thrilling ride of my life.' Sometimes, there is no pleasing today's youth.

It was during our travels that I was offered a job. Working our way up the Kauri coast and into the Hokianga region, we'd stumbled upon the small ferry town of Rawene. My mother, who can spot historic charm at ten paces, insisted we get out of the car to stroll about this quiet little place, soaking up its early settler atmosphere. My father, who can spot a bargain at fifty paces, got chatting to an affable 60-year-old Dutch guy selling Swedish antiques. Within mere minutes they'd bonded over their love of old Scandinavian crap, and when they discovered they'd both served in the merchant navy, there was no parting them. Not only were we staying for dinner at the sole restaurant in town, which Dutchman John happened to own, but we were also staying the night. It was during our meal, prepared by John's friend Dorothy that they mentioned they were looking for a new chef to change the style of the menu somewhat; my ears tingled and I suddenly found myself blurting out the words, 'I'll take the job.'

'Seriously?' asked a trio of voices incredulously: John and my parents.

'Sure. I'll have to check with Carl first, but I'm pretty sure he'd be okay with it.'

'Yes, but can you cook?' asked John.

'Well, I can do a million things with fish and shellfish, and there's always Swedish meatballs.' All three still looked doubtful. 'Tell you what; I'll cook you a three-course meal tomorrow morning. See what you think.'

The next morning, Dorothy and John sat down to my culinary delights: seafood salad with shrimp, peach and curried mayonnaise; oven-baked salmon stuffed with anchovy, dill and chives served with new potatoes and my secret sauce; lastly, a simple, palette cleansing raspberry sorbet. John laid down his spoon and winked at Dorothy. 'I think we've got ourselves our very own Swedish chef.'

But before I could accept the job, I had to ring Carl. 'So? What do you think? Is it okay if I take the job? The extra money will come in useful, but it will mean you'll have to work on *Albatross* without me. They want me to start after Christmas.'

There was a heavy sigh at the end of the phone. 'Oh, thank god, Yanne.' Carl's rich chuckle travelled down the line. 'Take the job. I wasn't sure I could survive six long months in port with you!'

I had a month before starting, so while Carl went off on a camping trip with his daughter Erica and her boyfriend, I started working my way through some of the jobs on the "effing to do" list. When Carl and his family returned, we celebrated Swedish Christmas together with Anders and Zara who arrived on Christmas Eve, bringing the essential seasonal dinner component of pickled herring without which a Swedish Christmas would just not be complete. The last time we'd seen Anders was twelve months before in St Lucia when he'd sailed with us to Union Island.

'*Hej!* It's the bullfrog. How's the diving going?' Anders asked Carl as they shook hands. 'Any better at keeping your arse below the water?'

'Probably better than your ability to remain on deck,' Carl deadpanned back. 'Fallen backwards off any boats recently?'

'Not since last New Year's Eve,' Anders replied.

'Well, it's only Christmas. Give it time,' Carl said. 'Skål!'

'Vell, I don't belief my ears!' a familiar voice shouted from the quayside. 'Dose damn Swedish are eferyvere!' We turned to see the familiar figure of Captain Dimitro Birioukovitch of *Bat'Kivshchyna*, the Ukrainian tall ship out of Kiev. He was now attempting to bring Ukrainian culture to New Zealand. Together with his crew and those of several other sailboats in the harbour, we made up a mismatched but merry band for the Christmas festivities with everyone contributing a national dish for the party.

Before signing on for work in Rawene, it was my turn for a little misadventure, so I joined my son Dino and his girlfriend Sofia on a trip south to Rotura where Dino insisted we experience extreme rafting on the river Waihuo, followed by extreme caving. I am usually reluctant to join anything preceded by the word "extreme," be it a religious group, club or activity. Nothing comes to any good when the word "extreme" is placed before it: weather, temperature and especially sports. But too proud to admit my fears to my son, I found myself in a rubber raft, with a yellow helmet tightly strapped on my head, looking at water gushing over rocks that had clearly been strategically placed to overturn, sink or just plain maim us. Finding myself the oldest person in a flimsy dinghy, I had to disguise my feelings by yelling loudly as if in orgasmic delight as we hurtled down the river. In a strange way, it was quite thrilling.

After that, squeezing myself into a dark hole where most rats wouldn't dare to venture in the fun-packed extreme cave exploration event was almost relaxing by comparison. At least I didn't scream as much, mostly because I'd lost my voice and was too shattered to find it again. Exhausted by so much extreme amusement, I was looking forward to starting my job.

I left Carl on *Albatross* in the company of Anders, Zara and several dozen cockroaches, and got a lift to Rawene to start my four-month stint as chef, busboy and washer-up, little knowing that my brief career in the catering industry was to add 125 pounds to my circumstances.

On my first day in the kitchen I was so nervous about cooking for paying customers that I could barely hold a potato peeler, but Dorothy quickly put me at ease with her sense of humour. By the end of the week, I was juggling the preparation of multiple dishes like a pro and creating my own signature recipes which gratifyingly were not sent back to the kitchen with comments of 'What the hell was the chef thinking?' It was rewarding work and I enjoyed the good natured atmosphere of friendly panic in the kitchen when we got rushed. *The Ferry House* was a popular restaurant with locals and tourists alike, and I became known in the area as the Swedish Chef; my meatballs with cranberry sauce was one of the specialities of the house. Less rewarding was cleaning up; the mountain of dishes which threatened to topple and crush me was a depressing sight at the end of a long day, but Dorothy and John often pitched in to help.

The small town of Rawene is one of New Zealand's oldest settlements, having prospered in the nineteenth century as a result of the booming timber industry and a healthy ship building business, but its population has never risen above 500. I'd joined a community so closely knit, that if you sneezed in the privacy of your bedroom, people would ask you the following day if your cold was improving. It was not dissimilar from small town Sweden, except the people of Rawene were not suspected of being drunk if they made eye contact. I thought I'd met all of the 450 residents of the town, so I couldn't help but notice as we were closing up one night John chatting with a woman at the bar I hadn't seen before. And she was the type I certainly would have noticed. I nearly dropped the stack of plates I was carrying when a pair of big brown eyes under long eyelashes sparkled in my direction. The owner of the brown eyes had a mass of dark hair, a wide smile, an infectious laugh and a pair of legs that seemed to have no end – I'm sure she also had arms and a torso, but these were the qualities that first struck me, and I was instantly struck. However, I'm a shy gentleman by nature and wouldn't have known how to flirt with the lady. In any case, my language skills were limited to talking about boats, boat maintenance, weather for boats and how best to get rid of cockroaches on boats, and I hadn't yet finished the washing up.

'Hey, Yanne.' John waved me over. 'Come over here. My friend would like to meet our very own Swedish Chef.'

'Well, you don't look like a Muppet,' said Brown Eyes. 'Hi. I'm Anita.' I dried my hands on my apron and held out a slightly clammy hand. She smiled a wide warm smile that after a while started to falter; I realized I was still clutching her hand and admiring her long fingers. 'And you are...?' she asked.

'Yes, I am,' I said. Anita looked confused. 'Oh, yes, I understand. I am Yanne,' I tried to answer confidently. It sounded as if I was announcing I was Yoda.

'Nice to meet you, Yanne,' Anita said.

'Yes,' I replied and racked my brain for something else to say. Nothing. So much for impressing the lady with my *savoir faire*.

'So how do you like living with us Kiwis?' she asked, gamely trying to continue the conversation.

'Yes, but I haven't seen many of them,' I said. 'I think they only come out at night.' *Good lord, how New Zealanders banged on about their birds.* Anita squinted at me, then giggled.

'Oh no! I mean "*us* Kiwis."' I must have continued to stare blankly at her. 'When we talk about "*us* Kiwis" I mean the people not the birds; that's what New Zealanders call themselves.'

I was speechless with my own ignorance. Mortified, I scuttled back to the safety of my dishes. But despite my ineptitude at making small talk, I sidled back to the bar when I'd finished cleaning the kitchen. John was stacking glasses.

'Anyone fancy going on for a drink somewhere?' Anita asked. Was it my hopeful imagination or was she looking directly at me?

'Sorry, it's been a long day,' John said. 'I'm off to bed.'

'I would like to go somewhere for a drink,' I said as clearly and swiftly as possible before the offer could be withdrawn.

'Great,' Anita said without hesitation, swooping up her bag. 'Let's go. I know a great place. We can take my car.'

I didn't resist but followed puppy-like, ready to give myself up to her charms should it be required. But all modesty aside, it seemed that I wasn't without my own endearing traits. We ended up sitting on the soft dunes of Opononi Beach, gazing at each other in the clear light of a full moon. Anita talked and I listened, understanding only half of what she said, but entranced by the way the moonlight made her skin glow, set the reds and browns of her hair alight and accentuated her long legs and full breasts. I had fallen in lust again.

'Isn't this romantic?' Anita said.

'Absolutely,' I said. 'It's like that film with the dogs.'

Anita's eyebrows furrowed slightly. 'What dogs?' she asked. '*Lassie?*'

'No, the film with the dogs in love.'

'*A Hundred and One Dalmatians?*'

'No, the film where the dogs eat spaghetti and meatballs under the moon.'

'Ah,' she said. '*The Lady and the Tramp*. Well, I hope you mean I'm the lady, not the tramp.'

'No, I'm sure you're not a tramp. I'm a tramp,' I gushed. Oh yes, I know how to romance a woman. And then I gave her the most passionate line in my repertoire. 'I'd give you my last meatball with my nose.' Although I grant you the romance of the sentiment may have got lost in translation. Nevertheless, my clumsy sweet talk didn't put Anita off; by the time the pink light of dawn had risen, we'd traded life stories. Anita had married young, had four children aged between twenty and three and was in the middle of a messy divorce, but hell, I could sympathize with all of that. She lived and worked in Auckland but was in the process of selling her Rawene house, hence her weekend visits back to the town.

'Will I see you again?' I asked as she drove me back to *The Ferry House* for my morning shift.

She smiled. 'Well, I certainly hope so. Otherwise I've wasted my time and a lot of moonlight taking you to the most romantic spot in New Zealand.'

And I'd naively thought I'd been seducing *her*. Never underestimate the cunning of a woman. But I hadn't yet played my master card.

'Change of lunchtime menu,' I announced to Dorothy as I flung myself around the kitchen with the energy of a hormonally charged teenager. I knew

Anita would shortly drive past and I particularly wanted her to see the midday special announced in large chalk letters on the board in front of the restaurant: *Sicilian style Spaghetti and Meatballs*. Never let it be said I don't know how to woo a woman.

While Anita and I were revelling in the heady days of little sleep and lots of nookie throughout that summer, the barometer was plummeting. But what did we care, until the fine weather ended not with a whimper but a bang as the mother of all storms swept in from the Tasman Sea. Raindrops fell like pebbles and the wind whipped itself into a frenzy, shaking the houses in Rawene so that the wood creaked and groaned. Carl reported that *Albatross* strained against her mooring ropes and whenever the cabin door was opened, rain poured into the cabin, drenching everything in the saloon. One storm would seem to abate, only for a more ferocious one to follow hot on its wet heels. This was cyclone season. Three tropical cyclones hit the South Pacific that year with winds of 130 miles per hour, resulting in 16 deaths and damage estimated at over US $200 million. Cyclone Heta, the deadliest of the three storms, all but devastated the little coconut island of Nuie we'd visited only three months earlier, and we wondered how the island's fragile economy would survive in the face of the constraints of limited air services, lack of skilled professionals and little entrepreneurial expertise. According to some of my friends in Rawene, it was the worst weather in over a hundred years, but as John dryly remarked to me, 'They say that every cyclone season.'

Nevertheless, I felt a rising panic one evening as the wind howled like an angry banshee and the rain hammered on the roof and windows of Anita's Rawene house. It was 6 February, the first day of the Waitangi Day weekend, and Anita and I had planned to spend the three-day national holiday together. We were halfway through dinner and a bottle of wine when I was overwhelmed with a feeling of dread or danger – I couldn't really say what, but I knew I had to trust my instincts.

'We can't stay here,' I suddenly announced, dropping my fork on my plate. 'We have to go.'

'Go? Now? Go where?'

I pushed back my chair and started to clear the table. 'I don't know. But it's just not safe here.'

Anita looked at me with bewilderment. 'Well, it's not safe out there, Yanne,' she said. 'Just look at that storm.'

'We have to go. We'll go back to Auckland and stay on *Albatross*.'

Anita half laughed. 'Are you out of your mind? Driving back in this weather will be impossible. We're safe here. This house has stood for a hundred years, it'll stand for another couple of hundred. And don't worry about *Albatross*. Carl said she's securely moored.'

But I insisted and eventually persuaded Anita to lock up the house and make the journey back to Auckland. She was right though, driving through the storm was treacherous; the lashing rain made visibility impossible and many roads were impassable due to fallen branches, forcing us to make detours and circuitous routes to the city. We eventually arrived at the marina at five in the morning and crept onto *Albatross*, careful not to wake Carl. Exhausted we got into bed and slept blissfully through the rest of the storm.

Hunger finally forced us up later that afternoon. I was rustling about in the galley when a man's high-pitched scream nearly caused me to drop the frying pan I was holding.

'Bloody hell, Calle! I know you're glad to see me but "hello" would have sufficed,' I said.

'But, but ...,' Carl's complexion was the colour of fog. He looked as if he'd had a rough night; his eyes were swollen and his face haggard.

'Well, you're looking messy. Been on a bender with some of your boat neighbours?' I asked, returning my attention to the contents of the frying pan.

'No,' he stammered. 'I've been mourning your death!'

'Who's dead?' asked Anita, entering the galley and looking fetching in one of my T-shirts.

'Aah!'

'Calle, for god's sake, stop screaming!' I said, rubbing my ear.

'You're both dead, you bloody idiot,' he shouted. He shakily sat down and told us what had happened. Anita and I had slept through a visit from two policemen who'd solemnly informed Carl that they'd suspected we'd perished in a house fire in Rawene. Anita's house had burned to the ground in the early hours of the morning, just as we were arriving in Auckland. Even now, as we stood in *Albatross*' galley, the police were sifting through the hot ashes of the villa looking for our remains and the cause of the fire.

'Oh my god,' cried Anita. 'My poor parents! I must let them know I'm alive.' She dashed for her phone.

'Well, reports of my death have been greatly exaggerated,' I said. I hadn't yet registered the full horror of what had transpired. I think I was slightly giddy at having cheated death.

Carl reminded me by muttering, 'Jesus, I was just about to call your family, Yanne. I was convinced I'd lost my best friend. Here I was picturing your bloody funeral.'

I was instantly sombre. 'You're right, Calle. Anita's lost her home. We're really lucky to be alive.'

'An understatement if ever there was one,' Carl said gravely. He looked at me. 'But why are you here? I mean, what made you leave and come back to Auckland?'

I couldn't answer him. And ten years later, I'm still not able to explain what instinct compelled me to insist on leaving the house that night, but ever since then I've come to believe in a sixth sense or a guardian spirit that watches over me. Call it intuition if you will, but some divine inspiration drove me to leave what could have been the site of my and Anita's untimely cremation. Investigation suggested that the fire had been deliberately set; a figure had been seen prowling around the property that night. More than ever, my damsel was in distress and needed a noble knight. I was going to gird my loins, polish up my armour and rescue her. But could I persuade her to join me in the land of meatballs, pine trees and flat pack furniture? And if I could tempt her, would she be prepared to wait another 18 months until I'd completed our circumnavigation?

Back in Rawene in the middle of March, happy and drunk on that singular cocktail of chemicals peculiar to those in love, I got a call from Carl. 'Yanne. I've got some bad news from Helsingborg.' His voice was sad and serious over the line. 'Ove's dead.'

Ove: my teacher, my mentor, my friend had died. Friends at Helsingborg Yacht Club reported that his body had been found in the icy water of the harbour. It was thought he'd capsized and drowned while test driving a new dingy. We'd pulled him out of the water on more than one occasion, but on a dark evening in early March there'd been no one to see or save him. He'd just turned 63 and I'd always hoped he'd be on the dock in Helsingborg, a glass of whisky in his hand, to toast to our return. We wouldn't have got this far without his help and knowledge, and he would have been so thrilled to have shared in our success. I was choked with sorrow, yet in my heart I'd always had an uneasy feeling that Ove would be taken by the sea: not a premonition, but the knowledge that he'd not really valued himself enough to care for his own safety.

The following weekend I returned to Auckland. Carl and I sat on the deck of *Albatross* and looked and laughed over photos of Ove we'd taken in Scotland during the Classic Malts Cruise and reminisced about the many moments we'd shared with our friend. Carl poured large measures of whisky and we raised our glasses. 'To Ove,' he said. 'Great boat mechanic, whisky connoisseur and cigar thief.'

'To Ove,' I agreed. 'And in his own words '"Whisky, a drink for men not boys. Cheers for this and the next one."' We took Ove sized gulps of our drinks and looked out across the bay towards the Auckland Harbour Bridge. 'This one's for you, Ove.'

While I was losing my heart to a pair of brown eyes, Carl had been dividing his time between making repairs on *Albatross* and touring the North Island with Eva who'd arrived from Sweden for a month. It was the end of March when I guiltily returned to Auckland for a weekend to help Carl with some of the heavier work on the boat. I was shocked on seeing Carl for the first time in a few weeks; one arm was held in a sling, both hands were covered in cuts and he had deep grazes and purple bruises on one side of his jaw.

'What the hell, Calle? What kind of fight did you and the wife have?'

'Oh, Eva left a week ago,' Carl said with a wince. 'I had a little accident.' He described how he'd been cycling along to the harbour showers when the towel he'd hung on the handlebars had become entangled in the front wheel, jarring the bike to a halt and shooting him across the tarmac like a human torpedo. 'I was lucky not to land on my nose,' he said. 'So I've kept my good looks. But I have to admit my arm hurts like the devil.'

I looked at the improvised silk scarf sling. 'And let me guess, you haven't seen a doctor about it!'

'Well, it'll probably be okay,' he mumbled. 'Although it might be broken.'

'Damn it, Calle! You're so tight you'd rather lose a limb than see a doctor! Haven't you learned anything from the last time when you nearly lost your leg?'

'All right, don't nag,' Carl said with a cringe, be it in pain or shame. 'I'll go tomorrow.'

The following day Carl returned from the emergency room at the North Shore Hospital in Milford with his left arm in a cast and a large smile. He'd fractured his wrist but hadn't been charged for the hospital care. 'They told me that as I was a guest in New Zealand, the cost was covered,' he said cheerfully. 'If I'd known that, I would have gone earlier.'

Fortunately, David Williams, a cracking bloke I'd got to know, had accompanied me to Auckland to see *Albatross* and help take our small diesel generator back to Rawene for overhauling. David owned a garage and repair shop in Rawene and had already helped us out when our Mitsubishi needed to pass its vehicle inspection. He was approaching 50 with the trepidation we all face at greeting a half century and had vowed to sail around the world when he was 55. Happy to assist anyone in pursuit of such an admirable goal, I'd suggested he sail with us to Fiji. We decided to cast off in early May if the weather forecast looked promising, although being a man in love I felt a pang at the thought of leaving Anita.

But before sailing any further, Carl and I had to pay attention to the most demanding woman in our life. *Albatross* required some major repairs before we put to sea. First, there was the problem of the roller furling system on the genoa, *Albatross*' main driving sail to windward. Fortunately we were put in touch with Peter Nordstrand, a third generation Swede who niftily refitted the roller by making a new cylinder to fit inside the outer casing. Our next problem was mounting the damn thing, not an easy task with three able hands as one of Carl's was still in plaster. Luckily Carl had found a good friend in Peter Häggert, another Swedish boat owner he'd got to know, who helped us install it. It was with great satisfaction that with the single tug of a rope we could finally quickly furl and unfurl the genoa. *Albatross'* sails were complete.

Our next major task was to repaint the hull. So in the first week of April we set sail for Gulf Harbour Marina, recommended to us for its haul-out and wash-down facilities. Located in a well-protected bay north of Auckland around 30 nautical miles from Bayswater Marina, we thought it would be a relatively quick and easy sail. Unfortunately, the wind turned northerly forcing us to tack the whole way against heavy swells in the Rangitoto Channel. The going was so slow we decided to use the engine for a bit more oomph, only to discover that the propeller had as much oomph as a hand whisk.

'Damn,' said Carl. 'It's probably dragging because of marine growth.'

But when the acrid smell of burning rubber stung my nostrils, I flung open the engine room doors to a cloud of thick smoke.

'Quick! Shut off the engine!' I shouted. After a few choice curse words, we waited for the smoke to clear and inspected the damage. It was a problem we'd encountered before on our way to the Galapagos Islands; the propeller shaft had become misaligned, probably as a result of broken engine bolts. We had no option but to turn south and head for a sheltered area where we could anchor for the night. With the wind behind us, we sailed into the Motuko-rea Channel and anchored in the shelter of the volcanic island of Rangitoto. There was nothing to do but sit back and wait for the wind to turn in our favour. As it was Maundy Thursday, we ate boiled eggs, crisp bread and pickled herring accompanied by cold beers and a few shots of snaps in the Swedish tradition. We might be far from home, but visits from friends had ensured a supply of Swedish delicacies for the season.

There was an autumnal nip in the air as the sun rose in an icy blue sky on Good Friday morning, but we were rewarded with a brisk westerly wind: perfect for raising the mainsail and continuing towards our goal. If only raising the anchor were as simple; frustratingly, the windlass kept slipping and we were forced to pull up the anchor by hand – a workout we could have done without. We sailed briskly towards Gulf Harbour but then limped into our pre-booked mooring with the engine doing a mere half a knot.

The last time our Hallberg-Rassy had been out of the water was two years earlier, and we were relieved to see the hull was sound and free from damage. Two men in outfits you'd expect to see on astronauts sprayed the hull with high-pressure water hoses, sending the accumulated plant growth flying. While Carl painted, polished and waxed with his one arm, I worked on the engine, replacing the broken engine bolts and realigning the propeller shaft. The smoke had been the result of the rubber seal getting hot and burning, a fortunate signal which had alerted us to the propeller shaft's misalignment, otherwise the problem might not have manifested itself until a critical moment miles from port. We then turned our attention to the windlass, the teeth of which were ground down to mere stubs. Ordering spare parts was out of the question as we were told, 'that thing should be in a museum!' The only option was to order a new windlass. Lastly, with Peter Häggert's help, we reinstalled our newly overhauled diesel generator. Happiness is turning the start switch and hearing the generator ticking away in the knowledge that it is charging the battery banks. Like other technologies we take for granted, you only fully appreciate electricity when you don't have it.

It was May and *Albatross* was now ready for the homeward bound leg of our journey, but my excitement at continuing was damped by my feelings for Anita. Bloody love, it's so damned inconvenient, but the heart wants what the heart wants and all that. Anita and I hadn't made any concrete plans about the future; we knew that one day we would be together; the real question was where: New Zealand or Sweden? If New Zealand was to be our home, it would be some years until I could return as I had to fulfil my commitment to my brother by managing the business for three years. But for Anita, moving to Sweden was a complicated affair as she had to consider her children and ex-husband. We decided to wait making any decisions until I'd returned to Helsingborg, believing we were above the problems usually associated with a long distance relationship; we felt completely secure in our commitment to each other.

'But you know what this means?' Anita said, looking at me gravely.

I rolled my eyes. 'Anything, darling,' I said, desperately hoping she wasn't referring to the immediate purchase of something involving karat, colour and clarity.

'You'll have to meet my family.'

'Happy to,' I lied. I was somewhat apprehensive about doing so, as Anita had already told her father about the Swedish love of her life who was attempting to sail around the world despite a massive gap in experience. Her father, who'd had a long career in the merchant navy, had dryly replied, 'What is he? Brave? Or stupid?'

I shook Harry's hand and we sized each other up, Harry eyeing me suspiciously as if he expected me to swig blood from a skull over dinner. I was momentarily tempted to introduce myself as "Yanne the Brave from Helsingborg" but that probably would have made me sound more stupid. Both Harry and I, rigorously instructed by our better halves, stayed on our best behaviour and rubbed along pretty well. I think he was relieved I didn't bash Anita over the head and carry her off over my shoulder while plundering the silverware from the dining room cabinet.

When we'd first arrived in New Zealand six months earlier, we'd originally intended to call at Opua in the Bay of Islands located northwest of the North Island, but the wind had driven us further south to Whangarei, so we decided to check out of the land of the long white cloud from Opua; Anita was joining us on the 140-nautical mile sail so we could spend our last week together.

'I don't get seasick on your boat,' she said cheerfully. *Must be love*, I thought to myself.

'But we haven't been out of port yet,' Carl pointed out. 'You might find it a bit rough once we get out on the ocean. I would recommend stocking up on some seasick tablets.'

The marina basin was mirror calm as *Albatross* slid out into the channel where the tide grabbed her and thrust her forward out on to the open water. My heart swelled with the waves and the joy of sailing again. We sailed into the Hauraki Gulf, home to 65 islands with colourful names like Beehive, The Noises, and Hens and Chickens, as well as Maori names that twisted my poor Scandinavian tongue into knots in my attempt to copy Anita's pronunciation. Some of the islands are developed and populated; others are inhabited only by birds, plants and reptiles. We headed for Shark Bay on Kawau Island where anchorage was easy. The sun was low in the horizon as we slowly sailed into the bay where we were the sole boat. All was eerily quiet until we heard the cry of a lone bird defending his territory.

'A kiwi,' Anita said with a mischievous smile. 'One of the feathered kind.'

The contours of the wooded slopes reflected dark green in the clear water broken suddenly by a ripple and a flash of white as a small flock of penguins swam to greet *Albatross*. They popped their sleek heads out of the water to regard us briefly with eyes as glossy as beads before diving under to feed on the fish that thrive in the gulf waters.

It was the blissful calm before the storm; by the following morning, the wind had increased to gale force, but fortunately we were well sheltered in the curve of the bay. We took the dinghy over to shore and tramped around for a bit. There are no public roads on the island, but the Kawau Island Historic Reserve has a network of pleasant walking tracks that cut through the woodland. Carl and I were surprised by the appearance of a troop of small kangaroos leaping past us.

'Look at all the baby kangaroos,' I whispered excitedly, scrambling for my camera.

'No,' Anita corrected me, 'they're wallabies. In the same family as kangaroos but smaller.'

'In other words, little kangaroos,' I said.

'No, not kangaroos. Wallabies, different kangaroos.'

I still didn't understand the difference but thought it prudent not to argue, a policy I still employ with most women; it proves easier in the long run.

The following day we headed to the Bay of Islands pushed north with a brisk wind and accompanied by a large whale as we entered the bay early on Friday morning. Of the 144 islands in the area, we were visiting Opua where we met David who would join us on our sail to Fiji. We'd hoped to spend a couple of days exploring the island and the area, but we heard from our Swiss friend Daniel on his sailboat *Shogun* that the weather window for sailing to Fiji and Tonga was closing due to an approaching storm front. We decided to set sail the following day, cutting short my plans for a last romantic weekend with Anita. We shopped for provisions and made the arrangements to check out of New Zealand. That evening Anita and I shared a last meal together in the purple twilight of Opua marina, gazing at each other with all the intensity of two cartoon dogs.

Anita's contribution to our logbook was as follows:

Opua 8th May 2004
Dear Carl and Yanne,
Thank you for all the love and friendship you have brought into my life and a big thank you to Albatross for sailing all the way to New Zealand. The last five months have been very special and to sail into Opua, your port for leaving New Zealand waters, was the 'icing on the cake.' But I admit I have never felt so frightened as when I awoke to the stormy sea upon leaving Kawau Island and for a while the journey stopped being romantic and was downright terrifying, until I looked at you both; how could I be so scared with two captains such as yourselves?

I look forward to sailing with you again. You are both very special, and I know you have touched many hearts on this quest of yours. There is no doubt in my mind that you are both the bravest men I have ever met – not stupid at all!

Yanne, you have made my life complete and I know this is just the start for us.
My love always, Anita.

Chapter 39

Cannibals and Crooks in the Garden of Eden

8 – 31 May 2004

Opua, New Zealand – Savusavu,Vanua Levu, Fiji – Lautoku, Viti Levu, Fiji

Experience: *In a storm, try for as long as possible to sail 60 degrees to the wind with greatly reduced sails. In really bad weather, heave to by reefing down as far as possible to slow the boat down for less unpleasant sailing.*

Tip: *Always hoist the dinghy from the water and stow it on deck making it difficult for thieves to steal; even paradise has its share of criminals.*

There was a sharp chill in the air as we weighed anchor and waited to check out of New Zealand. Low morning mist lay like a giant blanket over the masts of the sailboats in the marina, but by 8:30 the mercury had climbed, the sun had warmed the air and dissipated the mist.

Carl's tuneless whistling and David's broad grin indicated how excited they both were about our 1,500 nautical mile journey to Fiji. My own feelings were mixed; we'd enjoyed a wonderful six months in New Zealand, and although we were no closer to understanding the rules of rugby, we'd repaired our boat, Carl had made many good friends, and I'd met the love of my life whom I now had to leave behind. But we'd vowed that it wasn't to be for long; Anita would join us in Australia where we were scheduled to arrive in June, a month away.

'A *month*!' Anita had groaned.

'Don't worry. I'll ring you,' I said.

'Really?' she said, perking up. 'How?'

'From one of those,' I replied, pointing to a yellow buoy in the distance. 'It's a telephone buoy. They're lots of them all over the ocean.'

'Really? I didn't know that. That's brilliant.'

'Yes, but the only problem is finding them in a fog or getting close enough to stand on them if the sea's rough. And sometimes they're out of order.'

'But it would be wonderful if you could call me on your way to Fiji,' she said with a tender smile.

Carl may have rolled his eyes, but it's hard not to love a woman who unquestioningly believes every word you say.

After clearing customs and filling our diesel and water tanks, we headed out for open water. According to the GPS, 1,137 nautical miles lay between us and our next port of Savusavu on the island state of Fiji. Our start seemed propitious with the sea on its best behaviour, the tuna eagerly biting and a friendly breeze which picked up later in the afternoon. As we feasted on the tuna I'd caught, David gave a sigh of pleasure.

'Fantastic,' he said. 'This is just fantastic. But ...'

'But what?' Carl asked.

'Well, I mean, this is pretty easy sailing, isn't it? And if I'm going to sail around the world, I'll need to know how to sail in rougher weather. We could do with a little storm just to ...you know, liven things up a bit.'

While I often say "be careful what you wish for," I could also see David's point. I'd helped him in Rawene with the 30-foot sailboat he and his wife were planning to sail around New Zealand's coast. Once they'd achieved this, they were hoping to buy a bigger boat with which to venture further afield, so he really needed experience of heavy weather sailing. Lying back in the cockpit with a full stomach while *Albatross* flitted over gentle florescent waves wasn't going to teach him how to handle a crisis.

Twenty-four hours later, David got this wish when conditions definitely became a bit livelier; the wind was ranging between 40 to 50 miles an hour and we were being pounded by giant walls of water. We'd taken in the stay sail and reduced the main to two reefs and the genoa to 40 percent and were doing pretty well, holding our course and making five to six knots. We'd cut our teeth on worse we reckoned, and so we left David on watch to enjoy his experience of heavy weather sailing.

By three that morning, things had moved on from "a bit lively" to full-blown mayhem. David woke Carl and me with the understated words: 'I think we might have a problem.'

It was a problem all right: the genoa was completely unfurled and thrashing in the wind as if it would take off back to New Zealand. The six-millimetre steel reefing line to the sail had broken, so it was impossible to furl it in but vital to do so. Carl and I threw on our life vests, clipped on our safety harnesses and climbed up on deck. Icy waters swirled around us and towering waves nearly 30 feet high broke over the bow, threatening to wash us overboard. Standing was not an option, so we crawled slowly forward across the deck towards the bow: a feat which was not made any easier when my inflatable life vest suddenly inflated as a wave pounded over me and the sensor registered I'd fallen overboard. I was now being unhelpfully suffocated by my own life saving device; the technology of our newly purchased vests clearly required refinement. Crawling across the deck while wearing a bouncy castle in a gale-force storm presents certain challenges, not least of which was not being blown overboard, and the overinflated vest was squeezing the life out of me like a greedy python. Fortunately, we'd attached sharp knives to each device, and I used mine now to plunge it into my vest with all the vigour of a Samurai committing *hara-kiri*. Once deflated, I crawled painfully forward. It was as cold and dark as a Norwegian hell: numbness – and, I'll be honest, fear – threatened to paralyse my body. We reached the genoa and tugged hard to bring it down. David was clinging to the wheel, observing our struggle but unsure how to help us. We crawled slowly back to the cockpit.

'Lively enough for you, David?' Carl shouted against the howling wind. We hadn't talked about the concept of "brown boxer sailing" with our newest crew member, but I had a shrewd notion he grasped the concept fairly quickly that night.

For three days we battled a low pressure system that squirmed from the northeast to the northwest; the wind increased to a deafening howl, causing every rod, mast and sail on *Albatross* to screech and wine in protest. The waves grew higher making it impossible to prepare any hot meals. We ran four-hour watches around the clock, trying to snatch a nap if we could, but that too was unattainable; we were thrown out of our bunks the moment we relaxed into sleep. Nevertheless, despite the constant pounding from the waves and lurching unpleasantly up and down, the body will try to rest as best it can. My heavy eyelids would fall closed, my mouth would hang open and I'd catnap for a few minutes before waking in a pool of my own drool. David lived on a diet of seasick pills and bread with a side order of chocolate bars. He'd sleep upright for some moments then suddenly wake with a jolt, look around with wide eyes and yell, 'We're taking on water! Are we sinking?' We'd reassure him that *Albatross* was sound and his eyelids would close. Minutes later, he'd come to with an almighty start and shout, 'Water! We're taking on water! There's so much water!' It was like having an aquaphobic Lady Macbeth on board.

The wind finally abated on the fifth day so we could all catch our breath and inspect the damage on deck. Everything was intact with the exception of a few items: the flapping genoa had bent a lifeline on the port side of the bow; a guide rope on the windvane had to be changed as it had worn to breaking point; the turbine's propeller looked more like a clipped chicken wing, and the six-millimetre thick steel furling line to roll the jib had broken. But on the whole our Hallberg-Rassy had come through the latest showdown relatively unscathed.

'I understand now why the New Zealand ports attract so many vultures,' David said. After some confusion when I said I thought vultures only existed on African plains, he explained he was talking about the scavenging bastards who eyed the straggling yachts with tattered sails and multiple repairs that limped into the marinas of Auckland and Opua. They'd pounce on the physically and emotionally exhausted skippers and crew who having survived one cyclone didn't reckon their chances with another and decided to continue their journey home from the nearest airport. The vultures picked up boats on the cheap and laughed all the way to their nearest branch of the Bank of New Zealand.

After eight days at sea, conditions were finally calm enough to allow us to shower; the cabin – or rather its occupants – smelled rank. We all sat on the aft deck and took a long fresh water rinse and dried off in the sun. Then I prepared fish soup for dinner from the whopping barracuda we'd caught the day before; weighing over 60 pounds, it was one of the largest fish we'd caught and would keep us going for many meals.

'Ah,' sighed David, stroking his clean shaven chin. 'I feel human again. And as for the soup, I must say *puku ka pai*.'

'I hope that's a compliment and not a euphemism for a desire to vomit,' I said anxiously.

'No worries,' David replied. 'In Maori *puku* means stomach and *ka pai* means very good, so my stomach feels very good. And not too soon either!'

'I blame *you* for the weather,' Carl said. 'You did ask for a storm.'

'True, but I didn't ask for two in a row. I'll be happy to be on solid ground again.'

At dawn on the tenth day, we entered the Koro Sea, sighting Kadavu Island, the archipelago's fourth largest island, on our port side. We had just 160 nautical miles left to our destination of Vanua Levu. A brisk wind drove us forward and by midnight that evening we'd sighted the lighthouse at Point Reef marking the entrance to Savusavu Bay. Much as we were loath to sail into an unknown harbour in complete darkness, we felt confident enough in our detailed charts to navigate the broad inlet. Making sure to keep well away from the reef, and with David on the bow looking out for any obstacles, we slowly entered the bay. When the depth showed 30 feet, we dropped anchor. It was three in the morning. We sat on deck letting the warm tropical night wrap itself around us, each of us as excited as children on Christmas Eve keenly anticipating what joys the morning would bring. After a cold beer and a mooring snaps, we fell into our bunks.

Although not a verbose man, there are few things in this world which leave me speechless – tongue-tied, yes – but rarely am I completely lost for words.

But on Friday morning when we finally emerged from the cabin and surveyed the view before us, we were all struck momentarily dumb: it was extraordinarily beautiful. The three of us stared in silent wonder at the emerald clad volcanic hills sloping down to pristine palm-fringed golden beaches. The sea was every imaginable shade of blue. A shoal of small fish leapt out of the water making a shimmering silver streak over the gentle waves.

David spoke first. 'Welcome to the Garden of Eden,' he said softly as if afraid to break the spell.

The 330 islands of the Fijian archipelago – 100 of which are inhabited – are essentially the product of volcanic action and coral formations. They surround the Koro Sea in the South Pacific like a jade necklace. Viti Levu in the south and smaller Vanua Levu in the north are the two main islands, with most of the hustle and bustle happening in Suva, the country's capital on the south-western coast of Viti Levu. The total land area is slightly smaller than Wales or New Jersey. Despite being the most developed island nation in the South Pacific with an ever-expanding tourist industry, Fiji remains lovely and unspoiled: I don't believe the same can be said of either Wales or New Jersey.

We raised our yellow Q flag to indicate we wished to check in. An hour later a motor boat pulled upside *Albatross* and three uniformed officers presented themselves: '*Bula*,' said the customs officer; '*Bula*,' said the immigration officer and '*Bula, bula*,' said the third officer from the Fijian Ministry of Health. Thus we learned our first Fijian word, which we later discovered was an all-purpose expression meaning anything from "hello" or "have a good day" to "cheers, I'm enjoying this cold beer in the sunshine, want to join me?"

The officers presented us with a staggering pile of forms to complete. The immigration officer helpfully loaned me a pen which dried up after the fifteenth form; bureaucrats the world over love paperwork. After an hour of form filling, the customs officer finally presented us with the last sheet of paper, patting with relief his glistening forehead with a small blue handkerchief. This last form required us to itemize all the alcohol we had on board. We'd restocked considerably in New Zealand, as a bottle of wine there cost approximately the same as a box of matches in Sweden. The officer's eyebrows shot to his hairline when he saw how much we had.

'Are you going to have a very big party?' he asked.

'No,' we replied, mildly perplexed. 'This is just for daily consumption. How much can we bring in to the country?'

'As much as you need while you're in Fiji,' the officer replied with a broad smile, confirming that Fijians are a thoroughly sensible people. We immediately warmed to this friendly and wholly rational island nation.

For the price of a disposable razor in Sweden, we paid for an anchor buoy in Waitui marina for which we had use of toilets and showers. Although the marina looked a little shabby, it had a welcoming feel, and the small town of Savusavu exuded a faded charm; women in bright pink and orange sarongs leaned fetchingly in the shade of pale blue painted porches; they waved and smiled as if genuinely pleased to see us, calling out '*Bula!*' as we meandered past.

The first inhabitants of Fiji date back to ancient times: most experts agree that the original people to land on the islands were from Southeast Asia. Europeans found themselves in the archipelago more or less accidentally when Dutchman Abel Tasman nearly came to grief on a reef in 1643 during his search for the Great Southern Continent. Captain James Cook landed over a century later in 1774, although he only ever made it to Vatoa, one of the Lau islands. Captain Bligh was more familiar with these waters, having sailed them on his marathon 3,600-mile journey in an open boat after being cast adrift by the mutineers of *HMS Bounty* in 1789. Not that Bligh fancied his chances ashore: fear of ending up in a pot discouraged him from chatting with the natives. Although it's difficult to say how widespread cannibalism was in the South Pacific, it is certain that in an environment where access to red meat was rare, cannibalism was key to survival. Indeed, in the Fijian National Museum in Suva, one of the most compelling pieces of evidence of cannibalism is displayed alongside the only remaining part of the good ship *Bounty*: the sole of Rev Thomas Baker's left boot, all that was left of the unfortunate cleric after the Fijians ate him. Like the Maori and the Carib Indians, cannibalism between warring Fijian tribes was common. Deryck Scarr in *A Short History of Fiji* writes, "Ceremonial occasions saw freshly slaughtered corpses piled up for eating. 'Eat me!' was a proper ritual greeting from a commoner to a chief." Hardly surprising then that Captain Bligh didn't take a stroll on the islands.

The Europeans sorted out all that nonsense by first spreading Christianity and later deadly epidemics which all but wiped out the indigenous Fijian population in the late nineteenth century. Between 1875 and 1876, an epidemic of measles killed over 40,000 Fijians, so severely depleting the workforce required in the booming sugar industry that the British Government had to ship in indentured laborers from India three years later. When the indentured system was abolished in 1916, however, many Indians chose to stay in Fiji, the majority becoming independent farmers. Indians make up a significant part of the Fijian population and have impacted its culture and language despite facing years of deep discrimination.

Fiji finally gained its independence from Great Britain in 1970, trading one ruler for a different set of governmental and racial problems; there have been three military coups since 1987, the most recent as 2006. Relationships between ethnic Fijians and Indo-Fijians at a political level have often been strained and continue to dominate politics in the islands: a coup in 2000 toppled the government of Mahendra Chaudhry, the country's first Indo-Fijian prime minster following the 1997 constitution, and incited violent hostility against the Indo-Fijians for a time. It was hard to imagine such friendly, peaceful people driven to such acts of vandalism, but during the rioting there was apparently a clear case of them and us.

Vanua Levu, formerly known as Sandalwood Island because of its once rich quantity of sandalwood thickets, has a small population of 130,000 – only slightly more than my home town of Helsingborg. The main industry on the island is sugar cane production, but copra is also an important crop together with a burgeoning tourist industry owing to its diving and yachting facilities. Eager to remind ourselves about life on land and to get off the beaten track, we rented a four-wheel drive Toyota pickup which proved to be a robust choice for the abominable roads – clearly, a well maintained infrastructure was not a priority. This is presumably because cars are a considerable luxury; most of the rural population seemed to use horses or oxen to pull wagons and carts. Our drive proved to be quite a magical mystery tour; there were no signposts and "roads" would end abruptly in the middle of a field or a pothole too deep to navigate. Fortunately, there always seemed to be a local on hand to direct us with a smile and a handshake. We slowly made our way from the coast up into the hills of fertile jungle where villages huddled together. As we bounced past weather-beaten houses and ramshackle huts, men, women and children waved to us. When we stopped, villagers ran out of their houses to greet us as if we were Hollywood celebrities. Brown hands reached for our hands and arms to check if the pink on our skin was drying paint or if the colour could be rubbed off. We realized that there were still communities that had never seen white people and yet we were only 20 miles from a harbour full of international boats. Most of the villagers on the northern side of the island spent their whole lives living and working around the sugar cane plantations and never ventured far beyond their homes.

After a few days on sleepy Vanua Levu, we decided to sail on to Viti Levu, the largest island in the archipelago, and burial place of Ratu Udre Udre who holds the Guinness World Record for "most prolific cannibal" – a category I am horrified to think even exists, much less holds championships for the title. Udre Udre was known for practicing cannibalism even after Fiji had officially ceded to Great Britain and its people had widely accepted Christianity. During the nineteenth century, the world's most prolific cannibal reportedly ate more than 999 people, keeping a stone for each body he ate –

well, I guess you lose count after the first 20 or so – which were placed by his tomb in Rakiraki in the north of the island. According to Udre Udre's son, his father had a voracious appetite for human flesh and would keep beside him at all times a box of cooked and preserved human meat. Apparently, he was particularly fond of the head and didn't like to share. It's all disgustingly fascinating, but what I find most reprehensible is that he didn't share.

We set a course for Lautoka city, a 150-nautical mile journey which took us four days as we chose not to sail at night due to our dependence on "eyeball navigation" around the coral reefs. Instead we anchored overnight in the calm waters in the passages in the coral openings where we could explore another cosmos of colours and textures of the soft corals, something I never tired of.

Lautoka is known as Sugar City due its location in the heart of Fiji's prime sugar cane growing region. There the sugar mill is the city's largest employer, hiring some 1,300 workers. Built between 1902 and 1903 by the Colonial Sugar Refining Company, and now owned by the Fiji Sugar Corporation Limited, the building resembles a Victorian mill complete with a tall chimney, looking somewhat incongruous surrounded by palm trees and tropical plants: the lighter side of Victorian England's dark satanic mills. More interesting to me was the name of the city which is apparently derived from two Fijian words meaning "spear hit." Oral tradition has it that during a duel between two chiefs, one was hit by his opponent's weapon and cried "Lau toka!" Even more interesting was the Northern Club, a busy sporting and social club serving draught beer and great food at low prices – my favourite combination – encouraging us to immediately sign up for membership. As the sun went down and the tropical heat cooled, club members arrived for sundowners and to chat about their day, play tennis or relax in the club's pool.

'Strange, but I feel quite at home here,' Carl said.

'Calle, you'd feel at home wherever the beer is cheap and you can hear the sound of the sea,' I said.

David had decided to return home and bought a flight ticket back to Auckland, a simple process made hugely complicated by the number of extraneous people engaged in the operation. Six people were involved, starting with the first who painstakingly recorded all his personal details and which flight he required; the second checked these details thoroughly before passing the form on to a third assistant who covered it in stamps. He then passed it to a fourth person who scrupulously and slowly checked the details again should a mistake have been made by the first three. Once satisfied that the information was correct, he stamped the form and sent it along the counter to a fifth man who typed out the ticket, which was eventually handed to a sixth underling who checked it again, and finally handed it to David who'd grown a full beard during his wait. And all of this was achieved at Fiji speed; the pace of an exhausted, elderly slug. Fijians must have a terrible time trying to subtitle foreign films containing any dialogue such as 'Quick! Follow that taxi!' or 'Get me the crash cart! Stat!' as the concept of hurrying simply doesn't exist. But I suppose that's just as well, otherwise travellers like ourselves wouldn't be able to appreciate such tranquillity away from the usual frenzy of life.

The only place in town where there was a modicum of frenzy was the open air market where several hundred stallholders gathered daily to sell their local produce. The colourful array of items displayed was a feast for the eyes and the nose; everything that was farmed or fished on Viti Levu was for sale, and we salivated like Pavlov's dogs as we entered the fray of shouting and gentle jostling. What a joy to buy supplies here: mandarins that smelled tart and sweet the moment you stuck your thumb into the peel; apples that were juicy and crisp with each bite; brown eggs still warm from the chickens' backsides; fat peanuts in golden shells, bright red chillies and succulent limes. We hauled away 15 kilos of fresh produce for a pocketful of change. There was no chance of these sailors getting scurvy.

That evening we anchored off the small island of Vio. Dinner that night was a celebration of the abundance and bounty of Fiji's local produce, although we did our best to honour the New Zealand wine industry by drinking a couple of bottles of white. Never let it be said that we didn't do our best to support the local economies of the places we visited.

I was therefore enjoying a deep alcohol-enhanced sleep when I was rudely awoken by Carl bellowing like a bull undergoing the operation to become a bullock. I scrambled up on deck where a completely naked Carl was yelling furiously into the darkness. 'Get back here, you thieving bastards!'

'What the hell...?'

'Two blokes have just stolen our dinghy. They're over there somewhere in a red skiff.' Apparently, Carl had decided to sleep on deck where it was cooler and had been woken by the noise of the dinghy's outboard motor. We all stared morosely at the dark sea where we could just make out the silhouette of our vanishing dinghy. We fully expected the thieves to head for the outer reefs, but unexpectedly they changed course and went parallel to the coral.

'Quick,' said Carl. 'David, you start the engine and raise the anchor. We might just catch them. Yanne, you restart the computer and connect the navigation software and I'll try to keep my eye on their location.'

We rapidly put *Albatross* to sea and headed off with the engine going at full speed. Although visibility was minimal as the moon had gone down, the yellow sodium light from the quays gave us enough light to navigate by and keep our precious dinghy in sight which the bandits were directing along the overhanging mass of mangrove trees. We spotted three small white boats moored next to the bushes.

'There,' said Carl, pointing to the boats. 'There's our dinghy. Damn it! It's gone. Where the heck is it? Quick! Over to that island.' David threw the throttle on full.

'Shit, no!' I screamed from my post at the computer. 'Full reverse! There's only 60 feet until we run up on the reef!'

'Bugger, bugger, bugger,' screamed Carl, seriously angry at losing something he'd paid for. The hunter instinct in him was clearly riled and there was a bloodlust in his eyes I hadn't seen since he'd been overcharged in a 7-Eleven for a black coffee. Of course, he'd been clothed then so the effect had been less terrifying. 'This doesn't end here. I want my bloody dinghy back,' he growled. 'Yanne, you hold *Albatross* off the reef. David, radio the Coast Guard. I'm going in.' He hauled himself over the guard rail, not daring to dive in case the reef was too shallow.

'Take a knife with you,' I shouted.

'Forget it,' he yelled back. 'I'll use my fists.' I didn't doubt it, although the sight of an enraged Carl stamping naked through the undergrowth was probably sufficient to scare the thieves into submission. He shot through the water like Michael Phelps set on breaking an Olympic record, his only recently healed broken arm forgotten as he powered 500 yards towards the mangroves. Then he disappeared into the dense bush. I, meanwhile, started the blue rotating light on *Albatross*' mizzen mast; the glow of the emergency light illuminated the treetops and palm fronds. For good measure, I gave several prolonged blasts on the horn.

For a wretchedly long time, we heard nothing and I had to suppress dreadful images of a nude middle-aged man wrestling with two lithe Fijians. Then suddenly we heard the familiar hum of our dinghy's outboard engine. I immediately directed a light towards the sound. There in the halo of white light was a jubilant Carl sitting in the dinghy, slowly chugging towards us. David and I whooped and shouted with relief and joy: Carl had beaten the bandits and taken back our dinghy. We hauled him on board.

'Bloody well done, Carl! You did it!'

'Fantastic! That'll teach them not to mess with us Vikings!'

'But good lord, you look and smell like shit!'

Carl told us how he'd had to wade past the village's pig cages as he followed the thieves. Fortunately, it seems the blue emergency light and the horn blasts had scared them; to make a quick escape they'd abandoned the dinghy which had drifted out on the pull of the tide into open water where Carl had spotted it. Adrenalin fuelled, he'd swum a personal best to reach it and then heaved himself aboard.

'That's it, from now on, we bring the dinghy on board and suspend it from the aft davits,' I said. 'Even the Garden of Eden has its share of crooks.'

'I agree,' David said. 'Now for the love of god, will you both put some bloody underwear on? Stark bollocking naked Swedes! Have you no modesty?'

Did I forget to mention I also sleep *au naturel*?

The following morning we took the dinghy over to Vio Island. Just beyond the mangroves and pig cages was a large village of approximately 50 huts built out of recycled wood and roofed with corrugated metal. Many villagers stopped and stared at us while others smiled and waved, calling '*Bula*' in greeting. Word quickly spread that we were looking for the previous night's burglars and after a few minutes aimlessly tramping about, we were greeted by two youths who insisted we follow them to meet the village chief. Ponipate, a wiry but toned man, aged anywhere between middle and old age, and wearing a floral orange sarong, solemnly welcomed us to the village. He gently pushed forward his 12-year-old daughter Mereseini who recounted how she'd observed two men pulling a dinghy ashore and assumed they had been fetching water from the mainland while the tide was favourable. She'd recognised the young men's voices and was able to identify the thieves. Ponipate himself escorted us to the first culprit's hut where the father was fully aware of what his son had done. The son, meanwhile, had cannily done a runner. So we were lead to the second culprit's abode; his tactic was to act contrite and point a fat finger at his conveniently absent accomplice. His father fell at our feet to beg for leniency for his impressionable son and ask that we didn't report him to the police. Ponipate wasn't having any of it.

'The thieves must be punished,' he said, putting on an expression of gravitas worthy of a High Court judge. 'If the parents have not done their job in teaching their children right from wrong, then this must be done by those in authority.'

Having passed this judgement, he took the names of the boys and promised to refer the matter to the police. Then he invited us to join him and his family for Sunday lunch. We were shown inside the chief's hut where we perched uncomfortably on the "best" furniture – pieces of wood nailed together by a five-year-old – while the whole family waited on us, serving us copious amounts of orange juice. While the women laid out lunch on a tablecloth on the palm mat floor, Ponipate told us something of his life. He earned his living as a diver, collecting sea cucumbers, doing a total of 16 dives over four days, diving as deep as 180 feet around the reef to gather the cucumbers which were salted, boiled and sold to Japan and China as a substitute for Viagra. 'Oh, those crazy Japanese,' we all laughed superiorly. 'They'll buy anything if they believe it will guarantee them an erection!'

We were called to the lunch cloth where we sat crossed-legged on the palm mat floor with the rest of the family, Ponipate's son and three daughters. Then we tucked into the Fijian equivalent of a Sunday roast: cassava, pumpkin, yams and tarot roots boiled in coconut milk, octopus and reef fish, pineapples and tiny sweet bananas. In return for the family's hospitality, we invited them to visit us on the boat before we made sail for Vanuatu later that week.

A couple of days later, the family – which had doubled in size as six cousins had decided to come along – paddled their long skiff out to *Albatross*. All were dressed in what I suspected were their best sarongs in honour of the occasion. They clambered on board, thrilled to explore a sailboat for the first time. The children chattered excitedly and asked to press various buttons; they all tested the berths and marvelled at the heads and the showers; the Missus and the girls squealed over the galley and played with all the pots and pans. I suppose it was as fascinating to them as a NASA space station would have been to me. In lieu of offering fish to eat – as that would have been as embarrassing as serving ice to an Eskimo – we fed them all the chocolate and cake we had on board, the sugary effect of which made the children doubly hyper. As a parting gift, they presented us with a sea snail shell as big as a football and polished so it gleamed.

It was the perfect last evening in Fiji before starting the first leg of our long voyage to Australia. David signed off and would return to New Zealand having learned to be careful about what you wish for when it comes to storms at sea. He wrote us the following lines in our logbook:

I asked for one storm, not two! The wind screamed like a banshee around us while the sea was white with foam. The waves were huge and in the light of the full moon, we could really see the power of the ocean on Albatross. Sleep was impossible as I was tossed up and down in my bunk while my stomach was tossed in all directions. I survived on a diet of dry bread and got to experience a tough life at sea. Carl and Yanne have taught me so much about sailing on the high seas and in rough weather. It's been great fun to journey with Albatross and her two Vikings, and I look forward to meeting them again. Living with two blokes who I barely knew in such conditions was a real experience that I'll never forget. I wish them much luck for their journey home to Sweden.

My thanks, David.

(Incidentally, David hasn't yet managed his circumnavigation; his wife got a severe case of not wishing to end their lives prematurely by taking on such a dangerous undertaking: David, being the good soul that he is, has so far deferred to his wife.)

Chapter 40

Reasons to be Cheerful
in the Land Eternal

1 – 7 June 2004

Lautoka, Viti Levu, Fiji – Port Vila, Efate Island, Vanuatu – Cairns, Australia

Experience: *If you are going through hell, don't stop, just keep going.*

Tip: *Never throw anything away: it might be useful for repairs later.*

David turned to me, put his face very close to mine with our noses and foreheads touching. *Hello,* I thought. I started to pull away very slightly.

'No, don't,' David said. 'This is important.'

'Um, David. This is ..., well, this is...' It was bloody awkward. I like my personal space and David was not just in it but had invaded and was on the verge of planting a flag.

'This is a *hongi*,' he said, continuing to press his nose harder against mine. 'Now we share our breath.'

'Oh lovely,' I said, thinking *Oh must we?* A few more excruciatingly weird seconds passed before David let me go.

'There,' he said with a satisfied smile. 'Now we've said goodbye Maori style. A *hongi* is a very important symbolic greeting as it reflects the beginning of man when the god of life blew oxygen in to the nose to give life to the first human being. The gods will be with you now for a safe journey.'

'Good to know.' I wasn't being facetious; it was good to know. We'd learned a lot from David about New Zealand and the Maori culture, and would certainly miss our crewmate's informative company and good humour, not to mention his mechanical skills.

Our next leg was to sail 580 miles westwards to Efate Island in Vanuatu, where we'd planned a brief pit stop before continuing to Australia. Checking out required the same telephone directory sized pile of forms to be filled out at customs where they would be "filed" in tottering towers along the walls and down the centre of the office. I really wonder what the point is as I can't believe that the paperwork for a particular boat can ever be retrieved once it lands in one of these paper mountains. Digging out the forms for *Albatross* after a few months would require a mountain pick and a shovel. I picture some poor clerk disappearing for weeks in a stack of documents until a search party with tracker dogs is sent in after him.

Although we'd booked checkout with Emigration at 10 a.m., our officer was clearly on Fiji time and strolled up at midday, whereupon he put on an Oscar worthy performance of being the most stressed, hardest working government official in the whole of the South Pacific, which would have been more convincing had he not left the date on his stamping equipment set for three days earlier.

Locals had warned us of rough conditions around the reef, so we took the commercial shipping lane that leads southwest to the Malolo passage and out into open water. For the first five nautical miles we enjoyed classic blue water sailing, and then we braced ourselves. As we passed the Bounty and Treasure Islands in the stretch of water known as the Nadi Sea, the gates of hell opened.

'Oh crap,' Carl said. 'Here we go again. I'd better reef in the mainsail.'

Strong currents and a raw wind were colluding to push us onto the reef. I started the engine and Carl clipped on his safety harness and crawled towards the mast. The wind whipped at his thin T-shirt and shorts before a giant wave broke over *Albatross* swallowing Carl in the spray and foam. When the wave receded, I looked anxiously for signs of Carl; he was clinging for dear life to the mast like a wet stamp. Somewhat dazed he staggered to the rail and threw up. Then he stoically returned to business and started sheeting in the mainsail, pausing now and again to heave over the side. It took us nearly an hour to navigate the coral jungle with me at the helm and Carl at the bow where he alternated between calling out directions and feeding the fish.

It was just the beginning of four days of misery. We rolled and dipped in swells, buffeted by 40-mile an hour winds raging around us, lurching *Albatross* this way and that against 30-foot waves. It was fine riding the top of a wave but if we hit a trough, we plummeted into the chasm while our stomachs were momentarily suspended before rising into our throats. It was like a perpetual journey on one of those fairground rides that teenagers find so thrilling. Carl was misery personified, in the grip of seasickness so severe that by the second day he had nothing to vomit but bile.

'Think of the worse hangover you ever had,' he said to me weakly. The skin on his face hung slack and his complexion was an unappetising shade of vomit green. 'Multiple it by 20 and then add a severe case of bird flu plus a dose of gastroenteritis. A bloody picnic compared to the way I feel.' And off he went to dry heave over the rail again. He was so shattered, I took over his watch. I wasn't feeling particularly lively myself by the time Carl, his hue a somewhat healthier shade of beige, was fit enough to take over some 18 hours later.

Although our stomachs were at the mercy of the storm, one pleasing consequence was that *Albatross* held her course and was pushed forward like an express train covering 175 to 190 nautical miles a day. Eventually the wind slowed to a more friendly 25 miles an hour and Carl looked less like a bad extra from *The Night of the Living Dead* and had regained enough strength to stand watch. By the time we'd entered the inner reefs of Vila Bay, he was feeling almost perky, and as we dropped anchor in the still waters of Port Vila harbour, he'd rallied enough to consider a cold beer and a mooring snaps. The sun rose in the east, painting golden streaks across the sky and gradually waking the jungle. Across the bay we could see Iririki Island where travellers wealthier than ourselves were sleeping off the all-you-can-eat buffet in their luxury bungalows – unless, of course, they were being kept awake by the insistent and piercing crowing of every rooster on Efate Island.

Vanuatu, meaning "Land Eternal," is made up of a string of 83 islands spanning the Pacific Ring of Fire. Its people are mainly Melanesian with more than 115 distinctly different cultures and languages, which would make reading the nightly news hugely problematic but for the use of the national language of Bislama, a mostly English-based Creole language. Once known as the New Hebrides, the islands achieved independence from France and Britain in 1980 thus ending the Anglo-French condominium signed in 1906 and a two-century tussle between the colonizing nations. Of the 221,000 inhabitants, over 98.5 percent are Melanesian and the rest are a mixture of "others."

Once we'd cleared in, we took a stroll around Port Vila, the economic and commercial centre of Vanuatu, where our first experience was horror at how expensive the place was. Naively lured into a pub for a little liquid libation, Carl nearly lost the power of speech when he saw the price of a beer. 'Holy crap!' he stammered when he finally could use words again. 'I didn't want to buy the bloody brewery.' Order only the local beer: it's significantly cheaper.

Port Vila is a growing cosmopolitan town and draws Australian tourists seeking duty-free items like lemmings to a Norwegian cliff top, but neither Carl nor I were interested in tax-free cosmetics. This was the fastest of all pit stops, to make repairs and continue to Australia where Carl had 30 years of marriage to celebrate with Eva, and I had a date with Anita.

Nevertheless, I was sorry we were stopping only briefly in Vanuatu; this former Anglo-French colony has a number of eccentric traditions that I would have liked to have witnessed first-hand: a tribe that worships Prince Philip as a god – ironic given the number of politically incorrect gaffes the Duke of Edinburgh has made; an underwater post office manned by a scuba diver where you can buy special waterproof postcards to send home, and Yasur, one of the most accessible active volcanoes in the world which has been shooting out lava since Captain Cook sailed by on *HMS Resolution* in 1774. Vanuatu is also home to *kava*, the world's only legal narcotic drink and which I was desperate to try – purely in the name of research, you understand. Apparently, the suburbs of Port Vila contain hundreds of *kava* bars, some of which are little more than garden sheds; a coloured lantern outside indicates that *kava* is on sale. I was told a small shell of *kava* could be had for 50 Vatu, the price of a Mars bar.

And then, of course, there was the bungee jumping, or land diving as it is formerly known. Listed as one of the "must do" experiences in the best-selling adventure guide *100 Things to Do Before You Die*, I was keen to witness the *nagol*, the traditional ritual of land diving which takes place on Pentecost Island around the time of the yam harvest. Reading the full story of land diving explained the need for *kava*, which I can only assume divers consume in copious amounts before attempting this extreme sport. A 75-foot tower built out of wood cut from the jungle and bound together with vines is erected by 20 to 30 men. The rickety structure is then divided into 12 sections representing parts of the human anatomy from the feet to the forehead. Newly-circumcised boys jump from the lower levels to achieve the status of manhood, while the more experienced divers work their way up higher every year. With only vines attached to his feet and wearing nothing but a penis sheath – although personally I would have swopped the penis sheath for a crash helmet – the diver freefalls into space crossing his arms in a gesture of confidence, mostly in the bloke who cut and attached the vines to his feet: too long and the diver will slam into the ground: too short and he will crash into the tower. With only a leaf protecting the family jewels, there aren't many second chances.

I would also have liked to have explored the waters around the island of Espiritu Santo where the rusting carcass of World War II troop ship, the *SS President Coolidge*, now provides one of the best intact and accessible diving wrecks in the world.

And all this in a country which has twice been named the happiest place on earth. The Happy Planet Index released by the New Economics Foundation uses global data on life expectancy, experienced well-being and ecological footprint to rank countries: the lower the ecological footprint, the higher a country is likely to score. First released in 2006 and rating a total of 178 countries, Vanuatu then took first place: Britain, Sweden and the United States languishing in 108th, 119th and 150th places respectively in the same year. Certainly for the tourist there are many reasons to be cheerful on this South Pacific island; apart from drinking soup bowl sized shells of *kava*, there is outstanding scenery, great diving and the friendliness of the ni-Vanuatu as we experienced first-hand.

As for the ni-Vanuatu themselves: they are extremely poor, earning only what their garden produce will fetch at market, and it is no mean feat getting to market. Whole families make the gruelling journey over mud roads to the nearest main town, and once there, the families have to jostle for table space to sell their wares. Subsequently, they don't leave until they've sold everything they've brought, so markets stay open 24/7 with women and children sleeping under the tables. Yet despite such poverty, it isn't the abject poverty of say, Bangladesh; the people in Vanuatu rejoice in the fact they have abundant fresh water – it rains frequently and there are numerous freshwater rivers. Furthermore, as with all volcanic islands we'd visited, the soil is so rich in nutrients that you could drop a toothpick in the earth and it would grow. But there was a tangible sense of community that imbued the place: from the toddlers playing under the trestle tables as if it were the village hall mother and tots playgroup, to the boys kicking around an old sock stuffed with newspaper on a scrub of ground. Bright smiles and welcoming waves followed us everywhere. Or maybe they were just all happy on *kava*.

'Please can we see a *nagol* on Tanne?' I whined like a five-year-old to Carl.

He looked at me over the top of his glasses. 'No time. Too many repairs to do, Yanne.'

'But what about Mount Yasur and the volcano?'

'We've got to fix the Volvo Penta; the cooling system isn't working.'

'A quick dive to see the wreck?'

'We need to look at the diesel generator; it's been acting up.'

'The underwater post office?'

'The wire to the roller at the bow is tangled; the rolling mechanism needs sorting.'

'Ah, it never bloody ends! Can't we at least go to a *kava* hut and see what the fuss is all about?'

Carl put down his screwdriver. 'Yanne, we need to get these repairs done so we can sail on Monday. The sooner we get to Australia, the sooner you see Anita.'

I stopped sulking and brightened up at the thought of Anita. 'Fair point.'

'Besides, Eva will kill me if I don't get there for our wedding anniversary.'

So we spent the weekend mending gadgets and improvising repairs. Fortunately, we'd accumulated an assortment of equipment and had a well-stocked workshop on board: an essential requirement for any long distance yachtsman. On Tuesday morning, we made sail on the turning tide. Over 1,400 nautical miles of sailing lay before us and we fervently hoped it would be storm free; we were heartily sick of "lively" conditions.

But once out of the shelter of the bay, it was business as usual with 35-mile an hour winds and *Albatross* riding the waves like a bucking bronco on warp speed. There was nothing to do but grit our teeth and hold on for dear life. Conditions improved once we got out into deeper water, but the winds increased. After thousands of miles at sea, we were well practised at setting our sails; we reduced the sail area, reefing in the mainsail to the third reef. They may have laughed at us in Helsingborg but that stabilizing third reef was proving to be invaluable in the Pacific Ocean.

We hunkered down and set a schedule of six-hour watches, estimating that our journey to Australia would take us at least 10 days. For the first 48 hours we avoided cooking and lived on fruit and peanuts. Happily, our fishing skills had improved tremendously since the days of staring at broken lines, and I stocked the freezer with dorado and tuna filets. Once the rough weather passed, we ate heartily. Carl started his day with a large serving of porridge with raisins and yoghurt, while I like bread and cheese with a serving of sardines, some of which I'd share with the seabirds which flew around and above *Albatross*. We could watch their graceful aerial acrobatics for hours as they flitted over the foam, plunging below the waves now and again to snatch an inattentive fish. But then there was nothing else to watch; the birds were our only company.

We didn't sight another ship for days, a keen reminder of the vastness of the Pacific, making the achievements of the early explorers seem all the more remarkable. Here we were with the best in modern technology and design to help us cross this massive body of water while Balboa, Magellan, de Torres and Cook all stumbled about blindly like moles in the Gobi Desert trying to find land masses that didn't exist, missing ones that did or bumping into small islands where the reception was markedly unfriendly. To say being a naval explorer was a hazardous occupation in the sixteenth century is like saying the Pacific is big: it doesn't describe a fraction of it.

Exploration of the Pacific Ocean in the sixteenth, seventeenth and eighteenth centuries was generally geographical, after all captains and crew were too busy getting lost in it to consider what lay below. No one gave much thought to how deep it was, although Magellan did give it a shot in 1521 when he tried to measure it with a 2,400-foot weighted line, but it never reached the bottom. It wasn't until 1872 that the first real scientific attempt to determine ocean depth was initiated by *HMS Challenger* which laid the groundwork for an entire research discipline. But the astonishing fact is that even now about 95 percent of the ocean is unexplored; more astronauts have travelled into space than aquanauts into the deepest part of the ocean.

But we were finally leaving the Pacific Ocean and entering the Coral Sea. We'd sailed a total of 12,600 nautical miles across this colossal body of water, equivalent to 13,809 miles on land, equal to driving from New York to Los Angles five times. On the evening of the eighth day we sighted a lighthouse marking the far northern section of the Great Barrier Reef. Our level of excitement increased several notches. By midnight we were inching our way between the Holmes and Flora Reefs; there was no moon, and the sky and the sea were pitch black. We had to use the radar and computer to gauge our position before we came a cropper on the surrounding reef and set a new course to take us into Cairns via Grafton Passage.

The horizon was brightening as we sailed into Cairns; our first view of this new continent was illuminated by the morning sun, flooding the rich rainforest slopes with golden light and bringing into focus the city of Cairns.

Carl and I had arrived at the New World.

Chapter 41

Teeth, Tentacles and a Tornado Down Under

18 June – 17 September 2004

Cairns – Thursday Island – Darwin – Broome

Experience: *You can't outrun or out sail a tornado. Just hope you don't meet one.*

Tip: *Don't miss the Kimberley coast; it's astounding.*

I n 1788, Governor Arthur Philip sailed *HMS Supply* into Botany Bay carrying crew, the governor's staff and family, and around 700 petty thieves. His instructions were to found the first penal colony with those unfortunate enough to have travelled with him. What faced Philip and his motley band was a terrain so harsh that the good governor was completely bewildered as to why Captain James Cook, who had named the bay some 18 years earlier after the numerous plants he'd observed there, had given such an appealing description of the place. Instead of the natural meadows and the "safe and commodious" harbour Cook had described, they were faced with a dangerous anchorage, sand flies, marshy swampland and unpredictable natives who were amiable one moment but as likely to thrust a spear through you the next. Hardly the welcome they were hoping for after eight miserable months at sea.

Carl and I were also wondering what kind of reception we were in for: the infamous Australian Customs and Border Protection Service being notorious for their inclination to be more thorough than the Gestapo in their inspections. We weren't holding our breath that they'd be standing on the dock ready to greet us with a cheery "G'day, mate," and a couple of cans of Fosters. We glided cautiously towards the main wharf where four officers sporting more gold braid on their caps than cushions on a luxury hotel sofa were waiting, assorted forms and clipboards ready. They were already collectively annoyed with us: we'd blotted our copybooks by not announcing our ETA at least six hours ahead of our scheduled arrival.

'We tried,' we immediately protested, doing our best impressions of contrite. 'We radioed the Coast Guard early this morning, but we couldn't get an answer; he was probably sound asleep.'

'Hmm,' nodded the Customs officer with a frown. 'It happens all too frequently. We'll raise the issue with the Coast Guard.'

The mood mellowed after that, realms of paperwork flowed and the boat was systematically inspected. A few onions, some eggs, potatoes and two jars of mayonnaise were judged hazardous and confiscated, together with all our rubbish for incineration. The fish in our freezer was fine as they'd been caught in Australian waters. We waited nervously as our forms were scrupulously checked.

'Good on ya. She's apples,' said the Immigration officer, stamping the last form with a flourish rarely seen in a government official. 'Have a g'day and welcome to Australia.' Slack jawed, Carl and I watched them walk off down the wharf.

'So that was the infamous Australian Customs and Immigration. Not bad blokes after all,' I said.

'No,' Carl agreed. 'But what was all that about apples? We haven't got any.' It was to be the first of many linguistic confusions we encountered while we were down under.

We celebrated arriving at a new continent by indulging in a Chinese meal, not authentic Australian cuisine, I'll give you that – not that I knew much about Australian cuisine, if indeed there was such a thing beyond Vegemite and kangaroo burgers – but there was an abundance of Asian restaurants in Cairns, as well as dive shops, agents offering reef cruises, white water rides and rainforest tours, as well as every other shop selling souvenir T-shirts, fluffy koala bears and kangaroo key chains.

Cairns, once a mangrove swamp, grew out of the necessity for a port to service the goldfields discovered in the hills in the late nineteenth century, which prompted a minor rush once some fool shouted "Gold!" Today, the city sprawls 32 miles along the coast of northern Queensland and attracts over two million tourists each year, most of them backpackers desperate to tick diving on the Great Barrier Reef and walking in the Tropical Rainforest off their bucket lists. As indeed was I. Beatrice and her friend Franka were flying into Cairns from Germany; it had been two years since I'd last seen my daughter when she'd joined us on the Classic Malts Cruise in Scotland, and I was looking forward to spoiling and massively embarrassing her as only a father can.

We'd been in Cairns for a just 48 hours with our Swedish ensign flapping on the mizzen mast when Henry, a Swede who'd lived in Australia for so many years he spoke Swedish with a heavy Aussie twang, spotted our flag and strolled over to invite us to a midsummer party the following Saturday. We accepted the invitation without hesitation. And that's the strange but wonderful thing about the Swedish: back home, we might have lived in the same village, walked past each other for years and never made eye contact with Henry, and yet here a fellow countryman had gone out of his way to invite four people he'd never met, nor was ever likely to meet again when we left, to celebrate midsummer purely because we were Swedish.

A couple of days later Carl, Beatrice, Franka and I wandered along to a beach park where some 60 other Swedes resident in and around Cairns had gathered with the gusto typical of expatriate Scandinavians who anticipate getting together with the sole aim of getting plastered. (If you've forgotten the general rules for midsummer celebrations, please reread chapter 14.) We all helped decorate the 30-foot midsummer pole with tropical foliage and flowers cut from the surrounding rainforest, generally getting in the way of each other while taking a swig of snaps now and again to hinder the process further. Then we did the time-honoured dance of the little frogs around the pole, ate, drank and shrieked with laughter. We were becoming generally more raucous to the point where even the Aussies must have thought we were overdoing it, because a couple of burly types sporting sleeveless T-shirts and neck tattoos wandered over and said, 'G'day fellas. Not to be indelicate, but we were wondering if it was a bloke or a Sheila?' A group of onlookers waited at a distance for our answer.

'Bloke? What bloke?' I may have slurred.

'Who's Sheila?' asked Carl. 'Did I meet Sheila?' He looked around trying to recognize Sheila or just focus in general.

'Well, the fella or the Sheila that kicked the bucket.'

'No, no. We don't kick any buckets in Sweden,' Carl said, vigorously shaking his head. 'We kick footballs, bad dogs ...'

'Nah mate. I mean, who died?' the second man said.

'*Died*?' both Carl and I chorused in surprise.

'Yeah, well, what with the flowery cross and all, we reckoned she must have been a bonzer old Sheila who kicked the bucket, I mean, died.'

'Sheila Bonzer *died*!' croaked Carl, taking a consoling gulp of beer. 'Poor Sheila! And I never even met her.'

'Well, strewth, it's a weird way to have a funeral, with a barbie and all, but you dance away, mate.'

I don't know who was most confused at this point, but fortunately Henry arrived to untangle the misunderstanding on both sides; midsummer celebrations were explained to the Aussies, and Sheilas, kicking the bucket, bonzer and barbies were translated for us.

'Ah, holy strewth!' Carl moaned into his beer. 'We've got to learn the damn language all over again. It's exhausting.'

Carl also found dodging the attentions of an amorous lady whose eye he'd caught at the midsummer festivities equally fatiguing. The lady pursued him with a tenacity I could only admire, turning up at *Albatross* with home-cooked offerings and a determined glint in her eye. She was Swedish, around five years younger than Carl and, I have to admit, pretty darn hot: certainly out of Carl's league. I couldn't understand it; she must have been in the queue for legs and teeth when brains were being handed out.

'Have you been leading her on?' I asked him.

Carl snorted derisively. 'Of course not. It's just my natural charm.'

I found that very hard to fathom. 'Well, doesn't she know you're married?'

'Yes! And I talk about Eva all the time. But that doesn't seem to stop this woman, she just keeps showing up. I can't help it if she can't resist me.'

Statements like this would send me into peals of laughter, and Carl would mutter something about his George Clooney looks that would make me laugh until my stomach muscles hurt and I ran short of breath.

Carl escaped his stalker for three weeks to meet Eva in Bangkok where they planned to celebrate their 30-year wedding anniversary and visit their son Magnus, leaving me to work on *Albatross* which was quite bonzer by me; it would allow me to explore the area of Cairns with Beatrice and Franka and get some maintenance work done before Anita arrived.

But I was determined to discover something of this vast continent and desperate to see the Great Barrier Reef. Covering an area over 133,000 square miles, it is the largest single structure made by a living organism, although some would argue that it is not one continuous reef as it consists of nearly 3,000 individual reefs. Stretching nearly 1,400 miles, its gleaming fields of coral can be seen from outer space. The variety of marine creatures it supports is breath-taking: over 1,600 types of fish, 3,000 varieties of molluscs, 500 types of worms, 133 varieties of sharks and rays, and more than 30 species of whales and dolphins, not to mention the amount of seabirds which feed or nest on the reef. It is simply wonderful. Sell everything you own and go there at once.

The wonders of the Great Barrier Reef are rivalled only by those of the tropical rainforest, 11,000 square miles of which is to be found in North Queensland. We joined a tour at Cape Tribulation into the Daintree forest and enjoyed one of the most fascinating days on land I have ever spent. The atmosphere within the forest was immediately pervasive: only two minutes from the car park into the rainforest and it felt as if we'd retreated 135 million years into the past; immense plants and trees towered over us, cutting out the sunlight and intensifying the eerie quiet broken only by the whistles and whoops of birds; steamy mist swirled around the undergrowth and marshy ground. It was so humid my knees were sweating, attracting mosquitoes in their droves despite the thick layer of insect repellent I'd slathered on. 'Do not stray from the path,' our guide told us sternly. Only too happy to obey, we dutifully followed him along a well-worn trail as he narrated to us in hushed tones the perils of the rainforest. I began to realize he carried his machete not out of affectation but out of necessity.

'See that plant over there?' he said. Ten heads swivelled in the direction of his blade. A few feet from the path was an innocuous-looking green leafed plant about three feet tall. 'That is the Gympie-Gympie stinging tree, the most dangerous plant in the Daintree. You don't wanna touch that.'

'Um, vhy not?' a wide-bottomed German woman asked.

'Because the leaves and stems are covered in thick hairs that inflict a sting so painful people have compared it to being burnt with hot acid and electrocuted at the same time. The effects of the sting can last up to two years. There's no effective antidote and dogs that run into the plant have to be shot; best to put 'em out of their misery, you know?' Ten people stepped as one to the far side of the path. 'Careful there,' our guide said, causing ten heads to pivot in panic again. 'Baby scrub python overhead. Isn't he a beaut?' At least two of our party didn't think so, but uncertain what might be around the next tree to kill them, stood frozen on the path and shuddered.

'Anything else we should know about?' I asked casually. I wished I hadn't. By the time he'd finished detailing the dangers of ticks and leeches, salt water crocodiles, various other spiky plants that stung you just because they felt like it, not to mention the Cassowary bird which could slash open your abdomen with the murderous claw of its inner toe, I had all but lost the will to live.

'In 2003, there were 150 Cassowary attacks on humans, but mostly on drongos stupid enough to feed them. Ah, incidentally mate, I wouldn't sit on that tree stump,' he added. 'Red mites; their bite can lead to a nasty case of scrub itch.' I leapt from my resting place as if my whole arse was on fire. I was mildly surprised to get out of the rainforest alive.

But it wasn't all play and no work; I'd been busy on *Albatross*: sewing, welding, repairing, installing, replacing, mounting, tweaking, stripping down and polishing. By the time Carl returned from Thailand, our Hallberg-Rassy was gleaming. Glad as I was to see Carl, I was equally happy to see the back of him when he took off backpacking to Brisbane, leaving me to enjoy a little whoopee with Anita who I was exceptionally glad to see again. Beatrice and Franka flew back to Germany no doubt thoroughly embarrassed at the sounds of canoodling through the cabin walls.

Cairns is a real party city, full of people of all ages who come to visit the Great Barrier Reef and the rainforest by day and are ready to drink heartily by night. Anita and I loved it, and spent the three weeks of her visit in the most superficial way possible, doing nothing of merit other than socialising with people we'd probably never meet again, lying in the sun, eating and drinking, and repairing to the forward cabin of *Albatross*. Time is such an elastic entity and seemed to snap to its shortest length when Anita was with me; our three weeks together went by in a blink, but it served to confirm more than ever that we wanted to be together.

To celebrate completing our repairs and to bid farewell to Anita and the water-based assortment of people we'd got to know while in Cairns, we threw an impromptu party. Our guests included Paddy and Patrick Draper, and Mark Muir and his partner Gaye Bertacco, all of whom came from Nelson on New Zealand's South Island but had settled in Cairns some years earlier, swopping Kiwi slang for Aussie idioms. Even Carl and I were beginning to shorten words where we could; we talked about drinking a few tinnies, wearing our sunnies and boardies, watching the footy – although that seemed applicable for any game involving men in shorts running after a ball – and having the barbie in the arvo. We understood "the ditch" referred to the water between Australia and New Zealand, "ankle biters" were small children and that the prize in a "chook raffle" was likely to be a chicken. But we were still confused about why a redhead might be called a "bluey," and scratched our heads over "budgie smugglers" – not the meaning of the phrase as much as the need for such snug fitting swimwear. Mark, a bonzer bloke in his forties, could wear an earring without looking naff and regaled us for hours with stories of his fishing adventures on the rough west coast of New Zealand where he'd run a trawling company for many years. He and Gaye operated *Terri-too Calm Water Cruises* specialising in taking tourists up river crocodile spotting.

'Gotta watch those saltwater crocs,' he said. 'Salties are mean bastards, much more dangerous than sharks. A croc is really fast, and he'll take anything he fancies whether he's hungry or not. And you're food to a croc. He'll leap full length clean out of the water in a vertical position to catch you. Then he'll tear you to pieces by shaking you from side to side.' Mark gave a demonstration by furiously shaking his head, as if the picture wasn't already indelibly imprinted on my mind. And I wished he'd stop directing his narrative straight at me.

'I thought on average only one person a year is killed by a crocodile; more people die of bee stings,' I said.

Mark stared hard at me. 'Yeah, one *body* a year is retrieved. All I'm saying is that people are regularly attacked and frequently disappear. The trouble is they ignore the warning signs not to swim in creeks and rivers.'

'Are people really that stupid?' Paddy asked.

'Stupid or madder than cut snakes. They have a few tinnies and think they can out swim a saltie and let me tell you, you can't.'

'I wouldn't dream of trying,' Paddy said. He was a hefty bloke in his late forties and wisely recognized that his hundred-yard breaststroke was no match for a 15-foot crocodile.

'Anyway, Gaye and I are going to sell the business,' Mark continued. 'We've bought ourselves a couple of Harleys and we're going to spend a year riding around Australia. Then we're planning on buying a sailboat to sail around the world like you guys. We reckon we should dock in Sweden in about three years.' He seemed to have endless energy and nothing short of a saltie would have stopped him fulfilling his plans once he'd put his mind to it.

As we filled our plates with food and drank our wine in the velvety warmth of twilight, Mark asked Anita, 'So the roaches don't bother you then?'

'What roaches?' Anita asked.

'The cockroaches. They're everywhere.'

'I haven't seen any,' Anita said.

Mark pointed to a shadow on the cabin ceiling directly above her head. 'There's one, eyeing your fish soup.'

Anita looked up and dropped her spoon with a small shriek of disgust. 'Yanne! You never told me there were cockroaches on the boat.'

'Darling, I told you we had extra crew on board.'

'That's the "crew"! I thought with your dodgy English you meant something else!'

'We've always called them the crew,' Carl said blithely.

'The trouble is, once you've seen one, you start to notice them everywhere,' Mark said casually, and Anita duly spent the rest of the evening frantically counting the number of cockroaches that had previously been invisible to her.

'Don't worry, darling, there aren't any cockroaches in the bedroom,' I lied.

'Oh good,' Anita sighed, trusting me as always. I made certain to keep the lights off that night in case her love wasn't completely blind.

On the Friday of our departure we caught up with Max Brugger who'd left his native Switzerland for Australia some 40 years before. Max was a wiry 60-year old with grey hair and an ability to repair anything you threw at him. He'd helped us with all the stainless steel fittings on *Albatross* and was a mine of information about life in Australia. An avid fisherman, Max made his own lure for catching mackerel. He was also an excellent salesman as we immediately bought a few to try our luck out on the Great Barrier Reef. He talked about how much Australia had changed in the time he'd lived in the country. 'It's far more civilized around here than it used to be,' he said. 'It was like the Wild West until a few years ago. Cairns was an ugly town with grey mudflats and a shabby harbour. But in the 1990s the city got a makeover, the Esplanade was smartened up. There are family barbie areas, lawns, bike lanes and walking tracks. They even built a spanking new swimming lagoon. It's a great place now.'

On the first day of August we made sail for Darwin, which on a map of Australia looks as if we were just popping round the corner, but at 1,300 nautical miles was the equivalent of our journey from Helsingborg to Dublin. We'd refuelled, resupplied and had embraced Australia so wholeheartedly that when we saw an outfitters selling oilskin jackets and leather bush hats, Carl and I were convinced we both needed them, especially when Carl took the opportunity for a little boisterous haggling to get the price reduced. We thought we looked fair dinkum in them, although I have a suspicion that the charming shop assistant thought we looked like a couple of drongos.

Normally, once you have cleared into a country, you may sail freely in its waters, but this rule doesn't apply to Australia. Our plan was to sail over the top of Australia, round the peninsular of Cape York at the tip of Queensland, through the Torres Straight where we'd stop off at a couple of islands, and then on to Darwin. A good plan except that sailing in the waters north of Thursday Island in the Torres Strait is not permitted; the Australian Quarantine and Inspection Service were very specific about this.

'Don't even think about sailing north of Thursday Island,' an officer said to us sternly, wagging his finger at us like a boarding school headmistress. 'We have very tough controls. We're watching sailboats like you all the time.' The Australian authorities are terrified of pests entering from nearby Papua New Guinea which could decimate the extensive fruit and vegetable crops, so we submitted to the finger wagging without sulking.

We sailed on the outgoing tide with full rig, staying within the Great Barrier Reef and hugging the coast, the drawback being that we had to sail a zigzag course to avoid the numerous reefs that can rip a hull to shreds with one careless slip. For safety's sake we sailed only in daylight to navigate the treacherous corals, but there were many glorious small uninhabited islands in the windward shores of which we could anchor for the night. *Albatross* slipped over the water like a knife over soft butter, making good speeds of six to eight knots. Finding good anchorage was easy as there were many deserted white sand beaches, but once near Cooktown at the mouth of the Endeavour River, we were wary about dipping a toe in the water, particularly after what Mark had told us about the salties.

Early on the second afternoon of sailing we anchored in Watson's Bay on Lizard Island. Once again a perfect Eden of sandy beaches so white they made our eyes water appeared in the endless horizon of perfect shimmering blues. Soft grassy slopes rose to a stately pink granite peak, reef ribbons stretched from the island like streamers and schools of fish gleamed silver as they flitted below the sparkling surface. I apologize if I'm repeating myself, but there are only so many ways to describe paradise.

James Cook, however, didn't see it quite the same way during his exploration of Australia's northern coast, but then the good captain had probably lost his sense of humour as the *Endeavour* had run aground on the reef and required extensive repairs. The only reason he decided to even set foot on Lizard Island, so named because of the large number of monitor lizards he encountered, was because he was heartily sick of getting lost in the labyrinth of reefs and was "altogether at a loss which way to steer." Hence, he climbed to the island's highest point to find a channel between the islands. His mood probably didn't improve when he got to the summit to discover "a reef of rocks ... extending farther than I could see, upon which the sea broke in a dreadful surf." Nevertheless, he noticed a passage through which he navigated the *Endeavour* only to be so battered by the ocean beyond the outer reef that he turned the ship back again to seek shelter in the bay.

Watson's Bay was clearly a popular spot and there were already 15 or more yachts at anchor and snorkels dotted the surface of the water. A short swim from the beach lie the well-known Clam Gardens where giant clams the weight of Sumo wrestlers live in a mosaic of hard and soft corals, feather stars, sea pens, sponges and sea cucumbers. Pity the poor clam; it has an undeserved reputation as a man eater and only one chance to find a home on the sea bed where it hopes to sit quietly for a hundred years or so, until some berk comes along with a big knife to cut out its adductor muscle for – guess who – the Chinese who believe it to have – guess what – aphrodisiac properties.

An hour before sunset, we took the dinghy over to the beach where crews from other boats were gathering to grill and exchange sailing stories. As the heavenly smell of barbeque wafted over the beach, guitar music played by two blokes from Brisbane accompanied the gentle lapping of the waves against the shore. Maybe it was the alcohol, but we all became quite lyrical as the sun turned the horizon pink and gold. On second thoughts, it almost certainly *was* the alcohol, but in any event we decided to explore Lizard Island the following morning.

It was one of those ideas which was quite brilliant on the second bottle of wine, but lost its appeal in the scorching light of day when the lyrical thoughts I'd so carefully committed to paper at two in the morning revealed themselves to be incomprehensible twaddle. Clad in sturdy shoes, a pair of boardies and with enough water to sink a camel, Carl and I started the climb up the mountain to Cook's Lookout. After an ascent made unnecessarily strenuous due to a pounding headache, we arrived at the summit. The view was worth every wheeze and gasp I'd given to get there; the reefs stretched around the island in water of astonishing shades of turquoise and sapphire, and I came over all lyrical again.

Our descent was even tougher than the ascent, scrambling down rocks and through dense scrubby bush, grasses and small ravines on the south side of the island, surprising geckos, lizards and ourselves.

'Do you think there might be snakes about as well as lizards?' I asked Carl apprehensively.

'Probably. So I would get your foot out of that hole.' Advice I immediately followed. We later found out that pythons and tree snakes are common, but the only dangerous species on the island is the brown-headed snake described unreassuringly as "mildly venomous," which in Australian terms translates as not likely to kill you, but enough to send you into a jerky dance of pain after a nip on the ankle. Fortunately, we didn't meet any.

After four hours of picking our way down the hillside, we came to the Blue Lagoon, a 30-foot lagoon formed by Lizard Island, three other small islands and their fringing reef. We threw our clothes and caution to the wind and leapt into the silky turquoise water, trying to repress thoughts of saltwater crocodiles viewing us as a quick snack: even so, we didn't luxuriate in the water for long.

The following day we continued sailing along the long finger of the Cape York Peninsula, frequently entertained by residents of the Coral Sea; a whale showed off its breaching skills, creating a massive displacement of water as it thudded back into the ocean; three dugongs observed us with small mole-like eyes as they swam alongside us before disappearing below to feed on sea-grass, and Max's lure proved successful when we hooked a 10-pound Spanish mackerel. On our thirteenth day, we arrived in the strait between Thursday Island and Horn Island, the small town of Port Kennedy affording us the first sight of habitation since leaving Cairns. We were as far north in Australia as we could get.

Thursday Island is one of the larger of 274 small islands scattered over an area of 30,000 miles in the Torres Strait, named after Spaniard Vaez de Torres, the first European to navigate his way through them. The islands were once part of a land bridge between Australian and Papua New Guinea before rising seawaters submerged most of the land during the last big freeze some 12,000 years ago. Many of the islands are in fact the remaining peaks of this land bridge covered by the ocean rise, although today these are threatened by rising sea levels; islands which rise less than three feet above sea level could disappear altogether. Thursday Island, or Waiben (the place of no water) is the administrative heart of the Torres Strait and the most populated island with approximately 2,600 people living on less than one and a half square miles of land. Once a major pearling centre, the numerous cemeteries are evidence of the dangers of pearl diving; no doubt the unfortunate pearl fishermen were regularly picked off by saltwater crocodiles or marine stingers. Pearls are still farmed here on a much smaller scale, but the island's economy depends mostly on its role as an administrative centre and increasingly on tourism, despite the fact that for six months of the year you are unable to bathe in the ocean due to the proliferation of things with teeth or tentacles out to get you.

Those who would have it that sharks are the most dangerous predators in the water are scoffed at by crocodile specialists who are in turned scorned by marine stinger boffins who insist that the box jellyfish is the nastiest thing on the planet, packing twenty times more venom than a KGB's brolly tip. Although we were well outside the box jellyfish season which normally runs from October to June, the Australian Marine Stingers advisory services recommends the wearing of protective clothing or "stinger suits." Knowing that there is something invisible in the water capable of inducing intolerable pain for the three minutes before you meet your maker is enough to put many people off taking a paddle. Groups of tourists lined the shore staring morosely at the tempting turquoise water, wondering if they should risk it or not. Very few took the plunge. It seems grossly unfair to create a tropical climate, add crystal clear waters just begging you to take a refreshing dip and then stir in the world's most deadly creature. Popular beaches have stinger-resistant enclosures designed to prevent large box jellyfish from entering the enclosure. Notice, however, the use of the word "large." For some morbid reason I can't explain, I quite wanted to see one.

Once we'd anchored, we took a stroll along the main street through Port Kennedy, an easy- going little town with a cultural mix of Asians and Pacific islanders and still something of the nineteenth century pioneering spirit about it. Despite the fact that the island is so small you could walk the whole of it in under an hour, all the locals either hop in a car or on a bike to scoot around its 10 miles of road. It was Friday night on Thursday Island and the pubs on the main thoroughfare were starting to fill with fishermen and tourists from the surrounding islands to drink and gamble – most of the pubs' entertainment being online games with races displayed on monitors on every wall. Carl and I systematically visited all six of Port Kennedy's pubs, determined to learn something of island life, which we probably did but immediately forgot in the haze of an alcohol induced fog.

So once again I woke up with a pounding headache, trying to perform simple tasks my sluggish brain couldn't compute – beware of that XXXX beer, it creeps up on you and smacks you around the head. A new arrival, a 30-foot boat was trying to anchor but having problems due to the outgoing tide. We ran to help, catching ropes and advising him how to steer in. It was an old looking boat with a large, ungainly looking outhouse made of simple planks occupying most of the deck area.

'What the hell is that for?' Carl asked as we finished tying up.

'The fridge,' answered the skipper, a lean man with a Slavic accent underlying his Australian English. The boat was owned by Aldis Peyr from the Czech Republic who'd started his solo voyage from Townsville eight weeks early. He told us he was making his way back to his home country via the Suez Canal, across the Mediterranean and entering Europe's canal system at Marseille, hoping to arrive in the Czech Republic in the spring of 2005. Carl and I were immediately intrigued and asked him on board that evening to hear more of his story.

'Ah, splendid,' he said as he tucked into his fried chicken. 'Usually I just eat tinned food which I heat up on my one-ring stove.'

'So what's in the fridge?' I asked.

'Essentials,' he replied. 'Beer and milk, but mostly beer.' Carl and I nodded in sympathetic understanding.

Aldis was a self-taught sailor with even less experience than Carl and I'd had when he bought himself a very modest sailboat some three years before. He admitted that the 700-nautical mile journey along Australia's east coast had been a little hairy. 'I took a long break at Cape York,' he said between large bites of chicken – for a wiry man he could eat like a wolf – 'and learned how to read the electronic charts on my computer, but I still don't understand how the GPS works.'

So what was he doing in Australia, we wondered. 'Ah, a long story,' he sighed, wiping his grey beard. We refilled our glasses. 'In 1967, the Russians invaded my country, Czechoslovakia as it was then. We saw the tanks filling our streets and knew we would be under the steel thumb of the Russians. In 1953, when I was 19 and still idealistic, I'd been active in the underground resistance, fighting communist oppression, but when the Russians arrived I knew there was only one option: I left my home, my parents, my friends and my country. A year later I managed to get to Australia. For 40 years, I've lived a good life here: two wives, three married sons; I've had jobs in the construction and catering industries. I've been happy here, but now I'm 70 and it's time to be free: time to sail back to my homeland and fulfil my dream.'

What dream? Aldis' grey eyes misted for a moment and the frown lines in his forehead deepened. He took a deep gulp of wine and continued. 'We all have one great love, don't we? When I was 19, I met my great love, Anna, while I was in the underground resistance group. Our group conducted an attack against the dictatorship and, of course, the security police eventually tracked us down. We were questioned' – and here Aldis winced at the word – 'by the security police. I and many of my friends were found guilty; thank god, Anna was not. I refused to say anything about her.

'Our punishment was typically harsh: eight years imprisonment in the uranium mines. You can't imagine how miserable it was, but I survived. When I was free, I didn't dare contact Anna; I might have incriminated her. So when the Russian tanks came down the streets, I decided to leave for good; there was nothing to stay for. And I have loved Australia: such a beautiful country.'

'So why go back now?' I asked.

Aldis' smile crinkled the corners of his eyes. 'To meet my Anna. After all this time, I've managed to find her through the Red Cross. And she is single!' He slapped his hands on his thighs. 'And so am I!'

It was as heart-warming a story as anything thought up by Hollywood. And even at the age of 70, Aldis certainly seemed to have plenty of lead left in his pencil. I spent the following day teaching him the basics of navigation and how to use the GPS. It was astonishing he'd come this far without crashing his craft on the reef or colliding with other boats. With a little more knowledge and limitless optimism, Aldis continued his long journey home the next day. The man was a walking personification of the phrase, "You're never too old." I hope he and Anna are enjoying their golden years together wherever they may be.

Carl and I made sail the same day, ploughing briskly through Normanby Sound between Thursday Island and Prince of Wales Island, and entering the Arafura Sea, setting a westerly course towards Darwin. It was joyous sailing: a helpful breeze at our backs filled the spinnaker so we flitted over the water like a dragonfly. We were out on open water, away from the terrors and unpredictable waters of the reef, the Spanish mackerel were jumping onto our lure and we landed a hefty 25-pounder. Four days of breezy sailing later we came to Croker Island where we decided to anchor in Cambridge Bay to rest up and take a stroll on land. The sun was still high in the west when we launched the dinghy to explore. Although we later found out that around 300 people live on Croker Island, most of whom are gathered in an Aboriginal community at Mission Bay, the place had an uninhabited feel to it; the sound of the waves against the long white beach was intermittently interrupted by bird call from deep within the tropical rainforest. The sand looked as if it had never been walked on, although something heavy, predatory and much bigger than me had left worryingly large tail and claw marks starting at the water's edge, disappearing up the beach and into the undergrowth.

'A tropical abominable snowman?' Carl suggested.

'Look at the size of those bloody claw marks! I think we stay well away from the forest!' I said, my sense of survival beating out my curiosity. We turned and went in the opposite direction down the beach, checking behind us every now and again in case the crocodile was creeping up on us.

We stayed on Croker for two days, fishing and watching the giant tortoises swimming around *Albatross*; they seemed as curious about us as we were about them. The island seemed impossibly remote, and yet we read later how in 1940 a Methodist Mission built a shelter to house children of "mixed descent;" they were, in fact, children of the stolen generation. During 1909 to 1969, in a ludicrous policy designed to "breed out" Indigenous people, approximately 100,000 Aboriginal and Torres Strait Islander children were forcibly removed from their parents and raised by white families. It's a deeply shameful period in the country's history and for which the Australia government only finally apologized in 2008. In 1942, when the Japanese bombed Darwin, 95 children together with three missionary carers were trapped on Croker Island. Realizing they had to move their charges to safety themselves, the missionaries began a perilous 3,000-mile journey, travelling by boat, foot, canoe, truck and train to Sydney: it took them 44 days and all but one unfortunate child survived.

The most direct route under sail power to Darwin is via the Dundas Strait, across Van Dieman Gulf and then through the Clarence Strait. This requires sensible planning to catch the tides and our charts indicated strong tidal currents and dangerous areas. Lord knows, they were right; we spent forever trying to anchor near Burford Island but the currents spun *Albatross* around like a manic carousel. We gave up on the fourth attempt and headed further, finally dropping anchor on the west side of Greenhill Island where the currents were greatly reduced. As we neared Darwin, oil and gas platforms dotted the horizon like futuristic monsters; hourly radio warnings were issued to shipping approaching the channel to the city. As we passed Emery Point lighthouse at the entrance to Port Darwin, we began to relax. We'd arrived at the top end of Australia, the Northern Territory, home to one of the country's iconic natural landmarks, Uluru (Ayer's Rock).

Arriving at a new territory was like entering another country. We were told that prior to inspection, we had to anchor in the quarantine area and await an appointment with the Marine Pest Authorities or the Aquatic Pest Management or the Don't Bring your Pests in here Agency or whatever it was called.

'We're going to have to clean your bottom,' an official called Bengt said.

'I wasn't aware my bottom was dirty,' Carl said with a sniff.

'Sorry, mate, but all yachts must be inspected to prevent the spread of marine pests so I need to check your hull and clean your seawater systems. But don't worry, the Northern Territory government will cover the costs of both the hull inspection and the cleaning.'

'Oh, well in that case,' said Carl, smiling with relief, 'check away. What are you looking for?'

'Asian bag mussels, black-striped mussels and Asian green mussels.' All of which sounded like the ingredients for moules marinière, but are substantial threats to the biodiversity of the marine environment. In 2002, a plague of black-striped mussels in Cullen Bay marina caused AU $11 million in damage, so clearly the authorities were determined not to let such plagues reoccur. As Bengt got started on treating the internal seawater systems, we took a stroll around Cullen Bay marina, an attractive facility which was clearly popular with yachties and residents alike. Due to the very large tides, the marina has tidal sluice gates to maintain the waters inside at a constant level.

'Right,' Bengt said, on our return. 'I've added a dilute disinfectant solution into the piping of all onboard systems that draw seawater; that needs to stay in the pipes for a good 14 hours so it means you can't use the onboard systems. I'll send a diver out to inspect the hull later today. Once that's cleared, you can enter the marina.'

'But it's my birthday,' I said peevishly. Bengt wore the expression of a man who really didn't care.

'We were going to celebrate Yanne's birthday on *Albatross* tonight,' Carl explained.

Bengt's expression changed to one of mild surprise and he waved a hand airily towards land. 'Then I suggest you choose a bar to celebrate in. Strewth, there's about 40 of them.'

Bengt was way off: there are over 60 bars in Darwin, if you include nightclubs with dubious names such as *Throb*, which I'm sure didn't allude to the headache you develop from the music pumping loudly from the darkness within. For a population of around 128,000, dwelling in a climate which generally ranges from iron-scorching in its dry season to sauna steamy in its wet, beer is evidently to Top Enders what oxygen is to living organisms. Darwin has the highest annual beer consumption per capita of any city in the world and launched the world's largest beer bottle, the "Darwin Stubby" which holds two litres (three and a half pints) of amber gold. When the wall of heat belts you in the face, the need to quench your parched throat with large measures of cold beer is quite understandable. The local passion for beer also explains in large part the annual Darwin Beer Can Regatta: a perfect marriage of drinking and recycling in a competition which requires contestants to cross a finish line on a seaworthy vessel made of empty beer cans. The event attracts more than 15,000 spectators annually, along with contestants from as far away as Europe and North America. As descendants of a great boat building nation, world sailors and beer aficionados, Carl and I felt we could have drunk enough to build a winning craft, but disappointingly we'd just missed the regatta by a couple of weeks. Oh well, there's always something to aspire to.

Darwin, named after English naturalist Charles Darwin, has seen some hammering over the years – during the Second World War it was bombed 64 times by the Japanese, the first air attack by the same fleet that bombed Pearl Harbour, killing at least 243 people. Then on Christmas day in 1974, Cyclone Tracy flattened 70 percent of the town, killing more than 70 people and prompting the evacuation of 35,000 people out of a population of 45,000. The city was built all over again in a style I would describe as "fast and replaceable," so it was a mere 30 years old when we visited.

When *Albatross* was deemed mussel free and her pipes clean, the giant sluice lock gates opened for us and we entered Cullen Bay marina where we filled in numerous papers for a lock keeper who appeared to have been trying to raise the average beer consumption per capita all by himself the night before. We moored and plugged into the service pole, and as usual spent the first 48 hours of our arrival carrying out repairs. Then we went shopping.

The first item on our list was a new chart covering the Indian Ocean from Australia's west coast to South Africa as we'd decided the best way to South Africa was not to sail the usual route to the Christmas, Cocos Keeling and Chagos Islands, but instead to go along Australia's west coast, as we'd heard from other yachties that the Kimberley coastline is one of the most beautiful in the world: a claim we had to investigate for ourselves.

As we would be crossing the Indian Ocean – a voyage we estimated might take us a month – we headed to the largest supermarket in town where we quickly filled three trolleys with supplies. A friendly Indonesia taxi driver cheerfully deposited us and our load at Cullen Bay Marina where one of the lock operators lent us a large shopping trolley. With great care, we packed the trolley, stacking everything into a perilous mountain. When we'd run out of room, we hung more bags and wine boxes off Carl, then we proceeded, me pushing the trolley and Carl leading the way with his load, along the floating docks to where we were moored.

Now I'll readily admit that I may not have been concentrating as fully as I should have been, that my mind may well have been elsewhere, that I was enjoying a little flight of fantasy involving Anita and me, a bottle of champagne and a deserted beach. But some of the fault must also be placed on the fourth wheel of the trolley which refused to go in the direction of the other three; moreover, the mountain of food meant I couldn't see where the wayward trolley wheel was leading me. One moment I was pushing the heavy load in front of me and the next, everything went into free-fall; a loud splash as the trolley hit the water rudely woke me from my reverie. Carl turned to see gentle ripples pool as the handle slowly disappeared.

'Aargh!' I shouted eloquently. We both ran to the edge of the pontoon where a few of the contents of the trolley were rising to the surface: apples, potatoes, packets of biscuits, but most of our supplies had sunk to harbour floor. We threw ourselves prostrate on the dock to grab as much as we could.

'Holy crap and bloody strewth,' Carl said. 'Right, we'll have to dive for the rest.'

I rushed to *Albatross* to get on my diving gear and Carl dropped a spinnaker rope into the water. Visibility in the harbour was horrendous, it was like diving in pea purée, but the outline of the trolley appeared 15 feet down; there it was stuck in the soft silt of the seabed. By feel more than by sight, I found cans of food, bottles and jars and filled the shopping trolley. I gave the rope three quick tugs, the signal for Carl to start heaving. After two dives, we'd rescued most of our lost viaticum. We dumped everything out on the pontoon and washed it all clean. Fortunately, we bought pre-packed meat so we could salvage it. Never have I been so grateful for the wonders of cling film.

We'd drawn quite a number of spectators lunching at the waterside restaurants, so by the time Carl had cleaned up the trolley and was wheeling it back to the lock attendant, most of the marina had watched our misadventure with curiosity. There were approving whistles and shouts of 'Good on ya, mates,' as Carl strolled back to *Albatross*. With great aplomb, he took a slow bow, then indicated me, his other cast member, on deck where I also modestly received my applause with a shy bow.

'We Vikings never say die,' Carl shouted to his fans. There was an exchange of thumbs-up signs and we went back to stashing our cans. The only problem was the labels had worked loose in the water, so dinner for the next few weeks was a complete mystery; we would sit down to a series of taste bud-challenging meals – pork sausages with peaches in syrup or baked beans with pineapple chunks – served with whatever meat we pulled from the freezer, which I think is more or less how some restaurant chefs create their menus.

We were looking forward to cruising the Kimberley, famed for its striking rocky coastline, large bays and rivers, splendid fishing and countless calm anchorages. The few private craft who sail the area recommend taking a couple of months to explore. The Kimberley, one of the nine regions of Western Australia, covers an area of over 163,000 square miles – nearly three times the size of England – but is one of the most sparsely populated parts of the country with a population of only 41,000, many of whom are Aboriginal. The coastline itself stretches more than 8,000 miles including islands and bays and boasts over 2,633 islands in the archipelagos of Buccaneer and Bonaparte.

We set off with our usual optimism, sailing out on the tide into the Beagle Gulf, then west into the Timor Sea under a promising cloudless sky. A brisk wind scuttled us across Joseph Bonaparte Gulf towards Cape Londonderry; we raised the spinnaker and *Albatross* made good speed, her bow whooshing pleasantly through the clear turquoise waves. Every noon an Australian customs plane zoomed over our mast and radioed us to verify our name, home port, previous harbour and destination; the waters around Indonesia are strictly monitored by customs and coastguards to prevent the smuggling of drugs and people.

Like the middle of a disaster film, this idyll didn't last. All hell was about to be unleashed, not that Carl and I knew it when we welcomed the dark clouds of a rain storm.

'Oh goodie,' I said with the glee of a man who has no idea what he's in for. 'We can have a warm fresh water shower on deck. How nice.' The hero in such films never looks behind him and blithely goes about his business while the audience is frantically hissing at the screen, 'Look behind you, you idiot!' as the danger looms closer.

We eventually became aware of our looming danger when I suddenly glimpsed something strange in the distance; a long dark thread suspended between the sky and the ocean seemed to be moving over the water.

'Could you pass me the binoculars?' I asked Carl in a relatively calm voice considering the bolt of panic that was coursing through me.

'Why are you talking like a soprano?' Carl asked. He followed my shaky finger as I pointed at the dark thread which was rapidly becoming a solid black column. Even without the binoculars we could see that an almighty wind was whipping the sea into a monumental frenzy of thrashing waves. Carl and I said the word in unison.

'Tornado!'

We moved fast: we clipped on our safety harnesses; all sails were reefed in and secured; the engine was started and pushed to the max. Pictures of houses and cows being lifted and thrown across American states filled my mind. If a tornado could lift a 40-ton house in Alabama and chuck it into Mississippi, what could it do to a 16-ton sailboat?

'Let's get out of here!' Carl yelled, unnecessarily. I hadn't planned on staying.

'We can't outrun it!' I screamed back.

'Well, we've got to try!'

We'd survived the perils of the North Sea, narrowly escaped being mown down by a supertanker in the Bay of Biscay, thought our number was up when we took on water on the way to the Galapagos, and endured winds of 90 miles an hour that ripped our mainsail to shreds. But a tornado? A tornado was something we'd never reckoned with in all our "worst case scenario" planning. Though not quite sitting ducks, we were slow scuttling ones, even with the motor going as fast as it could without bursting into flames. The column was gaining on us, whirling only a nautical mile away, blacker and more menacing than ever.

We were staring down the barrel of a gun. We sat in the cockpit, in silence. I think both of us were praying to higher powers to protect us from the approaching peril. I thought of the last time I'd seen my parents, my children, Anita. Was this how it was going to end? With me whimpering in the cockpit? And if these were to be my final moments, shouldn't I spend them writing some meaningful last words to my nearest and dearest. Or at the least mixing a very strong gin and tonic and going down with a witty phrase?

Well, as the existence of this book testifies, *Albatross* wasn't swallowed up and thrown across the ocean. Long minutes passed as Carl and I watched that black column dance across the horizon before spinning out of energy and fading to a little wisp of mist. We slowly exhaled and relaxed all the muscles we'd been clenching.

'What'll it be? A strong drink or a change of underwear?' Carl eventually asked.

A day later we anchored in Brunei Bay on the uninhabited island of Maret where we spent the weekend playing Robinson Crusoe, combing the beach for shells, snorkelling, fishing and setting our lobster pots which as usual we hauled up empty. We cruised along this most spectacular coastline for 10 days, never seeing another soul or hearing anything except the sound of waves and the cries of the birds. The remote Kimberley islands have acted as ecological capsules; flora and fauna has remained safe from the threats of disease, fire and the introduction of feral herbivores such as donkeys and pigs. Species that are in decline on the mainland are flourishing on the islands. It may be one of the last bastions on the planet truly untouched by man, one of the last wildernesses left to us, so Carl and I were very careful not to leave anything that might disturb it. Our only contact with civilization was with the duty flight that radioed us every day at noon; we never saw another vessel. It was as if *Albatross* were the last boat on the face of the Earth and we the last two men on her.

So by the time we spotted the lights of the fishing boats off Broome, we were overexcited about having conversations with locals that consisted of more than 'Shall we reef in?' or 'Would you like your fish boiled or fried?' It was two in the morning when we finally anchored off Cable Beach in Broome. We sat in the dark, drinking our mooring snaps, listening to the Indian Ocean swell and roll into the shore, luxuriating in the knowledge that we'd success-fully completed the first stage of our journey towards South Africa.

Broome, known as the "pearl of the north," is a pearling town 1,400 miles north of Perth and 1,400 miles from Darwin to the east, officially locating it in the middle of nowhere. We woke up to a view as lovely as any we'd yet seen. Cable Beach is a 13-mile expanse of unblemished white sand, undulating dunes and turquoise water. We sighed with pleasure for a bit, then went in search of the town, taking the dinghy to shore, although shore seemed to get further away the more we went towards it; the tide was out and we had to haul the dinghy up the beach, something we are unused to doing in Sweden where the tide levels vary only by a few inches. The Kimberley coast experiences the biggest tides in the southern hemisphere with the difference between high tide and low tide close to 35 feet.

'Must be far enough, don't you think?' I said to Carl after bumping the dinghy up the beach towards the bush.

Carl agreed in the peevish tone of a man who has been denied breakfast and threw down his side of the dinghy. After trudging along on a single road for a bit, we came to a fork: no buildings or people were in sight.

'Which way?' I asked.

'How should I know?' asked Carl in that peevish tone again. Fortunately, before we broke into serious squabbling, a large four-wheel drive drove up the beach. We waved it down at the crossroads. Two fellows wearing bush hats low over their eyes turned their heads in our direction.

'Kin we halp ya fellas?' one asked, pushing his hat back on his head with a leathery hand.

'G'day,' I said, now fluent in the local dialect. 'Which way for Broome city?'

'We'll give ya a lift. Hop in the back and take a seat, though ya might have ta push the beers back a bit.'

Jim and John, two bonzer fellas, drove us into Broome and were good enough to give us a guided tour and a bit of information about the place, pointing out the pier, new hotels, Sun Pictures – the oldest operating outdoor cinema in the world – art galleries, Chinatown and the Chinese and Japanese cemeteries – a reminder of the early multi-cultural mix of people in Broome – and the Irish pub. Jim reckoned that the city's population numbered around 15,000 but tripled in the dry season. Broome had a charming, laid back feel to it, but then I imagine most of the time it's too hot to hurry. Jim told us it had been pretty dry of late: it hadn't rained in five months.

'Hope ya have a good time. And good luck with yer trip home, fellas. Oh, and just watch out for the irukandji on Cable Beach,' John said as he dropped us off in the centre of town.

'Irukandji?

'Yeah. A jellyfish, packs a thousand times more venom than a tarantula.'

'Okay. So what does it look like?' Carl asked.

Jim laughed. 'Nah, you won't see it, mate. It's the smallest jellyfish in the world, a tiny little bastard the size of a thumb nail. But you'll feel it.'

'Don't worry, fellas,' John said. 'We've only had a couple of deaths, but you should be okay this time of year. G'day.' He pulled his hat over his eyes and drove off leaving us to digest this latest nugget of doom-laden advice.

'*Should* be okay,' I said to Carl as we watched the car pull away. 'Is there anything in Australia that *doesn't* want to kill you?'

We wandered around the town, soaking up the pioneer flavour, admiring the streets of low houses and shops with wrap-around verandas from which flags hung limply for lack of breeze. The town was a strange fusion of back-packer type bars, cheap tourist shops and luxury boutiques offering expensive pearl jewellery for sale. Broome's heyday took place in the 1870s when the discovery of the Pinctada maxima – the world's largest pearl oyster – fuelled a mass stampede akin to that of the gold rush. Japanese, Filipino and Malay pearl divers arrived in their droves to make their fortunes, but paid dearly to do so, as the numerous cemeteries testify. In the early 1900's, Broome supplied 80 percent of the world's mother-of-pearl, in the process subjecting its pearl divers to appalling working conditions. Aborigines were kidnapped, enslaved and forced to dive for pearls, holding their breath for long periods. Pregnant Aboriginal women were believed to make the best divers as it was thought they could hold their breath longer.

The Indigenous people of Australia have endured the thinnest end of a very thin wedge during the country's history from the moment the British thought to stick a flag on a strip of land and declare it "terra nullius" – land belonging to no one. Of course, this was patently untrue as the Indigenous people already had a complex system for ownership belonging to different clans. A period began of systematic removal of Aboriginal people from their lands and their "integration" into the white man's society. While Australians celebrate Australia Day as the day the country was founded, Aboriginal people call it "Invasion Day."

Never have I witnessed a society in which a set of people were so invisible and seemed to wish to remain so. Aboriginal Australians make up three percent of the population, but few appear to be integrated into the country's society; I didn't meet any working in shops or restaurants. I glimpsed them huddled in the shade, sitting on benches, staring vacantly into space: there, but not there, making no eye contact as we passed. Not that this is their fault; over the ensuing decades since white settlers arrived, many governments have neglected basic services and infrastructure to assist the Aborigines. As a consequence of their treatment, Aboriginal communities and families break down; many live in abject poverty. It is a truly tragic problem of a people whose land, way of life and identity was taken from them. What is worse is that the damage done can never be repaired in the wake of the Stolen Generation. I got the impression that the average white Australian would prefer to ignore the problem because there is no easy solution to it.

Depressed by this, we sought to rally our spirits and quench our thirsts by visiting one of the pubs Jim and John had thoughtfully pointed out to us. We lubricated our throats with a large jug of XXXX beer, which fortified us enough to walk eight kilometres to the local marine store; we'd lost a propeller blade on the wind generator in the last storm and needed to order a new one. Craig at Moby Dick was very helpful and made a few calls to Sydney to order one for us.

'So you boys are anchored off Cable Beach then?' he said with a wide grin. 'Enjoying the view?'

'Yes, it's a beautiful bay,' we agreed.

'I guess you haven't taken a walk north of the rocks. The view's a bit different there.' Craig tapped his nose confidentially. 'All the nudies are there.'

'Newdies?' I asked. This was yet another new word to us. 'What kind of animal is that?'

'No, mate. It's a big nudist beach there.' Craig looked disappointed that we weren't more excited by his news. 'You know, clothes are optional? It's the most famous nudist beach in all Australia. Eleven miles of nakedness,' he added with a touch of pride

Carl and I struggled to look impressed. 'Ah yes,' said Carl, 'but you see, we're Swedish. Clothes are always optional to us. We're often newdie.'

Craig looked impressed. 'Bonzer!' he said.

Getting back to *Albatross* proved more challenging than we'd anticipated. The tide had come in: very, very far in, and powerful swells were rolling towards the beach.

'Where's the damn dinghy?' I asked.

Carl pointed to a speck in the distance bobbing on the waves. 'Guess that must be it over there. You'd better get "newdie" and swim out for it,' he said. The way he crossed his arms suggested that he would brook no further discussion. Swearing under my breath, I dumped my clothes at his feet and battled the waves and the possibility of irukandji, those tiny invisible plastic bags of death. The things I do for that man!

Jim and John had recommended a more protected anchorage near Broome Port, so we sailed 10 nautical miles around the corner and laid up there for a couple of days while we put the finishing touches to our repairs. Our three-month visa was running out and we would be illegal by Saturday, so on Friday morning we checked out *Albatross* and set a course for Rodriguez, 3,400 nautical miles away.

We were sad to leave Australia, feeling that we'd barely scraped the red surface of this remarkable continent. As sailors, it had been our mission to explore the coastline and of its 16,000 miles, we'd only covered approximately 3,500 miles in three months. We hadn't seen Uluru, nor the Sydney Opera House, nor Perth, nor Melbourne, nor Kakadu National Park. The rules of rugby and the reason to enjoy cricket were still unfathomable to us.

But on the plus side, we'd managed to avoid listening to anything by Kylie Minogue.

Chapter 42

A Paper Boat on the Indian Ocean

18 September – 16 October 2004

Broome, Australia – Port Mathurin, Rodrigues

Experience: *If it can break, it will break.*

Tip: *If you can't repair it, learn how to.*

Helsingborg, we have a problem. We're facing our longest sailing stretch yet, a passage over 3,500 nautical miles, the equivalent of flying from London to Chicago. The latter would only take around eight hours, but sailing across the Indian Ocean is going to take at least a month: a serious test not just of our sailing ability, but also of Carl's and my conversational skills. The trouble is we're slightly late out of the gate; we've missed the favourable trade August winds and now we risk having to sail most of the way against headwinds, as well as dodging seasonal storms.

Nevertheless, we aren't going to let a few headwinds get us down – heck, we've ducked a tornado and made it this far. So we sail out of Roebuck Bay with the tide and levels of optimism enjoyed by people who have no idea what they're in for. As we reach open water a humpback whale as big as a bus appears on our port side and puts on a tremendous display for us: breaching, rolling and slapping his, or her – I have no idea how to tell the sex of a whale – pectoral fins.

'I think it's in love with *Albatross*,' I say.

'You would, you lovesick fool,' Carl remarks dryly.

That night we sail against a spiteful headwind which drops to a lull by early morning. So much for the fair trade winds we'd hoped for.

Day 2

Sunday, a day of rest and it seems the wind is also having the day off; only the strong tidal current carries us westward. A humpback whale surfaces and studies us with a shiny brown eye the size of an orange.

'I think it's the same one who courted *Albatross* yesterday,' I say to Carl.

'Let's name him Paddy,' Carl says.

'How do you know it's a male?' I ask.

'How do you know it isn't?' Carl reasons. 'Anyway, he looks a bit like Paddy from Cairns.' He's right, there is a resemblance; Paddy is a big man.

Day 3

The new week starts with a welcome wind gusting up from the southwest. We set all the sails and *Albatross* speeds along at 6.5 knots. With something nearing overexcitement, we sight our first vessel astern of us: a huge container ship heading south towards Port Hedland, the main fuel and container port for the Pilbara region of Western Australia.

While we're digesting a meal of fresh-caught dorado later that evening, Paddy appears, greeting us with an effusive jet of water out of his blowhole. We wave hello and applaud his antics. 'So where do you come from then? Where are you going?' I wonder aloud.

Carl's salt and pepper eyebrows furrow as one. 'It's only our third day at sea and you're trying to have a conversation with a whale. Don't crack up on me, Yanne.'

Day 4

Gusty winds bounce us around like a tennis ball at Wimbledon and we continue to tack hard. The following day marks the equinox in the southern hemisphere; the sun is now at its zenith over the Equator making it too hot to stay on deck.

'Do you think it's possible to fry an egg on the deck?' I ask Carl. 'You know, like they do on stones in the desert?'

'I think I'd prefer my eggs fried properly in a pan and not messed about with on the deck,' is his response.

We settle into our routines like an old married couple, setting six-hour watches. Carl takes the graveyard shift from midnight to breakfast, whereupon I take over. This will be our schedule for the next three weeks: eat, sleep and stand watch.

Paddy appears in the evening to keep us company for half an hour before disappearing below the waves.

Day 6

The southeast trade winds finally start to blow, unfortunately casting up monstrous waves. But we're ploughing along pretty well, until at three in the morning when one of the guide ropes on the windvane breaks and *Albatross* immediately veers off course. The first I know of this is when Carl wakes me saying simply: 'Problem. Get up.' While Carl hand steers, I clip on my safety harness and crawl back in the stern to reattach the rope steering the rudder shaft. At times like these when it takes two of us to fix a problem, I wonder how solo yachtsmen cope.

Day 7

Albatross rushes through the waves like an express train. We sight another whopping container ship which we radio for a bit of a chat, but they don't reply; clearly they don't engage in idle banter with pleasure craft.

There's been no sign of Paddy for two days.

Day 8

The ocean is finally calm and we sleep well in our berths. For the first time on this passage we're able to make hot meals; we've survived so far mostly on breakfast, nibbling biscuits throughout the rest of the day until a cold dinner at six in the evening. I decide to make omelettes with Thai sauce for breakfast, but the first three eggs I crack release a smell so pungent, I gag. Unfortunately, *Carl* hadn't checked the best-by-dates on the eggs and a lot have gone off.

Day 9

Sulky clouds start to gather, obliterating the sunset; it looks like a storm is on the way, so we brace ourselves, lower the mizzen sail, reduce the jib by thirty percent and reef in the main to the third reef. Rain pelts us and the wind increases to fifty miles an hour: we're in for a night of it.

Disaster! Just before midnight, the self-steering system stops working; the turret tube has broken at two welding points and the whole servo rudder trails limply in the wake. Luckily, we'd fixed two safety lines on the rudder section so we're able to salvage the broken part. But the situation is pretty grim; it's like losing our best crew member. Our beloved windvane is essential to us. Here we are in the middle of the world's third largest ocean, surrounded by 28,350,000 square miles of water, enough to swallow Russia four times over. We're faced with the mammoth task of hand steering 2,500 nautical miles to Rodrigues: no picnic even in breezy conditions; in heavy weather it'll be damn near impossible, requiring total concentration and grim determination.

Our only hope is in the electronic self-steering, but we don't have much faith in the contraption as we've had so many problems with it. Nevertheless, for lack of anything else, we decide to test drive it at night, changing to three-hour watches during the day and taking turns to hand steer.

Day 10

Powerful winds and waves keep us in a stranglehold, but to our delight, the electronic self-steering is working well. During the day we plant ourselves firmly at the wheel looking grim and determined like characters out of a disaster movie, trying to keep our ship on course. It takes strength to be a good helmsman in violent weather and after a couple of hours my arms are burning with the effort. It also takes mental fortitude, the ability to stick it out, or go into the zone. My zone lasts approximately 30 minutes before I'm fed up of the pure drudgery of it. Although we've hand steered before, we haven't had to do so in the knowledge that 2,500 nautical miles lie before us. That in itself takes heroic stoicism or a very special zone.

I'm trying to immerse myself in my zone late on my evening watch when a swarm of powerful spotlights light up the stern side. I'm as blinded as a rabbit in car headlights and for a moment just as frozen.

'Calle! Massive boat on collision course with us,' I call, trying to sound calm. Carl comes up on deck, blinking in the glare of the lights. 'I can't tell how far away.'

'Is it a pirate ship trying to blind us with their lights? We can't let them board.'

We scramble for the knives when a red starboard light comes on. The vessel is a large trawler, probably out night fishing for shrimp. Panic over.

Day 11

One of our great joys is our onboard computer on which we have the software for receiving weather faxes via Getfax which produces clear 24-hour-forecast maps. We're just finishing lunch when the fax machine starts rattling out information, announcing wind speeds of up to 60 plus miles per hour: a powerful typhoon is forming in the South China Sea. 'Poor sods,' we think. 'Lord knows how tough it must be on a boat in a typhoon.'

Day 12

Fortunately, the electronic self-steering is still working at night while we manage to hand steer during the day. Conditions are becoming decidedly unfriendly; *Albatross* is pitched about by waves that slam into her port side with a resounding boom. Before our departure from Sweden, we talked with a yachtsman from Anchorage in Alaska who'd spent the best part of his sailing career exploring the world in his 42-foot Hallberg-Rassy. He'd given us a valuable tip, recommending that we replace all the plastic windows on the hull with more durable stainless steel ones as he'd discovered that heavy breakers could push in windows and water would gush into the boat.

Day 13

Great joy! The GPS indicates only 1,724 miles to Rodrigues. We're over half way. We celebrate by opening one of my birthday presents given to me by Swedish friends in Darwin: a tin of pea soup and a packet of Wasa crispbread. We sit in the cockpit and savour these Swedish delicacies, feeling a brief long-ing for home. Pea soup and crackers might not sound like much, but they bring us as much joy as baked beans and marmite on toast would to a Brit or peanut butter and jelly sandwiches to an American.

Day 14

Our fishing skills are challenged; we haven't had a bite since leaving port. We're faintly comforted by the fact that experienced fishermen told us that fish don't bite during a full moon. I still have no idea why this is.

Day 15

A wonderful day; the sea calms and the wind drops to a perfect speed, flit-ting *Albatross* over the rippling waves like a flying fish. After a week of beard growth – which on Carl is equivalent to a month on other men – and no showers, we luxuriate in washing ourselves, our clothes and our bedding. Tonight we sleep in fresh linen. What bliss to snuggle into our berths and snore in time with the murmurings of *Albatross'* hull as she ploughs on-wards.

Day 16

Of course, it was all too good to be true. We should have learned by now never to take anything for granted and that if it can go wrong, it will go wrong and we'll spend many minutes swearing about it. At 3:30 a.m. the electric wind-vane conks out. Carl steers manually until I take over my watch at six. The wind dies, the waves disappear and all is calm. We take down the sails and let *Albatross* drift with the current. We're as masterful as a paper boat.

Carl and I stand looking at the windvane with the bitter disappointment of two men whose winning racehorse has just dropped dead a few feet from the finish line.

'Well, we should have known it was going to give up on us sooner or later; they do on most boats,' I say sullenly. 'I was just hoping it would be later rather than sooner.'

'We better face the fact we'll have to hand steer the next 1,400 nautical miles to Rodrigues,' Carl says, resignation heavy in his voice.

We stare glumly at it for a bit; then we stare glumly at the glassy sea for a bit; finally, we stare glumly at each other.

'Oh bugger this!' I say. 'What have we got to lose? We might as well take it apart and see if there's anything we can repair.'

So we get to work. We quickly establish that all six power transistors aren't working because the contacts have corroded in the harsh saline elements. Then with a magnifying glass we examine the solder pads on the circuit boards; a further six soldered parts are worn. We solder the defective joints and clean everything of salt deposits. *Albatross'* cockpit looks more like an electronics workshop than an ocean-going sailboat.

After working with intense, hopeful concentration for the best part of the day, we carefully replace all the components and hold our thumbs. The wind-vane clicks into motion, the dial rotates and...

'Yes!' Carl and I high-five each other.

It works for a whole ten minutes before crashing once more, whereupon much unprintable swearing ensues. Then we stare glumly at each other again.

Day 17

After a calm night, we tackle the problem with renewed "sod-this-for-a-lark" determination. With the precision of surgeons, we dismount the entire drive unit and unscrew all the moving parts. Then we dismantle the gearbox, clean key parts in kerosene and grease everything in sight. The next problem is the drive motor. Using very fine grade sandpaper, we clean and polish the copper parts until they gleam. By the time the sun reaches its zenith, we have almost finished reassembling the unit. A propitious wind blows lightly from the south, so we raise the sails and send up a quick but fervent prayer to the powers that be. Carl very tentatively presses the button marked "auto" and we both hold our breath. Would the patient live or die?

'Yes!' I start to shout but Carl puts a restraining hand on my arm.

'Don't jinx it,' he says. 'How long will it run?'

The wind picks up and *Albatross* scoots over the waves true to course. After half an hour we're fairly confident that our lengthy operation has saved the invalid; although I notice that Carl's fingers are tightly wrapped around his thumbs. It isn't the first time I'm thankful for our chosen profession. If we'd been opticians, we'd never have made it this far.

Day 18

No complaints today. The electronic self-steering continues to function and we speed over the ocean. After spending so much time on deck in the sun, our faces and torsos are beginning to take on the appearance of cured ham.

Day 19

Enjoying the brisk wind, we continue directly towards Rodrigues under a sky heavy with grey clouds. We notice the fishing line is slack and to our great surprise discover that the Rapala hook and wire has disappeared. There's clearly been a tremendous tussle between fish and hook. I wouldn't want to meet whatever has bested a 250-kilo bearing Rapala hook.

Day 20

Our luck fishing finally returns and we land a 25-pound dorado. The dorado is an interesting fish; it appears a wonderful iridescent blue in the water but changes to a glittering greenish gold when landed. The fish thrashes and fights like a champion on deck, so we end its struggle by plunging a knife into the skull. As it dies, the scales fittingly turn corpse grey.

Day 21

The three weeks since we left Broome have passed surprisingly quickly. According to the GPS, we have only 837 nautical miles left to our goal. I allow myself to luxuriate in the warm glow of smug self-satisfaction.

Day 22

The fair weather continues. As it's Saturday, we both get ready for a night on the tiles – dinner in the cockpit while listening to our favourite tunes – by having a shower on the aft deck, shaving and attempting to comb our hair. Carl's mane grows at a frantic pace many men would envy, but becomes so thick and wiry he can't drag a fork through it. Although Carl and I trust each other implicitly, there's one thing we would never allow the other to do: cut hair. In the light of the fact that we're both ready to wield a scalpel to operate on one another in an emergency, it seems nonsensical not to let a shipmate use a pair of scissors for a quick trim. But as Carl says: 'One careless snip could ruin the whole effect.' Although the "effect" in Carl's case is clearly a tornado-battered haystack.

Day 23

'No! You've got to be kidding!' My enraged cry travels out across the dark ocean. The electronic windvane has packed up again, and we have to hand steer the entire night. At daylight, we're back to pulling apart the "black box" to identify the fault. We spend the best part of the day soldering contacts again and swearing creatively.

One of the most aggravating problems for a yachtsman is the quality of the some of the electronic equipment that is not intended for use in a harsh marine environment and yet is marketed for that purpose. Even cheap battery driven toys are better designed than many electronic gadgets. The correlation between quality and use is clear; the manufacturers make a poor product forcing the sailboat owner to stump up more cash for new merchandise or repairs in service centres. Carl puts it more succinctly: 'Thieving bastards.'

Day 24

Happiness is a well-functioning self-steering system. With only 484 nautical miles to Rodrigues, we let the electronic windvane take over while we begin a thorough cleaning session. But as one part of the boat is repaired, so another decides to bail on us; in the afternoon, the diesel generator starts to cough and splutter like a consumptive before eventually dying altogether. Sea water has penetrated the heat exchanger located under the engine, and it's up to me – being eternally nubile – to wriggle acrobatically around the machinery and sort it out. The inlet channel is blocked by heavy deposits of lime, so we use our entire stock of vinegar cleaning out the parts.

'No more vinaigrette on our salads,' Carl complains.

'So what? We ran out of fresh vegetables two weeks ago,' I remind him.

Day 25

Another day of repairs: the straps securing the lifebuoy that normally hang on the stern starboard side have become totalled pulverized. I whip out my sewing machine and run up new straps in more durable sail repair tape. Once again we're frustrated by the quality of certain goods for their intended environment. 'Bloody rubbish,' is Carl's verdict.

Day 26

Finally! A day free of electronic problems. Instead the wind disappears and to borrow Coleridge's words, we're "as idle as a painted ship upon a painted ocean." We lower all the sails and drift forward with the help of a westerly current.

Day 27

Still becalmed, gliding forward at a paltry two knots. The GPS indicates that only 269 nautical miles lie between us and Rodrigues. So close and yet so far.

The thermometer has been rising daily and the Indian Ocean lies smooth as a sheet before us. Having a swim in the unruffled blue waters is an irresistible temptation; we put out the diving ladder and I insist, partly out of courtesy but mostly out of self-preservation, that Carl go first while I keep a lookout for dorsal fins. Only as I float on my back, luxuriating in the warm silky water while Carl keeps watch, does it occur to me how the sharks have had time to pick up the scent of tasty Swedish sailor and are even now circling my inert form. Relaxation over.

Day 28

A light wind finally blows in from the south. We hoist all the sails and feel the gentle snap as the breeze presses against the sails and pulls the rigging taut. Later that night the wind increases and the sails billow full and round, so we set up the spinnaker and start to pick up some speed. The magical feeling of sailing returns. If the fine weather continues, we'll be carried to Port Mathurin on Rodrigues within a day. The notion of our imminent landfall suddenly seems strange after so long at sea. Excitement at reaching our destination competes with sorrow that the passage is soon ending. Despite our electronic problems, we've been happily cocooned on *Albatross*; it will be hard to disembark.

Day 29

On the morning of 16 October, we sight the tiny volcanic island of Rodrigues through a veil of grey drizzle. The island is surrounded by a large coral reef extending five nautical miles out into the ocean, so we approach via a long narrow inlet. Unfortunately, our charts appear to have nothing to do with what lurks beneath the hull; we risk impaling *Albatross* on the coral, so we resort to our well-practised technique of eyeball navigation. As we enter the inner harbour, a fisherman indicates we can moor alongside his boat and helps us to tie up. We like the place already.

We've reached terra firma after 30 days of sailing and a total of 3,808 miles, the longest passage we've accomplished to date. As I step ashore, the ground seems to tilt beneath my feet and I feel momentarily wobbly; it will take some time to lose my sea legs.

Or is it because after a month of not drinking, the mooring snaps I knocked back has gone straight to my head? Unthinkable.

Chapter 43

Politics on the Sleepy Isles

17 October – 3 November 2004

Port Mathurin, Rodrigues

Experience: *Phoenix beer: definitely the best beer in the world.*

Tip: *Invite a German for a Phoenix and you'll make memories for life.*

O ur arrival at Port Mathurin in Rodrigues marked a momentous point; we'd reached the tip of Africa, a new continent on our circumnavigation. The island, a volcanic bump measuring just 42 square miles, is the poor cousin to bigger and flashier Mauritius lying 350 miles to the west. Mauritius is lush and verdant with vast fields of sugar cane, whereas tiny Rodrigues is mountainous, drier and without sugar cane – ironic considering that 97 percent of the population are descendants of African slaves originally imported to work the plantations. The island has no industry and very little tourism, which was exactly what appealed to Carl and me; we wanted to avoid Mauritius' glitzy five-star hotels and beachside wedding ceremonies.

We moored alongside *Sealine*, a fishing boat owned by a German couple, Dirk and his wife Birgit. Although we'd radioed the authorities ahead to clear in, our calls had gone unanswered; meanwhile, several pairs of dark eyes followed us with interest from the shade of a small metal-roofed pier which had seen better days, before hurricanes had ripped the guttering from it. Further along, around 30 men appeared to have the ability to walk on water: not a multitude of messiahs but fishermen wading calf-deep on the coral reef, carrying either crude spears to catch squid or fishing rods not much of a step up from the stick, string and hook I'd used when I was in short trousers. Society and technology clearly hadn't evolved much in the last few centuries since the island's discovery in 1528 by its namesake Don Diégo Rodriguez.

We stood on deck and surveyed the scene for a bit, then huffed and puffed and looked at our watches, but no one arrived to clear us in. So Birgit on

Sealine called the port manager and in true Teutonic fashion gave them a verbal blasting along the lines of 'how dare they keep visitors waiting and to get off their arses and get over to *Albatross.*' I made a quick mental note never to mess with Birgit; she had all the cuddliness of a cobra.

Within mere minutes of her tongue lashing, a motley band of men representing the coast guard, the minister for health and Customs and Immigration appeared on the quay, stepping aboard for a speedy inspection. They flashed big smiles at us, signed and ticked boxes, and confiscated our spear gun.

'*Je suis desolé.* So sorry,' the coast guard said. 'We must take this. But it's no problem, we give it back when you leave.'

In return for their swift efforts, we gave them a 40-pound Spanish mackerel we'd caught the day before. All three were immensely grateful and shook our hands vigorously.

'Well, that was unexpectedly fast,' Carl said as we watched their departing backs.

Birgit jerked her chin at the officials with an expression usually reserved for chiding naughty children. 'Yes. The problem was they thought you were outside the lagoon. Once I told them that you were already in the harbour, they were happy to come out. You see, most of the locals are terrified to be in a dinghy or small boat in deep water beyond the coral reef: they've lost too many fishermen out there.' Then her face softened and she smiled. 'That big mackerel you gave them was a real treat.'

The first thing Carl did in port was to go in search of an establishment to cut his hair; the first thing I did was to phone Anita, reassure her that I was alive and mutter sweet nothings which are so nauseating except to those in love.

Port Mathurin, the island's small colonial style capital, had a sleepy Sunday feel about it except on market days when it seems the whole of Rodrigues turns up to sell its garden produce, fish and meat. The volcanic soil is perfect for vegetable growing and the reef is abundant with fish. The economy of the island relies heavily on that of Mauritius, and although the 37,000 inhabitants are undoubtedly poor, they are able to provide enough food for themselves and the tourists who visit. The tourism industry is even now limited to a few hotels and between 30 to 50 small family guesthouses or *chambres d'hôtes* offering homely (read "basic") comfort.

We were delighted to meet up with a sailing acquaintance in Port Mathurin: Piero Pierons on his fifty-foot schooner *Quo Vadis*. We'd last met Italian born Piero in French Polynesia on the tiny island of Nuku Hiva and we were glad to see him alive and gesticulating as wildly as ever. The 69-year-old was sailing alone and we'd been anxious for his safety during the bouts of bad weather we'd experienced, knowing how tough it must be for the solo sailor. He spotted us first and came over in his dinghy to welcome us to Rodrigues where he'd been for a month.

'I tella you,' he said in heavily accented English. 'It's very hard to leave disa beautiful island. It has a ...' he bunched the fingers of his right hand together as he searched for the word, 'it has a special flavour. De people, dey is so nice.'

Piero had just checked out *Quo Vadis* and was continuing to South Africa at sunrise the following morning, so we invited him, Dirk and Birgit for dinner on *Albatross* that evening. I grilled dorado and we enjoyed a pleasant evening eating and imbibing more than was strictly necessary: something I realized when I tried to lasso my bed to stop it from bouncing.

Dirk turned out to be both a mine of information and the type some might call a "character," but I would call a complete and utter nutter, mostly in a good way. He was the same age as Carl, but his scrappy salt and pepper beard, wiry frame and deeply lined faced made him look older: all the products of a misspent youth and middle age as he himself admitted. He and Birgit, whose 50-year-old bark we learned was much worse than her bite, had first visited Rodrigues as tourists seven years earlier, but they'd quickly fallen under its quiet spell and never left. On a whim, they'd sold everything they owned in Germany and settled on the island where they bought their boat *Sealine* with which to start their leisure activity company, taking angling fanatics on big game fishing expeditions. Although tourism was only in its infancy when we visited in 2004 – and, while on the incline, still hasn't developed much since then – it seemed business was booming. Rodrigues' greatest natural asset is the wide lagoon which surrounds the island and supports a variety of fish normally seen stuffed and mounted in natural history museums: dog tooth tunas, marlins, sailfish, sharks, wahoos, ignobilis kingfish to name but a few. And the game isn't just big, it's gargantuan; the island holds several world fishing records. Dirk had assisted a client in landing a blue marlin weighing 550 pounds – the weight of a Shetland pony. 'It was a hell of a battle,' Dirk said with casual pride in his voice. 'We hooked it at eight in the morning and finally hauled it on board as dawn was breaking the next day.'

'Sounds like hard work,' I said, my pride at my own fishing accomplishments shrivelling to the size of a raisin.

'I'll take you one day,' Dirk said. 'There's nothing like the thrill of the roar of Caterpillar engines and the scream of a tightly stretched line when you hook a big one.'

We hadn't intended to stay long on Rodrigues, but we too fell under the spell of its sleepy charm and vast blue skies. We discovered a mix of cultural oddities both charming and puzzling, remnants of the island's history. Rodrigues had initially been a place where ships could shelter from tropical storms and get fresh supplies of water and meat – the meat in question being that of the giant tortoise whose flesh was so delicious that during the nineteenth century the seamen of the Royal Navy ate them all, eradicating the entire species. Happily, the tortoises are back, reintroduced from Madagascar, protected and bred in a tortoise reserve.

After Don Diego Rodriguez' official discovery of the island, the first stab at colonisation was in 1691 when Francois Leguat and a few others attempted to flee religious persecution in their native country of France. For two years they cultivated land, grew crops and looked as if they might make a go of it, until they realized they'd failed to consider an essential component of island life which often guarantees happiness: namely women. Eventually, desperate for the charms of the fairer sex – or more probably sex – they built a raft out of driftwood and paddled to Mauritius, never to return. I'm surprised they lasted as long as they did.

During the eighteenth century, there was the usual tussle between the Dutch, French and British over who should own the island with the British eventually winning control. Together with Mauritius, Rodrigues gained independence from Britain in 1968, but signs of the British way of life remain, in the three-pin plugs, the sale of Weetabix, and driving on the left. However, it is the French culture that has endured: the official language is English but most locals speak French or Creole French; shops carry French names, and thankfully, the cuisine is determinedly French – albeit enhanced by the addition of cuisine imported by Indian and Asian immigrants – thus saving the inhabitants the horrors of overcooked vegetables and meat boiled to the colour and consistency of cardboard.

Dirk employed a full-time captain on *Sealine* to run the boat when he was off on one of his many benders. Soudin, an African descendant with skin a rich ebony black, had been in Dirk's employment for seven years and worked every day of the week preparing the boat for the forthcoming big game fishing season. He would arrive at five in the morning just as the sun was colouring the horizon and start his day by warming up the two diesel engines whose throaty gurgling we learned to sleep through. What we couldn't block out, however, was the loud music piped through the onboard speakers at a volume unkind to human ears. Soudin couldn't be separated from his Mauritian *séga*, a tropical party music with African roots, at any time of the day. And once he started singing along, Carl and I gave up trying to lie in, put on the coffee and invited Soudin over for a cup before we took our morning stroll to the bakery to buy fresh baguettes for breakfast.

We didn't mind the early start. Like the locals, we set our pace to the heat of the sun and found it better to work in the early part of the day before the mercury started to climb. We had numerous repairs to carry out on *Albatross*; the long voyage from Australia had taken its toll on some of her equipment. Dirk and Soudin were both a great help and great entertainment, particularly Dirk whose special brand of German humour was as hilarious as it was unexpected. Military blood ran through Dirk's veins as thickly as the love of raw herring and pine trees runs through a Swede's. During the First World War, his grandfather had been governor of a German colony in southern West Africa, now Namibia; his father had been a colonel and fought with Rommel during the Second World War, and Dirk had been an officer in the German Navy. His accounts of military life and his impressions of some of the types in the German forces had us rolling on the deck with laughter. To this day, I think he might be the wittiest German I have ever met, although I realize the humour bar is pretty low coming from a nation which has been voted least funny in Europe and still regards a cream pie in the face as the height of hilarity. As Mark Twain remarked: 'A German joke is no laughing matter.'

We'd been working on *Albatross* for nearly a week, checking the rigging, fitting a new diesel pump to the small generator and scraping the entire hull, when Dirk announced, '*Genug*! Enough! Time for some relaxation, guys. I invite you to accompany me on *Sealine's* season première; I have to make a test run.' Carl and I flung down our tools in our rush to accept. Early Saturday morning, we cast off with Dirk, Soudin and three experienced local fishermen, Francis, Gorge and René. Seven powerful looking rods with hooks that could have suspended a cow were mounted on the aft deck. The sun was burning fiercely in a sharp blue sky and a light north-westerly wind ruffled the waves over the reef. '*Ja*. A perfect day for fishing,' Dirk shouted over the roar of the engines. Soudin set a course for open water and as we steamed up the middle of the strait, the fishing reels began to whine as yards of lines spun out behind us. I was given the honour of being seated in the "fighting chair" on a wide rear platform where there was room to haul in a fish the size of a grand piano if the situation required. The rod was placed in the attachment tube adjacent to the chair. I felt a tug on the line and the showdown commenced. I reeled in 30 feet of line, the fish jerked and swam under, so I let out the line and started to reel in again. Sweat was running down the side of my face as this tug-of-war went back and forth for 30 minutes. I hung on desperately; it was a matter of pride now and surely this had to be a monster: maybe even a record-breaking fish. My arms were burning, my chest felt as if it would burst. By the time René hooked the fish on board, I was a puddle of perspiration. But instead of the giant marlin or sailfish I'd expected to see, a Spanish mackerel lay panting on the platform, looking considerably fitter than myself despite the large hook in its mouth.

'Fifty-five pounds,' announced René. 'Not bad.' Only 500 pounds below the world record, I thought to myself. Carl fared a little better and managed to land a 60-pound dorado. Overall, we bagged six fish weighing a total of 280 pounds. We were inordinately pleased with ourselves.

We didn't appreciate how lucky we'd been and how capable Soudin was at the helm until we happened upon a 32-foot fishing boat, *Blue Dynamite*, whose four Italian guests were more than a little rattled by their experience. A two-storey wave with the force of a wrecking ball had slammed into their craft, throwing it onto the reef and sending the passengers flying: one broke a leg, another broke an arm and a third was flung into the tackle box where he was unfortunately impaled on nine Rapala hooks, which makes me wince thinking about it even now: proof yet again of the perils of the waves around the reef systems and a reminder to close the tackle box when not in use.

We became acquainted with many local people through our friendship with Dirk and Birgit that allowed us an insight into the island life we wouldn't otherwise have had. On one occasion, we received a visit from Johnson Roussety, leader of the opposition party on the island, who was keen to see a Swedish boat. We gave him a tour of *Albatross*, in return for which he gave us a scenic tour of the island in his spanking new four by four. Johnson was a tall man in his early forties with a big voice and a bigger laugh, and I didn't doubt that he could throw his political weight around. From him we learned a tremendous amount about government on the island.

'And on your right is our only five-star hotel,' Johnson said as we passed a pristine whitewashed building with one of the best roofs I'd seen on the island. A 10-foot wall ran around the property's perimeter, a dodo like bird was painted on the wall beside a large pair of steel gates above which read "Rodrigues Prison." The efficacy of the steel gates was somewhat negated by the visitors' door standing wide open and a total absence of guards.

'Is there anyone inside?' I asked. The place had an air of complete abandonment, as if everyone, including the security guards, had done a runner.

'I think there are just a couple of guys in there at the moment. There's not much crime on the island, there's not really a lot to steal. I don't remember the last time there was a murder. Anyway, we ship off the mad and dangerous to Mauritius.'

That morning I'd wondered at the queues of elderly locals lining the pavements in front of the bank in Port Mathurin. I asked Johnson about it.

'It's the pensioners' payday,' he answered. 'Salaries and pensions are paid out during the last week of the month; on Monday the fishermen cash their cheques, the pensioners get their money on Tuesday, and workers from other sectors are paid on Wednesdays. You'll notice the bars are packed and by next week everyone will have spent their pay and be asking for credit at the Chinese and Indian supermarkets. It's the same every month: they get their money, pay off their debts, drinks all round and then start a new month of debt.

After seven years on Rodrigues, it seemed Dirk had adopted the local custom by doing the same, and we'd observed how he spent much of his time propping up his neighbourhood watering hole together with a sundry band of Chinese, Indian and African friends. And even though the local beer Phoenix – incidentally, one of the best beers we'd come across on our travels – was cheaper than dirt, Dirk's consumption was such that at the end of the month Birgit was obliged to go from bar to bar to settle her husband's bar tab. She wisely kept a firm hand on the purse strings.

Johnson also invited us to attend a session of the Rodrigues Regional Assembly. For the first time in two and half years we were obliged to don a suit and tie. After months of wearing shorts and T-shirts, it was odd to put on long trousers and my fingers fumbled with the unfamiliar strip of cloth around my neck. We sat in the visitors' box and watched with increasing amusement as the proceedings unfolded. The Assembly is of the Westministerian type with the minority facing the majority and a chairperson mediating the... I would like to use the word "discussion" but "fracas" is more appropriate. It began civilly enough, with objections being raised politely in English, but exchanges rapidly broke into heated French, whereupon the debate descended into a free-for-all with all 22 members screaming at each other in Creole while the chairperson tried futilely to bring them to order by banging his gavel and bellowing over the top of the din. I've seen football players behave with more decorum. And the matter being discussed? I believe it started out as a proposal about land sales, but I suspect dissolved into a completely different subject on a more personal level. At the very height of the chaos, the chairperson was compelled to show a red card to a member who, I can only assume, was particularly agitated. The member was required to leave the room until he'd recomposed himself, whereupon he was allowed to re-enter. It was one of the most bewildering and entertaining afternoons I'd spent since watching Anders teach Carl how to dive.

Johnson was eventually elected Chief Commissioner of the Rodrigues Regional Assembly in 2006, and held the position for five years until his resignation in 2011. Ironically, he blotted his copy book rather severely when in the same year he was found guilty of influencing a public official and received a three-month prison sentence. I wonder if he served it in Rodrigues prison or was shipped off to Mauritius. Nevertheless, according to his Facebook page he is back in politics.

We'd been on the island for two weeks and it was time to head on, much as we would have liked to have stayed. Dirk solemnly presented us with a parting gift as befitted only him: a pre-World War I German naval flag which we briefly hoisted on the spinnaker halyard to please him. Fearing misinterpretation of our political views, however, we quickly took it down and stowed it in a locker.

In return, we gave Dirk an old captain's hat that I'd trimmed with as much gold braid as I could rustle up. As we made sail and waved our farewells to all the friends who'd come to see us off, we realized how much Dirk appreciated our gift. There he was on the edge of the pier, standing to attention and wearing his cap, his beard newly trimmed in honour of the occasion. As we motored towards the channel, he clicked his heels together and gave us a smart naval salute.

Birgit later wrote to us: 'Dirk values that hat above all things, including me. He's very proud of it and only takes it off to shower. He even sleeps in the damn thing!'

Like I said, a complete and utter nutter.

Chapter 44

Rugged Beauty
in Reunion

4 November – 11 December 2004

Port Mathurin, Rodrigues – St Pierre, Reunion

Experience: *"Wine is life." Wise words from a wise Frenchman.*

Tip: *Avoid confusion and ensure all your navigation equipment is adjusted to the same north.*

'What do you mean, "You don't know where we are"?'

'Just what I said. I don't know where we are!'

'We're in the middle of the bloody Indian Ocean!'

'I know that, you old git. I just don't know exactly where in the middle of the bloody Indian Ocean we are!'

When you're in the middle of 28,350,000 square miles of water with nothing but an infinity of blue sky above and a vast ocean of darker blue below you, heated exchanges like this one do not bode well.

'Well, look at the damn GPS!'

'What do you think I'm doing? This is me, looking at the damn GPS, but the damn GPS is 20 degrees off from the Navtext and the computer navigation.'

'Ah.'

The GPS was one of the most important pieces of equipment on board, and to find it was suddenly "off" was bowel-tremblingly alarming. Sure, it had varied a degree or two with our other navigation equipment before but never by a whopping 20 degrees. If we didn't solve the problem, we could find ourselves bumping into an island or missing the whole continent of South Africa altogether, much like early explorers had failed to find the Americas for so long.

'What the heck? So we don't know where we are!'

'That's what I've been trying to tell you!'

After much frowning and twiddling of knobs and a generous smattering of curses, we managed to find our error. The discrepancy was that the GPS had been set up to show magnetic north, while the Navtext and the computer were indicating true north. We merely had to go into the GPS' main menu and select the same option for true north and suddenly all the equipment tallied. Crisis averted.

Our passage to the island of Reunion had so far been plain sailing – bar the little "where-in-god's-name-are-we" glitch. We'd zipped along on a strong easterly wind, passing Mauritius from where I swear we could hear the clink of champagne glasses and the beep of credit card machines on the beaches. By Sunday morning, we'd completed over 400 nautical miles and Piton de la Fournaise, the active volcano on Reunion, was dimly visible in the west.

'Bonzer!' Carl said, reluctant to let go of a phrase once he'd learned it. 'With any luck we'll be able to sail into Saint Pierre in daylight. Should be pretty simple.'

It wasn't. As we neared the coast, the wind started to climb and the wire stays began to scream in protest. The anemometer showed wind speeds of 50 miles an hour, force nine on the Beaufort scale. Friendly waves became giant beasts, breaking often over the deck and filling the cockpit. We'd never experienced so much water coming at us before and soon realized that our pump system was totally inadequate, so for much of our approach we were sloshing about the cockpit in water up to our knees.

Shortly after 10 a.m. we sighted Saint Pierre. Roger, a friend on the British schooner *Irena* we'd come across in various ports, had given us a simple hand sketch of the approach to the harbour together with the unnerving advice to "watch ourselves." We radioed the port captain for instructions, but after a garbled directive to contact him on channel nine, our calls went unanswered. Unwilling to test his limited English, I think the captain went for an early lunch.

The sea was hissing and thrashing like a monstrous serpent around us; we managed to bring down the mainsail and the mizzen, gunned the engine and locked our sights on the approach channel. Carl clipped on his safety harness and anchored himself to the mizzen mast from where he squinted through our well-worn binoculars to align the leading lines for the correct heading into port while shouting steering instructions to me. It was a hit and miss affair and we missed it on our first attempt. The inlet was narrow, surrounded by a treacherous reef on our port side. We were being pushed on the bow by the powerful current of an outflowing river, and bullied by waves on our starboard side crashing over the deck and drowning out Carl's instructions. We came uncomfortably close to being thrown up on the reef. Aligning the leading lines was as easy as threading a needle in a washing machine: just as we thought we'd got it, another wave would break over *Albatross* and we'd be knocked to port again. We were on the verge of cutting our losses and heading for Madagascar when we finally cracked it. It was with a dramatic flourish, a sense of enormous relief and very sweaty armpits that we motored into the relative calm of the inner harbour where we tied up between a French sailboat and *Born Free* out of Sweden whose skipper Hasse Faber helped us tie up.

'I think that calls for a very large snaps,' I said after we'd moored. But Carl was already pouring the *Gammel Dansk* with a trembling hand. He didn't wait to clink glasses but gulped his snaps down in one and poured another.

'*Fan!*' he said. I will not translate this, but I completely agreed with him.

We'd more or less stopped shaking when we received our first greeting from an elderly man who'd spotted our Swedish ensign and made a determined beeline for *Albatross*.

'*Hejsan! Välkommen till Reunion. Vad gör ni här?*' He introduced himself as Gérard Galloni, a Frenchman who'd lived in Sweden for 30 years. We naturally invited him on board to partake of a snaps and he swung himself over the guard rail with the sprightliness of a man half his age or an enthusiastic drinker who feared the offer might be withdrawn at any moment. He was a stocky man with a strong handshake, a grey buzz cut and matching grey chest hair.

'*Skål!*' he said, knocking back his snaps at an impressive speed. 'Not one, but two Swedish boats in the harbour. What's your story?'

We related ours, then as I prepared dinner, Gérard told us how he'd ended up in Sweden when he'd gone AWOL from the French army during his compulsory military service in 1960 during the Algerian War of Independence.

'Trust me, the war in Algeria was tough,' he said. 'Fighting is one thing, but the use of torture by the French was well known; I didn't want to be part of that. Anyway, I thought the Algerians should have their independence. So I discharged myself, went to Hamburg and took a boat to Copenhagen where I fell for a Swedish girl, so I found myself following her to Stockholm.' He smiled ruefully, deepening the lines around his dark eyes. 'But the love didn't last and I was out on the street. I got work washing dishes and then became a waiter, serving in some of the best hotel restaurants. I married and had a few children – eight at the last count. Fourteen years ago, I was advised by my doctor to move to a warmer climate because of my asthma, so I retired here. I wouldn't live anywhere else. Anything you want to know about the island, I'm your man. Once the weather clears, I'll show you around.'

The storm kept an iron grip on the island and Sunday dawned with white foam pouring over the coral reef.

'I'm glad we came in yesterday,' I said. 'I wouldn't want to try negotiating that inlet today.' We were pottering in the cabin, finishing breakfast and listening to the VHF radio when we heard a familiar voice trying to get hold of the harbourmaster. 'This is sailing yacht *Altair*,' the woman repeated. 'Please respond. We need instructions to get into port. Conditions are very rough out here.'

'That's Suzette.' We'd met her and her partner Paul several times around the islands. 'She'll be lucky; the harbourmaster's probably still in bed.' The strain in Suzette's voice was clear. Carl picked up the handset.

'Suzette. This is Carl from *Albatross*. Change over to channel nine and I'll guide you in. We know what it's like; we did the same yesterday.'

'Carl! Thank god. We're taking a beating out here.'

Fifteen minutes later, two very shaken Americans chugged into the inner harbour and we helped them tie up to the pontoon bridge. Their gratitude was effusive. 'We've got a bottle of whisky with your name on it,' Paul said. Much as we love whisky, we waved his offer away. That's sailing: we're family and we help each other out.

On Monday, the harbourmaster appeared like a genie out of a bottle after 100-year nap, so we were able to clear in: a swift process for us as Reunion is an overseas department of France and therefore part of the EU.

As this was our last chance to stretch our legs before the long sail to Cape Town, we decided to rent a car and explore this enchanting little island which the French have rather sneakily kept to themselves. Inviting Hasse and Gérard to join us, we packed a picnic of French cheeses, hams, fresh baguettes, local beers and a couple of bottles of impertinent reds, and set off after drawing straws for who would drive. I lost.

We drove up a winding road with more twists and turns than a Stig Larsson novel to Cirque de Cilaos, one of Reunion's three calderas that dominate the topography of the interior of the island. It's a hiker's dream with over 600 miles of trails, so we walked around the town for a bit, then tramped along on a well-maintained trail around the crater, through undergrowth and over rocks with our mouths hanging open – frequently swallowing the odd mosquito – at the sight of waterfalls, exotic plumed birds and fields of colourful flowers. Often described as rugged, Reunion's interior alternates between fantasy landscapes: lunar like around the volcanoes and calderas, and Jurassic Park type scenery with lush vistas where soaring peaks pierce the mist and jagged ravines plunge dramatically through forests of giant plants. Similar to the island of Hawaii, in that it is located above one of the hotspots in the Earth's crust, Reunion has an active volcano, Piton de la Fournaise, which rises more than 8,632 feet above sea level and has erupted over 100 times since 1640. Thankfully, it is constantly monitored so it was no surprise to anyone in the vicinity when it erupted two weeks before our arrival. The rain heavy air was thick with the smell of sulphur, and the lava that had poured out and burned a path through the thick forest towards the sea still sizzled.

The following day we visited the capital of Saint Denis on the north of the island, the Creole architecture of which gives the town a colonial flavour. Reunion was uninhabited when discovered by the Portuguese in the early sixteenth century, but it was the French who claimed it in 1643, established a colony and imported slaves from Africa to work the sugar plantations. Over the decades, the population was supplemented by Chinese, Malays and Indians, giving the island its cultural diversity, reflected in its cuisine. But with a boulangerie on every corner and the proliferation of Peugeots and Renaults, we could have been in Paris, except that there was a lazy carnival air about this small capital. Reunion ladies in exotic colours sashayed sedately along the roadside and lively folk music rang out from the cafés and bistros. The undercurrent of a relaxed rhythm of life was overlaid with the excited Creole chatter of women and children.

On Sunday, Gérard invited us to his home for lunch. His modest flat was set on the hillside above Saint Pierre. I was surprised to see that he didn't own a stove, fridge or television.

'I live as simply as possible,' Gérard explained. 'I buy my food fresh everyday so I don't need a fridge, I have a view that is better than anything on TV, and my rice cooker heats my food. What more do I need?'

He certainly knew how to lay a table with a spread of food and wine that was pleasing to the eye and the taste buds. In typical French fashion, lunch was long and leisurely, blending into the afternoon. It was early evening when we made the long walk back to the harbour where Hasse insisted we have a night cap on *Born Free*.

It was easy to fall into the casual step of the locals, but we had a number of preparations to make for our 2,500-nautical mile leg to South Africa. Our plan was to sail round the Cape of Good Hope and to Cape Town, avoiding Africa's wild coast between Durban and East London and the treacherous Agulhas Current, one of the world's strongest ocean currents which can achieve speeds of six knots an hour. This area of coastline is often the site of rogue waves or freak seas; south-westerly gales prevail against the southward flowing current, making swells steeper and more dangerous, overturning even cargo boats. When a chart contains the warning, "Abnormal waves of up to 65 feet in height, preceded by deep troughs may be encountered in the area between the edge of the continental shelf and 20 miles to seaward thereof," you can either hug the coastline or head offshore out of sight of land. We'd heard that the problem with the former was that a lot of north-bound shipping did the same, so we chose to do the latter. Even so, we could expect to encounter some very strong winds and rough seas. Moreover, the Antarctic waters would mean a temperature drop to about 10 degrees Celsius. It was time to batten down the hatches; we cleared the deck of any unnecessary equipment and got out the woollens and wet weather gear.

As we floated on our backs in the warm waters of the lagoon off Saint Gilles les Bains with the sun warming our faces, it was hard to imagine anything other than a benign ocean. Sadly, even the beaches of Reunion are no longer safe; in July 2013, a ban was placed on swimming, surfing and bodyboarding within a coastal strip 900 feet from shore following 12 shark attacks between 2011 and 2013, three of which were fatal. And only a few months after we left, the island was hit by a crippling epidemic of chikungunya – as nasty as its name suggests – a mosquito spread disease which affected over a quarter of the population and required the deployment of 500 French troops to eradicate the insects.

But Carl and I knew nothing of the unfortunate miseries to plague Reunion. In the middle of November, we sailed away with happy memories of a perfect island retreat.

Chapter 45
Wind, Waves, Water and an Albatross

22 November – 11 December 2004

St Pierre, Reunion – Cape Town, South Africa

Tip: *Make sure locks on hatches are good quality and keep on board the following materials for emergency windows: full-thread one meter stainless M8, M9 and M10 rods including "locking" nuts, and 15 mm plywood in cuts of one inch by four inch.*

Oceanographers have calculated that the maximum theoretical height for a wind-driven wave is 198 feet. It's difficult to imagine a wall of water the height of a 20-storey building coming at you, and I tried very hard not to. But sometimes these images come unbidden and no amount of whiskey will drown them, particularly when other sailors hearing of our plans kept saying: 'Whatever you do, stay near the coast.'

We'd discussed it with Hasse who'd set sail ahead of us. He intended to head first to Richard's Bay and then make his way round the coast to Cape Town. When we said, 'Stay in touch' to each other, it wasn't idly meant. Hasse was sailing solo on his 39-foot ketch *Born Free* and we agreed to radio each other twice a day. Meanwhile, he was concerned that our pure stubbornness was leading us not just into deep but dangerous water. Gérard was of the same opinion.

'As long as I've lived here, I've never known any other Swedes to set a direct course for Cape Town.' He scratched his chin thoughtfully. 'Or maybe you're just the first really stupid Swedes I've met.'

'Or just really brave,' I said, puffing out my chest with as much bravado as I could muster.

'But why not sail close to the coast and put into a couple of other harbours?' Gérard asked.

'I've got a hot date,' I answered.

'Well, I hope she's worth it,' Gérard said.

'Oh yes,' I said. It had been nearly two months since I'd last seen Anita and absence was proving to make the heart – not to mention the parts – grow fonder.

Day 1

On the day of our departure, the Indian Ocean is almost subdued; the sea is calm and only small waves roll towards land, but eventually the wind picks up and balloons out the sails, speeding us along at seven knots. I feel that rush of adrenaline as we rush across the water. Ah, it's good to be sailing again. We're on our way to new destinations.

Day 2

Never underestimate the power of the wind. A deck window above the toilet in the bow is blown out, shattering the window and scattering broken glass over the deck. Part of the problem is due to UV fatigue on the resin that holds the window. We clearly need to seal the window, so we cut two lengths of plywood and mount them crossways by drilling four holes through the boards, holding them with 10 millimetre thick rods threaded onto stainless steel discs. The result is a perfect emergency window which hopefully will stand up to whatever the ocean chucks at us. Large amounts of water pouring through a blown-out window can have devastating consequences for a boat.

Day 3

Throughout the day the ocean teems with an astonishing number of fish; enormous schools of tuna follow *Albatross*, driving up and feeding on small squid, which in turn attract flocks of hungry seabirds. At dusk a pod of dolphins arrives, chasing away the tuna and riding the bow wake.

Day 4

We've finally got our sea legs back and the feeling of queasiness has passed. So we settle down in the cockpit to ride the waves and read. Hasse from *Born Free* had leant us several books before we left.

Day 5

We read, write, fish and turn our skins crispy in the sun. The sea is blue and calm and our reading is disturbed only when we hook something big on the line. Carl is boning up on South Africa's history while I'm immersed in an adventure novel about Vikings.

We have radio contact with our American friends, Suzette and Paul from *Altair* who sailed two days before us and are on their way to Richard's Bay. It's important that Carl and I avoid the strong East Madagascar Current that flows southwards on the east side of Madagascar and feeds the Agulhas Current. Consequently, we are maintaining a safe distance of 200 nautical miles off the coast.

Day 6

A magnificent day of sailing that makes the soul and spirit soar, when the sky seems endless and the wind pushes us seven or eight knots over an undulating ocean. *Albatross* is visited by her namesake, the first we've seen. It is an astonishing bird, in flight as graceful as a prima ballerina, yet capable of surviving the harshest marine environments. It has been estimated that the royal albatross of New Zealand may travel a remarkable 200,000 miles a year, the equivalent of flying the equatorial circumference of the Earth eight times. Sadly, it is unable to survive man-made threats. According to the Royal Society for the Protection of Birds, 17 of the 22 species of albatross are threatened with extinction due to the proliferation of longline fishing, trawl fisheries and plastic debris. Unlike sailors of the past who feared the bird as a harbinger of bad luck, we feel privileged to have seen this incomparable bird. The sight of the albatross as it elegantly skims the water, rides the air and circles our mast is so uplifting we can't help but smile. Who knows how far it has travelled to join us.

Day 7

The fish are jumping on our lure at the moment and the freezer is full with our catches; today we hook a 45-pound dorado.

The wind has increased to 35 miles an hour and although *Albatross* makes great progress, it's difficult to keep a straight course as the wind rudder oscillates 15 degrees when buffeted by the heavy winds. We take down the mizzen, slowing our speed but keeping us on course with an oscillation of only plus-minus five degrees.

Day 8

Beware of the sun. Heed your mother and always wear sunscreen, and know that UV rays will destroy everything: plastic buckets rapidly degrade in the strong sunlight and the handles fall apart. Nevertheless, we give the buckets a new lease of life by reinforcing the handles and attaching a length of rope so we can throw them in the water, fill them and heave them on deck so we have plenty of water for cleaning our catches of fish.

We talk to Hasse on *Born Free* who is now on a westerly course into Richard's Bay having been forced to change course to a point 60 nautical miles northeast of the bay in order to avoid the strong Agulhas Current. Fortunately, he appears to have enjoyed good weather there. We hear this from Fred, a South African amateur radio enthusiast who gives a daily weather report for our area. Guys like Fred are invaluable and we thank them for the information and companionship they provide.

Day 9

Back in the doldrums. The wind disappears to a whisper in the middle of the night and for the rest of the day we are carried slowly on the southwest current.

There's nothing to do but read and fish, although I spend an unhealthy amount of time looking for Anita's face in the clouds and musing about her as I gaze at the water. I am abruptly woken from my reverie when a whopping 60-pound Spanish mackerel thrashes on the lure. The freezer is packed with fish and we can lay off fishing until we've eaten what we have, although about now I really fancy steak and chips.

Day 10

Fred reports that a low pressure system is moving westwards from the Cape of Good Hope into the South Atlantic. We hold our thumbs that it follows a path similar to other lows that have moved southeast, which could result in a favourable wind as we cross the Agulhas Bank on the way to the Cape. Both the wind and the waves have increased so we beam reach for more stability.

We receive a warning on the Navtext: "Container ship BBC China has lost numerous containers at sea. Dangerous area is 23-31S, 29-54E around port Saint John." This is an enormous area and is a real hazard to small sailboats; it's almost impossible to detect a container as they don't usually appear on the radar; crashing into 60,000 pounds of steel container and its contents would be like hitting an iceberg. It's an uncomfortable fact that somewhere between 2,000 and 10,000 containers a year are lost overboard due to bad weather. While many of these sink, some, filled with light cargo and packing material, stay afloat. During the day we can keep a look out, but at night we sleep in our lifejackets.

'They're probably full of 50-inch plasma TVs,' Carl says.

'I reckon we could get around 30 on the boat,' I muse. 'It could be a little earner for us.'

'You really live in hope, don't you, Yanne?' Carl remarks.

Day 11

A powerful solar flare has disrupted communication on the SSB radio. Our daily radio contacts with our safety net have been abysmal, so we help each other out by relaying messages, boat to boat. Our SailMail has also not been working so we suddenly find ourselves incommunicado.

Day 12

The humidity has increased significantly over the last few days; in the evening the deck oozes with condensation and during the day there isn't enough wind to dry it up. Below deck, the moisture is even worse, resulting in swampy papers, books and maps.

Day 13

A good news, bad news day.

Firstly, the good news: the SailMail is working again, so we can pick up our emails.

And now the bad news: we receive a weather fax indicating that the low pressure system west of Cape Town has intensified and is now moving east, warning of winds in excess of 60 miles an hour. It's hard not to be alarmed when the Navtext names the situation "cyclonic."

'Should we change course and head south?' I ask Carl.

'You mean, do a runner?' he says, and I nod.

Day 14

Good news from Hasse: he's put into Richard's Bay and is safely moored with 15 other sailboats waiting out the bad weather before continuing towards the Cape of Good Hope. We are approximately 900 nautical miles from the Cape, but the most difficult stretch still lies ahead of us: crossing the hazardous Agulhas Current where freak waves wreak havoc on boats, great and small. We have to head for the deep waters of the 9,000 foot trench south of the Agulhas Bank. We send up a fervent prayer to the weather gods. Although the low pressure over the Western Cape has moved southeast, a new low pressure system is forming in the South Atlantic and moving in our direction. Oh joy.

Day 15

We scuttle along at seven knots pulled by an easterly wind under a dark grey sky heavy with rain. For the most part during our long journey around the world we've been lucky enough to escape persistent rain and have only had to endure intense but cleansing showers. At noon the wind disappears, leaving us rolling unpleasantly on the heavy seas. Then suddenly a gale-force wind slams us with the sudden force of a giant wind machine. We quickly sheet in, lower the mizzen sail and reef in the mainsail to the third reef. In the few minutes it takes us to set the sails, the wind is already blowing 50 miles an hour, the rain is hammering down and the sea is a ferocious cauldron. The wind builds wave upon wave; *Albatross*' bowsprit plunges down into the foamy water and rises up again like a dolphin riding the bow wake.

'Right,' Carl says. 'We batten down and heave to.'

'Yup,' I agree, because there's really nothing else to do about it.

We check the sails for any luffing, lock the rudder to windward and tack on the mainsail about 30 degrees to the wind. While *Albatross* bobs on the waves like a cork, Carl and I can take a breather. We check the GPS, switch on the blue light atop the mizzen mast, then pull the cabin door closed and fall into our bunks to sleep. While we snore, our sailboat ploughs through the storm. By five in the morning, the wind has dropped to 40 miles an hour, the sea has fallen in sync with the wind and *Albatross* rides smoothly over the waves.

Not to blow our Swedish trumpets, but it's clear that *Albatross* comes from a long line of master boat-builders; our Hallberg-Rassy is as durable as a Viking long boat and we're exceptionally proud of her.

Day 16

The storm finally abates 28 hours later and the wind drops to a more agreeable 15 miles an hour. We continue tacking towards the Agulhas bank, buoyed by a favourable forecast for the next four days. Encouraged, we take the chance to sail over the Agulhas bank, saving ourselves a distance of 300 nautical miles.

The temperature is dropping and the nights are chilly as the southerly wind drives up the cold air from the Antarctic. We don hats, boots and gloves to keep warm, a sudden reminder that this is December weather in the real world we left behind two and a half years ago and that we are on our way back to the frozen north of Sweden where Stockholmers are digging out their cars after a night's snowfall.

Day 17

The capricious wind drops again and we have to use the engine to cover a few miles of ocean, but when we finally join the Agulhas Current we can feel its force under the hull as it pushes us forward at four knots. The forecast predicts a weak south-easterly wind for the next four days which is just perfect for us. We'd ideally like to round the Cape of Good Hope before the next storm forms. It's not for nothing that the Cape was originally named Cape of Storms by Portuguese explorer Bartolomeu Dias, the first European known to have sailed around the southernmost tip of Africa in 1488. Poor Dias eventually perished in a huge storm off the Cape 12 years later, leading me to think he'd be a bit ticked off to find that his name for the Cape had been changed to a more upbeat one.

Day 18

We are now sailing along the Agulhas Bank and it's suddenly as chaotic as the M25 or the New Jersey Turnpike at rush hour: shipping traffic is busy with numerous containers on their way to Asia. We spot a large oil tanker which appears to be heading straight for us. We immediately radio, but fortunately the skipper replies they've already changed their course to avoid us, as he must, but it is quite a manoeuvre for a 450,000-ton supertanker. We cross on our port side with a berth of a nautical mile; through the binoculars we see the bridge personnel waving to us. We wave enthusiastically in return. Good seamanship doesn't always prevail and you have to hold your bottle.

Day 19

There's still something magical about shouting "Land ahoy!" the eternal cry of the sailor, probably second to: "Are we out of toilet paper again?" At 15:00 we sight the rocky formation of Cape Agulhas through the haze. We are at Africa's southernmost tip, the official dividing point between the Atlantic and the Indian Oceans and a graveyard for many ships torn apart by rogue waves.

As we enter the Alphard Banks, dusk is falling. Mammoth oil platforms loom from the ocean like something out of the War of the Worlds, lighting up the darkness as their chimneys send 90-foot flames shooting into the sky. We sail between two of these giants using the radar to detect the numerous container ships and fishing boats that shuttle around them. At two in the morning we see the welcoming flash of the Cape Point lighthouse; we are so close to landfall, we can smell the grass and Carl chills a bottle of champagne given to us by a friend in Helsingborg. The wind blows up to 40-miles an hour as if to hasten us to our goal, and by dawn we are sailing in our home waters of the Atlantic. The sun rises like a spotlight over the famous Table Mountain, illuminating Cape Town nestling at its base. We are greeted by a welcome committee of dolphins, sleek and silver, effortlessly slicing through the waves around *Albatross* as we glide towards the harbour: the perfect welcome to one of the most perfect harbours in the world.

Chapter 46

Learning to Tackle in the Fairest Cape

12 December 2004

Cape Town, South Africa

Experience: *South Africa is a fantastic country, certainly one of the most interesting and naturally beautiful countries we visited during our trip around the world.*

Tip: *Keep your wits about you and beware of hobbit-sized pickpockets.*

Cape Town: a city by any other name would look as fair. In fact, the cape is sometimes referred to as the Fairest Cape and Cape Town is nicknamed the Mother City, some cynics say because it takes nine months to get anything done there. But to Carl and me it was a dream destination, and our pride at having made it this far, boat and crew still intact, competed only with our sense of awe as we approached our berth in the Royal Cape Yacht Club. We all but bounced from yacht to yacht as we motored in, as slack-jawed and wide-eyed as a couple of adolescents witnessing their first striptease. We were gawping in wonder at the magnificent Table Mountain backdrop. The San tribes called it *Hoerikwaggo*, the mountain of the sea, and as we motored towards Cape Town's Waterfront we could see why. Table Mountain's huge cliffs loomed 3,000 feet into cobalt skies bedecked with a necklace of snowy white clouds. If ever there was a harbour worthy of the "wow" factor appellation, Cape Town deserves it.

After 19 days at sea, we finally stepped ashore. It's surreal to walk on solid ground after thousands of miles of water under the keel and weeks of continuous motion, but it's a huge relief to be in command again – or at least to think you are – after being at the mercy of the capricious elements.

We'd emailed ahead to reserve a berth for two months at the Royal Cape Yacht Club where the staff were most helpful. The clubhouse was and still is a smart white-fronted building with jaunty navy trim and a token strip of lawn and hedge, but with the Table Mountain looming behind it like..., well, exactly like a giant table, we initially paid scant attention to the club. Later it would become our second home.

We were unsure what awaited us in the city; apartheid had ended over a decade earlier but it was still early days in terms of black, white and coloured integration. Eager to stretch our legs, explore and see something other than each other, Carl set off for the railway station in search of a phone card to ring the family, and I took a walk around the Victoria and Alfred Waterfront which I quickly realised probably had the highest rate of foreign tourists of anywhere in the country, attracted by luxury shopping and high-end entertainment. Carl had a more mixed experience at the central railway station. Six hours later he returned to the Royal Cape Yacht Club somewhat unroyally in the back of a police car.

'What the hell happened?' I asked as the uniformed men on either side of Carl marched him up the quayside to *Albatross*.

'Don't ever go back to the train station, ja,' the bigger, burlier policeman said. 'Yew can't show your face around there again.'

My mouth hung open. 'What in god's name did you do?'

It transpired Carl had ended up in Cape Town Railway Station, an old modernist building originally designed on the apartheid principles of control and race segregation. Carl, however, had experienced an afternoon of uncontrolled mayhem.

'So I buy myself a phone card and suddenly I'm surrounded,' he said, 'Half a dozen hobbit-sized Khoikhoi youths are all insisting on showing me how to use the phone card. Well, I'm no idiot, and I know they're trying to pick my pockets. But just as I'm telling them to "shove off," one of them shoots off like a bat out of hell, and I realize he's nicked my phone card. I scream "thief" at the top of my lungs and start after him.

'Well, the station security guards – guys built like Russian bouncers armed with batons as big as baseball bats – hear my shouts, and they start pelting after me. So now we're all running through the concourse: thieves, security guards and me. Anyway, I catch up to the slowest of the gang, and I rugby tackle him to the ground.

'The security bouncers reach us, and a guard asks me if they want him arrested. I answer, "Hell, yes!" Meanwhile, the rest of the gang are hiding around a corner watching what's going on. I guess they didn't expect me to give chase. Anyway, I leap up and start after them, scaring the shit out of them. I target the shortest and slowest and pounce on him with another rugby tackle, 'cos I've got the hang of it now, and I pin him to the ground. So now we've got two thieves, several security guards and a couple of policemen, and we all head to the police station. The thieves are cuffed, statements are taken, and in the middle of all this enters some big cheese – the chief of police or something – anyway, he's the first white man I've seen in all this.

'"You're a lucky man," he says and shows me an iron rod, sharpened to a very nasty point. "One of the thieves was carrying this: a homemade weapon they often use. You were lucky not to get stabbed in the stomach. Sometimes they use old bicycle spokes sharpened at the end to stab their victims in the neck. "'

'Strewth, Calle,' I said. 'What were you thinking?'

'Well, it never occurred to me they were armed. I just wanted my phone card back. Anyway, it turns out the guys I'd tackled had drugs, stolen credit cards and dozens of phone cards on them. The police chief says it probably isn't worth me bringing charges against them as I won't be in the country long enough to testify. Instead, they'll "teach them a lesson." Anyway, the police give me coffee at the station, and I tell them about how we're sailing around the world. When I get up to leave and say I'll take a train back to the waterfront, they all go nuts. "No way. The gang knows who you are now and will be out to get you. Best we drive you back to your boat." And here I am.' Carl smiled broadly. 'So how was your afternoon?'

Only Carl would try to take down a gang because they had the audacity to steal a 10-pound phone card, and I strongly recommend against rugby tackling members of the criminal classes. Fortunately, the central railway station was extensively refurbished at great cost for the 2010 World Cup, and there are fewer corners for gangs to hide in. Nevertheless, great poverty and the many social ills that South Africa continues to struggle with fuels the drug trade and violent crime. It's a city of huge contrasts: affluent villas, luxury boutiques and expensive cars on the one hand, and poor townships of ramshackle shelters where donkeys and carts are the means of transport on the other; the great divide created by a history of African slavery and a century of apartheid. I wondered if it were ever possible for the twain to meet. A decade after apartheid, South Africa had moved on: living restrictions had been removed, all white neighbourhoods were becoming integrated, and black and white customers were eating side by side in the waterfront restaurants. Yet, I was aware of a distinct tension, a wariness between the races that was palpable. Clearly, old ways of thinking die hard and would prevail while half the population of the city continued to live in the crowded, poverty-stricken townships where most of the buildings were cobbled together with scraps of metal and cardboard.

That evening we celebrated our arrival, and the fact that Carl hadn't been stabbed with a sharpened bicycle spoke, by indulging in an excellent dinner at the yacht club where we met other international sailors also making their way around the world from a variety of starting points. We exchanged our tall tales of bad weather, big fish and disasters, and it wasn't long before we found ourselves agreeing to crew for Harry Brehm on his yacht *Avanti* in the five-day Table Bay International Sailing Week. An opportunity to participate in some racing in the South Atlantic was too good to miss. We joined an international crew of eight others and competed against 75 boats in daily races around Robben Island. The freezing water was crowded with sailboats and sea life: dolphins, penguins, sea otters and seals dotted the ocean, frequently surfacing to observe *Avanti* before disappearing again to the fish-rich pantry below. The sailing was fierce, not just because we were a competitive crew, but due to the conditions; winds increased throughout the five days to storm strength, and several smaller boats had problems tacking back towards harbour and were pushed further out into the Atlantic, eventually requiring the assistance of tug boats to bring them back in. Two 38-foot sailboats lost their masts, and conditions were deemed so dangerous on the second day that sailing was cancelled all together.

We were luckier on *Avanti*, holding our course and coming fifth out of 15 in our "Cruising Class." But we all agreed that taking part is far more important than wining: the standard cry of a losing team. Nevertheless, the club's party, held for the participating crews on the final day of racing, went some way towards alleviating any disappointment at not wining. Indeed by the end of an evening of free food and drink, most of us were convinced we *had* won. The people of Cape Town certainly know how to put on a party, at least those who can afford to do so.

After getting to grips with some maintenance work and tackling a landfill-sized laundry pile, we took some time to explore, unloading the bikes and discovering Cape Town and its environs. The 3.74 million-strong city grew out of a victualing station established by Jan van Riebeeck in 1652 for Dutch East India Company ships and today is the second largest metropolis in South Africa.

There's a huge amount to see and do. As a keen gardener, Carl insisted on visiting the famous Kirstenbosch Botanical Gardens. While not as enraptured as Carl – who gets abnormally excited about soil pH values – I enjoyed a soothing afternoon wandering the hiking trails spread along the eastern slopes of the Table Mountain, admiring the variety of plant life and learning about the indigenous plants of the country.

A couple of days before Christmas, we were pleased to see our Italian friend, Piero Pierons, arrive safely in the harbour on *Qvo Vadis*. He'd had a tough solo sail along the coast, but was generous in his admiration of our choosing to sail a different course. His enthusiasm completed the seasonal cheer. The weather had settled, and the sun shone in a sharp blue sky. It was 25 degrees Celsius in Cape Town, and we were once again celebrating Christmas in shorts and T-shirts.

'Enjoy it while it lasts,' Carl warned. 'It'll be back to snow and ice next year.'

'Yes,' I agreed. 'But it'll be good to be back amongst friends and family.'

Not that we had any shortage of friends with whom to celebrate Christmas Day. The Royal Cape Yacht Club treated the harbour guests to a barbecue party where 40 long-distance sailors gathered to eat, drink, be merry and eventually fall down in a wine-sodden heap.

But while we were nursing our Boxing Day hangovers, the sea was about to unleash one of the deadliest natural disasters in recorded history. An earthquake in the Indian Ocean resulted in a devastating tsunami that sped towards land, swallowing coastal communities with 98-foot waves and killing over 230,000 people in 14 countries. We received an email from Birgit and Dirk whom we'd met in Rodrigues, telling us of the devastation and concerned about our safety. As bystanders, we were all horrified for those involved in the catastrophe; as people who sailed, we were concerned for fishermen and sailors out there on the ocean.

I was cheered by the arrival of my Christmas present by plane two days later when Anita arrived from Auckland. I do not intend to describe any unwrapping that went on; suffice to say we were overjoyed to see each other again, and I had a date for New Year's Eve.

It is not hyperbole to say that the chime of the clock at midnight when 2004 rolled into 2005 was a life changing moment. Carl, Anita and I had tickets for the party at the Royal Cape Yacht Club, a huge bash attended by 200 people. As champagne corks flew across the room, I took Anita's hand in mine and said earnestly, 'My darling, can I have your hand?'

Anita laughed – she gets very giggly on champagne. 'Yes, you're holding it.'

'No, I mean ...' I stumbled over the words; I'd never said this in English before. 'I mean can I marry your hand?'

'*Just* my hand?'

'No, I want to marry your body as well.'

A woman dolled up to the nines and wearing the contents of her jewellery box seated next to Anita said helpfully, 'I think you want say, "Can I have your hand in marriage?"'

'Yes, that's what I want to say!' I cleared my throat. 'Darling, can I have...'

'Yes! Yes, you can!' Anita flung her arms around me and kissed me.

'So have you got a ring?' the woman asked, less helpfully. 'She can't accept your proposal without a ring!' Anita looked at me questioningly. I hadn't thought about that; I'd been so focused on asking her to marry me that jewellery hadn't entered my head. I dived under the table.

'I take it he hasn't got a ring then,' I heard the woman say.

'Yanne,' hissed Anita. 'What the hell are you doing? It doesn't matter about a ring.'

But I was scrambling under the table in search of a temporary solution. I emerged with the metal cage from a champagne cork and twisted the wire into a loop around Anita's third finger. 'There,' I said jubilantly. 'One engagement ring.'

'I love it!' Anita said, proudly showing off her finger to everyone at our table. They all smiled and congratulated us, except for the bejewelled woman who looked as if Anita had just showed her a dog turd.

'I'll buy you a proper one soon,' I whispered.

'This is perfect,' she beamed. 'It's so romantic.'

Nevertheless, where better than in South Africa to shop for gold and diamonds, although my budget was still modest. I'd already told Anita that my part ownership in a 42-foot yacht and a three-year jaunt around the world was not an indication that I was a man of unlimited means. She'd looked at me quizzically and said, 'I knew better than to think a Swedish chef in a small restaurant in Rawene had a Rockefeller income.' We eventually found a jeweller who didn't look at Anita's improvised ring with contempt, but supplied us with an engagement ring and a length of 18 karat gold wire for me to make myself a copy of the champagne wire ring. This jeweller clearly recognized a master craftsman when he saw one. To my surprise, Anita wore the ring I'd made for her until the wire wore thin and broke. 'Why wouldn't I wear it?' she said. 'It's the most precious ring I've ever been given; it was the one you proposed to me with.'

I'd waited until Anita's arrival to visit the famous Table Mountain. Although Cape Town friends suggested it was better to visit in the morning before the tablecloth of clouds gathered and obscured the view from the summit, I decided to be more romantic. We Vikings have come a long way from our notorious rape and pillage days, and I hoped to show my sensitive side by being at the top of the mountain for the sunset.

Table Mountain rises 3,563 feet above sea level, and at approximately 260 million years old is some 10 million years older than the Andes and 200 million years older than the Rockies. The table itself is a level plateau approximately two miles from side to side, flanked by the cliffs of the Devil's Peak to the east and the Lion's Head to the west. The mountain was once home to roaming lions and leopards but is safer now, unless you are unlucky enough to come across one of the many very venomous snakes which inhabit it, including the Cape cobra, the puff adder, the boomslang, and the rinkhal, a nasty little piece of work that spits its venom into the face of anyone unfortunate enough to disturb it. After the fuss over the cockroaches on *Albatross*, I decided not mention the snakes to Anita.

The adventurous can hike to the summit, a four-hour round trip involving some steep and rocky sections through spiky bush and boulders, but the easiest and most popular option is to ascend in a cable car which rotates 360 degrees, affording unparalleled panoramic views and taking just five minutes to reach the top. Anita and I sensibly decided on this second option, thus avoiding any of the snakes likely to kill or hospitalize us.

'Wow!' Anita said.

There was certainly plenty to wow at on the plateau: a wildness totally unexpected in the middle of a city of nearly four million people. Although Table Mountain looks flat from below, there are hidden peaks and valleys on the table top dotted with colourful fynbos, a type of scrubland vegetation which blankets a narrow band of the Western Cape. There are 2,000 species of fynbos on Table Mountain alone, forming vibrant constellations of colour; white freesias and purple pelargoniums bloomed among feathery reeds and grasses; knots of hot pink erica clustered together with lobelias and campanulas, and spiky pink, orange and black proteas, the national symbol of South Africa, lit up the slopes like small fireworks.

And then there was the bird's eye view of the city and the ocean below. The sky was steel blue, a fresh breeze whipped at my cheeks and the sweet smell of the fynbos rose from the mountain slopes on the late afternoon air. The visibility was perfect; each peak of the Twelve Apostles mountain range stood out in sharp relief; the low townships of the Cape Flats sprawled to the southeast; we could see ships coming in and out of the berths at the Victoria and Albert Waterfront, and the green dot of Robben Island, the site of the former prison which had held political prisoners including Nelson Mandela, lay in the crescent-shaped Table Bay Harbour where the water twinkled as if the surface had been scattered with diamonds.

We gravitated to the wooden decks as the sun sank and threw crimson streaks across the sky. A pale moon rose and the city gradually seemed to come to life as lights flooded the valley below. Tellingly, the Cape Flats remained dark. The few of us left at the top spoke in hushed tones; it seemed wrong to disturb the tranquillity of the mountain. I cuddled up to Anita and we watched for shooting stars.

After romancing Anita on top of one of the New Seven Wonders of Nature, we returned to *Albatross*. Carl was reading in the cockpit, a bottle of wine by his side. He poured us a glass each and we compared notes for the day.

'Hey Yanne, is there any of that fish soup left? I'm a bit peckish,' Anita asked. 'It would go very well with this glass of white wine.'

'No problem, I'll heat some up.' I served us a bowl each and we sat in the cockpit to eat.

'You're a great cook, Yanne,' Anita said. 'But I think you forgot to peel a couple of the prawns before you put them in the soup.'

'Prawns?' I said. 'There aren't any prawns in the soup.'

'Then what's the crunchy thing I just ate?' Anita peered at her spoon. 'Oh my god!' A cockroach, or rather part of a cockroach, was sitting on her spoon. Anita flung it across the deck and ran to the side of the boat, simultaneously gagging and scraping her tongue with her fingers. I examined the contents of my bowl and discovered an uninvited guest reclining amongst the fish chunks, antenna weakly waving.

'I can't believe she ate the crew,' Carl remarked, looking up from his book. 'Why would she want to eat the crew?'

It took all my powers of romance, several glasses of wine and a promise to hunt down every last insect on *Albatross* to get Anita back on board after that.

While I was doing my utmost to persuade my fiancée to stay on board, Carl was doing all he could do to dissuade an uninvited guest from joining us for good. We were sitting in the cockpit having lunch when we heard a familiar voice calling, '*Hejsan*, Calle. Surprise!'

'What the hell...,' I said. It was the Swedish lady who'd been so smitten with Carl in Australia. There she was, standing on the quay, two hefty looking suitcases by her side. When Carl saw her, he was literally speechless, a phenomena I'd only once seen before when the doctor in Tobago had suggested Carl's infected leg be amputated. Carl appeared to be trying to move his mouth but no words came out.'

'*Älskling!* Darling!' she gushed as she clambered on board. 'I've come to stay. Yanne, can you take my bags?' she said, throwing them at me. She kissed a white-faced Carl on both cheeks. 'Isn't this a wonderful surprise? I've come to be your cabin girl.'

'Surprise ..., yes, surprise,' Carl stammered, clearly in a state of severe shock rather than happy wonder.

'Now, where's my cabin? Or are we sharing?' She gave him a playful elbow in the ribs which finally seemed to startle him into life.

'Hell no! There's no way you can stay here. My wife is coming in five days. Are you crazy? Did I say you could stay? When did I say you could stay with us? No way are you staying! NO! NO! NO!'

It seemed Carl's power of speech had returned.

'But you emailed me...,' the lady sniffed.

'No, you emailed me and I replied to your email,' Carl said, jabbing a finger in the air.

But then, of course, the lady began to pout and look tearful. After much discussion, Carl relented and said she could stay in the "popcorn cabin" for four nights. But the night before Eva was due to arrive, his admirer put up a fight to stay longer – she was tenacious, I'll give her that. Carl wasn't having any of it; he slammed her belongings into her bags, threw them on the dock and told her to go. She stomped off down the pier, livid at having been thrown off the boat.

'Was that wise, Calle?' I asked, as we listened to her swearing grow fainter as she marched off into the distance. 'Hell hath no fury like a woman scorned and all that.'

'Hell hasn't met Eva,' Carl said gravely.

Anita and I were keen to escape the city and see more of the Fairest Cape, so we hired a car and set off for the Garden Route and the Indian Ocean in search of quiet relaxation and water less likely to freeze one's dangly bits to snapping point. As we drove out of the city, we could see the low battered buildings of the townships sprawling far into the distance on the windswept Cape Flats, home to over a million people – the exact number isn't known. Referred to as "apartheid's dumping ground," the area was the site of townships created to house the displaced populations created by the 1952 mandate that black and coloured people live separately from whites. Initially, housing was built by the government, but unable to meet the demand, squatter camps of iron scraps, cardboard and plastic sheeting sprung up overnight like mushrooms. During the 1970s and 1980s, the government attempted to demolish these, but no sooner had the police left than the camps reappeared. The townships' people desperately persisted, eventually winning the right to stay. The government is currently attempting to improve conditions in the shantytowns, and many residents try to lead good lives, educate their children and run businesses amid the squalid detritus of humanity, where unemployment, gang warfare and drugs are rife. It's a far and desperate cry from the pristine villas of Camps Bay and the rarefied air of the smart restaurants of the Victoria and Albert Waterfront. Guided tours of the townships are now being offered to encourage an understanding of how communities are attempting to thrive in the face of extraordinary adversity. But back in 2005, entering as a white couple was unthinkable. In any case, I felt those who wanted to do so were in search of a lurid, voyeuristic form of entertainment with which I am uncomfortable.

In stark contrast, the 150-mile Garden Route stretching from Mossel Bay in the Western Cape to the Storms River in the Eastern Cape, offered some of the most glorious countryside I've ever seen: vistas of wide white beaches and bays of pounding surf to our right, and indigenous forests and majestic mountain ranges to our left. With a Mediterranean climate and plenty of rain, the profusion and variety of trees and flowering plants would rival the Chelsea Flower Show. It was 30 degrees Celsius, and as the car had no air conditioning, we drove with all the windows down, enjoying the heady bouquet of a thousand fragrant scents. We meandered along as the fancy took us, curious to see what was over the next crest or around the bend, taking unplanned turns off the road to appreciate a beautiful view or take a refreshing dip in the ocean. We overnighted in guesthouses we liked the look of where the owners seemed delighted to see us, making us feel more like long lost friends than customers and apologetically presenting us the bill at the end of our stay.

And then there were the vineyards. Although South Africa's best known vineyards are located further west, Route 62 takes you along the longest wine route in the Western Cape. The combination of fertile terrain and mild climate results in the production of some very quaffable wines. Anita and I managed to quaff numerous white and sparkling wines over lunches and dinners that make my gastric juices rumble with the delicious memory of them. Lounging around an outside table in a sunny courtyard, enjoying a bottle of the local produce, surrounded by views of the Tsitsikamma Mountains was the perfect antidote to the city and its problems. Nevertheless, both Anita and I noticed that all the patrons were white; those fetching and carrying under the blazing noon sun were African or coloured.

I was still concerned about Hasse on *Born Free* from whom we'd had no news since the tsunami had hit. When enquiries at the Cape Town yacht clubs hadn't yielded any news, it occurred to me that he might have put in to Port Elizabeth, 400 miles east of Cape Town. I wanted to ask for news of him at the yacht club there. Having read that Elizabeth was nicknamed "The Friendly City," I felt confident about taking a chance and driving around. We could stop overnight and get the flavour of the place.

If ever a place was misnamed, the hellhole that was Port Elizabeth was it. We entered on big wide roads where hundreds of people converged at the traffic lights ready to sell or steal whatever they could. Children's upturned hands reached towards the car, while lean youths slouched towards us, their expressions the very antithesis of friendly. I had never felt such raw hate or seen looks of pure menace. We quickly rolled up the windows, risking death by suffocation in the furnace-like heat of the car.

'Yanne, we have to get out of here,' Anita said. She was white with fear. 'This is all wrong.'

I've always been of the opinion that if you treat people with respect, you will receive respect in return, but in this instance I was ready to assume the worst of the youths thronging around the car. They didn't look as if they were part of the welcome wagon. I knew I enjoyed a privileged life, but never had I felt the proximity of such poverty-driven rage or known hatred based on my skin colour: it was a chilling insight into how the segregated masses must have felt for decades. The lights changed and I burned rubber as we raced down the road. Anita and I were both quite shaken by the near confrontation. We didn't stay the night but returned to the Garden Route and made for the nearest vineyard to settle our nerves with a couple of bottles of Chardonnay. We later learned that the Eastern Cape is one of South Africa's poorest provinces, with the highest infant mortality rate in the country and approximately 80 percent unemployment. We had entered the town on the wrong side, where more than a third of the population lived in crowded informal settlements. No wonder we felt unwelcome. Hasse, incidentally, turned up safely, blissfully unaware of the events surrounding our harrowing search for him.

Carl and Eva also visited the Garden Route where they'd been advised to visit Stilbaai, four hours out of Cape Town, and had booked self-catering accommodation over the phone. When Carl told me they'd got into "a bit of a muddle," I was hardly surprised, although the way Carl told it, this had been through no fault of their own. Apparently, they'd driven to the gated entrance to meet the woman from the tourist office with the key to the house, but after waiting what Carl thought was an unreasonably long time, they'd followed another resident's car through the gate and entered the house they'd believed they'd rented, only to find a naked man standing in the living room. There was some debate over who should be there, with Carl wondering if the man was a psycho with a hatchet, although just where he would have been concealing the hatchet Carl didn't explain. It turned out that he and Eva had barged in on the owner of another property. All was clarified and the owner offered to rent them a room in his house.

'It would have been rude to decline a naked man's offer,' Carl said with a shrug. 'We got a fabulous room with an ocean view and had a fantastic week, by the end of which we'd become such great friends he refused to let us pay.'

This sort of generosity must have brought tears to Carl's eyes.

The ladies left at the end of January, and Carl and I got back to the maintenance work on *Albatross* with renewed energy. Our loved ones could glimpse the light at the end of the tunnel; only five months remained until our scheduled arrival back in Helsingborg, but we had a lot of ocean to cross and *Albatross* needed to be ready to handle a long journey; the seventeen-year old compressor in the refrigeration unit had started to leak gas and needed repairing, and we finally bit the bullet and got a new mainsail at a fraction of the price we would have paid in Sweden. We were often guests on *Avanti* and at weekends were invited to Harry's villa on Bloubergstrand where we had the opportunity to see how one side of society lived, the side that was affluent and generous because it could afford to be.

And that's what South Africa seemed to be, two distinct societies; those who have and those who don't. It is a country endowed with all of God's gifts: a perfect climate, a staggeringly beautiful landscape, minerals and diamonds and countless natural bounties. But 20 years after Mandela first became president, the man-made evils of poverty, unemployment, drugs and violence continue to plague the country. It has some of the highest rates of murder, rape, violent crime and people living with HIV and AIDS of any country in the world. The disparity between the haves and have-nots seems to have grown ever wider. I am saddened to read that the situation in South Africa has improved only minimally since Carl and I visited.

Just before we were due to set sail, the Royal Cape Yacht Club invited us to give a talk to its members about our circumnavigation. Our audience was sedated with food and drink and settled down to listen as we talked about how we'd quit our jobs, taught ourselves to sail and how I'd sold my home to fund the purchase of *Albatross*. 'Bloody inspiring, man' said someone in the crowd. 'You guys should write a book.'

And that was the first time the words hit home, that I realized what Carl and I had done in following our dream – albeit it to some not so much a dream but a ludicrous middle-aged cry for help – was inspiring to others. The seed to share our story was sown, and if you've made it this far, you'll know that we did publish a book.

Of course, it's quite possible that the voice in the crowd came from someone who'd had one too many, was bored to tears by our talk and was being ironic. In which case, I apologize for wasting your time. Feel free to put this book down and dig the garden, scrape the hull or do whatever else I'm keeping you from.

We set sail a couple of days later after more than two months in a beautiful yet troubled country where we'd made many new friends. As the Table Mountain became a grey silhouette against a misty sky, I voiced a fervent hope: that South African would find a solution to its post-apartheid problems.

Carl and I had chosen to undertake a perilous journey which was nearing its conclusion, but South Africa's long road to democratization continues with no end in sight. To quote the great Nelson Mandela whose death occurred during the writing of this book: "I have discovered the secret that after climbing a great hill, one only finds that there are many more hills to climb. I have taken a moment here to rest, to steal a view of the glorious vista that surrounds me, to look back on the distance I have come. But I can only rest for a moment, for with freedom come responsibilities, and I dare not linger, for my long walk is not ended."

Chapter 47

In Search of Giant Squid and Life among the Saints

14 February – 6 March 2005

Cape Town, South Africa – Saint Helena

Experience: *Get a quality generator that can be repaired if need be in the middle of the ocean. Stock up with supplies in Cape Town; prices on the south Atlantic islands are high and the range of goods is limited.*

Tip: *When there's no room left in the freezer, dry any fish you catch. It's an easy and delicious way to preserve fish to eat later.*

The small island of Saint Helena, a 47-square-mile volcanic mound in the south Atlantic must be as remote as any place in the world gets. Lying approximately 1,200 miles from Africa and 1,800 miles from South America, this British Overseas Territory can only be reached by sea.

No surprise then that the island once served as a prison. When the Duke of Wellington stopped there on his return from India, its remoteness struck him as the perfect exile for Napoleon after his defeat at Waterloo in 1815. 'Ha, ha,' the Duke must have thought, remembering how his nemesis had escaped from his first exile on the island of Elba. 'Try and get back to France from here, you short Corsican git.' Or thoughts to that effect. In any case, it proved to be a devastating exile for the self-proclaimed Emperor of France. Images depict him staring morosely out to sea, no doubt contemplating how to get his own back on the Duke of Wellington. The best he came up with was to bequeath a not inconsiderable sum of money to the man who had tried to assassinate the duke in what seems to me a desperate attempt to have the posthumous last laugh.

Approximately 1,700 nautical miles lie between us and Jamestown on St Helena. We're entering the home stretch: a strange feeling, one of excitement tinged with melancholy; if all goes well our journey should come to an end in less than four months with just three stopping points to Sweden.

Day 1

According to Jimmy Cornell's *World Cruising Routes*, the sail from South Africa to Europe can be a pleasant one as the wind is off the starboard quarter once the trade winds are encountered. Jimmy may well have experienced an agreeable passage, but for the first couple of days, Carl and I feel dopey with seasickness; after two months in harbour it's proving hard to get our sea legs.

Just before lunch we hook a species of fish we haven't seen before: a long 10-pound gold-finned fish which I clean and refrigerate until our appetites return. For the moment we are unable to face anything more challenging than baked beans straight out of the tin.

Day 2

The wind has increased and we're shooting merrily along with that glow of pleasure that flows from the beauty of a sailboat converting passing air into forward motion.

And then, of course, something has to go wrong; the control pendulum on the wind rudder breaks and swings limply in the aft wake. The tube between the axle mount and the rudder has broken in half, a problem we experienced two years earlier on the crossing from the Canary Islands to the Caribbean. We heave the control panel on board, drill a new hole just below the broken area and repair it with a new M8 bolt and nut. When we remount the pendulum, *Albatross* seems to respond well to the wind again. We hold our thumbs tightly that the repair can withstand the force of the sea.

Day 3

During the night, *Albatross* crosses into Helsingborg's longitude; we have finally traversed every longitude, meaning we have travelled 360 degrees around the globe. We have only to cross the route we sailed between the Canary Islands and St Lucia to be able to legitimately call ourselves "circumnavigators."

Day 4

Our appetites finally return and I happily juggle my pots in the galley making concoctions with the fish we've caught. Although my fish fried in breadcrumbs, served with boiled beets is pretty tasty, both Carl and I have started to long for a hearty beef stew with root vegetables.

'Ah, beef,' Carl sighs as he washes the dishes. 'It's the stuff of my dreams.' He says it with such longing, I fear he might sink his teeth into the first cow he sees once on Swedish soil.

Day 5

Much as sailing can be a serene experience, it can also be extremely monotonous, particularly at night, so skippers and crew seek each other out to swop stories and experiences. At dusk, we sight what appears to be a giant white-tipped wave breaking along the horizon. As we get closer, it transforms into a colossal tower with white wings. A supertanker is sailing towards us. After a minute or so it changes course to starboard, passing us a mile off on our port side. Carl radios her and has a pleasant chat with Roy the captain. The super-tanker, named *Lucky*, is a big girl weighing in at 350,000 tons and measuring 1,200 feet. Roy tells us how they've just loaded her with crude oil in the Gulf and are heading back to the United States, completing the journey in 36 days at a steady speed of 14 knots. He's interested in our story, particularly as he has many good friends in Sweden with whom he worked in the shipping industry. He wishes us luck and signs off.

Half an hour later, Chief Officer Rouge radios. 'Hey! Roy told me about two crazy Vikings he's been talking to. You guys are pretty far from home. I guess the media must be following your circumnavigation with interest.' It's a chance for a little trumpet blowing.

'Well, we get about 700 visitors a day on our home page following our progress,' Carl says, trying to sound modest. 'We're not rock stars yet.'

'We certainly don't meet many small cruising craft out here,' Rouge says. 'It's interesting to hear your story.'

We feel exactly the same; a different voice, a new story, a thirty-minute chat breaks the tedium of the long sail and we're all grateful for it.

Day 6

And the kindness of strangers continues. Late in the evening we sight another supertanker which, after making a significant course change, passes us on our port side where we can clearly read her name, *Saga*. First mate Regio tells us they are also returning from the Gulf after loading up with crude oil.

'I guess you know you're in the middle of the "highway" for tankers on their way back to the U.S?' Regio says. 'Is all well on board? We can drop a package to you.'

'No, we're fine. But if you have an updated forecast for St Helena, we'd be grateful.' Regio comes from the Philippines but knows our home port of Helsingborg well. 'Hope you make it back, safely,' he says as he signs off.

As do we. Sunday doesn't start well: the fire alarm goes off. Carl initially blames me for burning breakfast, but realizes that black diesel smoke is pouring out of the engine room. The cause: a coin-sized hole in the exhaust pipe of the cylinder hose of the diesel generator; coolant gushes out like water out of a fire hydrant. The reason: damn salt water corrosion again. We have no means of repairing this as we don't have the resources to weld aluminium, so from now on we'll have to rely solely on the main Volvo Penta generator for electricity.

Later that evening the Volvo Penta stops working. Rude word upon rude word.

Day 7

We let *Albatross* sail herself while we spend most of the day stripping down the generator to a mere skeleton and then reassembling it. The water, which leaked from the small diesel generator, attacked all the electrical connections and the fine copper wires to the circuits have come loose. Unfortunately, we don't have access to a 220 volt socket to heat the soldering iron, having no generator. But as necessity is the mother of improvisation, we use the gas burners on the stove to solder the tips and manage to complete the repair. By afternoon, we've re-installed the generator. We hold our breath and turn the ignition key.

'Give it life!' I cry in Frankenstein like desperation. A pause and then the generator throbs noisily into action again. I begin to understand the thrill Doctor Frankenstein felt bringing his creations to life.

Day 8

Joy! The Volvo Penta is still working.

Day 9

During the night, we pass through the invisible line of the zero meridian. Finally, we are free of mechanical failures – although who knows for how long – but the weather turns sulky with heavy downpours, spiteful winds and powerful squalls that bump us around for the best part of the day.

Day 10

Happily, the squalls are short lived and the wind drops; the temperature rises to a pleasant 28 degrees Celsius, meaning we can wear T-shirts and shorts day and night. Not that we need to bother with clothes: this is a lonely part of the Atlantic; we haven't seen a boat for days and even the fish have deserted us; we haven't had so much as a nibble since that first day outside Cape Town.

I wonder if the absence of fish is due to the presence of the *Architeuthis dux*, more commonly known as the giant squid, which for centuries was the basis for tales of fearsome sea monsters. In 1848, Captain M'Quhae was guiding *HMS Daedalus* through the waters between the Cape of Good Hope and St Helena – more or less the same course we're in now – when the crew spotted what they described as a gigantic sea serpent, a 60-foot creature with "a maw full of large jagged teeth, sufficiently capacious to admit of a tall man standing upright between them." Either the crew had been overdoing the rum rations or they'd been treated to the sight of a colossal calamari. In any case, the captain's report was pooh-poohed, and the existence of such gigantic cephalopods remained the stuff of fanciful maritime myth until 1857, when Danish zoologist Japetus Steenstrup gave it scientific status by exhibiting a large squid beak – the only physical evidence that the creature existed at all. Even with today's sophisticated underwater technology, scientists are still not sure how many species are in the giant squid genus. Most of what is known comes from squid that have been hauled up in fishing nets or from beaks found in the stomachs of sperm whales. Two giant squid measuring 36 and 20-feet long are on display in the Smithsonian National Museum of Natural History in Washington, examples of the largest invertebrate ever to have lived on the face of the earth. In fact, examples of them are so rare precisely because they *don't* live on the face of the earth but at extreme ocean depths. In September 2004, two Japanese marine biologists hit the headlines when they captured the first underwater photographs of a live squid in the Pacific Ocean off the coast of Tokyo, proving that *Architeuthis dux* was alive and well and very aggressive.

Lord knows what lies beneath us in the depths of the ocean where no sunlight penetrates.

Day 11

No fish biting, but on the other hand no giant squid attacks. Curious as I am, I'm not thrilled about hooking something as long as *Albatross*. On the other hand, it would be quite a coup to land one...

Day 12

Only 145 nautical miles remain to our destination which we decide to approach from the north to the anchorage off Jamestown, thus keeping us in the windless lee of the island for the shortest time. Suddenly the fish start biting with a vengeance, and we land a whopping Spanish mackerel which I swiftly dispatch into fillets. As the freezer is full, I dry much of the catch following a recipe from the crew of a Swiss yacht we met in Cape Town. We have fish drying from every available surface making *Albatross* look like a Neapolitan street on washday.

Day 13

During our passage to St Helena we've been reading up on the place as both Carl and I know very little about the island other than what we've read in our pilot book; unsure of what language we'll be murdering there, we're relieved to find that St Helena, together with the Ascension Islands and Tristan da Cunha, are part of the British Overseas Territory and therefore is English speaking, although what form of English is another question. We've struggled with Scottish English, Irish accented English, New Zealand, Australian and South African slang, as well as the Pidgin English spoken on Caribbean islands .

'How many more types of English do we have to learn?' one of us grumbles, probably Carl. I have to give it to the English though, they'd didn't half get around, spreading the King's or the Queen's English, although in fairness St Helena was discovered and named by the Portuguese in 1502. It was effectively nicked by the English whose warships laid in wait ready to attack the Portuguese carracks as they returned to Europe. Surely, this goes against all the rules of fair play laid down by the British Empire as I'd learned them. The island remained a stopping-off point for ships using the trade winds, but its importance was diminished with the advent of steam ships and the opening of the Suez Canal.

When Napoleon and his 30-strong entourage first glimpsed the island in 1815, they were much dismayed, but then the disgraced emperor was probably not inclined to view his place of imprisonment positively, likening the island's rocks to the folded wings of a dragon rising out of the sea. As we sail along the eastern coast, a full moon illuminates the rocky cliffs, and they do indeed look like giant dragon wings. It's three a.m. when we finally drop anchor in Rupert's Bay off Jamestown bringing to an end a 13-day passage. Our mooring snaps is also our nightcap.

By the time we woke the next morning, the sun had already slipped behind the tip of Rupert's Hill casting a dark shadow over *Albatross* and Jamestown nestling in the long crevice lying between the jagged cliffs. Carl and I peered into water so clear restaurants could charge a premium to serve it.

'Nothing with pointy teeth to eat us here,' I remarked.

Carl grinned, threw off his T-shirt and dived in. For the first time since Fiji we could luxuriate in the warm waters without the fear of sharks or crocs snacking on our nether regions. Ah, serenity.

As it was Sunday, everything was closed. St Helena radio picked up our call to the harbourmaster and welcomed us to the island. 'Sorry, guys,' a friendly voice said to us, 'but you'll have to check in tomorrow. You're free to go ashore but you need to call Andrew on the ferry service on channel 14. He'll bring you over for a pound.'

Thirty minutes later, Andrew pulled up alongside us. Carl looked apologetic. 'Sorry, Andrew but we don't have any cash until we get to a bank.'

'Don't worry about it, fellas,' Andrew grinned. 'I'm sure you're good for it. Anyway we know where you are. Not much happens around here that somebody doesn't know about. There's virtually no crime on the island. We don't bother locking our doors and we leave the keys in the cars. I mean, if someone steals something, they can't go far with it, can they?'

We walked up the long main, and only, street of Jamestown, lined with handsome wooden colonial buildings. The town is sandwiched between the vertical cliffs that form James Valley, and with its quiet Sunday air, it felt as if little had changed in the last four hundred years since the capital was founded by the English East India Company. Along the cliff edges were visible the ruins of batteries and watch towers, testimony of the importance of the island's strategic position; it had effectively been a fortress run by the East India Company until the 1830s.

We took a pause at Donny's Place where the owner was wiping down tables and chairs.

'Any chance of a beer?' Carl asked idly.

Donny looked at his watch. 'Well, officially I'm closed. But I'll pour you a couple.'

'No problem. We haven't got any cash until we get to a bank anyway.'

'That's all right. Pay me later in the week.'

We'd been on the island less than an hour and had already run up two tabs. After a brief chat with Donny over our beers, we continued our meander through the town and were pondering the age of the church, when a middle-aged woman passed us, smartly dressed in what was clearly her Sunday best.

'Are you joining us Saints for the Sunday service?' she asked, tilting her head to one side, her optimistic smile daring us to say no. To refuse was to admit outright that we were ungodly heathens. I suppressed a beery burp while Carl nodded enthusiastically.

'Can't do us any harm,' he muttered under his breath as we took our places on a creaky pew in the back row. Which was all very well for him to say as he took an extended nap during the sermon. And Carl is not discreet when he naps; despite much elbow jabbing on my part, he snored and drooled for Sweden. The Saints did their best to ignore this but at a particularly loud snort, fifty heads turned in our direction. I put on an innocent expression, smiled at the rafters and kicked Carl's shin with all the vigour I could muster. Fortunately, his waking oath was in Swedish and thus incomprehensible to the rest of the congregation. To make up for Carl's transgression, we sang the final hymns as lustily as we could, thus emphasizing our mispronunciation of every word.

Despite Carl's dubious behaviour, we were invited to the hall for "a few refreshments." It was like something out of an Enid Blyton book: a large table in the centre of the room bowed under the weight of homemade cakes, pastries, pies, biscuits, fruit loaves and finger sandwiches. We were urged by the good ladies to fill our plates, refill them and when we could eat no more, had cakes thrust upon us to take back "in case you fancy a nibble later," as one old dear said to us.

'Maybe they think we look undernourished,' Carl said. Although glancing at his stomach, I very much doubted that was the case.

On Monday the island woke from its Sunday slumber and we could proceed with clearing in. We were warmly welcomed by the harbourmaster, "a born and bred Saint," as he told us. The procedure was quick and painless until we were asked for proof of health insurance to cover any costs incurred for an air ambulance in case of emergency. Lacking an airport, the island's needs are supplied by *RMS St Helena*, one of the last mail ships in service which shuttles between Cape Town and Jamestown bringing everything from wind turbines to car parts, groceries, furniture, alcohol, white goods and pharmaceuticals, as well as the mail and a hundred or so passengers. While we visited, there was much talk of the projected airport, the building of which was finally started in 2012, to boost St Helena's flagging economy and diminishing population which has wandered off the island in search of better paid employment in the UK or the Falklands. Fortunately, we remembered we'd taken out travel insurance which covered the cost of repatriation should we fall off a cliff.

Jamestown's main street was bustling and we browsed the shops, experiencing the sensation that time had stopped at some point in the 1950s: everyone said "good morning" to us or waved in greeting as they passed each other in the street; shops were fitted with long polished counters behind which goods were stocked on floor to ceiling shelves, although what was for sale seemed hugely unpredictable – a display case featured shoes surrounded by packets of fuses, light bulbs and flower seeds; antique cash registers went "kerching" instead of bleeping electronically. It reminded me of the corner shop of my childhood. The place was a mixture of quaint and otherworldly with an atmosphere of English country village thrown in. Within half an hour Carl and I had become infected and were waving to every adult and child we passed.

But during our stay we were to discover that St Helena's 1950s charm was also leading to its undoing. The small population, mostly descended from European settlers, Chinese itinerant workers and Madagascan, Asian and African slaves, has dwindled over the years. At the last count in 2012, it was a mere 3,800. Many youngsters talk of leaving the island as soon as they've finished their education. There is little opportunity for work and even those in employment can only expect to earn at most £5,000 per year while having to pay prices three times higher than in the UK for everyday goods. The economy is funded almost entirely by the British government as there is little commerce on the island apart from tourism and the St Helena Coffee Company, which produces one of the most expensive coffees in the world. Half the Saints we spoke with welcomed the building of an airport, believing it would bring with it employment opportunities and increased revenue from tourism; the other half were doubtful, saying that it would rob the island of its history and unique charm.

St Helena is certainly not the place for major yacht repairs, but we were directed to the local blacksmith who we hoped could repair the exhaust pipe for the diesel engine. His small shop floor was strewn with engines and parts from everything from lawn mowers to trucks.

'We're always desperate for spare parts,' the smithy explained. 'It can take months before a part arrives on the mail boat from Cape Town, so we often have to improvise. Show me what you've got and I'll do my best.' He examined our pipe and said he could have it ready for us in a couple of days.

We Swedes pop up in the most unlikely of places: it turned out that the operator of the island's radio station, *Saint FM*, was a fellow countryman. Mike Olsson had come to St Helena as a visitor nine years earlier, fallen prostrate under its spell and never left.

'*Fan! Jag har inte pratat Svenska i manga år,*' he said, delighted to speak Swedish again. 'Come over to the station and I'll put you on the air. You can tell us about your circumnavigation.'

So we became minor radio celebrities, at least for those Saints who listened to *Saint FM* on Tuesday morning. Mike was one of those techno geeks, happiest when surrounded by computers, cables and routers. He was an excellent source of information about the island and immensely proud of his radio station. (He is still manning the station although it closed briefly before reopening as *Saint FM Community Radio* in 2013.)

'What makes St Helena so special is the fact that it is so remote,' he said. 'Just look at the sky tonight: there's no light pollution; nowhere else will you see so many stars. Sure, you can't get a mobile phone signal, but that's the beauty of it.'

On Mike's recommendation we signed up for Corker's Tours, a father and daughter owned business taking tourists around the island in a 1929 open-top Chevrolet Charabanc. Colin Corker, who was 70 if he was a day, had inherited the car from his father who'd driven it as a 12-seater bus. We managed to recruit five other passengers to join us on a full-day tour and set off up one of the tortuously winding steep roads out of Jamestown. I'm not sure Colin ever changed out of first gear as we rumbled along the single lane road cut alongside the narrow ravine which rose 2,000 feet in under two miles. Of the few road signs I saw, one of the drollest appeared after Colin had negotiated several blind hairpin bends. As the road levelled out and my ears popped, a gentle curve was signposted "bend in the road." At least one Saint had a healthy sense of the absurd.

As we stopped at the first plateau to admire the panoramic view out over the Atlantic, we could also appreciate how the island was a planet in miniature, a smorgasbord of flora and fauna with a landscape that changed from one side of the island to the other: as desolate as the moon in one moment, lush and green in another. Grey volcanic cliffs gave way to undulating hills which in turn grew into rainforests of huge tropical plants. Every corkscrew turn around Diana's peak, the island's highest point, offered a new and wonderful view, even if my nose was beginning to bleed.

As interesting as the topographical diversity is the island's history. Our tour took in a visit to Longwood House, the former residence of St Helena's most famous prisoner. On a sunny day, it looked rather pleasant, surrounded by trees and a well-tended garden, although the building was somewhat dilapidated. (The house has since been renovated.) But when Napoleon and his retinue arrived at Longwood, they were horrified; situated on a windswept plain, at a distance from any other dwelling and crawling with mould and rats, the house was a far cry from the palaces the great military leader and ruler had enjoyed in his glory days. This was where, in his own words, he wore his "crown of thorns" from 1815 until his death in 1821. Worse than the accommodation was the food, which for a Frenchman must have been the final ignominy.

As I stood on the porch at the front of the house, unconsciously tucking my hand across my stomach, it was easy to picture Napoleon's final years and humanize the man behind the marble busts and grandiose portraits. This was the man who in 1804 had claimed: "Death is nothing. But to live defeated and without glory, is to die every day." He must have spent hours scanning the ocean for passing ships, cursing his captors and bemoaning his exile on the "cursed rock," as he called it. There were, in fact, several plots to rescue him that never came to fruition, including one to smuggle him off the island with a primitive submarine. Napoleon was not the only prisoner on St Helena; the British also kept the Zulu King Dinuzulu kaCetshwayo there in 1890, as well as 6,000 Boer prisoners from 1900 to 1902, all of whom I suspect would have welcomed an airport to freedom.

Colin drove us on down the road to Napoleon's tomb in Geranium Valley, a sheltered hollow where Napoleon apparently liked to picnic. But the neatly tended grave, ringed with dark iron railings, no longer contain his remains. In 1840, the coffin was unearthed and his remains returned to France where they now lie at Les Invalids in Paris.

If going uphill in a 1929 charabanc was challenging, taking the hairpin bends downhill was heart stopping. 'I hope Colin tests the brakes regularly,' I muttered to Carl. We got out shakily at Plantation House, the handsome residence of the governor of the island built by the East India Company – the opulence of which must have been an additional kick in the teeth to Napoleon.

'I'd like tew introduce yew tew Jonathan, the oldest resident on our island. Maybe he's even the oldest being in the world,' Colin said in his brand of St Helena English. 'He's 176 years old so he don't hear or see tew well.'

Good lord, I thought, *the governor is really hanging on to his job.*

Jonathan was in fact a giant tortoise who lives in the grounds of Plantation House together with five other tortoises, mere juniors at just a hundred years old.

'He's still pretty active for his age,' Colin told us. 'Still likes tew mate regularly with Emma and Myrtle there. Ah, la, there he goes.'

'Holy crap,' Carl said, in a tone that sounded envious. 'Hope I can get it up when I'm as old as him.'

I refrained from pointing out that in human to tortoise years, Carl *was* nearly as old as Jonathan. You had to admire his determination to get up and go – the tortoise's that is. While I felt distinctly awkward peeking, I did learn that tortoise sex is energetic and rowdy, or maybe that's just the way Jonathan prefers it. According to *St Helena Online*, he's still going strong, displaying a libido as healthy as ever, although he has since been given the privacy of a fenced enclosure, as it was feared the increased number of tourists arriving at the island via the new airport might put Jonathan off his stride.

One of the most visited sites on the island is the steep 699-step staircase known as Jacob's Ladder. In 1829, the St Helena Railway Company built a cableway to lift supplies from Jamestown port up to Ladder Hill Fort. When the cableway fell into disuse, the Royal Engineers rebuilt it as a long staircase. I stood at the top and peered down, feeling slightly giddy.

'Children slide down the rails to the bottom,' Colin told us, increasing my sense of nausea. 'And every two years, we have the ladder challenge at the end of the St Helena Festival of Running. The prize for the fastest to the top is a crate of beer.'

'What's the record?'

'About five and a half minutes.' Colin paused to consider this. 'I guess he really wanted that beer.'

Thanks to Colin we learned a lot about life on St Helena and I was beginning to understand why our Swedish compatriot, Mike Olsson, had fallen in love so quickly with the place and the Saints: unparalleled nature for walking and hiking, a superb coastline for wreck diving, a mild climate and a close-knit community steeped in British tradition yet decidedly un-British as reflected in its ethnic roots and cuisine. Restaurant menus featured Malay and Chinese dishes and the traditional British Sunday roast was served with a curry dish and sweet potatoes. English was the local language but with a particular lilt to the accent that was at first difficult to understand but charming when you did. And then there was the waving. If you didn't wave, you were considered ill, insane or plain rude. By the time we left, three weeks after our arrival, we were waving in our dreams.

Mike was also spot on about the night sky: never had I seen the heavens so bright with light. The Milky Way stretched overhead in James Bay in a great luminous arc, billions of stars studded the sky, and the two Magellanic Clouds swirled above us. St Helena's location at 16 degrees south of the equator means that virtually every constellation is on display at some time throughout the year. Was I being fanciful or did all the stars shine more intensely on our last night?

We checked out *Albatross* on Friday in preparation to sail that Sunday for the Azores. While I went ashore to present Mike at the radio station with a Swedish flag, Carl worked feverishly – his words, not mine – scrubbing the hull to remove the growth of lush vegetation that had accumulated above the waterline. By mid-morning we were ready to set sail; we weighed anchor and sounded the horn in farewell. It was with genuine regret that we left the island and waved our last goodbyes to the Saints who'd made us feel so welcome.

As the wind filled the sails and lifted *Albatross* over the waves, Carl and I turned back to admire a view Napoleon must have longed for: the aft wake of a departing boat in the Atlantic waters as the dragon wings of St Helena's shadowy cliffs receded into the distance.

Chapter 48
Fifty Shades of Green
6 March – 20 April 2005
Saint Helena, UK – São Miguel, the Azores, Portugal

Experience: *The Atlantic north of the equator offers many surprises, sometimes calm, sometimes stormy. A sailboat's average speed is approximately two knots less than when sailing in the southern hemisphere.*

Tip: *When becalmed, don't be tempted to drink your crew's urine: stick with your own.*

Between 30 to 35 degrees both north and south of the equator lie the regions known as the subtropical highs or horse latitudes. These areas of dry air and high pressure result in weak or no winds, giving rise to the notion that when sailing vessels were stalled and fearful of running out of supplies, sailors jettisoned their livestock overboard to save on provisions. That's one theory as to how the horse latitudes acquired their name; although, I feel it doesn't stand up to scrutiny, for surely the sailors would have eaten the animals rather than thrown them overboard. A more plausible idea is that when sailing from Europe, the horse latitudes were reached at around the same time the crews had worked off the period for which they had been paid in advance – their so-called "dead horse" time. Once they reached the horse latitudes, they would be working for future pay.

For whatever reason these latitudes had acquired their name, Carl and I were anxious about sailing due north, not just because if we became trapped in the doldrums I might be forced to throw Carl overboard, but because we were due to meet my parents, Anita and her younger children and Carl's wife in the Azores. We'd allowed time for quick stopovers at Ascension Island and Cape Verde, but we didn't have the luxury of sitting in the middle of the Atlantic gazing at our navels waiting for the wind to pick up.

'Don't worry about it,' Carl says. 'As long as we don't run out of beer or wine, we'll be fine.'

That at least is a comfort: we'll have to be in the doldrums for an extremely long time before thirst drives us to drink each other's urine.

We'd arranged to check in with two German yachts we'd met in James Bay. They were 50 nautical miles ahead of us and announced the wind was good.

Day 2

I hook a hefty-looking dorado, but it wriggles through my fingers and with an elegant backflip returns to the water.

'I swear that fish was smirking,' I say to Carl.

Carl narrows his eyes at me. 'We're near the Equator: your brain's softening in the sun. Wear your damn hat.'

We do end up jettisoning something overboard: a tray of 30 eggs we bought over a month ago in Cape Town. Fortunately, they hadn't cost us too much so we – or rather *I* – don't grieve too long over the waste.

'Wouldn't have happened if you'd let me buy those chickens in Santiago de Compostela,' Carl grumbles.

'Give it up, Calle,' I reply. 'That was over two years ago. They'd have ended up in the pot by now.'

Day 3

The wind drops to a whisper, reducing our speed to only three knots – the speed of a slow jog – so at dawn we raise the spinnaker; the sail billows in the wind and our speed immediately picks up to six knots.

The temperature is increasing by day to a very pleasant 30 degrees Celsius. A chain of fluffy clouds lazily hovers in an otherwise clear cerulean sky.

Day 4

Carl is not pleased: we have to jettison 15 of the 20 kilos of potatoes we bought in the Cape as they've become infected with a fungus and turned to mush. Carl's opinions on growers who wash their vegetables are long and bitter.

'There's nothing wrong with a potato with a bit of dirt on it. Muddy potatoes are the best.'

I'll never hear the end of it.

The wind vanishes late in the evening, and *Albatross* crawls forward at barely a knot with the help of the northwest current. The mercury rises with the sun and a light breeze sweeps in from the southeast, filling out the spinnaker and lifting us forward.

During the night Carl picks up Daytona radio station in Florida so we're able to download all our emails. News from friends cheers us no end.

Day 5

It's terribly lonely in these waters; we haven't encountered a single vessel since leaving Saint Helena until today when we sight a large cargo ship. We scramble for the radio in Robinson Crusoe like desperation to make contact with another living soul. Bob, mate on the *Fedrell Gipana*, a 150,000-tonne cargo ship out of Hong Kong, is happy to relieve our boredom and his. Our conversations are on the level of social chit-chat you make when you find yourself seated with people you don't known at a wedding reception: the "what do you do?" and "where are you from?" sort of dialogues to be forgotten the moment the party ends. But at sea, they are momentous enough to be recorded in the log.

We haven't seen many fish; we certainly haven't caught any. Fortunately, we're able to feast on our dried fish which has cured in the sun, turning white to golden brown and infused with peppers and chili spices.

We're making good headway with the spinnaker up, but when the wind increases, we take it down. Our German friends ahead of us on *Anke Two* are less lucky; their spinnaker collapsed over the bow, filled with water and sank under the keel, working itself around the rudder: a nightmare scenario. David and Ditmar struggled for several hours in rough conditions to pull up the sail again. It's a lesson for us all.

Day 6

Although we're close to Ascension Island, we decide not to stop there as weather reports warn of strong north-westerly swells rolling into Clarence Bay at Georgetown. Seasoned sailors in St Helena told us how such swells are common in March, releasing enormous amounts of energy as they roll into the bay and smash against the rocks and pier, forming 90-foot cascades: a real thrill to watch but not to attempt navigating in a small rubber dinghy.

A pity as we've been looking forward to experiencing St Helena's smaller sister island, another tiny volcanic mound rising from the Atlantic floor. I'm becoming something of an island aficionado: the smaller and more remote the land mass, the better I like it. Ascension is 700 miles from anywhere, a mere blip on a map, yet is strategically very important. Historically, it has been a safe haven for sailors and aviators, and for the last 70 years has been dominated by a U.S. military base. It is one of only six runways in the world capable of accommodating an emergency space shuttle landing. Until very recently, it was closed to tourism, but within its 34 square miles there is masses to see: 40 volcanoes, 32 sandy beaches home to nesting Green Turtles, colonies of seabirds and the island's National Park, Green Mountain.

If you can land there, which we can't. We pass Ascension in the early hours of the morning, a couple of lights twinkling weakly through the darkness, knowing exactly what we're missing.

Day 7

The sun beats down on us and the mercury climbs as we near the Equator. To combat the intense rays, we mount an additional screen on the cockpit roof.

Just before lunchtime, a huge shoal of bluefin tuna play alongside *Albatross'* hull. The tuna thrust up smaller fish out of the water which seabirds swiftly swoop upon to eat in flight. The tuna are jumping and turning somersaults in the spray of the waves.

'Never mind about the bloody acrobatics,' Carl growls. 'Just jump on the hook.' They don't.

Day 8

Sullen-looking clouds fill the sky and the sea turns rougher. We take down the spinnaker and set the main, the mizzen and the jib and *Albatross* zips across the ocean.

Day 9

We finally hook three beautiful 10-pound bluefin tuna for which the Japanese pay outrageous sums of money. Dinner is grilled tuna steaks with fried potatoes and onions, served with a tasty mayonnaise sauce seasoned with chillies and black pepper. They don't call me the Swedish chef for nothing, you know.

Throughout the afternoon and evening, the grey clouds that have followed us release a deluge we've not experienced since Colón. Carl and I strip off and enjoy a long shower in the warm tropical rain. What a fantastic sensation: to be completely naked and let the water pour over you. Being Swedish, we're very comfortable with nudity: surprising, I suppose given our inhospitable climate. All the more reason to enjoy being in our birthday suits when the weather permits.

Day 10

As I start my watch at dawn, a huge pod of dolphins appear on our port side. They spot *Albatross* and stream towards us in a huge silver streak as they compete to reach our bow where for the best part of an hour they race and play as if overjoyed to have found a new playmate, skilfully synchronizing their movements with one another.

Why is it that dolphins follow ships? Scientists believe that dolphins conserve energy by bow-riding, but I like to think they're just doing it for the pure joy of racing alongside a rushing hull. They're a social breed that live in groups of five to several hundred, often hunting together by surrounding a school of fish, trapping them and taking turns swimming through the school to snatch a snack. And did you know that to prevent drowning while sleeping, only half the dolphin's brain sleeps while the other half stays awake so it can continue to breathe? It's a remarkable animal that has been credited on several occasions for coming to the rescue of humans in distress in the water. Yet another reason, if one were needed, to halt the mass dolphin killings that take place in Japan every year.

Day 11

We sail sedately onwards, which is fine for a Spanish galleon but not for an ocean-going yacht. There's nothing to do but make the most of the wind we have and settle into a steady routine of chores, watches and reading. Then suddenly the small diesel generator stops working; the new drive belt we installed the previous week has completely worn out. Spare belts are packed away in the lockers in the bow, but typically we have to turf out bike gear, ropes, fenders, power cables and the like in order to access them.

At three in the morning, we cross the Equator; we're finally back in the northern hemisphere after 679 days of sailing south of the equatorial line.

Day 12

Heavy rain clouds loom over us and thunder booms intermittently in the north. Finally the wind increases and fills the sails, raising our speed to seven knots. Hurray!

Day 13

We consider landing on São Vicente, one of the 10 Cape Verde islands, if the wind continues in our favour; however, the weather is erratic: stormy and then calm.

The Atlantic also has its share of ugly eel-like fish we hooked in the Pacific and Indian Oceans.

'No matter how many times we catch one of those things, you'll never persuade me to eat it,' Carl says, shaking his head in revulsion.

'Don't worry,' I reply, equally repelled by its bulbous eyes and sharp protruding teeth. 'I'd rather eat you than this.' I chuck it back in the ocean to become food for something less discriminating than us.

Day 14

The ocean is completely desolate: no ships but at least we've had the company of dolphins; we receive visits from three individual pods that cavort around *Albatross*.

The night is completely still and we rock forward at barely two knots. Cape Verde lies some 800 nautical miles away. At this rate we'll never get there.

The darkness is lit up by flashes of lightning so bright we can read our books by them. Happily, we are well away from the eye of the storm; nevertheless, experience has taught us to take down all the sails during the night and let *Albatross* drift, as the wind blows in hurricane force gusts and then drops to nothing. We do everything possible to eliminate damage to our electronic equipment in case of a lightning bolt strike by disconnecting all the aerial wires, fuses and switches to the batteries and generators. Thor forbid we're on the end of a billion volts: we'd be toast.

Day 15

We're still in the grip of the storm but take advantage of the heavy rainfall to take cool showers on deck.

We're well into the doldrums, when navigation is a matter of luck not strategy and a patch of wind seems like a gift. We frequently have to use the engine to motor for an hour or so until the wind picks up just to trick ourselves into believing we're getting somewhere.

And then the engine starts leaking coolant; the copper pipe has corroded and salt water sprays out of a button-sized hole. We've previously been able to solder a repair, but this time we wrap self-vulcanising tape around the pipe: a stopgap measure that will have to do until we can replace it when we get home.

Day 16

We pick up an alarming email from Hans Faber on *Born Free*; two American sailing yachts were moving 30 miles off the coast of Aden to Oman when two motorboats with four armed men in each boat sped up to the yachts and started firing into their cockpits, obviously intending to kill those on board. Fortunately, one of the Americans was a former U.S. Marine and had a weapon of his own with which he managed to disable the engine of one of the pirates' boats, while the skipper of the second yacht had the presence of mind to ram the other. All on board the yachts considered themselves very lucky to have escaped unharmed.

The incident was the first piracy attack in Yemeni waters, marking the start of a reign of terror against ships and tankers in Somalia's surrounding waters. The frequency of such attacks has since prompted shipping companies to drill their crews in anti-piracy training. Our blue light and frying pan wouldn't have been much of a deterrent against pirates with automatic weapons, so our decision to sail the long way back to Europe via the Cape of Good Hope has been the right one.

Day 17

I'm sitting happily on watch, letting my imagination wander as I make new patterns out of the stars. The ancient Greeks imagined the heavens as a great, solid dome, forged of bronze upon which the heavenly constellations were fixed. Atlas was said to spin the dome around upon his shoulders, causing the stars to rise and set. If the ancient Greeks could see the forms of hunters, animals and other objects, surely I can see Anita's heavenly body in the heavenly bodies above: those stars to the north form the outline of her long hair over her shoulders, the swell of her bosom, and the full round curve of her... Suddenly, there's a wet smack in my face, followed by a swift thump in the groin.

'Ow' and 'what the hell?' are my simultaneous thoughts. I look up at the skies in pain and puzzlement. What magic is this? Thought transference? Has my wishful thinking miraculously transformed into ...

I look down, somewhat fearfully: a huge fish is wriggling in my lap. Mystery solved: a flying fish had flown into my face and landed in my groin. Nevertheless, I remain slightly spooked for some time and tried to keep my thoughts on a purer level. As Shakespeare said, "There are greater things in heaven and earth, Horatio, than are dreamt of in your philosophy."

Day 18

A Mayday alert is like the alarm bell in a fire station: everyone jumps and whoever is in the vicinity must respond. A hundred miles off the coast of Guinea a ship is on fire. Five cargo ships immediately go to assist, but the closest is an hour away at top speed. We listen intently throughout the day to the drama unfolding as various vessels try to assist the *Neptune*: cargo ships cool her hull with water cannons; a French warship goes at top speed to provide medical facilities for the crew suffering from burns and smoke inhalation. The fire is eventually brought under control with no loss of life. Another reminder that in a maritime crisis, help is not always close at hand.

Day 19

Another Mayday call comes over the radio; a ship has run aground and needs assistance. What the hell is going on here on the west coast of Africa?

Day 20

We're still tacking slowly and tediously north, hoping for the promised forecast of a change of wind. A stint of beam reaching would be very welcome.

Day 21

The wind increases, oscillating between 25 and 35 miles an hour, and the sea becomes angry; we're having difficulty staying on our set course for Cape Verde. We consequently decide to abandon our plan and sail instead directly to the Azores.

Day 22

In the evening we sight a large cargo ship on a direct course towards us. When we call her on the VHF no one answers. After several attempts to contact her, the ship suddenly changes course, and she silently disappears into the darkness as if guided by an invisible hand.

Day 23

The wind finally shifts slightly to the east but we still have to tack over some high waves.

Day 24

In the evening we establish radio contact with Bjarne, an amateur radio ham operating in Helsingborg. He gives us all the news from Sweden. We're closing the gap between us and home.

Day 25

Although the sea has been teeming with flying fish, resulting in having to clean the deck of stunned and dying fish, we've hooked nothing on our lines.

Day 26

A small shift in the wind towards the east is cause for renewed optimism that we might finally be able to sail directly towards the Azores. We've had enough of this continual weaving and tacking.

Day 27

Three cheers! We've finally come full circle. At 19:15 *Albatross* crosses the course we took on 3 December 2002 when we participated in the Atlantic Rally Cruise from the Canary Islands to St Lucia. Exactly 850 days have passed since the start of our voyage. We've officially sailed around the world. It's a tremendous feeling and we shout our joy to the empty sea and sky. As if to celebrate our achievement, eight dolphins join us, leaping and spyhopping – rising vertically out of the water and rotating to scan the area – around *Albatross.*

How do they know?

Day 28

The blasted wind drops again and with it our speed to just three knots. The Azores lie 1,070 nautical miles away.

Day 29

Our twenty-ninth day marks the longest continuous passage we've ever sailed – our previous record was 28 days on the way to Mauritius – and we're still speaking to each other. True, we don't discuss much other than sails, speeds, winds and waves, but we've settled into an easy rhythm like a couple on the verge of celebrating their golden wedding anniversary.

'Do you know what we haven't had so far on this passage?' I muse out loud to Carl. 'A really good soaking. We could do with a powerful rain storm to give *Albatross* a bit of a wash.'

Day 30

My loathing of cockroaches reaches an all-time high. The clipper speed log instrument suddenly stops working. We dismantle it and out pour a pile of dead roaches and their eggs. The instrument casing is also inhabited by live cockroaches which scatter when we open it. Carl and I recoil simultaneously in horror.

'I really hate those damn insects,' Carl says with a dark expression I've not seen since he chased down the dinghy thieves in Fiji. We clean out all the electronics and the circuit board; it works passably but doesn't register the correct speed. A more thorough repair will have to wait until we reach harbour.

Jupiter must have heard my remark about the lack of rain as Carl has a tough night of it when sudden squalls hit *Albatross*, throwing waves over her and drenching Carl with not one but two rainstorms. When I come on watch at six, his hair is hanging in wet clumps and he growls, 'I think you'll find the boat is spotless now. I'm bloody knackered,' before collapsing in his bunk.

Day 31

After the previous night's storms, Carl says he feels as if he went 10 rounds with Mike Tyson. Fortunately, the wind is light so we let out the sails and enjoy some broad reach sailing.

Day 32

Clear blue skies, a cool temperature of 18 degrees and a straight course to the Azores. We wonder why the fish haven't been biting; the answer is clear when we pull in the line.

'We can't bloody hook anything if we haven't got a hook!' I rant. Our heavy duty hook has disappeared. Whatever has taken it is probably something I wouldn't want to meet, much less eat.

Day 33

At dawn, the sea is so still I could slice it with a knife. There's nothing to do but dive from the guard rail into our own giant pool. At 12,000 feet deep, there's no risk of hitting our heads on the bottom.

To our great dismay, a swim round *Albatross* reveals how overgrown her hull has become; she looks more like a lush botanical garden below the waterline than a streamlined cruising machine. We sling ropes around ourselves, hang from the guard rail and spend the morning scraping away 33 days of growth as best we can. So much for the eco paint the hull was coated with a year earlier in New Zealand.

Day 34

The Atlantic is as lively as a fitted carpet, so we take to our berths and sleep long and soundly without worrying about our watches. After 34 days of around-the-clock six-hour shifts, it's a real luxury to sleep until the body wants to wake up. Unfortunately, my damn body is so attuned to our shifts that it wakes me after six and a half hours sleep.

Day 35

We have a conversationally active day, chatting with the first mate on a German freighter on her way from the Mediterranean to Puerto Rico, and for the first time in two years we hear from Gustav, a Swedish radio ham from Dalarna in central Sweden with whom we last spoke when we were in the Pearl Islands. He gives us the news and tells us how the spring weather in Sweden has finally warmed up to minus seven degrees Celsius: hard to imagine as we sit basking in 22-degree sunshine.

Day 36

So much for the sunshine; a ferocious storm rolls over the ocean and knocks us around for most of the night. Rain lashes down and the wind increases to gale-force, holding the sea in its grip, piling wave upon wave.

Day 37

After a brief respite and a chance to dry off, dark clouds loom and we're hit by a second storm with winds increasing to 50 miles an hour, making it damn near impossible to reef in the jib. It's at these moments I'm grateful not to be sailing alone, despite Carl's infernal snoring.

Day 38

The storm rages on, so preparing food becomes an Olympic event. Try cooking on a swing while someone throws buckets of salty water in your face. We make do by munching on crackers, sardines, cheese and bread.

But we take heart in the knowledge that the island of São Miguel, the largest of the islands in the archipelago of the Azores, is only 242 nautical miles away.

Day 39

And damn it all if the wind doesn't drop to the strength of ant's fart. Will we ever get there?

Day 40

We're beginning to lose the will to live after 40 long days. A feeble wind pushes us along at the heady speed of 0.9 knots. Unfortunately, we can't use the engine as we're running out of diesel and need to keep what is left to enter the harbour. The last time we fuelled was 5,908 nautical miles ago in Cape Town.

At least it's calm and clear enough to take a shower on the aft deck, but as the temperature has dropped to 14 degrees, it's manhood shrivellingly cold.

Day 41

Never have a few nautical miles seemed so far. A reluctant breeze edges us forward at two knots an hour. Despite having been so long at sea, the time has gone relatively quickly; we've been entertained by birds, dolphins, clouds and mechanical problems – if you consider the latter entertaining.

Day 42

Finally! At dawn on Sunday morning after 42 days of sailing we sight the breakwater off Ponta Delgarda harbour on São Miguel. We've sailed a marathon 6,061 nautical miles from Cape Town to the Azores with just one stop at St Helena; in fact, it's the equivalent of 266 marathons. We've made it into port by the skin of our teeth, a mere 23 hours before Anita, her children and my parents are due to arrive.

Our entrance into the harbour is less than graceful as we discover the reverse on the motor is shot. Harbour officials wave us over to moor alongside the far harbour wall but we can't position ourselves, so we sail directly towards another point where we calculate we can swing the boat round into the mooring. There's confused shouting and waving on all sides, with harbour officials running round the dock. The situation is probably not helped by my attempt to communicate we have no reverse by making gestures of cutting my throat, which are quite possibly misinterpreted as a threat. Furthermore, we probably resemble a couple of drug dealers on the lamb: after 42 days at sea, Carl's hair is as wild and woolly as a 1960s afro: an alarming sight on a 50-something Swede.

Carl chucks the mooring rope at the nearest harbour official, all but felling him in his haste to tie up. We both leap from the boat onto the pier, slap each other on the back, shake hands and laugh with pure relief at having finally made it to land after a long and tedious sail. Adrenaline courses through us.

'Where have you sailed from please?' asks a smartly uniformed port official in halting English.

'Cape Town, via St Helena,' Carl answers with a smile the size of the harbour.

'That's a long way. So in Cape Town, do you buy many alcohols? Gins and whiskies?'

'No, we only have a bottle or two. But we've got some wine.'

'Ah yes, and how much bottles of wine you have please?'

Carl scratches his head and looks at me. 'What do you think, Yanne?'

I do a quick calculation. 'Around 2,300. Give or take.'

The harbour official narrows his eyes. 'Very sorry, how *much* bottles?'

'About 2,300. Come to think of it, Calle, no wonder *Albatross* was so slow in the water.' We have cases of wine everywhere; in the popcorn cabin, in the shower, in any spare corner we can cram a case or bottle; if an unwary visitor opens a door, he's likely to be crushed by a cascade of falling bottles.

When the official registers the number, the poor fellow nearly drops his clipboard in the harbour.

'Over 2,000 bottles,' he says in a tight voice. 'One moment. How long you have been sailing?'

'Two years and ten months,' I reply.

'So you have sailed around the world?'

'Yup. That's right.'

The man pumps our hands. 'Congratulations Sweden. Welcome. Enjoy your stay in the Azores.' He is so impressed he doesn't charge us a penny in duty.

The Azores, a group of nine volcanic islands strung like a necklace across 370 miles of the Atlantic, are the beginning or the end of Europe, depending on which way you're going. Originally settled in the first half of the fifteenth century, the islands were squabbled over by the usual suspects, the British, the Spanish, the Dutch and the French, before being reclaimed by the Portuguese. São Miguel was a stepping stone for sailors on route to the

New World but the Portuguese cultivation and export of oranges to England made the island's capital, the architecturally handsome Ponta Delgada, hugely prosperous. The wealth generated by the orange trade is evident in the grand houses lining the city's smart black basalt and white limestone streets. Unfortunately, the orange production came to an abrupt end when the fruit groves were decimated by a blight; the islanders were forced to diversify into other crops such as tobacco, tea, chicory, sugar-beet and pineapples. Today, the population is 140,000, plus one cow to every person, and it's the only place in Europe that produces tea; an old tea factory in the mountains still operates using antiquated British belt-driven brass machines.

São Miguel is a popular holiday destination for Scandinavians taking advantage of the milder climate, so during the morning we were visited by many Danes, Finns and fellow Swedes who'd noticed our Swedish ensign. We basked unashamedly in their astonishment and admiration at how we'd sailed around the world. If we weren't careful, our self-inflated egos would blow us back to Sweden on a weak wind.

We went ashore for our mooring snaps; Carl knocked a couple back but after 42 days without a drink, I opted for a thimble full, which I sipped cautiously. All sense of judgement was immediately impaired. I was less restrained at dinner, which we ate in a quaint old restaurant in Ponta Delgada's city centre. We decided to treat ourselves to what Carl called "a white tablecloth meal," our reward for having lived on fish for over a month.

'Bring me beef!' Carl roared to the waiter, clearly recalling his Viking past. Carl tells me we had a fine meal, a couple of bottles of hearty red, coffee and deserts. I recall none of it; I was incomprehensively drunk after the second glass of wine, slurred at the other patrons something on the lines of being the first Vikings from Helsingborg to circumnavigate the globe and was assisted back to the boat by Carl. I awoke the following day with a hangover the size of the Pacific and shoes so scuffed at the toes it looked as if I'd scaled Everest in them: this apparently the result of Carl literally dragging my all but unconscious form down the road.

'You know what your trouble is, don't you?' said Carl as he watched me fall over as I tried to put on my trousers.

'Balance?' I said weakly.

'Lack of practise! If you drank as much as me, you wouldn't be in this state.'

I wanted to say if I drank as much as Carl, we wouldn't have got to the Azores, but I couldn't form the words. I clearly wasn't in the best state to meet my parents, my fiancée and her children off the plane. The situation was already complicated by the fact that Anita and my parents had met each other only 48 hours earlier: Anita didn't speak any Swedish, my mother spoke no

English and my father's command of the language was very old school and along the lines of "I wish to see my tailor to order a new evening suit." I had no idea how they'd got on.

My parents were too pleased to see me to worry about the fact that I was looking somewhat jaded, and I mumbled excuses about being tired after a month of sailing. I greeted the children and hugged Anita who confided in a low voice, 'God, Yanne. I feel terrible. Some of your friends insisted on celebrating my arrival with a champagne dinner. How do they put it away? I couldn't keep up with them. I'm so hung-over I think I might vomit.'

Ah, that's my girl, I thought.

My parents had booked a charter package for themselves and Anita, thoughtfully arranging a family room for Anita, the children and me – not quite the privacy we'd been hoping for – but for a week we enjoyed the luxury of hotel beds and continental breakfasts. It was a chance for me to get to know Anita's children and for my parents to get to know Anita and her family.

Poor Anita, she did her best, but she just wasn't Swedish enough for my mother – but then nobody's Swedish enough for my mother. Anita had already committed the horrendous error of repeating a toast Carl and I had taught her, lifting her glass of wine at dinner with my parents and exclaiming, '*Skål för fan!*' little realising that it didn't mean "Drink for fun," as she had assumed. Loosely translated it means "Cheers for fuck's sake" and therefore isn't a toast meant for potential in-laws' ears. Worse still, Anita had taught her children the phrase which they had proudly and very clearly enunciated to the horror of my open-mouthed parents. I'd unwittingly dropped her right in it.

The pace of the island suited my parents perfectly as many silver-haired couples in the tea-time of their lives come to the island in search of milder weather to relieve the aches and pains of old age. São Miguel is not a place for dancing in foam, although the islands were starting to offer adrenaline filled activities, such as swimming with sharks, to attract new visitors. My parents were not keen on jumping into the water with a bucket of bloody shark bait, although I suspect Anita's plucky 10-year-old daughter Antonia would have liked to given half a chance.

Instead, we squeezed ourselves into a hire car and toured the island, encouraging the children to admire the breath-taking scenery, which four-year-old Shaun and prepubescent Antonia were not inclined to do, even if the promise of an erupting volcano was dangled before them like a bucket of oats in front of a reluctant donkey. São Miguel is aptly known as the Green Island, and there are at least 50 shades of green: from the brilliant chartreuse of the tea bushes to the pea-green lakes, the lime of the tobaccos and the dark green of the verdant hillsides. The eruptions and earthquakes which had dominated the Azores' geological history are now silent, although in the town of Furnas, the hubble-bubble of caldera and the hiss of sulphuric steam escaping from fumaroles are reminders of the island's seismic origins. Exciting stuff, I thought.

'Smelly,' said Shaun, wrinkling his nose.

'We've got lots of these in New Zealand,' Antonia added, clearly unimpressed. 'Can we go for ice cream now? Shaun's hungry.'

The week passed quickly; Carl waved farewell to Eva and I to my extended family. The situation in New Zealand had become untenable for Anita – there was no going back for her now – so she and her two youngest children would return to Sweden and live in the tiny flat in which I'd stored my furniture. We were excited and apprehensive about the future; it was a huge step for Anita, but she was showing tremendous courage in following her heart and me. I was more than willing to do the same.

So it was easier all round to say goodbye; it was now only seven weeks until our scheduled arrival in Helsingborg. We were home free.

As our families left, so Ove Jöraas from the Helsingborg Yacht Club arrived; he would be signing on to crew with us on the passage to Scotland. Ove, a round-faced, easy-going guy in his early forties, was a welcome addition on *Albatross*, partly because Carl was fed up of doing the washing up and because he'd brought a large bag of spare parts we'd been desperate for. Service centres in the Azores were typically few and far between; I'd cycled around for a couple of days with the piece of corroded copper pipe from the engine, which we urgently needed repaired. After pantomiming my needs, I'd been directed to a small garage where a septuagenarian in overalls had looked at the pipe through glasses as thick as Coke bottles. He'd mused for a second or two, then said, 'Volvo Penta?' He knew his stuff. More gesticulating had followed from which I'd understood that the old fella would have it ready for us in two days. The repair cost us €10 and to this day, nine years after our return, is still going strong. I hope the old mechanic is, too.

With Ove's help we began to prepare *Albatross* for the long but tough sail up the west coast of Ireland to Tobermory on the west coast of Scotland where the likelihood of meeting the spring storms rolling in from Greenland and Iceland were high. I undertook to don my scuba gear and dive under the keel to scrub the hull clean, Carl's excuse being that he couldn't keep his buoyant arse under water. We lay on the dock and repaired the reverse and reinstalled the pipe in the engine. We were all set.

And then the fine weather vanished; the wind turned west, increased to gale-force bringing with it lashing rain. Waves rolled into the marina, pressing *Albatross'* starboard side hard against the floating pontoon bridge; the ropes, fenders, buoys and tyres creaked and groaned as they rubbed against the bridge. Fearing the worse as the storm increased in intensity, we moved to a fixed mooring on the harbour breakwater wall where we felt slightly safer. But for several days we were trapped off the Green Island.

Finally, the wind calmed to a mere 25 miles per hour. 'Right,' Carl said decisively. 'Sod it. Let's go. I've been waiting long enough for that whisky.'

Come hell or high water: that man will not let either prevent him from getting his favourite beverage.

Chapter 49
Show Me the Way to the Next Whisky Bar!

1 May – 4 June 2005

São Miguel, the Azores, Portugal – Tobermory, Scotland - Inverness – Skagen, Denmark

Tip: *When you can't adjust the wind, you have to adjust your mind and your sails.*

It took us 14 days to sail to Scotland: 14 of the most miserable, sodden, seasick-inducing, waterlogged, hateful days. The weather, the wind and the Atlantic waves conspired against us to make sure we didn't enjoy a single moment of it. It was enough to put us off sailing for good.

We'd started with our usual optimism, saying: 'We've been through severe weather before, surely it can't get much worse,' and the knowledge that we were nearing our journey's end doubled our confidence. We were pumped with the anticipation of arriving home as conquering heroes; furthermore, we had fresh crewing blood on board in the form of Ove who would help us out on the meanest ocean of them all. We cast off and waved cheerfully to the friends we'd made while in Ponta Delgarda, hoisted the mail sail and unfurled the jib. Scotland here we come.

We sped over frisky waves along the picturesque south coast of São Miguel, enjoying some brisk broad reach sailing.

At dusk we neared the island's most easterly point, passing the octagonal tower of the Ponta do Arnel lighthouse. Here the strong tidal current increased the size and strength of the waves which thundered over *Albatross'* foredeck. The dark ocean churned like a witch's cauldron and with it our stomachs.

We'd decided on four-hour watches; Ove was on at midnight, and Carl and I sunk into our bunks where I quickly fell into a deep dreamless sleep: our Hallberg-Rassy was in good hands, Ove knew what he was doing.

BOOM! BANG!

I woke in mid free-fall, suspended momentarily between my bunk and the cabin ceiling; then, a jolt as my head hit the ceiling and my body slammed down onto my bunk, punching the wind out of my chest and voice. Then the fear struck.

This was as frightened as I'd ever been. Scenarios of what had caused the devastating blast shot through my head. Had the engine exploded? Had the mast been ripped off? Had we hit a tanker? Had a tanker hit us? A dozen possibilities coursed through my brain in a flash, all of them bad and ending with us sinking. *Jesus, we're sinking!* I thought and leapt out of my bunk.

'What's happened? Have we hit something?' shouted Carl, stumbling forward.

Ove was lying spread eagled on the cabin floor, face down, one foot looped in the cabin ladder. For a split second I wondered if he'd shot himself to end the misery of seasickness, but then he lifted his head and said in a small shocked voice, 'What the hell was that?'

My heart was hammering hard in my chest as we waited for water to cascade into the cabin. But nothing. *Albatross* had managed to emerge from falling into the trough of one wave and was already climbing the crest of the next. Although this wasn't the first time a wave had dropped out from under her, it was the most dramatic plummet we'd experienced and it left us deeply shaken. None of us got much sleep for the rest of the night.

The following day our nerves had settled, just about, but Carl continued to battle with seasickness. I rustled up a hearty dinner of *pyttipanna*, which in Swedish means "small pieces in the pan," and consists of potatoes, bacon and whatever bits you have left over fried together. We all tucked in, but halfway through his plate Carl turned an unattractive shade of green and disappeared.

'Not to your liking?' I enquired. Carl didn't even have the strength for a comeback. As always it took his stomach three days to become accustomed to the roller coaster motion of the waves.

The misery continued; the wind was intent on driving us off course with the result we'd miss Ireland all together and hit Iceland instead, and the constant rough weather made cooking or showering an endurance test. We eventually changed course for an hour towards Greenland, a thousand nautical miles away, so I could cook a hot meal, returning to our original course once we'd done the washing up. There was an unsavoury pong about the cabin which after much finger pointing we realized was all of us; none of us had showered in four days. In milder weather we'd been able to shower on the aft deck, but as the temperature was dropping on our approach to northern latitudes we were back to using the forepeak shower cabin. Showering in something the size of a kitchen cupboard required the agility of a circus performer; if you dropped the soap, you needed to be as bendy as the incredible rubber man to retrieve it.

As we progressed north, it grew so cold Carl's stubble stopped growing. We ran the diesel heater to warm the cabin before showering. Even birds were desperate to take refuge on or even in *Albatross*; a sparrow settled on my head to rest for a while, digging small sharp claws into my skull to hang on. A few days later a finch arrived and made himself at home, flying in and out of the saloon, chirping happily as it settled on our heads and picked at the scraps on our plates. We named him or her – I'm no better at determining the sex of a finch than that of a whale – Eagle, because he or she seemed so proud and fearless. It slept at night in the saloon, gripping on the gallery railings. We were completely charmed.

Two days later our little Eagle expired; we found his small limp body resting in Carl's bunk. His death hit us surprisingly hard and we felt terribly melancholy for the rest of the day. We tried not to take it as a bad omen, but we all felt as if our good luck charm had given up the will to live.

The sea continued to thunder over us and 35-mile an hour winds kept us in a stranglehold.

'I must have lost my mind,' Ove said. 'Who really believes this is fun?'

We certainly began to question our sanity; maybe we weren't so much brave or stupid as insane and idiotic.

The wind had its hold on the sea, casting wave upon wave; *Albatross* rose up the side of one wave and plunged down again, and we slithered around the cabin like a knob of butter on a hot pan. At the top of a wave, Carl sighted a distant sail; another brave or stupid sailor was battling the Atlantic. After numerous calls, the skipper Ulf Lutzer answered. We detected a Danish accent to his English and discovered he was sailing his 50-footer from Saint Martin to Helsingør. 'Typical,' I joked to Ulf. 'All the way out here, and we bump into a Dane who lives four miles across the water from us in Helsingborg.'

'Come over for drinks in July,' Ulf said. 'We like to have the neighbours round.'

Ulf was on his way to Ireland to refuel, using the engine to try to make headway in the rough seas. While we understood his frustration in having to tack in the easterly wind pushing us ever westward, we thought it completely pointless to waste a full tank of diesel on motoring in such conditions. 'As useful as fly shit on a manure pile,' Carl said.

As for us, we'd long abandoned our plan of reaching the Irish island of Inishbofin, five miles off the Connemara coast. Instead we headed directly – or as directly as possible when tacking – for the small Isle of Coll lying west of Mull in the Inner Hebrides. To our great joy, after 13 days the wind finally turned and carried us straight to the Isles of Tiree and Coll. We put into the sheltered harbour of Arinagour at seven in the morning, mooring next to fishing boats and seagulls. Then we feasted on bread, ham, salami and cheese, with a beer and a toast of snaps.

Coll is as picturesque as any South Pacific island, as we discovered when we took the dinghy ashore to Arinagour village; low whitewashed fishermen's cottages huddled together against stone walls out of the wind of the sloping meadows; the church rose on a gentle hill above the harbour; fishermen were unloading their catch of crabs and lobsters on the pier. There was just one pub located in the smart white-facaded Coll Hotel, where we learned again to decipher the mangled vowels of Scottish brogue. A couple of pints of Guinness lubricated our linguistic skills enough to chat with the locals: fishermen and sheep farmers. We learned that the population stood at 129 souls – doubling in the summer with visitors drawn by whale, seal and bird watching – and that the nearest street light was in Tobermory on the neighbouring island of Mull, making Coll popular with stargazers. We stayed on for dinner and ate steaks with fresh vegetables that tasted extraordinarily good.

The island had been home to a branch of the Maclean Clan for five troubled centuries; their cousins, the Macleans of Duart invaded Coll in 1590, intending to take the island for themselves. A bloody battle was fought at Breachacha Castle where the Coll clan blithely slaughtered their would-be invaders, chopped off their heads and threw them in the stream, known today as "the stream of the heads." A forbidding fifteenth-century castle, indicative of the grim clan personality, still stands on the beach next to the "new" Breachacha Castle built in the eighteenth century. The Macleans of Coll died out in 1848 when the last Maclean decided he'd had enough and emigrated to the warmer climes of South Africa.

We'd hoped to walk around the island, visit the castles and the famed sandy beaches the following day, but unfortunately the wind increased again, making it impossible to take the dinghy out; large icy waves rolled into shore. Instead, we sailed 20 nautical miles to Tobermory. We were back on familiar territory, albeit the memory of which was slightly hazy; the last time we'd sailed around the Isle of Mull was during the whisky-fuelled Classic Malts Cruise in 2002, almost three years earlier.

Tobermory was as pretty as ever: the welcoming sight of brightly painted four-storey houses in raspberry pink, citrus yellow and royal blue lined the harbour wall. We tied up to a buoy in the bay and inhaled the promise of early summer forecast by the trees, heavy with blossom on this beautiful May morning. We'd found that after weeks at sea, our sense of smell was heightened; we could find the nearest pub blindfolded by literally following our noses, particularly Carl whose honker I believe is designed solely for this purpose.

We were sitting on deck, appreciating the loveliness of the view, the mirror calm of the bay, the green woodland-fringed hills beyond and listening to the solitary call of a cuckoo, when the whole effect was spoiled by the arrival of the harbourmaster brusquely demanding £12 per day for the buoy.

'Sod that,' Carl said with his usual diplomacy. 'We didn't just get off the boat yesterday, you know.' We untied *Albatross* from the buoy and dropped anchor a few feet away at a cost of nothing at all. Somewhere in the mud at the bottom of the bay there is supposed to be the wreck of a galleon; legend claims that the ship was part of the defeated Spanish Armada of 1588 and was fleeing the English fleet when she put into Tobermory to take on provisions. There was a spat over payment – the harbourmaster being just as tetchy back then as the one we'd encountered – during which the galleon rather handily "caught fire," resulting in the gunpowder magazine exploding. She was rumoured to be carrying £300,000 in gold when she went to the bottom, so locals starting jumping in after her in the hopes of salvaging a doubloon or two, although it's highly unlikely a war ship would have been carrying such a large amount of treasure. In any case, neither the wreck nor any treasure has ever been found; I think it's just a story put about to keep the gravy train of hopeful treasure hunters coming to the island to support the local hotels and pubs, and maintain a healthy ratio of people to sheep. Nevertheless, the Sound of Mull is a popular dive site; there are numerous wrecks to be explored in the cold but clear waters, many of which were cargo ships torpedoed in the First and Second World Wars.

The Isle of Mull is the second largest island of the Inner Hebrides, and Tobermory, originally built by the British Fisheries in 1788 to support the fishing industry, is Mull's main settlement. It's a thriving little town and the harbour was busy with fishing boats, yachts and the local ferry which chugs to and from Kilchoan. Mull is a popular holiday destination, particularly with wildlife enthusiasts keen to spot eagles, corncrakes and sea life, and the waters around the coast of Mull are vital feeding grounds for whales, dolphins and basking sharks.

And then of course, there's the whisky distillery, which in my opinion is the site of the *real* treasure. Tobermory distillery, established in 1798, takes inordinate pride on being the only one on the island and the oldest commercial distillery in Scotland. For us Swedes, it was a must do. We toured the distillery, our noses tingling at the aromatic whisky laden air, salivating more than any experimental dog in anticipation of a nosing.

'It's the peaty water that gives our single malt whisky its flavour,' our guide explained, as he swirled his glass and examined the colour in the manner of someone who takes his whiskies very seriously. 'This 15-year-old malt has a nice marmalade nose to it, a hint of smoke and a spicy finish. It's very easy to drink.'

Carl smacked his lips in true appreciation. 'Ah, that's the best whisky I've ever drunk.'

I wasn't sure about the marmalade business, but I can certainly testify that it was indeed very easy to drink, and it took me several attempts to articulate the word "delicious."

After a couple of days, Ove had to sign off to return to Helsingborg. But we received a new crew member, Staffan Wikström who would join us on our leg to Denmark. We'd last met Staffan in 2003 as a sailing virgin in the South Pacific when he'd lost his cherry travelling with us from Rarotonga to Auckland. Ever the sucker for punishment, he was keen to test his metal on the North Sea.

Later that evening, we were joined by three Swedish couples, friends whom we'd clearly bored so much by raving about the beauty of the Scottish islands and the potency of the whisky that they'd decided to visit, timing their holiday to coincide with our sojourn. It was a heck of a reunion and we celebrated with a party, much of which I can't recall. The following day, we drove around Mull. What a glorious island, steeped in history with turreted castles to visit and views to get lost in. The weather was warm and clear, and we picnicked with a view of the Sound of Mull, gazing upon the sight of soaring eagles and gorse bushes bursting golden on the surrounding slopes where the spring lambs gambolled fetchingly around sheep that looked as if they'd been freshly washed and fluffed for the occasion.

'Stunning,' Mona said with a deep sigh.

'I thought you guys were just drunk on the whisky when you described the Scottish islands,' Bo said. 'But this is truly magnificent.' And we all agreed there was no finer place than Mull and no finer drink than a single malt whisky.

Staffan, Carl and I put to sea the following day, sailing with the tide down the Sound of Mull twenty nautical miles to Craignure Bay on Mull's east coast. The publican at the Craignure Inn was good enough to allow us to moor on his buoy for free, in return for which we felt it only polite to drink as much as we could at his bar and to try the restaurant menu.

'What do you recommend?' I asked, in the full knowledge this was a risky question in a country where a deep fried chocolate bar is considered a culinary treat.

'Aye'd go fur the haggis, tatties and neeps,' the publican said.

I didn't recognize a single word, but did my best impression of a man who understands what is being said to him. When my plate of food arrived, I managed to work out that the tatties were potatoes, but toyed for a while with the bits of grey matter and orange mush before summoning the courage to stick my fork in them. Despite their appearance to the contrary, the haggis and turnips were surprisingly tasty. We got chatting with the locals, whose surnames without exception began with Mac: Macleans, MacLaines, MacKinnons, Macquarries and MacDonalds, all descendants of Mull's ancient clans.

The following day, on the publican's recommendation, I took a bus tour of the island and visited Duart castle, a thirteenth-century MacLean clan castle poised on a crag at the end of the peninsular jutting out in the Sound of Mull. It was the sort of setting and castle to inspire a burst of pride in a Scotsman's chest. Hell, the sight of it had me desperate to wear a kilt, do a Highland fling and shout from the parapets, 'Aye, but they will never take our freedom,' and even eat haggis again. In other words, it was as rousing a Scottish scene as any I'd come upon. Credit must be given to Sir Fitzroy MacLean, the twenty-sixth Chief who, in 1910 and at the ripe old age of 76, bought back the ruined castle and began the costly task of restoring the ancestral seat. The current owner and twenty-eighth Chief, Sir Lachlan McLean, regularly crops up on the guided tours of his home, kilt swinging jauntily and enthusiastically representing the clan today.

That's one of the most remarkable aspects of Scotland: the nation's determination to keep Scotland for the Scots and clan history alive and well. It has been estimated that there were once between 2,000 and 3,000 castles in Scotland, depending on your definition of a castle, but at least twice the amount built in England and Wales. Many have crumbled into ruins, but a considerable number have been restored with great love and at great cost. If you fancy yourself laird of the manor, you can pick up a ruin for a mere £300,000. If, however, you're looking for a modernized seventeenth-century bolthole with its original features, moat, turrets with arrow slots, battlements, vaulted crypt and so forth, that will set you back 10 times as much. As I fancy the latter, this book needs to sell extremely well, so please recommend it to friends, family or complete strangers, as necessary.

Early on Monday morning, we sailed further up the Lynn of Morvern with the tide, passed the long narrow island of Lismore and entered Loch Linnhe where *Albatross* was pulled forward on the rushing current into the loch. A cold wind blew steadily throughout the day speeding us towards Fort William. We moored for the night at the jetty in Corpach, a village lying at the entrance to the Caledonian Canal.

'Remember, Calle, how we were so nervous the first time we had to negotiate a canal lock?' I said.

Carl grinned. 'It seems a hundred years ago now, doesn't it? We've learned so much since then.'

We were full of ourselves as *Albatross* sailed down the canal with swan-like serenity; this was a piece of cake to us circumnavigators. At Banavie, just next door to Corpach, we decided to stretch our legs, taking a four-mile stroll to Fort William where we sniffed out the Ben Nevis Distillery located at the foot of the mountain. Once again we listened to a guide explain the whisky-making process, although by now we were so familiar with it, we could have given our own tours. At the nosing session, Carl was as appreciative as always, smacking his lips and claiming it to be the best whisky he'd ever tasted. I was beginning to detect a theme.

We sobered up and sailed up the canal, enjoying a strong westerly wind which pushed us six knots the length of Loch Lochy, stopping for the evening at the Letterfinlay Lodge where we watched the sun set over the loch and a loan osprey swooping over the water. I had a pint of beer in my hand and all was well with the world. It was the perfect way to end the day.

A storm was brewing over Loch Ness, churning up the moody waters. It was the first week of June and we had time to spare for our arrival in Helsingborg, so we decided to wait for better weather in Fort Augustus at the mouth of the loch. It was worth the two-day wait; the light west wind made for a beautiful sail to Urquhart Castle. We moored in the sheltered bay just north of the castle and took the dinghy ashore.

'Ah, can you smell it?' asked Carl, as we tied up

'Smell what?' asked Staffan. 'I can smell sheep and grass.'

'No.' Carl lifted his head and inhaled deeply. 'That way,' he said and set off at a determined pace over a bumpy field, scattering surprised sheep and lambs before him.

'Where the hell is he going?' Staffan asked me. 'What can he smell?'

'A pub or a distillery,' I said. 'His nose is like some kind of divining rod for hops and barely.'

After chasing the back of Carl's head and tramping a couple of miles over fields, dodging sheep droppings, we reached the village of Drumnadrochit where Carl steered us to the local watering hole.

'Ah,' he said, after taking a long gulp of his pint and wiping his foamy moustache with the back of his hand. 'Best beer I've ever tasted.'

As we arrived at Inverness, the weather started to blow up again, and storms in the North Sea were being forecast; conditions out there would be as miserable on the way home as they were when we'd sailed out to Peterhead three years earlier. Carl and I looked at each other and shrugged.

'I don't fancy that kind of journey again, do you, Calle?'

'Bugger it. We'll have to wait for the storm to blow over.' Carl looked sulky for a moment, then he beamed. 'Let's rent a car and tour the whisky distilleries. I'm sure Staffan would like to visit them.'

As if we needed Staffan as an excuse. We hired a small Ford Fiesta and for three days we pootled around the distilleries, becoming minor experts in nosings and tastings, colour and clarity. Familiar names became real places: Glen Moray, Glenfiddich and Glenmorangie, each with their own unique taste and history. At every nosing Carl would pronounce each whisky the best he'd ever drunk. I think he was quite disappointed when the storms cleared and favourable westerly winds were forecast. Time to face the North Sea again.

Chapter 50
Homeward Bound
10 – 18 June 2005

Inverness, Scotland – Skagen, Denmark – Helsingborg, Sweden

Experience: *East, west, home is best.*

Tip: *Don't sail too close to the oil and gas platforms in the North Sea: security gets very suspicious even of small sailboats.*

Just 500 nautical miles lay between us and our home port of Helsingborg; after travelling over 49,000 miles around the world to this point, it seemed like a mere spit in the ocean.

The Scottish weather was at its early summer best with cloudless skies and a fair wind as we cast off on the high tide on Sunday morning. We sailed towards Clachnaharrya and the remaining two locks of the Caledonian Canal, buoyed with a hearty breakfast and our usual dose of misplaced confidence.

'Nearly home, Calle,' I said as the last lock door slowly swung shut behind us and lowered us down to sea level.

'Plain sailing now, mate,' Carl replied with a broad grin.

If only. We'd barely sailed out onto the open water when the westerly wind capriciously dropped and turned to a light easterly breeze, forcing us to use the engine to make any headway against the inward flowing tide pushing us back towards Inverness. But by evening we'd left the Moray Firth and had progressed along the north coast of Scotland to Fraserburgh. The night sky was light, reminding us that midsummer was only two weeks away and for the first time in three years we'd be back in Sweden to celebrate it with friends and family. As dawn rose we passed the lighthouse on Kinnaird Head, the headland projecting into the North Sea where the town of Fraserburgh sits.

The world changes quickly, and in the time since we'd last crossed the North Sea, we noticed many new oil and gas platforms not marked on our charts.

'That shouldn't be there,' Carl kept saying as another mammoth structure loomed in the early morning mist.

We were in the Forties Oil Field, the largest oil field in the North Sea with an area of approximately 35 square miles. Discovered in 1970, this giant field was originally predicted to run dry by early 1990, but after producing over 2.65 billion barrels it is now expected to continue for another 20 years.

Drilling for oil at depths of two and three miles in the inhospitable North Sea is a perilous gamble. Since drilling there began over five decades ago, over 500 people have perished in accidents in oil rig explosions, helicopter crashes and drownings. Crews typically work two weeks on, two weeks off, but the North Sea is so rough personnel transfers must be made by helicopter; landing on the platforms' helipads is hugely dangerous and tragically, sometimes fatal. Furthermore, the very nature of the job of extracting volatile substances entails great risks. In 1980, a platform collapsed in a storm with a loss of 123 lives, and in 1988, 167 people died when a platform in the Piper Oil field exploded after a gas leak.

The rigs themselves are remarkable constructions, and I was interested in getting as close as possible to take photos and maybe shout a cheery greeting to the poor sods who work in such hostile conditions. But as soon as our approach was detected, the "bodyguards" immediately radioed to warn us to keep a distance of two nautical miles. I guess that given the importance of gas and oil platforms to the economy, security is tight, particularly in the wake of 9/11.

The following day the North Sea became its familiar self with a brutal north wind riling the waves to white foamy peaks.

'Here we go again,' Carl shouted, turning fifty shades of grey before emptying the contents of his stomach over the rail. The waves rose higher and faster, crashing over us and filling the cockpit knee high with water.

'I didn't expect to get trench foot on a sailboat,' Staffan yelled as he attempted futilely to duck another wave. We tried to reef in the jib but to our horror the clew broke and the sail fluttered out like a kite. After frantic work in the bow, I managed to rescue the sail. We sheeted in the staysail and let the shortened mainsail out to starboard in an effort to outrun the storm, but in vain; when a massive wave hit *Albatross'* port side, giving the hull a sudden bang, the preventer held the boom secure, but when she came round, the wind exerted such pressure on the sail that the stitches tore. We watched helplessly as a large tear opened like a wound all the way down to the boom.

Albatross looked like a giant scarecrow with fluttering rags for a mainsail. Luckily we'd bought a new one in Cape Town, but this was no time to be fiddling about and attaching sails. We salvaged what was left of the mainsail, our speed dropping significantly. We still had quite a distance to cover, approximately 150 nautical miles to Norway's south coast and around the same to the west coast of Denmark.

'Well, bugger this,' I yelled to Carl over the screaming wind. 'There's only one thing for it.'

'What?' shouted Staffan. 'Man the lifeboat? Hit the bottle? Say a prayer?'

'Heave to,' Carl answered.

I nodded. We'd found this was one of the best ways to sail more comfortably in rough weather during our passage from Reunion to Cape Town. We drove *Albatross* 40 degrees into the wind and tweaked the helm so she was riding comfortably and we could get some respite from the storm. For 35 hours we pushed ahead at a slow but solid one to two knots an hour – a slow walk – while the wind howled through the rigging. The wind subsided in due course but the waves still came fast and broke often, so we set the sails gingerly.

Eventually, we rounded the Skagen reefs and with relief entered the sheltered harbour on Tuesday morning as dawn was breaking. We drank our mooring snaps and watched the world slowly come to life as the sun climbed higher in the sky. We were back on our home shores where the perfume of the lilac bushes in bloom filled the air with the promise of summer, and long pale grasses rustled in the breeze. How different from the scent of jasmine and the view of palm trees titling in the Pacific wind.

On Wednesday, my son Dino arrived to join us on the sail to Gilleleje, where we would meet other members of the families, and make the very last part of our long journey, culminating in our triumphant – hopefully – entry into Helsingborg.

'Congratulations, Dad,' Dino said with a huge smile. 'You made it.'

'Nearly. Let's not jinx it,' I warned. 'It would be a real bugger to sink off the coast of Denmark now.'

And wouldn't you know it, but we nearly did. The weather was fickle, the wind was against us and we weren't helped by having a huge rip in the mainsail; we were unable to attach the new one we'd bought in Cape Town because we didn't have all the required parts. Nevertheless, we weighed anchor and set sail after optimistically hoisting the signal flags presented to us by Helsingborg's Yacht Club on our departure, slightly tattered after our first dreadful passage out of Sweden to Denmark. We'd also festooned *Albatross* with 32 courtesy flags from the countries we'd visited, some of which we'd been given and others we'd purchased. We wanted to make sure we looked good for our arrival and had dressed *Albatross* to impress.

'Are you having a party?' a passer-by in the harbour asked Carl.

Carl puffed out his chest like a courting frigate bird. 'No,' he said. 'We're going home.' As you could almost see the Swedish coast from Skagen, the passer-by saw no reason for the chest puffing and was duly unimpressed.

Dino looked at the choppy water anxiously. 'Are you sure we should sail to Gilleleje today?'

Carl and I smiled at him patronizingly, seasoned old salts that we now were. 'Ha! This is just a bit of a swell. No big deal. We've been through worse.'

For nine miserable hours we struggled through the Kattegat straits between Denmark and Sweden against a stubborn wind and an opposing current intent on driving us north to Gothenburg rather than sending us merrily on our way south to Gilleleje. We just couldn't do it without a functioning mainsail, and for the first time in our three-year journey we were forced to give up and turn back. After nine hours of battle, it took less than an hour to sail back to Skagen harbour.

'Back again so soon?' a Danish skipper moored in the harbour asked us.

'Yeah. Bit tricky out there,' Carl said in the irritated tone of a man who was missing his evening beverage and not in the mood for any jokes about his sailing prowess. The Dane didn't pick up on this.

'I thought you guys said you'd just sailed around the world. Yet you can't get to Gilleleje?'

'You try it without a mainsail, mate!' I distracted Carl from thumping the man with the happy clink of ice cubes in a glass.

The weather refused to play ball; the following day boded fine and clear without a whisper of wind; the weather gods were just toying with us now. At this rate we'd be stuck in Skagen and miss our conquering heroes' return. Our family and friends would be waiting for us in Gilleleje harbour, peering at the horizon wondering where we were. We were running out of time.

'Right,' Carl said decisively, scowling at the sea. 'No more piddling about. We've got a hundred litres of fuel, so let's use some of it to get out of here. The wind's bound to pick up out on the ocean.'

We ran the motor almost the entire way. Dino, Carl and I sat in the cockpit cursing to each other. 'Worse than the damn doldrums,' I grumbled. It looked as if we'd run out of fuel before we got there.

When we finally glimpsed the fishing boats outside Gilleleje on Friday morning, I all but danced a jig on the bowsprit. We were so close to home I could have swum the rest, not that I needed to as our family and friends arrived at *Albatross* only an hour after we'd tied up. We'd made it by the skin of our teeth.

It was one of those tearfully joyous reunions for all involved: chattering and hugging was punctuated by the popping of champagne corks. Carl was greeted by a tearful Eva and their daughters and partners. There were my parents, my brother and his wife and children, as well as Dino's girlfriend Sofia. And standing to one side, waiting patiently for my mother to finish asking me if I'd been eating enough was Anita, Shaun and Antonia with her: my new family. Anita's smile lit up her face and my heart. We were all going home.

The whole ensemble gathered at a restaurant where six years earlier we'd boasted of the yacht we'd just collected from Germany and told the owner how we intended to circumnavigate the world.

'I remember you guys,' he said. 'Thought you were either nutters or dreamers at the time. I certainly never thought you'd do it.'

'Nobody did,' Carl said proudly.

The following morning we were up at the crack of dawn; it was our big day and we had a lot to do to make *Albatross* look presentable for her grand entrance. Our families were travelling back to Helsingborg by train and ferry to await us there.

With just a few nautical miles left of our mammoth journey, Carl and I talked a lot; it was as if we knew it was our last chance to vocalize to each other what the past three years had meant to us. Once we arrived home, we'd be swamped by family and friends and there'd be little time for each other. And then there was the return to the daily grind; unlike Carl who had three months before he had to return to work and could therefore ease himself back into the norm slowly, I had a mere four days before I had to take over the photo lab for my brother; I owed him three years to pursue his goal. It was a deeply depressing realization: four days to come down from the high of coming home, four days to get myself organized, four days to sort out my home and life with Anita and the children, four days to get my head around the fact that it was all over. No, there wouldn't be much time for reflection once I was back in the real world as a working stiff stuck in a job in a shopping centre. It would be quite a reality check.

But I would go back to work a different man. Both Carl and I agreed that our journey had been as spiritual as it had been physical; our experiences had changed how we saw the world and how we prioritized our lives. I admit that I'd probably been more concerned with material possessions than was good for a person. This was no longer the case; I didn't give a damn about driving a shiny luxury car or wearing designer clothes. I'd given away all the clothes I'd intended to sell to help fund my journey; the rewards of a grateful smile, a meal eaten on the dirt floor of a hut, or a mound of fruit picked fresh from the jungle by barefoot children were worth more than dollars or deutschmarks.

Carl and I had learned so much – and I'm not talking just about sailing, although lord knows we'd learned a massive amount, much through trial and error, about that. That trite expression "the world is a small place" just isn't true. We'd learned that it is huge and diverse and exciting and dangerous and disappearing. We'd seen corners of the world untouched by the bulldozer, hotel conglomerates and the steady and irreversible tread of so-called progress.

We'd visited pristine beaches that had since vanished under oil spills, sailed to islands whose delicate ecosystems were being destroyed by tourism and seen tiny atolls that may be submerged by the time you read this.

In the process, I'd learned much about myself; a new man had emerged from within: a happier, more confident, less linguistically inept man. Carl had always maintained that I'd generally been fearful of life, of taking a risk, of getting things wrong and making mistakes. I'd been stuck in my middle-class comfort zone, tied to an occupation that paid the mortgage. By taking what many thought was a leap into the unknown, I'd grabbed an opportunity, the immeasurable value of which I was only beginning to appreciate.

By risking everything, we gained everything; we'd travelled the world, met its peoples and witnessed their humanity. We'd met villagers who'd rubbed our skin in wonder to see if it was painted pink, communities so poor they literally scratched a living out of the earth where the earth had little to give, men who'd presented us with pearls they'd risked their lives to get, women who shared food they'd cooked over simple fires, and children who'd given us shells they'd polished by hand. But we'd received so much more: memories of friendships that were given without expectation of anything in return, as well as an appreciation of a vanishing world.

'Yup,' Carl said. 'It's been one heck of a journey. We've learned a lot. You've learned to face challenges head on and speak your mind instead of bottling it up and letting things fester.'

I nodded. 'Fair enough. And you've finally learned that you don't need to sail with all the sails unfurled so the boat heels into the bloody water, and that it's just as effective to reef in occasionally.

Carl narrowed his eyes and said in a peevish tone, 'Now let's not start all that again, Yanne. More often than not ...'

I was wrong: apparently, he hadn't learned that. And so the discussion continues.

However, there was one vital thing on which we did agree: we couldn't have come this far without each other. Heck, we wouldn't have made it across the Öresund and back without each other's motivation. When Carl's conviction had failed, I'd encouraged him to keep our goal in sight. And when I'd doubted my ability, Carl's had been the voice of belief keeping the dream alive. Had we not goaded each other into believing we could succeed, we would surely have stumbled at the first post.

As we entered the Öresund, the final stretch of water between Denmark and Sweden, our excitement swelled. This was journey's end.

'Crap,' said Carl, looking at his watch. 'At this rate we're going to be early.'

It was imperative we arrived on the stroke of three. Even though our mainsail hung in three sad-looking strips of cloth and we had a two-knot counter current, we were still going too fast. We'd arrive at an empty harbour with no one to greet us apart from a couple of wandering tourists who wouldn't give a gnat's fart about our 49,500-nautical mile journey. We started the engine and threw it into reverse to slow down our progress. Anyone observing us must have wondered why we were trying to sail backwards.

We were just in sight of Viken harbour, a village approximately 10 miles from Helsingborg, when we were greeted by the first boat in a surprise welcome committee. It was Sven-Ingvar Bengtsson whom we'd last seen in Peterhead in Scotland. Not only had he been the last in Helsingborg to bid us farewell, but he'd made certain to be the first to meet us on our return, waving like a madman, sounding his boat's signal horn and shouting 'Welcome home' through a megaphone. Tears rolled down our cheeks, just as they had when we'd left three years ago. One by one, boats of every kind arrived to greet us, from small sailboats, dinghies with outboard motors carrying everyone it seemed we'd ever known, to a canoeist paddling like the devil to keep up with us. Then there was Martin, my former boat neighbour, with Kaiser his daughter, vastly grown in the years since we'd been away, both dressed as pirates. Sadly, my liveaboard neighbour and mentor, Ove would not be there, and I felt his absence as keenly as a knife to the chest; how I wished he could have shared in this. But as more and more boats arrived with tooting of horns and cheers and whistles, unhappy thoughts were pushed aside. Two dozen boats surrounded us to accompany us into harbour. We'd left Helsingborg as a single yacht, now we were returning with our own flotilla.

As if that wasn't overwhelming enough, the flyby of two jets was. Carl and I looked up as they shot past, dipped their wings and swerved around again a moment later.

'Who the hell are they out for?' I wondered, squinting into the sky. 'Surely not us?'

We later learned from friends that the Swedish air force base in Kallinge on the Baltic Sea had organized the flyby as part of the celebrations.

For that's what it was: a celebration for us, our family and friends, our home town and our yacht club. Six years earlier when we'd applied for a berth in the harbour for a boat we hadn't got and couldn't have sailed even if we'd had, we'd been told that no one from Helsingborg Yacht Club had ever attempted to circumnavigate the world, much less two idiots who didn't know port from starboard and were inclined to shout 'turn left' in a crisis.

Helsingborg was in sight, the city hall tower rose splendidly behind the marina, my and *Albatross*' old home. As we neared the dock, we could hear the crowd before we saw them, a roar of cheers, shouts and whistles rose to greet us. The piers were crowded with people, some waving the blue and yellow flag of Sweden, others waving the red and yellow flag of Skåne.

'Holy crap,' exclaimed Carl over the din. 'It's rent-a-crowd. Who the heck are all those people?'

It didn't seem to matter who they were, Carl dropped everything and starting grinning and waving to his public as if he were the Queen of Sweden on a royal visit.

'Calle,' I shouted. 'Fenders! Put out the damn fenders, you glorified fool.'

Brilliant! We were rushing into the harbour, no control, no fenders. At this rate we'd crash into the pier, gash a hole in our beloved boat and sink in front of a thousand-strong crowd, displaying an embarrassing lack of seafaring ability and leading everyone to the logical conclusion that we'd spent three years holing up in the first port in Norway. Carl eventually regained his wits, stopped his regal waving and we dashed about the deck, pulling ropes and throwing out the fenders. Hands reached out to grab mooring ropes, and as we stepped off *Albatross* more hands reached out to grab us, pat us on the back or shake our hands. It was chaos. Glorious, wonderful chaos. Crowns of flowers were put on our heads, garlands of summer blooms placed around our necks. We were rock stars. We were heroes. We were home.

I saw my father's face in the crowd, his cheeks glistening with tears of pride. Next to him was a man, approximately my father's age, whose face was familiar yet I couldn't quite place in the pandemonium of the moment. Both men pushed forward to greet me.

'Well done, son,' my father croaked. He was so moved he could barely speak.

The man beside him took my hand and shook it warmly. 'Congratulations to you both.' He winked. 'Not bad for beginners, but if you want to impress me, you'll have to do it a couple more times.'

And then I realized who it was: Kurt Björkland, my father's former helmsman and a legend in Helsingborg for his exploits. This was the man who in many ways had set the whole journey in motion, for had it not been for my telling Carl on a Normandy cliff top of Kurt's surviving the D-Day landings and his subsequent exploits, the seed of sailing around the world would never have been planted. This man had a lot to answer for.

I couldn't decide whether to punch him or kiss him.

Instead, I shook his hand warmly and thanked him from the bottom of my heart.

We passed through the crowd, shaking hands and accepting congratulations from friends we hadn't seen in three years, as well as people I'm pretty sure I'd never met before. A glass of champagne was pressed into my hand. Somewhere a brass band was playing. Cameras whirled and clicked. A microphone was suddenly shoved in front of my face; a television camera zoomed towards me.

'What are your thoughts on being back?' the reporter shouted at me.

My thoughts? I was a huge bundle of emotion pushing out any coherent thoughts. It felt amazing, wonderful, joyous, overwhelming. I felt like the luckiest man in the world. Few people get the opportunity to follow their dreams. I knew we'd been massively lucky; lucky in our chosen professions, able to tinker and repair anything electrical; lucky not to have been turned over by a rogue wave off the coast of South Africa; lucky not to have been hit by a container lost by a cargo ship in the Pacific Ocean; lucky not to have been in the direct path of a cyclone; lucky not to have been struck by a lightning bolt. Yes, although we'd often cursed the gods of wind and weather in the doldrums or in the North Sea storms, they'd also smiled benignly upon us.

But I'd been the luckiest of all; I'd had Carl without whose friendship and encouragement I might have faltered at the first step – getting on a boat. But even more: in following my dream, I'd met my dream girl, who'd bravely made her own journey halfway around the world to join me.

But I couldn't express any of that. I couldn't say anything; I was too choked with emotion, that such a huge crowd had turned out to welcome us, a couple of electricians who'd experienced a bit of a midlife crisis and gone off on a journey to find themselves. I looked for Carl in the throng; he'd know what to say.

'Calle,' I shouted. 'Get over here.'

Carl pushed his way over, wearing a lopsided crown of flowers and a huge smile. He threw an arm around my shoulders. Microphones and cameras swung in our direction.

'Tell us your thoughts,' the interviewer repeated to both of us.

'We did it!' Carl said without a second's hesitation. 'We bloody did it, didn't we, Yanne!' He threw back his head to the sky and roared his big hearty laugh with elation.

'Yes, we did,' I shouted. 'We did it! We really did it!'

Postscript
Home from the Sea

18 June 2005 – Present Day

Helsingborg, Sweden

Tip: *"Twenty years from now you will be more disappointed by the things that you didn't do than by the ones you did do. So throw off the bowlines. Sail away from the safe harbour. Catch the trade winds in your sails. Explore. Dream. Discover."*
Mark Twain

So were we brave or stupid? I leave my peers to decide which adjective is most applicable. However, of one thing I am certain: I've been very fortunate. On clear nights, when the wind has blown away the clouds, I gaze out across the dark waters of the Öresund. Then I look up to the stars and thank them.

By the time this book goes to print, it will have been nine years since Carl and I returned to Sweden, and the idly curious may be wondering what has happened in the meantime.

Anita made an honest man of me two months after our homecoming by marrying me on my fiftieth birthday. We've remained in Helsingborg ever since. Unfortunately, the relationship between the two women in my life is an uneasy one; Anita continues to turn an unpleasant shade of green whenever we set sail on *Albatross*. I fear they will never get along, but luckily my Kiwi understands my obsession and is not the jealous type to make demands along the lines of 'it's either me or the boat.' Anita is more inclined to stay on board in harbour now that the extra crew have disappeared. Rather than risk being frozen in northern climes, that repellent gang of glue sniffers jumped ship, leaving *Albatross* cockroach free to this day

As my relationship with Anita blossomed, so the corrosive effect of salt water unfortunately took its toll on Carl's and Eva's marriage; they decided to separate and divorced two years after his return. Carl had spread his wings and found a bigger world which Eva had been unable to share; she felt she needed to go in search of adventures of her own.

In 2010, Carl suffered a stroke which hospitalized him for six months, scaring the wits out of his nearest and dearest, not least himself. Fortunately, he made a full recovery – bar a dodgy leg – and is now enjoying his retirement. He is still trying to tame the North Sea with regular trips to Scotland to top up his whisky collection, but his long-term goal is to sail to Argentina, the Falklands and explore more of South Africa's coast. As he is nearing his sixty-fifth birthday, I keep reminding him his goal should be short-term rather than long-term. Since meeting Gerd, a lady who sets her sails just the way Carl likes them, he no longer expends unnecessary energy fending off amorous advances from the ladies; Gerd does that for him. As for the dodgy leg, he says it's useful for predicting cold weather.

In 2011, Carl's side of the story was published in Sweden under the title *Segla med Albatross* (Sailing with *Albatross*) which proved so popular we were asked for an English version: hence the book you are holding now, narrated from my perspective, so I have the luxury of carping about Carl, thus possibly allowing me to come off slightly better in this version.

Both Carl and I regularly give lectures and presentations about our adventures and sailing experience at boat shows and yacht clubs. More recently, we've been asked to give motivational speeches to companies on achieving one's goals. All these activities keep us busy at weekends and in drinks at the bar.

The real star of this story, our beloved Hallberg-Rassy, has turned 26 years old, and she's still a fine-looking boat. She continues to require pampering and a certain amount of money spent on her to keep her in shape; every autumn we check all the rigging, pack away the sails and clear everything from the deck; Carl and I are not keen winter sailors. In April when the weather is friendlier, we have a thorough spring clean, paying particular attention to the teak deck and the railings. Every other year, *Albatross* is sailed to a larger marina further up the coast and hoisted out of the water, so Carl and I can clean and polish the hull and service the motor. When we're not out on the ocean, she sits serenely in Helsingborg harbour and we congregate with friends in her cockpit, weather permitting, or below decks when it doesn't. I rustle up a meal in the galley, Carl opens a bottle of wine and we reminisce about the places we visited and the people we met, while *Albatross* sways ever so gently against her ropes and the sun sets behind Denmark.

Come and see us. Just ask around the harbour for Yanne, Carl or *Albatross*: I'm sure someone will point you in the right direction. If you're lucky, I might be making my famous meatballs and the *Gammel Dansk* will be on the table.

Skål för fan!

Useful Books and Websites

BOOKS

Bengtsson, Frans G.	The Long Ships: A Saga of the Viking Age
Bruce, Peter	Heavy Weather Sailing,
Cornell, Jimmy.	World Cruising Routes;
	World Voyage Planner
Cunliffe, Tom	The Complete Yachtmaster
Dashew, Steve & Linda	Offshore Cruising Encyclopaedia - II
Heyerdahl, Thor	Raroia: Happy Island of the South Seas
	Kon-Tiki: Across the Pacific by Raft
Michener, James	The Covenant; Tales of the South Pacific
Scarr, Deryck	A Short History of Fiji
Slocum, Josuah	Sailing Alone around the World
Strid, Steve & Andreasson, Claes	The Viking Manifesto
Wood, Charles & Margo	Charlie's Charts of Polynesia.

WEBSITES

Before you visit any other website, first take a look at ours on www.brave-orstupid.com for more information and photos about us, *Albatross* and our journey.

www.acp.gob.pa
An excellent website with news on the latest developments on the Panama canal.

www.americascup.com
History and competition news about the greatest racing cup of them all.

www.australia.com
The official site of tourism Australia, the glorious photos will inspire you to visit.

www.caribbeancompass
The online edition of Caribbean Compass Magazine covering marine and shore based topics in the Caribbean.

www.cornellsailing.com
Jimmy Cornell's site on
all things sailing.

www.hallberg-rassy.com
Hallberg-Rassy's excellent website
for information and brochures
on their boats.

www.helsingborg.se
Information on the
city of Helsingborg.

sthelenaonline.org
If you can't get there, St Helena's
website is so complete with news
and blogs, you'll feel as if you
are there.

www.galapagos.org
Focused on protecting the unique
ecosystems of the Galapagos
archipelago, the website contains
the latest news of activity on the
islands.

www.newzealand.com
The official site of New Zealand
tourism. Get yourself a Kiwi.

www.royalnavalmuseum.org
The story of the Royal Navy and
its people from earliest times to
the present.

www.tomcunliffe.com
Tom's website with links to his sailing
publications, videos and blogs.

www.scottishcanals.co.uk
Informative website on visiting
and sailing the canals of Scotland.

www.southafrica.net
Comprehensive website on
all things South African.

www.vasamuseet.se
The official website of the
Vasa museum in Stockholm.